GW01270701

THE LAW OF PUBLIC LEISURE SERVICES

AUSTRALIA AND NEW ZEALAND
The Law Book Company Ltd.
Sydney: Melbourne: Perth

CANADA AND U.S.A.
The Carswell Company Ltd.
Agincourt, Ontario

INDIA
N.M. Tripathi Private Ltd.
Bombay
and
Eastern Law House Private Ltd.
Calcutta and Delhi
M.P.P. House
Bangalore

ISRAEL
Steimatzky's Agency Ltd.
Jerusalem: Tel Aviv: Haifa

MALAYSIA: SINGAPORE: BRUNEI
Malayan Law Journal (Pte.) Ltd.
Singapore

PAKISTAN
Pakistan Law House
Karachi

THE LAW OF PUBLIC LEISURE SERVICES

By

Michael Scott, LL.M.

Foreword by

Charles Cross, M.A., LL.B.

London   Sweet & Maxwell   1985

Published in 1985 by
Sweet & Maxwell Limited,
11 New Fetter Lane, London.
Computerset by
Promenade Graphics Limited,
Cheltenham, Gloucestershire.
Printed by Robert Hartnoll (1985) Limited,
Bodmin, Cornwall.

British Library Cataloguing in Publication Data
Scott, Michael
 The law of public leisure services.
 1. Recreation—Law and legislation—Great Britain
 I. Title
 344.104'9   KD1105

ISBN 0–421–32680–8

All rights reserved.
No part of this publication may be
reproduced or transmitted, in any form
or by any means, electronic, mechanical, photocopying,
recording or otherwise, or stored in any retrieval
system of any nature, without the written permission
of the copyright holder and the publisher, application
for which shall be made to the publisher.

© Sweet & Maxwell 1985

dedicated

to poet and psalmist,

artist, musician and fell-walker

guides, who help men and women

to enjoy their leisure

Local Government Act 1985

Abolition of the Greater London Council and the six Metropolitan County Councils from April 1, 1986.

Note on Changes to Public Leisure Services

Since this book was typeset, the Local Government Act 1985 has received the Royal Assent. This means that the Greater London Council and six metropolitan county councils will cease to exist on April 1, 1986.

There are approximately 45 public leisure service areas of law touched on in this work. Of these, some are untouched by this reform. In Greater London, some 12 services are changed; the number affected is the same in the authorities outside London. (The numbers vary with the groupings of services.)

Whilst the extensive amendments to the text required to record these changes were, unfortunately, not possible in the publication timetable, it is not difficult for readers to follow the service changes. This is because, in general, all services currently allocated to one of the seven local authorities being abolished, are devolved to the adjacent district council or to the London borough and Common Council of the City of London, as the case may be. There are indeed, for our purposes, only four exceptions to this pattern, namely:

Subject or Service	*Transferee*
1. Green Belt land and control.	Boroughs or Shire Counties, according to situation. A statutory joint planning committee will advise on policy (s.7).
2. The South Bank arts complex.	The Arts Council.
3. Historic Buildings and related functions under the G.L.C.	The Historic Buildings and Monuments Commission for England.
4. The Horniman and Geffrye Museums.	The new Inner London Education Authority.

The full Destination Table for services affected by the above Act and dealt with in this book, is as follows:

NOTE ON CHANGES

Chapter No.	Service	Existing	Future
2	Commons registration	G.L.C. and Met. counties	Met. districts and London Boroughs
	Local Act services	GL.C. and Met. counties	Met. districts, London Boroughs and the Common Council
3	Archives	G.L.C. and Met. counties	Met. districts and London Boroughs. The Greater London Record Office goes to the City of London
	Metropolitan County museums	Met. counties	Met. districts and London Boroughs. The Chancellor of the Duchy of Lancaster may appoint trustees to take over any collection of national importance (s.46).
	Historic House Museums, i.e. Kenwood, Marble Hill and Rangers Houses London	G.L.C.	Historic Buildings and Monuments Commission for England
	Horniman and Geffrye Museums	G.L.C.	The new I.L.E.A.
	Ancient Monuments, Listed Buildings and Conservation Areas	G.L.C.	Historic Buildings & Monuments Commission for England
4	Street Playgrounds	G.L.C. & Met. Counties	Districts, London Boroughs and the Common Council
	Animals	G.L.C. & Met. Counties	Districts and London Boroughs
5	South Bank Complex (Royal Festival Hall,	GL.C.	The Arts Council

NOTE ON CHANGES

Chapter No.	Service	Existing	Future
	Q.E. Hall, the Purcell Room, the National Theatre, the National Film Theatre and the Hayward Gallery)		
	Historic Buildings Statutes and Monuments	G.L.C.	Historic Buildings and Monuments Commission for England
	Open Space and Recreation	G.L.C.	London Boroughs
	Green Belt land and control	G.L.C.	The Boroughs or Shire counties, according to location
	Commons registration	G.L.C.	London Boroughs
	Squares	G.L.C.	London Boroughs and the Common Council
	Entertainment licensing	G.L.C.	London Boroughs and the Common Council
	Recreation and Sport—Lea and Thames Valleys	G.L.C.	London Boroughs (No change *re* Lea Valley Park Authority)
6	Theatres (London)	G.L.C.	London Boroughs and the Common Council
	Cinemas (London)	G.L.C.	London Boroughs
	Greyhound Racing	G.L.C.	London Boroughs
	Athletic and Sporting Tracks	G.L.C.	London Boroughs and the Common Council
	Safety of Sports Grounds	G.L.C. and Met. Counties	London Boroughs and Met. districts
7	Pleasure boats	G.L.C.	London Boroughs
	School swimming pools (London)	I.L.E.A.	The new I.L.E.A.

ix

NOTE ON CHANGES

Chapter No.	Service	Existing	Future
8	Smallholders	G.L.C. and Met. counties	Lapses as a Met. authority function and properties pass to adjacent shire counties
	Wildlife	G.L.C. and Met. counties	Met. districts and London Boroughs
	National Parks participation	G.L.C. and Met. counties	Met. districts and London Boroughs
	Footpaths	G.L.C. and Met. counties	Met. districts and London Boroughs
9	Arts grants	G.L.C. and Met. counties	Met. districts and London Boroughs
	The South Bank complex	G.L.C.	The Arts Council

Foreword

This book will fulfill a long-held need in local government. There was a time when local authority leisure facilities consisted simply of public walks and pleasure grounds and public libraries. The law was simply and shortly expressed in several statutes. Those concerned with practice and administration could, by reference to a few sections and a small body of case law, discover what were the powers and duties of public authorities and what were the rights of the public.

Those days are passed. Public authorities are no longer limited in their activities: they now provide a wide range of sports and leisure services and many of these services are commercial in nature. It is a well established principle that as a service expands, so the law relating to that service expands, but to a more than proportionate degree. Similarly, as a service becomes more complex, the law relating to that service becomes more complex, but to a greater degree.

This principle applies to the law of public leisure services. The manager and administrators of a modern sports and leisure complex are now involved in many areas of law—commercial, employment, liquor and other licensing, health and safety, public liability, public entertainment, sex discrimination, sale of goods, as well as the torts of nuisance, negligence and trespass, and the law of parks and libraries.

The author of this work, by diligence and much research, has provided an exposition of law on all these and many other related topics, and in so doing will provide much needed guidance and advice to all concerned with sport and leisure.

460 The Royal Exchange,   Charles Cross
Manchester.
September 1985.

Preface

Leisure is the name of the golden thread which leads into the wonder world where we please ourselves. Sport is for our active moments, entertainment for our passive hours. Recreation overlaps both and also embraces the arts in all their forms, together with adult education and culture.

Leisure, sport, recreation and entertainment: language places limits on all these words. If "walking" can be a stroll by the river, a trek over the Downs or a sustained attack on the Pennine Way, so can "leisure" satisfy the multi-gym enthusiast or the lady who wants only a deck-chair on the promenade. "Leisure provision," said a recent report, "is concerned with much more than the facilities or opportunities for particular interests: its aim is the development of people's interests, their personal fulfilment and quality of life."* In recent years, this wave of interest has led to the description of a group of previously separate activities as the leisure services.

A dynamic law keeps pace with the needs of society, checking the excesses, supporting the enthusiasm, relieving the casualties. In our kind of society, with metropolis and village green, Milton Keynes and Keswick, city suburb and Shropshire hamlet, the public leisure service providers are essential. Picking out a tune on the lute in the Elizabethan barber's shop, whilst waiting one's turn, was very fine, but it has given way to the disco music in the unisex salon. So the law has sought to adapt to the needs of our mass leisure services. The common law from the courts and statute law from Parliament have been reshaped in recent years, to maintain a legal framework for these services.

This book is a response to that situation. It attempts to gather up the numerous branches of law that support the public leisure services and moves from libraries and museums, parks and sport to the National Parks, the National Trust and the Forestry Commission, the Arts and Sports Councils and eventually to beaches, boating, allotments and light railways. The selection has doubtless involved omissions which cannot please all. Likewise some items may seem to be given undue attention. The pattern followed is to consider first the underpinning of the leisure services by the general law, then to recognise the primary role of local authorities and then to outline thirty to forty other special parts of the law, which fall within the sweep of the public leisure services. Comments on the selection and balance of these subjects in this new book will be welcomed.

Not the least of the pleasures of research has been the fuller acquaintance with Commonwealth cases, especially about negligence, nuisance and copyright. They provide some stimulating judicial work on the ever-changing frontier between law and the leisure services of society.

* *Leisure Provision and People's Needs* (H.M.S.O., 1981), para. 3.2.

Preface

Lastly, it is pleasant to record my sincere thanks to busy colleagues from the local government field and others, who have given valuable time to scan those parts of this book which touched on their special areas of interest. Their range is a mark of the width of the subject and I am indebted to them all for their kindness.

They are Mr. R. S. Latham, with the National Trust; Miss M. A. T. Leckie and colleagues with the Forestry Commission in Edinburgh and her technical colleagues at the Research Station, Wrecclesham; Mr. J. A. Fox and Dr. A. L. Duggan of the Museums Association; Mr. D. Williamson, City Librarian, Leeds; Mr. J. A. Wilkinson, City Amenities and Recreation Officer, Cambridge; Mr. P. Crane, Director of Amenities, Bromley and his Chief Executive, Mr. N. T. Palk; Mr. R. A. Cameron of the Department of Sports and Recreation, Gateshead; Mr. W. N. G. Gilmore, Chief of the Department of Recreation, Culture and Health, South Yorkshire; Mr. A. Mahon of Kirklees and Mr. D. Wardman, Borough Treasurer, Blackpool from the besieged world of local government finance; and from the legal profession, in varied settings, Mr. L. A. Tawn at Wakefield; Mr. N. Gundhill at Pontefract; Mr. A. R. Sykes and Mr. J. S. Balsham at Bradford; Mr. M. D. Foster and Mr. R. M. Scott at Halifax; Mr. D. W. Riddle at Camden; Ms. A. E. Lomnika at University College London, and Mr. G. Tideswell of Manchester, for permission to use some earlier research.

I am also grateful for some kind comments from the Ministry of Transport, which endeavoured to keep me on the right gauge for light railways; Professor C. Drake of Leeds University for support and Mr. J. M. Porter, of their law library, for sustaining my research and enthusiasm. The publishers have encouraged and assisted at all times. I am also highly indebted to Mr. Charles Cross, of Counsel, for the initial inspiration to embark on the work and for contributing the Foreword.

The responsibility for errors remains with the author.

In conclusion, the concept of this book was to bring together those parts of our law which form the framework in which the public leisure services function. It is hoped that students in those services may find that it pinpoints the law they seek, that practitioners outside the town halls will find it useful as a chart to the law they meet and that perhaps a little of the experience garnered from the author's time in the public service will assist those for whom the law must needs be labour, rather than leisure.

The law is stated as at August 1985.

Halifax,
West Yorkshire.
September, 1985.

Michael Scott

Contents

	Page
Note on Local Government Act 1985	vii
Foreword	xi
Preface	xiii
Table of Cases	xxvii
Table of Statutes	xli

Chapter 1. General Legal Principles for the Providers of Leisure Services

Introduction	1
THE LEISURE SERVICES AUTHORITY AS PROPERTY OWNER	2
A. Duty to Visitors.	2
1. The Common Duty of Care	2
2. The Common Duty of Care in Relation to Special Classes	4
(1) Children	4
(2) Trespassers	5
(3) Persons Enjoying Easements over Land	6
(4) People Exercising Their Calling	6
(5) Warning Notices under the Unfair Contract Terms Act 1977	6
3. Other Aspects of the Common Duty of Care	7
(1) The Common Law Liability for Negligence	7
(2) The Common Duty of Care in Relation to the Intervention of the Independent Contractor	7
(3) The Common Duty of Care in Relation to the Limitation Acts	7
B. The Duty to Neighbours.	9
1. Nuisance	9
(1) Private Nuisance	9
(2) Public and Statutory Nuisances	9
2. The Rule in *Rylands* v. *Fletcher*	13
C. The Duty to Tenants and Tied Cottages.	13
Introduction	13
1. Residential Lettings	14
2. Agricultural Tenancies	16

3. Business Tenancies	18
(1) Businesses Affected	18
(2) Excluded Tenants	20
(3) The Protection of the Act	20
(4) Assignments	21
(5) New Tenancies	21
(6) Conclusion	21
D. Listed Buildings and Ancient Monuments.	21
1. Listed Buildings	22
2. National Heritage Act 1980	24

THE LEISURE SERVICES AUTHORITY AS EMPLOYER AND MANAGER

Introduction	25
A. The Contract of Employment.	26
B. Conditions of Work.	32
1. The Health and Safety at Work, etc., Act 1974	32
2. Discrimination	33
(1) Equal Pay for Men and Women	33
(2) The Sex Discrimination Act 1975	34
(3) Specific Exclusions by the Nature of the Job	35
(4) Unlawful Acts of Sex Discrimination	36
(5) General Unlawful Practices	37
3. Disabled Persons	39
4. Race Relations Act 1976	40
(1) The Actions of 1975 and 1976—Common Features	40
(2) Distinctive Features of the Act of 1976	41
5. Bribery and Corruption; Theft	42
(1) Bribery and Corruption	42
(2) Theft	43
C. Negligence.	44
1. The Duty	45
2. The Breach	46
3. Special Situations	46
(1) Negligent Statements and Economic Loss	47
(2) Liability of Professional Advisors	47
(3) Defective Premises	48
4. Consequences of the Breach	48
(1) Remoteness	48
(2) Nervous Shock	49
(3) Taking the Plaintiff as he is	50
5. The Burden of Proof	50
D. Defences.	50
1. Contributory Negligence	51
2. Volenti Non Fit Injuria	51

Contents

3. Statutory Powers	52
4. The Limitation Acts	53

THE LEISURE SERVICES AUTHORITY AS BUSINESS ORGANISER — 54

A. Contract. — 54
  1. Formation — 55
  2. Deviations — 56
     (1) Mistake — 56
     (2) Misrepresentation — 57
     (3) Duress — 58
  3. Void and Illegal Contracts — 58
  4. Capacity to Contract — 60
     (1) Minors — 60
     (2) Corporations — 60
     (3) Commercial Companies — 60
  5. Limits of the Lawful Contract — 61
     (1) Privy of Contract — 61
     (2) Assignments — 61
     (3) Contracts of a Personal Nature — 61
  6. Performance — 61
     (1) Substantial Performance — 61
     (2) Frustration — 62
  7. Breach — 62

B. The Unfair Contracts Terms Act 1977. — 63

C. Sale of Goods. — 64
  1. The Contract; Definitions and Formation — 64
  2. Effect of the Contract — 65
  3. Performance — 66
  4. Rights of the Unpaid Seller — 67
  5. Breach of Contract — 67

D. Consumer Protection. — 68
  1. The Fair Trading Act 1973 — 68
     (1) The Director General and the Consumer Protection Advisory Committee — 68
     (2) Current Activities — 69
  2. The Consumer Safety Act 1978 — 70
  3. Supply of Goods and Services Act 1982 — 71
     (1) The Framework of the Act — 71
     (2) Significant Detail — 72

E. Trade Descriptions. — 73

Chapter 2. Special Legal Principles — 78

Introduction — 78
A. Creatures of Statute. — 78
  1. Powers and Duties — 78

    2. Constraints   80
       (1) Breach of Statutory Duty   80
       (2) Judicial Review   80
       (3) Ministerial Control   82
       (4) The Local Government Commissioners   82
    3. *Ultra Vires*   84
       (1) When does an *Ultra Vires* Situation Arise?   84
       (2) Abuse of the Statutory Powers   86
       (3) What are the Consequences?   86
    4. Statutory Interpretation   87

B. Local Law Makers.   89
    1. Adoptive Acts   89
    2. Provisional Orders   89
    3. By-laws   90
    4. Local Acts   90

C. Land Transactions.   91
    1. Acquisition   91
    2. Appropriation   93
    3. Disposal   94

D. Open Space.   97
    1. Introduction   97
    2. The Open Spaces Act 1906   98
       (1) Acquisition   98
       (2) Management of Open Space   99
    3. Other Acts   100
       (1) Open Space on Housing Estates   100
       (2) Open Space Land of Local Education Authorities   100
       (3) Open Space under the Town and Country Planning Acts   101

E. Commons.   102
    1. Introduction   102
    2. Historical   102
    3. Public Rights Over Commons   107
    4. Caravan Sites and Commons   109

Chapter 3. Libraries and Museums   111

Introduction   111
A. Libraries.   112
  1. Library Provision and Management   112
     (1) The Public Libraries and Museums Act 1964   112
     (2) Legal Aspects of the Library Service   114
  2. Public Lending Right   115
     (1) A Legal Right   115
     (2) The Central Fund   115
     (3) Registration   116
     (4) The Library Authority's Role   116

3. Copyright	117
(1) Introduction	117
(2) The *Ames* Case	117
(3) The Earlier Cases	118
(4) Libraries: The Legal Copying Categories	120
(5) The Framework of the Copyright Act 1956	121
(6) EEC and Foreign Aspects	125
4. Performers Protection Acts 1958–1972	127
5. Archives	128
6. Art Galleries	129
(1) Provision	129
(2) Finance	129
(3) Art Gallery Liaison	129
(4) Works of Art—Customs, Excise and Tax	131
B. Museums.	132
Introduction	132
1. The Legal Framework for the Public Museum Service	133
(1) The Local Authority Service	133
(2) Finance	133
(3) Specimens Fund	134
(4) By-laws	134
(5) Community Activities	134
(6) External Grants	134
(7) Other Public Museums	135
2. Fieldwork	136
(1) Treasure Trove	136
(2) Wrecks and Whales	138
(3) Metal Detectors	140
(4) Wildlife Protection	142
3. Collections	143
(1) Contract	144
(2) Duties of a Bailee	144
(3) The Professional Duty	145
4. Ancient Monuments and Archaeological Areas	147
(1) Ancient Monuments	147
(2) Areas of Archaeological Importance	149

Chapter 4. Parks and Recreation Grounds 150

Introduction	150
A. The Creation, Management and Disposal of Public Parks.	151
1. Acquisition	151
2. Management	152
(1) Sport	152
(2) Seats, Games, Apparatus, Pavilions, Reading Rooms and Refreshment Rooms	153
(3) Legal Claims for Negligence and Nuisance	154

(4) Walls and Fences	156
(5) Metal Detectors	158
(6) Trepass	158
(7) Closure of Parks	158
(8) Car Parks	159
(9) Local Acts or Deeds of Transfer	160
(10) Park Wardens	161
3. Disposal or Changed Use of Parks	161
(1) Restrictive Covenants	162
(2) Local Acts	162
(3) Appropriation or Disposal	163
B. Parks and Rates.	164
1. The Statutes	164
2. The Cases	165
(1) The Extended Definition	165
(2) "Free and Unrestricted Use"	165
(3) "Dedicated in Perpetuity"	167
3. Conclusion	168
C. By-Laws.	168
1. The Statutes	169
2. The Cases	170
(1) Certainty	171
(2) Reasonableness	171
(3) Consistency with other Laws	172
(4) *Intra Vires*	173
3. The Practice	174
D. Miscellaneous Amenities.	175
1. Street Playgrounds	175
2. Diseases	175
(1) Dutch Elm Disease	175
(2) Fire Blight Disease	177
3. Wild Animals in Parks	177
4. Insurance and Bad Weather	178

Chapter 5. Special Cases — 180

A. The National Trust.	180
1. Introduction	180
2. Purposes	180
3. Powers	181
(1) General	181
(2) Commons	181
(3) Charges	182
(4) Local Authorities	182
(5) By-Laws	182

Contents

4. Special Properties		183
5. General Properties		183
6. Restrictive Covenants		185
7. Constitution		185
B. The Forestry Commission.		186
1. The Countryside Act 1968		186
2. By-Laws		186
3. Tree Planting for Amenity		187
4. General and Historical		188
5. Conclusion		188
C. London and the Public Leisure Services.		189
1. Historic Buildings, Statues and Monuments		190
2. Open Spaces and Recreation		191
(1) The Greater London Council (or relevant Successor Authority) and the London Borough Councils		191
(2) The Common Council of the City of London		194
3. Land		196
4. Commons		196
5. Squares		198
6. Libraries and Museums		199
7. The Royal Parks		199
8. Entertainment and Licensing		200
9. Recreation and Sport		200
(1) The Thames Valley		200
(2) The Lee Valley		201
10. The Countryside		201

Chapter 6. Public Entertainment   202

A. Theatres.	202
1. Licensing of Premises	202
2. The Nature of the Performance	203
3. Professional Contracts	205
(1) Restraint	205
(2) Non-Performance	205
(3) Management Discretion	207
4. The Premises	207
(1) Safety under the Health and Safety at Work Act 1974	207
(2) Safety under the Public Health Acts	208
(3) Safety at Common Law	208
(4) Coats of Arms	209
5. Young Persons Taking Part in Performance	209
6. Animals	210
7. Refreshments	211
8. Sunday Observance	211

Contents

B. Cinemas.	211
1. Licensing of the Premises	212
2. Enforcement	214
3. Exempted Exhibitions	214
4. The Safety of the Premises	215
5. The Safety of Children and Young Persons	215
6. Reputation of Film Renting and Exhibition	216
C. Local Authorities and Public Entertainment.	216
1. The Local Government Act 1972	217
2. Removal of Limitations	218
3. Private Covenants	218
4. Allied Provisions	219
5. Conclusion	220
D. Public Halls.	220
1. Entertainment Licences	221
(1) Scope of the Licence	221
(2) Pop Festivals	221
(3) The General Entertainment Licence	222
(4) Relation to Other Statutes	223
(5) Boxing and Wrestling	223
2. Hypnotism	223
3. Billards Licensing	224
4. Boxing and Wrestling	225
5. Breach of Copyright	225
6. Video Recordings Act 1984	226
E. Outdoor Entertainment.	226
1. Horseracing	226
(1) The Jockey Club	226
(2) The Horserace Betting Levy Board	227
(3) The Horserace Totalizator Board	227
(4) The Bookmakers Committee	227
2. Greyhound Racing	228
3. Athletic and Sporting Tracks	229
4. Safety of Sports Grounds	230
5. Pleasure Fairs	231
6. Local Authorities	231
7. Local Government (Miscellaneous Provisions) Act 1976	232
8. Ancient Custom	232
9. Animals	232
F. Sunday Observance, Licensing and Catering.	233
1. Sunday Observance	233
2. The Public Leisure Services and the Sale of Intoxicating Liquor	234
(1) Classes of Premises and Licences	235
(2) Obtaining a Licence	237

(3) Special Hours and Extensions	237
(4) Inspections and Alterations	239
(5) Young Persons	239
(6) Offences	240
3. Catering	241
G. Gambling.	241
1. Introduction	241
2. General Principles	242
3. Betting	243
(1) Betting Office	243
(2) Sporting Events	243
(3) General	244
4. Gaming	244
(1) Members Clubs	244
(2) Bingo Clubs	245
(3) Gaming with Machines	246
5. Lotteries	247
6. Prize Competitions	248
7. Amusements with Prizes and Gaming Machines	249
8. Competition for Prizes	250
H. Sex Establishments.	250
1. Statutory Code	250
2. Relation to Existing Law	252

Chapter 7. Sport 254

A. Managing Swimming Pools.	254
1. Provision	254
2. By-laws	255
3. Areas of Management Risk	256
(1) The Water	256
(2) Tickets	256
(3) The Surround	257
(4) The Pool	257
(5) The Diving Boards	257
(6) Children	258
(7) The Supervisors	258
(8) The Spectators	258
(9) Saunas	259
(10) Sales	259
(11) Loans of Swimming Equipment	259
(12) Lockers	260
(13) Car Parks	260
(14) Private Swimming Instructors	260
4. Finance	260
(1) Admission Charges	261
(2) Sales	261

B. Managing Sports Centres.	262
1. Provision	262
2. Running the Sports Centre	263
3. Cameo of a Sports Centre	264
C. Participating Sports.	264
1. The Parties	265
(1) The Players and the Organisers	265
(2) The Spectators	267
2. The Place of the Maxim: *Volenti Non Fit Injuria*	269
3. The Premises	270
4. Nuisance	271
5. Comparative Commonwealth Cases	272
6. The Safety of Sports Grounds Act 1975	275
7. Private Sports Clubs	275
D. Riding.	276
E. Water Recreation.	277
1. Boats	277
(1) Provision	277
(2) Licensing of Pleasure Boats and Boatmen	278
(3) By-laws	279
(4) Application	280
2. Fishing	280
(1) The Salmon and Freshwater Fisheries Act 1975	281
(2) Land Law and Fishing	283
3. Canals	284
4. Inland Waters	285
(1) National and Country Parks	285
(2) Other Inland Waters	287
(3) The Common Law and Water Rights	288
5. The Seaside	289
(1) Bathing	289
(2) The Foreshore	289
(3) Beach Activities	292

Chapter 8. Open Air Activity   293

Introduction	293
A. Allotments.	293
1. Historical	293
2. The Statutes	294
3. Terms of Letting	295
4. Offences	295
5. Termination	296
6. Compensation	296
7. Administration	297
8. The Present Day	297

B. Wildlife Preservation.	298
1. Protection of Birds	298
2. Protection of Animals	299
3. Protection of Plants	300
4. New Species	300
5. General	300
C. Light Railways.	301
D. National Parks and Access to the Countryside.	302
1. The Countryside Commission	303
2. National Parks	305
(1) Designation	305
(2) Duties in a Park	305
(3) Long Distance Routes	306
(4) Local Planning Authorities	306
(5) Powers of the Minister	307
(6) Administration of a National Park	307
3. Areas of Outstanding Natural Beauty	308
4. Country Parks	308
5. Access Arrangements and Local Authorities	309
(1) Reviews	310
(2) Access Orders and Agreements	310
(3) Land for Access	311
(4) Maps	313
6. Other General Local Authority Powers in relation to the Countryside	314
E. Footpaths.	315
1. Nature	316
2. Origins	316
3. Diversion and Closure	317
4. Maintenance and Obstruction	318
5. Danger from Bulls	319
F. Picnic Sites.	319
G. Litter.	320
H. Caravans.	320
1. Site Licensing	320
2. Exemptions	322
3. General	323

Chapter 9. Availability of Finance   324

Introduction	324
A. Local Government Finance.	324
B. Capital Expenditure Controls.	325

Contents

C. Government Grants.	327
1. Domestic Rate Relief Grant	328
2. The Block Grant	328
3. Rate Capping	331
(1) Selective Limitation of Rates and Precepts	331
(2) General Limitations	332
(3) Prescribed Consultations	333
D. Specific Grants.	333
1. Caravan Sites for Gypsies	333
2. National Parks	333
3. Local Lotteries	334
4. Derelict Land and National Parks	334
5. Countryside	334
6. Fees and Charges	335
E. Non-Local Authority Finance.	335
1. The Arts Council	335
(1) Aims and Objects	335
(2) Organisation	335
(3) Grant Aided Leisure Services	336
2. The Sports Council	336
(1) Aims	336
(2) Grants	337
(3) Organisation	337
(4) Conclusion	337
3. The Tourist Board	338
(1) The Development of Tourism Act 1969	338
(2) Hotel Development	339
(3) Local Authorities	339
4. Private Trust Funds	340
Index	341

Table of Cases

References throughout are to paragraph numbers.

Adamson v. Jarvis (1827) 4 Bing. 66; 29 R.R. 503, 12 Moore C.P. 241; 5 L.J.O.S.C.P. 68; 130 E.R. 693 .... 1.063
Addiscombe Garden Estates Ltd. v. Crabbe [1958] 1 Q.B. 513; [1957] 3 W.L.R. 980; (1957) 101 S.J. 959; [1957] 3 All E.R. 563 (C.A.); *affirming* [1957] 2 Q.B. 615 .... 1.046
Adelaide Corporation v. Australasian Performing Rights Society Ltd. [1928] 40 C.L.R. 481; Argus L.R. 127 .... 3.18
Amandarajah v. Lord Chancellor's Department (1984) 1 I.R.L.R. 131 .... 1.071
Anns v. Merton London Borough [1978] A.C. 728; [1977] 2 W.L.R. 1024; (1977) 121 S.J. 377; (1977) 75 L.G.R. 555; *sub nom.* Anns v. London Borough of Merton [1977] 2 All E.R. 492, H.L. 1.108, 1.130
Apple Corps Ltd. v. Lingasong Ltd. (1977) 121 S.J. 692; [1977] F.S.R. 345 .... 3.37
Appleton v. Cunard Steamship Company Ltd. [1969] 1 Lloyd's Rep. 150 .... 1.021
Application des Gaz S.A. v. Falks Veritas Ltd. [1974] Ch. 381; [1974] 3 W.L.R. 235; (1974) 118 S.J. 363; [1974] 3 All E.R. 51; [1974] 2 C.M.L.R. 75; [1974] F.S.R. 355; [1974] 2 Lloyd's Rep. 493; [1975] R.P.C. 421 (C.A.) 3.35
Arlidge v. Islington Corporation [1909] 2 K.B. 127; 78 L.J.K.B. 553; (1909) 93 J.P. 301; (1909) 7 L.G.R. 649; (1909) 100 L.T. 903; (1909) 25 T.L.R. 470 .... 4.49
Armorie v. Delamirie (1722) 1 Stra. 505; 93 E.R. 664 .... 3.53
Ashdown v. Samuel Williams and Sons Ltd. [1957] 1 Q.B. 409; [1956] 3 W.L.R. 1104; (1957) 100 S.J. 945; [1957] 1 All E.R. 35 (C.A.); *varying* [1956] 2 Q.B. 580 .... 1.011
Asher v. Seaford Court Estates [1950] A.C. 508; 66 T.L.R. (Pt. 1) 945; [1950] 1 All E.R. 1018; *sub nom.* Seaford Court Estates v. Asher, 94 S.J. 284 (H.L.); *affirming sub nom.* Seaford Court Estates v. Asher [1949] 2 K.B. 481 (C.A.) 2.24
Associated Provincial Picture Houses Ltd. v. Wednesbury Corporation [1948] 1 K.B. 223; [1948] L.J.R. 190; (1948) 177 L.T. 641; (1948) 63 T.L.R. 623; (1948) 112 J.P. 55; (1948) 92 S.J. 26; [1947] 2 All E.R. 680; (1947) 45 L.G.R. 635 (C.A.); *affirming* [1947] L.J.R. 678 .... 6.21, 7.19
Att.-Gen. v. Calderdale Borough Council, *ex p.* Sutcliffe (1982), unreported, L.G.C. November 11, 1982 (C.A.) 1.053
—— v. De Winton [1906] 2 Ch. 106; [1906] 75 L.J.Ch. 612; (1906) 70 J.P. 368; (1906) 54 W.R. 499; (1906) 22 T.L.R. 446; 4 L.G.R. 549 .... 2.22
—— v. Foster [1963] 2 Q.B. 477; [1963] 2 W.L.R. 658; 107 S.J. 154; [1963] 1 All E.R. 767 (C.A.), Petition for leave to appeal to H.L. dismissed *sub nom.* Mulholland v. Att.-Gen.; Foster v. Att.-Gen., *The Times*, March 7, 1963, *The Guardian*, March 7, 1963 (H.L.) 3.67
—— v. Hastings Corporation (1950) 94 S.J. 225 (C.A.) 1.026
—— v. Manchester Corporation [1931] 1 Ch. 254; 100 L.J.Ch. 33; 144 L.T. 112 .... 4.30, 4.40
—— v. Nissan [1970] A.C. 179; [1969] 2 W.L.R. 926; [1969] 1 All E.R. 629, *sub nom.* Nissan v. Att.-Gen. 113 S.J. 207 (H.L.); *affirming sub nom.* Nissan v. Att.- Gen. [1968] 1 Q.B. 286 .... 1.128
—— v. Overton (G. E.) (Farms) Ltd. [1982] Ch. 277; [1982] 2 W.L.R. 397; (1982) 1 All E.R. 524; (1981) S.J. 828 (C.A.) 3.51, 3.52, 3.61
—— v. P.Y.A. Quarries Ltd. [1957] 2 Q.B. 169; [1957] 2 W.L.R. 770; (1957) 101 S.J. 338; [1957] 1 All E.R. 894; (1957) 55 L.G.R. 208 .... 1.033
—— v. Southampton Corporation (1970) 21 P. & C.R. 281; (1970) 68 L.G.R. 288 .... 4.22
—— v. The Times Newspapers Ltd. [1974] A.C. 273; [1973] 3 W.L.R. 298; 117 S.J. 617; [1973] 3 All E.R. 54, H.L.; *reversing* [1973] 1 Q.B. 710; *reversing* [1972] 3 W.L.R. 855 .... 3.68
—— v. Todmorden B.C. (1937) 4 All E.R. 588 .... 4.16
—— v. Trustees of the British Museum [1903] 2 Ch. 598; 72 L.J.Ch. 743; 88 L.T. 858; 51 W.R. 582; 19 T.L.R. 555 .... 3.51

TABLE OF CASES

Att.-Gen. v. Westminster City Council [1924] 2 Ch. 416; (1924) 68 S.J. 736; [1924] 88 J.P. 145; (1924) L.G.R. 506; (1924) 131 L.T. 802; (1924) 40 T.L.R. 711 .... 3.06
Avais v. Hartford Shankhouse & District Workingmen's Social Club and Institute [1969] 2 A.C. 1; [1969] 2 W.L.R. 108; 133 J.P. 133; 113 S.J. 33; [1969] 1 All E.R. 130; 67 L.G.R. 217 (H.L.); *reversing* [1968] 1 W.L.R. 10; *sub nom.* Avias v. Hartford Shankhouse & District Workingmen's Club and Institute (1967) 111 S.J. 808 .... 6.86

Balfour v. Balfour [1919] 2 K.B. 571; [1919] 88 L.J.K.B. 1054; 63 S.J. 661 (1919) 121 L.T. 346; 35 T.L.R. 609 (C.A.) 1.135
Bartlett v. Tottenham [1932] 1 Ch. 114; [1932] 101 L.J.Ch. 160; (1932) 145 L.T. 686 .... 1.025
Baxendale v. Instow Parish Council [1982] Ch. 14; [1981] 2 W.L.R. 1055; (1981) 125 S.J. 289; [1981] 2 All E.R. 620 .... 2.77, 7.62
Beckett v. Cohen [1972] 1 W.L.R. 1593; (1972) 116 S.J. 882; (1972) 137 J.P. 116; [1973] 1 All E.R. 120 .... 1.182
Beckett Ltd. v. Lyons [1967] Ch. 449; [1967] 2 W.L.R. 421; 110 S.J. 925; [1967] 1 All E.R. 833; (1967) 65 L.G.R. 73; [1966] C.L.Y. 10932 (C.A.) 7.63
Beloff v. Pressdram Ltd. [1973] 1 All E.R. 241; [1973] F.S.R. 33; *sub nom.* Beloff (Nora) v. Pressdram [1973] R.P.C. 765 .... 3.30
Bents Brewery Co. Ltd. v. Hogan [1945] 2 All E.R. 570 .... 1.062
Beswick v. Beswick [1968] A.C. 58; [1967] 3 W.L.R. 932; 111 S.J. 540; [1967] 2 All E.R. 1197, (H.L.); *affirming* [1966] Ch. 538; *reversing* [1965] 3 All E.R. 858 .... 2.24
Bilston Corporation v. Wolverhampton Corporation [1942] 1 Ch. 391; 111 L.J.Ch. 268; [1942] 2 All E.R. 447; 167 L.T. 61; 106 J.P. 181; 40 L.G.R. 167 .... 2.30
Blake v. Hendon Corporation [1962] 1 Q.B. 283; [1961] 3 W.L.R. 951; (1961) 125 J.P. 620; 105 S.J. 666; [1961] 3 All E.R. 601; 59 L.G.R. 515; [1961] R.V.R. 552 (C.A.); *reversing* L.V.C./2265/1958 [1960] J.P.L. 429 .... 2.05
—— v. —— (No. 2) (1965) 109 S.J. 213; 63 L.G.R. 198; [1965] R.V.R. 160; 11 R.R.C. 119; [1965] R.A. 67 (C.A.); *reversing* LVC/173/1963 [1964] R.V.R. 149 .... 4.39
Blount v. Layard [1891] 2 Ch. 681; 4 T.L.R. 512 (C.A.); (1889) 5 T.L.R. 371 .... 7.58
Blyth v. Birmingham Waterworks Co. [1856] 11 Ex. 781; 25 L.J.Ex. 212; 26 L.T.O.S. 261; 20 J.P. 247; 2 Jur.N.S. 333; 4 W.R. 294; 156 E.R. 1047 .... 1.104
Bognuda v. Upton and Shearer (1972) N.Z.L.R. 741 (N.Z.L.A.) 1.025
Bolam v. Friern Hospital Management Committee [1957] 1 W.L.R. 582; 101 S.J. 357; [1957] 2 All E.R. 118 .... 3.76
Bolton v. Stone [1951] A.C. 850; [1951] 1 T.L.R. 977; [1951] 1 All E.R. 1078; 50 L.G.R. 32; *sub nom.* Stone v. Bolton, 95 S.J. 333 (H.L.); *reversing sub nom.* Stone v. Bolton [1950] 1 K.B. 201; *restoring* [1949] 1 All E.R. 237 .... 1.027, 1.100, 1.104
Bourgoin S.A. v. Ministry of Agriculture, Fisheries and Food, *The Times*, October 4, 1984 .... 7.36
Bourhill v. Young [1943] A.C. 92; 111 L.J.P.C. 97; 167 L.T. 261; [1942] 2 All E.R. 396; *sub nom.* Bourhill v. Young 86 S.J. 349 (H.L.) 1.114
Bowes Museum Park Trustees v. Cutts (V. O.) (1950) 43 R. & I.T. 881 .... 4.34
Bridge v. Deacons [1984] A.C. 705; [1984] 2 W.L.R. 837; (1984) 128 S.J. 263; [1984] 2 All E.R. 19; (1984) 81 L.S.Gaz. 1291; (1984) 134 New L.J. 723 (P.C.) 1.145
Brighton Corporation v. Packham [1908] 24 T.L.R. 603; (1908) 72 J.P. 318; 6 L.G.R. 702 .... 7.65
Brinckman v. Matley [1904] 2 Ch. 313; [1904–07] 73 L.J.Ch. 642; 48 S.J. 639; All E.R. 20; 91 L.T. 429; 68 J.P. 534; 20 T.L.R. 671; 2 L.G.R. 1057 (C.A.) 7.60
British Home Stores Ltd. v. Burchell [1978] 1 R.L.R. 379; (1980) I.C.R. 303 .... 1.099
British Library v. Palyza (1984) 128 S.J. 399; [1984] I.C.R. 504; [1984] I.R.L.R. 306, E.A.T. 1.089
British Railways Board v. Herrington [1972] A.C. 877; [1972] 2 W.L.R. 537; (1972) 116 S.J. 178; [1972] 1 All E.R. 749 (H.L.); *affirming sub nom.* Herrington v. British Railways Board [1971] 2 Q.B. 107; *affirming* (1970) 214 E.G. 561 .... 1.013, 1.016, 1.017
—— v. Pickin [1974] A.C. 765; [1974] 2 W.L.R. 208; 118 S.J. 134; [1974] 1 All E.R. 609 (H.L.); *affirming sub nom.* Pickin v. British Railways Board [1973] 1 Q.B. 219 .... 2.30

Table of Cases

Bromley L.B.C. *v.* Greater London Council [1983] 1 A.C. 768; [1982] 2 W.L.R. 92; (1982) 126 S.J. 16 (H.L.); *affirming* [1983] 1 A.C. 768 (C.A.) 2.02, 2.23
Brown *v.* Pelosi and St. Johnstone (1983) (unreported) 7.29
British Road Services Ltd. *v.* Crutchley (Arthur) Ltd. [1968] 1 All E.R. 811; *sub nom.* British Road Services *v.* Crutchley (Arthur V.) & Co. Factory Guards (Third Party) [1968] 1 Lloyd's Rep. 271 (C.A.) 3.73
Brutus *v.* Cozens [1973] A.C. 854; [1972] 3 W.L.R. 521; [1972] 2 All E.R. 1297; 56 Cr.App.R. 799; [1973] Crim.L.R. 56; *sub nom.* Cozens *v.* Brutus, 116 S.J. 647 (H.L.); *reversing* Cozens *v.* Brutus [1972] 1 W.L.R. 484 .... 7.34
Bunker *v.* Brand (Charles) and Son Ltd. [1969] 2 Q.B. 480; [1969] 2 W.L.R. 1392; 113 S.J. 487; [1969] 2 All E.R. 59; 6 K.I.R. 204 .... 1.006
Burnell *v.* Downham Market Urban District Council [1952] 2 Q.B. 55; 116 J.P. 168; 96 S.J. 165; [1952] 1 All E.R. 601; 45 R. & I.T. 166; 50 L.G.R. 286 (C.A.) 4.40
Burnley Borough Council *v.* England (1979) 77 L.G.R. 227 .... 4.47, 4.56
Butler Machine Tool Co. Ltd. *v.* Ex-Cell-O Corporation Ltd. [1979] 1 W.L.R. 401; (1977) 121 S.J. 406; [1979] 1 All E.R. 965 (C.A.) 1.134
Buttle *v.* Sanders [1950] W.N. 255; 66 T.L.R. (Pt. 1) 1026; 94 S.J. 369; [1950] 2 All E.R. 193 .... 4.31

Calder & Hebble Navigation *v.* Pilling (1845) 14 M. & W. 76; 3 Ry. & Can.Cas. 735; 14 L.J.Ex. 223; 5 L.T.O.S. 57; 10 J.P. 24; 9 Jur. 377; 53 E.R. 396 .... 4.51
Caldwell *v.* Sumpters (a firm) [1972] Ch. 478; [1972] 2 W.L.R. 412; (1971) 116 S.J. 15; [1972] 1 All E.R. 567 (C.A.); *reversing* [1971] 3 W.L.R. 748 .... 4.31
Callaghan *v.* Killarney Race Co. Ltd. [1958] I.R. 366; 90 I.L.T. 134 .... 7.32
Carlisle and Silloth Golf Club *v.* Smith (1913) 3 K.B. 75 .... 7.38
Cawley *v.* Frost (1976) 64 Cr.App.R. 20; [1977] Crim.L.R. 169; (1977) 64 C.A.R. 20 ..... 7.34
C.B.S. Inc. *v.* Ames Records and Tapes Ltd. [1981] 2 W.L.R. 973; (1981) 125 S.J. 412; [1981] 2 All E.R. 812; [1981] R.P.C. 407 .... 3.15, 3.18, 3.19
Cehave N.V. *v.* Bremer Handelsgesellschaft m.b.H.; Handsa Nord, The [1976] Q.B. 44; [1975] 3 W.L.R. 447; 119 S.J. 678; [1975] 3 All E.R. 739; [1975] 2 Lloyd's Rep. 445 (C.A.); *reversing* [1974] 2 Lloyd's Rep. 216 .... 1.157
Chapman *v.* Freeman [1978] 1 W.L.R. 1298; (1978) 122 S.J. 332, 594; [1978] 3 All E.R. 878; 247 E.G. 295; (1978) 36 P. & C.R. 323, C.A. 1.041, 1.046
Cheryl Investments Ltd. *v.* Saldanha [1978] 1 W.L.R. 1329; (1978) 122 S.J. 777; [1979] 1 All E.R. 5; (1978) 37 P. & C.R. 349; (1978) 248 E.G. 591, C.A. 1.046
Christie *v.* Davey [1893] 1 Ch. 316; 62 L.J.Ch. 439; 3 R. 210 .... 1.030
Churchwardens and Overseers of Lambeth Parish *v.* London County Council [1897] A.C. 625; 66 L.J.Q.B. 806; 76 L.T. 795; 46 W.R. 79; 13 T.L.R. 527; *sub nom.* St. Mary, Lambeth (Churchwardens and Overseers) *v.* London County Council, 61 J.P. 580, H.L.; *affirming* S.C. *sub nom.* London County Council *v.* Lambeth Overseers [1896] 2 Q.B. 25 .... 4.09
Coles *v.* Odhams Press Ltd. [1936] 1 K.B. 416; [1935] 105 L.J.K.B. 208; 79 S.J. 860; All E.R. 598; 154 L.T. 218; 100 J.P. 85; 52 T.L.R. 119; 34 L.G.R. 34 .... 6.85
Complaint against Liverpool City Council, *Re* [1977] 1 W.L.R. 995; 121 S.J. 223; [1977] 2 All E.R. 650; (1977) L.G.R. 817; [1977] J.P.L. 657, D.C. 2.14
Cooper *v.* Shield [1971] 2 Q.B. 334; [1971] 2 W.L.R. 1385; 115 S.J. 365; [1971] 2 All E.R. 917, D.C. 7.34
Costello *v.* Dacorum District Council (1980) 81 L.G.R. 1 (C.A.) 2.38
Coupe *v.* Guyett [1973] 1 W.L.R. 699; 117 S.J. 415; [1973] 2 All E.R. 1058; 71 L.G.R. 355; [1973] R.T.R. 518; [1973] Crim.L.R. 386, D.C. 1.182
Crowhurst *v.* Amersham Burial Board (1878) 4 Ex.D. 5; 48 L.J.Q.B. 109; 39 L.T. 335; 27 W.R. 95 .... 1.034
Cumings *v.* Birkenhead Corporation [1972] Ch. 12; [1971] 2 W.L.R. 1458; 115 S.J. 365; [1971] 2 All E.R. 881; 69 L.G.R. 444 (C.A.), *affirming* [1970] 3 W.L.R. 871; *sub nom.* Cumings *v.* Birkenhead Corporation (1970) 114 S.J. 786. .... 2.17
Cumming *v.* Danson (1943) 112 L.J.K.B. 145; 87 S.J. 21; 2 All E.R. 653; 59 T.L.R. 70; *sub nom.* Cumming *v.* Dawson, 168 L.T. 35 (C.A.) 8.09
Cunliffe *v.* Goodman (1930) 2 K.B. 237; (1950) 94 S.J. 179; [1950] 1 All E.R. 720; 66 (Pt. 2) T.L.R. 109 (C.A.) 1.048

Table of Cases

Cutler v. United Dairies (London) Ltd. (1933) 2 K.B. 297; 102 L.J.K.B. 663; 149 L.T. 436 (C.A.) 1.126
—— v. Wandsworth Stadium Ltd. [1949] A.C. 398; [1949] L.J.R. 824; 65 T.L.R. 170; 93 S.J. 163; [1949] 1 All E.R. 544 (H.L.), *affirming* [1948] 1 K.B. 291; *reversing* [1946] K.B. 501 .... 2.07, 6.53

Daimar Investments Ltd. v. Jones (1962) 112 L.J. 424 (Cty. Ct.) 1.046
Dawson & Co. v. Bingley Urban District Council [1911] 2 K.B. 149; 80 L.J.K.B. 842; 55 S.J. 346; 104 L.T. 659; 75 J.P. 289; 27 T.L.R. 308; 9 L.G.R. 502 (C.A.) 1.128
De Morgan v. Metropolitan Board of Works (1880) 5 Q.B.D. 155; 49 L.J.M.C. 51; 42 L.T. 238; 44 J.P. 296; 28 W.R. 489 (D.C.) 5.36
Derry v. Peek (1889) 14 A.C. 337; 58 L.J.Ch. 864; 61 L.T. 265; 54 J.P. 148; 38 W.R. 33; 5 T.L.R. 625 (H.L.); *reversing, sub nom.* Peek v. Derry (1887), 37 Ch.D. 541 (C.A.) 1.140
Deutsche Gramophone Case 78/70 Grammophon GmbH v. Metro, etc., [1972] C.M.L.R. 205 .... 3.36
Dickens v. Lee (1843) 8 Jur. 183 .... 3.14
Discount Inter-Shopping Co. Ltd. v. Micromet Co. Ltd. [1984] Ch. 369; [1984] 2 W.L.R. 919; (1984) 128 S.J. 260; (1984) 81 L.S.Gaz. 592 .... 3.29
Dodd & Dodd v. Wilson & McWilliam [1946] 2 All E.R. 691 .... 1.173
Dodsley v. Kinnersley (1761) 1 Amb. 403; 27 E.R. 270 .... 3.14
Donoghue v. Stevenson [1932] A.C. 562; 76 S.J. 396; 101 L.J.P.C. 119; 147 L.T. 281; 48 T.L.R. 494; 37 Com.Cas. 850 (H.L.) 1.100, 1.102, 1.106, 1.109, 1.128, 3.76, 7.15
Dover v. Prosser [1904] 1 K.B. 84; 73 L.J.K.B. 13; 48 S.J. 51; 89 L.T. 724; 68 J.P. 37; 52 W.R. 140; 20 T.L.R. 49; 2 L.G.R. 156 (D.C.) 1.039
Downs, The, Herne Bay, Kent, *Re* Ref. 219 D/2 [1980] C.L.Y. 246 .... 2.68
Dowty Boulton Paul Ltd. v. Wolverhampton Corporation (No. 2) [1976] Ch. 13; [1973] 2 W.L.R. 618; 117 S.J. 304; 71 L.G.R. 323; 25 P. & C.R. 282; *sub nom.* Dowty Boulton Paul v. Wolverhampton Corporation (No. 2) [1973] 2 All E.R. 491 (C.A.); *affirming* [1973] Ch. 94 .... 4.30
Dulieu v. White and Sons Ltd. [1901] 2 K.B. 669; 70 L.J.K.B. 837; 45 S.J. 578; 85 L.T. 126; 50 W.R. 76; 17 T.L.R. 555 (D.L.) 7.07
Dunne v. North Western Gas Board [1964] 2 Q.B. 806; [1964] 2 W.L.R. 164; 107 S.J. 890; [1963] 3 All E.R. 916; 62 L.G.R. 197 (C.A.) 1.128
Dunton v. Dover District Council (1978) 76 L.G.R. 87 .... 2.56

Edwards v. Dolin [1976] 1 W.L.R. 942; 120 S.J. 587; [1976] 3 All E.R. 705; (1976) 63 Cr.App.R. 218; [1976] R.T.R. 508; [1976] Crim.L.R. 580, D.C. 1.159
Elkenford Ltd. v. Stafford B.C. *See* Stafford Borough Council v. Elkenford.
Ellis v. Dubowski [1921] 3 K.B. 621; [1921] L.J.K.B. 89; [1921] All E.R. 272; 126 L.T. 91; 85 J.P. 230; 37 T.L.R. 910; 19 L.G.R. 641, 27 Cox. C.C. 107 (D.C.) 6.20
—— v. Fulham Corporation [1938] 1 K.B. 212; 107 L.J.K.B. 84; 81 S.J. 550; 157 L.T. 380; 101 J.P. 469; 53 T.L.R. 884; 35 L.G.R. 507; [1937] 3 All E.R. 454 .... 1.013, 7.09
Esdell Caravan Parks Ltd. v. Hemel Hempstead U.D.C. [1966] 1 Q.B. 895; [1965] 3 W.L.R. 1238; 130 J.P. 66; 109 S.J. 901; [1965] 3 All E.R. 737; 18 P. & C.R. 200; 64 L.G.R. 1; [1965] C.L.Y. 3785 (C.A.); *reversing* [1966] 1 Q.B. 895 .... 8.55
Esso Petroleum Co. Ltd. v. Harper's Garage (Stourport) Ltd. [1968] A.C. 269; [1967] 2 W.L.R. 871; 111 S.J. 174; [1967] 1 All E.R. 699 (C.A.); *reversing in part* [1966] 2 Q.B. 514; [1966] 2 W.L.R. 1043; *reversing* [1966] 2 Q.B. 514 .... 1.144
—— v. Kingswood Motors (Addlestone) [1974] Q.B. 142; [1973] 3 W.L.R. 780; 117 S.J. 852; [1973] 3 All E.R. 1057; [1973] C.M.L.R. 665 .... 1.142
—— v. Southport Corporation [1956] 1 A.C. 218; [1956] 2 W.L.R. 81; 120 J.P. 54; 100 S.J. 32; [1955] 3 All E.R. 864; 54 L.G.R. 91; *sub nom.* Southport Corporation v. Esso Petroleum Co. [1955] 2 Lloyd's Rep. 655 (H.L.); *reversing sub nom.* Southport Corporation v. Esso Petroleum Co. [1954] 2 Q.B. 182; [1954] 3 W.L.R. 200; [1954] 1 Lloyd's Rep. 446 (C.A.); *restoring* [1953] 3 W.L.R. 773 .... 1.013

TABLE OF CASES

Fanton v. Denville [1932] 2 K.B. 309; 101 L.J.K.B. 641; [1932] All E.R. 360; 147 L.T. 243; 48 T.L.R. 433 (C.A.)	6.13
Fielding v. Moisevitch (1946) 175 L.T. 265 (C.A.)	6.08
Fisher's Restaurant v. G.L.C. (1980) 18 L.G.R. 672 (D.C.)	6.02
Fitch v. Rawling (1795) 2 Hy.Bl. 393; 126 E.R. 614	6.59
Fitzhardinge (Lord) v. Purcell [1908] 2 Ch. 139; 77 L.J.Ch. 529; 99 L.T. 154; 72 J.P. 276; 24 T.L.R. 564	7.66
Geddis v. Proprietors of Bann Reservoir [1878] A.C. 430; 3 App.Cas. 430	1.128, 2.04
Gee v. National Trust [1966] 1 W.L.R. 170; 109 S.J. 935; 17 P. & C.R. 6 (C.A.); *reversing sub nom.* Gee (Gordon's) Application, *Re* LP/25/1964 [1965] C.L.Y. 3350; [1965] J.P.L. 308	5.11
General Cleaning Contractors Ltd. v. Christmas [1953] A.C. 180; [1953] 2 W.L.R. 6; 97 S.J. 7; [1952] 2 All E.R. 1110; 51 L.G.R. 109; *affirming sub nom.* Christmas v. General Cleaning Contractors; Same v. Caledonian Club Trust [1952] 1 K.B. 141	1.019
Gibaud v. G. E. Railway Co. [1921] 2 K.B. 426; 90 L.J.K.B. 535; 65 SJ. 454 (C.A.)	3.74
Gibson v. Manchester C.C. [1979] 1 W.L.R. 294; (1979) 123 S.J. 201; [1979] 1 All E.R. 972; (1979) 77 L.G.R. 405; [1979] J.P.L. 532 (H.L.); *reversing* [1978] 1 W.L.R. 520	1.134
Gilbert v. Spoor [1983] Ch. 27; [1982] 3 W.L.R. 183; (1982) 126 S.J. 260; [1982] 2 All E.R. 576; (1982) 44 P. & C.R. 239 (C.A.)	4.27
Gill v. El Vino Co. Ltd. [1983] Q.B. 425; [1983] 2 W.L.R. 155; (1982) 126 S.J. 769; [1983] 1 All E.R. 598; [1983] I.R.L.R. 206 (C.A.)	1.079
Glasgow Corporation v. Johnstone [1965] A.C. 609; [1965] 2 W.L.R. 657; 129 J.P. 250; 109 S.J. 196; [1965] 1 All E.R. 730; 63 L.G.R. 171; [1965] R.V.R. 111; 11 R.R.C. 127; [1965] R.A. 49	1.041
—— v. Muir [1943] A.C. 448; 112 L.J.P.C. 1; 87 S.J. 182; [1943] 2 All E.R. 44; 169 L.T. 53; 107 J.P. 140; 59 T.L.R. 266; 41 L.G.R. 173 (H.L.)	1.006
—— v. Taylor [1922] 1 A.C. 44; 91 L.J.P.C. 49; 126 L.T. 262; 86 J.P. 89; 38 T.L.R. 102; 20 L.G.R. 205 (H.L.)	1.013
Goldman v. Hargrave [1967] 1 A.C. 615; [1966] 3 W.L.R. 513; 110 S.J. 527; [1966] 2 All E.R. 989; [1966] 2 Lloyd's Rep. 65; *affirming sub nom.* Hargrave v. Goldman (1963) 37 A.L.J.R. 277	4.15
Goodman v. Saltash Corporation (1882) 7 A.C. 633; 52 L.J.Q.B. 193; 48 L.T. 239; 47 J.P. 276; 31 W.R. 293 (H.L.); *reversing, sub nom.* Saltash Corpn. v. Goodman (1881) 7 Q.B.D. 106 (C.A.)	2.77
Grandel v. Mason [1953] 3 D.L.R. 65	1.030
Grand Junction Canal Co. v. Petty [1888] 21 Q.B. 273; 57 L.J.Q.B. 572; 59 L.T. 767; 52 J.P. 692; 36 W.R. 795 (C.A.)	7.53
Grant v. Australian Knitting Mills [1936] A.C. 85; 105 L.J.P.C. 6; 79 S.J. 815; 154 L.T. 18; 52 T.L.R. 38	7.15
Gray v. Holmes [1949] T.R. 71; 41 R. & I.T. 117; 30 T.C. 467	1.041
Greenhalgh v. British Railways Board [1969] 2 Q.B. 286; [1969] 2 W.L.R. 892; 113 S.J. 108; [1969] 2 All E.R. 255 (C.A.)	1.017, 1.018
Griffiths v. Liverpool Corporation [1967] 1 Q.B. 374; [1966] 3 W.L.R. 467; 130 J.P. 376; 110 S.J. 548; [1966] 2 All E.R. 1015; 64 L.G.R. 407 (C.A.)	7.09
Halifax Building Society v. Registry of Friendly Societies [1978] 1 W.L.R. 1544; (1978) 122 S.J 523; [1978] 3 All E.R. 403	2.24
Hall v. Beckenham Corporation [1949] 1 K.B. 716; [1949] L.J.R. 965; 65 T.L.R. 146; 113 J.P. 179; 93 S.J. 219; [1949] 1 All E.R. 423; 47 L.G.R. 291; 42 R. & I.T. 247	4.10, 4.11, 4.13, 4.57
—— v. Brooklands Auto-Racing Club [1933] 1 K.B. 205; 101 L.J.K.B. 679; 147 L.T. 404; 48 T.L.R. 546 (C.A.)	1.124, 7.30, 7.36
—— v. Green [1853] 9 Exch. 247; 23 L.J.M.C. 15; 22 L.T.O.S. 122; 17 J.P. 777; 2 C.L.R. 427	6.34
—— v. Nottingham and Others (1875) L.R. 1 Ex.D. 1; 45 L.J.Q.B. 50; 33 L.T. 697; 24 W.R. 58	6.59

Table of Cases

Hargreaves *v.* Diddams [1875] L.R. 10 Q.B. 582; 44 L.J.M.C. 178; 32 l.T. 600; 40 J.P. 167; 23 W.R. 828 .... 7.58

Harman *v.* Butt [1944] K.B. 491; 114 L.J.K.B. 99; [1944] 1 All E.R. 558; 170 L.T. 355; 108 J.P. 229; 60 T.L.R. 341; 42 L.G.R. 158 .... 6.21

Harris *v.* Harrison (1914) 111 L.T. 534; 78 J.P. 398; 30 T.L.R. 532; 12 L.G.R. 1304 (D.C.) 5.36

Harrison *v.* Vincent [1982] 1 R.T.R. 8 (C.A.) 7.27

Hartley *v.* Mayoh [1954] 1 Q.B. 383; [1954] 1 W.L.R. 355; 118 J.P. 178; 98 S.J. 107; [1954] 1 All E.R. 375; 52 L.G.R. 165 (C.A.); *affirming in part and reversing in part* 117 J.P. 369 .... 1.020

Harvey *v.* Tivoli Manchester Ltd. (1907) 23 T.L.R. 592 (D.C.) 6.08

Harwood *v.* Borough of Reigate and Banstead (1980) 43 P. & C.R. 336; 80 L.G.R. 660 .. 8.09

Haseldine *v.* Daw [1941] 2 K.B. 343; [1941] 111 L.J.K.B. 45; [1941] 3 All E.R. 156; 165 L.T. 185; 58 T.L.R. 1 (C.A.) 1.023

Havering Borough Council *v.* Stevenson [1970] 1 W.L.R. 1375; [1971] R.T.R. 58; *sub nom.* London Borough of Havering *v.* Stevenson, 114 S.J. 664; [1970] 3 All E.R. 609 (D.C.) 1.177

Haynes *v.* Harwood [1935] 1 K.B. 146; 104 L.J.K.B. 63; 78 S.J. 801; 152 L.T. 121; 51 T.L.R. 100 (C.A.) 1.126

Hedley Byrne *v.* Heller and Partners [1964] A.C. 465; [1963] 3 W.L.R. 101; 107 S.J. 454; [1963] 2 All E.R. 575; [1963] 1 Lloyd's Rep. 485 (H.L.); *affirming* [1962] 1 Q.B. 396; *affirming The Times*, December 21, 1960 .... 1.106, 1.108, 3.73

Hensher (George) Ltd. *v.* Restawhile Upholstery (Lancs.) Ltd. [1976] A.C. 64; [1974] 2 W.L.R. 700; 118 S.J. 329; [1974] 2 All E.R. 420; [1974] F.S.R. 173; [1975] R.P.C. 37 (H.L.); *affirming on different grounds* [1973] 3 W.L.R. 453 .... 3.27

Heron Service Stations *v.* Hunter [1981] Crim.L.R. 418; [1981] 79 L.G.R. 679 (D.C.) .. 1.180

Hilder *v.* Associated Portland Cement Manufacturers Ltd. [1961] 1 W.L.R. 1434; 105 S.J. 725; [1961] 3 All E.R. 709 .... 1.104

Hill *v.* Hill (William) (Park Lane) Ltd. [1949] A.C. 530; [1949] L.J.R. 1383; 65 T.L.R. 471; 93 S.J. 587; [1949] 2 All E.R. 452 (H.L.) 1.142

Hirst *v.* Sargent [1967] 65 L.G.R. 127; 111 S.J. 54; 12 R.R.C. 234; [1966] C.L.Y. 10255; [1966] R.A. 605 (D.C.) 1.041

Hivac Ltd. *v.* Park Royal Scientific Instruments Ltd. [1946] Ch. 169; 115 L.J.Ch. 241; 90 S.J. 175; [1946] 2 All E.R. 350; 174 L.T. 422; 62 T.L.R. 231 (C.A.) 1.062

Home Office *v.* Dorset Yacht Co. [1970] A.C. 1004; [1970] 2 W.L.R. 1140; [1970] 2 All E.R. 294; [1970] 1 Lloyd's Rep. 453; *sub nom.* Dorset Yacht Co. *v.* Home Office, 114 S.J. 375 (H.L.); *affirming sub nom.* Dorset Yacht Co. *v.* Home Office [1969] 2 Q.B. 412 .... 1.128

Houghton-le-Touzel *v.* Mecca [1950] 2 K.B. 612; [1950] 1 All E.R. 638 .... 6.62

Hubbard *v.* Vosper [1972] 2 Q.B. 84; [1972] 2 W.L.R. 389; (1971) 116 S.J. 95; [1972] 1 All E.R. 1023 (C.A.) 3.30

Imperial Chemical Industries Ltd. *v.* Shotwell [1965] A.C. 656; [1964] 3 W.L.R. 329; 108 S.J. 578; [1964] 2 All E.R. 999 (H.L.); *reversing sub nom.*, Shotwell *v.* Imperial Chemical Industries, *The Guardian*, July 17, 1963; [1963] C.L.Y. 2377 (C.A.) 7.33

Imperial Tobacco *v.* Att.-Gen. [1981] A.C. 718; [1980] 2 W.L.R. 466; (1980) 124 S.J. 271; [1980] 1 All E.R. 866 (H.L.); *reversing* [1979] Q.B. 555; *reversing* [1979] Crim.L.R. 315 .... 6.85, 6.86

I.R.C. *v.* National Federation of Self Employed and Small Businesses [1981] 2 W.L.R. 722; (1981) 125 S.J. 325; [1981] 2 All E.R. 93; [1981] S.T.C. 260 (H.L.); *reversing sub nom.* R. *v.* I.R.C., *ex p.* National Federation of Self Employed and Small Businesses [1980] Q.B. 407 .... 4.06

Johnson *v.* Nottinghamshire Combined Police Authority; Dutton *v.* Same [1974] I.C.R. 170; [1974] 1 W.L.R. 358; (1973) 118 S.J. 166 .... 1.059

Jones *v.* Vernon Pools Ltd. (1938) 2 All E.R. 626 .... 1.135

Kay (John) Ltd. *v.* Kay [1952] 2 Q.B. 258; [1952] 1 T.L.R. 766; 96 S.J. 212; [1952] 1 All E.R. 813 (C.A.); *affirming* (1951) 102 L.J. 123 .... 8.09

TABLE OF CASES

Kearney v. Waller (Eric) Ltd. [1967] 1 Q.B. 29; [1966] 2 W.L.R. 208; 110 S.J. 13; [1965] 3 All E.R. 352 .... 1.007
Keehan v. Walters [1948] K.B. 19; 177 L,T. 552; 63 T.L.R. 483; 91 S.J. 494 (D.C.) 6.84
Kennedy (R.) v. Birmingham Licensing Planning Committee, ex p. [1972] 2 Q.B. 140; [1972] 2 W.L.R. 939; sub nom. Kennedy v. Birmingham Licensing Committee [1972] 2 All E.R. 305 (C.A.); affirming [1972] 1 W.L.R. 281 (D.C.) 2.05
Kennaway v. Thompson [1981] Q.B. 88; [1980] 3 W.L.R. 361; (1980) 124 S.J. 378; [1980] 3 All E.R. 329; [1980] J.P.L. 515 (C.A.) 7.44
Kings Norton Metal Co. Ltd. v. Eldridge Merritt & Co. Ltd. (1897) 14 T.L.R. 98 (C.A.) 1.137
Kingston-upon-Hull Corporation v. Clayton [1963] A.C. 28; [1961] 3 W.L.R. 497; 125 J.P. 585; 105 S.J. 630; [1961] 3 All E.R. 118; 59 L.G.R. 460; [1961] R.V.R. 478; affirming sub nom. Clayton v. Kingston-upon-Hull Corporation [1961] 1 Q.B. 345 .... 4.37
Kirkham v. Marter (1819) 2 B. & A. 613; 106 E.R. 490 .... 1.135
Klyne v. Bellegarde [1978] 6 W.W.R. 743; [1979] C.L.Y.B. 1870 .... 1.100, 7.36
Knipe v. British Railways Board [1972] 1 Q.B. 361; [1972] 2 W.L.R. 127; (1971) 116 S.J. 16; [1972] 1 All E.R. 673; [1972] 1 Lloyd's Rep. 122 (C.A.) 1.024
Kruse v. Johnson [1898] 2 Q.B. 91; 67 L.J.Q.B. 782; 42 S.J. 509; 79 L.T. 647; 62 J.P. 469; 46 W.R. 630; 14 T.L.R. 416; 19 Cox. C.C. 103 (D.C.) 4.46, 4.47, 5.36

Ladbrokes (Football) v. Perret [1971] 1 W.L.R. 110; (1970) 114 S.J. 930; [1971] 1 All E.R. 129 (D.C.) 6.85
Lagan Navigation v. Lambeg Bleaching Co. [1927] A.C. 226; 96 L.J.P.C. 25; 136 L.T. 417; 91 J.P. 46; 25 L.G.R. 1 (H.L.) 1.031
Laird v. Briggs (1881) 16 Ch.D. 663; 44 L.T. 361 (C.A.) 7.63
Lally & Weller v. George Bird (1980) (unreported) (Q.B.D.) May 23, 1980 .... 1.173
Lamb v. Newbiggin [1844] 1 Car. & King 549 .... 7.58
Lambeth Overseers v. London County Council [1897] A.C. 625; 66 L.J.Q.B. 806; 76 L.T. 795; 46 W.R. 79; 13 T.L.R. 527; sub nom. St. Mary, Lambeth v. L.C.C. 61 J.P. 580 (H.L.); affirming sub nom. L.C.C. v. Lambeth Overseers [1896] 2 Q.B. 25 .... 4.37, 4.38, 4.40
Latchford v. Spedeworth International Ltd. (1984) 134 New L.J. 36; The Times, October 11, 1983; (1983) C.L.Y. 2584 .... 7.27, 7.28, 7.31
Lazenby Garages v. Wright [1976] 1 W.L.R. 459; 120 S.J. 146; [1976] 2 All E.R. 770; [1976] R.T.R. 314; 19 Man.Law 19 (C.A.) 1.163
Leaf v. International Galleries (a firm) [1950] 2 K.B. 86; 66 T.L.R. (Pt. 1) 1031; [1950] 1 All E.R. 693 (C.A.) 1.136, 1.140
Leakey v. National Trust for Places of Historic Interest and Natural Beauty [1980] Q.B. 485; [1980] 2 W.L.R. 65; (1979) 123 S.J. 606; [1980] 1 All E.R. 17; (1979) 78 L.G.R. 100, C.A.; affirming [1978] Q.B. 849; [1978] 2 W.L.R. 774; (1978) 122 S.J. 231; [1978] 3 All E.R. 234; (1978) 76 L.G.R. 488 .... 1.029
Lee Cooper Ltd. v. Jeakins (C. H.) and Sons Ltd. [1967] 2 Q.B. 1; [1965] 3 W.L.R. 753; 109 S.J. 794; [1965] 1 All E.R. 280; [1964] 1 Lloyd's Rep. 300 .... 3.73
Lee Verhulst (Investments) Ltd. v. Harwood Trust (1972) 1 Q.B. 204; [1972] 3 W.L.R. 722; 116 S.J. 801; [1972] 3 All E.R. 619; 24 P. & C.R. 346 (C.A.) 1.047
Lerose v. Hawick Jersey International [1973] C.M.L.R. 83; [1973] F.S.R. 15; [1974] R.P.C. 42 .... 1.142
Leon v. Casey [1932] 2 K.B. 576; 101 L.J.K.B. 578; 147 L.T. 165; 48 T.L.R. 452; 37 Com.Cas. 330; 18 Asp.M.L.C. 300 (C.A.) 4.65
Lewis v. Averay (No. 2) [1973] 1 W.L.R. 510; 117 S.J. 188; [1973] 2 All E.R. 229 (C.A.); reversing [1972] Q.B. 198 (C.A.) 1.137
Lilley v. Doubleday [1881] 7 Q.B. 510; 51 L.J.Q.B. 310; 44 L.T. 814; 46 J.P. 708 .... 3.74
Lister v. Romford Ice & Cold Storage Co. Ltd. [1957] A.C. 555; [1957] 2 W.L.R. 158; 121 J.P. 98; 101 S.J 106; [1957] 1 All E.R. 125, sub nom. Romford Ice & Cold Storage Co. v. Lister [1956] 2 Lloyd's Ref. 505; affirming sub nom. Romford Ice & Cold Storage Co. v. Lister [1956] 2 Q.B. 180 (C.A.) 1.062, 1.063
Liversedge v. Anderson [1942] A.C. 206; 110 L.J.K.B. 724; 85 S.J. 439; 116 L.T. 1; 58 T.L.R. 35 .... 7.19

Table of Cases

Llandudno Urban District Council v. Woods [1899] 2 Ch. 705; 68 L.J.Ch. 623; 43 S.J. 689; 81 L.T. 170; 63 J.P. 775; 48 W.R. 43 .... 7.65
Llanfyllin Rural District Council v. Holland (1964) 62 L.G.R. 459; 16 P. & C.R. 140 (D.C.) 8.55
Lock v. Rank Leisure Ltd. (1984) 148 J.P. 340; (1984) 148 J.P.N. 315 .... 6.81
London and Westcliff Properties Ltd. v. Ministry of Housing and Local Government [1961] 1 W.L.R. 519; 125 J.P. 229; 105 S.J. 208; [1961] 1 All E.R. 610; 12 P. & C.R. 154; 59 L.G.R. 244 .... 2.19
London County Cycling and Athletic Club Ltd. v. Beck [1897] 3 Commercial Cases 49 .... 4.65
London County Council v. Robinson & Lambeth B.C., LVC/192/1954 [1955] J.P.L. 607; 48 R. & I.T. 455; 105 L.J. 460; 166 E.G. 9, Lands Tribunal 4.38
London Theatre of Varieties Ltd. v. Evans (1914) 31 T.L.R. 75 (C.A.) 6.07
Loose v. Castleton (1978) 122 S.J. 487; (1978) 41 P. & C.R. 19 (C.A.) 7.64
Lord Warden and Admiral of Cinque Ports v. H.M. in His Office of Admiralty [1831] 166 E.R. 304; 2 Hagg. 438; 2 St.Tr.(N.S.) App. 1014 .... 3.59

M.F.I. Warehouses Ltd. v. Nattrass [1973] 1 W.L.R. 307; (1972) 117 S.J. 143; [1973] 1 All E.R. 762; [1973] Crim.L.R. 196 (D.C.) 1.181
McCafferty (T.) v. Metropolitan Police Receiver [1977] I.C.R. 799; [1977] 1 W.L.R. 1073; (1977) 121 S.J. 678; [1977] 2 All E.R. 756 (C.A.) 1.131
McComisky v. McDermott [1974] I.R. 75 .... 7.32
McCutcheon v. MacBrayne [1964] 1 W.L.R. 125; 108 S.J. 93; [1964] 1 All E.R. 430; [1964] 1 Lloyd's Rep. 16; 1964 S.C. (H.L.) 28; 1964 S.L.T. 66; *reversing* [1963] 1 Lloyd's Rep. 123; *affirming* [1962] 1 Lloyd's Rep. 303 .... 1.173
Magee v. Prairie Dusters Motor-cycle Club, Laurence & Dunn [1975] W.W.D. 165 .... 7.36
Manchester Corporation v. Farnworth [1930] A.C. 171; [1929] 99 L.J.K.B. 83; [1929] All E.R. 90; 73 S.J. 818; 46 T.L.R. 85; 94 J.P. 62; *sub nom.* Farnworth v. Manchester Corpn. 142 L.T. 145; 27 L.G.R. 709 (H.L.) 1.128
—— v. Manchester Palace of Varieties [1955] P. 133; [1955] 2 W.L.R. 440; 119 J.P. 191; 99 S.J. 150; [1955] 1 All E.R. 387; 53 L.G.R. 269 .... 6.14
—— v. Markland [1936] A.C. 360; [1935] 104 L.J.K.B. 480; All E.R. 667; 153 L.T. 302; 51 T.L.R. 527; 33 L.G.R. 341; *sub nom.* Markland v. Manchester Corporation 99 J.P. 343 (H.L.) 1.128
Manuel v. Att.-Gen.; Nottcho v. Att.-Gen. [1983] Ch. 77; [1982] 3 W.L.R. 821; (1982) 126 S.J. 642; [1982] 3 All E.R. 822; (1982) 79 L.S.Gaz. 1411 (C.A.); *affirming* [1982] 3 W.L.R. 821; [1982] 3 All E.R. 786 .... 2.30
Marquess of Zetland v. Driver [1939] Ch. 1; 107 L.J.Ch. 316; 82 S.J. 293; 158 L.T. 456; 54 T.L.R. 594; [1938] 2 All E.R. 158 (C.A.) 5.11
Marriage v. East Norfolk Rivers Catchment Board [1950] 1 K.B. 284; 66 T.L.R. (Pt. 1) 225; 114 J.P. 38; 94 S.J. 32; [1949] 2 All E.R. 1021 (C.A.); *affirming* [1949] 2 K.B. 456; [1949] L.J.R. 1473 .... 1.128
Mason v. Provident Clothing and Supply Co. Ltd. [1913] A.C. 724; [1911–13] 82 L.J.K.B. 1153; 57 S.J. 739; All E.R. 400; 109 L.T. 449; 29 T.L.R. 727 (H.L.); *reversing sub nom.*, Provident Clothing & Supply Co. Ltd. v. Mason [1913] 1 K.B. 65 (C.A.) 1.062
Masters v. London Borough of Brent [1978] Q.B. 841; [1978] 2 W.L.R. 768; (1977) 122 S.J. 300; [1978] 2 All E.R. 664; (1977) 76 L.G.R. 379; (1977) 245 L.G. 483 .... 1.028
Mellor v. Walmsley (1905) 2 Ch. 164; 74 L.J.Ch. 475; 49 S.J. 565; 93 L.T. 574; 53 W.R. 581; 21 T.L.R. 591 (C.A.) 7.61
Meux's Brewery Co. v. City of London Electric Lighting Co. [1895] 1 Ch. 287; 64 L.J.Ch. 216; 39 S.J. 132; 72 L.T. 34; 43 W.R. 238; 11 T.L.R. 137; 12 R. 112 (C.A.); *subsequent proceedings* [1895] 2 Ch. 388 (C.A.) 1.025
Miller v. Jackson [1977] Q.B. 966; [1977] 3 W.L.R. 20; (1977) 121 S.J. 287; [1977] 3 All E.R. 338 (C.A.) 1.026
Ministry of Defence v. Jeremiah [1980] Q.B. 87; [1980] I.C.R. 13; [1979] 3 W.L.R. 857; (1979) 123 S.J. 735; [1979] 3 All E.R. 833; *sub nom.* Jeremiah v. Ministry of Defence [1979] I.R.L.R. 436 (C.A.); *affirming* [1978] I.C.R. 984 .... 1.079

TABLE OF CASES

Mitcham Common Conservators v. Cox; The Same v. Cole [1911] 2 K.B. 854; 80 L.J.K.B. 1188; 104 L.T. 824; 75 J.P. 471; 27 T.L.R. 492; 9 L.G.R. 843 (D.C) 5.36
Mixnam's Properties v. Chertsey U.D.C. [1965] A.C. 735; [1964] 2 W.L.R. 1210; [1964] R.V.R. 632; *sub nom.* Chertsey Urban District Council v. Mixnam's Properties, 128 J.P. 405; 108 S.J. 402; [1964] 2 All E.R. 627; 15 P. & C.R. 331; 62 L.G.R. 528 (H.L.); *affirming* [1964] 1 Q.B 214 (C.A.); *reversing* 107 S.J. 175 ..... 8.55
Moore v. C. and A. Modes [1981] 1 R.L.R. 71, E.A.T. 1.099
Moorhouse and Angus and Robertson (Publishers) Property Ltd. v. University of New South Wales [1976] R.P.C. 151; *sub nom.* University of New South Wales v. Moorhouse and Angus & Robertson (Publishers) Pty. (1975) 49 A.L.J.R. 267, Australia High Ct. *affirming in part, reversing in part* [1975] R.P.C. 454 .... 3.18
Morris v. Martin (C. W.) & Sons Ltd. [1966] 1 Q.B. 716; [1965] 3 W.L.R. 276; 109 S.J. 451; [1965] 2 All E.R. 725; [1965] 2 Lloyd's Rep. 63 (C.A.) 3.73
Morrissey v. Galer [1955] 1 W.L.R. 110; 99 S.J. 113; 53 L.G.R. 303; *sub nom.* Galer v. Morrissey, 119 J.P. 165; [1955] 1 All E.R. 380 (D.C.) 4.50
Murray v. Harringay Arena [1951] 2 Q.B. 529; 95 S.J. 529; 2 All E.R. 320 (C.A.) 1.124, 7.30
Musik-Vertrieb GmbH and K Tel International v. G.E.M.A. (No. 92/78) [1982] 1 C.M.L.R. 630; [1982] F.S.R. 355; [1982] F.S.R. 477 (German Federal Ct.) 3.36

Nagle v. Fielden [1966] 2 Q.B. 633; [1966] 2 W.L.R. 1027; 110 S.J. 286; [1966] 1 All E.R. 689 (C.A.) 6.48
Nash v. Finlay (1901) 85 L.T. 682; 66 J.P. 183; 18 T.L.R. 92; 20 Cox. C.C. 101 (D.C.) ... 4.47
Nettleship v. Weston [1971] 2 Q.B. 691; [1971] 3 W.L.R. 370; 115 S.J. 624; [1971] 3 All E.R. 581; [1971] R.T.R. 425 (C.A.) 3.76
New Windsor Corporation v. Mellor (1975) Ch. 380; [1975] 3 W.L.R. 25; 119 S.J. 440; [1975] 3 All E.R. 44; 73 L.G.R. 337; 30 P. & C.R. 429 (C.A.); *affirming* [1974] 1 W.L.R. 1504 .... 2.76
Nicholls v. Mitford [1882] 20 Ch.D. 380; 51 L.J.Ch. 485; 30 W.R. 509 .... 2.62
Nobilo v. Waitemata County (1961) N.Z.L.R. 1064 .... 1.025
North Riding of Yorkshire County Valuation Committee v. Redcar Corporation etc. Committee [1943] 1 K.B. 114 .... 4.11, 4.38

O'Connor v. Isaacs [1956] 2 Q.B. 288; [1956] 3 W.L.R. 172; 120 J.P. 325; 100 S.J. 432; [1956] 2 All E.R. 417 (C.A.); *affirming* 2 W.L.R. 485 .... 1.130
O'Reilly v. Mackman; Millbanks v. Secretary of State for the Home Department [1983] 2 A.C. 237; [1983] 3 W.L.R. 1096; (1982) 126 S.J. 820; [1982] 3 All E.R. 1124 (H.L.); *affirming* O'Reilly v. Mackman, etc., [1982] 3 W.L.R. 604 .... 2.09
Oliver v. Court [1820] 146 E.R. 1152; Dan. 301; 8 Price 127 .... 4.31
Overseas Tankship (U.K.) Ltd. v. Miller Steamship Co. Pty. [1967] 1 A.C. 617; [1966] 3 W.L.R. 498; 110 S.J. 447; [1966] 2 All E.R. 709; [1966] 1 Lloyd's Rep. 657 (P.C.) *reversing sub nom.* Miller Steamship Co. Pty. v. Overseas Tankship (U.K.); Miller (R. W.) & Co. v. Same, The Wagon Mound (No. 2) [1963] 1 Lloyd's Rep. 402 .... 1.113, 7.27
—— v. Morts Dock & Engineering Co. (The Wagon Mound) [1961] A.C. 388; [1961] 2 W.L.R. 126; 105 S.J. 85; [1961] 1 All E.R. 404; [1961] 1 Lloyd's Rep. 1 (P.C.); *reversing sub nom.* Mort's Dock and Engineering Co. v. Overseas Tankship (U.K.) (The Wagon Mound) [1959] 2 Lloyd's Rep. 697 (C.A.); *reversing* [1958] 1 Lloyd's Rep. 575 .... 1.113, 7.27

Page Motors v. Epsom and Ewell Borough Council (1981) 125 S.J. 590 (C.A.); (1982) 80 L.G.R. 337; [1982] J.P.L. 572 (C.A.) *affirming The Times,* July 11, 1981 .... 1.031
Paine v. Colne Valley Supply Co. Ltd. and British Insulated Cables Ltd. (1938) 83 S.J. 115; [1938] 4 All E.R. 803; 160 L.T. 124; 55 T.L.R. 181; 37 L.G.R. 200 .... 1.063
Pannett v. McGuinness & Co. [1972] 2 Q.B. 599; [1972] 3 W.L.R. 386; 116 S.J. 335; [1972] 3 All E.R. 137 (C.A.) 1.014
Paris v. Stepney Borough Council [1951] A.C. 367; [1951] 1 T.L.R. 25; 115 J.P. 22; 94 S.J. 837; [1951] 1 All E.R. 42; 49 L.G.R. 293; 84 Ll.L.Rep. 525 (H.L.); *reversing* [1950] 1 K.B. 320 (C.A.) 1.102

Table of Cases

Parker v. British Airways Board [1982] 2 W.L.R. 503; (1982) 125 S.J. 119; [1982] 1 All E.R. 834; [1982] Q.B. 1004 (C.A.) 3.53

Payne & Payne v. Maple Leaf Gardens Ltd., Stewart and Marucci [1949] 1 D.L.R. 369 .... 7.36

Peake v. Automotive Products Ltd. [1978] Q.B. 233; [1977] I.C.R. 968; [1977] 3 W.L.R. 853; (1977) 121 S.J. 644 [1978] 1 All E.R. 106; *sub nom.* Automotive Products *v.* Peake [1977] I.R.L.R. 365; *reversing* [1977] Q.B. 780 .... 1.079

Performing Rights Society Ltd. v. Ciryl Theatrical Syndicate Ltd. [1924] 1 K.B. 1 (C.A.); [1923] 2 K.B. 146; 39 T.L.R. 143 .... 3.17

Perkowski v. Wellington Corporation [1959] A.C. 53; [1958] 3 W.L.R. 564; 102 S.J. 794; [1958] 3 All E.R. 368; *affirming* [1957] N.Z.L.R. 39 .... 1.008

Pett v. Greyhound Racing Association (No. 1) [1969] 1 Q.B. 125; [1968] 2 W.L.R. 1471; 112 S.J. 463; [1968] 2 All E.R. 545 (C.A.) 6.53

Phillips (J.) v. Brookes Ltd. (1919) 2 K.B. 243; [1918–19] 88 L.J.K.B. 953; All E.R. 246; 121 L.T. 249; 35 T.L.R. 470; 24 Com.Cas. 263 .... 1.137

Phipps v. Rochester Corporation [1955] 1 Q.B. 450; [1955] 2 W.L.R. 23; 119 J.P. 92; 99 S.J. 45; [1955] 1 All E.R. 129; 53 L.G.R. 80 .... 1.005

Pickwell v. Camden London Borough Council [1983] Q.B. 962; [1983] 2 W.L.R. 583; (1982) 126 S.J. 397; [1983] 1 All E.R. 602; (1982) 80 L.G.R. 798 (D.C.) 2.21

Polemis and Furness Withy & Co., *Re* [1921] 3 K.B. 560; *sub nom.* Polemis v. Furness, Withy & Co. 90 L.J.K.B. 1353; 126 L.T. 154; 37 T.L.R. 940; 15 Asp.M.L.C. 398; 27 Com.Cas. 25 (C.A.) 1.111, 1.112

Poole Stadium and Fearman v. Squires (1982) 125 S.J. 134; [1982] 1 All E.R. 404; [1982] Crim.L.R. 39 (D.C.) 6.53

Popperwell v. Cockerton [1968] 1 W.L.R. 438; 132 J.P. 231; 112 S.J. 175; [1968] 1 All E.R. 1038n. (D.C.) 3.65

Prescott v. Birmingham Corporation [1955] Ch. 210; [1954] 3 W.L.R. 990; 119 J.P. 48; 98 S.J. 886; [1954] 3 All E.R. 698; 53 L.G.R. 68 (C.A.); *affirming* [1954] 3 W.L.R. 600 .... 7.19

Public Prosecutor v. Yuvaraj [1970] A.C. 913; [1970] 2 W.L.R. 226; (1969) 113 S.J. 737 (P.C.) 6.03

Quaglieni v. Matthews [1865] 6 B. & S. 474; 29 J.P. 439; 122 E.R. 1270; *sub nom.* Gauglieni *v.* Matthews 34 L.J.M.C. 116 .... 6.34

Quinnen v. Hovell [1984] I.C.R. 525; (1984) 128 S.J. 431; [1984] I.R.L.R. 227; (1984) 134 New L.J. 360; (1984) 81 L.S.Gaz. 1438, E.A.T. 1.074

R. v. Bogdanov (Michael) [1982] (unreported) 6.03
—— v. Bromley Licensing Justices, *ex p.* Bromley Licensed Victuallers Association [1984] 1 W.L.R. 585; (1984) 128 S.J. 264; (1984) 148 J.P. 495; [1984] 1 All E.R. 794; (1984) 81 L.S.Gaz. 663 .... 6.68
—— v. Bromley London Borough Council and Others *ex p.* Lambeth London Borough Council [1984] *The Times,* June 16, 1984 (D.C.) 2.09
—— v. Brown [1895] 1 Q.B. 119; 64 L.J.M.C. 1; 39 S.J. 64; 72 L.T. 22; 59 J.P. 485; 43 W.R. 222; 11 T.L.R. 54; 18 Cox. C.C. 81; 15 R. 59 (C.C.R.) 6.80
—— v. Calder & Boyars [1969] 1 Q.B. 151; [1968] 3 W.L.R. 974; 133 J.P. 20; 112 S.J. 688; [1968] 3 All E.R. 644; 52 Cr.App.R. 706 (C.A.) 6.03
—— v. Chester City Council *ex p.* Quietlynn, *The Times,* March 22, 1984 .... 6.88
—— v. Dacorum Gaming Licensing Committee *ex p.* E.M.I. Cinemas & Leisure Ltd. (1971) 115 S.J. 810; [1971] 3 All E.R. 666 (D.C.) 2.03
—— v. Electricity Commissioners [1924] 1 K.B. 171 .... 2.08
—— v. Essex County Council *ex p.* Clearbrook Contractors Ltd. (1981) (unreported) ... 4.31
—— v. Flintshire County Council Licensing County (Stage Plays) Committee *ex p.* Barrett [1957] 1 Q.B. 350; [1957] 2 W.L.R. 90; 121 J.P. 80; 101 S.J. 87; 55 L.G.R. 53; *sub nom.* R. v. County Licensing (Stage Plays) Committee of Flint County Council, *ex p.* Barrett [1957] 1 All E.R. 112 (C.A.); *reversing* [1956] 1 W.L.R. 1415; *sub nom.* R. v. County Licensing (Stage Plays) Committee, etc., *ex p.* Barrett [1956] 3 All E.R. 535 (D.C.) 6.20

TABLE OF CASES

R. v. Herrod *ex p*. Leeds City Council etc., [1976] Q.B. 540; [1976] 2 W.L.R. 18; 119 S.J. 867; [1976] 1 All E.R. 273; (1975) 74 L.G.R. 70 (C.A.); *reversing* [1974] 1 W.L.R. 1275; 118 S.J. 613; [1974] 3 All E.R. 362; 73 L.G.R. 9 (D.C.) 6.83
—— *v*. Huntingdon District Council *ex p*. Cowan (1984) 1 All E.R. 58 .... 6.36
—— *v*. H.M. Inspector of Taxes *ex p*. Clarke [1974] Q.B. 220; [1973] 3 W.L.R. 673; 117 S.J. 815; [1972] 1 All E.R. 545; *sub nom.* R. v. General Commissioners of Income Tax for Freshwell, *ex p*. Clarke (1971) 47 T.C. 691 (C.A.) 2.03
—— *v*. Leicester Gaming Licensing Committee *ex p*. Shire [1971] 1 W.L.R. 1648; 115 S.J. 772; [1971] 3 All E.R. 1082 (C.A.); *affirming* [1971] 1 W.L.R. 1216; 115 S.J. 465; [1971] 2 All E.R. 1329 (D.C.) 2.03
—— *v*. Local Commissioner for Administration for the North and East Area of England, *ex p*. Bradford Metropolitan City Council [1979] 1 Q.B. 287; [1979] 2 W.L.R. 1; (1978) 122 S.J. 573; [1979] 2 All E.R. 881; (1978) L.G.R. 305; [1978] J.P.L. 767 (C.A.); *affirming* [1978] J.P.L. 706 .... 2.14
—— *v*. L.C.C. *ex p*. The Entertainment Protection Association [1931] 2 K.B. 215 (C.A.); (1930) 47 T.L.R. 111 (D.C.) 1.144, 6.21
—— *v*. Mills (1978) 68 Cr.App.R. 154; [1979] Crim.L.R. 457 (C.A.) 1.097
—— *v*. Pontypool Gaming Licensing Committee, *ex p*. Risca Cinemas [1970] 1 W.L.R. 1299; 114 S.J. 705; [1970] 3 All E.R. 241 (D.C.) 2.03
—— *v*. Secretary of State for the Environment *ex p*. Brent London Borough Council [1982] Q.B. 593; [1982] 2 W.L.R. 693; (1982) 126 S.J. 118; [1983] 3 All E.R. 321; (1982) 80 L.G.R. 357 (D.C.) 9.07
—— *v*. Secretary of State for Social Services and Another, *ex p*. G.L.C., *The Times*, August 16, 1984 .... 2.09
—— *v*. South West Water Authority, *ex p*. Cox, *The Times*, January 2, 1981 .... 7.47
—— *v*. Sunair Holidays Ltd. [1973] 1 W.L.R. 1105; 117 S.J. 429; [1973] 2 All E.R. 1233; 57 Cr.App.R. 782; [1973] Crim.L.R. 587 (C.A.) 1.182
—— *v*. Thomas and Willett (1863) Le. & Ca. 313; 3 New Rep. 141; 33 L.J.M.C. 22; 9 L.T. 488; 28 J.P. 5; 12 W.R. 108; 9 Cox. C.C. 376 (C.C.R.) 3.52
—— *v*. Wood (1855) 5 E. & B. 49; 119 E.R. 400; *sub nom.* R. v. Rose 24 L.J.M.C. 130; *sub nom.* R. v. Stafford shire JJ. *ex p*. Wood 25 L.T.O.S. 127 .... 4.52
Radstock Co-operative and Industrial Society v. Norton-Radstock Urban District Council [1968] Ch. 605; [1968] 2 W.L.R. 1214; 132 J.P. 238; 112 S.J. 135; [1968] 2 All E.R. 59; 66 L.G.R. 457 (C.A.); *affirming* [1967] Ch. 1094; *sub nom.* Radstock Co-operative & Industrial Society v. Radstock U.D.C. (1967) 111 S.J. 398 .... 1.128
Read v. Lyons (J.) & Co. Ltd. [1947] A.C. 156; [1947] L.J.R. 391; 175 L.T. 413; 62 T.L.R. 646; [1946] 2 All E.R. 471 (H.L.); *affirming* [1945] K.B. 216 .... 1.019
Reese v. Coleman and 27 Others [1976] 3 W.L.R. 739 .... 7.36
Rhyl Urban District Council v. Rhyl Amusements Ltd. [1959] 1 W.L.R. 465; 103 S.J. 327; [1959] 1 All E.R. 257; 57 L.G.R. 19 .... 2.20
Rimmer v. Liverpool City Council [1984] 2 W.L.R. 426; (1984) 128 S.J. 225; [1984] 1 All E.R. 930; (1984) 47 P. & C.R. 516; (1984) 269 E.G. 319; (1984) 82 L.G.R. 424; (1984) 12 H.L.R. 23; (1984) 81 L.S.Gaz. 664 (C.A.) 1.103
Roberts v. Hopwood [1925] A.C. 578; 94 L.J.K.B. 542; 69 S.J. 475; [1925] All E.R. 24; 133 L.T. 289; 89 J.P. 105; 41 T.L.R. 436; 23 L.G.R. 337 (H.L.); *reversing sub nom.* R. v. Roberts, *ex p*. Scurr [1924] 2 K.B. 695 (C.A.) 2.17, 7.19
Robinson v. Graves [1935] 1 K.B. 579; [1935] 104 L.J.K.B. 441; 79 S.J. 180; All E.R. 935; 153 L.T. 26; 51 T.L.R. 334; 40 Com.Cas. 217 (C.A.) 1.174
Roe v. Harrogate Justices (1966) 110 S.J. 673; (1966) L.G.R. 465; [1966] C.L.Y. 6612 (D.C.) 6.63
—— *v*. Minister of Health; Woolley v. Same [1954] 2 Q.B. 66; [1954] 2 W.L.R. 915; 98 S.J. 319; [1954] 2 All E.R. 131 (C.A.); *affirming* [1954] 1 W.L.R. 128; 98 S.J. 30 .... 3.76
Rolls Royce Ltd. v. Walpole [1980] 1 R.L.R. 343, E.A.T. 1.098
Rootes v. Shelton [1968] A.L.R. 33 .... 7.27, 7.36
Rother Valley Rail Co. Ltd. v. Ministry of Transport [1971] Ch. 515; [1970] 3 W.L.R. 909; 114 S.J. 845; [1970] 3 All E.R. 805; 21 P. & C.R. 953 (C.A.); *reversing* [1970] 2 W.L.R. 1041 .... 8.16

TABLE OF CASES

Royal College of Nursing of the United Kingdom v. D.H.S.S. [1981] 2 W.L.R. 279; (1981) 125 S.J. 149; [1981] 1 All E.R. 545; [1982] A.C. 800; [1981] Crim.L.R. 322 (H.L.); *reversing* (1980) 124 S.J. 813 (C.A.); *reversing* (1980) 124 S.J. 615 .... 2.24
Russian Commercial and Industrial Bank v. British Bank for Foreign Trade Ltd. [1921] 2 A.C. 438; 90 L.J.K.B. 1089; 65 S.J. 133; 126 L.T. 35; 37 T.L.R. 919; *sub nom.* British Bank for Foreign Trade v. Russian Commercial & Industrial Bank, 38 T.L.R. 65 .... 2.09
Rylands v. Fletcher (1868) L.R. 3 H.L. 330; 37 L.J.Ex. 161; 19 L.T. 220; 33 J.P. 70 (H.L.); *affirming sub nom.* Fletcher v. Rylands (1866) L.R. 1 Exch. 265; *reversing* (1865) 3 H. & C. 774 .... 1.001, 1.034, 1.120, 1.122, 7.57

St. Helen's Smelting Co. v. Tipping (1865) 11 H.L.Cas. 64, 35 L.J.Q.B. 66; 12 L.T. 776; 29 J.P. 579; 11 Jur.N.S. 785; 13 W.R. 1083; 11 E.R. 1483; *sub nom.* Tipping v. St. Helen's Smelting Co. (1864) 4 B. & S. 616 Ex.Ch. 1.025
Said v. Butt [1920] 3 K.B. 497; 90 L.J.K.B. 239; 124 L.T. 413; 36 T.L.R. 762 .... 6.10
Saunders (Executrix of the Estate of Rose Maud Gallie) v. Anglia Building Society [1971] A.C. 1004; [1970] 3 W.L.R. 1078; *sub nom.* Saunders v. Anglia Building Society, 114 S.J. 885; *sub nom.* Saunders (Executrix of the Estate of Rose Maud Gallie) v. Anglia Building Society [1970] 3 All E.R. 961 (H.L.) 1.138
Schroeder Music Publishing Co. Ltd. v. Macaulay (formerly Instone) [1974] 1 W.L.R. 1308; 118 S.J. 734; [1974] 3 All E.R. 616 (H.L.); *affirming sub nom.* Instone v. Schroeder (A.) Music Publishing Co. [1974] 1 All E.R. 171 (C.A.) 1.062
Scott v. London and St. Katherine's Docks Co. [1865] 3 H. & C. 596; 5 New Rep. 420; 34 L.J.Ex. 220; 13 L.T. 148; 11 Jur.N.S. 204; 13 W.R. 410; 159 E.R. 665 .... 1.117
Scruttons Ltd. v. Midland Silicones Ltd. [1962] A.C. 446; [1962] 2 W.L.R. 186; 106 S.J. 34; [1962] 1 All E.R. 1; *sub nom.* Midland Silicones v. Scruttons [1961] 2 Lloyd's Rep. 365 (H.L.); *affirming sub nom.* Midland Silicones v. Scruttons [1961] 1 Q.B. 106 (C.A.); *affirming* [1959] 2 Q.B. 171 .... 3.73
Sedley-Denfield v. O'Callaghan [1940] A.C. 880; (1940) 84 S.J. 657; [1940] 3 All E.R. 349; 164 L.T. 72; 56 T.L.R. 887; *sub nom.* Sedley-Denfield v. St. Joseph's Society for Foreign Missions 109 L.J.K.B. 893 (H.L.) 4.14, 4.15
Seekings v. Clarke (1961) 105 S.J. 181; 59 L.G.R. 268 (D.C.) 8.49
Sheffield Corporation v. Tranter [1957] 1 W.L.R. 843; 55 L.G.R. 351; 2 R.R.C. 61 (C.A.); *affirming* [1956] J.P.L. 385; 49 R. & I.T. 216; 106 L.J. 253; 167 E.G. 319; 1 R.R.C. 17; [1956] C.L.Y. 7257 .... 4.38, 4.39
Shelfer v. City of London Electric Lighting Co. (1895) 1 Ch. 287; 64 L.J.Ch. 216; 39 S.J. 132; 72 L.T. 34; 43 W.R. 238; 11 T.L.R. 137; 12 R. 112 (C.A.); [1895] 2 Ch. 388 (C.A.) 1.025
Showboat Entertainment Centre Ltd. v. Owens [1984] 1 W.L.R. 384; (1984) 128 S.J. 152; [1984] I.C.R. 65; [1984] 1 All E.R. 836; [1984] I.R.L.R. 7; (1984) 134 New L.J. 37; (1983) 80 L.S.Gaz. 3002 E.A.T. 1.089
Simkiss v. Rhondda Borough Council (1983) 81 L.G.R. 460 (C.A.) 1.013
Simms v. Leigh Rugby F.C. Ltd. [1969] 2 All E.R. 923 .... 1.008, 1.124, 7.26, 7.27
Sims v. Foster Wheeler (Plibrico Third Party) [1966] 1 W.L.R. 769; 110 S.J. 189; [1966] 2 All E.R. 313; 1 K.I.R. 1 (C.A.) 1.173
Singette Ltd. v. Martin [1971] A.C. 407; [1971] 2 W.L.R. 13; 114 S.J. 951; [1970] 3 All E.R. 938 (H.L.); *affirming* [1970] 2 Q.B. 565 (D.C.) 6.87
Slater v. Clay Cross Ltd. [1956] 2 Q.B. 264; [1956] 3 W.L.R. 232; 100 S.J. 450; [1956] 2 All E.R. 625 (C.A.) 1.021
Smith (V. O.) v. St. Albans City and District Council (LVC/880/1975) (1977) 244 E.G. 391; [1979] J.P.L. 110 .... 4.41
Smith v. Baker [1891] A.C. 325; 60 L.J.Q.B. 683; 65 L.T. 467; 55 J.P. 660; 40 W.R. 392; 7 T.L.R. 679 (H.L.) 1.063
—— v. East Elloe R.D.C. [1956] A.C. 736; [1956] 2 W.L.R. 888; 120 J.P. 263; 100 S.J. 282; [1956] 1 All E.R. 855; 54 L.G.R. 233; 6 P. & C.R. 102 (H.L.); *varying* [1955] 1 W.L.R. 380 (C.A.) 2.19
—— v. Leech Brain & Co. Ltd. [1962] 2 Q.B. 405; [1962] 2 W.L.R. 148; 106 S.J. 77; [1961] 3 All E.R. 1159 .... 7.07

TABLE OF CASES

Solle v. Butcher [1950] 1 K.B. 671; 66 T.L.R. (Pt. 1) 448; [1949] 2 All E.R. 1107 (C.A.)	1.136
Solloway v. Hampshire County Council (1981) 258 E.G. 858; [1981] 79 L.G.R. 449 (C.A.)	1.028, 1.029
Sowler v. Potter [1940] 1 K.B. 271; [1939] 109 L.J.K.B. 177; 84 S.J. 115; 4 All E.R. 478; 162 L.T. 12; 56 T.L.R. 142	1.137
Springfield v. Thame (1903) 8 L.T. 242; 19 T.L.R. 650	3.12
Stackpoole v. The Queen (1875) I.R. 9 Eq. 619	3.54
Staden v. Tarjanyi (1980) 78 L.G.R. 614 (D.C.)	4.47
Stafford Borough Council v. Elkenford [1977] 1 W.L.R. 324; [1977] J.P.L. 170; (1976) 19 Man. L. 36; (1976) 75 L.G.R. 337 (C.A.)	4.56
Stewart v. Reavell's Garage [1952] 2 Q.B. 545; [1952] 1 T.L.R. 1266; 96 S.J. 314; [1952] 1 All E.R. 1191	1.173
Sturges v. Bridgman (1879) 11 Ch.D. 852; 48 L.J.Ch. 785; 41 L.T. 219; 43 J.P. 716; 28 W.R. 200 (C.A.)	1.026
Sutton v. Bootle Corporation [1947] K.B. 359; 177 L.T. 168; 111 J.P. 81; [1947] 1 All E.R. 92 (C.A.)	1.013
Sutton Common, Wimborne, Re [1982] 1 W.L.R. 647; (1982) 126 S.J. 329; [1982] 2 All E.R. 376; (1982) 44 P. & C.R. 99	2.71
Taylor v. Caldwell (1863) 3 B. & S. 826; 2 New Rep. 198; 32 L.J.Q.B. 164; 8 L.T. 356; 27 J.P. 710; 11 W.R. 726; 122 E.R. 309	3.73
Teasdale v. Walker [1958] 1 W.L.R. 1076; 102 S.J 757; [1958] 3 All E.R. 307 (C.A.)	1.046
Terry v. Brighton Aquarium Co. (1875) L.R. 10 Q.B. 306; 44 L.J.M.C. 173; 32 L.T. 458; 39 J.P. 519	6.63
—— v. Variety Theatres Controlling Co. (1928) 44 T.L.R. 451 (C.A.)	6.08
Theatre de Luxe (Halifax) Ltd. v. Gledhill [1915] 2 K.B. 49; [1914–15] All E.R. 166; 112 L.T. 519; 79 J.P. 238; 31 T.L.R. 138; 13 L.G.R. 541; 24 Cox. C.C. 107 (D.C.)	6.21
Thompson v. Smiths Shiprepairers Ltd. [1984] Q.B. 405; [1984] 2 W.L.R. 522; [1984] I.C.R. 236; [1984] 128 S.J. 225; [1984] 1 All E.R. 881; [1984] I.R.L.R. 93; (1984) 81 L.S.Gaz. 741	1.103
Thompson's (Funeral Furnishers) Ltd. v. Phillips (1945) 2 All E.R. 49 (C.A.)	1.071
Thornton v. Kirklees Metropolitan Borough Council [1979] Q.B. 626; [1979] 3 W.L.R. 1; (1979) 77 L.G.R. 417; sub nom. Thornton v. Kirklees Metropolitan District Council (1979) 123 S.J. 285; [1979] 2 All E.R. 349; [1979] J.P.L. 459 (C.A.)	2.07
Tito v. Waddel (No. 2); Tito v. Att.-Gen. [1977] Ch. 106; [1977] 2 W.L.R. 496; [1977] 3 All E.R. 129; judgment on damages [1977] 3 W.L.R. 972 (N.)	7.61
Trendtex Trading Corporation v. Credit Suisse [1981] 3 W.L.R. 766; (1981) 125 S.J. 761; [1981] 3 All E.R. 520; [1982] A.C. 679; [1981] Com.L.R. 262 (H.L.); *affirming* [1980] Q.B. 629; [1980] 3 W.L.R. 367; (1980) 124 S.J. 396; [1980] 3 All E.R. 721 (C.A.)	1.151
Tweddle v. Atkinson (1861) 1 B. & S. 393; 30 L.J.Q.B. 265; 4 L.T. 468; 25 J.P. 517; 8 Jur.N.S. 332; 9 W.R. 781; 121 E.R. 762	1.149
Universal Corporation v. Five Ways Properties Ltd. (1978) 123 S.J. 33; [1979] 1 All E.R. 552; (1979) 38 P. & C.R. 687; (1978) 250 E.G. 447 (C.A.); *reversing* [1978] 3 All E.R. 1131	2.24
Verrall, Re, National Trust for Places of Historic Interest or Natural Beauty v. Attorney-General [1916] 1 Ch. 100; 85 L.J.Ch. 115; 66 S.J. 141; 113 L.T. 1208; 80 J.P. 89; 14 L.G.R. 171	5.03
Wakefield Corporation v. Wakefield and District Light Railway Co. [1908] A.C. 293; 77 L.J.K.B. 692; 52 S.J. 497; 99 L.T. 1; 72 J.P. 315; 24 T.L.R. 603; 6 L.G.R. 647; 2 Konst.Rat.App. 433 (H.L.)	8.15
Wallis Son & Wells v. Pratt & Haynes [1911] A.C. 394; [1910] 2 K.B. 1003; 79 L.J.K.B. 1013; 103 L.T. 118; 26 T.L.R. 572 (C.A.)	1.157

TABLE OF CASES

Wandsworth London Borough Council *v.* Winder (1984) 128 S.J. 838; (1985) 82 L.S.Gaz. 201 (H.L.); *affirming* [1984] 3 W.L.R. 563 (C.A.) 2.23
Ward *v.* Hertfordshire County Council [1970] 1 All E.R. 535; (1969) 114 S.J. 87 (C.A.); *reversing* [1969] 1 W.L.R. 790; 113 S.J. 343; [1969] 2 All E.R. 807; 67 L.G.R. 418 .... 1.013
—— *v.* Tesco Stores [1976] 1 W.L.R. 810; 120 S.J. 555; [1976] 1 All E.R. 219; *sub nom.* Tesco Stores *v.* Ward [1976] I.R.L.R. 92 (C.A.) 1.118
Wessex Dairies Ltd. *v.* Smith [1935] 2 K.B. 80; [1935] 104 L.J.K.B. 484; [1935] All E.R. 75; 153 L.T. 185; 51 T.L.R. 439 (C.A.) 1.062
Westminster City Council *v.* Ray Alan (Manshops) [1982] 1 W.L.R. 383; (1982) 126 S.J. 115; [1982] 1 All E.R. 771; [1982] Crim.L.R. 309 (D.C.) 1.181
White *v.* Blackmore [1972] 2 Q.B. 651; [1972] 3 W.L.R. 296; 116 S.J. 547; [1972] 3 All E.R. 158 (C.A.) 7.31, 7.32
Whitehouse *v.* Jordan [1981] 1 W.L.R. 246; (1980) 125 S.J. 167; [1981] 1 All E.R. 267 (H.L.); *affirming* [1980] 1 All E.R. 650 (C.A.) 3.76
Whiting *v.* Hillingdon London Borough Council (1970) 114 S.J. 247; 68 L.G.R. 437 ...... 7.09
Wilks *v.* Cheltenham Home Guard Motor-Cycle and Light Car Club [1971] 1 W.L.R. 668; 115 S.J. 309; *sub nom.* Wilks (formerly An Infant) *v.* The Cheltenham Home Guard Motor Cycle, etc., Club [1971] 2 All E.R. 369 (C.A.); *reversing* 115 S.J. 127 .... 7.31, 7.36
Williams *v.* Compair Maxam Ltd. [1982] 1 I.R.L.R. 83; [1982] I.C.R. 156, E.A.T. 1.068
—— *v.* National Theatre Board [1982] I.C.R. 715; [1982] I.R.L.R. 377 (C.A.); *affirming* [1981] I.C.R. 248; [1981] I.R.L.R. 5 E.A.T. 1.072
Wilson *v.* Quastel (Danny) (Rotherhithe) Ltd. [1966] 1 Q.B. 125; [1965] 3 W.L.R. 774; 129 J.P. 393; 109 S.J. 372; [1965] 2 All E.R. 541 (D.C.) 6.79
Wilsons and Clyde Coal Co. Ltd. *v.* English [1938] A.C. 57; 106 L.J.P.C. 117; 81 S.J. 700; 157 L.T. 406; 53 T.L.R. 944; [1937] 3 All E.R. 628 .... 1.063
Windsors (Sporting Investments) *v.* Oldfield; Boulton *v.* Coral Racing [1981] 1 W.L.R. 1176; [1981] 2 All E.R. 718; (1981) 125 S.J. 607; [1981] Crim.L.R. 619 (D.C.) 6.79
Winkfield, The (1902) P. 42; 71 L.J.P. 21; 46 S.J. 163; 85 L.T. 668; 50 W.R. 246; 18 T.L.R. 178; 9 Asp.M.L.C. 259 (C.A.) 3.74
Winstone *v.* Wurlitzer Automatic Phonograph Co. of Australia Ltd. [1946] V.L.R. 338 .... 3.17
Withers *v.* General Theatre Corporation Ltd. [1933] 2 K.B. 536; 102 L.J.K.B. 719; 149 L.T. 487 (C.A.) 6.09
Wombwell Urban District Council *v.* Burke [1966] 2 Q.B. 149; [1966] 2 W.L.R. 669; 130 J.P. 282; 110 S.J. 311; [1966] 1 All E.R. 911; 64 L.G.R. 151 (C.A.) 8.06
Woodward *v.* Hastings Corporation [1945] K.B. 174; 114 L.J.K.B. 211, 218; 2 All E.R. 565; 172 L.T. 16; 109 J.P. 41; 61 T.L.R. 94; 43 L.G.R. 29 (C.A.) 1.023
Wooldridge *v.* Sumner [1963] 2 Q.B. 43; [1962] 3 W.L.R. 616; 106 S.J. 489; [1962] 2 All E.R. 978 (C.A.); *reversing The Times*, December 7, 1961 .... 7.12
Worsley (Ben) *v.* Harvey [1967] 1 W.L.R. 889; (1967) 131 J.P. 376; 111 S.J. 541; [1967] 2 All E.R. 507; 65 L.Q.R. 373 (D.C.) 1.177

Table of Statutes

References throughout are to paragraph numbers.

Year	Statute	Para
1677	Statute of Frauds (c. 3)—	
	s. 4	1.135
1780	Sunday Observance Act (20 Geo. 3, c. 49)	6.62, 6.63
1824	Vagrancy Act (5 Geo. 4, c. 83)	6.03
1831	Civil List Act (1 Will. 4, c. 25)—	
	s. 2	3.60
1832	Allotments Act (2 & 3 Will. 4, c. 42)—	
	s. 8	8.03
1836	Inclosure Act (6 & 7 Will. 4, c. 115)	2.61
1837	Civil List Act (1 & 2 Vict. c. 2)	3.60
1845	Museums Act (8 & 9 Vict. c. 43)	3.01, 3.02
	Protection of Works of Art, etc., Act (8 & 9 Vict. c. 44)	3.39
	Gaming Act (8 & 9 Vict. c. 109)	6.43, 1.142
	Inclosure Act (8 & 9 Vict. c. 118)	2.63
1848	Public Health Act (11 & 12 Vict. c. 63)—	
	s. 74	4.03
1850	Public Libraries, etc., Act (13 & 14 Vict. c. 65)	2.26, 3.01, 3.02, 3.06, 3.44
1851	Crown Lands Act (14 & 15 Vict. c. 42)	5.39
1852	Inclosure Act (15 & 16 Vict. c. 79)	2.63
1854	Public Statutes (Metropolis) Act (17 & 18 Vict. c. 33)—	
	ss. 5, 7	5.23
1855	Metropolis Management Act (18 & 19 Vict. c. 120)	5.37
1856	National Gallery Act (19 & 20 Vict. c. 29)	3.40
1857	Inclosure Act (20 & 21 Vict. c. 31)	2.63
	Burial Act (20 & 21 Vict. c. 81)	2.41
1859	Recreation Grounds Act (22 & 23 Vict. c. 27)	4.03
1860	Public Improvements Act (23 & 24 Vict. c. 30)	4.03
1863	Town Gardens Protection Act (26 & 27 Vict. c. 13)	2.47, 2.55, 4.03, 5.37
1866	Metropolitan Commons Act (29 & 30 Vict. c. 78)	2.64, 5.36
	ss. 6–10	5.35
1868	Regulation of Railways Act (31 & 32 Vict. c. 119)—	
	s. 28	8.16
1869	Metropolitan Commons Act (32 & 33 Vict. c. 107)	5.36
1871	Bank Holidays Act (34 & 35 Vict. c. 17)	4.20
1872	Parks Regulation Act (35 & 36 Vict. c. 15)	5.39
1873	Poor Allotments Act (36 & 37 Vict. c. 19)—	
	ss. 3–4	8.03
1874	Infants Relief Act (37 & 38 Vict. c. 62)	1.146
1875	Public Health Act (38 & 39 Vict. c. 55)	1.040, 2.55, 4.01, 4.02, 4.03, 4.05, 4.22
	s. 164	1.040, 2.05, 2.35, 2.68, 4.02, 4.03, 4.09, 4.12, 4.26, 4.30
	s. 165	5.22
	s. 172	7.40
1876	Commons Act (39 & 40 Vict. c. 56)	2.65, 2.72
	s. 7	2.60, 2.65
	s. 8	2.60
	ss. 10, 12	2.65
	s. 20	5.05
	s. 29	2.65
	Cruelty to Animals Act (c. 77)	4.64
1877	Destructive Insects and Pests Act (40 & 41 Vict. c. 68)	4.62
1878	Metropolitan Commons Act (41 & 42 Vict. c. 78)	2.64
	Corporation of London (Open Spaces) Act (41 & 42 Vict. c. cxxvii)	5.32, 5.33
	Epping Forest Act (41 & 42 Vict. c. ccxiii)	5.32
1882	Ancient Monuments Protection Act (45 & 46 Vict. c. 73)	1.052
1889	Public Bodies Corrupt Practices Act (52 & 53 Vict. c. 69)	1.094, 1.096
	s. 1 (1)	1.095
	(2)	1.095

Table of Statutes

Year	Act	Ref
1889	Public Bodies Corrupt Practices Act—*cont.*	
	s. 2	1.096
	s. 7	1.096
1890	London Council (General Powers) Act (53 & 54 Vict. c. ccxliii)	5.30
	s. 16	5.30
	Public Health Acts (Amendment) Act (53 & 54 Vict. c. 59)	4.01
	s. 37	6.55
	s. 42	5.22
	s. 44	4.20, 5.31
	(2)	4.06
	s. 45	4.02
	s. 46	5.22
1892	Public Libraries Act (55 & 56 Vict. c. 53)	3.03, 5.06
	s. 15 (1)	3.03
1894	Finance Act (57 & 58 Vict. c. 30)—	
	s. 15	3.43
	Merchant Shipping Act (57 & 58 Vict. c. 60)	3.54
	s. 72	3.55
	s. 184	3.57
	s. 523	3.54
	s. 566	3.55
	Sched. 22	3.57
	Local Government Act (57 & 58 Vict. c. 73)—	
	s. 33	8.03
1896	Light Railways Act (59 & 60 Vict. c. 48)	8.15
	ss. 2, 7	8.16
	s. 2 (*b*)	8.16
	s. 3	8.16
	s. 9	8.16
	s. 12	8.16
	s. 28	8.16
1898	Metropolitan Commons Act (61 & 62 Vict. c. 43)	2.64
	Library Offences Act (61 & 62 Vict. c. 53)	3.08, 3.09
1899	Commons Acts (62 & 63 Vict. c. 30)	2.66, 2.67, 2.72, 5.15
	s. 1	2.66, 5.35
	s. 2	5.35
1900	Burial Act (63 & 64 Vict. c. 15)—	
	s. 10	4.17
1901	Public Libraries Act (1 Edw. 7, c. 19)—	
	s. 3	5.06
1906	Open Spaces Act (6 Edw. 7, c. 25)	1.040, 2.46, 2.48, 2.51, 2.54, 2.55, 2.70, 4.01, 4.04, 4.22, 4.26, 4.34, 5.24, 5.29
1906	Open Spaces Act—*cont.*	
	s. 2	2.49
	s. 3	2.50
	s. 4	2.51
	s. 5	2.52
	ss. 7, 8	2.53
	s. 10	2.35, 2.54, 4.30
	s. 14	4.05
	s. 15	2.55
	s. 20	2.48
	Prevention of Corruption Act (6 Edw. 7, c. 34)	1.094
	s. 1	1.095, 1.096
	(2)	1.096
1907	Destructive Insects and Pests Act (7 Edw. 7, c. 4)	4.62
	National Trust Act (7 Edw. 7, c. cxxxvi)	5.01, 5.03, 5.07, 5.08
	s. 4	5.02
	(2)	5.04
	s. 21 (2)	5.08
	s. 29	5.05
	s. 30	5.05
	s. 31	5.05
	s. 33	5.06
	s. 36	5.05
	Sched. 1	5.07
	Public Health Acts (Amendment) Act (7 Edw. 7, c. 53)	4.01, 4.06, 4.07, 7.41–7.43
	s. 76	4.06, 4.07
	(4)	4.07
	s. 77	4.25
	s. 94	7.41
	(7)	7.41
1908	Small Holdings and Allotments Act (8 Edw. 7, c. 36)	8.03, 8.04, 8.09
	s. 8	8.08
	s. 23	5.43, 8.04
	s. 25	8.04
	s. 26	8.05
	s. 28	8.05, 8.08
	(4)	8.05
	s. 35	8.08
	s. 41	8.04
	s. 49	8.08
1909	Cinematograph Act (9 Edw. 7, c. 30)	5.40, 6.19, 6.24
	s. 2	6.20, 6.21
	s. 7	6.24
1911	Protection of Animals Act (1 & 2 Geo. 5, c. 27)	6.60
1912	Light Railways Act (2 & 3 Geo. 5, c. 19)	8.15
1916	Prevention of Corruption Act (6 & 7 Geo. 5, c. 64)	1.094
	s. 1	1.096
	s. 2	1.097

TABLE OF STATUTES

1919	Forestry Act (9 & 10 Geo. 5, c. 58) 5.13, 5.17
	Land Settlement (Facilities) Act (9 & 10 Geo. 5, c. 59) 8.04
	s. 16 .... 8.04
	s. 28 .... 5.10, 8.04
	National Trust Charity Scheme Confirmation Act (9 & 10 Geo. 5, c. lxxxiv) 5.08
	s. 12 .... 5.08
1921	Railways Act (11 & 12 Geo. 5, c. 55) 8.16
	s. 68 (1) (*b*) 8.16
1922	Allotment Act (12 & 13 Geo. 5, c. 51) 8.03, 8.04, 8.09
	s. 1 .... 8.06
	(1) (*b*) 8.06
	(*c*) 8.06
	(*d*) 8.06
	(*e*) 8.06
	s. 2 .... 8.07
	s. 10 .... 5.10
	s. 11 .... 8.06
	s. 19 .... 8.05
	s. 22 .... 8.03
1925	Law of Property Act (15 & 16 Geo. 5, c. 20) 2.73, 2.75
	s. 40 .... 1.135
	s. 84 .... 4.27
	s. 189 (2) 2.69
	s. 193 .... 2.73, 8.26, 8.36
	(1) (*b*) 2.74
	(5) 2.75
	s. 194 .... 2.75
	Performing Animals (Regulation) Act (15 & 16 Geo. 5, c. 38) 6.16
	Allotments Act (15 & 16 Geo. 5, c. 61) 8.03, 8.04
	s. 1 .... 8.03
	Public Health Act (15 & 16 Geo. 5, c. 71) 4.01
	s. 56 .... 4.06
1926	Parks Regulation (Amendment) Act (16 & 17 Geo. 5, c. 36) 5.39
1927	Destructive Insects and Pests Act (17 & 18 Geo. 5, c. 32) 4.62
	Landlord and Tenant Act (17 & 18 Geo. 5, c. 36) 1.037, 1.051
	s. 19 .... 1.049
1931	Agricultural land (Utilisation) Act (21 & 22 Geo. 5, c. 41) 8.04
1931	London Squares (Preservation) Act (21 & 22 Geo. 5, c. xciii) 5.29, 5.37
1932	Sunday Entertainments Act (22 & 23 Geo. 5, c. 51) 6.21, 6.39, 6.63
	Administration of Justice Act (22 & 23 Geo. 5, c. 55) 4.27
	s. 4 .... 3.39
1933	Children and Young Persons Act (23 & 24 Geo. 5, c. 12)
	s. 12 .... 6.15, 6.31
	s. 23 .... 6.15
1934	Protection of Animals Act (24 & 25 Geo. 5, c. 21) 6.16
	Whaling Industry (Regulation) Act (24 & 25 Geo. 5, c. 49) 3.57
	Betting and Lotteries Act (24 & 25 Geo. 5, c. 58) 6.53
1936	Public Order Act (26 Geo. 5 & 1 Edw. 8, c. 6)—
	s. 5 .... 7.34
	Public Health Act (26 Geo. 5 and 1 Edw. 8, c. 49) 7.02
	s. 59 .... 6.12, 6.55
	s. 92 .... 4.50
	s. 221 .... 7.02
	s. 223 .... 7.05
	(1) 7.05
	(2) 7.05
	s. 224 .... 7.02
	s. 226 .... 6.31, 7.02
	s. 228 .... 7.02
	s. 229 .... 7.02
	s. 231 .... 7.60
	(1) (*d*) 7.60
	s. 298 .... 4.56
	Pt. VIII 7.01, 7.02
1937	Physical Training and Recreation Act (1 Edw. 8 & 1 Geo. 6, c. 46) 4.01
	National Trust Act (1 Edw. 8 & 1 Geo. 6, c. lvii) 5.11
	s. 3 .... 5.03
	s. 8 .... 5.11
1938	Street Playgrounds Act (1 & 2 Geo. 6, c. 37, repealed 8 & 9 Eliz. 2, c. 16) 4.57
	Green Belt (London and Home Counties) Act (2 & 3 Geo. 6, c. xciii) 2.36, 5.34
	s. 3 .... 5.34
	s. 5 .... 5.34
	s. 27 .... 5.34
1939	National Trust Act (2 & 3 Geo. 6, c. xxxvi) 5.08
	s. 8 .... 5.08

1943	Law Reform (Frustrated Contracts) Act (6 & 7 Geo. 6, c. 40) 1.152	1948	Agricultural Holdings Act —*cont.*
			s. 1 .... 1.043
1944	Disabled Persons (Employment) Act (7 & 8 Geo. 6, c. 10) 1.087		(1) 1.043
			s. 2 (1) 1.043
			s. 94 .... 1.042
	s. 1 .... 1.087	1949	Lands Tribunal Act (12, 13 & 14 Geo. 6, c. 42) 4.27
	s. 6 .... 1.087		
	s. 9 .... 1.087		War-Damaged Sites Act (12, 13 & 14 Geo. 6, c. 84)—
	(2) 1.087		
	s. 11 .... 1.087		s. 1 .... 5.10
	s. 14 .... 1.087		National Parks and Access to the Countryside Act (12, 13 & 14 Geo. 6, c. 97) 1.009, 8.18, 8.19, 8.26, 8.32, 8.40, 8.46
	s. 17 .... 1.087		
	s. 19 .... 1.087		
	Agriculture (Miscellaneous Provisions) Act (7 & 8 Geo. 6, c. 28)—		
			s. 1 .... 7.55
	s. 1 .... 8.18		s. 3 .... 8.20
	Education Act (7 & 8 Geo. 6, c. 31) 2.51, 6.31, 7.01, 7.03		ss. 5–7 .... 8.21
			s. 5 .... 7.55, 8.20
	s. 9 .... 8.08		s. 6 .... 8.20, 8.22
	s. 41 .... 6.31		s. 7 .... 8.21
	s. 52 (2) 7.03		s. 11 .... 8.40
	s. 53 .... 2.51, 7.01		s. 12 .... 8.40
	(1) 7.03		(5) 7.55
	s. 68 .... 2.10		s. 13 .... 7.55, 8.40
	s. 120 .... 8.08		s. 14 .... 8.24
1945	Law Reform (Contributory Negligence) Act (8 & 9 Geo. 6, c. 28) 1.122		s. 21 .... 8.40
			ss. 51–57 .... 8.23
			s. 51 .... 8.34
	Forestry Act (8 & 9 Geo. 6, c. 35) 5.17		s. 52 .... 8.23
			s. 54 .... 8.23
	Statutory Orders (Special Procedure) Act (9 & 10 Geo. 6, c. 18) 5.09		s. 59 .... 8.32
			s. 60 .... 8.35–8.38
			(1) 8.37
1946	Roosevelt Memorial Act (9 & 10 Geo. 6, c. 83) 5.23		s. 61 .... 8.33
			s. 62 .... 8.33
1947	Forestry Act (10 & 11 Geo. 6, c. 21) 5.17		s. 63 .... 8.33
			s. 64 .... 8.34
	Civic Restaurants Act (10 & 11 Geo. 6, c. 22) 6.76		s. 65 .... 8.34
			(2) 8.34
	s. 3 .... 6.76		(5) 8.34
	Agriculture Act (10 & 11 Geo. 6, c. 48)—		s. 66 .... 8.38
			s. 69 .... 8.34
	s. 109 .... 1.043, 8.03		s. 70 .... 8.38
	Transport Act (10 & 11 Geo. 6, c. 49)—		ss. 72, 73 .... 8.38
			s. 74 .... 7.55, 8.32
	s. 12 .... 7.52		s. 76 .... 8.35
	Sched. 3 .... 7.52		s. 77 .... 8.24, 8.35
	London County Council (General Powers) Act (10 & 11 Geo. 6, c. xlvi)—		s. 78 .... 8.39
			s. 81 .... 8.39
			s. 82 .... 8.42
	s. 59 .... 5.38		s. 85 .... 8.29
1948	Local Government Act (11 & 12 Geo. 6, c. 26) 6.27		s. 86 .... 8.22
			s. 89 .... 8.41
	s. 132 .... 6.29		s. 90 .... 8.41
	Agricultural Holdings Act (11 & 12 Geo. 6, c. 63) 1.042–1.043		s. 91 .... 8.41
			s. 92 .... 8.25
			s. 97 .... 9.21

1949	National Parks and Access to the Countryside Act—*cont.*	
	s. 99	8.42
	ss. 112–113	8.32
	s. 114	7.56
	(1)	7.56
	Sched. 2	8.37
	para. 1 (*a*)–(*b*)	8.37
	(*f*)	8.37
	Pts. II and III	5.10
	Pt. V 5.10, 7.55, 8.32, 8.37, 8.41, 8.73	
	Pt. VI	5.10
1950	Shops Act (14 Geo. 6, c. 28)	6.17
	s. 3	6.17
	Allotments Act (14 Geo. 6, c. 31)	8.04, 8.09
	s. 3	8.07
	s. 4	8.07
	s. 9	8.04
	s. 10	8.05, 8.09
	s. 11	8.09
	s. 12	8.05
	s. 27 (6)	8.05
1951	Forestry Act (14 & 15 Geo. 6, c. 61)	5.17
	London County Council (Crystal Palace) Act (14 & 15 Geo. 6, c. xxviii)	5.31
1952	Customs and Excise Act (15 & 16 Geo. 6 & 1 Eliz. 2, c. 44)	6.82
	Hypnotism Act (15 & 16 Geo. 6 & 1 Eliz. 2, c. 46)	6.41, 6.42
	s. 6	6.42
	Cockfighting Act (15 & 16 Geo. 6 & 1 Eliz. 2, c. 59)	6.60
	Cinematograph Act (15 & 16 Geo. 6 & 1 Eliz. 2, c. 68) 6.19, 6.24, 6.25, 6.39	
	s. 2 (1)(*a*)	6.24
	s. 3	6.25
	s. 5	6.23
	(2)	6.25
	London County Council (Holland House) Act (15 & 16 Geo. 6 & Eliz. 2, c. v)	5.31
	London County Council (General Powers) Act (15 & 16 Geo. 6 & Eliz. 2, c. viii)—	
	s. 20 (3)	3.41
1953	Emergency Laws (Miscellaneous Provisions) Act (1 & 2 Eliz. 2, c. 47)—	
	s. 5	8.04
1953	Historic Buildings and Ancient Monuments Act (1 & 2 Eliz. 2, c. 49)	1.056
1954	Law Reform (Limitation of Actions) Act (2 & 3 Eliz. 2, c. 36)	1.024, n. 43
	Landlord and Tenant Act (2 & 3 Eliz. 2, c. 56) .1.037, 1.046, 1.047–1.049, 1.051	
	s. 23	1.046
	(4)	1.046
	s. 30	1.048
	s. 38	1.046
	s. 41A	1.047, n. 1
	s. 42 (1)	1.047
	s. 43	1.046
	s. 57	1.046
	Pt. II	2.45
	National Gallery and Tate Gallery Act (2 & 3 Eliz. 2, c. 65)	3.40
	s. 2	3.40
	s. 4	3.40
	(5)	3.40
	s. 5	3.41
	Sched. 2	3.40
	British Transport Commission Act (2 & 3 Eliz. 2, c. lv)—	
	s. 16	7.52
1956	Administration of Justice Act (4 & 5 Eliz. 2, c. 46)—	
	s. 1 (1) (*s*)	3.58
	s. 3 (2)	3.58
	Copyright Act (4 & 5 Eliz. 2, c. 74) 3.15, 3.20, 3.24, 3.26, 3.27, 3.35, 6.45	
	s. 1	3.15, 3.26, 3.27
	s. 2	3.27
	s. 2 (3)	3.34
	s. 3 (4)	3.34
	s. 4	3.28
	s. 5	3.28
	s. 6	3.29, 3.30
	s. 7	3.20, 3.21
	(5)	3.22
	s. 8	3.29
	s. 9	3.30
	s. 11	3.28
	s. 12	3.15
	s. 15 (4)	3.23
	s. 17	3.31
	(2)	3.31
	(4)	3.31
	s. 18	3.31
	s. 19	3.31
	s. 20	3.32
	s. 21	3.32, 6.45
	s. 22	3.32

Table of Statutes

1956 Copyright Act—*cont.*
    s. 23 .... 3.33
    s. 24 .... 3.33
    s. 36 .... 3.34
    s. 37 .... 3.34
    s. 40 .... 3.26
    s. 41 .... 3.34
    Scheds. 2, 3 .... 3.28
    Sched. 5 .... 3.34
        Pt. II 3.30
        Pt. IV 3.33
    City of London (Various Powers) Act (4 & 5 Eliz. 2, c. i)—
        s. 10 .... 5.32

1957 Occupiers' Liability Act (5 & 6 Eliz. 2, c. 31) 1.003, 1.006–1.010, 1.013, 1.014, 1.022–1.023, 1.025, 7.10, 7.12, 7.23
    s. 1 (1) 1.006, 1.021
        (2) 1.005, 1.007, 1.021
        (4) 1.009
    s. 2 (1) 1.011
        (2) 1.004, 7.10, 7.11
        (3) 1.013
            (*a*) 7.10
            (*b*) 1.019
        (4) (*b*) 1.023
        (5) 1.008
    s. 5 (1) 1.010
    Parish Councils Act (5 & 6 Eliz. 2, c. 42) 4.03
    Housing Act (5 & 6 Eliz. 2, c. 56) 2.56
    s. 47 .... 2.19
        (2) 2.19
    s. 93 .... 2.56
    Pt. V 1.040
    London County Council (General Powers) Act (5 & 6 Eliz. 2, c. xxxv)—
        s. 31 .... 5.22

1958 Disabled Persons (Employment) Act (6 & 7 Eliz. 2, c. 33) 1.087
    Litter Act (6 & 7 Eliz. 2, c. 34) 8.52
    Dramatic and Musical Performers Protection Act (6 & 7 Eliz. 2, c. 44) 3.37
    s. 1 .... 3.37
    s. 2 .... 3.37
    s. 3 .... 3.37
    s. 4 .... 3.37
    s. 5 .... 3.37
    s. 6 .... 3.37
    s. 7 .... 3.37

1958 London County Council (General Powers) Act (6 & 7 Eliz. 2, c. xxi)—
    s. 36 .... 5.38
    Waltham Holy Cross U.D.C. Act (6 & 7 Eliz. 2, c. xxxvii) 4.24
    City of London (Various Powers) Act (6 & 7 Eliz. 2, c. xlvii)—
        ss. 7–10 .... 5.34

1959 County Courts Act (7 & 8 Eliz. 2, c. 22)—
    s. 84 .... 3.67
    Eisteddfod Act (7 & 8 Eliz. 2, c. 32) 6.29
    Obscene Publications Act (7 & 8 Eliz. 2, c. 66) 6.03, 6.90
    Halifax Corporation Act (7 & 8 Eliz. 2, c. xlviii)—
        s. 24 .... 3.46
    City of London (Various Powers) Act (7 & 8 Eliz. 2, c. xlix)—
        s. 17 .... 5.32

1960 Films Act (8 & 9 Eliz. 2, c. 57) 6.26
    Charities Act (8 & 9 Eliz. 2, c. 58) 4.31
    s. 39 .... 4.03
    Caravan Sites and Control of Development Act (8 & 9 Eliz. 2, c. 62) 8.53, 8.56
    s. 3 (3) 8.53
    s. 4 .... 8.53
    s. 5 (2), (5) 8.54
    s. 7 .... 8.55
    s. 8 .... 8.55
    s. 9 .... 8.56
    s. 12 .... 8.57
    s. 19 .... 8.54
    s. 23 .... 8.58
    s. 24 .... 9.18
    s. 25 .... 8.58
    s. 26 .... 8.56
    s. 28 .... 8.58
    Sched. 1 .... 8.57
    Sched. 2 .... 8.58
        Pts. I, II 8.53
    London County Council (General Powers) Act (8 & 9 Eliz. 2, c. xxix)—
        s. 10 .... 5.35
    Bournemouth Corporation Act (8 & 9 Eliz. 2, c. xliii) 4.24
    s. 44 .... 4.24
    s. 58 .... 4.24

Table of Statutes

Year	Statute	Page
1960	Hertfordshire County Council Act (8 & 9 Eliz. 2, c. xlix)	4.24
	s. 7	4.24
1961	Consumer Protection Act (9 & 10 Eliz. 2, c. 40)	1.168
	Crown Estate Act (9 & 10 Eliz. 2, c. 55)—	
	s. 19	2.48
	Public Health Act (9 & 10 Eliz. 2, c. 64)	4.01, 7.43
	s. 4 (6)	6.12
	s. 51	8.52
	s. 52	4.25
	(3)	4.06
	s. 53	4.20, 5.31
	s. 54	4.06, 7.40
	(4)	4.06
	s. 75	6.56
	s. 76	7.43
1962	Town and Country Planning Act (10 & 11 Eliz. 2, c. 38)—	
	s. 83	4.29
	Transport Act (10 & 11 Eliz. 2, c. 46)	7.52
	s. 10 (1) (a)	7.52
	Local Government (Records) Act (10 & 11 Eliz. 2, c. 56)	3.38
	ss. 1, 2	3.38
	City of London (Various Powers) Act (10 & 11 Eliz. 2, c. xliii)—	
	s. 5	5.38
1963	Betting, Gaming and Lotteries Act (c. 2)	6.50, 6.51, 6.54, 6.77, 6.79, 6.85
	s. 1	6.49, 6.79
	s. 5	6.53
	(1) (b)	6.53
	s. 6	6.54
	s. 8	6.79
	s. 9	6.79
	s. 10	6.79
	s. 11	6.79
	s. 13	6.49
	s. 14	6.50
	s. 17	6.53
	s. 23	6.54
	s. 55	6.54
	Sched. 1	6.79
	Sched. 2, para. 1 (a)	6.53
	Sched. 3, para. 7	6.54
	para. 13	6.54
	Sched. 4	6.79
	para. 2	6.79
	para. 4	6.79
	para. 5	6.79
1963	Betting, Gaming and Lotteries Act—*cont.* Sched. 4—*cont.*	
	para. 6	6.79
	Local Authorities (Land) Act (c. 29)	2.18, 2.83
	London Government Act (c. 33)	5.19, 5.20
	s. 2	5.38
	s. 40	5.22, 5.43
	s. 48	5.24
	s. 52	5.40
	s. 53	5.40
	s. 55 (4)	5.43
	s. 57 (2) (e)	5.31
	s. 59	5.34
	Sched. II, para. 16	5.38
	para. 18	5.22
	Deer Act (c. 36)	8.12
	Children and Young Persons Act (c. 37)—	
	s. 37	6.15
	s. 38	6.15
	s. 39	6.15
	s. 40	6.15
	Water Resources Act (c. 38)	7.57, 7.58
	s. 21	7.57
	s. 24	7.58
	Performers Protection Act (c. 53)	3.37
	s. 1	3.37
	s. 3	3.37
	s. 4	3.37
1964	Licensing Act (c. 26)	6.39, 6.43, 6.68, 6.75
	s. 1	6.66
	s. 2	6.65
	s. 4	6.67
	s. 6	6.67
	ss. 10, 11	6.67
	s. 19	6.73
	s. 20	6.73
	s. 26	6.67
	s. 74 (4)	6.37
	s. 79	6.72
	s. 88	6.63
	s. 168	6.74
	s. 169	6.74
	(4)	6.74
	s. 170	6.74
	s. 174 (4)	6.72
	s. 180	6.67
	s. 199 (c)	6.17
	Sched. 1	6.73
	Pt. IV	6.67
	Harbours Act (c. 40)	7.57
	Riding Establishment Act (c. 70)	7.39, 17.69

TABLE OF STATUTES

1964	Riding Establishment Act —cont.	
	s. 1	7.39
	(4)	7.39
	(5)	7.39
	(7)	7.39
	s. 2	7.39
	s. 3	7.39
	s. 4A	7.39
	Public Libraries and Museums Act (c. 75)	2.03, 2.16, 3.03, 3.06, 3.39, 3.45, 3.47, 5.06
	s. 2	3.03
	s. 3	3.03
	s. 4	3.03, 3.39
	s. 7	2.03, 3.03
	(2)	3.04
	s. 8	3.05
	(2)	2.03
	s. 9	3.03, 3.06
	s. 10	3.06
	s. 12	3.39, 3.45
	s. 13	3.39, 3.46
	(2)	3.46
	s. 14	3.46
	s. 15	3.46
	s. 17	3.06
	s. 18	3.06
	s. 19	3.06, 3.47, 5.06
	s. 20	3.06, 3.47
	s. 23	3.06
	s. 25	3.39, 5.38
	s. 26	5.06
	Sched. II	3.39, 3.46
	Sched. III	3.06
1965	Finance Act (c. 25)—	
	s. 31	3.43
	Commons Registration Act (c. 64)	2.60, 2.68, 2.69, 7.62
	ss. 1–3	2.69
	s. 2	5.35
	s. 7	2.71
	s. 8	2.70
	s. 11	2.72
	s. 13	2.71
	s. 14	2.71
	s. 16	2.72
	s. 22	2.68
	Rent Act (c. 75)—	
	s. 33	1.045
1966	Sea Fisheries Regulation Act (c. 38)	7.45, 7.70
	Local Government Act (c. 42)	9.07
	s. 4	9.07
	Greater London Council (General Powers) Act (c. xxviii)—	
	s. 21	5.40
1966	Lee Valley Regional Park Act (c. xli)	5.42
	s. 26	5.42
	s. 38	5.42
1967	Road Traffic Reğlation Act (c. 1)—	
	s. 26	4.58
	(6)	4.58
	s. 27	4.58
	s. 46	4.22
	s. 56A	4.58
	s. 84	4.58
	s. 84B	4.57
	s. 84C	4.58
	s. 84D	4.58
	Misrepresentation Act (c. 7)—	
	s. 2	1.140
	Plant Health Act (c. 8)	5.17
	ss. 3, 5	4.59
	General Rate Act (c. 9)	4.34, 4.41
	s. 44	4.35, 4.36, 4.41
	(1)	4.35
	(2) (a)	4.35
	s. 48	9.08
	s. 263	8.05
	Forestry Act (c. 10)	4.59, 4.60, 5.15, 5.17
	s. 1 (4)	5.17
	s. 3	5.16
	s. 9	4.60
	s. 40 (4)	5.10
	s. 46	5.15
	(3) (a)	5.15
	s. 46 (5)	5.15
	s. 47	5.15
	s. 48	5.15
	s. 49 (1)	5.10
	Private Places of Entertainment (Licensing) Act (c. 19)	2.26, 6.34
	s. 7	5.40
	Leasehold Reform Act (c. 88)—	
	s. 16 (1)	1.046, n. 92
	s. 32	5.10
	Ministry of Housing and Local Government Provisional Order Confirmation (Greater London Parks and Open Spaces) Act (c. xxix)	5.24, 5.35
	s. 6	5.24
	(1)	5.35
	s. 7	5.24, 5.25
	s. 8	5.26
	s. 9	5.26, 5.35
	s. 10	5.27
	s. 11	5.27

Table of Statutes

1967	Ministry of Housing and Local Government Provisional Order Confirmation (Greater London Parks and Open Spaces) Act—*cont.*	
	s. 11—*cont.*	
	(4)	5.27
	s. 12	5.35
	s. 13	5.28
	(1)	5.28
	s. 14	5.29
	s. 15	5.29
	(2)	5.29
	s. 16	5.29
	s. 17	5.29
	s. 18	5.29
	Sched. II	5.35
	City of London (Various Powers) Act (c. xlii)	5.32
	ss. 26–27	5.32
1968	Rent Act (c. 23)	1.044
	s. 9 (3)	1.046
	Trade Descriptions Act (c. 29)	1.176, 1.179
	s. 1 (1) (*a*), (*b*)	1.177
	s. 3	1.179
	s. 4	1.178
	(3)	1.178
	s. 6	1.177
	s. 11	1.180
	s. 14	1.181
	s. 19	1.185
	s. 23	1.177
	s. 24	1.183
	ss. 28, 29	1.184
	s. 33	1.184
	Countryside Act (c. 41)	2.59, 5.14, 5.16, 5.38, 7.56, 8.18, 8.20, 8.26, 8.30, 8.32, 8.40, 8.43, 9.22
	s. 1	8.20
	s. 2	8.20
	(5)	8.20
	s. 4	8.20
	s. 6	8.30
	(3)	8.30
	s. 7	8.31
	(5)	8.31
	(7)	8.31
	s. 8	7.55, 7.61, 8.31
	s. 9	8.31, 8.51
	s. 11	8.18
	s. 12	7.55, 8.27
	s. 13	7.55, 8.28
	s. 16	7.56
	(4)	7.56
	s. 18	8.36
	s. 20	8.42
	s. 22	7.57
1968	Countryside Act—*cont.*	
	s. 23 (2)	5.14
	s. 24	5.16
	(4)	5.15
	(5)	5.15
	ss. 33, 34, 36	9.22
	s. 34 (1)	9.22
	s. 36	9.21
	(3)	9.22
	(6)	9.22
	s. 37	8.18
	s. 41	8.25, 8.41
	s. 42	8.25
	s. 43	8.43
	s. 49	7.55
	Sched. 3	8.46
	Theatres Act (c. 54)	6.01–6.04, 6.11, 6.39, 6.42
	s. 2 (1)	6.03
	(2)	6.03
	(3)	6.03
	(4)	6.03
	s. 5	6.04
	s. 6	6.04, 6.17
	s. 7	6.05
	s. 8	6.05
	ss. 12–14	5.40
	s. 12	6.02
	s. 13	6.02
	s. 14	6.02
	s. 16	6.05
	s. 18	6.03
	s. 28	5.40
	Sched. 1	6.02
	para. 7	6.02
	Sched. 3, para. 11	6.81
	Hovercraft Act (c. 59)—	
	ss. 3, 4 (3)	7.40
	Theft Act (c. 60)—	
	Sched. I, para. 21	7.51
	Gaming Act (c. 65)	2.03, 6.80, 6.81
	s. 1	6.81
	s. 3	6.81, 6.86
	s. 11	6.81
	ss. 16–18, 24	6.86
	s. 16	6.86
	(1) (*c*)	6.86
	s. 18 (1)	6.86
	s. 20	6.82
	s. 24 (2)	6.86
	s. 27	6.83
	s. 30	8.44
	s. 31	6.83
	s. 32	6.83
	s. 33	6.83
	(2)	6.86
	s. 36	6.83
	s. 37	6.83
	s. 38	6.83

Table of Statutes

1968	Gaming Act—*cont.*		1970	Equal Pay Act—*cont.*	
	s. 39	6.83		ss. 4, 5	1.077
	s. 40	6.81		s. 7	1.077
	s. 42	6.78		Trees Act (c. 43)	5.17
	s. 43	6.78, 8.51		Indecent Advertisements	
	s. 44	6.78		(Amendment) Act (c.	
	s. 52 (1)	6.80		47)	6.90
	Sched. 1	6.81		Conservation of Seals Act (c.	
	Sched. 3	6.81, 6.86		70)	8.12
	paras. 7–9	6.81	1971	Consumer Protection Act (c.	
	para. 12	6.81		15)	1.168
	para. 14	6.81		Betting, Gaming and Lotteries	
	para. 20	6.81		(Amendment) Act (c.	
	Pt. II	6.81, 6.83, 6.86		26)—	
	Pt. III	6.83		s. 1	6.53
	Race Relations Act (c. 71)	1.088		Fire Precautions Act (c.	
	Town & Country Planning			40)	6.39, 6.55
	Act (c. 72)—			s. 30	6.12
	s. 49 (4) (*a*)	1.054		Wild Creatures and Forest	
	Transport Act (c. 73)	4.58		Laws Act (c. 47)	5.17
	s. 104	7.52		Pool Competitions Act (c.	
	s. 105	7.52		57)	6.87
	(2), (3)	7.52		Town and Country Planning	
	s. 107	7.52		Act (c. 78)	1.053, 2.34, 2.36, 2.38, 8.47–8.48
	s. 110	7.52		s. 54	1.053
	s. 114	7.52		s. 54A	1.054
	s. 121 (4)	8.16		s. 56 (3)	1.053
	Sched. 12	7.52		s. 58 (1)	1.054
	Pt. VII	7.52		s. 112	2.83
	Sea Fisheries Act (c. 77)	7.45		(1A)	2.83
1969	Development of Tourism Act			(1B)	2.83
	(c. 51)	9.32		(3)	2.83
	s. 2 (9)	9.32		s. 113	2.34
	s. 3 (1)	9.32		ss. 114–117	5.21
	(2)	9.32		s. 119 (4) (*d*)	5.21
	(3)	9.32		s. 121	2.35
	s. 4	9.32		(2)	2.35
	s. 19	9.33		s. 122	2.37
	Sched. II	9.32		s. 123	2.38
	Pt. II	9.33		(7)	2.38
	Law of Property Act (c.			s. 128	2.41, 2.42
	59)	1.047, 2.45, 4.27		(2)	2.41
1970	Riding Establishments Act (c.			s. 129	2.42
	32)	7.39, 7.69		s. 210	8.47
	s. 1	7.39		s. 290	1.053
	s. 2	7.39		Pt. VI	2.32, 2.41, 2.42
	s. 3	7.39		National Trust Act (c. vi)	5.07, 5.11
	Local Authorities (Goods and			s. 24	5.06
	Services) Act (c. 39)	2.16		s. 27	5.11
	Agriculture Act (c. 40)	8.18		s. 28	5.07
	s. 29	8.18		Pt. IV	5.07
	s. 38	5.43		City of London (Various	
	s. 99	1.045, n. 83		Powers) Act (c. clxi)	5.32
	Equal Pay Act (c. 41)	1.076, 1.077, 1.079, 1.085		Pt. IV	5.32
	s. 1	1.077	1972	Sunday Cinema Act (c. 19)	6.63
	(1)	1.077		Betting and Gaming Duties	
	(2)–(5)	1.077		Act (c. 25)	6.82
	s. 2	1.077			
	s. 3	1.077			

Table of Statutes

1972 Sunday Theatres Act (c. 26) ... 6.63
Performers' Protection Act (c. 32) 3.37
Trade Descriptions Act (c. 34) 1.176
Defective Premises Act (c. 35) 1.105, 1.109
   s. 3 .... 1.109
Agricultural (Miscellaneous Provisions) Act (c. 62)—
   s. 20 .... 4.59
European Communities Act (c. 68)—
   s. 2 (1) 3.35
   s. 4 .... 4.59
Horserace Totalisator and Betting Levy Boards Act (c. 69)—
   s. 5 .... 6.49
Local Government Act (c. 70) 1.147, 2.21, 2.27, 2.32, 2.38, 2.40, 2.60, 3.39, 6.28, 7.20, 8.04, 8.25, 9.07, 9.34
   s. 72 .... 7.61
   s. 101 .... 2.57, 6.84
   s. 111 .... 2.18, 7.20
   s. 112 .... 2.35
   s. 120 (2) 2.83
      (4) 2.83
   s. 121 .... 2.83, 4.02
      (2) 2.83
   s. 122 (6) 4.26
   s. 123 .... 2.27, 2.38
      (2) 2.38
      (3) 2.38
   s. 125 .... 2.40
      (5) 2.40
   s. 126 .... 2.40
   s. 127 .... 2.40
   s. 137 .... 2.18, 6.84
   s. 144 .... 9.34
   s. 145 ... 6.28, 6.29, 6.31, 6.57, 6.76, 9.05
      (2) 4.21
      (3) 6.30
   s. 180 .... 5.22, 7.02
   s. 204 (6) 6.01
   ss. 206–208 .... 3.38
   s. 206 .... 3.03, 3.45, 5.38
   s. 207 .... 3.03
   s. 215 .... 4.17
   s. 222 .... 2.09
   s. 235 (1) 4.44
      (3) 4.44
   s. 236 .... 4.54
   s. 238 .... 4.57
   s. 239 .... 2.30
   s. 240 (1) (c) 2.27
   s. 245 .... 2.02

1972 Local Government Act—cont.
   s. 251 .... 6.53, 8.08
   s. 262 .... 2.29, 2.58
   s. 270 .... 4.57
   s. 273 .... 6.53
   Sched. 14, Pt. II, para, 1 ...... 7.02
      para. 27 .... 4.05
   Sched. 17 .... 8.25
   Sched. 29 .... 8.04
      para. 14 .... 8.53
      Pt. II 8.04
      Pt. VII 2.83
Museums and Galleries Admission Charges Act (c. 73) 3.49
1973 Gaming (Amendment) Act (c. 12) 6.81
Supply of Goods (Implied Terms) Act (c. 13)—
   s. 7 (2) 1.158
Protection of Wrecks Act (c. 33 .... 3.56, 3.78
   s. 1 .... 3.56
Water Act (c. 37) 5.41, 7.47, 8.19
   s. 20 .... 5.41, 7.57
   s. 22 .... 5.41, 8.18
   s. 24 .... 5.41
   ss. 25, 26 .... 5.41
   s. 27 .... 5.41
   Sched. 1 .... 7.47
   Sched. 2, para. 4 .... 7.47
   Sched. 7 .... 7.48
Fair Trading Act (c. 41) 1.165
   s. 1 .... 1.165
   s. 2 (3) 1.165
      (4) 1.165
   s. 12 .... 1.165
   s. 21 .... 1.165
   s. 35 .... 1.167
   ss. 36–38 .... 1.167
   s. 42 .... 1.167
   Sched. 1 .... 1.165
      Pt. II 1.166
      Pt. III 1.165
National Conservancy Council Act (c. 54) 8.14, 8.19
Badgers Act (c. 57) 8.12
Powers of Criminal Courts Act (c. 62)—
   s. 35 .... 1.184
1974 Local Government Act (c. 7 .... 2.11, 2.14, 9.07
   s. 7 .... 9.19
   s. 24 .... 2.11
   s. 26 .... 2.11, 2.14
   s. 29 (6) 2.14
   s. 31 (1) 2.13
   s. 32 .... 2.14

Table of Statutes

1974	Local Government Act—*cont.* s. 32—*cont.*	
	(3)	2.14
	s. 34	2.11
	Sched. 2, para. 5	9.08
	Prices Act (c. 24)	1.156
	Parks Regulation (Amendment) Act (c. 29)	5.39
	Finance Act (c. 30)	7.57
	Scheds. 6, 13	3.43
	Health and Safety at Work, etc., Act (c. 37)	1.001, 1.021, 1.073, 1.075, 6.11
	s. 1 (2)	1.073
	s. 2	6.11
	(1)	1.074
	(2)	1.074
	(*a*)	6.11
	(3)	1.074
	(7)	1.074
	s. 6 (4) (*a*)	1.074
	s. 17	1.075
	s. 33	1.075
	s. 47	1.075, 6.11, 6.13
	(1) (*a*)	6.11
	(2)	6.11
	(4)	6.11
	s. 82	1.074
	Consumer Credit Act (c. 39)	1.156
	ss. 137–140	1.156
	Control of Pollution Act (c. 40)—	
	s. 24	8.52
	Insurance Companies Act (c. 49)—	
	s. 83 (6)	4.65
	Road Traffic Act (c. 50)—	
	s. 21 (1)	4.58
	Greater London Council (General Powers) Act (c. xxiv)—	
	ss. 3–6	5.43
1975	Reservoirs Act (c. 23)	7.57
	Prices Act (c. 32)	1.156
	Conservation of Wild Creatures and Wild Plants Act (c. 48)	8.12
	Salmon and Freshwater Fisheries Act (c. 51)	7.45, 7.46, 7.48, 7.50
	s. 15 (1) (*a*)	7.46
	s. 17	7.46
	ss. 23, 24	7.47
	s. 25	7.47
	(7)	7.47
	s. 26	7.47
	(4)	7.47
	(5)	7.47
	s. 27	7.47

1975	Salmon and Freshwater Fisheries Act—*cont.*	
	s. 28	7.48, 7.49
	(3), (4)	7.49
	ss. 31–36	7.50
	s. 41 (2)	7.47
	Sched. 1	7.47
	Sched. 2	7.47
	para. 9–14	7.47
	Sched. 3	7.48
	Sched. 4	7.50
	Pts. I, II	7.46
	Pt. II	7.47
	Safety of Sports Grounds Act (c. 52)	6.55, 7.12, 7.24, 7.25, 7.37, 9.31
	s. 9	6.55
	Limitation Act (c. 54)	1.131
	Sex Discrimination Act (c. 65)	1.076, 1.078, 1.080, 1.088, 1.089, 1.092
	ss. 1–4	1.083
	s. 1	1.079
	s. 2	1.079, 1.080
	s. 3	1.079
	s. 4	1.079
	s. 6	1.079
	s. 7	1.080, 1.089
	s. 9	1.089
	s. 29	1.079, 1.081
	(1)	1.081
	(2)	1.081
	(*b*)	1.081
	(*e*)	1.081
	(*f*)	1.081
	(*g*)	1.081
	s. 30	1.081
	s. 34	1.081
	s. 35 (1) (*c*)	1.082
	(2)	1.082
	s. 38	1.083
	s. 39	1.083
	s. 40	1.083
	s. 41	1.083
	s. 48	1.084
	s. 66	1.085
	s. 77	1.085
	Pts. I, II	1.079
	Pt. II	1.083
	Pt. III	1.083, 1.085
	Pt. IV	1.083
	Pt. VI	1.085
	Pt. VII	1.085
	Employment Protection Act (c. 71)	1.059
1976	Congenital Disabilities (Civil Liability) Act (c. 28)—	
	s. 1 (5)	3.76
	Fatal Accidents Act (c. 30)	1.024

TABLE OF STATUTES

1976	Lotteries and Amusements Act (c. 32)	6.86
	ss. 1, 2	6.84
	s. 3	6.84
	(d)	6.84
	s. 4	6.84
	ss. 5, 11	6.84
	s. 6	6.84
	s. 8 (3)	9.20
	s. 14	6.84, 6.85
	Sched. 4	6.83
	Pt. II	6.84
	Restrictive Trade Practices Act (c. 34)	1.142
	Dangerous Wild Animals Act (c. 38)	4.64
	s. 7	4.64
	Resale Prices Act (c. 53)	1.156
	Local Government (Miscellaneous Provisions) Act (c. 57)	2.56, 4.01, 6.56, 7.01, 7.02, 7.04, 7.19, 9.34
	s. 9	2.56
	s. 15	7.24
	s. 19	4.34, 6.57, 7.01, 7.19, 7.40
	(1)	7.22
	(a)	7.04
	(e)	7.22
	(f)	4.22, 7.22
	(2)	7.04
	(3)	7.38
	s. 20	6.58
	s. 22	6.56
	s. 81 (1)	9.34
	s. 224	7.02
	Sched. 2	9.34
	Race Relations Act (c. 74)	1.076, 1.088, 1.089, 1.090–1.092
	s. 3.	1.090
	s. 5	1.091
	s. 47	1.092
	s. 71	1.092
	Rent (Agriculture) Act (c. 80)	1.044
	s. 1	1.045
	s. 5 (3)	1.044
1977	Protection from Eviction Act (c. 43)—	
	s. 4	1.045
	Housing (Homeless Persons) Act (c. 48)—	
	s. 3 (4)	2.07
	Unfair Contract Terms Act (c. 50)	1.012, 1.020, 1.175, 7.07, 1.127, 1.155
	s. 1 (3)	1.012
1977	Unfair Contract Terms Act —cont.	
	s. 2	7.07
	(2)	7.07
	s. 6	1.158
	ss. 12, 13	1.158
	City of London (Various Powers) Act (c. xv)	5.32
	s. 5	5.32
	s. 6	5.32
	s. 7	5.32
	s. 8	5.32
	s. 9	5.33
1978	Interpretation Act (c. 30)	2.24
	s. 14	4.45
	s. 17 (2) (a)	5.06
	Protection of Children Act (c. 37)—	
	s. 5	6.90
	Consumer Safety Act (c. 38)	1.168
	s. 1	1.168
	s. 2 (4)	1.168
	(6)	1.169
	(8)	1.168
	s. 3 (1) (a)	1.168
	(b)	1.168
	(c)	1.168
	s. 5	1.169
	s. 6	1.169
	s. 9 (1)	1.170
	(2)	1.170
	(4)	1.070
	Sched. 1, Pt. I	1.168
	Pt. III	1.168
	Employment Protection (Consolidation) Act (c. 44)	1.061–1.072
	s. 1	1.061
	s. 4	1.067
	s. 49	1.064
	s. 53	1.064
	s. 54	1.065
	s. 57 (1)	1,070
	(2)	1.068, 1.070
	(3)	1.070
	s. 58	1.065, 1.066
	(3A)	1.066
	(4)	1.067
	(5)	1.067
	s. 59	1.06
	s. 60	1.069
	s. 62 (4)	1.072
	s. 63	1.071
	s. 64 (1) (a)	1.071
	(b)	1.071
	s. 141 (2)	1.071
	(5)	1.071
	s. 144 (2)	1.071
	s. 145 (2)	1.071

Table of Statutes

Year	Statute	Page
1978	Employment Protection (Consolidation) Act—*cont.*	
	s. 146 (1)	1.071
	Sched. 9, para. 2 (1)	1.072
	Greater London Council (General Powers) Act (c. xiii)—	
	s. 12	5.31
	Parochial Registers and Records Measure (No. 2)—	
	s. 7 (4)	3.38
1979	Customs and Excise Management Act (c. 2)—	
	Sched. 3	6.90
	Public Lending Right Act (c. 10)	3.10, 3.12
	s. 1	3.11
	s. 3 (8)	3.13
	s. 4 (5)	3.13
	(7)	3.13
	Capital Gains Tax Act (c. 14)	3.42, 3.43
	s. 147	3.43
	Forestry Act (c. 21)	4.59
	Ancient Monuments on Archaeological Areas Act 1979 (c. 46)	3.62, 3.65, 3.78
	s. 1	3.78
	(4)	3.78
	s. 2	3.79
	s. 5	3.80
	s. 6	3.80
	ss. 7–9	3.80
	s. 10	3.80
	ss. 11, 13	1.056
	ss. 12–18	3.65
	ss. 15, 16	3.80
	s. 17	3.80
	s. 18	3.78
	s. 21	3.80
	s. 28	3.79
	s. 33	3.80
	s. 35	3.80, 3.81
	s. 37	3.81
	s. 39	3.81
	s. 42	3.61, 3.65, 3.81
	s. 57	3.79
	s. 61	5.22
	s. 64	3.81
	Pt. I	3.65
	Sched. II, para. 13	3.80
	Pt. II	3.65
	Sale of Goods Act (c. 54)	1.156, 1.159, 1.160, 1.162, 1.171–1.172
	s. 2	1.156
	s. 4	1.156
	s. 5 (3)	1.156
	s. 6	1.156
	s. 10	1.157
1979	Sale of Goods Act—*cont.*	
	s. 11	1.157
	(2)	1.157
	(3)	1.157
	s. 12	1.158
	s. 13	1.158
	(2)	1.158
	(6)	1.158
	s. 15 (1)	1.158
	(2)	1.158
	s. 16	1.159
	s. 17	1.159
	s. 18	1.159
	s. 20	1.159
	s. 22	1.160
	s. 23	1.160
	s. 24	1.160
	s. 25	1.160
	s. 27	1.161
	s. 30	1.161
	s. 31	1.161
	s. 32	1.161
	s. 34	1.161
	s. 35	1.161
	s. 36	1.161
	s. 37	1.161
	s. 41	1.162
	ss. 44–46	1.162
	s. 48	1.162
	s. 49 (1)	1.163
	s. 50	1.163
	s. 51	1.163
	s. 52	1.163
	s. 53	1.163
1980	National Heritage Act (c. 17)	1.056
	s. 2	1.056
	s. 3 (2)	1.056
	(3)	1.056
	(5)	1.056
	(6)	1.056
	s. 16	1.056
	Pt. I	1.056
	Betting, Gaming and Lotteries (Amendment) Act (c. 18)—	
	s. 1	6.53
	Limitation Amendment Act (c. 25)	1.024
	Employment Act (c. 42)	1.067
	Magistrates Courts Act (c. 43)	6.65
	s. 97	3.67
	Finance Act (c. 48)—	
	s. 8	6.82
	Housing Act (c. 51)	1.040, 1.041
	s. 1	1.040
	s. 28	1.040, 1.041
	s. 48	1.041
	Sched. 3	1.040, 1.041

Table of Statutes

1980	Limitation Act (c. 58)	1.024, 1.129, 1.154, 4.17
	s. 2	1.129, 1.139
	s. 5	1.154
	s. 8	1.154, 4.17
	s. 11 (1)	1.129
	ss. 22, 38	1.130
	s. 23	1.154
	s. 28	1.130, 1.154
	s. 29	1.154
	s. 32	1.130
	s. 33	1.131
	s. 36	1.154
	Local Government, Planning and Land Act (c. 65)	1.052, 2.32, 2.66, 3.37, 4.30, 7.38, 9.07, 9.15
	s. 1	2.66, 9.08
	s. 3	2.66
	s. 4	9.08
	s. 10	2.66
	s. 12	2.66
	s. 55	9.08
	s. 56 (1)	9.09
	(6)	9.09
	(8)	9.09, 9.10
	s. 57 (1)	9.09
	(2)	9.14
	s. 59	9.10, 9.12
	s. 60	9.08, 9.14
	(3)	9.14
	s. 61	9.14
	(7)	9.14
	s. 62	9.12
	s. 70	9.18
	s. 71	2.11, 9.04
	s. 72	9.05
	s. 73	9.06
	(2) (b)	9.06
	s. 77	9.05
	s. 78	9.06
	s. 98	2.11
	s. 116	2.11
	s. 122	2.34, 4.30
	s. 123	4.30, 4.31, 7.02
	s. 123A	4.34
	s. 186	7.41
	Sched. 9	9.08
	Sched. 15 (5)	1.054
	para. 8 (a)	1.053
	Pt. XVI	7.40
	Sched. 34	2.66
	Pt. VIII	9.04
	Pt. X	4.27
	Highways Act (c. 66)	4.17, 8.45, 8.47–8.49
	s. 25	8.45
	s. 26	8.45
	s. 31	8.45

1980	Highways Act—*cont.*	
	s. 31—*cont.*	
	(6)	8.45
	s. 32	8.38
	s. 38	8.45
	s. 41	8.49
	s. 42	8.49
	s. 56	8.49
	s. 116	8.47
	ss. 118–119	8.47
	s. 120	8.47, 8.48
	s. 130 (3)	8.49
	ss. 219–225	2.26
	West Midlands County Council Act (c. xi)	6.30
	s. 85	6.30
	Cheshire County Council Act (c. xiii)—	
	s. 16 (1)	6.30
	s. 145 (3)	6.30
	West Yorkshire Act (c. xiv)	6.30, 6.52
	s. 70 (5)	6.30
	s. 71	6.30
	South Yorkshire Act (c. xxxvii)	6.52
1981	Zoo Licensing Act (c. 37)	4.63, 4.64
	s. 4 (5)	4.63
	ss. 10–12	4.63
	s. 13	4.63
	s. 17 (1) (a)	4.63
	(b)	4.63
	Forestry Act (c. 39)	4.59, 5.17
	Indecent Displays (Control) Act (c. 42)	6.90
	Contempt of Court (c. 49)	3.67, 3.68, 3.70
	s. 1	3.68
	s. 2	3.68
	s. 5	3.68
	s. 10	3.69
	Sched. 1	3.68
	Supreme Court Act (c. 54)—	
	s. 31	2.08
	Acquisition of Land Act (c. 67)	2.36, 5.09
	s. 18	5.09
	s. 121	2.36
	(4)	2.83
	Wildlife and Countryside Act (c. 69)	8.10, 8.12–8.14, 8.18, 8.19, 8.21, 8.32, 8.40, 8.46
	s. 1 (1)	8.10
	(5)	8.11
	s. 2	8.11
	s. 27	8.11
	s. 39	8.42
	s. 40	8.20

Table of Statutes

1981 Wildlife and Countryside Act
—*cont.*
s. 41	8.18
s. 42	8.24
s. 43	8.24
s. 44	8.42
s. 46	8.25
s. 47	8.19
s. 48	8.18
s. 49	8.41
s. 53	8.46
s. 54	8.44, 8.46
s. 56 (1)	8.45
s. 59	8.50
s. 62	8.26
Sched. 13	8.19
para. 2	8.19
para. 5	8.19
para. 13	8.19
paras. 14, 15	8.19
Pt. III	8.50

Greater Manchester Act (c. ix)—
s. 163	2.58

1982 Gaming (Amendment) Act (c. 22) 6.43, 6.81

Supply of Goods and Services Act (c. 29) 1.171
s. 1	1.174
s. 2 (3)–(5)	1.174
ss. 3–5	1.174
ss. 7–10	1.173
s. 9	1.174
s. 11	1.174
s. 12	1.175
(2)	1.175
s. 13	1.173
s. 14	1.173
s. 15	1.173
s. 16	1.174
Pt. I	1.174
Pt. II	1.175

Local Government (Miscellaneous Provisions) Act (c. 30) 2.18, 5.40, 6.20, 6.34, 6.35, 6.41, 6.44, 6.72, 6.88, 6.89, 6.90
s. 2	5.40
s. 8	8.54
s. 18	4.41
s. 19 (1) (*f*)	4.22
s. 32	2.18
s. 44	2.18
Sched. 1	6.34, 6.39
para. 13	6.72
para. 21 (*b*)	6.20
Sched. 2	5.40
Sched. 3, para. 3 (2)	6.90
para. 4	6.89

1982 Local Government (Miscellaneous Provisions) Act
—*cont.*
Sched. 3—*cont.*
paras. 6, 8–10	6.89
para. 12	6.89
(3)	6.89
para. 13	6.89
paras. 20–23	6.89
paras. 25, 26	6.89
para. 27	6.89
Pt. III	6.88

Local Government Finance Act (c. 32) 9.07, 9.15
s. 19	2.21
Pt. II	9.10, 9.12

Cinematograph (Amendment) Act (c. 33) 6.19, 6.22, 6.90
s. 2	6.23
s. 3	6.20
s. 5	6.22
(3)	6.22
s. 6	6.21, 6.22
s. 7	6.21, 6.22

Copyright Act 1956 (Amendment) Act (c. 35) 3.26
Derelict Land Act (c. 42)—
ss. 1, 5	9.21
s. 1 (6)	9.21
(11)	9.21

Employment Act (c. 46) 1.064
s. 3	1.065

Criminal Justice Act (c. 48)—
s. 39	5.15
Sched. 3	5.15

1983 Water Act (c. 23) 7.57
s. 3	7.57

Licensing (Occasional Permissions) Act (c. 24) 6.68
s. 2	6.68
s. 3	6.68
s. 9	6.69
s. 21	6.69
s. 50	6.69
s. 59	6.70
s. 60	6.70
s. 61	6.70
(1) (*b*)	6.72
s. 62	6.71

Litter Act (c. 35) 8.41, 8.52
s. 1	8.52

National Heritage Act (c. 47) 1.056, 3.48
s. 3	3.48

1984 Occupiers Liability Act (c. 3) 1.014, 1.020, 1.025, 4.19, 7.23
s. 1	1.014–1.017

1984	Occupiers Liability Act—*cont.* s. 1—*cont.*		1984	Rates Act (c. 33) .... 9.07, 9.15 ss. 1, 2 .... 9.15	
	(3)	1.009		s. 3	9.15
	s. 2	1.020		s. 5	9.15
	Lotteries (Amendment) Act			s. 7	9.15
	(c. 9)	6.84		ss. 9, 10, 11	9.16
	Betting, Gaming and Lotteries (Amendment) Act (c.			s. 13	9.16
				Pt. I	9.16
	25)	6.79		Pt. II	9.16
	Housing and Building Control			Video Recordings Act (c. 39) ..	6.46
	Act (c. 29)	1.040		s. 2	6.46
	s. 31 .... 1.040, n. 74			s. 12	6.89
	Food Act (c. 30) 6.17, 7.14		1985	Gaming (Bingo) Act (c. 35)	6.82
	s. 16	6.17		Sporting Events (Control of Alcohol, etc.) Act (c. 57) .	6.55

Chapter 1

GENERAL LEGAL PRINCIPLES FOR THE PROVIDERS OF PUBLIC LEISURE SERVICES

"If we would but adhere to principle, the law would be what it ought to be – a science"

Alderson B. in *Ingate* v. *Christie* (1850) 3 Car. and K. 61.

Introduction

This book is designed as an outline of so much of the law of this country as falls within the area of activity connoted by the public leisure services. Chapters 3 to 9 embrace some 45 areas of law selected with that gauge in mind. In this and the next Chapter, an outline is given of those branches of the general law which affect the management, the practice and the legal problems associated with the public leisure services.[1] Necessarily, in this Chapter this involves some treatment of the torts of nuisance, negligence and trespass, the rule in *Rylands* v. *Fletcher* and the principles of remoteness of damage.   **1.001**

This Chapter will also deal with the Health and Safety at Work Act, the Race and Sex Discrimination Acts, and those Acts embodying our laws concerning the sale of goods, and employment law. All these branches of law combine, in varying degrees, law based on cases in the courts and law primarily laid down in Parliament. The law of contract, also to be discussed, is now an admixture from these two sources. Occasionally, law deriving from custom is touched upon. The whole will be selected in the light of the subject of this work: only so can it be reasonably limited; but only so, it is hoped, can some unity emerge in place of what might otherwise be a miscellany of selections from that extensive library constituted by English law at the present time.[2]

The various branches of law can conveniently be grouped as those met when the public leisure services authority is acting as property owner, secondly as employer and manager, and thirdly as business organiser.   **1.002**

"Public leisure services" is an expression intended to extend beyond

---

[1] *Halsbury's Statutes* currently extend to 56 volumes; *Halsburys Laws*, the library of textbooks, which range over the whole field of English law, contains 60 volumes.
[2] *Ibid.*

local authorities to other public bodies which operate in this field. The Forestry Commisssion, with its holiday chalets, the Water Authority, with its promotion of fishing and boating and the Countryside Commission are examples. If in the text local authorities are referred to more than the others, that is a matter of convenience and is not intended to be an exclusive term. The term "public authorities" was not used, since it would seem to suggest branches of government and as such it would be misleading, since those departments and their branches are not normally involved in the provision of leisure services.

THE LEISURE SERVICES AUTHORITY AS PROPERTY OWNER

A. The Duty to Visitors

1.003 The Occupiers' Liability Act 1957 was a watershed in the law of tort. It sought to create order where there was confusion. It stemmed from a report of the Law Reform Committee[3] and was thus a considered and in fact a considerable measure of codification. It was not a consolidating Act, since it repealed no earlier statutes. The previous law had been case law and that Act of 1957 gathered together compactly what hitherto had been diffused. Its subject matter is of importance for all in the public leisure services, since nearly all are occupiers of property to which visitors resort throughout the year. The Act of 1957 deals with the variety of situations created in law by the status of those visitors, the variety of those premises and the occasions which bring them together.

1. The Common Duty of Care

1.004 "The common duty of care is a duty to take such care as in all the circumstances of the case is reasonable, to see that the visitor will be reasonably safe in using the premises for the purposes for which he is invited or permitted by the occupier to be there."[4]

This duty, it will be observed, is owed to *visitors* and that term gives rise to the first of seven glosses upon expressions in this foundation definition:

1.005 The persons who are to be treated as visitors in relation to the occupier are the same as the persons who would, at common law, be treated as his invitees or licensees.[5]

Invitees and licensees were visitors lawfully on the premises. Whilst invitees were present for a purpose in which the occupier had a material interest, such as a customer in a cafe, in the case of licensees no such material interest existed. People taking a stroll in the local public park

---

[3] Third Report (Occupiers' Liability to Invitees, Licencees and Trespassers 1954), Cmd. 9305.
[4] Occupiers Liability Act 1957, s.2(2).
[5] *Ibid.* s.1(2).

would be licensees of the local authority for this purpose.[6] There were different legal duties owed by the occupier to these two classes and these have now been united in "the common duty of care."

1.006 This duty arises in respect of "dangers due to the state of the premises or to things done or omitted to be done on them."[7]

As the word "premises" is not defined in the Act, difficulties oblige litigants to turn to the courts for assistance. Earlier, in 1943, Lord Wright said that the word "premises" embraces "places and structures of all sorts on which persons may be invited to come."[8] O'Connor J., in 1968, said that the word includes "fixed and moveable structures."[9] In the context of such words, it would seem that in a recreation ground, whilst a slide would be a fixed structure, a swing would not, in the normal use of the words, be a "moveable structure." It is a piece of playground equipment.

1.007 The common duty of care, the Act further provides, rests upon the same persons as at common law.[10] These arise out of a person's occupation or control of premises. This can mean that if, say, a museum was closed for a month for stone-cleaning, then the cleaning contractor could legally be in occupation of the premises for that period and accordingly bear the common duty of care in relation to visitors.[11]

1.008 This common duty of care does not, moreover, impose on an occupier "any obligation to a visitor in respect of risks willingly accepted as his by the visitor."[12]

The Act says that the question whether that risk has been willingly accepted is to be settled on the same principles as in other cases where one person owes a duty of care to another. For instance, a player in a rugby match accepts a risk of being thrown in a tackle[13] and a swimmer who uses a diving board over the sea accepts risks resulting from different depths of water caused by the ebb and flow of the tide.[14]

1.009 A person who enters premises under rights conferred by an access agreement under the National Parks and Access to the Countryside Act 1949, is not to be treated as a visitor of the occupier of those premises, for the purposes of the Act of 1957.[15]

1.010 On the other hand, a person who visits premises pursuant to a contract with the occupier, as a spectator at a sports ground, is entitled to the benefit of the common duty of care. This provision is included to remove the

---

[6] *Phipps* v. *Rochester Corporation* [1955] 1 Q.B. 450.
[7] Act of 1957, s.1(1).
[8] *Glasgow Corporation* v. *Muir* [1943] A.C. 448 at p. 461.
[9] *Bunker* v. *Brand (Charles) and Son Ltd.* [1968] 2 Q.B. 480 at p. 486.
[10] Act of 1957, s.1(2).
[11] *Kearney* v. *Waller (Eric) Ltd.* [1967] 1 Q.B. 29.
[12] Act of 1957, s.2(5).
[13] *Simms* v. *Leigh Rugby F.C. Ltd.* [1969] 2 All E.R. 923.
[14] *Pertiouski* v. *Wellington Corporation* [1959] A.C. 53.
[15] s.1(4) of the Occupiers Liability Act 1957. The Act of 1949 says that a person going on to land for open air recreation, while an access agreement is in force, is not, by reason only of such entry, to be treated as a trespasser (s.60 of the 1949 Act). Being neither a trespasser, nor a visitor, he must, one infers, be "another," as that expression is euphemistically used in the Occupiers Liability Act 1984, s.1(3).

1.010 GENERAL LEGAL PRINCIPLES

old distinctions, which were somewhat fine, about the respective duties owed to such visitors compared with others who did not have a contract.[16] (The Act says that the common duty of care is to be a term implied in a contract which is silent on this point.)

1.011 The last and by no means least important of these seven glosses on the common duty of care, is the provision that the occupier can "extend, restrict, modify or exclude his duty to any visitor or visitors by agreement or otherwise."[17]

Those last two words "or otherwise" import ways in which, before 1957, occupiers would limit their legal duty to visitors by warning notices. So in *Ashdown* v. *Samuel Williams and Sons Ltd.*[18] where a visitor to land was injured by a railway truck engaged in shunting work, a claim for damages failed since a notice warning visitors of this type of danger was on the land and of a nature and in a situation which would be reasonable to achieve its aim.

The Unfair Contracts Terms Act 1977

1.012 The Unfair Contracts Terms Act 1977 prohibits the use of contract terms and warning notices to limit liability in relation to death or personal injury due to negligence. The term or notice must pass the test of reasonableness for other loss or damage.[19]

2. The Common Duty of Care in Relation to Special Classes

(1) *Children*

1.013 The Act of 1957 expressly deals with an occupier's duty to visitors who are children: "an occupier must be prepared for children to be less careful than adults."[20]

The courts look for dangers known to the occupier and for which he is liable and which would be alluring, or even traps, for children. There are cases which relate to glass in a paddling pool,[21] poisonous berries in a public park,[22] a hillside used for children's slides,[23] a finger injury on a swing in a recreation ground,[24] and a head injury against a school playground flint wall.[25]

---

[16] Act of 1957, s.5(1).
[17] *Ibid.* s.2(1).
[18] [1957] 1 Q.B. 409.
[19] Note the definition of "business" liability in s.1(3) of the Act of 1977, as the prohibition is limited to this class.
[20] Occupiers' Liability Act 1957, s.2(3).
[21] [1938] 1 K.B. 212.
[22] [1922] 1 A.C. 44.
[23] (1983) 81 L.G.R. 460.
[24] [1947] 1 K.B. 359.
[25] [1970] 1 All E.R. 535; *British Railways Board* v. *Herrington* [1972] A.C. 877.

(2) Trespassers[26]

1.014 This group of persons, unlawfully on land, has recently been the subject of Parliamentary attention. The Act of 1957 did not deal with trespassers but the Occupiers' Liability Act 1984 is devoted to the subject. The code laid out in section 1 of the Act of 1984 embodies these principles, which may be elaborated as follows:

(a) The occupier owes a duty to "persons other than his visitors," *i.e.* trespassers.

(b) The duty is to take such care as is reasonable, in all the circumstances of the case, to see that the trespasser does not suffer injury on the premises by reason of the danger concerned.

(c) And what is the "danger"? It is the risk of suffering injury by reason of any danger due to the state of the premises or to things done or omitted to be done on them.

(d) The occupier's duty arises "if he is aware of the danger or has reasonable grounds to believe that it exists," and if "he knows, or has reasonable grounds to believe, that the other is in the vicinity of the danger concerned or that he may come into the vicinity of the danger." Both these crucial new prerequisites are to be satisfied before the new duty exists. So also is a third condition, that the risk must be "one against which, in all the circumstances of the case, he may reasonably be expected to offer the other some protection." This is presumed to connote dangers akin to traps, known to the occupier, but indiscernible, even to a wide awake nocturnal prowler.

1.015 (e) How is the duty discharged? The Act continues that this can be done, in an appropriate case, by giving warning of the danger or "taking steps to discourage the persons from incurring the risk."

(f) Lastly, by way of clarification, the section states that the duty is not in relation to persons using a highway, or to risks willingly accepted by the trespasser, or to loss or damage to property but only to personal injury.

1.016 The aim of the new Act of 1984 is to offer the non-visitor some protection, and obviously cases will develop this guideline. It will be of the greatest interest to occupiers and their advisers to see whether the law has been changed from that embodied in the common law. In the House of Lords debates on the Bill, the Lord Chancellor said: "This is not a charter for trespassers."[27] From those debates and the wording of the Act, it is at least clear that one avenue opened by the last leading case of *British Railways Board* v. *Herrington*[28] has been closed. That was the suggestion in one judgment that the duty to trespassers, who still entered land of others at their peril, might best be described as taking such steps "as common sense or common humanity would dictate."[29]

---

[26] After the subject was referred to the Law Commission which reported (No. 75) in March 1976 and suggested a statutory duty to "unwanted entrants" in a draft Occupiers Liability Act. The case of *Pannett* v. *McGuinness* [1972] 2 Q.B. 599 still merits study.
[27] Second Reading, July 12, 1983, H.L.
[28] [1972] A.C. 877.
[29] *Ibid.* at p. 767*d*.

1.017 The facts of *Herrington*'s case are worth recapitulating. An electrified railway line ran through property of the National Trust, to which the public had access. Because of the poor state of the fencing, it was possible to gain access to the track and there was evidence that visitors to the National Trust properties did cross the track. The infant plaintiff was injured when crossing the line. At first instance, in the Court of Appeal and finally in the House of Lords, British Rail were held liable. They had allowed the fence to fall into disrepair, knowing that children were in the habit of trespassing on the line. Whilst none of the courts suggested that the occupier had an obligation to ensure that trespassers could not enter, the salient elements in the local circumstances which led to the finding for the plaintiff were the proximity of a public path, the land being open to the public, the ease with which a child could pass through the fence and the fact that a child would not appreciate the danger of a live rail.

It is pure conjecture what steps British Rail might have taken in the above circumstances in order to discharge the newly defined occupier's duty in the Occupiers' Liability Act 1984. It seems evident that, at the least, the plainest and boldest warning notice would not suffice.

(3) Persons Enjoying Easements over Land

1.018 This group of persons are not "visitors" and the case of *Greenhalgh* v. *British Railways Board*[30] exemplifies this distinction. It concerned a lady injured whilst exercising a right of way over a railway bridge.

(4) People Exercising their Calling

1.019 "An occupier may expect that a person, in the exercise of his calling, will appreciate and guard against any special risks ordinarily incident to it, so far as the occupier leaves him free to do so."[31]

The principle embodied in this provison may be exemplified in a case relating to an injured factory inspector and another case involving a window cleaner who was injured whilst traversing parts of premises outside his usual route and knowledge.[31a]

(5) Warning Notices under the Unfair Contract Terms Act 1977

1.020 This important Act of 1977 has been mentioned as the location for statutory provisions about the nature of disclaimers of legal liability. The subsections mentioned above raise questions from time to time about the form and content of warning notices and their effectiveness in limiting an occupier's legal liability to persons injured on his land.[32]

---

[30] [1969] 2 Q.B. 286.
[31] The Act of 1957, s.2(3)(*b*).
[31a] *Read* v. *J. Lyons and Co. Ltd.* [1947] A.C. 156; *Christmas* v. *General Cleaning Contractors Ltd.* [1953] A.C. 180.
[32] *Hartley* v. *Mayoh* [1954] 1 Q.B. 383, is instructive.

1.020

Attention is therefore drawn to the recent Occupiers' Liability Act 1984, where a modification of the Act of 1977 is effected. Parliament wishes to achieve two objectives:

(i) Encourage, *e.g.* farmers to permit ramblers to cross their lands. To do this, farmers had not to be subject to some new liability to those persons for natural and obvious risks, like rocks, lakes, "pots" for pot-holing. They should continue to be able to exclude any liability for that sort of feature of their land.

(ii) Retain within the general control of the Act of 1977 all terms restricting liability as regards business premises, where recreational facilities are part of a commercial proposition, to use the words of Lord Hailsham when explaining the new measure in the House of Lords. Holiday camps and safari parks were the two examples he gave.[33] Perhaps the final comment on this change of law should be that it is about the state of the premises and not about dangerous activities carried out there.

3. Other Aspects of the Common Duty of Care

(1) *The Common Law Liability for Negligence*

1.021
"If a landowner is driving his car down his private drive and meets somebody lawfully walking upon it, then he is under a duty to take reasonable care so as not to injure the walker; and his duty is the same, no matter whether it is his gardener coming up with his plants, a tradesman delivering goods, a friend coming to tea or a flag seller seeking a charitable gift."[34]

As Lord Denning's utterance, above, was in a case in 1956, it may be reasonably treated as a last minute protest at undue niceties in the law about visitors, before the first Occupiers' Liability Act reached the statute book. But, nearly 30 years later, it is not universally accepted that the Act of 1957 embodies the total existing common law of duties to lawful visitors. The position is, indeed, rather the reverse. Cases come before the courts where the choice between two or more bases of claim is canvassed, and that under the Act of 1957 is regarded as only one option. Useful examples are found in cases relating to a fall on the Queen Elizabeth liner[35] and an injury on a toboggan slide in Canada.[36] This arises because the Act lays down the rules discussed in the previous sub-sections

> "in place of the rules of the common law, to regulate the duty which an occupier of premises owes to his visitors in respect of dangers due to the state of the premises or to things done or omitted to be done on them."[37]

---

[33] See O.L.A. 1984, s.2.
[34] Lord Denning M.R. in *Slater* v. *Clay Cross Ltd.* [1956] 2 Q.B. 264 at p. 269.
[35] [1969] 1 Lloyd's Rep. 150.
[36] [1969] 3 D.L.R. 649.
[37] Act of 1957, s. 1(1).

1.021 But the Act proceeds to state that the new rules

> "regulate the nature of the duty imposed by law in consequence of a person's occupation or control of premises."[38]

1.022 The view is taken by some textbook writers, that the Act of 1957 does not deal with claims arising out of an occupier's neglect towards his visitor in doing something like shunting an engine, or riding a horse or putting a bull into a field: what have been called "activity duties."[39]

One can only conclude that those responsible for the public leisure services, with premises open to the public, have to guard also against this second limb of liability, based on negligence.

(2) *The Common Duty of Care in Relation to the Intervention of the Independent Contractor*

1.023 The Act of 1957 contains a provision about the occupier's duty to the visitor when the accident occurred due to the intervention of an independent contractor engaged by the occupier.[40] Examples which may be studied relate to a lift[41] and a snow-covered step at a school.[42]

(3) *The Common Duty of Care in Relation to the Limitation Acts*

1.024 The law governing the limits on the time within which legal action in the courts can be commenced is, unfortunately, technical and complex. It is nonetheless vital and as a possible pitfall for litigants, can give rise, rightly, to charges of negligence against their advisers if its provisions are overlooked.

Public property owners are at risk from injured claimants for a basic period of three years from the time when the action could be brought. This is sometimes described as the time when the breach of duty took place.

Unhappily, from the point of view of those seeking certainty, the above statement is clouded by recent statutory provisions which seek to allow latitude to plaintiffs when latent damage prevents their taking prompt action on some injury or accident. The statutory provisions must, in these circumstances, be consulted.[43]

---

[38] *Ibid.* s.1(2).
[39] "Not one which would have been encountered in the normal use of the premises," is the Law Reform Committee's wording for what they wished the Act to cover in this situation.
[40] s.2(4)(*b*).
[41] *Haseldine* v. *Daw* [1941] 2 K.B. 343.
[42] *Woodward* v. *Hastings Corporation* [1945] K.B. 174.
[43] See now the Limitation Act 1980; also the Law Reform (Limitation of Actions) Act 1954, the Fatal Accidents Act 1976 and the Limitation Amendment Act 1980. In one exceptional case, a man was permitted to sue in relation to an injury suffered 20 years previously: *Knipe* v. *British Railways Board* [1972] 1 Q.B. 361.

B. THE DUTY TO NEIGHBOURS

1. **Nuisance**

(1) *Private Nuisance*

The Occupiers' Liability Acts 1957 and 1984 have given a pattern to the law about a property owner's duty to his lawful and unlawful visitors. There is, as yet, no comparable statute for this section of our survey, relating to the occupier's duty to his neighbours. It is the law of nuisance which embodies the legal principles to be applied to that situation.

Nuisance is a tort with the prestige of antiquity and experience. Unfortunately, the pressure it has come under, from the chemical and other industrial nuisances of our society, on the one hand, and on the other, from the inroads made by statutes dealing with public nuisances, have left a mishapen body of case law and an ill-assorted set of rules for litigants.

By way of entry into this territory, from the point of view of the public leisure services, we shall take the subjects of cricket matches and trees. This is partly because they happen to have some special relevance to the subject but also because they are areas where the benefit of recent significant court decisions, provides a modern conspectus of the law, as it responds to social changes and pressures.

The law of nuisance is, indeed, very much a matter of balance. It is in essence concerned with that use of one's own property to an extent which constitutes an unacceptable interference with the use and enjoyment of his land by the neighbour. Thus the interference suffered by the neighbour must be appreciable. Whether the nuisance consists of smell,[44] vibration,[45] noise,[46] subsidence,[47] flooding,[48] or other ways in which the use and enjoyment of one's own property can be impaired, the courts only intervene when "damage of a material kind" is suffered, to take a phrase from a typical case.[49]

(a) **Cricket matches**

In the case of *Miller* v. *Jackson*[50] an action was brought by a householder against a cricket club. This alleged (*inter alia*) nuisance, and it was said that the frequent hitting of cricket balls into the garden of the house and against the house and its roof, interfered with the householder's use and enjoyment of the house and its curtilage. The club had offered various forms of physical protection for the house, as well as the 14 feet 9 inch boundary wall and surmounting fence. What the club could not do was to

---

[44] *St. Helen's Smelting Co.* v. *Tipping* (1865) 11 H.L.C. 642.
[45] *Meux's Brewery Co.* v. *City of London Electric Lighting Co.* [1895] 1 Ch. 287.
[46] *Shelfer* v. *City of London Electric Lighting Co.* [1895] 1 Ch. 187.
[47] *Bognuda* v. *Upton and Shearer* (1972) N.Z.L.R. 74.
[48] *Bartlett* v. *Tottenham* [1932] 1 Ch. 114.
[49] *Nobilo* v. *Waitemata County* (1961) N.Z.L.R. 1064.
[50] [1977] Q.B. 966.

1.026 GENERAL LEGAL PRINCIPLES

guarantee that balls would not be hit on this residential property, which was only 34 yards from the square in the centre of the cricket pitch. At a first hearing, an injunction against the playing of cricket was granted but on appeal the Court of Appeal did not maintain the injunction. The Court of Appeal decision comprised:

1. Agreement (by two of the three judges) that the club's activities amounted to an actionable nuisance.

2. It was no defence to the complaint that the cricket club has been active for 70 years and the plaintiffs had moved into a new house a few years before the court case was begun. The case of *Sturges* v. *Bridgman*[51] should be followed on that point.

3. The borderline between the tort of nuisance and the tort of negligence is not always easy to see but at least in the remedies available to a successful plaintiff, there is a difference. An injunction is possible for nuisance, though not for negligence.

4. However, an injunction to stop the cricket was not held to be the appropriate remedy. A payment of damages in respect of past and future damage to the plaintiff's property was held to be the right remedy.

5. In considering whether the cricket club's activity was an unreasonable interference with the plaintiff's enjoyment of his house and garden, a balance had to be maintained between the right of the individual to enjoy his house and garden without the threat of damage and the rights of the public in general or a neighbour to engage in lawful pastimes. There was, in the view of the majority in the Court of Appeal, a real risk of serious injury.

This case usefully illustrates certain basic principles in the tort of nuisance:

  (i) The interference has to be significant.[52]
 (ii) The question of the remedy for the nuisance is crucial. An injunction to restrain the nuisance is not automatic: damages may be appropriate.
(iii) The principle of *Sturges* v. *Bridgman*,[53] a leading case, 100 years old, is still important. It is no defence to say: you came to the nuisance.

1.027   (iv) It was the continuing cricket activity which precipitated the case and led the court to concentrate on the tort of nuisance. This provides a contrast between this case and another one where a person was hit by a cricket ball struck by a batsman 100 yards from the highway where the injured plaintiff was walking. That case[54] turned on negligence and, in particular, the reasonable

---

[51] (1879) 11 Ch.D. 852.
[52] See, *e.g. Att. Gen.* v. *Hastings Corporation* (1950) 94 S.J. 225, where the Court of Appeal upheld an injunction to stop organised speedway racing.
[53] (1879) 11 Ch.D. 852.
[54] *Bolton* v. *Stone* [1951] A.C. 850.

foresight of the reasonable man that such damage as ensued might occur.

(b) Trees

If games of cricket exemplify the approach of the courts to activities on land, then the spread of tree roots and branches illustrates, in relation the law of nuisance, the perils possible from the natural state and condition of the land. Two cases are of particular interest. **1.028**

Masters v. London Borough of Brent[55]

The roots of a lime tree spread beneath the plaintiff's land and caused subsidence of his house. The Corporation as owners of the tree, were held responsible for the cost of remedying that damage.

Solloway v. Hampshire County Council[56]

The roots of a horsechestnut tree, standing in the highway, spread under the plaintiff's house and caused subsidence. Though the house stood, for the most part, on plateau gravel with clay beneath, there were pockets or outcrops of clay in the gravel beneath the house. These were dehydrated by the roots and thus subsidence occurred earlier than might otherwise have happened.

As the risks to the plaintiff's house were not found to be such that the Corporation should reasonably have foreseen them, the plaintiff lost his case. The case of *Leakey v. National Trust*,[57] a year previously, had developed this area of the law by providing a definition of the duty of the property owner in relation to the foreseeable risks of damage to his neighbour's property. These cases about trees thus illustrate important principles in the law of nuisance: **1.029**

    (i) A continuing nuisance carries continuing liability.
    (ii) Things naturally on the land still carry liability in nuisance, if consequential danger to adjoining land is foreseeable and can reasonably be averted.

(c) General

It remains to outline the other main points affecting the public leisure services in relation to the law of nuisance: **1.030**

(1) A property owner who engages in otherwise reasonable use of his land, does not thereby become liable in nuisance merely because a neighbour embarks upon an extraordinary or specialised use of adjoining land. So when mink farmers wished their neighbours to desist from allegedly

---

[55] [1978] Q.B. 841.
[56] (1981) 79 L.G.R. 449.
[57] [1980] Q.B. 485.

noisy activities during the whelping season, the tort of nuisance did not avail the mink traders.[58]

(2) Malice by a property owner in relation to some activity on his land, which provokes an action for nuisance by his neighbour, is not relevant to liability. However it can stop a defendant in such an action alleging that his use of his land is reasonable.[59]

1.031 (3) The plaintiff in an action for nuisance must "occupy" the land allegedly affected. However, this occupation may be as freeholder, lessee, ordinary licensee or as a licensee in exclusive occupation.

(4) There must be a legal link between the defendant and the alleged nuisance on his land. Thus gypsies were legally on land of the local authority[60] against whom a nuisance action was brought on account of the activities of the gypsies. Again, a landlord from whose property a slate fell and caused injury, had a legal right in his tenancy agreement to enter that property and carry out repairs.

(5) The three legal remedies for a nuisance suffered to land are:
  (i) damages.
  (ii) injunction.
  (iii) abatement, without legal process. This is the justification for lopping overhanging branches. It is not a recourse to be taken except with care and reasonableness. It is a privilege and its use precludes an action for damages.[61]

(2) Public and Statutory Nuisances

1.032 The main discussion hitherto has been devoted to what are called private nuisances. That is the "unlawful" interference with a person's use and enjoyment of his property. In the interests of completeness, we add a short note on these two other legal areas where the word nuisance is also used.

(a) **Statutory nuisances**

This is a criminal offence, created by statute. The Public Health Acts create such offences for foul deposits, noises and odours which are of such consequence that they call for abatement or other control: local authorities as public health authorities exercise these powers in the public interest.

(b) **Public nuisances**

1.033 These too are criminal offences which "materially affect the reasonable comfort and convenience of life of a class of Her Majesty's subjects."[62]

---

[58] *Grandel* v. *Mason* (1953) 3 D.L.R. 65.
[59] *Christie* v. *Davey* [1893] 1 Ch. 316.
[60] *Page Motors* v. *Epsom and Ewell B.C.* (1982) 80 L.G.R. 337.
[61] *Lagan Navigation* v. *Lamkeg Bleaching Co.* [1927] A.C. 226 at p. 244.
[62] *Att. Gen.* v. *PYA Quarries Ltd.* [1957] 2 Q.B. 169 at p. 184.

The sphere of the nuisance is said, in one case, to be "the neighbourhood" and the class of persons affected is a question of fact in each case.

Examples of public nuisance are quarrying to the discomfort of a neighbouring village,[63] a pop festival,[64] obstructing public highways and allowing oil to wash onto the shore.[65]

To prevent a multiplicity of legal actions, it is normal for legal process for a public nuisance to be in the hands of a local authority or the Attorney General. Only when special damage is suffered by the individual can he sue.[66]

2. The Rule in Rylands v. Fletcher

This subsection has considered those situations where a property owner can be liable in nuisance due to unreasonable behaviour on his part. For a hundred years, these cases have been complemented by a special group of situations where the property owner's liability is strict, *i.e.* not dependent upon his negligence. They all involved a non-natural use of land and an "escape" to the neighbour's land. The series began with a bursting reservoir in the case of *Rylands* v. *Fletcher*[67] and were extended to "escapes" of methane gas from a refuse tip and yew tree leaves[68] which harmed a neighbour's cattle. The rule has been less and less used. It was always subject to exceptions for act of god, act of a stranger, the consent of the plaintiff and the case of the default of the plaintiff.

1–034

C. The Duty to Tenants and Tied Cottages

Introduction

A public leisure services authority from time to time finds itself, legally, not only an occupier in relation to visitors and a property owner in relation to neighbours, but also a landlord in relation to tenants.

1.035

This role may well be slight, compared with those so far considered. There would indeed seem to be three groups of such tenants in normal experience. The first will be those town flats that Victorian forefathers or thoughtful successors have built in out of the way corners of civic theatres, libraries or museums. These premises call for residential tenancies, perhaps slightly specialised. Secondly, most parks and recreation authorities

---

[63] *Ibid.*
[64] See Department of the Environment Report, "Pop Festivals and their Problems." (H.M.S.O., 1978).
[65] *Southport Corporation* v. *Esso Petroleum Co. Ltd.* [1954] 2 Q.B. 182 at p. 196.
[66] There are full dicussions of this subject in the standard textbooks on the Law of Torts; *e.g. Winfield and Jolowicz* (12th ed., 1984) and *Salmond and Heuston* (18th ed., 1981), at p. 260.
[67] (1868) L.R. 3 H.L. 330.
[68] *Crowhurst* v. *Amersham Burial Board* (1878) 4 Ex. D.5; 48 L.J. Ex. 109; 39 L.T. 355; 27 W.R. 95.

1.035 will have cottages hidden away in some of the large Victorian parks, former lodges perhaps of town estates. Similar cottages will be found in woods and forests laid out with tourist attractions, such as nature trails or orienteering activities. Thirdly, non-residential lettings will proliferate, not least with the catering facilities that accompany leisure services. Of course, many of these may be licences, franchises, tenuous legal permits to provide or use kiosks, hoardings, piers, seaside entertainment of all sorts. The aim on the one side is to achieve security, so that money can be committed to an entrepreneur. On the local authority side, whilst acknowledging the reasonableness of this object, is a desire to retain some scope for manoeuvre should future policy call for early repossession of the property in question.

1.036 The important feature of the first two groups of lettings described, is that they are lettings to employees of the authority. Their work will be so related to the location of the cottage or flat that the dwelling is "tied" to the work.[69] When the work ends, so should the tenancy. Whilst the law now contains elaborate restraints on the landlords of both residential and agricultural tenancies, on the general market, the local authority will be seen to be in a different position.

1.037 Non-residential lettings and licences on the other hand, call into play the law relating to business tenancies, contained in the Landlord and Tenant Acts of 1927 and 1954, for the greater part.

In both fields, common law and custom and practice fill in the interstices left by the series of statutes, though it must be emphasised that this whole area of the law is now very much one of statute law.[70]

1. Residential Lettings

1.038 On the basis that the residential lettings in which we are interested will be confined to individual houses, cottages or flats, away from the municipal housing estates, we turn to consider them in two groups. The first is where an employee is *required* to occupy a particular house or flat, to enable him to perform his job effectively. This arrangement is appropriate for the lodge in the forest, the flat in the sports centre,—anywhere, indeed, where location is vital. The agreement is a licence to occupy the residence, whilst the employment continues. It will deal with payments for the occupancy, rates, repairs, alterations to the premises, nuisances, non-assignment and any other special terms. The main legal provision, however, will be that when the employment ends, the right to occupy that property ends too. This is on the reasoning that the real occupation is that of the employer, not the employee. The employer arranges the occupancy, so that his work can be done effectively by his employee. This means that, in the final

---

[69] "House with job," as a former Archbishop of Canterbury is alleged to have said of the episcopal situation.
[70] The account given here has been designedly kept free of the various complex statutory systems which do not apply to the properties with which this book is primarily concerned.

analysis, the authority[71] could resort to the County Court and secure an order for possession. They would have to give evidence of the background as above and also satisfy the court that their attitude and their action had been reasonable. They would be expected to show that they had allowed some time for the existing employee to vacate the premises and that there was a real need for the incoming employee to occupy it.

On the other hand, when a house is *made available* to an employee as an emolument and so is part of the benefits of the employment, but its location is not vital in order to carry out that employment, then the agreement is a tenancy.[72] This means that it is an agreement which will deal with the items mentioned above. It will also refer to the employment which the tenant provides for the landlord and will then set out the rent, the period of notice to terminate the agreement and other terms common to tenancies. These will include a covenant for quiet enjoyment, given by the landlord, a covenant to permit the landlord to enter and inspect and terms about painting and about the permitted use of the premises. These are to regulate the occupation so that both parties understand what is expected of them. If the situation alters and the landlord needs possession for another person, he will have to give the proper notice to quit and if necessary satisfy a court that he had reasonable grounds for requiring possession.

1.039

The difference between the employee's licence to occupy and the ordinary tenancy is heightened by the terms of the Housing Act 1980, and the right of a tenant to buy his property from his landlord. The Housing and Building Control Act 1984 extends that line of legislation. By the Act of 1980, and later amendments, such a right to buy is given to large numbers of local authority tenants but these are precisely those houses which are held by the council in question under Part V of the Housing Act 1957. This provides the powers and duties for a local authority to provide housing accommodation. All municipal housing estate houses and flats are normally held on that legal basis.

1.040

However, the houses and flats for public leisure services will not normally be so held. They will be held, perhaps, under the Public Health Act 1875 and its successors or the Museums and Libraries Acts and a variety of other Acts. What the Housing Act 1980 does is to confer on the Part V tenants, as explained above, the status of "a secure tenancy," and it is from this status that the right to buy stems. The Act schedules local authority employees with others as not coming into that class.[73]

---

[71] *Thompsons (Funeral Furnishers) Ltd.* v. *Phillips* [1945] 2 All. E.R. 49. A chauffeur was placed in occupation of a residence, to be available for orders. The money allowance by his employers was a complicating factor but the court agreed that it was a licence rather than a tenancy they were construing. Forty years ago, terminology was a problem. The first judge called it a "service occupancy" (Lawrence L.J. at p. 51A); the second "a service licence" (Mackinnon L.J. at p. 51F); and the third, "a mere service occupation" (Morton L.J. at p. 52D). The editor of this volume of Halsbury appeals to practitioners to abstain from the ambiguous "service tenancy" and stay with licence and tenancy as the alternatives. 4th ed, (1981 Vol. 27, para. 14).
[72] *Dover* v. *Prosser* [1904] 1 K.B. 94.
[73] s.1 deals with "secure tenants"; s.28 and Sched. 3 with exempted tenancies.

Though the Secretary of State in 1983 exercised a power under the Housing Act 1980 to extend the right to buy to houses of local authorities held otherwise than under the Housing Act 1957, Pt. V, he qualified that extension. It was limited to "secure tenants" and thus still leaves untouched by that legislation the employees with which we are currently dealing.[74]

1.041 Another relevant provision in the Housing Act 1980 must be mentioned. Section 28 and Schedule 3 define tenancies which are not "secure tenancies," as mentioned above, in terms which restrict the provision to employee's licences rather than tenancies. In other words, the provision is only about those "required" to occupy "for the better performance of his duties," to quote the statute. This phrase was used to define only "strictly tied accommodation"[75] and the case of *Gray* v. *Holmes* may be referred to for an indication of the implications of that concept.[76]

Whilst section 48 of the Housing Act 1980 confers on the holder of a licence to occupy a dwellinghouse the status of secure tenancy, the Schedule 3 to that Act clearly leaves such occupants where they were before the Act. This is reassuring but it emphasises the difference between the employee's licence and the general tenant with which this discussion began.[77]

The difference between these two types of agreement, *i.e.* the licence and the tenancy, is important, mainly in relation to recovering possession: it is easier in the case of the licence. The difference has been put in the form of the test: "Has the employee exclusive occupation for his own purposes or does he occupy the premises in order to carry out his employment obligations on the premises?"

2. Agricultural Tenancies

1.042 It was pointed out above that some of the lettings of houses and cottages will be in rural locations. Whilst the above basic distinction in house lettings applies also to these houses, the legal provisions relating to agricultural tenancies are covered by different legislation.

Farm labourers' cottages are the archetype of the tied cottage and there are several statutes on that subject. Basically, local authority houses are

---

[74] S.I. 1983 No. 672, the Housing (Extension of the Right to Buy) Order 1983. This Order in terms defines a group of tenant employees of local authorities, *i.e.* those with tenancy agreements dated before October 3, 1980. But it does not affect the exclusion from the right to buy, of this group of employees on licence, conferred by the Housing Act 1980, Sched. 3. The Housing and Building Control Act 1984, s.31, is relevant, insofar as it releases from the public trust status, the lands held under s.164 of the Public Health Act 1975 and s.10 of the Open Spaces Act 1906 (see Chap. 4, on these groups of land holdings). But the Act of 1984 does not change the position of employees occupying houses or flats under licence, as discussed in para. 1.038 above.
[75] Hansard H.L. Vol. 412, col. 115.
[76] [1949] T.R. 71.
[77] See also *Hirst* v. *Sargent* (1967) 65 L.G.R. 127; *Glasgow Corporation* v. *Johnstone* [1965] A.C. 609, and *Chapman* v. *Freeman* [1978] 1 W.L.R. 1298.

1.042

outside that area of law but it is still desirable to indicate briefly what that area of law comprises.

"Agriculture" is defined in the Agricultural Holdings Act 1948[77a] as including[78]:

> "Horticulture, fruit growing, seed growing, dairy farming, livestock breeding and keeping, the use of land as grazing land, meadow land, osier land, market gardens and nursery grounds and the use of land for woodlands where that use is ancillary to the farming of land for other agricultural purposes."

1.043 This Act affords protection to the tenant of an agricultural holding for a term of years or from year to year, and an agricultural holding is the aggregate of land used commercially for agriculture for such a letting.[79] The definition has given rise to interesting borderline problems about the inclusion of cottages and buildings. The courts take a broad view: is it in substance a tenancy of agricultural land?

The protection begins with a restriction; legal termination can be achieved only by notices to quit of 12 months duration. The Act then makes essential the adjudication of the Agricultural Land Tribunal, to safeguard continuity in the cultivation and husbandry of agricultural holdings. There are elaborate codes to encourage improvements and guard against the division of viable farms.[80]

Recovery of possession of houses used by persons employed in agriculture is the only topic on which it is proposed to embark in detail. Section 1(1) of the Agricultural Holdings Act 1948 excludes "a contract under which the said land is let to the tenant during his continuance in any office, appointment or employment held under the landlord," from being an agricultural holding. This excludes that class of tenancy agreement from the provisions mentioned above.

1.044 Again the Rent (Agriculture) Act 1976 contains a detailed pattern of law by which agricultural workers are given in relation to their houses the same sort of protection as has been conferred for many years on urban houses under the Rent Acts.[81] But where the landlord's interest belongs to a local authority and a number of other public bodies, the tenants do not acquire statutory tenancies[82] and thus the Act is not relevant from that point of view. (Local authorities as housing authorities were given new duties but that falls outside the purview of this book.)

[77a] As amended, most recently by the Agricultural Holdings Act 1984.
[78] The Agricultural Holdings Act 1948, s.94.
[79] *Ibid.* s.1, and the Agriculture Act 1947, s.109.
[80] See Jackson and Muir-Watt, *Agricultural Holdings* (Sweet and Maxwell). Also Yates and Hawkins, *Landlord and Tenant Law* (1981, Sweet and Maxwell). Agricultural Holdings Act 1948, s.2(1).
[81] See now the Rent Act 1968 as the latest consolidating Act, repealing (*inter alia*) 12 earlier ones.
[82] Rent (Agriculture) Act 1976, s.5(3).

1.045 However, the Protection from Eviction Act 1977, s.4 contains a provision which does affect the agricultural tenants of local authorities.[83] The effect is as follows:

1. The house is occupied under the terms of his employment as a person employed in agriculture.

2. Procedure to recover possession of such a dwelling begins with service of the appropriate notice to quit. The court which hears a subsequent application for an order of possession, has a general power to suspend such an order. However, that court, under the above Act, must suspend the order unless satisfied.

3. (i) Other suitable accommodation will be available or
   (ii) efficient management of agricultural land or the efficient carrying on of any agricultural operations[84] will be seriously prejudiced unless the premises are available to be occupied by a person employed by the owner or that greater hardship will be caused by suspending the order than by executing it in the period in question or that the occupier has been causing damage to the property or been a nuisance to neighbours and also that it would be reasonable not to suspend the order for possession.

4. The section contains ten subsections in all, which elaborate the main provisions summarised above. It will be evident that it is at the commencement and the termination of their occupancies that the legal position of employees in agricultural and forestry tied cottages is particularly critical.

3. Business Tenancies

1.046 The Landlord and Tenant Act 1954 introduced a code to regulate the legal management of business tenancies which has operated without significant amendment for 30 years. It affects local authority lettings. An outline of the framework created by the Act of 1954 is set out below.[85]

(1) *Businesses Affected*

The Act excludes the following:
 (a) Agricultural holdings.[86]
 (b) Mining leases.[87]

---

[83] It is the current re-enactment of a provision first in the Rent Act 1965, s.33, as amended by the Agriculture Act 1970, s.99.
[84] The definition from the Rent (Agriculture) Act 1976, s.1, includes forestry.
[85] Lord Denning said it should be called "the Business Tenancy Act" (*Cheryl Investments Ltd. v. Saldanha* [1978] 1 W.L.R. 1329 at p. 1332B. For a detailed study see Woodfall, *Landlord and Tenant* (28th ed. by V.G. Wellings and N. Huskinson) and Hill and Redman's *Landlord and Tenant* (16th ed. by M. Barnes and others). A recent compact study is Yates and Hawkins, *Landlord and Tenant Law*, (1981, Sweet and Maxwell).
[86] Landlord and Tenant Act 1954, s.43.
[87] *Ibid.*

The Duty to Tenants and Tied Cottages 1.046

(c) Part-residential use.[88]
(d) Licenced premises.[89]
(e) Service tenancies.[90]

(f) Public interest tenancies, where the landlord is a government department, a local authority, a development corporation, statutory undertaker or certain health service authorities. But this exclusion applies only when a certificate of the relevant government department, under section 57 of the Act of 1954, has been given that a change of use from business is requisite for the body concerned.[91] This provision, whilst no doubt a necessary safeguard for occasional critical situations, does not appear to be used very much.

(g) National security cases.
(h) Extended leases.[92]
(i) Short leases.[93]

(j) Commercial licences, where the licence is genuine and the ramifications of a legal business tenancy are not appropriate for the wishes of the parties, *e.g.* a tea kiosk, in a park, or sometimes a franchise for deckchairs perhaps, on the promenade at the seaside.

Whilst contracting out of the Act is forbidden, a joint application to the court to exclude the Act is in order.[94]

The Act itself applies to "any tenancy where the property comprised in the tenancy is or includes premises which are occupied by the tenant and are so occupied for the purposes of a business carried on by him or for those and other purposes." The definition of "business" is wide:

> "a trade, profession or employment and includes any activity carried on by a body of persons."[95]

The business to be within the Act must not be:
(i) unlawful[96]; or
(ii) sporadic[97]; or
(iii) on premises convenient, though not necessary, for the conduct of the business.[98]

---

[88] This exclusion was introduced by the Rent Act 1968, s.9(3).
[89] See n.86, *supra*.
[90] For an example of one identified by the court as a sham, see *Teasdale* v. *Walker* [1958] 1 W.L.R. 1076.
[91] These s.57 certificates are, in practice, not greatly used, so that exclusion, apparently maximal, is minimal.
[92] Leasehold Reform Act 1967, s.16(1).
[93] See n.86, *supra*.
[94] Act of 1954, s.38.
[95] Act of 1954, s.23. The word "activity" gave rise to *Addiscombe Garden Estates Ltd.* v. *Crabbe* [1958] 1 Q.B. 513, where a members' tennis club was held to be a business within the Act.
[96] Act of 1954, s.23(4), *e.g. Dairner Investments Ltd.* v. *Jones* (1962) 112 L.J. 424, where a tenancy was held to be under a "prohibition" when it lacked planning permission for business use.
[97] *Cheryl Investments Ltd.* v. *Saldanha* [1978] 1 W.L.R. 1329.
[98] *Chapman* v. *Freeman* [1978] 1 W.L.R. 1298.

(2) *Excluded Tenants*

1.047 If the tenant sub-lets the whole of his tenancy he loses the protection of the Act; though his sub-tenant may acquire that protection.[99]

Where several persons are tenants but only one or two run the business, then those only are identified for the purposes of the Act of 1954.[1]

A series of subsidiary companies gives rise to another situation where the statute provides a formula to resolve the question: who is now the tenant?[2]

(3) *The Protection of the Act*

1.048 The main provision of the Act of 1954 is to give the lawful tenant of the lawful business the right to a new tenancy on the expiry of the existing one, unless that renewal is successfully resisted by the landlord on one of the following seven grounds[3]:

(i) The state of repair of the premises due to the tenant's failure to fulfil his repairing obligations.
(ii) Persistent delay in paying the rent.
(iii) Other substantial breaches of the tenant's obligations.
(iv) Suitable alternative accommodation is available.
(v) Possession is required of the whole of the premises, of which this is only a subletting.
(vi) The landlord intends to demolish or reconstruct the property.
(vii) The landlord wishes to occupy the property himself.[4]

This list serves to focus the court case on the central issue between the parties: who should have possession? That stage is not reached without other procedural steps. For instance, the landlord will normally terminate the tenancy, it will continue as the tenant serves notice requesting a new tenancy. This in turn obliges the landlord to state if he will do so and, if not, on which of the above seven grounds he is resisting the tenant's request.

The timetable for these exchanges is very important. The landlord has to give six months' notice, the timing of which is critical; but ultimately it is the attitude of the landlord on the request for renewal which is decisive.

---

[99] Yates and Hawkins, *supra*, at p. 471, n. 46, *i.e. Lee Verhulst (Investments) Ltd.* v. *Harwood Trust* [1972] 1 Q.B. 204.
[1] An amendment to the Act of 1954 by the Law of Property Act 1969 achieved this situation, which was unclear hitherto. Act of 1954, s.41A, now covers the matter.
[2] Act of 1954, s.42(1).
[3] Act of 1954, s.30.
[4] The Act refers to the landlord's intention. Proof that this is firm is sometimes difficult, *e.g.* Asquith L.J.: "It must have moved out of the zone of contemplation, out of the sphere of the tentative, the provisional and the exploratory, into the valley of decision." (*Cunliffe* v. *Goodman* [1930] 2 K.B. 237).

(4) *Assignments*

This is another feature of the Act of 1954 which requires comment. Many tenants wish to assign their tenancy and the agreement may be expected to contain a term which forbids this outright or, in the alternative, says that consent to an assignment should not be unreasonably withheld. The strict position on assignments in the first form may have been agreed only at the expense of a reduced rent and other terms favourable to the tenant, who has accepted this major imposition. The latter alternative is more common and has been the subject of interpretation in the courts. What might the word "unreasonably" mean? The courts have said that the word limits an enforceable objection to assignments by the landlord to one objectively related to the proposed assignee or to the premises. What is not acceptable, the courts have said, is a refusal of a quixotic character, say, in relation to the race or sex of the proposed assigneee.[5] Nor can the request for consent be made the occasion for the landlord to demand a premium.[6]

(5) *New Tenancies*

Where a new tenancy has been sought by a tenant, refused by the landlord, taken to court and resolved in the tenant's favour, that court is empowered to lay down not only the term and rent of the new tenancy but also other relevant terms.[7]

(6) *Conclusion*

Attention has been drawn to those areas in operating the Landlord and Tenant Acts of 1927 and 1954 which, in practice, often prove contentious. The machinery and indeed the text of the Acts allow for these disputes to be resolved. For a local authority with possibly hundreds of business tenancies, the use of the procedure of the Acts is constant. It can only be emphasised that, despite these remarks, it behoves managers of public leisure services to ensure that their commercial lettings do not come within the procedures of the Acts if the lettings are inherently unsuitable for that tight control, whether because of the mixed property content, the slight amount of property involved or possibly the ephemeral nature of the letting.

D. LISTED BUILDINGS AND ANCIENT MONUMENTS

Most public leisure service authorities own some listed buildings and ancient monuments, whether they are Victorian libraries or museums

---

[5] Landlord and Tenant Act 1927, s.19.
[6] See Yates and Hawkins, *supra*, footnotes at p. 482.
[7] Landlord and Tenant Act 1954, s.35.

1.052　General Legal Principles

with statues in the forecourts, former town houses, country houses in parkland or recent buildings displaying "technological innovation," to quote a recent circular.[8]

The law about these edifices has been developed since 1882[9] and the last major Act was in 1980.[10] At the start of the century, 29 monuments were the subject of legal protection in England and Wales: now there are some 260,000 listed buildings and 12,000 scheduled ancient monuments.[11] The legal aspects of this subject to which attention is drawn here are:

(i) The scheduling of ancient monuments.
(ii) The listing of buildings.
(iii) The designation of areas of archeological importance.

These provide the basic legal framework within which property owners have to work. This outline does not attempt to move into detail: it seeks only to help the owners of the buildings and monuments in question when changes affecting that property have to be made. *The Scheduling of Ancient Monuments* and *The Designation of Areas of Archeological Importance* will be found in Chapter 3 in relation to the law for museums authorities, being the service most closely affected.

1. **Listed Buildings**

1.053　"Buildings," for this purpose, range from lampposts and horse troughs to railway viaducts and textile mills, bandstands, and model villages, market crosses and stocks, caves and archways, towers and stables and the Tower of London. The definition in the Town and Country Planning Act 1971 states that it includes "any structure or erection and any part of a building, structure or erection, but does not include any plant or machinery comprised in a building."[12]

In addition to the building is its curtilege and its setting. Curtilege is a word used in many conveyances of buildings: it connotes land associated with the occupation or use of a building or needed for its comfortable enjoyment.[13] The "setting" of a building is also now referred to in the statute containing the criteria for listing a building and thus preserving it.[14]

---

[8] D.O.E. Circular 23/77, Historic Buildings and Conservation Areas—Policy and Procedure.
[9] Ancient Monuments Protection Act 1882.
[10] Local Government, Planning and Land Act 1980.
[11] These figures are taken from a comprehensive outline of this subject by R.W. Suddards, *Listed Buildings: The Law and Practice* (1982, Sweet and Maxwell), which is recommended for detail on all aspects of this subject.
[12] s.290.
[13] *Att. Gen.* v. *Calderdale B.C., ex.p Sutcliffe* (1982), C.A., unreported. See L.G.C., November 26, 1982. The case illustrated a broad approach to s.54 of the Town and Country Planning Act 1971 in construing "curtilage," so that the effective decision about demolition of a building connected to the main listed building rests with the Department of Environment on a Listed Building Consent application and not with the courts on construction of a word.
[14] Local Government Planning and Land Act 1980, Sched. 15, para. 8 (*a*) and s.56(3) of the Town and Country Planning Act 1971.

1.054 "The List" is the list kept by the Department of the Environment of all listed buildings. It grades buildings into I "of exceptional interest" and II "of special architectural or historic interest which warrant every effort being made to save them."[15] The List is compiled both by systematic geographic survey and also by spot-listing. Listing is not appealable but the List can be amended.

Once a building is listed, then before works of demolition, alteration or extension can be carried out, listed building consent must be obtained.[16] This gives rise to public notice, occasional objection, public enquiry and final decision from the Department of the Environment. It may be an episode of considerable public interest and even furore. It is sometimes important that financial considerations are taken into account in deciding whether to give listed building consent, though not, it is emphasised, in deciding to list a building. It is now possible to seek immunity from listing for five years, but such a course of action is by no means easy to recommend to a property owner: delicate considerations affect both advantages and disadvantages.[17]

The criteria currently in use for selecting buildings built between 1914 and 1939 cover a range of buildings and of nine classes, the second is "cinemas, theatres, hotels and other places of public entertainment" and the seventh class is "municipal and other public buildings."[18]

A building preservation notice can be made by a local authority as an emergency procedure to prevent works of demolition or alteration.[19] The notice delays those works until the Department of the Environment has considered whether the building should be listed. It is designed to freeze the situation for six months whilst that consideration takes place.

1.055 In conclusion, it is emphasised that the listing of a building, whilst it has important legal consequences—and, indeed, criminal sanctions for breaking the law, is intended as a control mechanism. It does not represent a final or considered judgment on the architectural or other merits of the building. It allows, to quote Sir H. Casson, at a public enquiry, "time for study and second thoughts."[20]

---

[15] Circular 23/77, *supra*, gives criteria for listing buildings by reference to their age; *e.g.* before 1700 all are listed if in anything like their original condition. Then most buildings of the 1700–1840 range are to be listed.
[16] Town and Country Planning Act 1968, s.49(4)(*a*).
[17] The immunity certificate is dealt with in the Local Government, Planning and Land Act 1980, Sched. 15(5), and s.54A of the Town and Country Planning Act 1971. Application to the Department of the Environment can be made on condition that planning permission has been given or sought. The certificate is the recognition that expenditure can safely take place; for five years there will be no listing nor any Building Preservation notice. A copy of the application has to be served upon the local planning authority.
[18] D.O.E. Circular 23/77, *supra*, and D.O.E. Circular 12/81.
[19] Town and Country Planning Act 1971, s.58(1).
[20] R.W. Suddards, n.11, *supra*. The text does not attempt to embark on a description of Conservation Areas. These, too, lead to the need to seek consent to demolish a building in such areas. They differ from Listed Building and Building Preservation procedures described above in referring to areas rather than individual buildings.

2. National Heritage Act 1980

1.056 Public leisure service authorities need to know of this national fund, which can sometimes assist projects which have national tourist attraction. Part I of the Act of 1980 contains the following provisions:

The National Heritage Act 1980 sets up the National Heritage Memorial Fund. "Memorial" refers to its memorial nature in relation to those who have died for the United Kingdom. The fund is managed by trustees.[21] Grants and loans are made from the fund:

(a) To acquire, maintain or preserve any land building or structure of outstanding scenic, historic, aesthetic, architectural or scientific interest.

(b) Similarly, to acquire, maintain or preserve any object or collection or group of objects of outstanding artistic, historic or scientific interest and

(c) Similar powers in relation to lands or objects connected with (a) or (b) and also for rights over land being rights considered desirable for the benefit of the land mentioned above.[22]

In each case of a grant or loan, the supported object has to be "of importance to the national heritage."[23]

The securing of public access or public display, as the case may be, is an aspect to which the trustees are required to have regard.[24]

There are wide powers about the conditions which the trustees can impose on their advances, including if necessary, repayment in the event of a breach.

A grant can be made to an existing trust, if it will advance one of the stated objects of the fund.[25]

Eligible recipients for payments from the fund are listed in the Act, *i.e.*

(a) a museum, an art gallery or some institution having the purpose of preserving for the public benefit a collection of historic, artistic or scientific interest;

(b) some body with the purpose of providing, improving or preserving amenities or land to be enjoyed by the public or acquiring land to be used by the public;

(c) any body whose purpose is or includes nature conservation,[26]

(d) the Secretary of State, when acting under section 5 of the Historic Buildings and Ancient Monuments Act 1953 or section 11 or 13 of the Ancient Monuments and Archeological Areas Act 1979.[27]

Trustees can use monies from the fund on related expenses other than

---

[21] It succeeded the National Land Fund, which was set up in 1946 as a "public war memorial" and which had been operated under the auspices of the Treasury.

[22] s.3. This is supported by a useful provision in s.16. This allows the Secretary of State to give an indemnity to a museum for a collection maintained for the public benefit, whilst it is on loan to another similar museum.

[23] s.3(2).

[24] s.3(3).

[25] s.3(5).

[26] s.3(6).

[27] *i.e.* respectively, buildings or objects of outstanding historic or architectural interest, and acquiring or maintaining ancient monuments.

grants *e.g.* transport or repairs. They are expressly forbidden to hold property without the consent of the Minister. In other words, they are not to build themselves into a holding company. They can accept gifts for the fund; they can make investments from the fund when prudent to do so; they are required to present annual reports.

The above summarises those parts of the Act relevant to the subject of this book and does not embark upon the remainder.[28]

THE LEISURE SERVICES AUTHORITY AS EMPLOYER AND MANAGER

Introduction

1.057 Public leisure services gather into their ranks many who can be described as employers and managers. An essential element in services which use artistes, advertisers, and enterprise of all sorts, are those persons who engage and dismiss staff, who arrange for the payment of the large labour force, deal with its health, safety and general welfare, its mischief and misconduct, and determine the legal implications of its activities.

1.058 The legal aspects of taking people into employment have never been more complex. It has been estimated that over 100 statutes on aspects of employment law have come onto the statute book in the last century.[29] But collective bargaining, by national agreements of employers and employees, has transformed the pattern and the content of the contract of employment, especially for the individual employee. His contract will often incorporate terms from such a national agreement; their enforcement may be complicated.[30]

1.059 Again the European Economic Community dimension of this subject has to be taken into account. Some of the British employment laws have been enacted to give effect to standards embodied in international charters or conventions, to which the British government is a party.[31] Provisions about closed shops in the European Convention on Human Rights and Fundamental Freedoms were the subject of litigation before the European Court. The Treaty of Rome, Article 118, states that the aim of members is to produce close collaboration in relation to "employment, labour law and working conditions . . . and collective bargaining between workers and employers." Provisions in the Employment Protection Act 1975 gave effect to the Directive of the EEC on collective redundancies, but the overlap between the two documents is not always complete.[32]

---

[28] This Act of 1980 is not linked with the National Heritage Act 1983, which set up trustees for Kew Royal Botanic Gardens, and for the Victoria and Albert Museum, and also dissolved the Historic Buildings Council and replaced it by the Historic Buildings and Monuments Commission for England.
[29] See, *e.g.* Hepple and O'Higgins, *Employment Law* (4th ed., 1981, Sweet and Maxwell).
[30] *Ibid.* Chap. 8.
[31] See, *e.g.* the right of disabled persons to rehabilitation and resettlement in the European Social Charter (1965).
[32] See Hepple and O'Higgins, *ibid.* p. 343, and *Johnson* v. *Nottinghamshire Combined Police Authority* [1974] 1 W.L.R. 358.

1.060 These comments will indicate the growth of this branch of law in recent years. For the purposes of this book, the outline will necessarily be limited in the first place to the basic elements in the general contract of employment to which employers and managers should be alert.[33]

A. THE CONTRACT OF EMPLOYMENT

1.061 A convenient starting point is the Employment Protection (Consolidation) Act 1978 (the Act of 1978). This requires an employer within 13 weeks of the start of a person's employment, to give his employee a written statement containing basic facts about the terms of his contract of employment. These are:
1. The wage or salary, how it is calculated and when it will be paid.
2. Terms and conditions about the hours of work, and also about holidays, sickness, injury and pensions.
3. Particulars of the notice required to terminate the contract.
4. The title of the job.[34]

Common law requirements

1.062 The common law has evolved a number of conditions in a normal contract of employment, which help to fill out the terms listed above. These include the following:

Duties on the employee

The employee is to serve faithfully and obey instructions. The employee is prohibited from working for a trade competitor, whilst in the employment in question.[35]

The employee is responsible to his employer for the consequences of his negligence, whilst engaged in his employer's work.[36]

An employee is to show good faith to his employer[37] and not, for instance, canvass his employer's customers to induce them to become his customers if and when he should end his existing employment.[38]

The employer's secrets

Leisure services can be an area of work where it is important that an employer's secrets are preserved, *e.g.* about negotiated terms for artistes or

---

[33] The provisions in the Treaty of Rome about the free movement of workers (Articles 48–50) have continuing implications for contracts of employment.

[34] Act of 1978, s.1. Some jobs are excluded and not relevant to this book. There are also some exempted short-time jobs, *i.e.* less than 16 hours per week and subject to another rule when 16 to 26 hours per week.

[35] *Hivac Ltd.* v. *Park Royal Scientific Instruments Ltd.* [1946] Ch. 169.

[36] *Lister* v. *Romford Ice & Cold Storage Co. Ltd.* [1957] A.C. 555 at p. 572.

[37] *Bents Brewery Co. Ltd.* v. *Hogan* [1945] 2 All E.R. 570.

[38] *Wessex Dairies Ltd.* v. *Smith* [1935] 2 K.B. 80 at p. 85.

sports teams to appear or commercial companies to provide goods in the locality. A term in a contract of employment which seeks to restrain an employee from competing against the employer for a stated period and in a defined area, after the employment in question ends, is one which needs careful drafting if it is to be effective in the courts. The general view taken is that such covenants are an undue restraint on a man's freedom in the market place, unless the covenant is reasonable both between the two parties and also reasonable in the public interest.[39]

Duties on the employer

The employer's general duty, apart from any arising from statute and discussed below, is to provide competent staff, adequate materials, a proper system of work and effective supervision.[40] This statement is meant to define a duty lower than that of an insurer of his employee's safety. An employee is expected to accept the reasonable risks of his employment and this limits the employer's obligations.[41] **1.063**

On the other hand, this is not a duty which the employer can delegate to an independent contractor. Where a kiosk was the place in which a workman had to work close to live electrical equipment, his employer was liable for his death, since it was no defence to say that he had entrusted the manufacture of the inadequate kiosk to another person. The employer had the primary duty and also had the opportunity to examine the kiosk and decide if it was safe for his workman.[42]

Lastly, from the employer—employee relationship is implied a term that the employer will indemnify the employee against losses incurred in carrying out the duties of his employment reasonably.[43] This obligation of the employer does not, however, extend to any consequences of the employee's misconduct.[44]

Dismissal

Dismissal has become legally complex, coupled as it is with redundancy law, compensation and numerous statutory provisions. **1.064**

The Employment Protection (Consolidation) Act 1978, amended in part by the Employment Act 1982, stipulates periods of notice related to the term of years served as an employee, *e.g.* 1 week of notice for every year served between 2 and 12 years, and 2 weeks notice if more than 12 years has been served. The calculation of the period of continuous employment

---

[39] *Mason* v. *Provident Clothing and Supply Co. Ltd.* [1913] A.C. 724 at p. 733. See also for a void contract due to unreasonableness. *A Schroeder Music Publishing Co. Ltd.* v. *Macaulay* [1974] 3 All E.R. 616.
[40] *Wilsons and Clyde Coal Co. Ltd.* v. *English* [1938] A.C. 78.
[41] *Smith* v. *Baker* [1891] A.C. 325 at p. 360.
[42] *Paine* v. *Colne Valley Supply Co. Ltd. and British Insulated Cables Ltd.* [1938] 4 All E.R. 803.
[43] *Adamson* v. *Jarvis* (1827) 4 Bing. 66.
[44] *Lister* v. *Romford Ice Cold Storage Co. Ltd.* (*supra*).

1.064 GENERAL LEGAL PRINCIPLES

for the above formula is itself intricate and the cases upon it must be studied. Changes of employer complicate that issue.[45]

A written statement of reasons for the dismissal is to be given if requested.[46]

Unfair dismissal in relation to trade union activities

1.065 An employee must not be dismissed unfairly. To do so gives rise to the right of the employee to seek redress, including, possibly, reinstatement, from an Industrial Tribunal.[47] The reasons given in the amended Act of 1978 which are stated to make the dismissal "unfair" are:

(a) that the employee was or proposed to become a member of an independent trade union;

(b) that the employee had taken or proposed to take part at any appropriate time in the activities of an independent trade union;

(c) that the employee was not a member of any trade union.

This reason is elaborated in the Act; so also are the various circumstances in which the reason is not to apply, so that the Act has to be looked at carefully if this situation is relevant.[48]

Fair dismissal in relation to trade union activities

1.066 The new section 58 provides that a dismissal is fair if, in brief:

(a) it is the practice, within the closed shop at the establishment in question, to join a specified independent trade union; and

(b) a principal or substantial reason for the dismissal is that the employee was not a member of such a trade union; and

(c) the closed shop had the status of having been approved by a postal ballot, complying with the Act and held within five years preceding the dismissal.[49]

(The Act sets out the various percentages for the ballot in question to be acceptable for this purpose.)

1.067 The Act of 1978, as amended, then provides that the above shall not apply if one of the following five conditions is met:

(i) The employee was a non-trade union member for the stated five year period[50]; or

(ii) the employee objects on conscientiously held grounds to joining a trade union[51]; or

(iii) the employee participated in the ballot by which the closed shop

---

[45] Act of 1978, s.49.
[46] *Ibid.* s.53.
[47] *Ibid.* s.54.
[48] *Ibid.* s.58. This is an amended s.58; see Employment Act 1982, s.3.
[49] *Ibid.* s.58(3A).
[50] *Ibid.* s.58(5).
[51] *Ibid.* s.58(4).

agreement at this establishment came into existence after August 14, 1980, and has not been a member of a trade union since that time; or
(iv) an employee's declaration of unreasonable expulsion from a trade union existed or was the subject of proceedings before an industrial tribunal at the time of the dismissal[52]; or
(v) the employee's refusal to take part in a strike (giving rise to his expulsion) or to join a trade union was due to the terms of a written code of conduct for employee's of his qualifications and (ii) or (iv) do not apply.

This is admittedly complex and no attempt is made here to summarise the ballot provisions. The inclusion of this subject matter is intended to alert employers and managers in the public leisure services to the points that will be relevant in a dismissal situation with which they may have to deal.

Unfair dismissal in relation to redundancy

After these three reasons relating to an employee's trade union membership, the Act turns to the question of redundancy.[53] It says that the dismissal shall be unfair if, though the principal reason for the dismissal is that the employee was redundant, the employer has not dismissed other employees who were in virtually the same situation as the one dismissed. In addition it has to be shown that the employer either was departing from an agreed practice governing redundancy (without special reasons for so doing) or that his real reason was the trade union membership one outlined above. The employer has the option to provide evidence that the employee could only have been in contravention of some enactment if he had been retained at work, as a driving disqualification when he has to drive at work. Finally the employer may show some other "substantial reason" for the dismissal.[54] This is wide-ranging, covering the deliberate misleading of the employer about a material fact when applying for the job and an irreconcilable conflict of personalities mainly caused by the dismissed employee. Two statutory "substantial reasons" may also be adduced by the employer:
(i) The person being dismissed is the temporary replacement of a permanent employee and he was told this would happen when appointed;
(ii) the person being dismissed was a temporary replacement for a pregnant employee and, again, was told at the time of appointment what would happen.

---

[52] s.4, Employment Act 1980.
[53] Act of 1978, s.59. Attention is drawn to the leading case of *Williams* v. *Compair Maxim Ltd.* [1980] 1 I.R.L.R. 83, for guidelines in dealing with this situation. These relate to warnings, consultation, objective criteria for selection, considering suggestions by the union on selection and offering alternative employment.
[54] *Ibid.* s.57(2).

Unfair reasons for dismissal—pregnancy

1.069 The last of the statutory situations dealt with in detail in the Act of 1978 is a dismissal related to an employee's pregnancy.[55] Such a dismissal is unfair, unless:
  (i) at the time in question, the employee will, because of her pregnancy, have become unable to do her work adequately; or
  (ii) some statutory provision would be contravened if she continued in work when pregnant.

Even if able to substantiate one of the above reasons, the employer must still be in a position to show that he is offering the lady in question a new and equivalent job, in circumstances detailed in the Act.

Valid reasons for dismissal

1.070 In assessing the merits of the employer's reasons in the situations described above, the tribunal has to comply with the following general provisions:
  (i) The employer has to show the reason for the dismissal.[56]
  (ii) He does this by showing that the reason related to the conduct of the employee or his capability or qualifications in relation to his particular job. Alternatively he can show that it was because the employee was redundant or could only continue in work if in conflict with some enactment.[57]
  (ii) Lastly, "the determination of the question whether the dismissal was fair or unfair, having regard to the reason shown by the employer, shall depend on whether, in the circumstances (including the size and administrative resources of the employer's undertaking), the employer acted reasonably or unreasonably in treating it as a sufficient reason for dismissing the employee; and that question shall be determined in accordance with equity and the substantial merits of the case."[58]

Exceptions

1.071 There are 8 classes of employees outside the above provisions:
  1. Employees who at the time of termination had not been employed for at least two years.[59]
  2. An employee who at the time of termination has reached his normal retiring age.[60]
  3. Where there is no prescribed retiring age, that he has reached pensionable age, *i.e.* 65 for men and 60 for women.[61]

---

[55] *Ibid.* s.60.
[56] *Ibid.* s.57(1).
[57] *Ibid.* s.57(2).
[58] *Ibid.* s.57(3), as amended by the Employment Act 1980, s.6.
[59] *Ibid.* s.64(1)(*a*) and S.I. 1985 No. 782.
[60] *Ibid.* s.64(1)(*b*).
[61] *Ibid.*

4. Persons employed by their husbands or wives.[62]
5. Dockworkers.[63]
6. Persons working in fishing vessels as non-profit sharers.[64]
7. Persons working under contracts which normally involve their working outside the United Kingdom.[65]
8. Persons employed on ships registered in Great Britain but whose employment is normally outside Great Britain, or who are not normally resident in Great Britain.[66]

General

A general exemption is also prescribed for a case where a dismissal is certified by a Minister that it was required for the purpose of safeguarding national security.[67]

The pressure upon an employer by a strike or other industrial action is to be ignored when a tribunal is considering whether a dismissal was fair or unfair.[68]

The Employment Protection (Consolidation) Act 1978 has a series of provisions about strikes and lock-outs. One of these gave rise to a case in the Court of Appeal concerning thirty employees at the National Theatre who went on strike, for reasons worth noting.

The case is *Williams* v. *National Theatre Board*.[69] At the conclusion of a damaging strike, which involved the cancellation of eight performances, there was a claim for unfair dismissal. The employers succeeded in their defence by showing that the employees had been offered re-engagement in the same jobs as before. It was that word "jobs" which engaged the main attention of the court. The only real difference in the situation was that the employees were told that they would be regarded as being in a second warning situation. The question for the court was whether this feature altered the "jobs" done by the men, so that they were not the same as before. Lord Denning M.R. giving the leading judgment, studied the definition of "job" in the Act of 1978.[70] This referred to place, nature and capacity and as place and nature were the same, without argument, the critical question was whether the "capacity" had altered. Shaw L.J.

---

[62] *Ibid.* s.146(1).
[63] *Ibid.* s.145(2).
[64] *Ibid.* s.144(2).
[65] *Ibid.* s.141(2).
[66] *Ibid.* s.141(5).
[67] Sched. 9, para. 2(1), *ibid.*
[68] Act of 1978, s.63. Generally, attention is drawn to recent remarks of the President of the Employment Appeals Tribunal, Waite J. in the case of *Amandarajah* v. *Lord Chancellor's Department* (1984) 1 I.R.L.R. 131. A warning was given against "pre-occupation with guideline authority" by Industrial Tribunals in unfair dismissal cases. "Industrial Tribunals are not required . . . to subject the authorities to the same analysis as a court of law searching in a plethora of precedent for binding or persuasive authority." The aim of Parliament had been "to banish legalism" in the Industrial Tribunals, the statement continued.
[69] [1982] I.R.L.R. 377.
[70] s.62(4) of the Act of 1978.

1.072 summed up the view which supported the employers: "Capacity," he said, "goes to conduct in his position and not performance in his task."[71]

B. Conditions of Work

1. The Health and Safety at Work, etc., Act 1974

1.073 This Act contains a comprehensive legal code for the health, welfare and safety of persons at work. The code is regularly updated and with the associated regulations, and codes of practice, provides a flexible system for inspecting, repairing and improving the physical environment of employees. Its scope extends to the protection of non-employees against risks to their health and safety arising from the activities of persons at work.

It contains one unusual feature. It schedules over 30 statutes which it is planned to have progressively replaced by a system of regulations and approved codes of practice, operating in conjunction with the other provisions of the Act.[72] The main provisions are as follows.

(1) Duties of Employers

1.074 A general duty is laid down to ensure the health, safety and welfare of all their employees, so far as is reasonably practicable.[73]

This is, in particular, to cover plant and systems of work, the use, storage and transport of substances, health education and work training, safe working conditions and facilities for welfare at work for the employees.[74]

Employers must prepare and bring to the notice of employees a written statement of their general policy in relation to health and safety at work.[75]

Employers must consult safety representatives of the employees and set up a safety committee, if requested.[76]

They must ensure that substances used at work are safe, so far as possible, by testing and examining them.[77]

(2) Duties of Employees

1.075 They must take reasonable care for the health and safety of themselves and others affected by their acts or omissions at work.

---

[71] para. 47.
[72] Act of 1974, s.1(2). Reference should be made to the treatment of the Act in relation to work in theatres (Chap. 6, s.1).
[73] Health and Safety at Work, etc., Act 1974, s.2(1).
[74] *Ibid.* s.2(2).
[75] *Ibid.* s.2(3). The Act of 1974 includes a definition of the contract of employment, in s.82, and cases go to the Tribunals on this issue. A recent case of *Quinnen* v. *Howell* (March 13, 1984, E.A.T. Law Society Gazette, May 23, 1984), in allowing an appeal from an Industrial Tribunal, decided that self-employed persons were within the definition, in s.82, of a "contract to execute any work or labour."
[76] *Ibid.* s.2(7).
[77] *Ibid.* s.6(4)(*a*).

They must co-operate with the employer, in relation to the duties under the Act.

(3) Breach of Duties

Breach of these duties gives rise to liability for a fine in the criminal courts but not to civil liability.[78]

(4) Codes of Practice

The Health and Safety Commission can promulgate codes of practice. There is consultation and ministerial approval to be obtained before that is done. The codes are, however, an integral part of the legal framework for this comprehensive legislation. They can, indeed, be used as support for prosecutions for dereliction of duties under the Act.[79]

2. Discrimination

1.076 There are currently three statutes embodying, respectively, the principle of equal pay for men and women doing equal work, and prohibiting discrimination in terms and conditions of employment in relation to sex and race. They are:
(1) The Equal Pay Act 1970.
(2) The Sex Discrimination Act 1975.
(3) The Race Relations Act 1976.

The first two are the measures by which Article 119 of the Treaty of Rome and associated Directives have been implemented in this country, in relation to the principle of equal pay for equal work.[80] The Race Relations Act, on the other hand, stems from an earlier Act of 1968 and represents the stance of Parliament on a social problem considered to need legislative aid.

(1) Equal Pay for Men and Women

1.077 The Equal Pay Act of 1970 provides that an equality clause shall be deemed to be included in every contract of employment, at an establishment in Great Britain, where a woman is employed.[81]

An equality clause is then defined as being to ensure that existing terms shall be modified so that they are no less favourable to a woman than a term of a similar kind in the contract under which a man is employed on like work in the same employment.[82]

This is to operate in a situation where a woman is employed on like

---

[78] *Ibid.* ss.33 and 47.
[79] *Ibid.* s.17.
[80] EEC Directives 75/117 and 76/207.
[81] Equal Pay Act 1970, s.1.
[82] *Ibid.* s.1(1).

1.077 work with a man in the same employment or on work rated as equivalent with that of a man in the same employment.

It is not to apply when the employer can show that the different treatment of men and women is "due to a material difference" other than sex.[83] The Act proceeds to elaborate ways of checking that a "like work" situation exists, or a "work rated as equivalent" situation exists.[84]

Recourse to an industrial tribunal is then prescribed to resolve problems created by the Act.[85]

Other principles are designed to implement the equal pay principle in the fields of collective pay agreements,[86] the armed forces[87] and existing wages regulation orders.[88]

From the point of view of providers of leisure services, the principle of equal pay for equal work between men and women has received parliamentary approval and is to be applied in all matters relating to terms and conditions of employment.

(2) *The Sex Discrimination Act 1975*

1.078 The Act makes unlawful certain acts of discrimination against either men or women on grounds of sex. It sets up an Equal Opportunities Commission, which is to promote equality of opportunity for men and women generally and work towards the elimination of discrimination as mentioned.

Basic principles

1.079 These are contained in Parts I and II of the Act of 1975 and are as follows:

It is discrimination against a woman when, for the purposes of circumstances relevant to any provision in the Act, she is treated "on the ground of her sex" less favourably than a man. If a condition or requirement is applied to a woman which is to her detriment, then again that is discrimination for the purposes of the Act of 1975.[89] In the case, for example, of *Gill* v. *El Vino Co. Ltd.*, it was held to be unlawful discrimination when ladies were not served drinks at the bar, as men were, but restricted to service at tables. The Court of Appeal said: "This is not a technical statute, and, therefore, is not of a kind where one should or need go for the meaning of words to other decided cases. It is a simple statute seeking to deal with ordinary everyday behaviour and the relative positions of men and women."[90] The decision was that there had been a breach of section 29 of the Act of 1975.

---

[83] *Ibid.* s.1(2)–(5).
[84] *Ibid.* s.2.
[85] *Ibid.* s.2.
[86] *Ibid.* s.3.
[87] *Ibid.* s.7.
[88] *Ibid.* ss.4 and 5.
[89] Sex Discrimination Act 1975, s.1.
[90] [1983] 1 All E.R. 398 and Eveleigh L.J. at p. 401e.

If a person treats a man differently, according to "his marital status," then his treatment of a woman, for the purposes of this provision, is to be compared to the treatment of a man with the "like marital status."[91] In the earlier case of *Peake* v. *Automotive Products Ltd.*[92] the Court of Appeal said it was not discrimination to allow women to leave a factory 5 minutes before men, in order to avoid being hurt in the rush through the factory gates, when work finished for the day.

In *Jeremiah's Case*,[93] the Court of Appeal said that certain expressions in *Peake's Case* (above) were "too forceful." *Jeremiah's Case* is very useful in understanding the Act.

The underlying principle is to apply to men, as it does to women, with such verbal modifications as are needed to make it read correctly.[94]

Special treatment of a woman in relation to pregnancy or child birth is not to be taken into account, when looking for discriminatory practices.[95]

It is unlawful discrimination within the Act of 1975 to treat a married person of either sex, in the circumstances of Part II of the Act relating to employment, less favourably than an unmarried person of the same sex.[96]

It is unlawful discrimination to victimise a person who has brought legal proceedings against the victimiser, given evidence or otherwise exercised his or her legal rights and powers under the Equal Pay Act 1970.[97]

In relation to employment by himself, at an establishment in Great Britain, it is unlawful for a person to discriminate against a woman in either the arrangements for filling a vacant post or in relation to the conditions on which the post is offered or, indeed, by refusing or deliberately omitting to offer her employment.[98]

(3) *Specific Exclusions by the Nature of the Job*

1.080 Certain areas of employment and social life are excluded from the operation of the Act. Some of these, like mining, are outside the ambit of this book. Some are specifically within it, *e.g.* where being a man is a genuine occupational qualification for a job, then it is not unlawful to discriminate. The eight areas thus excluded from the operation of the Act are as follows:

(1) Where the essential nature of the job calls for a man for reasons of physiology (excluding physical strength or stamina), or in dramatic performances or other entertainments for reasons of authenticity, so that the

---

[91] See n. 89, *supra*.
[92] [1978] 1 All E.R. 106.
[93] *Ministry of Defence* v. *Jeremiah* [1979] 3 All E.R. 833. This case has important comments on the principles embodied in s.1 of this Act of 1975. The Court found a "detriment," adverse to men examiners, existing in an ordnance factory. Their work conditions, in relation to colour bursting shells, were different from those of women inspectors. Lord Denning M.R. said "Equality is the order of the day. In both directions. For both sexes." (at p. 836a).
[94] Sex Discrimination Act 1975, s.2.
[95] *Ibid.*
[96] *Ibid.* s.3.
[97] *Ibid.* s.4.
[98] *Ibid.* s.6.

1.080

essential nature of the job would be materially different, if carried out by a woman;

(2) where it is necessary to preserve decency or privacy and physical contact or the circumstances are such that men might reasonably object to the job being done by a woman;

(3) where the nature or location of the place of work makes it impracticable for the employee to live elsewhere than on the employer's premises and it would be unreasonable to expect the employer to provide sleeping accommodation and sanitary conveniences for both men and women in privacy from each other;

(4) where the job is part of a prison or hospital or other establishment for persons requiring personal care and attention and all the persons are men and it is reasonable, "having regard to the essential character of the establishment," that the job should not be held by a woman;

(5) where the holder of the job provides personal services for individuals, which promote their welfare or education or other similar personal services and those services can most effectively be provided by a man;

(6) where the job needs to be held by a man, because of restrictions imposed by the laws regulating the employment of women;

(7) where the job involves work in a country whose laws or customs preclude easy discharge by a woman;

(8) where the job is one of two to be held by a married couple.

In respect of items (1) to (7) above it is stipulated that the Act is not to preclude an employer from filling the post with a man in his employment if he can reasonably do so, having regard to the number of available men and the switch can be made without undue inconvenience.[99]

(4) *Unlawful Acts of Sex Discrimination*

1.081 Persons engaged in the public leisure services should be aware of certain other actions rendered unlawful by the Act of 1975, *i.e.*

(i) Discrimination against a woman by a person providing goods, facilities or services to the public, when that woman seeks to obtain or use those goods, facilities or services. This discrimination, to constitute an unlawful act under the Act of 1975, involves:

> refusing or deliberately omitting to provide the woman with them; or refusing or deliberately omitting to provide the woman with goods facilities or services of the like quality manner or terms normal for men.[1]

Examples of these discriminatory acts, given in the section, include:
(a) "Access to and use of any place which members of the public or a

---

[99] *Ibid.* s.7. The Act is to apply to both men and women, though it does not print "or men" every time after the word "women" (s.2).
[1] *Ibid.* s.29(1).

section of the public are permitted to enter." This could be relevant to many leisure facilities.[2]
  (b) Accommodation in an hotel, boarding house, or other similar establishment.[3]
  (c) Facilities for entertainment, recreation or refreshment.[4]
  (d) Facilities for transport or travels.[5]
  (e) "The services of any profession or trade or of any local or other public authority."[6]

(ii) The Act also prohibits discrimination against a woman when engaged in disposing of premises or affording to a woman in premises occupied by her any benefits or facilities.[7]

(iii) An exception to the offences contained in sections 29 and 30 of the Act (*i.e.* (i) and (ii) above), is given in favour of a voluntary body where its membership or facilities are restricted to one sex.[8]

(iv) A further exception, of importance to managers of bathing pools or similar facilities, is provided where "the facilities or services are provided for, or are likely to be used by, two or more persons at the same time, and
  (1) the facilities or services are such that male users are likely to suffer serious embarrassment at the presence of a woman, or
  (2) the facilities or services are such that a user is likely to be in a state of undress and a male user might reasonably object to the presence of a female user."[9]

(5) *General Unlawful Practices*

Part IV of the Sex Discrimination Act 1975 deals with a number of unlawful practices which can be found in specific areas of employment and commerce. These are:

1. Advertisements indicating a discrimination against women. The examples given in the Act of 1975 are postman, waiter, sales girl and stewardess "unless the advertisement contains an indication to the contrary."[10]

2. Instructing another person to do an action unlawful under the Act of 1975.[11]

---

[2] *Ibid.* s.29(2).
[3] *Ibid.* s.29(2)(*b*).
[4] *Ibid.* s.29(2)(*e*).
[5] *Ibid.* s.29(2)(*f*).
[6] *Ibid.* s.29(2)(*g*).
[7] *Ibid.* s.34.
[8] *Ibid.*
[9] *Ibid.* s.35(1)(*c*) and s.35(2).
[10] *Ibid.* s.38. The unlawful act is the publication of an advertisement which indicates "an intention by a person to do an act which is, or might be, unlawful, by virtue of Part II, or Part III of the Act of 1975." By reference, this lists all the general acts of discrimination in ss. 1, 2, 3, and 4 of the Act, as outlined at para. 1.079 above, and also refers to the specific field of employment.
[11] *Ibid.* s.39.

3. Putting pressure on a person to carry out a discriminating act by offering some benefit or threatening some detriment to make him do so.[12]

4. An employer is equally guilty with his employee of an unlawful action, under the Act of 1975, when that action is done in the course of employment by his employee "whether or not it is done with the employer's knowledge or approval." The statutory defence available to the employer is that he took such steps as were reasonably practicable to prevent the employee doing the act in question.

A principal is equally guilty with his agent under the Act of 1975 of an unlawful action done with his authority.[13]

Training

1.084 5. Every manager in the public leisure services becomes involved in training recruits to the service from time to time. It is important to take note of an exception contained in the Act of 1975 for what would otherwise be discriminatory training. Section 48 deals with this activity and the exemption is described as limited to the situation where there was a shortage of persons of the sex in question for the job or activity in question.[14]

Enforcement

1.085 6. Part VII of the Act of 1975 deals with enforcement of its provisions. This rests generally upon action through industrial tribunals. When satisfied that a complaint brought before them is well founded, such a tribunal may take one of three courses:
  (i) Declare the rights of the parties before it.
  (ii) Order payment of compensation, as if it were damages in the County Court.[15]
  (iii) Recommend action the respondent should take to obviate the damage he has caused.

The High Court may still be approached for orders of prohibition, mandamus and certiorari.[16]

Acts of discrimination under Part III of the Act may be the subject of civil proceedings like any other claim in tort but only in the County Court, which in this instance may give the same remedies as the High Court might do.[17] Such remedies, if including damages, may include an item for injury to feelings, in addition to any other head of claim.

---

[12] *Ibid.* s.40.
[13] *Ibid.* s.41. This authority can be express or implied and can be given before or after the act in question.
[14] The words in the Act are that, in the preceding twelve months, there were either no persons "of the sex in question" among those doing that work, or the number of that sex was "comparatively small."
[15] The present limit is £7,500. (Unfair Dismissal (Increase of Compensatory Limit) Order 1982, S.I. 1982 No. 1868).
[16] For details, see Chap. 2.
[17] *Ibid.* s.66.

The Equal Opportunities Commission is constituted in Part VI of the Act of 1975, to secure enforcement of the Act.

A term in a contract is void under the Act of 1975, if it embodies an action rendered unlawful by this Act. Also a term is unenforceable if it purports to limit or exclude any provision in this Act, or the Equal Pay Act of 1970. These principles can be taken to the length of a County Court Order if desired; such an order could, for example, have the offending clause removed from the contract in question.[18]

3. Disabled Persons

Providers of leisure services constantly have to meet the special needs of disabled persons. This relates to access to entertainments, personal needs, ramps rather than stairs, physical dangers on premises to which the public resort, the use of lifts and numerous other situations. The legislation on the subject is slight: common sense and humanity govern the approach to most situations. It may be useful to itemise such legislative guidance as exists.

This is centred upon the Disabled Persons (Employment) Acts 1944 and 1958, in which the main points of interest are as follows:

1. Employers of more than a substantial number of persons are obliged to give employment to a quota of disabled persons from the official register.[19] This quota is currently 3 per cent.[20]

2. The two additional obligations imposed by the Acts upon employers are:
   (i) not to dismiss such a disabled person from his employment without a permit from the Minister, if such action would take him below his statutory quota[21]; and
   (ii) not to engage a non-disabled person if a vacancy arises when he is still below his legal quota[22];
   (iii) to keep suitable records.[23]

3. The Secretary of State for Employment may authorise criminal proceedings for breaches of the Act.[24]

4. Under his power to designate suitable employments for disabled persons, the Secretary of State has so designated passenger electric lift attendant and car park attendant.[25]

5. District Advisory Committees ("Disablement Advisory Committees"

---

[18] *Ibid.* s.77. (This is a large Act of 87 sections and 4 Schedules. It is outlined in the text to the extent considered suitable for those engaged in or with the public leisure services.)
[19] Act of 1944, s.9.
[20] Disabled Persons (Standard Percentage) Order 1946 (S.R.O. 1946 No. 1268).
[21] Act of 1944, s.11. Figures published in May 1983 showed only one in ten of district councils were meeting their quota. The figures were no better for larger authorities.
[22] *Ibid.* s.9(2).
[23] *Ibid.* s.14.
[24] *Ibid.* s.19.
[25] Disabled Persons (Designated Employments) Order 1946 (S.R.O. 1946 No. 1257). The Disabled Persons (General) Regulations 1945 (S.R.O. 1945 No. 1558) are also important.

in practice) are set up by the Secretary of State and provide a point of contact for the employer, together with the Employment office.[26]

6. A person suffering from mental disorder can be "disabled" for the purposes of these Acts.[27] Like others, he has to be registered.[28]

4. Race Relations Act 1976

1.088 An outline of the Race Relations Act 1976 is easier in the light of the above outline of the Sex Discrimination Act 1975. This is because the drafting of the 1976 Act followed the framing of the 1975 Act. There had been a Race Relations Act 1968 but the Act of 1976 makes what its preamble calls "fresh provision" and the shape of the Act of 1976 is remarkably similar to that of the Sex Discrimination Act.[29]

It may assist the reader to identify those parts of the Act of 1976 in which the wording follows the Act of 1975 and then to turn to those differences which are important for the providers of public leisure services.

(1) *The Acts of 1975 and 1976—Common Features*

1.089 1. Discrimination by employers is defined in similar terms in both Acts by reference to applications, appointments and dismissals (paragraph 1.079, above).

2. Contract workers are dealt with in the same way in both Acts.[30]

3. Discriminatory practices are defined in similar terms relating to advertisements, giving instructions,[31] exerting pressure, aiding unlawful acts and liability as employer or as principal (paragraph 1.083 above).

4. Charities are given a similar exemption in both Acts (paragraph 1.081 above).

5. Education, training and welfare by an employer (paragraph 1.084 above).

6. The composition and powers of the Commission for Racial Equality set up under the Act of 1976 are very similar to those of the Equal Opportunities Commission (paragraph 1.085 above).

7. Enforcement of the Act of 1976 follows a pattern very similar to that in the Act of 1975, in relation to County Courts, industrial tribunals, non-discrimination notices and assistance for persons, whether aggrieved in fact or as prospective claimants.[32]

---

[26] Act of 1944, s.17.
[27] *Ibid.* s.1. (Definition of disabled person.)
[28] *Ibid.* s.6.
[29] Introducing the Race Relations Bill (2R) the Home Secretary said it was "closely modelled" on the Sex Discrimination Act 1975 (Hansard, March 4, 1976).
[30] Sex Discrimination Act 1975, s.9; Race Relations Act 1976, s.7.
[31] See *Showboat Entertainment Centre Ltd.* v. *Owens* [1984] 1 W.L.R. 384, for a case on unlawful instructions to discriminate, *i.e.* to exclude black persons from an entertainment centre.
[32] It is often vital to obtain sight of documents in the possession of the other side in these cases. The recent case of *British Library* v. *Palyza* (E.A.T. February 28, 1984; L.S. Gaz., February 18, 1984), decided that a decision of an Industrial Tribunal about discovery can be reviewed and, if necessary, reversed by the E.A.T.

(2) *Distinctive Features of the Act of 1976*

Definition of Discrimination

Whilst the basic definition of discrimination is identical, the Act of 1976 has two necessarily distinctive points: **1.090**

(a) The social ill against which the Act is directed is discrimination "on racial grounds," a term defined as connoting "colour, race, nationality, or ethnic or national origins."[33]

(b) The term "racial group" is used in the basic definitions of discrimination, *i.e.* treating a person differently from those of another racial group. This term is defined as "a group of persons defined by reference to colour, race, nationality or ethnic or national origins and references to a person's racial group refer to any racial group into which he falls." The fact that a racial group comprises two or more distinct racial groups does not prevent it from constituting a particular racial group for the purposes of this Act."[34]

Again it is laid down that a comparison of the case of a person of a particular racial group with that of a person not of that group must be such that the relevant circumstances in the one case are the same, or not materially different, in the other.

Exclusions

There are fewer exclusions in the Act of 1976, but they are interesting: **1.091**

(a) A dramatic performance or entertainment, where a person of that racial group is required as a matter of authenticity.

(b) Being an artist's or photographer's model and needed on account of authenticity.

(c) Where the setting for the provision of food and drink requires persons of that racial group in the interests of authenticity.

(d) "The holder of the job provides persons of that particular group with personal services promoting their welfare and those services can most effectively be provided by a person of that racial group."[35]

Codes of Practice

The Code for Race Relations[36] published by the Commission for Racial Equality in 1984 is an example of an exercise of one of the Commission's powers in the field of education and public relations. The wording for this section of the Act of 1976 has been adapted from the Act of 1975. **1.092**

---

[33] Act of 1976, s.3.
[34] *Ibid.*
[35] *Ibid.* s.5.
[36] *Ibid.* s.47. The new publication provides a useful summary, directed to employers, employees, trade unions and employment agencies.

1.092

Local Authorities

Local Authorities are required to promote equality of opportunity and the elimination of discrimination.[37]

5. Bribery and Corruption; Theft

(1) Bribery and Corruption

1.093 The public leisure services involve large commercial contracts; sometimes in catering, sometimes in entertainment in all its forms, sometimes in relation to gambling. An extensive licensing system is also integral to the public leisure services. Furthermore, building contracts often involve large sums of money. In all these spheres human frailty can give rise to situations where this small but vital branch of the law is involved.

The Acts

1.094 The Acts are the Public Bodies Corrupt Practices Act 1889, the Prevention of Corruption Act 1906, and the Prevention of Corruption Act 1916.

Main Offences

1.095
(1) Members of public bodies receiving corrupt gifts.[38]
(2) Giving or offering corrupt gifts to members of a public body.[39]
(3) Corrupt acceptance of gifts by an agent in relation to his principal's affairs.[40]
(4) Giving or offering corrupt gifts to an agent in relation to his principal's affairs.[41]
(5) Giving to an agent, or using as an agent, a false receipt, account or other document, in order to mislead the principal.[42]

1.096 "Public body" means the council of a county or of a town or city—and generally the body which has power to administer money raised by rates.[43]

"Public office" means any office or employment of a person as a member, officer or servant of such public body.[44]

"Consideration" includes "valuable consideration of any kind."

"Agent" includes any person acting for another and "principal" includes an employer.[45]

The current sanction for these offences is imprisonment for not more

---

[37] *Ibid.* s.71.
[38] Act of 1889, s.1(1).
[39] *Ibid.* s.1(2).
[40] Act of 1906, s.1.
[41] *Ibid.*
[42] *Ibid.*
[43] Act of 1889, s.7.
[44] *Ibid.*
[45] Act of 1906, s.1(2).

than two years or a fine of £500, or both, when tried on indictment: if tried summarily, four months imprisonment or £200 or both. These punishments relate to offences (3), (4) and (5) above.[46]

For the two offences (1) and (2), the punishment is imprisonment for not more than two years, or £500 fine, or both. In addition, a person convicted of either of these two offences may be ordered to restore the gift and forfeit[47] the office in question for five years.

If the offence is committed in connection with a contract with a Government department, then the maximum period of imprisonment is increased, for a conviction on indictment, to not less than three years and not more than seven years.[48]

1.097 There is a very important provision about onus of proof in the Act of 1916. Where the money, gift or other consideration is proved to have been given, it is deemed to have been given and received corruptly, unless the contrary is proved.[49]

In the light of these provisions, it would be normal for those responsible to insert in appropriate contracts a clause providing for the avoidance of the contract if found to have been tainted by corruption.

An example of the onus provision in practice is *R. v. Mills*,[50] where a person was convicted of accepting free holidays in connection with a lucrative contract. He sought to show an intention to double-cross the donor for the future, but did not discharge the statutory onus of proof which lay upon him, when the acceptance of the holidays had been proved.

(2) *Theft*

1.098 Theft is universal; it is, in law, simple and yet may be complicated in the extreme.

Theft from the employer or fellow-worker, at work, is normally a justification for summary dismissal, as constituting gross misconduct.

The discovery of a thief, red-handed, is not the most difficult situation for an employer but the loss of bar takings at a sports centre, where several employees are under suspicion; the probability that two employees are involved in the theft of an expensive grass mower, though only one has confessed; the quiet young man who spends long hours in a corner of the reference library and provides no tangible evidence to justify an allegation that he is connected with the disappearance of valuable books, whose subject matter is unconnected with travel—these are all serious employer problems. The courts have met them all.

The employer should have a published disciplinary code, which covers theft and the existence of which is known to all employees.[51]

---

[46] Act of 1906, s.1.
[47] Act of 1889, s.2.
[48] Act of 1916, s.1.
[49] *Ibid.* s.2.
[50] (1978) 68 Cr.App.R. 154.
[51] See ACAS Code of Practice on Disciplinary Practice and Procedures.

1.098

He must act reasonably at all times. He should bear in mind a test suggested by the court in the case of *Rolls Royce Ltd.* v. *Walpole*[52]: Was dismissal within the reasonable range of responses open to a reasonable employer in those circumstances?

1.099 Employment law differs from criminal law. The employer is entitled to take account of the feelings of other employees when theft is discovered and thus is entitled to take action when police might not take a case to court. A test in the case of *British Home Stores Ltd.* v. *Burchell*[53] is important:

(i) The employer must honestly believe in the guilt of the employee.
(ii) The employer must have in his mind reasonable grounds to support that belief.
(iii) At the final stage when he formed that belief, the employer must have carried out as much investigation into the matter as was reasonable in all the circumstances of the case.

This reasonable investigation must include hearing the employee's account of the situation, as well as carrying out his own code of discipline.[54]

Conclusion

This is not comprehensive. It endeavours to indicate the approach to the problem of theft in its various forms, which Industrial Tribunals have been encouraging in recent years.[55]

C. Negligence

Introduction

1.100 The tort of negligence is of great importance to the providers of leisure services. It can arise when a cricket ball injures a passer-by after being struck in the adjoining cricket ground[56]; or where a spectator is injured at a hockey match[57]; or a consumer of ginger beer finds her drink tainted with a foreign body.[58] It is at once simple and yet subtle. It consists in the breach of a duty of care and consequent injury, not necessarily physical, suffered by an aggrieved person. Yet the duty is not universal, the breach is not always easy to agree and the injury is sometimes complex and has to be dissected into that within and that outside the duty in law. A working

---

[52] [1980] I.R.L.R. 343.
[53] [1978] I.R.L.R. 379.
[54] *Moore* v. *C. and A. Modes* [1981] I.R.L.R. 71, was a case where the "reasonable belief" of the employer was critical.
[55] A difficult area not discussed above is that of offences not connected with the work situation but which render the employee less suitable for his work or unacceptable to his fellow employees. The author is indebted to an article in (1983) L.S.Gaz. by Mr. M. Edwards at p. 892, which considers this further problem.
[56] *Bolton* v. *Stone* [1951] 1 All E.R. 1078.
[57] *Klyne* v. *Bellegarde* [1978] 6 W.W.R. 734; [1979] C.L.Y.B. 1870.
[58] *Donaghue* v. *Stevenson* [1932] A.C. 562.

definition comes from the leading case of *Donoghue* v. *Stevenson*, in the judgment of Lord Atkin:

> "The rule that you are to love your neighbour becomes, in law, you must not injure your neighbour, and the lawyer's question: Who is my neighbour? receives a restricted reply.
> You must take reasonable care to avoid acts and omissions which you can reasonably foresee would be likely to injure your neighbour. Who then, in law, is my neighbour? The answer seems to be—persons who are so closely and directly affected by my act, that I ought reasonably to have them in contemplation as being so affected, when I am directing my mind to the acts or omissions which are called in question."[59]

1.101 It is convenient to consider the subject of negligence under the following headings:
1. The duty.
2. The breach.
3. Special situations:
   (i) Negligent statements and economic loss.
   (ii) Liability of professional advisers.
   (iii) Defective premises.
4. Consequences of the breach.
5. The burden of proof.

1. The Duty

1.102 This is a duty to exercise care to avoid acts and omissions which can be reasonably foreseen to be likely to cause damage, as later discussed.

The degree of care varies according to the circumstances. In *Paris* v. *Stepney B.C.*[60] a one-eyed garage mechanic suffered injury to his eye whilst working. The House of Lords held that the special risk of injury was part of the matters the employer should consider and the failure to provide goggles was negligent, so that damages should be paid to the workman. "The test is what precautions would the ordinary, reasonable and prudent man take?"[61] "These included the foreseeable consequences of an accident and their seriousness for the person to whom that duty was owed."[62] *Donoghue's* case came into the argument before the court in that case.

1.103 The degree of care also results from keeping abreast of current knowledge. The recent case of *Thompson* v. *Smiths Shiprepairers Ltd.*[63] was a test case on the extent of an employer's duty, and consequential damages, for avoiding deafness to labourers in ship repair yards. The period of work extended over 40 years and knowledge of the growth of deafness due to

---

[59] *Ibid.* at p. 580.
[60] [1951] A.C. 367.
[61] *Ibid.* Lord Normand at p. 380.
[62] *Ibid.* p. 381.
[63] [1984] Q.B. 405. It was said to be the test case for 20,000 others. See especially Mustill J. at p. 531.

1.103 that work had increased due to certain publications and events in that period.

A second recent case, *Rimmer* v. *Liverpool City Council*,[64] usefully illustrates a third aspect of the duty of care, namely knowledge of the materials and potential danger in a building. The Council let a flat to the tenant, which included a glass panel 3mm thick as part of an internal wall opposite to the lounge door. A panel twice as thick was initially specified by the project architect. The plaintiff suffered serious injury when his hand went through the glass panel. The landlord's duty was defined by the court as being "to take reasonable steps to see that the premises were reasonably safe."[65] They had failed and were thus held liable in negligence.

2. The Breach

1.104 The test was put a century ago by Baron Alderson: "Negligence is the omission to do something which a reasonable man, guided by those considerations which ordinarily regulate the conduct of human affairs, would do or doing something which a prudent and reasonable man would not do."[66]

The reasonable man, the man on the Clapham omnibus, is a creation of law and is used as a yardstick in many legal problems. What would he do? Of course, the question is hypothetical but it helps to focus the problem on a person who is detached from those in the case before the court.

In *Bolton* v. *Stone*,[67] the possibility of injury to a lady in the adjacent highway was not a risk a reasonable man would have contemplated. The attitude of the cricket club was upheld and the plaintiff lost her case.

In *Hilder* v. *Associated Portland Cement Manufacturers Ltd*,[68] a football kicked into a road from adjoining ground where youngsters were allowed to play, struck a passing motor cyclist, who suffered injury. The likelihood of injury in this way was real and, said the court, should have been foreseen and the plaintiff won his case.

3. Special Situations

1.105 The law of negligence has the capacity to develop to meet new customs and social pressures. There are three particular areas of social life where the growth of this tort in recent years has been marked and should be noted briefly here. They relate to negligent statements causing economic loss, negligent professional loss and, lastly, the situation now covered by the Defective Premises Act 1972.

---

[64] [1984] 2 W.L.R. 426.
[65] *Ibid.* at p. 431.
[66] *Blyth* v. *Birmingham Waterworks Co.* [1856] 11 Ex. 781 at p. 784.
[67] [1951] 1 All E.R. 1078.
[68] [1961] 1 W.L.R. 1434.

NEGLIGENCE   **1.106**

(1) *Negligent Statements and Economic Loss*

This is an interesting development of the principle in *Donoghue's* case. It shows the courts as ready to uphold a claim for damages, due to a negligent statement.   **1.106**

Hedley Byrne and Co. Ltd. v. *Heller and Partners Ltd.*[69] has proved a watershed in cases of its kind. It was a decision of the House of Lords, on a claim for £17,000 lost by the plaintiffs in reliance on negligent statements of the defendants. There was no physical injury and there was no contract. It was a case where the plaintiffs sought references at second hand from the defendants, who were bankers, about a company with whom the plaintiffs were having business dealings. There was no doubt that the defendants' advice was crucial and would be relied upon. In that situation, favourable references were given carelessly. The decision of the court, although the actual claim was dismissed, was important because it showed acceptance of this principle, namely that in order to be liable at law for a false statement which gives rise to economic loss, the defendant must be shown to have assumed some responsibility to those who will act on his information or advice. "This creates a duty of care towards them,"[70] said the court.

The court cases on this subject are generally from the business and commercial world: mortgages, debentures, architects certificates, hire-purchase agreements. In the leisure services field, if a significant block booking of seats for a football match or a play were made on the basis of a statement by the defendant that a particular player or actor would be appearing in that match or play, without disclaimer, then the duty of care would arise, with the consequences indicated above.   **1.107**

(2) *Liability of Professional Advisers*

Another series of cases has developed, of which *Anns* v. *Merton London Borough*[71] is the leading case. The House of Lords decided that a duty of care was laid upon a local authority and its staff, when discharging their statutory functions in relation to a builder's deposited plans under the building by-laws. That duty covered the question of whether and how inspection of the new building should be done and also the level of competence of the staff detailed to carry out that inspection, if indeed it were to be arranged. When, therefore, the foundations of a building gave way and were found to have been constructed differently from the plans submitted to and approved by the local authority, the local authority was held responsible for the failure of its inspecting staff to exercise reasonable care, in ensuring that the building by-laws were complied with and that the building matched its plans.   **1.108**

This may seem a little way from leisure services and will not be elabor-

---

[69] [1964] A.C. 465.
[70] *Ibid.* Lord Devlin at p. 529.
[71] [1978] A.C. 728.

ated. Its importance, in this context, is the underpinning it gives to the principle of the duty of care, the acceptance of economic loss for damages, as in the *Hedley Byrne* case, and, particularly, the authoritative and extended discussion of the proximity of relationship between defendant and plaintiff. That was critical, due to the time lapse between the inspector's action, or inaction, and the development of the defect in the building. That could be relevant for anyone who became responsible for a new building, whether it be a multi-million pound sports centre, or a new canteen block.

(3) *Defective Premises*

1.109 This is noted as a signal instance of the principle in *Donoghue's* case, being embodied in a statute in relation to one special social and legal problem.

Under the Defective Premises Act 1972, where work of construction, repair, maintenance or demolition or any other work is done on or in relation to premises, then any duty of care owed, because of that work, to persons who might reasonably be expected to be affected by the doing of that work, is not ended when the premises are subsequently disposed of to another owner or occupier.

A plaintiff, in other words, can still base his claim on the negligence of the builder.[72]

The Act has a number of other provisions which are not of relevance to this section.

4. Consequences of the Breach

1.110 The consequence, in the tort of negligence, of breach of the duty of care, is liability for a claim for damages. As indicated above, this comprises monetary compensation for the physical injury suffered by the plaintiff, as well as the economic consequences of that injury in loss of wages and other expenses directly associated with the act which gives rise to the claim. There are three aspects of damages and they can be critical. They are the question of remoteness, the question of nervous shock and finally, the question of the special characteristics of the plaintiff.

(1) *Remoteness*

1.111 What damage is too remote to be attributed to the defendant's breach of duty? There are two classic cases. An American one concerned a person on a railway station, injured when an explosion caused scales to fall and injure her. The explosion was caused by a parcel which fell from a passenger who was boarding a train: a railway company employee had negligently dislodged the parcel, which was believed to contain fireworks. The plaintiff's injury was held to be too remote.[73]

---

[72] s.3.
[73] *Palgcaf* v. *Long Island Railway Co.* (1928) 284 N.Y. 339.

In the second case, a Greek ship in Casablanca harbour was a total loss after a fire had been started by a spark from a falling plank, which ignited petrol vapour in the hold.[74]

Both cases demonstrate a sequence of totally unexpected events.

For a century, two views have been canvassed: **1.112**
  (i) Consequences are too remote, if a reasonable man could not have foreseen them.
  (ii) A man is responsible for all the direct consequences of his action, whether a reasonable man would have foreseen them or not.

The above shipping case, *Re Polemis*, was settled in 1921, on the basis of the second principle above. But in 1967, another shipping case, known as the *Wagon Mound*, caused the Judicial Committee of the House of Lords to lay down the first principle above as the one to be followed. This time the accident occurred in Sidney harbour, involving heavy damage to two ships and the adjacent wharf. Oil had gathered on the water near the vessels, due to carelessness while bunkering oil was loaded. Repairs on one boat by oxy-acetylene welding led to hot pieces of metal flying out over the water and igniting the oil.

> "It is the foresight of the reasonable man which alone can determine responsibility. The *Polemis* rule, by substituting 'direct' for 'reasonably foreseeable' consequences, leads to a conclusion equally illogical and unjust,"

1.113

said one of the judges in the *Wagon Mound* case. One merit of "reasonable foreseeability" as a test of remoteness of damages, is that this is also the test used when considering the first question of breach of duty.[75]

(2) *Nervous Shock*

It has been established for some years, that damages available to a successful plaintiff in a negligence action can include an item for nervous shock. In the leading case of *Bourhill* v. *Young*,[76] a motor cyclist in Edinburgh, driving at an excessive speed, collided with a motor car and was killed. The plaintiff, a fishwife standing 45 feet away, was unloading her basket. She heard the noise, suffered nervous shock and, being eight months pregnant, her child was still-born a month later. She failed in an action against the driver's estate for, the court said, she was outside the area of those the motor-cyclist should reasonably have foreseen would be affected by his actions.

1.114

The case is, however, a focus for the law and various cases on either side of success or failure have turned on the formulations it contains. In brief, the plaintiff may recover when the fear for his own safety is reasonable, in the light of the foreseeability test. This has been extended to a fear also for the safety of his close relatives.

1.115

---

[74] In *Re Polemis and Furness Withy & Co.* [1921] 3 K.B. 560.
[75] *The Wagon Mound* [1961] A.C. 388 (P.C.), *No. 1 case* at p. 424 (*supra*); [1967] A.C. 617, *No. 2 case*. Full title: *Overseas Tankship (UK) Ltd.* v. *Miller Steamship Co. Property.*
[76] [1943] A.C. 92.

(3) *Taking the Plaintiff as he is*

1.116 The defendant in an action for damages for negligence, may be surprised to discover that the injured plaintiff had an egg-shell skull and died from a fall which would have bruised a robust person. But the law is that the defendant takes the plaintiff as he finds him. Whatever the physical frailty of the plaintiff, that is part of the situation. In other words, the law looks for a real person. This aspect of a claim is treated in practice as part of the process of assessing damages. Likewise, when turning to that part of a claim that relates to loss of earnings and loss of expectation of life, the discovery by the defendant that the plaintiff is a pop star or a professor or a cleaner or a canteen assistant is all part of the situation, for which he has responsibility.[77]

5. The Burden of Proof

1.117 A plaintiff in a claim for damages for negligence, has to prove the duty of care, the breach and the consequent damages.

Sometimes the facts encourage the plaintiff to invite the court to say that the negligence is clear. This step is associated with the maxim *res ipsa loquitur*.[78] Even so, the courts have emphasised that this maxim is just a neat way of summarising the plaintiff's case: these are the facts; can the defendant rebut the inference of negligence which the court is invited to draw? The defendant may well be able to do so.

1.118 As a recent example, in a commercial setting, see *Ward* v. *Tesco Stores*.[79] A lady slipped on spilt yoghurt in a supermarket and was injured. She sued the owners who gave evidence that they cleaned the floor five or six times a day, so the yoghurt could not have been there long. They claimed that they exercised reasonable care for their customers. The case turned on whether the owners had left the spillage for an unreasonable period of time. In the absence of more cogent evidence from the owners, they lost.

The burden of proof is at all times upon the plaintiff.

D. Defences

1.119 The defences available for an action in tort may be conveniently considered under four headings:
  (i) Contributory negligence.
  (ii) The plaintiff voluntarily accepted all the risks involved in the action of which he complains: *volenti non fit injuria*. Contributory negligence pre-supposes a breach of duty by the defendant. *Volenti* does not. It alleges that because the plaintiff saw and accepted what was happening and what might happen, the defendant had no duty to protect the plaintiff.

---

[77] See further discussion in Chapter 7.
[78] *i.e.* the facts speak for themselves. *Scott* v. *London and St. Katherine's Docks Co.* [1865] 3 H. & C. 596.
[79] [1976] 1 All E.R. 219.

DEFENCES   1.119

(iii) The statutory powers of the defendant.
(iv) The Limitation Acts.

These defences are those generally available. This does not alter what 1.120
has been said above about the *Rylands* v. *Fletcher* defences, *i.e.* the unforeseeable act of a stranger, Act of God and default of the plaintiff. Nor, indeed, nuisance, where 20 years' prescription may legalise a private nuisance, though not a public one.

1. Contributory Negligence

This defence is available when it can be established that the plaintiff is 1.121
partly at fault when sustaining his injury. The "contribution" of the plaintiff is not to the negligence of the defendant (since that has to be settled on the principle of breach of the duty of care) but to the injury or damage he has suffered. For example, the plaintiff may have been partly responsible for the accident which caused the injury (perhaps a traffic accident at a cross roads) or his injury may be more serious than it need have been because of his own conduct (not wearing a seatbelt).

The Law Reform (Contributory Negligence) Act 1945 provides that 1.122
where a person suffers damage, as the result partly of his own fault and partly of the fault of any other person, the damages recovered shall be reduced as the Court thinks fit, having regard to the claimant's share in the responsibility for the damage. Where several parties are involved in the accident, the damages are apportioned among them according to their respective faults. The assessment of relative fault will take into account all relevant factors, including the age or disability of the claimant.

Contributory negligence is not only a defence to an action based on negligence. It is also available as a defence to actions brought for nuisance, under *Rylands* v. *Fletcher* and for occupier's liability.

2. Volenti Non Fit Injuria

A person who assents to an injury cannot sue for it. The defence is also 1.123
known as the voluntary assumption of risk by the plaintiff. In normal circumstances, whether or not the defence will apply is to be judged from the surrounding facts of the case, but some decisions of the courts are of assistance in stating the general principles underlying the defence. Participants in games are expected to accept the normal risks inherent in the playing of the games and spectators at sporting events assume the risk of injury caused by the playing of the game they are watching. The occupier of premises on which games are being played can thus avail himself of the defence both as against the players and the spectators.

Examples from three cases about different sports may be helpful.

A rugby player failed in an action based on his injury when thrown 1.124
against a boundary wall in a tackle.[80] A spectator at a motor race failed

---
[80] *Simms* v. *Leigh Rugby Club* [1969] 2 All E.R. 923.

1.124

when injured by a car that crashed through a boundary railing.[81] A boy, injured by an ice hockey puck, failed after being struck when the puck came through boundary netting. All three claimants were met by the *volenti* defence.[82]

1.125 There may be circumstances when the voluntary assumption of the risk of injury does not disentitle the plaintiff from his remedy. The cases in which this applies are usually called the "rescue cases." They arise when the plaintiff has voluntarily responded to a moral duty to go to the assistance of another person, who has been injured or is in danger of being injured as a result of the negligence of a third party. There are cases which illustrate this principle.

1.126 In one, (*Haynes* v. *Harwood*), the plaintiff was a policeman who was injured when he grabbed a bolting horse of the defendant, as it was heading for a crowded street. He succeeded in an action, the court holding that he had responded reasonably to an emergency created by the defendant's negligence.[83] But another claimant failed when injured after helping to hold a bolting horse in a field. The emergency was over, and the plaintiff had voluntarily accepted a risk of injury.[84]

1.127 It should be noted that the defence can only be used when it is established that the plaintiff has voluntarily assumed the risk of injury. Knowledge of the danger is not by itself the equivalent of the assumption of the risk of injury; knowledge of a potential danger may be relevant to the defence of contributory negligence but mere knowledge will not constitute a total defence.

For the effect of the Unfair Contract Terms Act 1977 on exclusion clauses, as one aspect of the *volenti* defence, see para. 1.155 of this Chapter.

3. Statutory Powers

1.128 Public providers of leisure services include local authorities, who will invariably be acting under statutory powers. It may be that these afford a good defence to some of the claims in tort brought against them. That defence would bear upon liability; even though it were successful, the plaintiff could conceivably be entitled to statutory compensation—outside his claim in tort—for injury or damage suffered, due to the exercise of the powers in question. There are two associated points which bear upon the defence, that statutory powers have been employed:

(i) The courts lean towards the citizen, in the sense that they will not impute to the legislature an intention to take away private rights without clear language.[85] Being satisfied on the point, the courts, of course, do not put obstacles in the way of a duly authorised activity.[86]

---

[81] *Hall* v. *Brooklands Auto-Racing Club* [1933] 1 K.B. 205.
[82] *Murray* v. *Harringay Arena* [1951] 2 All E.R. 320.
[83] *Haynes* v. *Harwood* [1935] 1 K.B. 146.
[84] *Cutler* v. *United Dairies (London) Ltd.* [1933] 2 K.B. 297.
[85] *Farnworth* v. *Manchester Corporation* [1929] 1 K.B. 533.
[86] *Att.Gen.* v. *Nissan* [1970] A.C. 179 at p. 229, *per* Lord Pearce.

(ii) Many of these cases arise in the field of nuisance.[87] The statutory powers may exonerate the authority from a claim in nuisance[88]; they do not exempt the authority for the consequences of using those powers negligently.[89] One or two examples will assist.

1. Blackburn J. in the leading case of *Geddis* v. *Proprietors of Bann Reservoir*[90] said:

> "No action will lie for doing that which the legislature has authorised, if it be done without negligence, although it does occasion damage to anyone; but an action does lie for doing that which the legislature has authorised, if it be done negligently."

2. In the case of *Home Office* v. *Dorset Yacht Co.*[91] the court was able to review these principles. Seven boys had escaped from Borstal custody, seized a yacht and damaged a boat of the plaintiff's in a collision. The main issue, considered by the House of Lords, was whether the Home Office owed a duty of care to the plaintiffs, and the answer was in the affirmative. Lord Reid rested his argument on *Donoghue* v. *Stevenson* in an authoritative judgment.[92]

(iii) Naturally a defence of statutory powers has to be supported by evidence that those powers have been correctly exercised. The aggrieved party will, reasonably, seek evidence of any weak link in the long chain which runs from the Act of Parliament, through assignment of the duty of decision, a minute of a properly constituted committee, to the way in which the work, perhaps, was authorised to be put in hand.[93] Finally, the court will often be invited to scrutinise whether the action taken comes within the four corners of the parent statute.

4. The Limitation Acts

The facts sometimes give a defendant the opportunity to plead the Limitation Acts; the plaintiff, he can say, has not come to the courts soon enough.[94] It is not a popular plea but it is legal. With regard to actions in tort, these Acts lay down:

(i) A basic period of six years from the date when the right of action arose.[95]

---

[87] *Marriage* v. *E. Norfolk Catchment Board* [1950] 1 K.B. 284.
[88] *Manchester Corporation* v. *Farnworth* [1930] A.C. 171, (*supra*, on appeal).
[89] *Dunne* v. *N.W.Gas Board* [1964] 2 Q.B. 806.
[90] [1873] 3 A.C. 430 at p. 455.
[91] [1970] A.C. 1004.
[92] Further instances of local authorities' negligence in carrying out statutory duties are *Dawson & Co.* v. *Bingley U.D.C.* [1911] 2 K.B. 149, *Manchester Corporation* v. *Markland* [1936] A.C. 360.
[93] *Radstock Co-op. and Ind. Society* v. *Norton-Radstock U.D.C.* (1968) Ch. 605; *Allen* v. *Gulf Oil Refining Co. Ltd.* (1981) A.C. 1001.
[94] The main consolidating Act is now the Limitation Act 1980.
[95] The Limitation Act 1980, s.2.

1.129

(ii) A reduction in the basic period to three years in cases of personal injuries. The wording is important:

> "This section applies to any action for damages for negligence, nuisance or breach of duty (whether the duty exists by virtue of a contract or of provision made by or under a statute or independently of any contract or any such provision) where the damages claimed by the plaintiff for negligence, nuisance or breach of duty consist of or include damages in respect of personal injuries to the plaintiff or any other person."[96]

The Act must be pleaded if it is to be relied on.

1.130 The period of six or three years above, runs from the date when the cause of action accrued. This is sometimes a matter of difficulty. For instance, if the cause of action for defective house foundations is the negligent inspection by a building inspector, it would be unfair to make the date of that inspection the start of the limitation period, if the defect in question did not become apparent for more than six years.[97] In a case of this nature, the court decided that the time should run from the date when the plaintiff, with reasonable diligence, might have discovered the defective state of the property. (The expression in section 32 of the Limitation Act 1980 is "discovered or might with reasonable diligence have discovered it," in relation to periods of limitation which have a starting date delayed by fraud, mistake or concealment of facts. A comparable formula seems to be emerging for this other situation—the latent defect.)[98]

If, as in nuisance, the tort is of a continuing nature, a limitation period is not relevant, since while the nuisance continues, each day can found a new period.[99]

There are special rules for persons under a disability, due to infancy, or mental illness or for the case of the death of the plaintiff.[1]

1.131 There is also a power available to the court, since the Limitation Act 1975, to override the starting time limits, if it appears equitable to do so in the light of prejudice to the parties if the ordinary rules were enforced.[2]

THE LEISURE SERVICES AUTHORITY AS BUSINESS ORGANISER

A. Contract

Introduction

1.132 This is a subject that runs through the whole of public leisure services. There is a basic framework for the English law on the subject which is not

---

[96] *Ibid.* s.11(1).
[97] [1978] A.C. 728.
[98] *Anns* v. *Merton Borough Council* [1977] 2 W.L.R. 1024.
[99] *O'Connor* v. *Isaacs* [1956] 2 Q.B. 288.
[1] Limitation Act 1980, ss.22, 28 and 38.
[2] Limitation Act 1980, s.33. And see *T.McCafferty* v. *Metropolitan Police Receiver* [1977] 2 All E.R. 756.

difficult. How is a legal contract formed? What are its essential elements? How can it be terminated? What residue of responsibility remains when that is done? Are some contracts forbidden? What effect on the formation of a contract have mistake, misrepresentation, duress or fraud? Are there some people who cannot make a legal contract?

Like a number of other branches of the law, however, the law of contract has become increasingly subtle. This may be looked on in one sense with satisfaction; the law should meet the needs of society and if those needs have changed, the law can do so too, by grafting on exceptions and nuances. In a real sense, nevertheless, it is regrettable if the law to be applied to a new set of facts is not easily predictable by legal advisers. That has become the case in more and more fields of contract law in the last 40 years.

It will be convenient to divide this subject into the following sections: **1.133**
1. Formation.
2. Deviations—Mistake, Misrepresentation, Duress.
3. Void and Illegal Contracts.
4. Capacity to Contract.
5. Limits of the Lawful contract.
6. Performance.
7. Breach.

1. Formation

A contract has been defined as "a promise or set of promises which the law will enforce."[3] It is complete when a valid offer has been matched by a valid acceptance and the two are bonded together by valid consideration. Offer and acceptance takes place in many ways. In a recent Manchester City Council case,[4] there was a series of letters between the Council and a tenant about a possible sale to him of the house he occupied. The House of Lords was called upon to analyse the legal effect of the correspondence at the critical moment when political control of the Council changed and the new Council wished to stop this sale. The House ruled that a contract had not then been concluded, after applying the classic principles for contract formation.

Acceptance may be made in the form appropriate to the nature of the offer. Both use of the post and oral communication, have in the past given rise to difficulties. Acceptance must be reasonably prompt or the offer may lapse. Again, the offer may be withdrawn before acceptance has occurred. Death of the offerer cancels the offer.

Consideration has been defined as the price paid by the plaintiff for

---

[3] Sir F. Pollock.
[4] *Gibson* v. *Manchester C.C.* [1979] 1 All E.R. 972. It was a test case for 350 others and the House overruled the two lower courts. In *Butler Machine Tool Co. Ltd.* v. *Ex-Cell-O Corporation Ltd.* [1979] 1 All E.R. 965, another case about the effect of letters, the approach which seeks "the area of consensus," to avoid too mechanical an attitude, is usefully discussed.

the defendant's promise. It is fundamental for a legal contract. It can take many forms, as well as money, *e.g.* giving employment, withholding opposition to a sale, and others.

The courts do not audit the value of consideration but if slight, the consideration may indicate lack of serious intent in the agreement. Moral considerations and past consideration do not rank as adequate legal consideration.

A valid agreement, under seal, does, however, rank as a valid legal contract, without the need for consideration.

Legally enforceable relations

An agreement is sometimes made without any intention thereby to enter into legally enforceable relations. The law respects this position and examples from the reports include football pools,[5] family arrangements and even an industrial compact, which, said the court, embodied "undertakings binding in honour."[6]

Two classes of contract formation must comply with statutory requirements. In this respect they differ from the general principles for contract formation under common law as described above. The two cases are as follows:
  (i) The sale or other disposition of land is to be in writing and signed by the party to be charged. See the Law of Property Act 1925, s. 40, which has widespread and detailed implications.
  (ii) The Statute of Frauds 1677, s.4, relates to a promise to answer for "the debt default or miscarriage" of another person. In one case, a man promised the owner to reimburse him for the horse injured by his son. Under this Act, he was held to his promise by the court.[7]

2. Deviations

(1) *Mistake*

1.136 Many of the cases of contract law taken to court turn on a mistake by one or both of the parties. We now consider:
  (a) Mutual mistake.
  (b) Unilateral mistake.
  (c) Documents mistakenly signed.

(a) **Mutual mistake**

This can arise in connection with the subject matter of the contract, *e.g.* who was the artist of the painting being sold[8] or whether the flat being let

---

[5] *Jones* v. *Vernon Pools Ltd.* [1938] 2 All E.R. 626.
[6] *Balfour* v. *Balfour* [1919] 2 K.B. 571.
[7] *Kirkham* v. *Marter* (1819) 2 B.& A. 619.
[8] *Leaf* v. *International Galleries* [1950] 2 K.B. 86.

was outside the Rent Acts.[9] Such a contract, being voidable in equity, can be set aside or rectified to achieve the real agreement between the parties.

Sometimes the mistake concerns the intentions of the parties and neither is aware of the misunderstanding. The courts start with the aim of upholding the agreement if possible. Secondly, if one party has made a mistake, he must abide by it and pay for it. The principle applied is to ask what agreement the reasonable man would infer from the evidence of the circumstances relating to the formation placed before the court.

(b) Unilateral mistake

1.137 Here the mistake by one party is known to the other. Most cases in the reports on this topic stem from mistaken identity of the parties. The principle here is that the concluded agreement can only be upset if the aggrieved party satisfies the court that he intended to agree with M, that the identity of M was important to him, that the other party knew this and, finally, that he took reasonable steps to verify the identity of the other party.

Cases of trickery in the reports concern false letter heads,[10] disguises when valuable jewellery is purchased[11] and false names when a letting of premises is obtained for immoral use by the tenant and her customers.[12]

(c) Documents mistakenly signed

1.138 When a person has signed a document by mistake, thinking it was something else, the general approach of the courts is to uphold the signature. He must have been careless, say the courts, and we cannot relieve him on that account.

In the House of Lords, recently, the test applied in this situation was: What was the object of the exercise?[13] When the document signed was so different from the one intended that it would be inequitable to hold a man to it, the courts will give equitable relief.

(2) *Misrepresentation*

1.139 Under the Misrepresentation Act 1967, s.2, liability in damages can follow misrepresentation which leads to a contract and consequential loss. The misrepresentation does not have to be fraudulent and the defendant is relieved of his penalty only if he believed in its truth on reasonable grounds up to the time when the contract was made.

This is intended to allow an aggrieved party to obtain damages for a misrepresentation negligently made, which led him to enter into the con-

---

[9] *Solle* v. *Butcher* [1950] 1 K.B. 671.
[10] *Kings Norton Metal Co.Ltd.* v. *Eldridge Merritt & Co.Ltd.* (1897) 14 T.L.R. 98.
[11] *Phillips* v. *Brooks Ltd.* [1919] 2 K.B. 243.
[12] *Sowler* v. *Potter* [1940] 1 K.B. 271; [1939] 4 All E.R. 478. As a recent decision see also *Lewis* v. *Averay* [1972] 1 Q.B. 198. A useful article on unilateral mistake is S. Tromans, "Careless Slips and Greedy Snaps" October 18, 1984, L.S. Gaz.
[13] *Saunders* v. *Anglia Building Society* [1969] 2 Ch. 40 (C.A.), and [1971] A.C. 1004 (H.L.).

1.139 tract. A misrepresentation is a statement, or conduct, or even silence, at a critical juncture in pre-contract discussion, which induces a party to go forward and enter into the contract. The relevant legal principles are:

1.140 1. If it was made fraudulently, the aggrieved party can sue for rescission of the contract and compensation in the form of consequential damages.[14]

2. Under section 2 of the Act of 1967, he can now take the same step for negligent misrepresentation.

3. But an undue delay in seeking his legal remedy can limit that remedy. Where, in *Leaf* v. *International Galleries*, a man bought a fake, believing the picture to be Constable's Salisbury Cathedral, and delayed 5 years before taking legal process to rescind the contract, he was denied that remedy and limited to damages only. As they were not claimed, the plaintiff lost his case.[15]

4. The contract is only voidable and not void, where there has been misrepresentation.

5. A condition is a statement which, as well as inducing the contract, is embodied in it. "That car has only done 20,000 miles," may induce a sale. But if it is no condition in the contract, it is a warranty only. For a false warranty, the legal remedy is damages only and not rescission; with a broken condition, both are available.

6. Rescission is not granted by the court, if (i) there has been an undue lapse of time or (ii) restoration to the pre-contract situation is impossible or (iii) it would adversely deprive an innocent third party of the subject matter of the contract or, finally, (iv) if the aggrieved party has effectively affirmed the contract.

It is the view of many commentators that the Act of 1967, making only a partial reform, has made the existing law more complex.

(3) *Duress*

1.141 A contract induced by duress can be set aside. Whilst physical duress is encountered infrequently, it is, nevertheless some pressure of a physical nature that the courts look for, if this extreme situation is to give rise to rescission.[16]

3. **Void and Illegal Contracts**

1.142 Certain contracts are not enforceable in the courts:

1. Wagering contracts, *e.g.* about a greyhound race or other uncertain event. Under the Gaming Act 1845, these are void, though not illegal. No legal rights derive from them.[17]

2. Restrictive trading agreements. These are, under the Restrictive

---

[14] *Derry* v. *Peak* (1889) 14 A.C. 337 is the leading case.
[15] [1950] 1 All E.R. 693.
[16] Cheshire & Fifoot, (10th ed., 1981) at p. 265; J.C. Smith and J.A.C. Thomas, *A Casebook in Tort* (7th ed., 1982) at p. 281.
[17] See *Hill* v. *William Hill* (*Park Lane*) *Ltd.* [1949] A.C. 530.

Trade Practices Act 1976, in the realm of agreements for both goods and services, where two or more parties agree about restrictions on prices, charges, terms or conditions or other matters. These agreements must be duly registered and if that is not done, the agreements are not enforceable in the courts.

3. The Treaty of Rome, article 85 deals with trade restrictions embodied in agreements and affecting trade between states.[18]

4. There are six classes of contract which, on account of public policy, are illegal. These are contracts:

  (a) prejudicial to the administration of justice;
  (b) to defraud the revenue;
  (c) which tend to corruption in public life;
  (d) to the prejudice of public safety;
  (e) to commit a crime;
  (f) that are sexually immoral.

1.143

5. Then there is an important group of three which may be described as void, since the courts will not enforce them:

  (a) Contracts to oust the jurisdiction of the courts.[19]
  (b) Those to the prejudice of marriage.
  (c) Those in restraint of trade. This is the most complex of the three groups. It was illuminated by a recent case that went to the House of Lords, *Esso Petroleum Co. Ltd.* v. *Harper's Garage (Stourport) Ltd.*[20] This emphasises that two separate questions must not be confused. First is the question: Is the contract void, because the restraint is so restrictive? Then, secondly, can the restrictive clause be thought reasonable? This case is a store of information and guidance on these points.

1.144

6. A last group is of interest to those in the leisure services, where it is inevitable that staff will acquire great knowledge about commercial customs and negotiating practices. They can thus be made subject to contracts seeking to restrain them from working in the immediate area when they change their work.

1.145

The courts, it must be emphasised, are not sympathetic to such agreements, unless there is clear evidence that they are needed to protect some trade secret or the employer's business connection. There are cases in the reports about professional footballers and cricketers, as well as the Jockey Club. One of the most recent cases concerned a solicitor with a firm in Hong Kong. A covenant was upheld, to restrain him from practising in Hong Kong for five years or dealing with persons who had been clients of the firm during the three years before his departure.[21]

---

[18] As examples see *Esso Petroleum Co.* v. *Kingswood Motors (Addlestone)* [1974] Q.B. 142; *Lerose* v. *Hawick Jersey International* [1973] C.M.L.R. 83.

[19] A cinema case is *R.* v. *London County Council, ex p. The London Entertainments Protection Association* [1931] 2 K.B. 215.

[20] [1968] A.C. 269.

[21] *Deacons* v. *Bridge* [1984] 2 All E.R. 19. This was despite the fact that the employee had a strong case, based on the completely specialised nature of his work in an extremely large firm.

1.145   General Legal Principles

In the background, as creatures of statute, are the Monopolies and Mergers Commission and the Restrictive Trade Practices Court. These exercise a specialised role.

4. Capacity To Contract

(1) *Minors*

1.146 A person under 18 years, known in the law as a minor, cannot generally make legally binding contracts. The Infants Relief Act 1874 declares 3 such classes void and the common law has also developed 3 groups of exceptions to the general prohibition.
- (a) Void contracts under the Act of 1874 are accounts stated, agreements to repay loans or to pay for goods which are not "necessaries."
- (b) Exceptions to the normal ban on infants' legally enforceable contracts are:
  - (i) "necessaries," such as food, clothes, shelter and tools of the trade.
  - (ii) contracts of service, such as a young boxer contracting with the Boxing Board of Control; and
  - (iii) contracts about a class of subject matter of a permanent nature, such as the tenancy of a bed-sitter or a call on shares.

(2) *Corporations*

1.147 The capacity of a statutory corporation to enter into contracts is governed by its powers. Local authorities, being now creatures of statute, are governed by the relevant statute.

Functions such as providing swimming pools, country parks or libraries, are dealt with in empowering statutes about those subjects.

The power to take action to achieve those objects is then supplemented by the Local Government Act 1972, or similar general Act. This not only authorises all action "reasonably incidental to the discharge of their functions" by local authorities. It also widens what might seem tightly drawn legal powers to cover expenditure when it is, in the opinion of the authority, in the interests of their area or part of it or all or some of its inhabitants.

The challenge relating to the powers of the local authority may not, initially, relate to a contract; it would be strange however, if in the train of a policy decision, some contract was not eventually needed.

(3) *Commercial Companies*

1.148 The capacity to contract by a limited liability company is governed by the terms of its memorandum of association. This can often be widely drawn so that there need not in practice be great risk of challenge on the ground of its *vires*, when contracting for trade or business.

CONTRACT   **1.149**

5. **Limits of the Lawful Contract**

We note next three legal limits placed on the making and dealing in contracts.   **1.149**

(1) *Privity of Contract*

Only a party to a contract can sue upon it and be bound by it.[22] This does not gainsay the ability to assign powers under a contract, nor the ability to appoint or become an agent. An assignee steps into the shoes of the party from whom he took his assignment; an agent exercises such powers as are conferred upon him in the agency agreement.

(2) *Assignments*

A party to a contract may assign his interest in whole or in part to a third party. Thus a party due to receive £1,000 under an insurance policy could assign the right to receive all or part of that sum to a third party. It is sometimes obligatory but always wise to notify the other party to the initial contract that an assignment has taken place. Such notification may indeed be a compliance with a term in the original contract. Failure to give notice would prejudice the assignee in respect of payments made to his assignor after the assignment and in ignorance of it.   **1.150**

(3) *Contracts of a Personal Nature*

It is not permitted to assign contractual rights that depend on personal skill and confidence, nor certain rights to pensions and alimony. The main bar on assignment is the right to litigate, sometimes called the "bare right of action."[23] This distinguishes it from a right to litigate, that arises from and goes with some right in property. In that situation the right to litigate would go with the property without restraint.   **1.151**

6. **Performance**

When has a contract been "substantially performed?" When has a contract been frustrated, so that performance is not possible? These are the two most common legal problems associated with performance.   **1.152**

(1) *Substantial Performance*

It is common practice in building contracts to refer to the point of substantial performance. It is not to be expected that every screw and grummet will then be in position. It means that the purpose of the building is substantially achieved, so that the major payment to the builder can be

---

[22] *Tweddle* v. *Atkinson* (1861) 1 B.& S. 393.
[23] *Trendtex Trading Corporation* v. *Credit Suisse* [1980] Q.B. 629.

1.152   GENERAL LEGAL PRINCIPLES

completed and the customer take possession and start shop-fitting or whatever it might be. Substantial performance is a desirable and important milestone in the execution of a contract.

(2) Frustration

Sometimes a contract, though well intentioned and well made, simply cannot be performed. The ship sinks, the procession is cancelled, the weather is so bad that the match is postponed, the concert hall is burned down.

Before 1943, the courts handled this situation by seeking to define that which was essential to the performance of the contract or, as said in one case, "the state of things going to the root of the contract."

Under the Law Reform (Frustrated Contracts) Act 1943, monies paid before the date when the frustration occurred, may be recovered, with a set off for agreed expenses incurred by the other party. A *quantum meruit* calculation is then allowed for the benefit of the work done up to the time of discharge of the contract. This Act has created the climate in which the courts now seek a reasonable solution to the new situation created by the unexpected happening.

7. Breach

1.153   There are three principal legal remedies for breach of contract.

(1) **Quantum meruit** is "as much as he deserves." One may sue for the value of the benefit conferred, or money expended, under the contract before the breach occurred.

(2) **Damages** are the normal remedy. The classic measure for damages for the aggrieved party is
- (a) those which may fairly be considered to arise naturally from the breach; and
- (b) that which may reasonably be supposed as having been envisaged by the parties as the probate result of the breach, at the time when they entered into the contract.

(3) **Specific performance** is the equitable remedy, to be pursued when damages are considered to be inadequate. Whilst damages are a right, specific performance is discretionary. It is not allowed by the court if it would be complex to carry out, such as the supervision of a contract involving personal service. But it is available if practicable, in a situation where damages are simply not an adequate recompense for the injury caused by the breach.

Limitation Acts

1.154   It has always been a principle that persons seeking legal remedies in the courts should do so in a reasonable time. Statute has codified practice and currently the Limitation Act 1980 sets out the limitation periods for various types of action.

CONTRACT   1.154

1. For an action based on breach of contract, the action must be commenced within six years of the date when the right of action accrued.[24]

2. If the action is based on a "speciality," *i.e.* a document under seal, the comparative period is 12 years.[25]

3. An action based on an account is subject to the same period of limitation as the subject matter of the account.[26]

4. In addition:
  (i) In the case of an action for a specific sum of money, like a debt, the period runs from the date of the last part-payment, as a visible acknowledgment, or the date of a document constituting a valid acknowledgment. This means that it is in writing, signed by the debtor and admits liability to pay the sum in question.[27]
  (ii) Where the plaintiff has a disability, when his cause of action accrues, the period of limitation does not start to run until the disability is removed, possibly even by death.[28]
  (iii) Since specific performance, and sometimes injunctions, are historically equitable remedies, these statutory limitations do not apply to them.[29] Nonetheless, courts of equity always took a firm line against undue delay in coming to court—*laches* was the old word—and at the present day the courts maintain that principle when equitable remedies are sought. The doctrine of laches, as it is called, is preserved in the Limitation Act 1980.[30]

B. THE UNFAIR CONTRACTS TERMS ACT 1977

Restraints upon the use of unfair contract terms are to be found in the Act of 1977 of that name, passed to carry into legislation recommendations of the Law Commission. The terms in question form a somewhat untidy group; the Act itself is in the nature of an interim one; and it is arguable that the piece-meal nature of its reforms has left the body of contract law more complex. Managers in the public leisure services can only be guided, in this work, to the items with which the Act of 1977 deals. These are as follows: 1.155

1. Notices and contract terms cannot be used to exclude or limit a person's business liability for death or injury due to negligence, *e.g.* on recreation ground equipment or from the diving board of a swimming pool.

2. A test of reasonableness is applied to similar terms or notices relating to loss or damage; also to contract terms which seek to limit a person's obligations to a consumer or in a situation where his written terms of business are used; and to indemnity clauses in a contract with a consumer.

---

[24] Act of 1980, s.5.
[25] *Ibid.* s.8.
[26] *Ibid.* s.23.
[27] *Ibid.* s.29.
[28] *Ibid.* s.28.
[29] *Ibid.* s.36.
[30] *Ibid.* s.36.

1.155   GENERAL LEGAL PRINCIPLES

3. Specious guarantees are prohibited. These are the ones which take away a customer's statutory or common law rights, whilst offering to remedy defects in the goods sold.

C. Sale of Goods

1.156   The Sale of Goods Act 1979, and associated cases in the courts, govern this subject. It can conveniently be considered as follows:

1. The Contract; Definitions and Formation

(1) The contract of sale of goods is a contract by which the seller transfers, or agrees to transfer, the property in the goods to the buyer for the price, *i.e.* the money consideration.

(2) If the transfer is to take place in the future, it is an agreement to sell.[31]

(3) The contract may be valid, whether made in writing, or by word of mouth or may be part written and part oral; it may indeed be inferred from conduct.[32]

(4) The "goods" may exist or be planned to come into existence after the contract is made, when they are known as "future goods." A present contract for the sale of future goods takes effect as an agreement to sell.[33]

(5) If the goods have perished at the time the contract is made, the parties being ignorant of this, the contract is void.[34] Likewise, with an agreement to sell, if the specific goods perish before a transfer of the risk to the buyer, the agreement is at an end.

(6) The price may be fixed but if it is not, guidelines in this Act are that the price be simply "reasonable" and "according to the circumstances." Other statutes have increasingly been used to determine prices in particular areas of commerce, such as the Prices Acts 1974–75, the Resale Prices Act 1976 and the Consumer Credit Act 1974.[35]

Conditions and warranties

1.157   (7) When the parties wish time to be a condition of the contract—default in which can give rise to action for breach—they must state that time is of the essence of the contract.[36]

(8) A condition in a contract is an important term, breach of which gives rise to a right to reject the contract and ask for the return of the price paid. A warranty is collateral, often about quality, and gives rise only to a

---

[31] Sale of Goods Act 1979, s.2.
[32] Act of 1979, s.4.
[33] *Ibid.* s.5(3).
[34] *Ibid.* s.6.
[35] ss.137–140 of the 1974 Act on extortionate credit bargains, permits the court to reopen a credit agreement.
[36] Act of 1979, s.10.

claim for the appropriate damages.[37] The buyer is empowered to waive a condition or to treat a breach of condition as a breach of warranty.[38] The fact that a term is called a warranty in the contract is not to be regarded as conclusive: it may be still found, on analysis, to be a condition.[39]

The Goods

(9) Section 12 of the Act defines legal implications about the title which the seller possesses and is able to pass to the buyer.   **1.158**

(10) Goods are to correspond with the description of them in the terms of sale. The correspondence of the bulk of the goods with a sample used in the bargaining does not relieve the seller of this condition in relation to the description.[40]

(11) The goods are deemed to be of "merchantable quality" when sold in the course of business. The statute makes this an implied condition in the contract.[41] The expression "merchantable quality" means as fit for the purpose, for which goods of that kind are bought, as it is reasonable to expect, having regard to the circumstances.[42]

(12) Sale by sample is a method which is the subject of an express or implied term in the contract.[43] A condition is implied in three parts in such a sale, namely that the bulk corresponds with the sample, that reasonable examination of the sample will reveal any defect of a nature that would render the goods unmerchantable, and, thirdly, that the buyer will be able to compare the bulk with the sample.[44]

2. **Effect of the Contract**

The Act of 1979 has four rules for the passing of the property under a contract for the sale of goods: **1.159**

(i) No property passes until the goods are ascertained. (With a large quantity of goods, ascertainment occurs when part is allocated to the contract.)[45]

(ii) In other cases, property passes when the parties intend it to pass.[46] The Act then sets out rules for ascertaining that intention.[47] In sum, they

---

[37] *Ibid.* s.11. Two of the leading cases on the distinction are: *Wallis Son & Wells* v. *Pratt & Haynes* [1911] A.C. 394; *Cehave N.V.* v. *Bremer Handelsgesellschaft m.b.h.* [1975] 3 All E.R. 739.
[38] Act of 1979, s.11(2).
[39] *Ibid.* s.11(3).
[40] *Ibid.* s.13.
[41] *Ibid.* s.14(2).
[42] *Ibid.* s.14(6). The Unfair Contract Terms Act 1977, s.6, forbids any exclusion or restriction of liability for this obligation, as against a person dealing as a consumer. The subsection (6) is from the Supply of Goods (Implied Terms) Act 1973, s.7(2). The same prohibition applies to ss.12 and 13 relating to the title and description of goods sold.
[43] Act of 1979, s.15(1).
[44] *Ibid.* s.15(2).
[45] Act of 1979, s.16.
[46] *Ibid.*s.17.
[47] *Ibid.* s.18.

1.159

provide for the immediate passing, in the case of "deliverable goods," on the making of the contract; transfer on completion of acts of the vendor, where the contract depended on such acts[48]; and transfer on the buyer notifying his approval or acceptance of the goods, where, *e.g.* they were in his possession "on approval" or "on sale or return."

(iii) Even if the property is in the possession of the buyer, the property will not pass, if the seller has reserved the right of disposal on conditions and that fetter has not been removed.[49]

(iv) The risk passes with the property.[50]

Transfer of Title

1.160 The Act then turns to the subject of the transfer of title. This is complex and moves into the questions of theft and fraud cases, where goods which are not legally owned are disposed of. The Act deals with sales in the open market, being one of the means by which a person without a title of his own can confer a good title on the buyer[51]; goods retained in the possession of the seller after the sale is complete and then coming into the possession of a third party[52]; the purchase of goods under a voidable title, when a buyer in good faith can acquire a title[53]; or the difficult case when the buyer acquires premature possession and then parts with the goods, but again in certain circumstances a third person can obtain a good title if he is acting in good faith.[54] All these are cases where legal advice would of necessity be sought and fuller enquiry made than can be embarked upon in this work.

3. Performance

Rights on delivery

1.161 The seller is under a duty to deliver the goods and the buyer to accept and pay for them, under the normal contract for the sale of goods.[55] Variations from normal expectancy are for the parties in their contract, *e.g.* if delivery is to be elsewhere than the normal place of the seller's place of business.

When wrong quantities are delivered, the contract rate obtains, if the buyer decides to accept larger or smaller quantities than those covered by the original contract.[56]

---

[48] This could be the allocation of goods to the contract or testing them.
[49] A case about the sale of petrol at the filling station is *Edwards* v. *Ddin* [1976] 3 All E.R. 705.
[50] Act of 1979, s.20.
[51] s.22. The goods have to be purchased in good faith and without notice of the defect or want of title on the part of the seller.
[52] Act of 1979, s.24.
[53] *Ibid.* s.23.
[54] *Ibid.* s.25.
[55] *Ibid.* s.27.
[56] *Ibid.* s.30.

Sale of Goods   1.161

Unless agreed, the buyer is not bound to accept delivery by instalments.[57]

Delivery by the seller to a carrier, if contracted, is deemed delivery to the buyer.[58]

Acceptance normally follows inspection by the buyer; he should be afforded a reasonable opportunity to do so.[59] Acceptance is inferred from the buyer's conduct if he does not communicate with the seller.[60] If the buyer rejects the goods for a reason stated and tells the seller, he is not obliged to return the goods.[61]

On the other hand, if the buyer is told that the seller is ready and willing to deliver and he declines to take delivery, the buyer is responsible for the deterioration in the goods due to his so acting.[62] In addition the seller can treat the buyer as having put an end to the contract and then sue him for damages.

4. Rights of the Unpaid Seller

The Act of 1979 sets out three rights of the unpaid seller: 1.162
  (i) He has a lien on the goods, *i.e.* a right of retention until paid.[63]
  (ii) He has a right to stop the goods in transit, if the buyer becomes insolvent.[64]
  (iii) He has a right of resale if he has notified the buyer of his intention to do so, because he has not been paid. If he exercises this right of resale, the seller may recover any loss resulting, from the buyer.[65]

5. Breach of Contract

1. Once the property has passed and no due payment is made, the seller   1.163
can sue for the price.[66]

2. If the buyer refuses to accept the goods, he may be sued for damages for non-acceptance.[67] The Act provides that such damages are to be "the estimated loss directly and naturally resulting in the ordinary course of events from the buyer's breach of contract." This can *prima facie* be the difference between the contract price and the market price—if there is one—at the time when the goods should have been accepted.[68]

---

[57] *Ibid.* s.31.
[58] *Ibid.* s.32.
[59] *Ibid.* s.34.
[60] *Ibid.* s.35.
[61] *Ibid.* s.36.
[62] *Ibid.* s.37.
[63] *Ibid.* s.41.
[64] *Ibid.* ss.44–46.
[65] *Ibid.* s.48.
[66] *Ibid.* s.49(1).
[67] *Ibid.* s.50.
[68] s.50. See *Lazenby Garages* v. *Wright* [1976] 1 W.L.R. 459.

1.163 GENERAL LEGAL PRINCIPLES

3. Likewise, the buyer can sue for non-delivery, if the seller declines to do so; the basis of damages will be as in 2 above.[69]

4. Specific performance may be ordered by the court, in either of the situations in 2 and 3 above, if "specific or ascertained goods were involved,"[70] as an alternative to damages.

5. An action for damages for breach of warranty is a final legal resource for parties facing a breach of contract situation.[71]

D. CONSUMER PROTECTION

1.164 Consumer Protection has become the umbrella term to cover the statutes which provide rights and duties for the citizen as consumer. Some branches of this area of law extend beyond the purview of this book; the field of mergers and monopolies is part of the remit of the Office of Fair Trading, but we shall deal only with Consumer Protection as the other major element in that remit. Again, consumer credit is the subject of major legislation which takes in hire purchase. Undoubtedly the need for greater coherence in these laws is well appreciated in the right quarters and the coming decade may see more moves in that direction.

1. **The Fair Trading Act 1973**

1.165 This Act can conveniently be considered in relation to:
    1. The Director General and the Consumer Protection Advisory Committee.
    2. Current activities.

(1) The Director General and the Consumer Protection Advisory Committee

A Director General of Fair Trading is appointed under the Act of 1973.[72] His duties are to:

(a) keep under surveillance commercial activities in the United Kingdom in relation to goods supplied to consumers, goods produced in order to be so supplied and services provided for consumers;

(b) collect information about these activities in order to be aware of circumstances about "Practices which may adversely affect the economic interests of consumers in the United Kingdom." He is to receive and collate "evidence" about both the economic interests of consumers and "interests with respect to health safety or other matters" concerning consumers. This remit could hardly be wider[73];

(c) to inform the Secretary of State regularly on the above matters; submit to him an annual report and receive his directions on work priorities[74];

---

[69] *Ibid.* s.51.
[70] *Ibid.* s.52.
[71] *Ibid.* s.53.
[72] Act of 1973, s.1. The 1st Schedule sets out the main terms of the appointment.
[73] *Ibid.* s.2(1).
[74] *Ibid.* s.2(3).

(d) consider action under Part III of the Act of 1973 against any person "in relation to any course of conduct on the part of a person carrying on a business, which appears to be conduct detrimental to the interests of consumers in the United Kingdom and to be regarded as unfair to them"[75];

(e) produce an annual report and submit it to the Secretary of State[76];

(f) take general and detailed directions from the Secretary of State on priorities for his work and otherwise.[77]

The Consumer Protection Advisory Committee

1.166 Though active for four years, this appointed committee has had no references about undesirable trade practices, from Ministers or the Director General, since 1977. Consequently, since 1982, its membership has been allowed to lapse.

(2) *Current Activities*

1.167 These stem from Part II of the Act of 1973 and it is evident, from the disbandment of the Consumer Protection Advisory Committee and the latest annual report of the Director General, that this is the field for fruitful activity under the Act at the present time. Part II allows the Director General to take action, not against trade practices, but against individual traders. His annual reports now regularly list such persons who have been called to give legally binding assurances to desist from adverse practices or who have been prosecuted (*e.g.* 407 assurances taken since the procedure began, 47 being in 1983).[78]

The cases go to the Restrictive Practices Court[79]: an appeal can be taken to the Court of Appeal.[80]

These steps are under section 34, which calls on the Director General to deal with traders who "persist in a course of conduct which is detrimental to the interests of consumers" and is to be regarded as "unfair to consumers."

As well as action in the courts, the Office of Fair Trading continues to promulgate information about the best trading practices.[81] A Code of Practice about travel agents is part of this work; a similar Code about holiday caravans is reported to be under negotiation.

---

[75] *Ibid.* s.2(4).
[76] The 10th such report appeared in July 1984, covering 1983. It was significant that a current listed research report, by Newcastle University, is about "consumer problem identification and rationales for intervention" (p. 119).
[77] *Ibid.* s.12.
[78] Annual report, Office of Fair Trading (1983), p. 21.
[79] s.35. ss. 36–38 relate to evidence, Orders of the Court and corporate bodies in these procedures.
[80] *Ibid.* s.42.
[81] The 1983 annual report of the Office of Fair Trading, says that a draft has been circulated and "attracted considerable interest." It could give legal backing to the voluntary standards hitherto embodied in the Codes of Practice. *Ibid.* p. 14.

2. The Consumer Safety Act 1978

1.168 A successor to the Consumer Protection Acts 1961 and 1971, this Act authorises legal action to safeguard consumers from dangerous goods. The action takes the following forms:

(1) Prohibition Orders.[82]

For 12 months these Orders can ban the supply or possession for supply of listed goods considered to be "not safe." They apply to all traders.

(2) Prohibition Notices.[83]

These measures, of unlimited duration, place a ban on one trader in respect of listed products.

(3) Safety Regulations.[84]

These are designed to follow in the wake of Prohibition Orders and be permanent.

(4) Notices to Warn.[85]

These are the fourth type of stricture available against dangerous goods. They are used when the goods are in circulation and their receipt obliges a trader to take all reasonable steps to alert all persons in his trade outlets about the deemed danger of named goods.

Contravention of the above Regulations, Orders and Notices gives rise to offences which can be the subject in the courts of fines to a maximum of £2,000 or three months imprisonment.[86] The offences are created by the Act and not by the subordinate legal documents described above.[87]

1.169 A statutory defence is "that the accused took all reasonable steps and exercised all due diligence to avoid continuing the offence."[88] If the accused blames another person for the essential offence, he must notify the prosecutor at least seven days before the relevant court hearing.[89]

Enforcement of the Act of 1978 lies with the inspectors of the weights and measures authority.[90]

The Act of 1978 provides a special remedy for aggrieved persons, *i.e.* the victims of dangerous goods. They may sue for breach of the statutory duty. The right thus created is "subject to the defences and other incidents applying to actions for breach of statutory duty.[91]

Any contract to exclude or restrict this legal right is void.

---

[82] s.3(1)(*a*) and Sched. 1, Pt. I.
[83] s.3(1)(*b*) and Sched. 1, Pt. II.
[84] Act of 1978, s.1. *e.g.* Novelties (Safety) Regulations 1980 (S.I. 1980 No. 958), maintains the prohibition on balloon-making kits from substances containing benzine. The Dangerous Substances and Preparations (Safety) Regulations 1980 (S.I. 1980 No. 136) concerns the chemical "Tris" on textiles, and chloroethylene as an aerosol propellant.
[85] s.3(1)(*c*) and Sched. I, Pt. III.
[86] Act of 1978, s.2(4).
[87] *Ibid.* s.2(8). The earlier £1,000 was raised by the recent Criminal Penalties, etc., (Increase) Order 1984 (S.I. 1984 No. 447) of May 1, 1984.
[88] *Ibid.* s.2(6).
[89] *Ibid.* s.2(6).
[90] *Ibid.* s.5.
[91] *Ibid.* s.6.

Lastly, what area of commerce comes within this Act, and is there anything in the field of public leisure services which is outside its purview? **1.170**
  (i) The Act of 1978 covers all goods except food, animal feed, fertilizer, medicines and drugs.[92]
  (ii) The goods have to be supplied or in possession for supply. The word "supply" is defined to limit it to an action "in the course of carrying on a business (whether or not dealing with the goods in question) and either as principal or agent."[93]
  (iii) The activity of "supplying" can be in the form of a sale, hire-purchase, an exchange or a gift.[94]

3. Supply of Goods and Services Act 1982

Managers in the public leisure services may well be involved in contracts for the provision of a new tennis court, the construction and equipment of a new trim trail, or the building of a new swimming pool, with its diving boards, seating, lockers and associated equipment. **1.171**

The common feature of these contracts is that they arrange for both goods and work to be provided by the contractor. The type of contract is of frequent occurrence but the Law Commission found a gap in the law in relation to such contracts. The Sale of Goods Act 1979 dealt with the goods. This Act of 1982 deals with the combined agreements for both goods and services, as well as one or two other items.[95]

(1) *The Framework of the Act*

These goods and services contracts are made subject to four provisions almost identical with corresponding terms in the Sale of Goods Act 1979, discussed above. They require sound title to the goods, their conformity with any contracted description and their compliance with any standard of merchantable quality and fourthly, if supplied with a sample, their compliance with the three Sale of Goods Act stipulations for that situation (see para. 1.158, (12)). **1.172**

These four terms are implied conditions. The same four terms, about good title, reliability of the description, merchantable quality and correspondence of bulk with sample, are applied in the Act of 1982, to a second type of contract, *i.e.* for the hiring of goods.[96] This was because the Law Commission had found considerable difference of view among judges in earlier cases about the legal obligations laid upon a hirer, where the contract is silent on that point. **1.173**

The third class of contracts dealt with in this Act relates purely to ser-

---

[92] *Ibid.* s.9(4).
[93] *Ibid.* s.9(1).
[94] *Ibid.* s.9(2).
[95] Law Commission Report No. 95. Implied Terms in Contracts for the supply of goods, July 17, 1979.
[96] *Ibid.* ss.7, 8, 9 and 10.

1.173 GENERAL LEGAL PRINCIPLES

vices. Instances which might be met by leisure service managers and which have been before the courts in the past include: transporting goods on land[97] or water,[98] erecting scaffolding,[99] inoculating cattle,[1] or repairing motor vehicles.[2] There are, of course, many more.

In these contracts to perform a service, the Act of 1982 now implies three terms:
(i) The supplier will carry out the service with reasonable care and skill.[3]
(ii) The service will be carried out within a reasonable time.[4]
(iii) A reasonable charge will be paid for the service.[5]

What is "reasonable" in (ii) and (iii) is "a question of fact."

(2) *Significant Detail*

1.174 We turn now to a little greater detail about some of the provisions.

Excluded contracts

To define the group of contracts for work and materials with which Part I of the Act of 1982 is concerned, it is necessary to exclude contracts for the sale of goods, hire-purchase agreements, contracts with no consideration but which, being sealed, are enforceable, and trading stamp transfer agreements.[6]

Title

The section about the implied condition of a good title also refers to the case where a transferor wishes to give only a qualified, or cautiously guarded, assurance of his title, perhaps because of the continuing interest in the goods of a third party.[7] The Act gives the transferee the benefit of a warranty, rather than a condition, and holds the transferor to a full disclosure of the charges or encumbrances affecting the property.

The new implied term about the merchantable quality of the goods is not to commit the transferor to liability for defects to which he draws

---

[97] *Lally & Weller* v. *George Bird*, May 23, 1980, QBD (unreported).
[98] *McCutcheon* v. *MacBrayne* [1964] 1 W.L.R. 125.
[99] *Sims* v. *Foster Wheeler* [1966] 1 W.L.R. 769.
[1] *Dodd & Dodd* v. *Wilson & McWilliam* [1946] 2 All E.R. 691.
[2] *Stewart* v. *Leavell's Garage* [1952] 2 Q.B. 545.
[3] Act of 1982, s.13.
[4] *Ibid.* s.14.
[5] *Ibid.* s.15.
[6] *Ibid.* s.1. The Law Commission called the Part I contracts "analogous to sale." G.F. Woodroffe in his book on the 1982 Act, *Goods and Services—The New Law* calls them "quasi-sales" (para. 2.01).
[7] *Ibid.* s.2(3) (4) and (5). This section and ss. 3, 4 and 5 can also apply to a contract of barter. The law reports contain a case on portrait painting, which nicely illustrates the difficulties which this section is designed to eliminate, *i.e. Robinson* v. *Graves* (1935) 1 K.B. 79.

attention, or those to which an inspection, reasonably carried out, should have alerted the transferee.[8]

The terms implied in a contract for the transfer of goods or the hire of goods are not to be exclusive, with the exception of those about quality and fitness.[9] The same principle applies to a contract for a service.[10]

Excluded services

Excluded from Part II of the Act of 1982 concerning the supply of services are: 1.175
(a) An apprenticeship.
(b) A contract of service, *i.e.* a contract of employment.[11]
(c) Any services subsequently excluded by Orders made by the Secretary of State.[12]

The definition of a contract of service for the purposes of this Act is simply: "a contract under which a person agrees to carry out a service."[13]

The Act contains a provision to harmonise its main provisions about implied terms with the Unfair Contract Terms Act 1977.

E. Trade Descriptions

Introduction

There are two Trade Descriptions Acts, the main one passed in 1968 and a short Act of 1972. They are part of the group of Acts which deal with consumer protection in its many aspects. The two Trade Descriptions Acts replace six Merchandise Marks Acts, which had constituted a growing body of cohesive law on this important subject. Anyone engaged in the public leisure services needs to be aware of the main provisions of these Acts. 1.176

Offences

The Acts initially create two main offences: 1.177
(a) A person who in the course of a trade or business applies a false trade description to any goods; and
(b) a person who in the course of a trade or business suplies or offers to supply any goods to which a false trade description is applied.[14]

There are a number of comments to be made on these offences:
1. "Offering to supply" has been held to include not only having avail-

---

[8] *Ibid.* s.9.
[9] *Ibid.* s.11.
[10] *Ibid.* s.16.
[11] *Ibid.* s.12(2).
[12] *i.e.* the Secretary of State for Trade and Industry. One such Order (The Supply of Services (Exclusion of Implied Terms) Order 1982 (S.I. 1982 No. 1771)), excludes from s.13 the services of an advocate in courts or similar situations, such as tribunals. A later Order, S.I. 1983 No. 902, excludes the services of a director of a building society to the society. This followed an earlier Order about company directors.
[13] *Ibid.* s.12.
[14] Trade Descriptions Act 1968, ss.1(1)(*a*) and (*b*).

able for sale in a shop but also having goods in store on the premises and available for supply.[15]

2. If it transpires that the offence is due to some other person than, *e.g.* the salesman, then the Act also allows the prosecution of that other person.[16]

Definition

1.178   3. A trade description is defined as "an indication direct or indirect and by whatever means given of any of the following matters with respect to any goods." "These matters" then include quantity, size, suitability, performance, behaviour, accuracy, tests and the results of such tests, method of manufacture, date of manufacture, and other history about the ownership or use of the goods.[17]

4. "Applying" the trade description is defined comprehensively, to include the various ways in which a trade description of the nature mentioned can be understood by a customer as referring to the goods in question. Thus the description has been "applied," if it is not only on the goods themselves but on a container, or if the goods in question are with other goods which bear a trade description.[18]

If the handing over of the goods, from seller to customer, is in response to a request which embodies a trade description, then the law infers that the conduct of the supplier amounts to the application of that trade description to those goods.

Falsity

1.179   5. It is the "false" trade description that breaks the law. When is it false? The Act of 1968 states that the description must be false "to a material degree."[19]

False prices

1.180   The definition of trade description did not include price. That element in a trade description is dealt with separately in section 11 of the Act of 1968.[20] There are three sorts of false statement which can ground an offence:
  (i) one that suggests that the price offered is less than that actually being charged;
  (ii) one that suggests that the price offered is less than or equal to a recommended price;

---

[15] Act of 1968, s.6. But see *Ben Worsley* v. *Harvey* [1967] 2 All E.R. 507.
[16] Act of 1968, s.23, and *Havering B.C.* v. *Stevenson* [1970] 3 All E.R. 609.
[17] Act of 1968, s.4.
[18] *Ibid.* s.4(3).
[19] *Ibid.* s.3.
[20] *Heron Service Stations* v. *Hunter* (1981) 79 L.G.R. 679, shows that an actual sale is not necessary in order to complete this offence.

(iii) one that suggests that the price offered is less than a price at which he previously offered those goods.[21]

False statements about services

Another section[22] defines two offences for making false statements about services, accommodation and facilities. 1.181

1. One offence is to make such a statement, which he knows to be false, about any specified matter, in the course of a trade or business.

2. The second offence is to make a statement recklessly[23] in the course of a trade or business, which is false about any specified matters.

These specified matters are the provision in the course of a business, of the services, accommodation or facilities being provided, or the nature of those three items, or the time at which those three items were being provided, or that approval has been given to them or, finally, about the location or amenities of any accommodation so provided.

Two comments are offered on these important provisions: 1.182

(a) A statement about the future is not one about which a section 14 allegation as to its truth or falsity at the time it is made, can be sustained.[24] Thus "I will erect this garage for you in ten days" cannot be said to be true or false, if in fact the ten days was exceeded as the building period for the garage. "Parliament did not intend to make a criminal offence out of what is really a breach of warranty," said Lord Widgery.[25]

(b) Guilty knowledge by an identified defendant is required for these offences—not simply by the firm.[26]

Defences

There is a statutory defence comprising two elements: 1.183
 (a) one of the following five, that the commission of the offence was due to:
  (i) a mistake; or
  (ii) reliance on information supplied to him; or
  (iii) the act or default of another person; or
  (iv) an accident; or
  (v) some other cause beyond his control.
   AND
 (b) that he took all reasonable precautions and exercised all due dili-

---

[21] This is now reinforced by the Price Marking (Bargain Offers) Amendment No. 2 Order 1979 (S.I. 1979 No. 1124).
[22] Act of 1968, s.14. A recent case, *Westminster City Council* v. *Ray Alan (Manshops)* [1982] 1 W.L.R. 383, shows that "facilities" in s.14 does not extend to "sales."
[23] On "recklessly" see *M.F.I. Warehouses Ltd.* v. *Nattrass* [1973] 1 All E.R. 762. It connotes an attitude of mind, indicating that "he did not have regard to the truth or falsity of his advertisement"—Lord Widgery, *ibid.* p. 768c.
[24] *Beckett* v. *Cohen* [1973] 1 All E.R. 120.
[25] *Ibid.* p. 122b; this was followed in *R.* v. *Sunair Holidays Ltd.* [1973] 2 All E.R. 1233.
[26] *Coupe* v. *Guyatt* [1973] 2 All E.R. 1058. For the niceties of argument on this section, see G. Stephenson, "A Review of Appeal Cases" July 11, 1984 L.S. Gaz., p. 2006.

1.183

gence to avoid the commission of the offence by himself or by any person under his control.[27]

If part of a defence is to draw attention to the act or default of a person other than the defendant, the defence must give to the prosecution in writing such notice, at least seven clear days before the hearing, as will identify that person or help to identify that person.

3. If the offence charged should relate to a false trade description in an advertisement, then it is a defence for the defendant to show that he received it in the course of ordinary business and did not know or have reason to suspect that the publication would amount to an offence. This means that the defence is for the owners of advertising media, the billboards, the newspapers, television, and not for advertising agents; they are in a different category.

Enforcing authorities

1.184 The weights and measures authorities are charged with enforcing the Acts. These are the county councils and, in London, the Common Council and the London borough councils.

Their powers include entry for spot-checks, seizure when an offence is suspected, and entry and seizure under warrant when they have reason to expect to be refused entry.[28]

Current penalties for conviction of the offences described are a maximum fine of £2,000 summarily and two years' imprisonment and an unlimited fine when tried on indictment.[29]

The practice of making Compensation Orders is common in Trade Descriptions cases, under the Powers of Criminal Courts Act 1973, s.35. (A maximum figure of £2,000 applies to such orders at the present time.

If, when a case is taken before the courts the owner of goods is not convicted, the authority or government department which brought the case is liable to compensate the owner if those goods are lost, damaged or deteriorate.[30]

Limitation periods

1.185 No prosecution for an offence under these Acts may be started more than three years after the commission of the offence.[31] The alternative period is one year from the discovery of the offence by the prosecutor and the earlier of these two periods is the effective one, in any particular case.

There is a twelve months' limit, rather than the usual six months, on laying an information in a magistrates court.

This Act is designed to catch foreign goods which are given names or trademarks which are likely to be taken as United Kingdom ones. An

---

[27] Act of 1968, s.24.
[28] Act of 1968, s.28. There are associated offences for obstructing such officers (s.29).
[29] S.I. 1984 No. 447 (May 1, 1984).
[30] Act of 1968, s.33.
[31] *Ibid.* s.19.

offence is committed by the supplier, unless he ensures that the real place of production is conspicuously indicated on the goods or, at the other extreme, the offending name is so inconspicuous that a purchaser is unlikely to be aware of it or be influenced by it. There are various forms of defence and relief provided in the Act.

Chapter 2

SPECIAL LEGAL PRINCIPLES

"It is better that the law should be clear than that it should be clever"
Sir A. Clarke (*Parsons* v. *B.N.M. Laboratories Ltd.* (1964) 1 Q.B. 95 at p.102)

Introduction

2.01   This Chapter leaves the general legal background, against which the public leisure services operate. Local authorities are responsible for many of those services and this Chapter looks at certain branches of the law which affect their role in this field.

Initially we shall consider the statutory framework within which they must work. The domestic law connoted by local Acts and by-laws is the subject of the following section. There follow three sections about the large specialist territories in which there are laws for local authorities. These are commons, open space land and the slightly vaguer but very important subject of land purchase, appropriation and disposal.

A. Creatures of Statute

2.02   Many former local authorities were the creations of charters; all are now creatures of statute.[1] The great reorganisation of 1974 saw a rationalisation of the functions of local authorities. There was a considerable effort made to regulate practice and function more effectively. Then and thereafter a large number of unnecessary statutes were repealed.

Yet amid this reshaping and reform, the central legal core of local authority activity remained. It is the powers conferred by Parliament which determine the powers of local government. "Without those powers, it has no power."[2]

1. **Powers and Duties**

2.03   Local authorities are managers of legal functions, some of which are duties and some powers. For instance, in the Public Libraries and Museums Act 1964: "It shall be the duty of every library authority to provide a compre-

---

[1] The Local Government Act 1972, s.245, is the authority under which district councils have petitioned for charters to acquire borough status.
[2] Watkins L.J. in *Bromley L.B.C.* v. *Greater London Council* [1983] 1 A.C. at p. 768.

hensive and efficient library service . . . ." But: "A library authority may make a charge for notifying a person that a book . . . (is) . . . available for borrowing."[3] The difference is traditional and necessary.

A simple example of the difference between the statute which prescribes and the statute which permits relates to the statutory timetable for the application for a bingo club licence in the Gaming Act 1968. The case is *R. v. Pontypool Gaming Licensing Committee*.[4] The Act requires a copy of the newspaper advertisement about the application to be sent to the clerk of the licensing committee within seven days of publication. In the event, it was 13 days before it was sent, 15 before it was received. All else was in order. The authority did not object in principle to the application. But it was declined because the mandatory requirements of the Act of 1968 had not been fulfilled. On appeal it was argued that a mere administrative inconvenience had occurred. The High Court held otherwise: "Parliament has laid down the entire procedure, with specific limits of time." The court refused an application for an order that the licensing committee should hear and determine the licence application. This could not be done: the application was not lawful.[5]

2.04 In exercising both powers and duties, local authorities come under the scrutiny of the courts if they depart from the principle that in exercising those statutory functions, they must not inflict on others damage that might, with reasonable care, be avoided. Provided that they carry out the functions Parliament has entrusted to them, without negligence, they incur no liability. In the well-known words of Lord Blackburn in the case of *Geddis* v. *Proprietors of Bann Reservoir*, "No action will lie for doing that which the legislature has authorised if it be done without negligence but an action does lie . . . if it be done negligently."[6]

2.05 There are two other principles established by the cases, which underline this prime duty of local authorities to operate competently within the statutes:

(a) They cannot by deed or contract limit themselves not to fulfil their obligations under the statutory functions.[7]

(b) They may make internal rules to guide themselves in executing

---

[3] ss.7 and 8(2).
[4] [1970] 1 W.L.R. 1299.
[5] In other cases on the same Schedule, a court has excused the printing of ABE for ABC as an obvious error (*R. v. Dacorum Gaming Licensing Committee ex p. EMI Cinemas & Leisure Ltd.* [1971] 3 All E.R. 666), but another court declined to uphold another notice, which whilst containing the correct items, added several superfluous ones. It was an invalid public notice, said the court. The Schedule is mandatory on these matters (*R. v. Leicester Gaming Licensing Committee ex p. Shine* [1971] 1 W.L.R. 1648. Depending on the context, courts have held time requirements to be directory only, and thus a mistake in that respect has not been fatal to the statutory procedure. See *R. v. Inspector of Taxes ex p. Clarke* [1974] Q.B. 220.
[6] [1878] A.C. 430 at p. 455.
[7] See *Blake* v. *Hendon Corporation* [1962] 1 Q.B. 283, for an illuminating discussion by Devlin J. of this principle in relation to s.164 of the Public Health Act 1975. To dedicate land for a public park was not, said the court, binding themselves to flout a statutory duty. It was compatible with the main objects for which the land was acquired.

2.05

those functions, provided that those rules are not arbitrary but are relevant and consistent with the enabling legislation.[8]

2. Constraints

2.06 The main sanctions against local authorities which depart from these principles, have emerged over the years. They include (i) breach of statutory duty, (ii) judicial review, (iii) ministerial oversight, and (iv) the Ombudsman. Audit is, of course, another, most important, control and this is discussed in Chapter 9.

(1) *Breach of Statutory Duty*

2.07 This is a sanction which has often received acceptance in the courts, paradoxically, by the claims based upon it which are dismissed, rather than those which succeed. It was, however, upheld as recently as 1979 in *Thornton* v. *Kirklees M.B.C.*[9] The Court of Appeal supported a claim for damages for breach of the statutory duty to secure housing accommodation for the plaintiff, which arises under the Housing (Homeless Persons) Act 1977, s.3(4). They rested their decision on being satisfied with the application to the facts of that case of three tests, which emerge from a House of Lords decision in 1949 (*Cutler* v. *Wandsworth Stadium*)[10]:

(a) Is this claim for the kind of harm the statute was intended to prevent?
(b) Was the plaintiff one of the class of those for whom the protection of the statute was intended?
(c) Was the special remedy provided by the statute adequate for the protection of the person injured?

The general principle is that where a statute imposes a duty on a public authority, for the benefit of a specified category of persons, but prescribes no special remedy for breach of that duty, it is to be assumed that a civil action for damages will lie for such a breach.

(2) *Judicial Review*

2.08 An application for judicial review is a general form of appeal to the High Court against alleged breach of some duty in law, by any body of persons granted legal authority to determine questions affecting the rights of subjects. This somewhat general description certainly brings many of the decisions taken by local authorities into the category of those which can be brought before the courts for examination and possible corrective action.

---

[8] See *Kennedy* v. *Birmingham Licensing Committee* [1972] 2 Q.B. 140, where it was held that an "equation of barrelage" required by the Committee from an applicant for a new on-licence was invalid because it was unreasonable.
[9] [1979] Q.B. 626.
[10] [1949] A.C. 398.

It arises precisely under the terms of Order 53 of the Rules of the Supreme Court and for detail that Order should be consulted.[11] It originated in 1977 and has been described as providing a uniform, flexible and comprehensive code of procedure for the exercise by the High Court of its supervisory jurisdiction over the proceedings and decisions of other bodies of persons charged with the performance of public acts and duties.[12]

There have been many cases when this procedure has been employed, for example:

2.09

In *O'Reilly* v. *Mackman*,[13] certain prisoners brought an ordinary action for damages against the Board of Visitors for Hull Prison. The defendant raised the question of appropriate procedure and succeeded in the House of Lords. That House said that Order 53 should have been used, due to the nature of the case. "It would be contrary to public policy and, as such, an abuse of the process of the court, to permit a person seeking to establish that a decision of a public authority infringed rights to which he was entitled to protection under public law, to proceed by way of ordinary action and by this means to evade the provisions of Order 53 for the protection of such authorities."

The case of *R.* v. *Bromley L.B.C. and others, ex p. Lambeth L.B.C.*,[14] was important in showing that the Order 53 powers and procedures were available for litigants when a declaration was sought, even though no decision was being challenged and none of the three prerogative orders was being sought. The subject of the declaration sought in that case was whether a subscription to the Association of London Authorities was lawful. Before ruling in the affirmative on this question, the High Court required to be satisfied that:

(a) The plaintiff council had a real and not simply an academic interest in the matter,[15] and

(b) There was a real "contender," (*i.e.* in the person of Lambeth

---

[11] This came into operation under the Supreme Court Act 1981, s.31.

[12] The extent of this procedure is indicated in *R.* v. *Electricity Commissioners* [1924] 1 K.B. 171 at p. 205.

[13] [1983] 2 A.C. 237.

[14] *The Times*, June 16, 1984 D.C. The three prerogative orders, formerly known as writs, are *mandamus*, which commands the body or person to do that which it is his legal duty to do; *prohibition*, which forbids, e.g. a lower court from doing that which it should not do; and *certiorari*, which brings into the High Court in order to quash them, judicial (in its widest sense) proceedings which have gone wrong, or are going wrong, because, *e.g.* fair trial is not likely due to bias, or jurisdiction is exceeded. More than one of these orders may issue for a particular complaint.

[15] The status of being an "aggrieved person," and thus entitled to pursue litigation, received a further refinement in *R.* v. *Secretary of State for Social Services and another, ex p. Greater London Council*, *The Times*, August 16, 1984, before Woolf J.

The court held that the local authority, *i.e.* the G.L.C., had no standing but the Child Poverty Action Group did have sufficient standing to seek and obtain a Declaration under Order 53 procedure against the Secretary of State and his chief Supplementary Benefits officer, on behalf of unidentified claimants for arrears of Supplementay Benefit. A local authority could not simply assume this role, under s.222 of the Local Government Act 1972.

2.09   SPECIAL LEGAL PRINCIPLES

L.B.C.), "a proper contradictor," as Lord Dunedin had once said.[16]

(3) *Ministerial Control*

2.10 Local authorities have always been subject to the control of a Minister of the Crown for some of the many services they administer. For dereliction of duty by a local education authority, the Secretary of State has the clearest reserve default power:

> "If the Secretary of State is satisfied that they . . . have failed to discharge the duty imposed upon them, the Secretary of State may make an Order declaring . . . to be in default and giving such directions as may be expedient for enforcing that duty."[17]

For general local government oversight and leaving until Chapter 9 the financial controls, there are still a variety of controls, such as inspection, obtaining information, consenting to appointments, giving directions,[18] making regulations, not to mention the extensive areas of local government decisions, *e.g.* for large urban redevelopment where development plans and compulsory purchase orders go to one Minister or another for confirmation.

Whether used rarely or frequently, these controls and reserve powers create the climate of opinion in which local authorities work.

(4) *The Local Government Commissioners*

2.11 The Ombudsman, to use the popular term, was introduced to local government by the Local Government Act 1974. England has three and Wales one. Each Local Commissioner has a territorial responsibility.

These Ombudsmen investigate complaints, duly lodged, into "injustice in consequence of maladministration."[19] The decision to investigate is discretionary, so that, for instance, an Order of Mandamus by the High Court to a Local Commissioner would be inapt.[20] (This discretionary element is fortified by section 34 of the Act of 1974: "It is hereby declared

---

[16] *Russian Commercial and Industrial Bank* v. *British Bank for Foreign Trade Ltd.* [1921] 2 A.C. 438 at p. 447.

[17] s.68 of the same Act of 1944 gives even stronger control over actual or potential failure by an education authority to carry out its duties in a reasonable manner.

[18] *e.g.* Local Government Planning and Land Act 1980, ss.71, 98 and 116 about the restriction on capital expenditure, the disposal of land not put to good use and the assessment of land suitable for residential development.

[19] These reports are submitted to "representative bodies," being committees with representatives from the local authority associations and the National Water Council. They in turn circulate reports throughout the country: s.24, Local Government Act 1974. Whilst the Act of 1974 says that the maladministration is to have occurred "in the exercise of the administrative functions of the authority," (s.26), any exclusion of, *e.g.* law-making activities such as by-laws, or executive functions, seems in practice difficult to discern.

[20] *Re Fletchers' Application.* This is about the Parliamentary Commissioner but the wording is the same and is thus relevant.

2.11 that nothing in this Part of this Act authorises or requires a Local Commissioner to question the merits of a decision taken without maladministration by an authority in the exercise of a discretion vested in that authority.")

The Ombudsman affords to the local authority, against which the complaint is levelled, a chance to comment, even to try to negotiate a local settlement of the grievance. The annual report is a useful record of the scale and effectiveness of this new control over local government.[21]

2.12 The emphasis is on the *way* in which the local authority handled the problem, whether it be housing, or town planning (which still head the list of subject areas calling for investigation), or compensation, or a variety of others.

The Ombudsman is likely to find maladministration if he finds evidence of unfairness, neglect, bias, unreasonable delay, failure to follow prescribed procedures, or arbitrariness.[22]

2.13 An Ombudsman can recommend a culpable authority to take action to remedy their failure, perhaps pay compensation, repair a house, rehouse someone, and the findings are given the pressure of publicity to induce some favourable, positive, response. The local authority is required to inform the Local Commissioner of the action they have taken on his report. On receiving this, the Commissioner may decide to issue a second report.[23]

2.14 After ten years' experience of this system, one or two points have been ventilated in the courts and additional legal provisions in the code of practice followed by the Ombudsmen are worth emphasis.

  (a) Communications to and from an Ombudsman as part of an investigation are, for the purposes of the law of defamation, absolutely privileged.[24]
  (b) The case of *R. v. Local Commissioner for Administration for the North and East Area of England, ex p. Bradford M.B.C.*[25] illuminates the selection by an Ombudsman of complaints for investigation, in the light of a restriction in section 26 of the Act of 1974 that this is not to cover:
    (i) an action in relation to which a person has a right of appeal to a tribunal under an enactment, or to a Minister of the Crown;
    (ii) likewise, an action in which a person has a remedy by way of process in a court of law.

---

[21] In the latest annual report, "The Local Ombudsman," covering 1983/1984, it is stated that some 3,000 complaints were considered of which housing and town planning matters accounted for two thirds and leisure/recreation for just over 1 per cent. Formal investigation reports were issued in 322 cases. The Commission has maintained a dialogue with the Secretary of State for the Department of the Environment about possible extensions of the subjects investigated in non-leisure service fields. The Government has held out no hope that such a step is likely.
[22] H.C. Debates, (1966) Vol. 754, c. 51; Mr. R. Crossman in Second Reading debate on the Bill.
[23] Act of 1974, s.31(1).
[24] *Ibid.* s.32.
[25] [1979] 1 Q.B. 287.

2.14   Special Legal Principles

(c) The case of *Re A Complaint against Liverpool City Council*[26] is a useful test of the effect of the statutory notice served by a local authority, under investigation, under section 32(3) of the Act of 1974, that the production of certain papers to the Ombudsman would be contrary to the public interest. In that case, the papers related to the fostering of a child. Under the Act of 1974, the Secretary of State has power to "discharge" such a notice by a local authority but he had not done so. In these circumstances the refusal of the council was upheld in the Divisional Court.

(d) Obstruction of an investigation gives rise to an Ombudsman's certificate to the High Court, which is empowered to deal with the offender as if he were before that Court. The offence has to be "such that it would constitute contempt of court" if the Ombudsman's investigations were a proceeding in the High Court.

(e) An Ombudsman can call in expert advice.[27]

3. Ultra Vires

2.15 As local authorities are creatures of statute, they are not allowed to act outside the powers conferred by those statutes. To do so is *ultra vires* (beyond the powers). The application of the doctrine of *ultra vires* provides a particular example of circumstances in which actions and decisions of local authorities may become subject to judicial review, which is referred to above. This question may be approached by asking:

(1) When does an *ultra vires* situation arise?
(2) What are its consequences?

(1) *When Does an Ultra Vires Situation Arise?*

The territory

2.16 If a local authority seeks to spend money outside its own area, it is likely to be acting *ultra vires*. The Public Museums and Libraries Act 1964 empowers the authority to provide a service for people resident in the area or in full time education there. This is the normal situation—a service for the rate payers. It has been modified to the extent, *e.g.* that the Local Authorities (Goods and Services) Act 1970 allows agreements between adjoining authorities for the provision of a joint service, joint use of plant or the carrying out of maintenance. As social development has reduced the likelihood that any authority will be selfcontained, this is an area of risk to be kept under review.

The money

2.17 The local authority by law works within its annual budget. Differing political opinions can lead to an *ultra vires* decision in the field of staff pay-

---

[26] [1977] 2 All E.R. 650.
[27] Act of 1974, s.29(6).

ments or contracts to be made. This happens if prudence is stretched to breaking point, as in *Roberts* v. *Hopwood*[28] when the courts held *ultra vires* wages paid to a class of employees of a London borough which went significantly beyond nationally negotiated levels.

An acceptance by a local authority of a tender for goods or services which is not the lowest has normally to be justified by giving "special reasons," within the authority's standing orders. This kind of internal ruling is a good way of starting to meet an *ultra vires* challenge to such expenditure: it evidences an intent to act with financial prudence.

For the approach of the courts in the field of education policy to such internal guidelines, see *Cumings* v. *Birkenhead Corporation*.[29]

Easing the ultra vires rule

A number of statutory provisions should be noted which enlarge an authority's powers at points where the *ultra vires* rule would have applied. **2.18**

By the Local Government Act 1972, s.111, "a local authority shall have power to do any thing . . . which is calculated to facilitate, or is conducive or incidental to, the discharge of any of their functions." The words "conducive or incidental to" can give rise to keen debate.

By the same Act of 1972 the power in section 137 to spend money, up to the product of a two penny rate, "in the interests of their area or of all or some of its inhabitants" on purposes not specified or authorised in any other enactment, gives a measure of leeway to members frustrated by the limits of their portfolio of enabling statutes.[30]

The Local Government (Miscellaneous Provsions) Act 1982 has extended two earlier powers:

(i) The power above in section 137 of the main Act of 1972 is widened to include "power to incur expenditure in giving financial assistance to persons carrying on commercial and industrial undertakings."[31]

(ii) A power in the Local Authorities (Land) Act 1963 is extended so that the local authority can advance money to enable a person to acquire land or erect buildings or carry out work on land.[31a] (The former provision was limited to land sold or let by the local authority or to land where the council was a party to a building agreement.[32])

---

[28] [1925] A.C. 578.
[29] [1971] 2 All E.R. 881.
[30] This was the power under which Hackney L.B.C. successfully resisted a challenge to their action in giving financial help to the costs of the British Olympic team in Moscow in 1980. The Council said that their action was based on the involvement of local inhabitants in the Olympics.
[31] Act of 1982, s.44.
[31a] *Read* v. *J. Lyons & Co. Ltd.* [1947] A.C. 156; *Christmas* v. *General Cleaning Contractors Ltd.* [1952] 1 All E.R. 39.
[32] *Ibid.* s.32.

(2) *Abuse of the Statutory Powers*

2.19 In addition to the primary question, have the powers been exceeded?, there is a more general and searching question: have the powers been abused?[33]

Though the House of Lords has held that bad faith as such is not a ground for a challenge to a decision as being *ultra vires*, the jurisdiction of the courts in the face of an abuse of legal powers, is evidenced by *London and Westcliff Properties Ltd.* v. *Ministry of Housing and Local Government*.[34] The local authority came to an arrangement with the freeholders of a site to dispose of the leasehold interest in that site to them, when the authority's compulsory purchase order on that leasehold interest had been confirmed. The financial arrangements to achieve this destination of the valuable leasehold interest were agreed before the public enquiry into an objection by the leaseholders to the order. The order was confirmed by the Ministry but quashed by the High Court as *ultra vires*. Ashworth J. said: "The proposal and the agreement involved the council in as plain a contravention of s.47(2) of the Housing Act 1957 as can be imagined. This was a bargain which . . . the Minister's officials should at once have detected as improper . . . it was acting ultra vires."[35]

Ultra Vires and Estoppel

2.20 There is a final point to be made, illustratrated by *Rhyll U.D.C.* v. *Rhyll Amusements Ltd.*[36] A local authority granted a 31 year lease of a marine lake and pleasure grounds to a company, without taking the necessary first step of obtaining consent from the Ministry for the transaction, as the lease was longer than seven years. Some 20 years later, desiring to renegotiate terms, the Council advanced the argument that the original lease was void, for the reason explained above. In court, the company lessee sought to hold the council estopped from presenting that point, having by conduct honoured the lease for many years. The court did not agree with the company. Harman J. said that to allow that argument would be to gloss over the *ultra vires* act. "Otherwise such a body," he said, "could by this means confer on itself a power which it had not got and the *ultra vires* doctrine would be reduced to a nullity."

(3) *What are the Consequences?*

2.21 By audit, unlawful expenditure can be challenged, both at the level of an elector, who examines the books of account and raises questions on them and also at the level of the authority's professional auditor.

The position of the latter has altered radically under the Local Govern-

---

[33] *Smith* v. *East Elloe R.D.C.* [1956] A.C. 736, a compulsory purchase order case.
[34] [1961] 1 W.L.R. 519.
[35] *Ibid.* at p. 529. S.47, referred to by the court, requires the best price to be obtained for land thus bought. The arrangement with the freeholders breached this requirement.
[36] [1959] 1 All E.R. 257.

ment Act 1972. From being one who raised a surcharge upon a council on the basis of his audit, he has been "placed in the invidious position of a quasi-prosecutor, with responsibility for deciding to launch and for conducting the proceedings in this court." These are the words of Ormrod L.J. in *Pickwell* v. *London Borough of Camden*,[37] where the court dismissed an application by a district auditor for a declaration that a pay settlement of the local authority was *ultra vires*. The council paid increased monies to their staff, who were on strike, and could have paid less if, like other local authorities, they had waited for the result of national negotiations on that very matter. The Court held the authority to have been justified, by the dire effects upon essential public services, in not waiting for a national settlement. The power to apply to the court is now in section 19 of the Local Government Finance Act 1982.

2.22 A local authority treasurer has a duty to refuse to incur unlawful expenditure "If an order is made on the county treasurer to pay expenses wholly disconnected with county matters, such an order is without jurisdiction and one which the county treasurer would be bound to disobey." This is a quotation from the leading case of *Att. Gen.* v. *De Winton*,[38] which laid down the role of the council's treasurer as being "not merely the servant of the council; he owes a duty and stands in a fiduciary relation to the burgesses as a body . . . He cannot plead the orders of the council as an excuse for an unlawful act." This is the second sanction against an *ultra vires* act; the authority's treasurer may decide that he cannot implement the financial aspect of it.

2.23 The important case of *Bromley L.B.C.* v. *Greater London Council*[39] illustrates the role of the courts as a third sanction. The fares reduction policy decided and implemented by the defendants was declared *ultra vires* at the level of the House of Lords. Thus an application by way of judicial review for a declaration about the legality of a decision, coupled with an injunction, if appropriate, would take the lines discussed earlier in this Chapter about the new judicial review procedure.

As indicated at the start of this Chapter, local authorities, as creatures of statute, are subject to certain resulting restraints. The *ultra vires* rule enshrines one of these and it is evident from recent decisions in the courts that it is still being regularly exercised.[40]

4. Statutory Interpretation

2.24 "A judge should ask himself this question. If the makers of this Act had themselves come across this ruck in the texture, how would they

---

[37] [1983] 1 All E.R. 602.
[38] [1906] 2 Ch. 106.
[39] [1983] 1 A.C. 768.
[40] *The Times*, April 5, 1984. *Wandsworth London Borough Council* v. *Winder*. The fundamental point was about the reliance on judicial review as the established method of challenging a local authority decision. The court held that a challenge could be made, based on private law rights, by raising the question of the *vires* of the local authority.

have straightened it out? A judge must not alter the material of which it is woven but he can and should iron out the creases."

This is an extract from the judgment of Denning J. in *Seaford Court Estates v. Asher*.[41] It is not a view held by all courts. There have clearly been different approaches to statutory interpretation and only a small part of the topic has been codified into statute. When one text book has some 75 rules for different problems raised by this subject,[42] clearly all that can be collected here is a series of some of the main ones.

1. The making of law is for the legislature, not the courts.

> "There is one course the courts cannot take; they cannot fill the gaps. They cannot, by asking the question 'What would Parliament have done in this case?—one not contemplated—if the facts had been before it?' attempt themselves to supply the answer, if the answer is not in the terms of the Act itself."[43]

2. Many Acts of Parliament have their own interpretation section. In addition there is an Interpretation Act of 1978. These often help.

3. Where a statute is ambiguous, the court should seek the intention of Parliament:
   (a) in the statute itself;
   (b) in other related legislation;
   (c) in contemporaneous circumstances;
   (d) then in the rules of law:
      (i) What was the common law before this Act?
      (ii) What was the defect or mischief for which the common law did not provide?
      (iii) What remedy had Parliament resolved upon?
      (iv) What was the purpose—the aim—of the remedy?[44]

4. The words of the statute should be construed to give them a sensible meaning.

5. Words should be given their ordinary meaning if there is nothing to alter or modify the language.

6. Where general words follow specific words, the general words ought to be confined to things of the same kind as those specified.[45]

7. When construing a consolidating Act, there is a presumption that it was not intended to alter the law. This must give way to a contrary intention.

If this subsection began with a challenging point of view of Denning J., it may end with an equally searching one from Templeman J. in *Halifax Building Society v. Registrar of Friendly Societies*[46]

> "There are no reasons why I should officiously strive to limit the

---

[41] [1950] A.C. 508.
[42] *Halsbury* (4th ed.), Vol. 44, Statutes, paras. 840–915 incl.
[43] *Royal College of Nursing* v. *D.H.S.S.* [1981] A.C. 800 at p. 822E, *per* Lord Wilberforce.
[44] Cited in *Universal Corporation* v. *Five Ways Properties Ltd.* [1978] 3 All E.R. 1131 at p. 1136.
[45] *Beswick* v. *Beswick* [1968] A.C. 58 at p. 87.
[46] [1978] 1 W.L.R. 1549 at p. 1550.

CREATURES OF STATUTE **2.24**

scope of section 43 in order perversely to forbid that to be done which plainly must and ought to be done, namely, the safeguard of the investors in a building society from loss."

B. Local Law Makers

Local authorities operate within a framework of legal powers and duties; **2.25** hence the reality of *intra vires* and *ultra vires* discussed above. For the most part, that framework is contained in the general law of the land, *i.e.* Acts of Parliament: Housing Acts, Finance Acts, Town and Country Planning Acts, Public Health Acts, Local Government Acts and others.

A local authority can acquire more legal powers in the following ways: (1) adoptive Acts, (2) provisional Orders, (3) by-laws and (4) local Acts. These are the classic methods and this subsection explains their present standing and usefulness.

1. **Adoptive Acts**

These are important Acts of Parliament which are operative only in those **2.26** parts of the country where, by the prescribed method, they are "adopted."[47] Examples are the Private Places of Entertainment (Licensing) Act 1967, and The Highways Act 1980, insofar only as the Advanced Payments Code in sections 219–225 is concerned. Whilst this class of legislation was used from time to time in the nineteenth century, and allowed for some flexibility in the application of special laws, it has now ceased to fulfil any ongoing useful purpose, as general law has become comprehensive. Its use is infrequent.

2. **Provisional Orders**

These are Orders employed to give legal authority for a special and **2.27** limited activity, *e.g.* adjusting a harbour, or local authority boundaries, or arranging for joint local authority functions, perhaps for a regional art gallery or sports centre, in a boundary area. They are akin to Orders subject to special parliamentary procedure, both being within the same section of the Local Government Act 1972.[48] They are procedures used occasionally, for "special" occasions, and an example from the public leisure services relates to the disposal of land within a public park. By section 123 of the Act of 1972, only 250 square yards of such land could be disposed of and this special procedure was then necessary. (That particular stipulation has now been amended.)

---

[47] The Adoptive Act itself prescribes the procedure for adoption. Sometimes it is a vote of the local authority but, instead, it might be a majority vote of the inhabitants. For the first Libraries and Museums Act 1850, a two-thirds vote of the voting burgesses in favour of the Act was stipulated.
[48] Local Government Act 1972, s.240, especially subs. (1)(*c*).

2.28   SPECIAL LEGAL PRINCIPLES

3. By-Laws

2.28 These have been mentioned above. They provide detailed powers of control in a limited area of legal activity. To that extent only, they enhance a local authority's powers. They are in regular use by all local authorities. A full discussion will be found in Chapter 4 in the context of public parks.

4. Local Acts

2.29 This form of local law is in decreasing use.[49] There are good reasons for this situation:

(a) The scope for Local Acts has been greatly reduced because of the vast range of public and general Acts. (A glance at the volumes of Local Acts for recent years shows their use by one authority which required to build a footbridge over the river Severn, another which needed to secure powers to deal with stray dogs in Scotland, a third which sought to rationalise the legality of its market undertaking, and a fourth which desired to be able lawfully to compensate householders discomforted by the noise of its airport.)

(b) The Government, after the local government reorganisation of 1974, stimulated a close scrutiny of Local Acts, as part of the consolidation of the new authorities by amalgamating their Local Acts. This exercise was demanding and rigorous but worthwhile and necessary. It called for a certain amount of legal spring cleaning and when the exercise was complete, the calls for new Local Act powers were few.[50]

(c) A Local Act is still an expensive venture for a local authority and thus not embarked upon lightly.

Procedure

2.30 The essential procedure for obtaining a Local Act is contained in the standing orders of each House of Parliament:

(a) A petition for the Bill is presented. This is supported by special resolutions of the authority passed before and after the deposit of the Bill.

(b) The procedure in Parliament then, as Erskine May says:

> "partakes of a judicial character. The persons who are applying for powers or benefits appear as suitors for the Bill, while those who apprehend injury are admitted as adverse parties in the suit. Many of the formalities of a court of justice are maintained . . . if the parties do not sustain the Bill in its progress, by following every regulation and form prescribed, it is not forwarded by the House in which it is pending."[51]

This is in a section headed: "Distinctive character of Private Bills."

---

[49] In 1977, 6 out of 23 were local government Bills; in 1978, it was 12 out of 21; in 1980, the figure was 14 out of 43; in 1981 15 out of 35 and in 1982, it was 8 out of 29. The proportions are not large and neither are the overall totals.
[50] Local Government Act 1972, s.262.
[51] *Parliamentary Practice* (20th ed.), p. 893.

(c) As an adjunct of this judicial character, private bills were subject for some time to a jurisdiction exercised in the Chancery Court, to restrain persons from petitioning for or against them.[52]

A full examination of the position of the courts in relation to private bills took place in the recent case of *British Railway Board* v. *Pickin*[53] and the House of Lords ultimately decided that Parliament, and not the courts, was responsible for rectifying any irregularity in procedure in relation to an Act passed by Parliament.[54]

(d) Even though this examination of Private Bills takes on a judicial atmosphere, with counsel and witnesses and cross-examination, the essential procedure corresponds to that for Public Bills. They have their First and Second Readings, and the important scrutiny takes place in Committee. Two committees are available, one when the Bill is opposed and the other when unopposed. The preamble and each clause of the Bill are considered, particularly in the light of any petitions also before Parliament, from interested pressure groups or formal objectors in the country.

The Bill is then reported to the House and given its Third Reading. Then the other House embarks upon the same procedure leading in due course to the Royal Assent. By convention between the two Houses, the major scrutiny takes place in the first House: this serves to share out the Private Bill work between the two Houses.[55]

(e) The general power to oppose or promote Private Bills, in the interests of the area in question, is now contained in section 239 of the Local Government Act 1972.

C. Land Transactions

The statutory provisions relating to the land transactions of local authorities are to be found in the Local Government Act 1972, as amended by the Local Government, Planning and Land Act 1980. Supplementary powers in connection with town and country planning are contained in Part VI of the Town and Country Planning Act 1971 (the 1971 Act).

1. Acquisition

Very wide powers to acquire land are given by the 1972 Act.[56] These powers for acquiring land inside or outside their areas are given to princi-

---

[52] See this asserted as recently as 1942 in *Bilston Corporation* v. *Wolverhampton Corporation* [1942] 1 Ch. 391. Though the Court there found Wolverhampton Corporation acting in breach of an agreement in opposing a Private Bill, the court declined to grant an injunction, as being outside its proper jurisdiction. The remedy lay with Parliament, said the court, not with the courts.
[53] [1974] 1 All E.R. 609, where the House of Lords, overruling the Court of Appeal, held that the Courts have no power to examine proceedings in Parliament in order to see whether the passing of an Act had been obtained by means of an irregularity or fraud. This was followed by the important case on the Canada Act—*Manuel* v. *Att. Gen.* [1982] 3 All E.R. 822.
[54] Erskine May, *ibid.* at p. 895.
[55] *Ibid.*, especially Chap. 38.
[56] Part VII.

2.32 pal councils (local authorities other than parishes) for the purposes of any of their functions under the 1972 or any other Act and for the benefit, improvement or development of their areas. Land may be acquired in advance of requirements and until required for the purpose for which it was intended, the land may be used for any of the Council's functions.[57] Two or more Councils acting together can arrange for one of them to acquire land required for the joint project.[58]

2.33 Principal councils are empowered to acquire land compulsorily, with the approval of the Minister concerned with the function for which the land is required.[59] The power of acquisition by compulsory purchase exists where there is a power to acquire by agreement except in three cases, namely (i) where in any case the power to acquire land is limited to acquisition by agreement, (ii) purchases under the Local Authorities (Land) Act 1963 and (iii) where the land is to be acquired for the benefit, improvement or development of their area.[60] Two or more councils can act together through one of them being nominated for the purpose. The procedure to be followed in the compulsory purchase of land is prescribed by the Acquisition of Land Act 1981.[61]

2.34 The 1971 Act enables county, London Borough and district councils and Joint Planning Boards (Peak Park Joint Planning Board and Lake District Special Planning Board) to acquire compulsorily any land which they require, for certain purposes[62]:

(a) land in their area which is suitable for and is required in order to secure the carrying out of one or more of the following activities, namely development, re-development and improvement;

(b) any land in their area which is required for a purpose which it is necessary to achieve in the interests of the proper planning of an area in which the land is situated.

In deciding what land is suitable for development, redevelopment or improvement, account has to be taken of the provisions of the development plan, any planning permissions in force and any considerations which would be material in dealing with a planning application.[63] The power to acquire compulsorily extends to any adjoining land which is required for facilitating the development of the former land and to any land required for the purpose of being given in exchange for any common land or open space required for development.[64]

The Greater London Council have power to acquire land compulsorily, but where they propose to acquire land by agreement within one of the

---

[57] s.120(2).
[58] s.120(4).
[59] s.121.
[60] s.121(2).
[61] s.121(4). A useful full treatment of compulsory purchase procedure is in C.A. Cross, *Principles of Local Government Law*, (6th ed. 1981), and the *Encyclopedia of Compulsory Purchase and Compensation* (Sweet and Maxwell).
[62] s.112.
[63] s.112(1A).
[64] s.112(1B).

boroughs, the consent of the Borough Council is required or, if it is refused, the consent of the Minister.[65]

The Secretary of State for the Environment has power under the 1971 Act to acquire compulsorily land "necessary for the public service."[66] "Public service" is not defined and the power appears to have the widest scope. Section 122 of the 1980 Act extends this power by authorising the acquisition of other land which in the Minister's opinion should be acquired in the interests of the proper planning of the area concerned, for the better or most economic development of the other land, or for exchange for common or open space land. "Public service" is to be construed as including activities of international bodies.

2. Appropriation

Land belonging to a principal council which is no longer required for the purpose for which it is held, may be appropriated for any purpose for which the council may acquire land by agreement and the appropriation takes effect, subject to the rights of any person with an interest in the land.[67] Land forming part of a common (for which a procedure is described under section 121 of the 1971 Act) may not be appropriated unless its area does not exceed 250 square yards and a notice of the intention to appropriate is advertised for two weeks in a local paper, after which the council consider any objections to the proposed appropriation. In the case of open space land, a similar procedure has to be followed and where the land appropriated is held for the purposes of section 164 of the Public Health Act 1875, or under section 10 of the Open Spaces Act 1906, the land ceases to be subject to the trusts which arise by reason of those statutory provisions.[68]

2.35

The appropriation of commons open space and fuel and field garden allotments, (other than green belt land within the meaning of the Green Belt (London and Home Counties) Act 1938), is dealt with under section 121 of the 1971 Act. The procedure requires the Order of the local authority, which is confirmed by the Secretary of State. The special provisions of the Acquisition of Land Act 1981, relating to the compulsory purchase of commons, are applied to Orders under section 121.

2.36

Land for the time being held for planning purposes, may be appropriated under section 122 of the 1971 Act, as amended by the 1980 Act. The consent of the Secretary of State is required for the appropriation of land which consists of a common, part of a common or which formerly consisted of a common or part thereof. The advertisement procedure of

2.37

---

[65] s.112(3).
[66] s.113.
[67] L.G.A. 1972, s.112. Appropriation is the change of the legal purpose for which the land is held. It is effected by resolution of the council, and is, normally, subject to confirmation by a Government department.
[68] T.C.P.A. 1971, s.121(2). See Chap. 4.

2.37   Special Legal Principles

the Act has to be followed where the land in question consists of or forms part of an open space.

3. Disposal

2.38 Principal councils may dispose of land in any way they wish but unless the consent of the Secretary of State has been obtained or the disposal is by way of the grant of a lease not exceeding seven years or the assignment of a lease with not more than seven years to run, the authority must obtain the best consideration that can reasonably be obtained.[69] In the case of land which consists of, or forms part of, an open space, the advertisement procedure described above has to be followed and when the land is sold, any trusts which arise solely by reason of the statutory power under which the land was held, cease to be applicable.[70] Section 123 of the 1971 Act enables land held for planning purposes to be disposed of, subject to the consent of the Secretary of State in the case of land which is or was part of a common. It is a condition that this land is held by a local authority, under a local Act and the disposal is for a consideration less than the best that can reasonably be obtained.[71] Land held for planning purposes, which consists or forms part of an open space, is subject to the same constraints as to disposal as are described above in relation to land whose disposal is governed by the 1972 Act. The 1971 Act specifically authorises the disposal of planning land in such manner and subject to such conditions as appear to be expedient in order to secure the best use of that and other land or to secure the construction of buildings needed for the proper planning of the area.

2.39 The phrase "for a consideration less than the best that can reasonably be obtained" does not necessarily mean the highest price that can be obtained.[72] Local authorities can often attain their purposes by arrangements with other persons and one particular means of achieving this objective is by the sale or lease of land, subject to covenants requiring the execution of specified works or restricting the use to a specified one. The imposition of covenants of this nature can in themselves reduce the value of land, especially where the commercial prospects of a proposed venture are diminished and the land has to be valued subject to the restrictions on the use or the requirements imposed by the authority. It is a matter of policy for the authority to determine whether such a course of action is justified in the particular circumstances. Statutory recognition of this principle is given in the case of the disposal of land which has been acquired or appropriated for planning purposes involving the develop-

---

[69] L.G.A. 1972, s.123. For a case where a lease was *ultra vires* because for the veiled purpose of evicting caravans and not simply an open space lease, see *Costello* v. *Dacorum* D.C. (1980) 79 L.G.R. 133.

[70] L.G.A. 1972, s.123(3).

[71] This does not apply to the grant of a lease or an assignment, where, in each case, there is less than seven years of the term to run.

[72] *Ibid.* s.123(2).

ment, redevelopment or improvement of an area.[73] Land may be disposed of to its former owners living in the area or carrying on businesses there, who wish to return there on terms which reflect the price at which the land had been acquired from them.

Parish Councils

The provisions of the 1972 Act are applied to parish and community councils with certain adaptations which allow for their relationship with the district councils covering their areas, and their different constitutional position.[74] Their powers of acquisition by agreement parallel those of principal councils, but in the case of compulsory purchase, a special procedure is provided involving the intervention of the district council which, if the proposal is approved by the Secretary of State, carries into effect the provisions of the order.[75] A particular feature of the procedure is the need to give consideration to the land holdings of certain owners and to the avoidance, so far as possible, of taking an undue or inconvenient quantity of land from any one owner. The powers of appropriation and disposal by a parish or community council closely follow those applicable to principal councils under the 1972 codes, including the requirements relating to commons and open spaces.[76]

Church Land and Burial Grounds

A most useful power which enables consecrated land and burial grounds to be developed or used for other purposes is contained in section 128 of the 1971 Act, which applies to purchases by a Minister, local authority or statutory undertaker. For the purposes of the section "land" includes a building. The section applies to land acquired under Part VI of the 1971 Act or compulsorily under any Act and to land appropriated by a local authority for planning purposes. In the case of burial grounds, (defined as including any churchyard of consecrated land or land, including buildings, used for religious worship or a cemetery or other ground, whether consecrated or not, which has at any time been set apart for the purposes of interment) the powers of the section do not have effect in respect of land which has been used for burial of the dead, until the prescribed requirements relating to the removal and reinterment of human remains and the disposal of monuments have been complied with. This means obtaining the faculty of the bishop of the diocese, in respect of consecrated ground or a licence of the Home Secretary under the Burial Act 1857 in other instances.[77] Subject to the procedural requirements of the section and the Regulations made thereunder, the land acquired may be

---

[73] T.C.P.A. 1971, s.123(7).
[74] L.G.A. 1972, s.125.
[75] *Ibid.* s.125(5).
[76] *Ibid.* ss.126 and 127.
[77] T.C.P.A. 1971, s.128(2). See the Town & Country Planning (Churches, Places of Religious Worship and Burial Grounds) Regulations 1950, S.I. 1950 No. 792.

used by a Minister in any manner by him or on his behalf, for any purpose for which he acquired it. In the case of purchase by any other body under the section, the land may be used in accordance with planning permission.

Commons and Open Spaces

2.42 A similar power is contained in section 129 of the 1971 Act enabling land consisting of or forming part of a common, open space, or fuel or field garden allotment to be used by a Minister or another person on his behalf for any purpose for which the land was acquired or by a local authority or statutory undertaker in accordance with planning permission. As in the case of section 128, the power applies to land which has been acquired under Part VI of the 1971 Act or compulsorily under any other Act, or which has been appropriated for planning purposes. This provision avoids any difficulty which might otherwise arise in the use of commons or open space which are subject to strict limitations in their use.

Reference was made in the previous Chapter to the powers of local and other authorities to make land available for use by other persons. Apart from outright disposal, as described earlier in this Chapter, the choice in making land available for use by others is by licence or by lease.

Licences

2.43 A licence constitutes the permission of the owner or occupier of land to another person to enter the land. A licence is granted for the personal benefit of the person or group of persons intended to enter the land, as opposed to a lease, the effect of which is to create an interest in the land, giving a right of possession to the lessee to the exclusion of the person granting it (the lessor). Licences should normally be the vehicle for granting the use of land or buildings where the use is of a transient kind or for a limited period. Examples are:

> the hire of a hall for a few days for a flower show or concert,
> a franchise to sell refreshments in a theatre or park;
> the use of a sports facility (bowls, tennis, football) on a seasonal basis or for one day per week;
> an agreement to place boats on a boating lake or on a canal;
> stationing an ice-cream kiosk or van on the foreshore or at a picnic site or in a country park.

2.44 Licences of these types are normally incorporated in agreements which contain relevant conditions in respect of usage, provision for termination at a specified date or on notice being given, safety of the public or users, restrictions on works having an effect on the land or building, indemnity for damage to land and building or injury to third parties, avoidance of nuisance, and compliance with any licensing requirements. Because licences are matters of agreement between the parties, there is no limitation on their content: it is for the parties to agree on the relevant terms. The grant of a licence may follow an advertisement seeking tenders for the operation of a facility and the licence will normally embody the advertised terms which are central to the agreement.

Leases

Whilst licences have the advantage of flexibility, leases tend to be more formal in structure and are subject to the applicability of a number of statutes. Contravention of any term of a licence can usually be remedied quickly or the licence can be terminated in the more serious cases. Any contravention of a covenant in a lease (with limited exceptions) will normally require the service of a formal notice on the lessee, who may have the right to serve a counter notice resulting in the intervention of a court, which can be a costly and lengthy process. **2.45**

The grant of a lease for premises or land, which the tenant occupies for the purpose of a business carried on by him, is subject to the provisions of Part II of the Landlord and Tenant Act 1954 as amended by the Law of Property Act 1969. This has been considered in the last Chapter.

D. Open Space

1. Introduction

The Open Spaces Act 1906 (the Act of 1906) is the statutory foundation of a group of powers and duties of local authorities. The Act of 1906 provided a badly needed code of law, which allowed open space land, as it was called, to be taken into the ownership of municipal and other councils and maintained for the benefit of the community. This class of land supplemented the parks, which were usually fenced, and remedied an unsatisfactory area of law, as well as land. **2.46**

Previously, customary rights over open areas of land were only for the benefit of limited groups, such as "the inhabitants of the village of Ambridge," and not for the use of the public at large. Again, when a donor wished to ensure that his bequest of open space land was kept by a local authority for that ongoing use, he was able, by use of the Act of 1906, to escape from the restraints of the conveyancer's obstacle race, the Perpetuities Rule[78]; for a local authority, in 1906 at least, did not perish. Finally, a benefit of the Act of 1906 was the by-law making power. This helped to control nuisances and other unsocial conduct on the public open spaces.

It is true that, in the more affluent areas, houses were often built round squares, which were laid out as gardens for the benefit of the house owners. Unfortunately, as time passed, many of these areas became neglected, as interest in their upkeep waned or its cost became prohibitive. The Town Gardens Protection Act 1863, which is still in force, enabled local authorities to take remedial action in that situation. They could vest **2.47**

---

[78] This restricts the period during which the destiny of land can be controlled by will to the sum of 21 years plus the number of years actually lived by a chosen living person.

the garden land in management committees of the local residents or, ultimately, in themselves. By-laws could then be made to regulate these areas and penalties were available as a sanction against those who caused damage.

2. **The Open Spaces Act 1906**

2.48 It was the Open Spaces Act 1906, however, which marked a major advance in dealing with an issue much wider than town squares. The Act of 1906 defined "Open Space" as

> "Any land, whether enclosed or not, on which there are not buildings or of which not more than one twentieth part is covered with buildings and the remainder of which is laid out as a garden or is used for purposes of recreation or lies waste and unoccupied."[79]

The powers in that Act are available to all local authorities,[80] including the Greater London Council and the London Boroughs and to those powers we now turn. It will be convenient to consider them in relation to the acquisition of land, and the powers of management.

(1) *Acquisition*

2.49 A group of powers enables open spaces to be transferred to local authorities by various classes of trustees:

(a) **Statutory trustees**

Trustees holding open space land under statutory[81] trusts with a view to its preservation as a garden, or some other open space, are empowered, with the consent of the occupiers of any houses fronting to the open space, or who are liable to be rated for its upkeep, to convey the land, with or without consideration, to the local authority. Alternatively, they can transfer the right of management to the authority; again, they can make an agreement with the authority to open up the land to the public; a fourth option is to grant a lease or a lesser right to the local authority; lastly, they may themselves open up the land to persons not entitled to its use under the terms of their own holding statute. If the freehold of the land, or the greater part of the houses about the space, is held by the same person, his consent must be obtained. Any purchase money is to be held by the trustees for the benefit of the persons originally intended to benefit from the use of the open space.

---

[79] s.20.
[80] The Act of 1906 does not apply to the Royal Parks, Crown land, land owned by the Duchy of Lancaster, metropolitan commons, land belonging to the Societies of the Inner and Middle Temple, gardens managed by the Secretary of State for the Environment, or lands managed under the Crown Estate Act, s.19.
[81] *Ibid.* s.2.

OPEN SPACE   **2.50**

(b) **Non-statutory trustees**

2.50   Where land is held by trustees not appointed by statute, for the purpose of public recreation, they may transfer it to the local authority or grant a lease of it to the local authority, which will then hold it subject to the same trusts, unless they should be legally varied by a scheme which has been approved by the procedure set out in the Act.[82]

(c) **Charitable trusts**

2.51   Land held by trustees other than those described above, for any charitable purpose as an open space, may be conveyed or leased to the local authority, subject to such conditions as may be agreed. The Charity Commissioners and High Court or County Court might well be involved in the approvals needed for such a transfer and the details of such authorisations are described in the Act of 1906.[83]

(d) **Open space with adjoining houses**

2.25   Where the right to use open space is limited to the owners or occupiers of houses round or near the open space, the owner of the freehold in the open space may, with the consent, expressed in special resolution of those owners and occupiers, convey or lease the land to the local authority in trust for the enjoyment of the public. Alternatively, he can make an agreement with the authority to open up the land for use by the public, under the management of the local authority. If that is done then the freeholder is discharged from his obligations to those persons originally entitled to the rights of user.[84]

(e) **Sales by groups**

2.53   Sections 7 and 8 of the Act of 1906 authorise groups of persons or individuals to sell land to local authorities, in order to enable it to be preserved as open space.

In these ways the old difficulties were overcome and wide use, enduring and effective control were achieved, so that open spaces could be provided for everyone to enjoy.

(2) *Management of Open Space*

2.54   Having acquired the open space from the trustees, or a disused burial ground from the ecclesiastical authority,[85] the local authority has a clear,

---

[82] *Ibid.* s.3.
[83] *Ibid.* s.4. The court is the High Court or County Court.
[84] *Ibid.* s.5. Two meetings are needed, with a two-thirds majority for the resolution at each one.
[85] For local authority powers to hold on trust a disused burial ground for enjoyment by the public as an open space, see the Act of 1906, s.10.

2.54   SPECIAL LEGAL PRINCIPLES

if broad, duty laid down in the Act of 1906 for keeping the land as "open space":
- (i) It is to be held in trust to allow, and with a view to, the enjoyment thereof by the public, as an open space and under proper control and regulation and for no other purpose.
- (ii) It is to be kept in a good and decent state.
- (iii) The authority may spend money on drainage, levelling the land, railings, plants, lights, ornaments, seats and improvements.[86]

By-laws

2.55   One of the principal powers given by the Act of 1906 is to allow local authorities, subject to the usual confirmation at the level of Government, to make by-laws, under section 15, to regulate the use of open spaces, ensure the maintenance of order and the prevention of nuisances, the removal of persons offending against the by-laws and finally, fixing the days and times of admission. Since these regulatory powers are similar to those normally used in relation to public parks and pleasure grounds provided under the Public Health Act 1875, it is not unusual for a common set of by-laws to be in force within a local authority's area for these two sorts of open space for the public. The same type of by-laws may also be made by the trustees or other owners of land to which the public have been given access under the earlier provisions of the Act of 1906 or under the Town Gardens Protection Act 1863.

3. Other Acts

(1) Open Space on Housing Estates

2.56   Recreation grounds are often provided by housing authorities on their larger housing estates. Power to make this provision is contained in the Housing Act 1957.[87] This is one of the "ancillary facilities" which the Secretary of State may approve in conjunction with housing projects; it may also be the subject of a direction by the Secretary of State, when considering such a project, that other statutory powers, appropriate to the facilities in question, should be used.

A specific power to make by-laws for such lands is now available, under the Local Government (Miscellaneous Provisions) Act 1976.[88]

(2) Open Space Land of Local Education Authorities

2.57   Local education authorities are required, under the Education Act 1944, to provide adequate facilities for recreation for pupils in their schools.[89]

Large areas of land have, in consequence, been acquired and laid out as

---

[86] Open Spaces Act 1906, s.10.
[87] s.93 and see *Dunton* v. *Dover District Council* (1978) 76 L.G.R. 87.
[88] s.9.
[89] s.53.

school playing fields. These lands are often heavily used by the pupils and many local education authorities have been reluctant to see sports clubs and the general public add to the wear and tear suffered by the playing fields.

The arguments for and against such dual use have been well rehearsed over the years and the outcome turns on policy, rather than law.

The legally flexible ways for the discharge of a local authority's functions, introduced by section 101 of the Local Government Act 1972, permit a variety of ways to achieve co-operation between their interested departments.[90]

Some local education authorities, in permitting (or taking no steps to prevent) the casual use of school playing fields, have found it difficult to establish a basis for regulating such use and indeed bringing it to an end, if that is desired. The employment of playing field wardens is expensive and the civil remedy of proceedings for trespass both heavy handed and ultimately ineffectual. There are problems of identifying the persons playing the games and the award of damages or even an injunction does not solve the real problem. The answer attempted in some local Acts, promoted during the consolidation of local legislation enjoined under the Local Government Act 1972, s.262,[91] has been to make it an offence to play games on school playing fields, when a notice prohibiting such use is displayed. Such notices need not be continuously displayed: they can be used in the above way from time to time and area to area, as a form of regulation dependent on the condition of the various playing fields.[92]

(3) *Open Space under the Town and Country Planning Acts*

Extensive powers of land acquisition are given to local authorities by the Town and Country Planning Acts. These were noted earlier in this Chapter. These powers include one to purchase land required as exchange land for any part of a common, open space or field garden which is being acquired. The current series of Town and Country Planning Acts gives considerable scope to local authorities to create open space land in urban areas as part of redevelopment schemes and elsewhere. Specific powers are now available to local authorities to establish country parks under the Countryside Act 1968[93] but even without going to that stage, local authorities can use their powers under these Acts to good advantage by acquiring and improving open land in their areas, clearing unsightly land, restoring derelict land and reclaiming waste or polluted land.

The final reference must be to the areas of open space which probably have the greatest popularity—the foreshore round our coasts. This particular subject is dealt with in Chapter 7.

---

[90] The four methods set out in s.101 are discharged by a committee, by a sub-committee, by an officer or by another local authority.
[91] These joint authority Local Act promotions in metropolitan areas obliged each authority to consider which powerws were of vital interest in the post-1974 regime.
[92] An instance is the Greater Manchester Act 1981, s.163.
[93] See Chapter 8.

E. Commons

1. Introduction

2.60 Local authorities are closely linked with the commons in their area. On behalf of the inhabitants, they have a right to appear at public enquiries about commons and make representations. They may contribute to the cost of improvements in the commons and, if necessary, compensate commoners in exchange for acquiring greater privileges for the townsfolk. Also, the local authority can inititiate an application for the legal regulation of a common.[94]

The creation of larger local government units by the Local Government Act 1972 brought commons from the purview of rural and county authorities into the management of district and urban councils. Furthermore, the pace engendered by the registration and thus the rationalisation of commons, under the Commons Registration Act 1965, has stimulated interest in and clarification of the legal problems associated with them. It is not surprising that volumes of collected law reports in recent years regularly include some on this subject.

It has to be admitted that the law relating to commons and the town and village greens, with which they are usually associated, is complex and it is not the purpose of this book to expound it in detail.[95] However, in order to understand the current position, it is desirable to give some historical background of the law relating to commons, their enclosure over the years and ultimately the rights now enjoyed by the public.

2. Historical

2.61 The nature and extent of the rights of villagers over common land can best be understood by reference to social history.[96] After many years in which the existence of much common land was an accepted part of the manorial system of land holding, improved agricultural methods in the seventeenth and eighteenth centuries led to an increasing speed of enclosing common land. No less than 4,000 Inclosure Acts were passed in the century before the general Inclosure Act of 1836.[97] The agricultural revolution saw many

---

[94] Commons Act 1876, s.8.
[95] Commons were originally for cropping grazing and turfing. The classic rights are pasture, turf (turbary), timber (estovers), beechmast and acorns for pigs (pannage) and fishing (piscary). Village greens, on the other hand, were for recreation. The two uses have in many areas dovetailed. Recreation as a desirable usage of commons is mentioned in the Commons Act 1876, s.7. The modern reader will think of "commons" as *areas of land* for the use of commoners and the public. In earlier days, commons were the *rights* over common land. The specialist book, *The Law Relating to Common Land* by B. Harris and G. Ryan (1967, Sweet and Maxwell) uses "common land" consistently but Parliament—the Commons Registration Act 1965—and law report editors stay with "commons" as both land and rights.
[96] G.M. Trevelyan, *English Social History* is a useful starting point.
[97] *Halsbury's Statutes* (3rd ed.), Vol. 3, p. 679.

commons converted into rectangular fields, where scientific rotation of crops could be practised.

The extinguishment of common rights was possible by agreement with the lord of the manor and those persons entitled to exercise rights of common. This was difficult because agreement had to be reached between many parties.

2.62

The lord of the manor could also exercise rights of approvement to terminate commons rights.[98] This meant taking superfluous manorial waste into his possession and use and leaving unenclosed sufficient common land for the owners of the common rights. In many cases the lord of the manor was able in this way to extinguish common rights physically, without agreement from those entitled to exercise rights of common.

However, the principal means of extinguishing common rights for a lengthy period of time was by the use of Inclosure Acts. The Acts tended to be in common form and after the Inclosure Act 1845, a code of these clauses normally used was approved and this facilitated inclosures without the need for full individual statutes. That Act of 1845 generally made all land which was the subject of rights of common, available for inclosure; but whilst that Act remains the regulatory Act on the subject of inclosures, the procedure it lays down is nowadays regarded as obsolete.[99]

2.63

The pressure on commons is further evidenced by the practice of Inclosure Commissioners, when making their awards, in diverting land from its agricultural use to that of recreation for the local inhabitants, or public purposes such as roads or schools, or individuals such as churchwardens or overseers and some land for field gardens for the labouring classes. Later in the nineteenth century, additional protection was afforded to commoners, particularly by the Inclosure Acts of 1852 and 1857. A range of offences was also created in relation to town and village greens, such as wilful damage to their fencing, driving animals onto the green or interfering with the enjoyment of people using the greens.

(a) **The metropolis**

The first effective legal move to protect commons was taken in the metropolitan police district, by the Metropolitan Commons Act 1866. As strengthened by later Acts in 1878 and 1893, the Act of 1866 effectively prevented any further inclosure of metropolitan commons. The first of those three Acts made it obligatory to obtain the consent of the Secretary of the State for the Environment (to substitute the present ministerial counterpart) before either inclosures or approvements could be lawful.[1]

2.64

---

[98] *Nicholls* v. *Mitford* [1882] 20 Ch.D. 380 illuminates this practice.
[99] G.M. Trevelyan (*supra*) identifies the decade 1865–1875 as the time when this practice was halted. He ascribes it less to protests by commoners than to agitation, eventually via the Commons Preservation Society, by town dwellers who were loathe to lose these opportunities for air and exercise.
[1] See Law of Commons Amendment Act 1893, s.2: "not valid unless . . . with the consent of the Board of Agriculture."

(b) The Commons Act 1876

2.65 The Commons Act 1876, which marked the turning point in public attitudes to commons outside London, made provision for the regulation, inclosure and improvements of commons. The Act is still in force and the Secretary of State for the Environment exercises the powers it conferred upon the Inclosure Commissioners. He is required, in considering the expediency of any application for inclosure, to take into account the question whether the inclosure would be for the benefit of the neighbourhood. He is also empowered to include in any Order under the Act requirements about free access, reservation of recreation areas, safeguarding of trees or historical objects, the provision of roads, footpaths and bridleways and indeed any other matters deemed to be of advantage to the neighbourhood. It will be evident that this marked a significant break with earlier legislation.[2]

This policy guidance is supplemented in the Act of 1876 by detailed procedural conditions to be met before a Provisional Inclosure Order reached its final stage.[3] A Provisional Order under the Act of 1876 required the approval of Parliament and had no validity until the appropriate procedure had been completed.[4]

An interesting protection afforded to town and village greens by this Act was the section which said that any erection thereon or disturbance or interference with the land, otherwise than with a view to the improvement of the town or village green or recreation ground, was to be deemed a public nuisance.[5]

(c) The Commons Act 1899

2.66 The Commons Act 1899 marked a further step towards the present position. It enables district councils to make Schemes and Provisional Orders for the regulation and management of commons in their area with a view to expenditure on the drainage, levelling and improvement of the common.[6] It also empowers those councils to make by-laws and regulations for the prevention of nuisances and preservation of order on the common.

After due public notice, deposit for inspection of the draft Scheme and consideration of objections made in a three month period, the Council may decide to make the Scheme. The need for ministerial approval was dispensed with by the Local Government, Planning and Land Act 1980.[7]

Having made the Scheme, the Council becomes responsible for the management of the common. They can make by-laws[8] and take a contri-

---

[2] Act of 1876, s.7.
[3] *Ibid.* ss.10 and 12.
[4] *Ibid.* s.12.
[5] *Ibid.* s.29.
[6] Commons Act 1899, s.1.
[7] ss.1 and 3 and Schedule 34.
[8] *Ibid.* s.10.

bution towards the costs of management from any neighbouring Council whose inhabitants benefit from the Scheme.[9]

An indication of the contents of a Scheme of Management under the Act of 1899 is illuminating.[10] It has to cover the following:

2.67

(i) Any works of drainage, fencing, treeplanting, providing seats and otherwise improving the common as a place for exercise and recreation.

(ii) Except as provided by the Scheme, the authority are forbidden to alter the natural features of the common or interfere with free access to any part thereof.

(iii) In particular the authority are prevented from erecting any buildings or similar erections on the common without the consent of the landowner.

(iv) The authority must deal with all problems associated with the prevention of trespass and the making of encroachments.

(v) A statement must be published of the rights of the local inhabitants to free access to all parts of the common and the privilege of playing games and enjoying other kinds of recreation thereon, subject to by-laws made by the Council.

(vi) Any features on the common requiring preservation.

(vii) The maintenance and construction of any paths or roads over the common.

(viii) The provision of parking places on the common and making charges for parking.

(ix) A statement about the purpose of by-laws is to be made by the Council. The by-laws would aim to prevent conduct or behaviour which interfered with the rights of enjoyment of the common by the public.

(x) Finally, the Scheme is to provide for protecting the rights of the landowner or any rights over or under the common for game, mines and minerals. The Scheme must not adversely affect the commoners' rights nor the lawful use of any highway over the common.

(d) **Definitions**

All the powers in relation to commons considered above may give the impression that it is easy to define common land. The two definitions now appended are taken from the last major Act of Parliament on this subject, the Commons Regulations Act 1965. They indicate how in this area of the law, definitions are built out of history:

2.68

"**22.**—(1) In this Act, unless the context otherwise requires,—
"common land" means—

---

[9] *Ibid.* s.12.
[10] Local authorities are required in the current Regulations (S.I. 1982 No. 209) to ensure, when laying out games areas, that they are not so near any dwelling houses or road that they will create a nuisance or be an annoyance to the inhabitants of the houses or to persons using the road.

2.68 SPECIAL LEGAL PRINCIPLES

(*a*) land subject to rights of common (as defined in this Act) whether those rights are exercisable at all times or only during limited periods;

(*b*) waste land of a manor not subject to rights of common; but does not include a town or village green or any land which forms part of a highway; [. . .]

"town or village green" means land which has been allotted by or under any Act for the exercise or recreation of the inhabitants of any locality or on which the inhabitants of any locality have a customary right to indulge in lawful sports and pastimes or on which the inhabitants of any locality have indulged in such sports and pastimes as of right for not less than twenty years."[11]

(e) The Commons Registration Act 1965

2.69 The Act of 1965 requires the registration of common land, rights of common and town and village greens in registers maintained by county councils and the Greater London Council as registration authorities.

Two separate registers are kept, one being for common land and the other for town and village greens.[12]

Periods for provisional registration of commons and greens are prescribed[13] and at the end of those periods, no land capable of being registered shall be common land or a town or village green, unless duly registered and likewise, no rights of common shall be exercised over such land unless those rights are duly registered under the Act of 1965 or, in this instance, under the Land Registration Acts.[14]

2.70 When objections to provisional registration are resolved and registrations are final, then if no person is duly registered as owner, the registration authority must refer the issue to the Commons Commissioner, unless the land is registered under the Land Registration Acts. If the owner is known or can be found, the land will be vested in him. If the land is town or village green, with an unknown owner, the appropriate local authority becomes the effective owner and can exercise powers of management under the Open Spaces Act 1906.[15] Where the land is unclaimed common land, again, local authorities are empowered to take steps to protect it.

2.71 The final registration of the land and the rights, as described above, is conclusive evidence of the matters so registered.[16] There is provision for

---

[11] s.22. A decision of the Commons Commissioner was obtained that land acquired under the Public Health Act 1975, s.164, for "pleasure grounds" was not "allotted for exercise and recreation" under s.22. "Acquiring was not apt for 'allotting'," he said, *Re The Downs, Herne Bay Kent*, Ref 219D/2 [1980] C.L.Y. 246.

[12] Act of 1965, ss.1, 2 and 3.

[13] *Ibid.* s.1.

[14] Law of Property Act 1925, s.189(2).

[15] The Act of 1965 provides for ultimate vesting in the local authority, if no owner is apparent to the Commissioner: s.8.

[16] Act of 1965, s.7. An objection to the registration of common land puts in issue its validity as a whole. When the Commons Commissioner has the issue referred to him, he should make the person who made the registration prove its validity: *Re Sutton Common, Wimborne* [1982] 1 W.L.R. 647.

due amendment of the two registers on change of circumstances.[17] Further, the High Court has a residual power to rectify the registers.[18]

2.72 The Act does not apply to the New Forest, Epping Forest or the Forest of Dean or where it is exempted by Order of the Minister.[19] This power of the Minister is circumscribed. It is not to be exercised unless the land is regulated by a Scheme under the Commons Act 1899, or by the Metropolitan Commons Acts, or by a Local Act or by an Order made under the Commons Act 1876 and, in each case, no rights of common have been exercised there for at least 30 years and the landowner is known. (The Act allows for certain interruptions in that period of prescription, as it is called, and these can be ignored, *e.g.* where the land was requisitioned or where the land could not be used by those with rights due to steps taken in connection with animal health.)[20]

3. Public Rights Over Commons

2.73 Members of the public have the right of access for air and exercise to any land which is a metropolitan common or is manorial waste[21] or a common which is wholly or partly situated in an area which, immediately before the major local government reorganisation at April 1, 1974, was a borough or an urban district. Lastly, the rights of access apply to land which on January 1, 1926, was subject to rights of common. It is a section of the Law of Property Act 1925 which confers these important rights of access and that section has to be formally applied to the last mentioned class of land by the deposit with the Minister of a deed to that effect, given by the lord of the manor or some other owner of that land over which the rights of common have been exercised.[22]

2.74 The above rights are subject to four qualifications:

1. The provisions of any Act, Scheme, Provisional Order, By-law, Regulation or Order made under statutory authority.

2. Any conditions affecting access imposed by the Minister to prevent the land being injuriously affected, particularly in relation to any object of historical interest or other rights over that land.[23]

3. The rights do not include the right to draw or drive any carriage, cart, caravan, truck or other vehicle over the common or to camp there or to light a fire.

4. Those rights terminate if (1) the common rights are extinguished under any statutory provision or (2) if any land is excluded from public access by resolution of the local authority managing it, and that resolution is duly confirmed by the Minister.

---

[17] Act of 1965, s.13.
[18] *Ibid.* s.14.
[19] *Ibid.* s.11.
[20] *Ibid.* s.16.
[21] That part of the manor subject to the tenants' rights of common.
[22] Law of Property Act 1925, s.193.
[23] *Ibid.* s.193(1)(*b*).

2.75 The existence of public rights over commons does not affect the legal rights of any persons to win and remove mines and minerals.

These Law of Property Act rights of access do not apply if commons are being held for military purposes and the rights of common have been extinguished or otherwise cannot be exercised.[24]

(a) **Building on commons**

The Law of Property Act 1925 also prohibits the erection of any building or fence whereby access to the commons is prevented or impeded, unless the consent of the Minister is obtained.[25] An exemption from this provision is granted for works carried out under the authority of an Act of Parliament or an Order having the force of an Act or in relation to the working of minerals or the placing of a telegraphic line.

(b) **Custom**

2.76 The right of the public to use town and village greens was examined by the Court of Appeal in *New Windsor Corporation* v. *Mellor*.[26] The land in that case was owned by the local authority and had been registered in the register of town and village greens under the Commons Registration Act 1965. This was done on the basis of enjoyment of customary rights to indulge in lawful sports and pastimes on the site from the middle of the seventeenth century. From time to time, the land had become neglected but groups of inhabitants, including one known as the "Bachelors of Windsor," had joined together to improve it, so that it could be enjoyed by all local inhabitants. Attempts had been made a hundred years before to inclose the land but these had been successfully resisted by the inhabitants. The last local authority before 1964 had let the land for pasture, subject to the rights of "the Bachelors of Windsor who are entitled to use the land for all lawful recreations and amusements." Many other attempts over the years to use or sell the land had shown determination by local inhabitants to retain the rights quoted above. It was when the position as thus set out was affirmed by a Commons Commissioner, after registration under the Commons Registration Act 1965, that the local authority took the opportunity to test the matter in an appeal to the Court of Appeal. The legal ground taken by the local authority was that, in the light of earlier cases, the customary right was not lawful. It was not enjoyed by the residents of a specific locality. Being either for the Bachelors of Windsor or the inhabitants at large, it did not subsist for the inhabitants of a specific locality.

In its judgment the court said that Parliament was presumed to have intended that all registered greens should be available for sports and pastimes for the local inhabitants and that all commons should be opened to

---

[24] *Ibid.* s.193(5).
[25] Law of Property Act 1925, s.194. The same restraint applies if "other work" will have the same effect.
[26] [1975] 3 All E.R. 44.

the public, subject to the rights of the commoners. The decision was to uphold the registration by the Commons Commissioner of the land as a green; the court found that the right in question had been enjoyed for 300 years.

(c) **The foreshore**

2.77 Difficulties in the definitions of commons and town and village greens, have arisen where claims have been made for the registration of parts of the foreshore as commons or greens. (Rights over the foreshore are discussed in Chapter 7.) Sometimes the right to registration has been claimed on the basis of alleged public rights to fish or to collect wood. Rights of common have then to be distinguished from public rights at common law, which do include the rights of fishing and navigating in tidal waters.[27] In short, the legal position is that where the foreshore is owned by the Crown, the Crown Estate Office dispute the possibility of its being waste of the manor. Where the foreshore has been disposed of to a local authority or private owner, the position will fall to be determined by the terms of the conveyance or lease.

4. Caravan Sites and Commons

2.78 Finally there are two modern statutory provisions relating to commons which should be noted.

The Caravan Sites and Control of Development Act 1960 contains a code for the regulation of caravan sites.[28] Under the Act, a District Council may make an Order which prohibits, either absolutely or subject to the terms of the Order, the stationing of caravans on common land for the purposes of human habitation. Contravention of the Order is punishable by fine. The making of exceptions to the Order does not in itself give a right as against the landowner to station caravans on the common.

2.79 The second and rather more important provision in recent years is in the Countryside Act 1968.[29] Certain authorities are given powers to provide or improve opportunities for the enjoyment of the countryside and in the interests of people resorting to the common land. These include facilities for meals and refreshments, parking places, shelters and public conveniences. However, accommodation and refreshments are only to be provided by the authorities to the extent that existing facilities are inadequate.

To the extent also that the local authorities require land as sites for some of these facilities, they may be authorised by the Minister to acquire land and this can include parts of the common. If the common land should thus be needed, the authority will normally be expected to give

---

[27] See *Goodman* v. *Saltash Corporation* [1882] 7 A.C. 633. For a recent case see *Baxendale* v. *Instow Parish Council* [1981] 2 W.L.R. 1055.
[28] s.23 has certain exclusions, which need to be studied.
[29] s.9.

2.79 SPECIAL LEGAL PRINCIPLES

equal land by way of exchange; the Minister again may decide that in special circumstances this is not necessary.

The exercise of these powers by local authorities is not to be prevented by reason of general restrictions applying to common land or restrictions affecting particular land or by any trusts affecting common land.

It will be recalled that the acquisition, appropriation and disposal of land subject to common rights is subject to special rules, which were considered earlier in this Chapter.[30]

---

[30] Paras. 2.32–2.45.

Chapter 3

LIBRARIES AND MUSEUMS

"Short cuts are sometimes attractive but frequently lead one into a morass"
Edmund Davies L.J. (*Pannett* v. *McGuinness and Co.* [1972]
2 Q. B. 599 at p. 608G).

INTRODUCTION

If parks and recreation grounds are the oldest form of public leisure service provided in this country, then libraries and museums must be ranked second. The first general Act was passed in 1850, though there were earlier local Acts. The Public Libraries Act 1850 was described in the preamble as being "for the Instruction and Recreation of the people," and it authorised the collection, though not the purchase, of books and maps and, in addition, specimens of art and science. This was so that both public libraries and public museums of art and science might be established.[1] The Act was adoptive in municipal boroughs having a population of more than 10,000. The money to be devoted to this new public service was not to be greater than the product of a halfpenny rate, though power to borrow monies with Treasury consent was also contained in the Act.   **3.01**

From such tentative beginnings arose the present libraries and museums services of this country. It is true that the expression "lending library" does not appear in a statute until an Act of 1887[2] but the principle of a collection of books in a library, to which public admission was obliged to be free, was established in the Act of 1850.   **3.02**

It will be convenient to consider libraries' and museums' law separately, and to turn first to libraries.

---

[1] There had first been Parliamentary authority to set up public museums in the Museums Act 1845, which was consolidated and repealed by the Libraries Act 1850.
[2] It seems that three authorities, Canterbury, Salford and Warrington, were beginning to operate libraries under the Museums Act 1845. Mr R.J.B. Morris, in his perceptive study *Parliament and the Public Libraries* (1977), p. 18, offers the view that the three authorities took advantage of ambiguities in the scope of the terms of the Museums Act 1845 to establish combined museums and libraries and so made the Act of 1845 "a Libraries Act of a sort."

3.03 LIBRARIES AND MUSEUMS

A. LIBRARIES

1. **Library Provision and Management**

(1) *The Public Libraries and Museums Act 1964*

3.03 The Public Libraries and Museums Act 1964 now contains the basic law about this subject. It can be conveniently summarised as follows:—

(1) The Chancellor of the Duchy of Lancaster is responsible for superintending and promoting the improvement of the public library service provided by local authorities in England and Wales.[3]

(2) The Library and Information Services Councils, one for England and one for Wales, act under the above Minister to advise him.[4]

(3) The whole of England and Wales is divided into library region areas. A council is established for each such area and it operates under a Scheme made by the Chancellor.[5] The primary duty of a council is to encourage co-operation between library authorities.

(4) The library service to the public is provided by library authorities who are, in England, non-metropolitan county councils, London borough councils and the City of London Common Council and metropolitan district councils.[6] In Wales it is the county and district councils who are the library authorities. These authorities operate under a duty set out in the Act of 1964, to "provide a comprehensive and efficient library service for all persons desiring to make use thereof and for that purpose to employ such officers, to provide and maintain such buildings and equipment, and such books and other materials, and to do such other things, as may be requisite."[7]

(5) This duty extends only to residents in the area of the library authority and persons undergoing full-time education in that area.[8]

3.04   (6) The general duty is then made specific in three fields:
   (i) There should be sufficient books, pictures, films, gramophone records and other materials to meet both general requirements and the special needs of adults and children.

---

[3] The Act of 1964 designated the Secretary of State for Education and Science as the responsibile minister. However the duties were transferred to the Chancellor named in the text by S.I. 1979 No. 907 as from September 1, 1979; there is a qualification in that Order (art. 3) about s.9 of the Act of 1964, relating to contributions and grants, in that those functions are to be exercised jointly. The Department of Education and Science also (art. 8) retains a specific duty in relation to the Library Advisory Council for Wales.
[4] Public Libraries and Museums Act 1964, s.2.
[5] *Ibid.* s.3.
[6] *Ibid.* s.4 and Local Government Act 1972, ss.206 and 207.
[7] *Ibid.* s.7. Now that gramophone records have become an integral part of the library service, it is no longer necessary to show the fine ingenuity of Counsel in a pre-1964 Opinion. Basing himself on the Public Libraries Act 1892, which allowed collections of "specimens of art and science," he argued "As music is both a science and an art and a gramophone record is undoubtedly a specimen of music, the Council have power under s.15(1) of the Act of 1892 to form a lending library of gramophone records"!
[8] *Ibid.* s.7 (proviso).

(ii) There should be encouragement to both adults and children to use the service fully.
(iii) The library authority should ensure full co-operation with any other authority whose functions are exercisable in the library authority area.[9]

(7) The Act then provides some useful detail about the services for which it is lawful to make a charge.[10] These are: **3.05**
   (i) When notifying the borrower that the book or any other article he has reserved is available.
   (ii) When taking action for the non-return of a book or other article.
   (iii) For borrowing any article except a book, journal, pamphlet or similar article or a reproduction thereof.
   (iv) Supplying book catalogues and indexes.
   (v) Generally, for providing a facility which "goes beyond those ordinarily provided by the authority as part of the library service."

(8) The library authority may make grants and contributions to other library authorities or other persons who provide library facilities for members of the public.[11] **3.06**

(9) The Chancellor has default powers in the event of failure of a library authority to fulfil its duties.[12]

(10) The library authority has the power to make by-laws about its services. These are subject to confirmation by the Chancellor.[13]

(11) The library authorities can be authorised by the Chancellor to purchase land for their functions by compulsory purchase procedure.[14]

(12) There is a provision setting out the duties of the local authority under this Act in relation to any duties or powers the authority may possess under a local Act. The public Act is to prevail where the two are inconsistent with each other but otherwise the local Act is to continue in force.[15]

(13) The Chancellor is placed under a duty to provide an annual report to Parliament upon the discharge of his duties under this Act.[16]

(14) A section empowers a library authority to use or allow the use of its premises for meetings, exhibitions or other events of an educational or cultural nature. This is in keeping with the trend to make libraries into attractive community buildings rather than simply quiet bookish retreats.[17]

---

[9] *Ibid.* s.7(2).
[10] *Ibid.* s.8.
[11] *Ibid.* s.9.
[12] *Ibid.* s.10. The section goes into some detail on this process.
[13] *Ibid.* s.19.
[14] *Ibid.* s.18.
[15] *Ibid.* s.23.
[16] *Ibid.* s.17.
[17] *Ibid.* See Sched. III. (Att.Gen.)

(15) The Act repeals five earlier Library Acts from 1892 onwards.[18]

The Act of 1964 is thus comprehensive and consolidating. It was necessarily amended at the time of local government reorganisation in 1974 to take account of the new library authorities. Otherwise it has withstood well the wear and tear of twenty years.

(2) *Legal Aspects of the Library Service*

3.07 (i) There are certain legal aspects of this service which are common to all who manage staff and buildings. These include the torts of nuisance and negligence, trespass and the legal defences to those issues, and also the subject of damages consequent upon breaches of the law. These have all been discussed in the first two chapters of this book. Those branches of the law deal with the situations which arise when visitors to premises suffer injury or persons enter premises without authority. Again, buildings may give rise to complaint from the occupier of a neighbouring building, perhaps because of damp from escaping rainwater or weakened foundations of a building due to the roots of a tree in the library curtilage. These are problems which lead into the general legal areas covered in Chapter I. Again, the implications of the Health and Safety at Work legislation, and those statutes which embody terms to be built into the employer-employee contracts have been discussed in the earlier chapters. In particular the engagement of staff and termination of their contracts of service is, in these days, very much a matter for expert legal advice.

3.08 (ii) The basic service of lending books and other articles is free of legal worries for the greater part of its time. But there will be persons who keep books too long and they will sometimes have to be taken to the County Court on claims to recover the property or damages in lieu. There will be other persons who damage the authority's property, both the personalty and the realty. The extreme case may call for reference to the Police for prosecution. The extensions of the service to records and pictures and perhaps video cassettes will open up different problems for the staff of the authority, particularly relating to the causes of damage to goods borrowed, but experience will enable most of these to be handled satisfactorily.

(iii) Parliament has retained the Library Offences Act 1898 for its power to deal with four troublesome areas of conduct. These are being disorderly, using violent, abusive or obscene language, gaming in the library or remaining after closing time, after proper warning. All four offences

---

[18] *Ibid.* s.20. The case of *Att.-Gen.* v. *Westminster City Council* [1924] 2 Ch. 416, illustrates the perils of treating library premises as available for any use to which the local authority choose to put them. An injunction was issued to restrain their use for office purposes. In his judgment Sargant L.J. said:

"Their powers in respect of these premises are powers under the Public Libraries Act as the library authority and not as an authority having a whole number of other powers under other Acts, relating to other properties; otherwise, illimitable confusion may be caused." (p. 425).

have as a constituent element "to the annoyance or disturbance of any person using the same." No doubt they are a weapon of last resort for the staff of our public libraries: it is nonetheless significant that the Act was not repealed when such major consolidating legislation was undertaken in 1964.

(iv) By-laws supplement the Act of 1898. They cover the conduct of persons using libraries which, whilst falling short of the four specific acts mentioned above, is nonetheless to be discouraged. Remaining on the premises for an undue time or consuming food and drink on the premises are two simple examples. **3.09**

2. Public Lending Right

After several unsuccessful Bills and a campaign lasting more than 20 years, one Bill succeeded and became the Public Lending Right Act 1979. It represented the culmination of much public debate on the grievance of authors at the loss of royalties on the copies of their books read by the public after purchase by the public libraries. The Act has been set in motion: it is unusual in several ways but it depends for its effectiveness on the co-operation of the public libraries. As an adjunct of the public library service, it is of interest to append a short outline of the basic features of the Public Lending Right scheme.[19] **3.10**

(1) *A Legal Right*

The Public Lending Right is a legal right. It can be owned by a registered author of a book available for borrowing from public libraries. It is a right to receive payments "from time to time" out of a Central Fund.[20] This right can be assigned as personalty.[21] The document of transfer bears stamp duty and must be produced to the Registrar appointed under the Act. The right can also be bequeathed or otherwise pass on death. It lasts for 50 years from the year when the author died.[22] As a legal right, it can also be renounced.[23] **3.11**

(2) *The Central Fund*

The Central Fund was created with a sum of £2 million and a current rule that the maximum annual or other periodic payment to an author for loans of his registered books is £5,000.[24] The payments are made by the **3.12**

---

[19] The skeleton scheme in the Act is filled out by S.I. 1982 No. 719, with 52 articles and 4 Scheds. The outline in the text combines the provisions of both Act and Order.
[20] s.1., Act of 1979.
[21] S.I. 1982 No. 719, article 19.
[22] *Ibid.* art. 20.
[23] *Ibid.* art. 32.
[24] *Ibid.* art. 46.

3.12 LIBRARIES AND MUSEUMS

Registrar. He operates the whole scheme set up by the Act.[25] The amount of an individual payment is proportional to the number of times the books of the author in question have been borrowed through the public libraries of this country.[26]

(3) *Registration*

Registration is effected by an author giving a Statutory Declaration to evidence his authorship.[27] "Author" for the purposes of the Act, includes an illustrator but does not include a reviser, editor, compiler or translator.[28] A book is not registrable if it had more than four authors. The current minimum size of a book for the purposes of the Act is 32 pages (unless it is drama or poetry, when special rules apply).[29]

(4) *The Library Authority's Role*

3.13 The part played by library authorities in the scheme is as follows. Sixteen authorities at any one time are designated by the Registrar as sampling points. They are selected in order to constitute a variety of library authorities.[30] The numbers of loans at those libraries are recorded and extrapolated by the Registrar in order to calculate his periodical payments. The costs incurred by the library authorities in acting as sampling points are reimbursed by the Registrar.[31]

A book can be removed from the Register by the Registrar if no sum under the scheme has been due to an author in respect thereof for ten years.[32]

There is an offence, for which a maximum fine of £1,000 is the present sanction, for making false statements in connection with an entry in the register.[33]

The Secretary of State is to report annually to Parliament on the working of the scheme.[34]

---

[25] *Ibid.* art. 49.
[26] *Ibid.* art 46. The formula to be used in calculating the periodic payment is set out in this article.
[27] *Ibid.* art. 18.
[28] *Ibid.* article 6. An interesting case on the meaning of "author" is *Springfield* v. *Thame* (1903) 8 L.T. 242. Though the idea in a book may have come from another person, the person who actually wrote the book was held to be the "author." In that case, it was a sub-editor who created an amended script and was held to be the "author" rather than the original journalist who had submitted the "story" to the newspaper. The case has implications for the "ghosted" autobiographies of sportsmen and others.
[29] *Ibid.* art. 6.
[30] *Ibid.* art. 38.
[31] *Ibid.* art. 44.
[32] The Act of 1979, s.4(5).
[33] *Ibid.* s.4(7).
[34] *Ibid.* s.3(8). The first annual report published in July 1984, states that 7,750 authors and 1 million books were registered for the scheme. The maximum payment of £5,000 was attained by 46 authors. (Cmnd. 9303, The Public Lending Right Scheme 1983/84).

3. Copyright

(1) Introduction

An action by Charles Dickens to restrain the breach of his copyright in his story "The Christmas Carol" provides a suitable introduction to this section.[35] Dickens' classic was published by Messrs. Chapman and Hall on December 19, 1843, six days before Christmas. On January 6, 1844, a fraudulent imitation of half of the book was published as "A Christmas Ghost Story—re-originated from the original, by Charles Dickens Esq. and analytically condensed expressly for this work." It was in a series called *Purley's Illuminated Library*. The story and characters were the same as in the Dickens book, except that "Fizziwig" became "Fuzziwig." It sold for 1d. instead of 5s. The case was heard before Knight-Bruce V.-C. and the argument for the defendant is of interest since it is still relevant whenever the question of plagiarism or pirating arises. Although Lee, the defendant, got his ideas and names from Charles Dickens, it was said he had bestowed "so much mental labour" on the story for the weekly library, "that it is not a colourable imitation nor a piracy" but "a fair abridgement." Using principles established in an earlier case,[36] it was argued that it had become a new work, since "a fair application of mind and talent has been made to the labours of another." The defendant said further that Charles Dickens had acquiesced in similar treatment of his earlier works in the same publication.

The judge did not find the defendant's publication "deserving the character of an original work" nor did it exhibit a "fair exercise of mental operation." Dickens won his case.

(2) *The Ames Case*

Librarians are now expected to hire out pictures, gramophone records, video cassettes as well as books. The law of copyright is thus part of the legal framework within which they work. A modern writer on library legislation says: "The problem of copyright runs like a thread throughout the whole modern history of the distribution of literature."[37] The relevance of this branch of the law is well indicated by a recent authoritative case in the High Court: *C.B.S. Inc.* v. *Ames Records and Tapes Ltd.*[38] A record lending library was established by the defendant in his shops in Burnley and Blackburn. It resembled the record lending schemes of the public libraries apart from two respects: firstly, in the *Ames* scheme, the hirer had a right to purchase the records borrowed; secondly, the proportion of "pop" records was somewhat greater than might be found in a public record library.

---

[35] *Dickens* v. *Lee* (1843) 8 The Jurist, p. 183.
[36] *Dodsley* v. *Kinnersley* 1 Amb. 403.
[37] R.J. Morris, *Parliament and Library Law*, p. 175.
[38] [1981] 2 All E.R. 812.

3.15   The case put by the plaintiffs was that the defendant had infringed the copyright held by the plaintiffs in the records, by authorising home taping of those records whilst on hire from his shops. By the Copyright Act 1956, only the owner of the copyright has the right "to make a record embodying the recording."[39] Hence during the hearing and in his judgment the judge, Whitford J., considered the evidence about the knowledge of the shopkeeper that persons hiring his records might tape-record the music from them. The shopkeeper has given evidence that his sales of records had increased, in order to counter any inference that his businesses were solely devoted to pushing the hiring of records. With regard to tape-recording, the defendant said that he could not stop it but did not encourage it. "Can it be said," asked the judge, "that Ames have 'authorised' such home taping? I cannot believe that anybody other than a lawyer would have any difficulty in saying No."

3.16   Whitford J. mentioned the various sources from which records for home taping might be acquired – including public libraries – and declined to say that the shopkeeper "authorised" home taping by running his record-lending library. (Evidence had been given that, at the time of the trial, warning notices existed in the libraries and on the record sleeves to dissuade hirers from breaching copyright in the music).

(3) The Earlier Cases

3.17   In the *Ames* case, the judge reviewed a number of cases which had raised the same question that he had to determine *i.e.* had the act which constituted an infringement of the copyright in the music been "authorised" by the defendant? The copyright "thread" can usefully be followed through a number of these cases:

(i) When an infringing performance of music was given by a band engaged by a company, then the managing director of that company, being abroad and unaware that the music in question would be performed, was not liable for a breach of copyright.[40]

(ii) The above case was considered by the Supreme Court of Victoria in *Winstone* v. *Wurlitzer Automatic Phonograph Co. of Australia Ltd.*[41] A jukebox in a coffee bar played the tune "Pony Express" composed by the plaintiff. The court held that the coffee bar proprietor had "authorised" the performance. There were no relevant circumstances to distance him in law from the simple operation of the jukebox, and the playing of the music. The defendant indeed provided the jukebox, and selected the records to be placed in it. He did everything except place the coin in the jukebox and

---

[39] Copyright Act 1956, ss.1, 12.
[40] *Performing Rights Society Ltd.* v. *Ciryl Theatrical Syndicate Ltd.* [1924] 1 K.B. 1 (C.A.). The company was liable and the band was liable but the case is important in allowing a distinction to be made about the position of the managing director. One of the defendant's letters to the plaintiff said: "I engage an orchestra who provide their own music; if they are infringing any copyright, you must look to them and not to me."
[41] [1946] V.L.R. 338.

the Court did not consider that this one element relieved the proprietor of his legal responsibility for copyright infringement.

3.18 (iii) *Moorhouse and Angus and Robertson (Publishers) Property Ltd. v. University of New South Wales*[42] an Australian case, was then examined by Whitford J. in the *Ames* case, since it was strongly urged upon him by the plaintiffs that it supported their case. It concerned not a record-player but a photocopying machine in the University. It was available for use by students. Not only the machine but also all necessary materials to photocopy their own scripts were provided by the University. The incident which gave rise to the case was the photocopying by a graduate on the machine, not of his thesis or other legitimate work, but a published book of short stories. This act infringed the copyright of the author. Had the University "authorised" the infringement? In that case, the Court said: Yes. The word "authorise" was treated as meaning "sanction, approve, countenance," as in the other cases in this series. The judge, Hutley J.A., was not prepared to exclude authorisation when the evidence indicated mere passivity by the University. On appeal, his decision was upheld. McTiernan A.C.J. said:

> " 'authorise' connoted a mental element and so, in addition to having the power to prevent the copyright infringement, it was necessary to be able to infer from the circumstances that the University knew or had reason to anticipate or suspect that the particular act is or is likely to be done."

That judge's own summing up of the principle involved is helpful:

> "A person who has under his control the means by which an infringement may be committed, – such as a photo-copying machine – and who makes it available to other persons, knowing, or having reason to suspect that it is likely to be used, for the purpose of committing an infringement and omitting to take reasonable steps to limit its use to legitimate purposes, would authorise an infringement that resulted from its use."[43]

3.19 In the *Ames* case, Whitford J. concluded that the shopkeeper had not authorised the infringement of copyright. Apart from the gloss on "authorised" established by the above cases, it would seem that the judge was influenced by the fact that the plaintiffs had sold their records to the defendant "who was then perfectly entitled to sell them, give them away, hire them or destroy them."[44] Thus the limit of legal control residing with the plaintiffs over the defendant's use of the records lay in the Copyright Act protection.

The normal lending activities of public libraries relate to goods which they own – books, records, pictures and cassettes – and the above cases

---

[42] [1975] R.P.C. 454.
[43] *Ibid.* at p. 487 (quoting Knox C.J. in the case of *Adelaide Corporation* v. *Australasia P.R. Society* 40 C.L.R. 481).
[44] *Ames* case, *supra.* no. 38 at p. 830.

3.19   Libraries and Museums

show that, provided the library stays short of authorising a breach of copyright when engaging in that lending activity, its activities are not at risk of legal challenge.

(4) *Libraries: The Legal Copying Categories*

3.20   We turn now to some important provisions in the Copyright Act 1956, which prescribe classes of copying of documents which are within the law for library authorities, provided that the relevant conditions are honoured.

(a) **Periodicals**

The librarian of a library falling within the Regulations made under the Act of 1956, is entitled to supply a copy of a periodical publication, subject to the following conditions:
  (i) The library is not one run for profit.
  (ii) The copies are supplied for the purposes of private study or research and a declaration to that effect is completed by the person taking the copy.[45]
  (iii) Only one copy is supplied.
  (iv) The copy should not extend to more than one article in the publication.
  (v) Payment in respect of the cost is made for the copy supplied.[46]

(b) **Parts of published works**

3.21   A librarian of the class of library mentioned in (a) above may supply a copy of part of a published literary, dramatic or musical work. This sanction, in section 7 of the Act of 1956, does not apply, however, when the librarian knows the name and address of the copyright holder or he could, by reasonable enquiry, ascertain those particulars.[47] Furthermore the part copied must not amount to "more than a reasonable proportion" of the work in question.[48]

The three safeguards in (i), (ii) and (v) in (a) above must be met.

(c) **Complete works for other libraries**

3.22   A copy of a literary, musical or dramatic work may be supplied to the librarian of another library if it is in the classes covered by the above Regulations. When he makes such a copy, and the document copied is a periodical publication, the librarian is released from the obligation about ascertaining the copyright owner set out in (b) above.[49]

---

[45] The form of Declaration is contained in the Copyright (Libraries) Regulations 1957 (S.I. 1957 No. 868).
[46] Act of 1956, s.7. School and university libraries, as well as public libraries enjoy these exemptions.
[47] *Ibid.* and S.I. 1957 No. 868.
[48] *Ibid.*, regulation 4(c).
[49] Act of 1956, s.7(5).

(d) Typographical Arrangements

3.23 This class comprises the typographical arrangement of a published edition of a literary, dramatic or musical work in the United Kingdom. In this case also, the librarian is excused from conferring with a known copyright owner.[50]

(e) Publication of original work

3.24 The fifth and final exception in favour of librarians making copies is interesting and exceptional. Libraries and archive authorities often act as the repository of literary, dramatic or musical works which have not been published. Conditions attached to the transfer into the custody of the library may touch on the question of publication. Subject to that point and the manuscript being one open to public inspection, it may be desired to publish some of the works. The Act of 1956 deals with this situation. Though the finer details are not reproduced here, the basic procedure cannot begin until 50 years have elapsed from the death of the author. In addition 100 years must have elapsed since the work came into existence. Due notice of intention to publish has then to be given on two occasions in newspapers with national circulations, so that copyright owners, if existing, have an opportunity to come forward.[51]

3.25 The Act contemplates the situation that such an original manuscript might be published as part of a larger work which contains new commentary or other material explanatory of the old work. It also encourages the broadcasting, public performance or recording of the new publication, as the case may be, by exempting all three from the infringement sanctions in the Act.

(5) *The Framework of the Copyright Act 1956*

3.26 The law of copyright is here outlined only to the extent that those seeking to work with or within the public leisure services will need to understand its extent and structure.[52] The framework of the Act of 1956 itself gives a useful perspective within which to set the important provisions contained in the previous sub-sections of this chapter.[53]

---

[50] Act of 1956, s.15(4).
[51] S.I. 1957 No. 868.
[52] A practitioner's text book of over 2,000 pages such as *Copinger and Skone James on Copyright* (12th ed., 1980, Sweet and Maxwell) is an indication of the depth and range of the full subject.
[53] The Copyright Act 1956 was a consolidating Act, repealing 4 earlier Acts completely and the major consolidating Act of 1911 for all except 4 sections. The Act of 1956 has stood the test of nearly 30 years' use. However, with new technology now greatly facilitating the reproduction of copyright material, the Act has recently came under criticism for ineffectiveness. The only statutory amendments in that time have been the Copyright (Amendment) Act 1982, to amend s.40 *re* broadcasts, and an Act, similarly titled in 1983, to increase fines for pirating sound recordings and films and giving greater powers of seizure of infringing material.

3.26

The definition

"Copyright is the most natural of all titles, because it is a tenure by creation." Thus speaks Benjamin Disraeli, no mean author himself, seeking to elucidate the nature of copyright.[54] The definition in the Copyright Act 1956 is less colourful. Copyright, it states in section 1, "means, in relation to a work, the exclusive right, by virtue and subject to the provisions of this Act, to do and to authorise other persons to do, certain acts in relation to that work" in the United Kingdom, or other countries.

3.27 The strangely colourless nature of the definition is paradoxically due to the rich variety of works in which the right exists. These are, quite simply, all literary, dramatic, artistic and musical works. In addition, sound recordings, cinematograph films, TV and sound broadcasts all give rise to copyright. In essence, the object of copyright law is to protect the writer, composer and artist against the unlawful reproduction of his material.[55] The purpose of the above statutory definition is to allow its adaptation to all the above areas of artistic creation. The Act indeed provides some elaboration of each of those seven areas but the section 1 definition is the starting point.

The statutory prohibitions

In relation to a literary dramatic or musical work, the acts restricted by the existence of copyright are reproducing the work in a material form, publishing it, performing it in public, broadcasting it, transmitting it via a diffusion radio or TV service or doing any of the above to an adaptation of it. The final prohibition is against making an adaptation of the work.[56] An artistic work, defined in section 3, includes paintings, sculptures, engravings, photographs, works of architecture, (both buildings and models) and works of artistic craftsmanship not falling within the above.

The four infringing acts in relation to artistic work are (1) reproducing it in a material form; (2) publishing it; (3) including it in a TV broadcast, and (4) causing the TV broadcast which includes the work to be transmitted to subscribers to a diffusion service.

3.28 The Act then explains the significance of copyright in particular types of artistic work, lays down rules for ascertaining the ownership of copyright in artistic dramatic and musical works,[57] and provides special rules for works published anonymously, pseudonymously or by joint authors.[58]

The dealings in artistic dramatic and musical works, by way of import

---

[54] See R.F. Whale, (1969) Comment on Copyright, published by the British Copyright Council. Because the word "copyright" is so impersonal, the above author takes the view that "author's property right" would have been better.

[55] In the case of *George Hensher Ltd.* v. *Restawhile Upholstery (Lancs) Ltd.* [1976] A.C. 64 at p. 98, there is approval for this definition, found in Copinger and Skone James (n. 52 *supra*), at p. 3.

[56] Act of 1956, s.2.

[57] *Ibid.* s.4.

[58] *Ibid.* s.11 and Scheds. 2 and 3.

LIBRARIES 3.28

from abroad[59] or by way of sale in this country, are the subject of provisions which describe the points at which copyright is infringed.

Permitted Acts

The Act then sets out the special circumstances in which copyright in records of musical works is not infringed.[60] Similarly it sets out the circumstances in which the copyright in literary, dramatic and musical works is not breached. These are important and are (1) reproduction for the purposes of judicial proceedings,[61] (2) fair dealing in those works for the purposes of private study or research, criticism or review, or (3) for reporting current events.[62] (The reading in public of a literary or dramatic work or the inclusion of a short passage of the same in a book for schools, can be exempt if the proper steps and safeguards are fulfilled). 3.29

The use of a dramatic literary or musical work for the purposes of a broadcast is subject to special provisions.[63]

Fair dealing

"Fair dealing" is again protected and this expression is clearly important; it emphasises in this field how important are the judicial interpretations that have gathered about some of the other key expressions above.[64] 3.30

The copyright provisions in relation to cinematograph films, sound recordings, TV and sound broadcasts must be studied in detail by those particularly involved in those areas.[65]

Litigation

Part III of the Act contains the legal rights of copyright owners in protecting their copyright and also the defences that can be raised to their claims: 3.31

Damages, an injunction and the taking of accounts are three of the remedies that can be secured by a justifiably aggrieved copyright owner.

The flagrancy of the infringement can lead to increased damages.[66]

Proof by a defendant, on the other hand, of his ignorance that he was

---

[59] *Ibid.* s.5.
[60] *Ibid.* s.8 and see *Discount Inter-Shopping Co. Ltd.* v. *Micrometer Ltd.* [1984] 2 W.L.R. 919 for s.8 in a practical situation.
[61] *Ibid.* s.6.
[62] *Ibid.* s.6.
[63] *Ibid.* s.6.
[64] *Ibid.* ss.6 and 9. Two recent interesting cases in which interpretation of "fair dealing" was involved are *Hubbard* v. *Vosper* [1972] 2 Q.B. 84 and *Beloff* v. *Pressdram Ltd.* [1973] F.S.R. 33.
[65] See Part II of the Act of 1956.
[66] Act of 1956, s.17.

breaching a copyright can limit an otherwise successful plaintiff to an account for profits rather than damages.[67]

Building plans

A special case is where the copyright relates to the construction of a building. Here no order is to be made, in relation only to the copyright breach, that would stop a building being completed or have it demolished if it has been completed.[68]

A copyright owner is entitled to the same rights in an infringing copy of his work, or in a plate for use with such copies, as if he were the actual owner of those articles. This is to enable him to remedy any conversion or detention of those articles by the person infringing his copyright. These rights are subject to the Limitation Acts.[69]

The relation between the copyright owner and the holder of an exclusive licence from him are regulated by section 19 of the Act. The distinction between such a licence and an assignment is important and has been evolved in case law.[70]

Legal action

3.32 The Act makes provision for the onus of establishing copyright in legal actions[71]; lays down penalties for various offences, in each of which knowledge of the copyright infringement in question is an important ingredient[72]; and prescribes steps available to a copyright owner in literary, dramatic or musical works, to secure the prohibition, by the Commissioners of Customs and Excise, of printed copies of his work, being copies which, if printed in the United Kingdom, would be infringing copies.[73]

Performing Rights Tribunal

3.33 The Performing Rights Tribunal and its jurisdiction are described in Part IV of the Act.[74] This Tribunal is available to determine three kinds of disputes:
    (i) Those relating to the right to perform in public or to broadcast a literary, dramatic or musical work or an adaptation from it.
    (ii) Those relating to a right to cause a sound recording to be heard in public or to be broadcast.

---

[67] *Ibid.* s.17(2).
[68] *Ibid.* s.17(4).
[69] *Ibid.* s.18.
[70] *Ibid.* s.19. The subtleties are discussed in *Halsbury's Laws of England* (4th ed.), Vol. 9, paras. 879–881.
[71] Act of 1956, s.20.
[72] *Ibid.* s.21.
[73] *Ibid.* s.22.
[74] *Ibid.* s.23.

(iii) Those about the right to cause a TV broadcast to be seen or heard in public.[75]

The Tribunal, constituted of a legal Chairman and two to four others,[76] is to determine disputes between licensing bodies and persons seeking licences, and organisations representing such persons.[77] For the finer points about the Tribunal, the licence schemes upon which it can adjudicate, the effects of its Orders, and its handling of licences for TV broadcasts, specific sound recordings and the diffusion of foreign broadcasts, the interested reader must be referred to the text of the Act.[78]

Finally the Act of 1956 has several miscellaneous points to which attention is drawn:
(1) Copyright can be transmitted by assignment, by will or otherwise as personal property.[79]
(2) The BBC and ITV possess copyright in TV and sound broadcasts but can deal with the performing rights in those broadcasts only strictly in accordance with a procedure laid down in the Act.[80]
(3) A saving provision protects the use of copyright material in schools. Such use, including the performance of literary dramatic or musical work "if in the course of the activities of school," is not to be deemed to be in public.[81]
(4) The normal term for copyright extends from the date of publication until 50 years after the author's death.[82] There are some fine modifications to this general provision, relating to photography, sound recordings, cinematograph films, broadcasts and others for which the Act should be consulted.

(6) *EEC and Foreign Aspects*

Copyright is a branch of British law in which the law of the European Economic Community is integrated.[83] It is therefore necessary to take account of any decisions of the European Court of Justice in this field, in so far as they have a bearing upon the practice of those engaged with the law of the public leisure services. EEC law is a specialist area, as is the other international aspect, *i.e.* the impact of the Berne and other Conventions upon the operation of the British copyright law.[84]

---

[75] *Ibid.* s.24.
[76] *Ibid.* s.23.
[77] *Ibid.* s.24.
[78] Part IV of the Act or, of course, a specialised text book as mentioned in n. 52, *supra*.
[79] Act of 1956, s.36.
[80] *Ibid.* s.37 and Sched. 5. At present these are dealt with in the two separate organisations.
[81] *Ibid.* s.41. But contraventions of this permission for, *e.g.* school orchestra scores, have led to enforcement of their legal rights by the Music Publishers Association.
[82] See, *e.g.* in the Act of 1956, s.3(4) and s.2(3), *re* literary dramatic, musical and artistic works.
[83] European Communities Act 1972, s.2(1).
[84] See, *e.g. Halisbury's Laws of England* (4th ed.), Vol. 9, § 6. It is necessary for Acts of Parliament to embody the provisions in terms which can then be applied by the courts of this country. As an instance, the Copyright Act 1956 itself followed an international convention at Brussels.

3.35   LIBRARIES AND MUSEUMS

One instance only is given of a copyright case dealt with under EEC law, as a pointer to a developing situation.[85]

(a) **Treaty of Rome**

The law of copyright makes its appearance in the foundation document of the EEC, the Treaty of Rome, where it refers to "the protection of industrial property," in Article 36. This is part of a complex section of the Treaty which places qualifications upon the broad declaration of Article 30:

> "Quantitative restrictions on imports and all measures having equivalent effect shall, without prejudice to the following provisions, be prohibited between the member states."

(b) **The Gema case**

3.36   The case in question raised the interpretation of these Articles in connection with the import of gramophone records to Germany. It was the German *Gema*[86] case of 1981 where 100,000 records had been placed in free circulation in the United Kingdom, and the Performing Rights Society or its equivalent had collected royalties when that took place. The records had been manufactured in the United Kingdom and the rate of royalty was based upon that fact. The records were then imported into Germany and that circumstance led *Gema* – the German counterpart of the Performing Rights Society in this country – to claim an additional royalty. In so far as this could be regarded as a financial restriction within Article 30, it led to *Gema* going before the EEC Court of Justice. The German national court, which first heard the case, had raised the point, whether such an exercise of copyright, being lawful under German domestic law, was compatible with the requirements of the EEC Treaty on the free movement of goods.

In the event, the claim of *Gema* was not upheld by the Court of Justice. That court held that copyright raised the same question as any other industrial or commercial property right. The case law of the EEC Court showed that the holder of such a right, which was protected by the law of a member state, might not rely on that law to prevent the marketing of a product on the market of another member state, when that marketing results from a lawful distribution of the product. The product here was the gramophone record and the final conclusion of the European Court of Justice was that this lawful distribution was either by the proprietor of the right or, alternatively, with his consent. *Gema* argued that its claim was not a restriction on marketing but only the collection of the balance of licences paid for all such distribution on the German market. This case is

---

[85] But see also a U.K. case where the court allowed defences to be added, based on Articles 85 and 86 in the EEC Treaty, concerning undue restriction of competition and abuse of dominant position. (*Application des Gaz S.A.* v. *Falks Veritas Ltd.* [1974] Ch. 381).
[86] *Musik-Vertrieb GmbH and K Tel International* v. *GEMA* [1981] E.C.R. 147.

mentioned as a cameo of EEC legal complications for British leisure service staff involved in *e.g.* gramophone record commercial dealings with the Continent.[87]

4. Performers Protection Acts 1958–1972

The three Acts collectively known as the Performers Protection Acts 1958–1972 are an important adjunct of copyright law.[88] They are designed to protect performers from having records made of their performances and distributed commercially, without their consent. Thus a literary, dramatic, or artistic performance, whilst not itself having the benefit of copyright, is given a degree of protection against others benefitting commercially from it, without payment or other consent from the performers. An outline of these provisions is set out below[89]: **3.37**

(1) There are three offences, namely, making the record, selling or distributing the record commercially and, thirdly, using the record for a public performance.

(2) In relation to the first of the above offences, it is a defence to prove that the record was made only for private or domestic use.

(3) A similar set of three offences is then applied to the making of a cinematograph film of a musical or dramatic work, without consent. For these the defence of non-commercial use, as in (2) above, is available.[90]

(4) To complete the net, an offence is created for broadcasting either a film without the consent in writing of the performers, or for broadcasting a performance by any actors, singers, dancers or other persons, who "act, sing, deliver, declaim, play in or otherwise perform" literary, dramatic, musical or artistic works, without that like consent in writing of the performers.[91]

(5) To be in possession of a printer's plate to make records in contravention of the Act is another offence.[92]

(6) A court dealing with one of these offences, is empowered to order

---

[87] The EEC Court is developing the Continental concept in copyright of distinguishing between the existence or substance of the right and the exercise of the right. This has been described in a leading case in that court by saying that Article 36 permits restrictions on freedom of trade only to the extent that they are justified "for the protection of the rights that form the specific object of that property." Clearly this concept has to be developed further in U.K. terms. (*Deutsche Gramophone Case* 78/70 *Grammophon GmbH* v. *Metro etc.* [1971] E.C.R. 487).

[88] The three Acts are the Dramatic and Musical Performers Protection Act 1958, the Performers Protection Act 1963 and the Performers Protection Act 1972.

[89] Act of 1958, s.1.

[90] *Ibid.* s.2.

[91] *Ibid.* s.3, as amended by the Act of 1963 s.1. By s.3 of the Act of 1963, the transmission of that broadcast via a diffusion service, or otherwise to be seen or heard in public, is an offence.

[92] *Ibid.* s.4.

3.37   Libraries and Museums

        the destruction of files or records made in contravention of the Acts of 1958–1972.[93]

(7) There are two special defences. These are for:
   (a) Making the recording or film only to report current events.
   (b) Satisfying a court that the recording or film in question was only incidental or by way of background to the principal matters dealt with in the record, film or broadcast.[94]

(8) The consent of the agent of a performer is to be as effective for the purposes of the Act as the consent of the performer, provided that the consent is genuine.[95] A recent case has underlined the difference that might arise between the nature of the consent needed merely to tape a performance and that required to make and sell commercial records based upon that tape.[96]

(9) The punishments for offences under these Acts are now maximum fines of £20 for each record and up to £400 maximum fine for offences in (3) above, from £50 to the same maximum of £400 for the various offences in (4) above, and also the plate offence in (5) and the final two offences described in sections 3 and 6 of the Act of 1958.

5. Archives

3.38   The archives of a locality have been recognised as a suitable accompaniment to the collection of books to be found in public libraries, since Parliament began to interest itself in the matter in the mid-nineteenth century. Plans, muniments, documents of all sorts, collections of family and estate papers, newspapers – all were part of the public heritage which some members of the community in each generation would wish to study. The public library has come to be regarded as a natural centre for the storing and inspection of this specialised collection.[97]

Legally, a period of concurrent powers for county and district councils in the metropolitan counties followed local government reorganisation.[98] The demise of those counties will leave the metropolitan district councils

---

[93] *Ibid.* s.5.
[94] *Ibid.* s.6.
[95] *Ibid.* s.7. If the agent was not so authorised to give consent, then he himself is guilty of an offence. See s.4 of the Act of 1963.
[96] See *Apple Corps Ltd.* v. *Lingasong Ltd.* [1977] F.S.R. 345, a colourful and instructive case. The circumstances in which a court might grant injunctions in respect of "bootlegging" of recordings of live broadcasts are discussed in *Copinger and Skone James on Copyright* (12th ed., 1980, Sweet and Maxwell), para. 692.
[97] The Local Government (Records) Act 1962 deals specifically with the subject of archives. It describes them, identifies the various tasks needed to keep them available for study and exhibition to the public, and empowers local authorities to accept and store them (ss.1, 2).
[98] Whilst the Act gave this last power to counties and London boroughs, it was available only to such county districts as are approved by the Secretary of State for the Environment. (Local Government Act 1972, ss.206–208).

as archive authorities. Elsewhere, the service goes with the library service.[99]

6. Art Galleries

(1) *Provision*

Local authorities are empowered by the Public Libraries and Museums Act 1964 to provide art galleries.[1] These are an important feature of any public leisure service and have featured in legislation since 1845.[2]

By agreement of the Secretary of State, a local authority may transfer an art gallery and its collections to another local authority.[3]

(2) *Finance*

A charge for admission may be made by the managing local authority, on condition that, before imposing such a charge, the authority has taken into account the position of its school children and students and also the need for itself, as the local authority, to take its full part in the promotion of education in the area.[4]

Local authorities maintaining art galleries may make financial contributions to persons who are maintaining art galleries in England and Wales or who are providing an advisory service, or some other service, for the benefit of an art gallery. Thus public money could provide support for a private art gallery.

There is a further financial power for library authorities. This is to establish an Art Fund. With the Secretary of State's consent, such a Fund may be amalgamated with an existing Local Act fund.[5]

(3) *Art Gallery Liaison*

Since art collections are frequently on loan from gallery to gallery, with a view to exhibition, co-operation between local authorities and also with the national galleries is an essential feature of this public leisure service.[6]

---

[99] A repository provided by a local authority under the above Act of 1962 may be designated as a diocesan record office, by virtue of the Parochial Registers and Records Measure 1978, s.7(4).

[1] In England the authorities are shire counties, metropolitan districts, London Boroughs and the Common Council and in Wales, county and district councils and joint boards, if constituted. See Act of 1964 ss.4, 25, and the Local Government Act 1972.

[2] Whipping thrice and hard labour were deemed to be suitable penalties for persons damaging pictures or other works of art, whether the damage were done out of malice or not. (Protection of Works of Art, etc., Act, 8 & 9 Vict. c. 44).

[3] Act of 1964, s.12.

[4] Act of 1964, s.13. Under the Sunday Entertainment Act 1932, s.4, there is exemption from Sunday closing requirements for art galleries.

[5] The second Schedule to the Act of 1964 sets out the procedures for managing such a fund.

[6] Handling collections involves the law of bailment, on which see Museums, below, para. 3.44 *et seq.*

(a) The National Gallery and National Portrait Gallery

3.40 This is the gallery which initially receives pictures or other works of art which have been given or bequeathed to the nation for public benefit and in the absence of any direction to the contrary by the donor. The management is in the hands of a director, working with ten trustees. The trustees have a power of selection in the case of bequests: they select only those deemed fit for a national collection; the rest fall back into the residuary estate of a testator.[8] The Secretary of State can direct that a picture or work of art which would otherwise have gone to the National Gallery trustees, shall go the the Tate Gallery trustees or some other specified institution.[9] The Act of 1956 directs regular consultation between the trustees of the National Gallery and the Tate Gallery, in order to facilitate decisions on the making of loans or transfers. It was the National Gallery and Tate Gallery Act 1954 which had given independent legal status to the Tate Gallery and that Act contained three important guiding principles[10]:

(i) To maintain at the National Gallery a collection of pictures of established merit or significance.

(ii) To maintain at the Tate a collection of British pictures and a collection of modern pictures.[11]

(iii) To ensure that each picture is in that collection where it will be available and on view in the best context.

Before agreeing to let a picture go on loan from the National Gallery, the trustees are to satisfy themselves that it is proper to expose the picture to the incidents of the journey and also that it will not be exposed to special risks.

A picture appearing to have been painted by a foreign artist before 1700 cannot be loaned for exhibition outside the United Kingdom, without Parliamentary procedure. There is also a fifteen year period[12] to run before a recent bequest can be loaned at all, save with the consent of the owner's representatives.[13] In this situation, if the proposed transfer out-

---

[7] The general rule in this book is to deal with features of the London situation in the London section, below, paras. 5–19 *et seq.*

[8] See the National Gallery Act 1856 and the National Gallery and Tate Gallery Act 1954, Sched. 2.

[9] See the Transfer of Functions (Cultural Institutions) Order 1965 (S.I. 1965 No. 603), art. 2(1). Thirteen major museums are listed in the Schedule to the Act of 1954. These include the National Portrait Gallery and the National Gallery of Scotland.

[10] Act of 1954, s.2.

[11] Act of 1954, s.4(5). Speaking on the second reading debate (October 29, 1954) Mr. Henry Brooke said it was designed to "start the Tate Gallery on a new life, give it new status and new strength."

[12] Act of 1954, s.4.

[13] *Ibid.*

side the country involves some departure from conditions laid down by the donor, then the above 15 year period becomes a qualifying period of 25 years. Again, the owner's representatives can give consent, as above.[14]

Finally, the Act of 1954 requires the trustees to give students and others engaged in research reasonable opportunities to view pictures and works of art, whilst on public display.

(b) **The Tate Gallery**

This gallery dovetails with the National Gallery in a number of ways, as indicated above. Now established with its own trustees and director, the Tate is maintained as a gallery for modern foreign art and British paintings, as well as modern sculpture.

The powers available to its trustees for loans are subject to similar constraints as those laid upon the National Gallery, in relation to physical hazards to the pictures, the justification for releasing them on loan, meeting the claims of students and researchers, and other matters. The proportion of the number of their pictures and works of art which the trustees can lend for display is one tenth of the total in their charge.[15]

(c) **Sir John Soame's Museum**

By way of contrast with the restrictions on the movement of art treasures described above is the permission granted by statute for the famous Hogarth and other pictures kept at Sir John Soame's museum in Lincoln's Inn Fields, London, to be moved for display near Hampstead Heath, at Kenwood, the former estate and mansion of Lord Iveagh, and which is now maintained as a period home for public viewing by the Greater London Council.[16]

(4) *Works of Art—Customs, Excise and Tax*

The legal provisions to which attention is drawn, are those associated with the potential high value of certain works of art. The current legal framework is found in the Customs and Excise and Finance Acts, as follows:

(a) **Import and export control**

Under the Import Export and Customs Powers (Defence) Act 1939 s.1, the Board of Trade was authorised to make orders to prohibit or regulate the importation into or exportation from the United Kingdom of "all goods or goods of any specified description."

Since 1945, a series of Export of Goods (Control) Orders has been used by the Government to maintain control over (*inter alia*) the export of works of art. The current Order is S.I. 1981 No. 1641.

---

[14] *Ibid.*
[15] Act of 1954, s.5.
[16] London County Council (General Powers) Act 1952, s.20(3).

3.42   Libraries and Museums

The actual legal control is:
  (i) Goods[17] as scheduled are prohibited to be exported to any destination, unless a licence has been given by the Secretary of State (article 2).
  (ii) There are severe penalties for fraud or any other contravention of this procedure (article 5).[18]

EEC Regulations also relate to this subject. They permit collectors pieces, and works of art not intended for resale, to be imported without payment of duties under Commission Customs Tariff. Galleries, museums and other institutions seeking this relief have to obtain approval as institutions from the Department of Trade and Industry, after which relief from the duty is granted by H.M. Customs and Excise.[19]

(b) **Gifts**

3.43 Library and museum authorities are sometimes offered gifts or bequests of works of art. In certain circumstances, donors can obtain tax exemptions.[20] In the Finance Acts, the relevant category of "goods" is "works of national, scientific, historic or artistic interest."

Under the Capital Gains Tax Act 1979, a gift can be made of a work of art, as above, if the Treasury direct that it falls into the above category. The consequence is that a gain accruing on the disposal is not a chargeable gain on which the donor would pay Capital Gains Tax. As a matter of practice, the Treasury will expect an undertaking from the recipient that the item will remain in the United Kingdom.

The same approach is made by the Treasury in the case of a bequest.

B. Museums

INTRODUCTION

3.44 The modern museums service demonstrates the immense expansion in the

---

[17] Whilst earlier Orders said "works of art," a recent assimilation of the Schedule of "goods" to EEC categories led the 1970 Order (S.I. 1970 No. 1288) to use the expression "Articles not elsewhere specified, manufactured or produced more than 100 years before the date of exportation, including works of art but not including postage stamps of philatelic interest and similar articles." The 1981 Order goes a stage further in elliptical reference to Old Masters. Its wording is "Any goods manufactured or produced more than 50 years before the date of exportation" (with certain exceptions not relevant to the subject), Pt. 1, Sched. 1, Group B. Thus the expression "works of art" is no longer in the Order, though the control described above continues in force. The Department Notice No. 361 of 1980 gives detailed procedural guidance.

[18] Additionally, since October 4, 1982, all works of art exported from Argentina and imported into the U.K., directly or indirectly, require a Department of Trade and Industry licence, unless the goods are bona fide personal effects not for re-sale.

[19] Such goods may only be lent, hired out or transferred to other institutions if those are themselves approved institutions and prior permission for the loan has been obtained from the D.T.I.

[20] The current statutes are the Finance Act 1965, s.31., Finance Act 1975, Sched. 6, 13, and the Capital Gains Tax Act 1979, s.147. V.A.T. is dealt with currently in H.M. Customs & Excise Notice No. 712 (Feb. 1973 plus amendments).

concept of the museum, since that first tentative Public Libraries Act of 1850. Wrecks and folk museums, metal detectors and treasure trove, natural history and regimental museums, as well as national monuments and memorials, are all within its accepted range. Art galleries move a little arbitrarily from museums to libraries as one moves from town to town; on this occasion we have dealt with them in the Libraries section.

1. The Legal Framework for the Public Museum Service

(1) *The Local Authority Service*

The museums service provided by local authorities in this country works within a legal framework contained in the Public Libraries and Museums Act 1964 (the Act of 1964). There is no national directive on policy or provision, as with the library service. Instead, the Act of 1964 simply enjoins a local authority "to provide and maintain museums . . . within its administrative area or elsewhere, in England and Wales . . . and to do all such things as may be necessary or expedient in connection with the maintenance or provision thereof."[21] **3.45**

Local authorities, in England, for the purposes of the museums service, means London Boroughs and the Greater London Council, the Common Council, county councils, district councils and the Council of the Isles of Scilly. In Wales, the relevant local authorities are the county and district councils.[22]

(2) *Finance*

Charges may be made for admission to a museum.[23] At one time, it was the practice to obtain local Act powers in order to charge for such admissions. In those days, it was thought that charges should be made only for special museums and not, generally, for all municipal museums.[24] Even now, though the general power of charging is available, it is discretionary. A local authority is required, nonetheless, before using those powers, to consider how far it can be said that the museum in question plays its full part in the promotion of education for the people in the area. The local authority is, secondly, to have particular regard to the interests of children and students when determining to impose museum entrance charges.[25] Education is one aspect of museum provision; the above section in the Act of 1964 does not rule out consideration of leisure service aspects of the service when charging is under review. **3.46**

The local authority is empowered to make contributions to the expenses

---

[21] Act of 1964, s.12.
[22] Local Government Act 1972, s.206.
[23] Act of 1964, s.13.
[24] See, *e.g.* Halifax Corporation Act 1959, s.24, where only Shibden Hall Folk Museum was deemed suitable for such a step.
[25] Act of 1964, s.13(2).

3.46   Libraries and Museums

of "some other person" in providing a museum.[26] Those expenses can include the cost of advisory and financial help in running that museum.

(3) Specimens fund

A fund can be set up to purchase objects to exhibit in the museum. Guidelines, additional to those in the Act, will normally be laid down by a council for such a fund.[27]

(4) By-Laws

3.47 By-laws can be made about the use of the facilities provided in museums. The Secretary of State has to confirm these.[28] The conduct of visitors and maintenance of good order in the premises will normally feature in such by-laws, together with the avoidance of nuisances in and around the premises.[29]

(5) Community Activities

A local authority can permit its museums to be used for community events, of a cultural or educational nature.[30] If a museum shop is provided, the Trades Description Acts, discussed in chapter I, are relevant.

(6) External Grants

3.48 Many public museums will qualify to be considered as recipients of grants or loans from the National Heritage Memorial Fund.[31] Within the context of an Act passed to preserve property of importance to the national heritage, the trustees of the fund thereby created are authorised to make grants or loans to "eligible recipients." These advances will be to secure the preservation of collections or groups of objects which "taken as a whole, are of outstanding historic, artistic or scientific interest."

A museum entering into an arrangement with the National Heritage Memorial Fund trustees will need to be ready to discuss:
    (i) Conditions about public access to, or display of, the property in question.
    (ii) Its repair, maintenance, safekeeping and insurance.
    (iii) Its lending or disposal.

---

[26] Act of 1964, s.14.
[27] Act of 1964, s.15, Sched. 2, which governs the financial arrangements.
[28] Act of 1964, s.19. The full discussion in this work is in Chap. 4.
[29] The Act of 1964 authorises by-laws. These can deal with all aspects of behaviour by the public on museums premises, *e.g.* creating a disturbance, holding an unauthorised meeting, eating and drinking, creating a nuisance by deposits of foul matter, or stink bombs or fireworks. The police can assist in enforcing the by-laws, if the museums staff cannot deal with breaches on their own.
[30] Act of 1964, s.20.
[31] See National Heritage Act 1983, s.3.

(iv) The conditions governing repayment of the grant or loan if the conditions are broken.[32]

(7) *Other Public Museums*

There are, in addition to local authority municipal museums, many individual museums available to the public. These are frequently specialised in character, varying from industrial museums or those devoted to the possessions and property of a famous person or family, to the arts and crafts museums and folk museums which have been created in recent years. Many of the national museums have some enabling Act of Parliament in their history and it must suffice here to list the main national museums and indicate those Acts, to assist those who wish to study the subject in greater detail.

3.49

	Museums	*Enabling Act*
1.	British Museum	British Museum Act 1963
2.	British Museum Natural History Museum	British Museum Act 1963
3.	Museum of London	Museum of London Act 1965
4.	Guildhall Museum	Museum of London Act 1965
5.	National Maritime Museum	National Maritime Museum Act 1934
6.	The Wellington Museum	Wellington Museum Act 1947
7.	Imperial War Museum	Imperial War Museum Acts of 1920 and 1955
8.	Imperial Institute	Commonwealth Institute Act 1958
9.	Horniman Museum	London Government Act 1963, s. 7 and London County Council (General Powers) Act 1901, s. 46
10.	Sir John Sloane Museum	London County Council (G.P.) Act 1952, s. 20
11.	Geffrye Museum	London County Council (G.P.) Act 1959, s. 20
12.	Victoria and Albert Museum	National Heritage Act 1983

(The above Act of 1983, in addition to setting up the National Heritage Memorial Fund, constituted a Board of Trustees for this famous museum in South Kensington, London. The Act distinguishes between those objects which are to be transferred to the new Board and those which remain with some Minister of the Crown.[33] The Victoria and Albert Museum also illustrates the complexity of museum management at cer-

---

[32] *Ibid.*
[33] The Victoria and Albert Museum (Excepted Objects) Order 1984 (S.I. 1984 No. 226).

tain levels, for that museum also manages the Wellington Museum, and the Theatre Museum, as well as including the National Art Library).[34]

The power to make admission charges for certain of these national museums was contained in the Museums and Galleries Admission Charges Act 1972. The power was exercised for some months, aroused intense public dislike and the charges were discontinued.

2. Fieldwork

(1) *Treasure Trove*

3.50 Gold or silver, in the form of coin, plate or bullion, which is found, having been hidden, in the earth or other secret place, is Treasure Trove and thereby belongs to the Crown, under Royal prerogative. If the owner should be found, then it belongs to him.

The times when this part of our law was laid down seem ancient; the activity in our time, whether excavation for buildings, highways or general redevelopment of land, has yielded a crop of cases which have tested and to some extent modified the principle stated above.

The main legal elements illuminated by the cases are:
(a) Was it hidden?
(b) Was it gold or silver?
(c) Has the onus been fulfilled?

(a) **Was it hidden?**

3.51 In the most recent case, *Att.-Gen.* v. *G.E. Overton (Farms) Ltd.*[35] Dillon J. at first instance, and the Court of Appeal, on appeal, dealt with a claim by the Crown for 7,811 third century Roman coins. Found in a field on a Lincolnshire farm, they were below the level at which a plough-share would catch them. A broken Roman earthenware urn was close to the coins. Both courts readily accepted the inference from these circumstances that the coins had been "hidden."

Old English authorities have described this requirement. Sir Edward Coke,[36] used the words "of an ancient time hidden" and Chitty "concealed . . . in a house or in the earth, or other private place."[37]

In an important Irish case, a gold bowl, a necklace, torques and a collar and chain were found in a ploughed field. The circumstances were accepted by Farwell J. as showing that this treasure had been "hidden."

---

[34] The Tower of London is a national museum in its own right, with its safe-keeping of the Crown Jewels and other famous national items. Regimental museums, sometimes managed on an agency basis by the local authority, are to be found in many of the towns with close army links.
[35] [1982] 2 W.L.R. 397.
[36] Coke 3rd Inst. p. 132 (1628–1644).
[37] *Prerogatives of the Crown*, Joseph Chitty, 1820 p. 152.

The circumstances included not only the location but the history of the site, which had suffered a great Norse invasion in the ninth century.[38]

(b) **Was it gold or silver?**

This was the main issue in the *Overton Farms* case.[39] Samples were analysed from the large number of coins found. These sample coins were said to have silver contents as low as 1.6 per cent. but some reached 18 per cent. After a good deal of expert evidence had been given the Court of Appeal reviewed earlier authorities and held that in order to be treasure trove, the metal must be gold or silver. Furthermore, the proportion of gold or silver in the treasure claimed must be "substantial." Lord Denning, indeed, said that he would treat that word as connoting more than 50 per cent. before it could be described as a gold or silver object.[40]

3.52

(c) **Has the onus been fulfilled?**

Normally the finder of property on the land he owns can claim it; thus treasure trove forms an exception to the general law.[41] One of the elements in treasure trove law is that the original owner is unknown. This is invariably the position simply due to the time which has elapsed since the hiding of the treasure.[42] Nowadays it is the practice of the Crown to reward, with the full market value, the finder of the treasure, when it has been determined by the coroner's inquest to be treasure trove in law. Alternatively, if the objects, for one reason or another, are not retained by the Crown or a museum, then they will be returned to the finder.

3.53

---

[38] *Att.-Gen.* v. *Trustees of the British Museum* [1903] 2 Ch. 598. The court found the above conclusion easier to reach since it had been presented with an alternative, more romantic, theory for the location of the treasure. This relied on the site having formerly been sea-bed. The treasure, it was said, must have been votive offerings to a sea god: this must have happened between 300 B.C. and 700 A.D., and it must have been the custom for the kings or chiefs to make such votive offerings. The court found the evidence offered on these limbs of the museum's argument "of the vaguest description" (at p. 610).
Other examples of treasure "hidden" are given in an interesting article by C.S. Emden. "The Law of Treasure Trove-Past and Present" (1926) L.Q.R. 368. This was quoted by Denning M.R. in the *Overton Farms* case.

[39] See *supra*, n. 35.

[40] *Ibid.* at p. 530(e) The case of *R.* v. *Thomas and Willett* (1863) 169 E.R. 1409 has some interesting details. Rings discovered in a ploughed field in Sussex had to be gold, not brass, it was determined, if treasure trove law was to be satisfied. Twentieth century documentation on this subject includes two Home Office circulars (12/6/31 and Ho. 68/1955) which restrict the duties of coroners in connection with treasure trove to gold and silver.

[41] *Armorie* v. *Delamirie* (1722) 1 Stra. 505; *Parker* v. *British Airways Board* [1982] 2 W.L.R. 503, contains a recent examination by the Court of Appeal of finder's rights in relation to those of occupiers. The occupier has the prior title, said the court, when the object is in the soil, as, for instance, embedded in the mud; he also enjoys the prior title when he has shown an intention to exercise control over anything which might be on the premises and his intention is manifest.

[42] Thus if a member of the museum staff made a discovery of treasure trove, this belongs to the Crown if it is silver or gold, it was hidden and the owner is not known. If the Crown has to be eliminated from the title, then the owner of the soil has a claim, as indicated in n. 41, *supra*.

3.53   Libraries and Museums

The correct practice, therefore, when a finding of potential treasure trove occurs, is to report it to the police, who alert the coroner. He holds an inquest, takes evidence and obtains a verdict on whether the articles in question are treasure trove.

(2) *Wrecks and Whales*

(a) **Wrecks**

3.54   The work of the public museums service of this country is not confined to buildings. It extends to fieldwork, such as that described in the last sub-section, and also the exploration and exhibition of Viking and Roman artifacts, as at York, Bath, London and elsewhere. From time to time, it is further extended to take in wrecks.

(i) *Basic principle*

A wreck is, in law, a ship or her cargo cast ashore after shipwreck and which thus has ceased to float.[43] By virtue of the prerogative, a wreck belongs to the Crown, in Cornwall to the Duke of Cornwall and in Wales to the Lords Marchers.[44] The Merchant Shipping Act 1894 now embodies this ancient legal custom in statutory form.[45] As a result of this principle, it is within the power of the Crown to grant a right to wreck, as it is called, and this right can be accompanied by the soil or not, as the case may be.

(ii) *Legal practice*

3.55   The Secretary of State for the Environment is entitled to be notified whenever a wreck is found and to require the wreck to be handed into the custody of the receiver of wrecks, when the finder is not the owner.[46] The receiver holds the wreck for 12 months before disposing of it and accounting for the net proceeds, in accordance with the above Act and Regulations made under it.

---

[43] It can include a hovercraft if sunk, stranded or abandoned on a navigable river or the foreshore. (See Hovercraft (Application of Enactments) Order 1972 (S.I. 1972 No. 971). A quaint Irish case of 1875, *Stacpole* v. *The Queen* I.R. 9 E. 619, concerned two logs from a wrecked ship, which floated on to the Clare beach. Though marked by a finder with his "A," one log floated away with another tide. The Lord Chancellor, before whose court the case came, first quoted Lord Coke and Lord Hale and said:
> "Had it been floating between high and low water mark, it would have been a droit in Admiralty. If taken and carried away when the beach is dry, it is clearly a wreck .... Goods vary in their character according to the circumstances ... wrecks while the tide is out, and they lie on the beach, but when the tide is in and they are again floated, droits in Admiralty" (at p. 622).

[44] See *Halsbury* (4th ed.), Vol. 8, para. 1505 *et seq.* where it seems there could be a possible claim by a subject in Cornwall. Flotsam, jetsam and ligan go to the first finder.

[45] s.523.

[46] Merchant Shipping Act 1894, ss.72, 566. The law contains a number of subleties about presumed grants and grants by prescription, which are outside the scope of this work. The York-Antwerp Rules of 1974 are also essential reading for anyone wishing to pursue this topic in detail. (*Halsbury* (4th ed.), Vol. 25, para. 923).

MUSEUMS   3.56

(iii) *Protection of Wrecks Act 1973*

Under the Protection of Wrecks Act 1973, the Secretary of State is   3.56
empowered to designate, by Order, wreck sites for two purposes. Firstly,
sites which are regarded as of historic, archaeological or artistic importance. These wrecks can be thus protected against unauthorised interference. Secondly, sites which are considered to be potentially dangerous to
life or property can be safeguarded by one of these Orders.[47]

The Orders designate an area about the wreck which does not exceed
the high water mark of the ordinary spring tides.

Once made, the Orders allow entry to the area to take place only with
the consent of the Secretary of State. For his part, he grants such consent
only to persons who are considered competent and who have a legitimate
reason for the activity in question. Fines, both at the level of summary jurisdiction and on indictment, are the sanction in the Act for offences of
damaging the wreck or objects formerly contained, or for various other
acts which imperil the wreck. There is also an offence for simply entering
the area.[48]

(b) **Whales**

A note on whales may be of interest to curators. A dead whale is indeed   3.57
sometimes cast up on the beach, like a wreck, and to that extent, the topics
are allied. Whales are, in law, an interesting and special case.

(1) A whale, like the sturgeon, is a royal fish:

> "Also the King, shall have throughout the realm, whales (and stur-
> geons) taken in the sea or elsewhere within the realm, except in cer-
> tain places privileged by the King."[49]

The seas are "within the realm" if in territorial waters.[50]

(2) Whales are, legally, in a group of things found derelict on the sea, as   3.58
flotsam and jetsam, and which are called droits in Admiralty.[51] The
Admiralty jurisdiction of the High Court deals with claims on behalf of
the Crown to determine the rightful ownership of such things.

(3) Payment akin to salvage is payable to captors of royal whales. The
procedure for recovery of such payments is that of an Admiralty action for
salvage.

(4) A vivid account in the law reports relates to a whale found three   3.59

---

[47] Protection of Wrecks Act 1973, s.1.
[48] At the present time, Orders protecting wrecks have been made under the Act of 1973 for the *Mary Rose*, the *Grace Dieu*, the *Amsterdam*, the *Mary*, *HMS Assurance* and *HMS Dartmouth*. Four of the sites are on the south coast, one in Anglesey and one in the Sound of Mull.
[49] De Prerogativa Regus (of the King's prerogative), 17 Ed. II, time uncertain. Words which included wrecks at sea in this section about the Royal Prerogative were repealed when the Merchant Shipping Act 1894 incorporated a modern procedure for wrecks, as described above:s. 184, Sched. 22.
An interesting list of 31 types of whale is to be found in the schedule to the Whaling Indus-
try (Regulation) Act 1934.
[50] See Chapter 7, para. 7.61 about the Seaside and Crown rights on the foreshore.
[51] Administration of Justice Act 1956, s.1(1)(*s*), s.3(2).

3.59

miles from the shore and towed onto Whitstable beach by the masters and crews of seven oyster smacks in 1829.[52] They claimed and were granted salvage from the proceeds. The report also records the conclusion of the court that in the jurisdiction of the Lord Warden of the Cinque Ports, on the south coast, the Lord Warden had been granted the right to royal fish by the sovereign and, therefore, enjoyed the title to the whale in question.

3.60 (5) The present law has succeeded centuries in which the position was more confused. Lords of the Manor, in towns possessing Admiralty jurisdiction, enjoyed these droits. Then the creation of the Court of Admiralty ended this diffusion of rights, for some of the Admiral's patents included droits, both fish and flotsam and jetsam, where these had not been granted to other persons. The sovereign resumed the right to the royal fish in the nineteenth century and the present position is as summarised above.[53]

(3) *Metal Detectors*

3.61 The leading case of the *Overton Farms* treasure trove[54] took its place in the law reports after a man had used his metal detector on a Lincolnshire farm. Metal detectors have indeed been for some time an element in the fieldwork interests of museums authorities in this country.

Legally the subject can be considered conveniently in relation to the timing, the method and control exercised over the practice by the museum authorities. There is also a special provision on this subject in the Ancient Monuments and Archaeological Areas Act 1979, s.42.[55]

(a) **Timing**

3.62 The occasion for metal detectors to be used in an area may be prompted by impending development or it may simply be due to inspired curiosity by the practitioners of this pastime. It is likely that the town planning department at local authority level will be the first to learn of the wish of a metal detector club to survey a site, when that survey is linked to projected development. Thus liaison of the museums and planning departments at all times becomes important. The consent to enter land, and avoid a charge of trespass, will not normally concern the local authority, when privately owned land is involved. (However, if the site is "ancient" it may be that the Ancient Monuments and Archaeological Areas Act 1979 will impinge, and this is discussed below).

---

[52] *Lord Warden and Admiral of the Cinque Ports* v. *H.M. in his Office of Admiralty* (1831) 166 E.R. 304; 2 Hagg. 438.
[53] See Holdsworth A. *History of English Law*, Vol. 1, pp. 559–561. Both the Civil List Act 1831 (1 Will 4, c. 25), s.2 and the Civil List Act 1837 (1 & 2 Vict. c. 2)), s.2 contain the phrase "the produce of the hereditary casual revenues arising from any droits of Admiralty or droits of the Crown." These monies were to go into the Consolidated Fund "for the support of H.M. Household and the Honour and Dignity of the Crown."
[54] See [1982] 2 W.L.R. 397.
[55] See paras. 3.78 *et seq.*, below.

MUSEUMS   3.63

(b) **Control**

When the local authority wish to permit entry by a club, as envisaged   3.63
above, then the normal conditions would cover matters such as:
(1) Limits upon the time allowed for the survey.
(2) An indemnity against damage or nuisance to third parties or the landowner and against claims for injury by club members, if the site has hazards.
(3) Possible financial consideration for the concession.
(4) A stipulation that artifacts or objects of any sort discovered and recovered from the site are the property of the landowner.

Since metal detector clubs have come into being, they have come to expect such arrangements.

(c) **Method**

A complex site to be surveyed in advance of town centre development   3.64
may well require detailed specification about the parts of the surface to be disturbed and phasing may be introduced at this point. Limitation to Sundays or special holidays would be another consideration before final consent was given to entry by a club.

The Ancient Monuments and Archaeological Areas Act 1979 deals with   3.65
the use of metal detectors in a "protected place" and this covers three sorts of property:
(i) A monument scheduled under the Act.
(ii) A monument under the ownership or guardianship of the Secretary of State or a local authority by virtue of that Act of 1979.
(iii) Areas of archaeological importance.[56]

The Schedule is maintained and published from time to time by the Secretary of State.[57] The guardianship of ancient monuments is a practice embodied in the above Act of 1979, whereby privately owned monuments, after a guardianship agreement has been executed, pass into the guardianship of the Secretary of State or the relevant local authority.[58] With a view to controlling carefully the investigation of areas of archaeological importance, the local authority and Secretary of State are given powers to designate such areas. There are sanctions, in the form of offences created for investigating those areas without prior notice to the authority in question obtaining, due consent and complying with other statutory requirements.[59]

The Act of 1979 makes it an offence: (1) to use a metal detector in one of the protected places; (2) to remove an artifact ("object of archaeological or historical interest") which he has found in a protected place by the use of a metal detector; and (3) to break a condition imposed in a consent to enter into a protected place. To the above three offences, the Act provides two particular defences: (a) When charged with "using" the instrument,

[56] Act of 1979, s.42.
[57] See Pt. I of the Act of 1979.
[58] See Act of 1979, ss.12–18.
[59] Act of 1979, Pt. II.

3.65   Libraries and Museums

that it was being used for a purpose other than to locate or detect objects of historical or archaeological interest; and (b) in relation to the second and third offences above, that he had made reasonable enquiries to ascertain if the location was a protected place and in good faith did not believe that it was such a place.[60] The definition of metal detectors is important: "any device designed or adapted for detecting or locating any metal or mineral in the ground." The expression "or adapted" covers the situation discussed in connection with the adaptation of a motor van in the case of *Popperwell v. Cockerton*.[61]

(4) *Wildlife Protection*

(a) **Legislation**

3.66   This is a further area of fieldwork for a modern museums authority.

In this book, consideration of the specific legislation on the subject is to be found in Chapter 8, at paragraphs 8.10 to 8.14.

(b) **Preservation of secrecy**

3.67   A museums curator is occasionally in possession of important secrets and it may be useful to summarise the law, in the light of the recent Contempt of Court Act 1981. The curator's secrets may be about the nest of a golden eagle or the location of some treasure trove or other items. There may have been a campaign to secure disclosure, which he can resist. It is only in the face of court proceedings that the pressure to reveal reaches its legal ultimate. It is that situation which, among other important matters, is dealt with in the above Act of 1981.

(i) It has always been a common law contempt of court to refuse to answer a question of the court, relevant to the proceedings, without lawful excuse. Fine and imprisonment are the sanctions to enforce compliance in that situation.[62]

3.68   (ii) The Act of 1981, enacted after a special committee had studied the problem,[63] defined certain actions as subject to a "strict liability rule." This meant that the action was regarded as contempt of court, though no intent to commit the offence was proved.[64] (Intent is a normal ingredient in a criminal offence). This rule is limited to publications to the public which create a "substantial risk that the course of justice, in the proceedings in question, will be seriously impeded or prejudiced."[65]

(iii) A condition is that the proceedings are "active," an expression which is carefully defined in terms of judicial process, *e.g.* the summons has been served, the accused has been arrested and likewise for other situ-

---

[60] *Ibid.* s.42.
[61] [1968] 1 W.L.R. 438.
[62] *Att.-Gen.* v. *Foster* [1963] 2 Q.B. 477; in the County Court, the County Courts Act 1959, s.84; in the Magistrates' Court, the Magistrates' Court Act 1980, s.97.
[63] Report of the Phillimore Committee, Cmnd. 5794, 1974.
[64] Contempt of Court Act 1981, s.1.
[65] *Ibid.* s.2.

ations.[66] It is a defence that the defendant did not know that the proceedings were "active," though he had taken reasonable steps to find out.

(iv) "A publication made as, or as part of, a discussion in good faith of public affairs or other matters of general public interest, is not to be treated as a contempt of court, under the strict liability rule, if the risk of impediment or prejudice to particular legal proceedings, is merely incidental to the discussion."[67]

(v) The effect of the provisions referred to so far is that the museums curator, in our imaginary situation, would be moving towards a position of peril in relation to the law, only if:
   (a) His statement was in relation to court proceedings.
   (b) Those proceedings were "active."
   (c) He published his statement to the public.
   (d) He is not within the protection of section 5, above.
   (e) His remarks went beyond normal comment and reflected on the court.

The perilous statement would therefore be of the nature of: "he did not trust the court: he would not help the court: he would never yield up the secret about the nest or what ever it might be."

(vi) At that point, the curator's attention must be drawn to section 10 in the Act of 1981, headed "Disclosure" and reading as follows:

> "No court may require a person to disclose, nor is any person guilty of contempt, for refusing to disclose, the source of information contained in a publication for which he is responsible, unless it is established to the satisfaction of the court that disclosure is necessary in the interests of justice or national security or for the prevention of disorder or crime."

(c) **Conclusion**

It is evident that firstly the publication in a newspaper or other organs of the media by a journalist or reporter and secondly the recalcitrant journalist in the witness box, are the orthodox problem situations to which this Act of 1981 is directed. But other persons and other situations could lead to the Act being invoked. It might be that bizarre circumstances could demand a revelation from a museum curator and then, being at the centre of a controversy, he would have to determine his attitude to the court in the light of the above Act of Parliament.

3. **Collections**

The acceptance, display, and transmission of collections of ethnographic, artistic or cultural material is the lifeblood of many museums. We turn now to the legal framework wthin which this activity takes place.

---

[66] *Ibid.* Sched. 1.
[67] *Ibid.* s.5 and *Att.-Gen.* v. *The Times Newspapers Ltd.* [1974] A.C. 273.

3.72

(1) *Contract*

3.72 Contracts may be made between the transmitting and receiving authorities, when a collection is "on loan" at a museum. It may be that those terms will be adequate to cover any problems that may arise from the transaction. Basic contract law has been discussed in Chapter 1. Perhaps formal contracts have not been used, but there has been an exchange of letters, which will serve as the starting point in assembling the terms of the implied contract, if that should, at some controversial stage, be necessary. Whilst in the possession of the museum, the collection is bailed with that museum and the law of bailment cannot be ignored, when one enquires about the rights and responsibilities of the museum authority in relation to the sometimes extremely valuable collection.[68]

(2) *Duties of a Bailee*

3.73 The prime duty of a bailee of goods is to take "proper care" of them[69]:

(a) The bailee must protect the goods against theft.[70]

(b) If the goods are lost, the burden of proof is upon the bailee to satisfy a court that either he took appropriate care of the goods or that his failure to do so did not contribute to their loss.[71] This onus is an important one: it is different from the claim in negligence as described in Chapter 1, where the burden of proof lies upon the plaintiff, he who brings the action at law. (In the circumstances envisaged, the museum's curator would be the defendant in an action brought by the aggrieved owner of the goods).

(c) Proper care of the goods by the bailee may be adjudged by the degree of benefit or reward that the bailee is deriving from possession of the goods. In the case of a museum collection, this would involve holding a keeper responsible, on behalf of his employer, for slight neglect.[72]

(d) Sometimes there can be a clause in the agreement between the bailee and the person to whom be passes the collection, *i.e.* the sub-bailee, designed to end further liability for the collection when possession passes into the hands of the sub-bailee. Cases show that such an exclusion clause, as it is called, may be effective, as against the original bailor, despite the lack of any agreement by him about such an arrangement.[73]

(e) A bailor can sue for the full value of goods lost or destroyed by the bailee's negligence. Normally, in tort, a claim for loss following negli-

---

[68] "It represents a conveyance of personal property, created by contract and enforceable in tort" N.E. Palmer, *Bailment* (1979), p. 1.
[69] *Morris* v. *C.W. Martin & Sons Ltd.* [1966] 1 Q.B. 716, *per* Salmon L.J. at p. 738. Also Diplock L.J. at pp. 731–732.
[70] *Lee Cooper Ltd.* v. *C.H. Jenkins and Sons Ltd.* [1967] 2 Q.B.1.
[71] See, *e.g. B.R.S. Ltd.* v. *Arthur Crutchley Ltd.* [1968] 1 All E.R. 811, *per* Sachs L.J. at p. 822.
[72] See *Taylor* v. *Caldwell* (1863) 3 B. & S. 826, *per* Blackburn J. at p. 839, see also *Hedley Byrne* v. *Heller and Partners* [1964] A.C. 465, where gratuitous advice carried the onus of a duty of reasonable care.
[73] *Scruttons Ltd.* v. *Midland Silicones Ltd.* (1962) A.C. 446 at pp. 489–490, *per* Lord Denning M.R. and *Morris* v. *C.W. Martin and Sons Ltd.*, *supra* at pp. 729–730.

gence, would be limited to the extent of the plaintiff's personal loss. Bailment is here again, different.

(f) The bailment comes to an end with the redelivery of the goods to the bailor or to another person to whom he has agreed to deliver them.

(g) Finally, reference should be made to two important principles: **3.74**
  (i) The bailee, here the museum authority, is in possession. If the collection is stolen or damaged, he may sue the wrongdoer in trespass or for the full value of the chattel taken or the full cost of its damage. "As against a wrongdoer, possession is title."[74]
  (ii) If the bailee departs from the terms on which he received the goods into his possession, he loses the benefit of terms in the contract of bailment. This might be an exclusion clause or something else of great importance.

Sometimes called "the four corners rule," this principle was authoritively stated by Scrutton L.J. in a leading case, *Gibaud* v. *G.E. Railway Co.*[75]:

> "The principle is well known and perhaps *Lilley* v. *Doubleday*[76] is the best example, that if you undertake to do a certain thing in a certain way, or to keep a thing in a certain place, with certain conditions protecting it; and have afterwards broken the contract by not doing the thing contracted for or not keeping the thing in the place in which you have contracted to keep it, you cannot rely on the conditions, which were only intended to protect you if you carried out the contract in the way in which you had contracted to do it."

Though there are no cases on museum collections in the reports, there have been and will continue to be legal problems resulting from the loan, display and transport of collections of exhibits. "Permanent loan" or some similar method for the display of a collection is one more setting in which the rights and liabilities of the law of bailment can be brought into full play.

(3) *The Professional Duty*

Though the law of bailment, as set out above, touches on most problems raised by the reception, display, care and transmission of a collection by a museum, it is impossible to ignore one final question: what was the proper, professional care required in the circumstances of that case? **3.75**

An anti-Gainsborough maniac in the town may have broadcast evil intentions in the week before the collection reached the museum for display; the lock system universally used in Scrimpshire for display cases, may have been found faulty by a neighbouring museum a day or two

---

[74] *The Winkfield* (1902) P. 42 at p. 60, *per* Collins M.R.
[75] [1921] 2 K.B. 426 at p. 435.
[76] [1881] 7 Q.B. 510.

3.75 LIBRARIES AND MUSEUMS

before the collection arrived; the senior keeper may have shown signs of mental instability at a bridge club contest the week before, as bruited in the local paper; the technique of mounting paintings without the use of the recently advertised thief-proof clasps may be suspect; an article in the *Museums Journal* about the theft of a Van Gogh in Melbourne Art Gallery two months previously, may have disclosed a new technique by international art crooks, a combination of vapourising and neo-reductionism. These are purely imaginary examples of local circumstances and professional knowledge which might bear upon the appraisal of a museum curator's professional standards, when some crisis casts a spotlight upon his competence. How do the courts approach that question? There being, happily, no evident museum case to draw upon, we will touch on the general principles and then apply them to this situation.

(a) **General principles**

3.76 The standard of reasonable care expected of a professional man or woman has been discussed in Chapter 1. It stems from *Donoghue* v. *Stevenson*[77] and is the duty to take reasonable steps to avoid reasonable harm to his neighbours. The "neighbours" are those he can foresee as likely to be affected by his acts. The foreseeable harm is the "conceivable" harm.[78] He is not an insurer against all risks. The question is judged by the standards of knowledge in his profession at the time. In *Roe* v. *Minister of Health*[79] the court considered the precautions to be observed in a hospital in relation to the use by the anaesthetist of ampoules of nupercaine. Knowledge changed between 1947, when the accident happened and 1954, when the case was in court. "We must not look at a 1947 accident with 1954 spectacles," said Lord Denning.

The standard is objective. It does not vary with the competence or experience of the professional person. If he is inexperienced, he should seek advice. He cannot say: "I was doing my best and I could not help it."[80] He is judged by the standard of skill and care knowledgeable members of his profession bring to their professional duties.[81]

---

[77] [1932] A.C. 562.
[78] See, *e.g.* A.M. Dugdale & K.M. Stanton, *Professional Negligence* (Butterworths, 1982), para. 23.06. This area may be looked on as one application of the general principles described in relation to Negligence in Chap. 1. It could apply equally to many of the professionals involved in the public leisure services.
[79] [1954] 2 Q.B. 66.
[80] *Nettleship* v. *Weston* [1971] 2 Q.B. 691 at p. 699.
[81] Some words of McNair J. in *Bolam* v. *Friern Hospital Management Committee* [1957] 1 W.L.R. 582 have become the accepted principle, having been approved in the House of Lords (*Whitehouse* v. *Jordan* [1981] 1 W.L.R. 246, and embodied in the Congenital Disabilities (Civil Liability) Act 1976, s.1(5). McNair J. said:
"Where you get a situation which involves some special skill or competence, then the test . . . is the standard of the ordinary skilled man exercising and professing to have that special skill . . . . There may be one or more perfectly proper standards . . . if a medical man conforms with one of those proper standards, then he is not negligent . . . . That does not mean that a [medical] man can obstinately and pig-headedly carry on with some old technique, if it has been proved to be contrary to what is really substantially the whole of informed (medical) opinion . . . ."

MUSEUMS   3.77

(b) **Competence and the curator**

To apply these standards to the museums director is to seek to turn   3.77
principles into practical tests; these questions are simply indicative and
not exhaustive:
   (i) Was it a task where a consultant would normally be brought in?
   (ii) Were the premises secure, ventilated, safe for the objects in the collection, safe for visitors?
   (iii) Were there enough staff? Were they competent, briefed on special features of the exhibition? Had his delegation been reasonable? What had he kept as his own role?
   (iv) Ultimately, how far was he abreast of the shared knowledge of his profession, nationally and, nowadays, internationally?
   (v) Was the mishap, the catastrophe, due to an error of judgment or was it due to negligence?
   (vi) Is his insurance cover in force and adequate?

4. Ancient Monuments and Archaeological Areas

(1) Ancient Monuments

The law relating to ancient monuments was consolidated and changed in   3.78
the Ancient Monuments and Archaeological Areas Act 1979 (the Act of 1979). As a major Act of 65 sections and 5 Schedules, a full study is outside the scope of this work but the main legal provisions that will be of concern to museum authorities are set out below.[82]

The Secretary of State now keeps a statutory list of all scheduled monuments. These are the monuments which he considers to be of national importance.[83] (A dwelling house not occupied by the caretaker of the adjacent monument and his family cannot be included in the list.[84])

The above group of *Scheduled* monuments are all by the Act of 1979, deemed to be *ancient* monuments. So also are other monuments which the Secretary of State considers to be of historical, architectural, traditional, artistic or archaeological interest. The width of this definition may be gauged if we mention that it includes not only Hadrian's Wall and the Tower of London but also bridges, deserted villages, castles, crosses, inscribed stones, Roman remains and camps and settlements.

A guardianship system is retained, whereby an ancient monument can

---

[82] For a full, helpful and specialist treatment of the Act of 1979, see *e.g.* R.W. Suddards, *Listed Buildings, the Law and Practice* (1982, Sweet and Maxwell).

[83] Act of 1979, s.1. The list is published and local portions can be inspected at the offices of town planning authorities.

[84] *Ibid.* s.1(4). The definition of monument is now any building, structure or work, or the site thereof, a cave or excavation or any site comprising the remains of a vehicle, vessel or aircraft. It does not include a wreck protected by Scheduling in the Protection of Wrecks Act 1973.

3.78 be placed in voluntary guardianship with the Secretary of State or the relevant local authority.[85]

3.79 A *protected* monument can now be defined as one which is either scheduled, as described above, or is under guardianship.[86]

Having established these groups of monuments, the Act proceeds to buttress them by laying down a number of offences:

- (a) To execute or cause or permit the execution of works damaging a scheduled monument, unless authorised by the consent of the Secretary of State.[87]
- (b) Destroying or damaging a protected monument.[88]
- (c) Failing to give information about interests in land.[89]

3.80 There is a whole range of associated statutory powers which can be used by the Secretary of State or local authorities to support the above basic framework:

- (i) Compulsory acquisition of the monument, adjacent land or supporting easements by the Secretary of State or use of ordinary transfer.[90]
- (ii) Entry in the Local Land Charges Register of scheduled monuments.[91]
- (iii) Entry upon the site of a monument by the Secretary of State to carry out urgent works for its preservation.
- (iv) Extensive powers of entry for the Secretary of State to ascertain by inspection works needed to a scheduled monument.[92]
- (v) Agreements by the Secretary of State with the owners of ancient monuments to maintain them.[93]
- (vi) Transfer of monuments between local authorities and the Secretary of State.[94]

The Secretary of State may be obliged to pay compensation where consent for works to be carried out to an ancient monument is refused or, again, where there is damage to a monument within a guardianship order.[95]

At all times the Secretary of State can provide advice on works to monuments for the benefit of local authorities and can provide supervision for those works.[96]

---

[85] *Ibid.* s.18.
[86] *Ibid.* s.28.
[87] *Ibid.* s.2.
[88] *Ibid.* s.28. This provision of two offences—s.2 and s.28 one for scheduled and one for protected monuments—exemplifies the importance of the two categories under the Act.
[89] *Ibid.* s.57.
[90] *Ibid.* s.10.
[91] *Ibid.* s.5.
[92] *Ibid.* s.6.
[93] *Ibid.* s.17.
[94] *Ibid.* s.21.
[95] *Ibid.* ss.7–9.
[96] *Ibid.* s.25.

MUSEUMS 3.80

(2) *Areas of Archaeological Importance*

Part II of the Act of 1979 contains a code for protecting these areas. Legal action begins when the area is designated in an Order[97] made by the Secretary of State or by a local authority, subject to his confirmation.[98] The immediate consequence is that it becomes an offence to carry out any works, which disturb the ground or cause flooding or tipping in that area, unless an operations notice has first been served[99] upon the district or the London borough council.

The aim of the procedure is not to "freeze" the site for all time. Rather it is to delay development until adequate archaeological investigation has taken place. An initial four week period for the investigating authority to give notice that it will be excavating the site, can be extended to 18 weeks. A little detail will usefully fill out this picture: 3.81

(1) The person to carry out the archaeological investigation must be duly appointed.[1]
(2) A local authority can use the procedure of an injunction to combat operations in contravention of section 35 (the operations notice) in urgent cases.
(3) There is power for the Secretary of State to relax section 35 in certain cases.[2]
(4) There is also power for the investigating authority to move faster, and pay compensation for damage caused, where a site has been acquired compulsorily.[3]
(5) Use of metal detectors in an archaeological area without consent is an offence.[4]
(6) There are certain statutory defences to the offence created by section 35, *i.e.*:
　(i) That all reasonable precautions were taken and due diligence exercised.
　(ii) The defendant did not know and had no reason to believe that he was in an archaeological area.
　(iii) The operation was urgently necessary in the interests of health or safety and that due notice was given.

---

[97] Act of 1979, s.33.
[98] *Ibid.*, Sched. 2, para. 13.
[99] *Ibid.*, s.35.
[1] *Ibid.*, s.64.
[2] *Ibid.*, s.37.
[3] *Ibid.*, s.39.
[4] *Ibid.*, s.42 and see above paras. 3.61–3.65.

CHAPTER 4

PARKS AND RECREATION GROUNDS

*"That is, after all, the
beauty of the Common Law,
that it is a maze and not a
motorway."*

Diplock L.J. [1965] 3 W.L.R. 286.

INTRODUCTION

4.01 The law relating to parks and recreation grounds has not yet been consolidated. The Law Commission regularly recommends parts of the law of this country which would benefit from consolidation but so far the Commission has not reached this branch.

Thus the main legal authority for the provision of public parks and recreation grounds is to be found in a statute of 1875.[1] That was the time when urban authorities were creating these leisure outlets in all our towns and cities; like the statute itself, many parks then brought into being still serve their communities.

This branch of the law well reflects changing trends. The related Public Health Acts, which, with the Act of 1875, contain the legal framework for modern parks management, were passed by Parliament at intervals, 1890, 1907, 1925, 1961 and 1976, to reflect the call from town halls for powers to provide an ever wider range of these facilities.[2]

In this chapter, the main legal provisions affecting parks management will be described in section A.[3] Historically those provisions have been

---

[1] Public Health Act 1875. The expression there is "public walks and pleasure grounds."
[2] The Local Government (Miscellaneous Provisions) Act 1976, whilst replacing the Physical Training and Recreation Act 1937, also exemplifies the major enlargement of powers to meet this area of need.
[3] The full titles of the series of Acts referred to in this chapter are as follows:
    Act of 1875 Public Health Act 1875
    Act of 1890 Public Health Acts (Amendment) Act 1890
    Act of 1906 Open Spaces Act 1906
    Act of 1907 Public Health Acts (Amendment) Act 1907
    Act of 1925 Public Health Act 1925
    Act of 1961 Public Health Act 1961
    Act of 1976 Local Government (Miscellaneous Provisions) Act 1976

glossed by a series of rating cases, which will be discussed below. By-laws play their part in the management of parks and these will be dealt with in section C.[4] The fourth section gathers up several otherwise unrelated items of law affecting parks, including animals, zoos and safaris, insurance against bad weather, elm disease and fire blight and, as a related facility to recreation grounds, street playgrounds.

A. The Creation, Management and Disposal of Public Parks

1. **Acquisition**

Local authorities[5] may acquire land by purchase or lease and lay it out for use as parks by the public.[6] They may do this, directly, themselves, or, indirectly, by other persons and contribute to that provision. The necessary ancillary power to maintain and improve those parks is also available to local authorities.[7]

The expression "public walks and pleasure grounds" in the parent Act of 1875 has now been in operation for over a century. Though it does not include the words "parks" or "public parks," those amenities are recognised as coming within the statutory expression. The variety of lands laid out for public walks and pleasure grounds is immense, both in size and in treatment and it is remarkable that the somewhat vague statutory phrase has stood the test of time so well.

The Victorian Acts

The power to provide parks in the Act of 1875 was the culmination of a series of Victorian statutes, each of which dealt with a small aspect of the total subject. First the Public Health Act 1848, s.74, was in virtually the same terms as section 164 of the Public Health Act 1875, which replaced it. An Act of 1859, the Recreation Grounds Act, extended the powers of public authorities to grounds which the National Playing Fields Association has inherited.[8] The Town Gardens Protection Act 1863 was concerned with special public walking areas in towns, such as gardens and lawns in squares and crescents. A Public Improvements Act 1860, adop-

---

[4] This account is referred to in other parts of this book, when by-law making powers of other bodies, *e.g.* the Forestry Commission, come under consideration.
[5] Local authorities include county and district councils, London boroughs, parish councils and both the Greater London Council and the Common Council of the City of London.
[6] Acquisition can be made by use of compulsory powers, under the Local Government Act 1972, s.121. The general power is in the Act of 1875, s.164, supplemented by the Act of 1890, s.45. This later Act added lands outside the authority's area to those described in the Act of 1875, provided that the lands outside the authority's district can be 'conveniently used" by the inhabitants of the district engaging these powers.
[7] Act of 1875, s.164.
[8] The Charities Act 1960, s.39 repealed the Recreation Grounds Act 1859 as "no longer required." Trusts set up by the 1859 Act may however still be met, as they were preserved.

4.03 Parks and Recreation Grounds

tive in nature, had taken the provision further; ratepayers in townships with 500 or more inhabitants, could spend money to provide parks, exercise or playgrounds.[9]

Other open space

4.04 Public parks are a form of public open space. Chapter 2 deals with the operation of the Open Spaces Act 1906 and also with commons, an important additional open space. Village greens are themselves a type of common. If it appears to a local authority that a public park can suitably be used as a "country park," then, from the date of the authority's decision, it must be so treated. Country parks are described in Chapter 8. Open spaces associated with the sea or inland waters will be found in Chapter 7 as an aspect of sport.

2. Management

4.05 The initial power in 1875 extended to "laying out, planting, improving and maintaining" the parks. Soon, the precise meaning of those six words was tested, as local authorities sought sanction from government departments to borrow money for amenities considered reasonable in their parks. Under a sympathetic administration in Whitehall, sanctions were granted for greenhouses, reading rooms, bandstands, bowling greens, shelters, cycle tracks and gymnastic appliances. Nevertheless, the desire to extend these amenities, to charge for some of them and to place some in the temporary care of clubs and societies, led to the need for clarifying legislation over a period of 100 years (see paragraph 4.01). The resulting portfolio of powers available in parks to local authorities is as follows.[10]

(1) *Sport*

(a) **Boating lakes**

4.06 Pleasure boats can be provided, let for hire or licensed to some person or persons for letting for hire.[11] The provision of the pools and associated buildings and equipment is also authorised.[12]

---

[9] Repealed by the Parish Councils Act 1957.
[10] Local authorities in 1875 meant urban authorities. This was extended in 1906 (Act of 1906, s.14) to county councils and to rural authorities generally in 1931 (Rural District Councils (Urban Powers) Order 1931 (S.R. & O. 1931 No. 580)). Finally, by the Local Government Act 1972, Pt. II, Sched. 14, para. 27, all current local authorities were given the power of managing public parks. The Act of 1875 was kept in being when functions were defined but not codified.
[11] See, *e.g.* the Act of 1890, s.44(2).
[12] Act of 1961, s.54. Where the existence of a boating pool is likely to interfere with any water flowing directly or indirectly out of or into any watercourse vested in or controlled by a River Board, or other public water authority, the local authority is required to confer with that body, before providing the new pool (Act of 1961, s.54(4)).

THE CREATION, MANAGEMENT AND DISPOSAL OF PUBLIC PARKS **4.06**

(b) **Ice skating**

A power exists to enclose not more than one quarter of the area of ice for skating and then to charge for admission to that area.[13]

(c) **Cricket, football and other games**

Sports pitches involve some exclusion of the public and this has been authorised since 1907.[14] Power to charge the persons granted the use of those pitches is also authorised.[15] Nevertheless, the local authority must ensure that exclusive use, as above, does not extend to more than one third of any one park or pleasure ground. Nor must they allow more than one quarter of the total area of their parks to be the subject of exclusive use. Parliament has also laid down that the local authority must satisfy themselves that they have not unfairly restricted the space available to the public for games and recreations.[16] An obvious instance of such unfairness might be the exclusive letting of sports pitches, up to the legal maximum at the weekend, when experience had shown that public demand at that time was so great that it could not be met by the three-quarters of the total area which would, at those weekends, be available.[17]

The statutory principle set out above affects public rights and is thus the sort which is suitable for enforcement by an aggrieved ratepayer by judicial review in the High Court.[18]

(2) *Seats, Games, Apparatus, Pavilions, Reading Rooms and Refreshment Rooms*

These are five amenities found in parks, different in nature but related in **4.07** law. All were listed in the Act of 1907[19] as amenities which local authorities were in future authorised to provide. A power to charge for the use of such amenities was added, in the case of the apparatus, the reading rooms and the pavilions. That power, in the case of these two buildings, is not to be used on more than 12 days in one year, nor on more than four consecutive days.[20]

The Act of 1907 specifically safeguards terms imposed by a donor or lessor of a public park. The powers described above are not to be exercised so that they would contravene any condition or covenant imposed by such

---

[13] Act of 1907, s.76.
[14] *Ibid.* The exclusion is, of course, only for the period of play and cannot be carried through to tenancies or leases. If the land is really surplus, it could now be appropriated and then let.
[15] Act of 1925, s.56.
[16] Act of 1961, s.52(3). These general powers can be varied by local acts.
[17] Act of 1961, s.52(3).
[18] But see the qualifications on this procedure under R.S.C. Order 53, as to the standing of the applicants or otherwise, in *I.R.C. v. Federation of Self Employed* [1981] 2 All E.R. 93 (H.L.).
[19] s.76.
[20] *Ibid.*

4.07 PARKS AND RECREATION GROUNDS

persons, unless consent has been obtained from the persons currently able to enforce them.[21]

(3) *Legal Claims for Negligence and Nuisance*

4.08 Those responsible for the management of public parks have particular hazards in the field of potential litigation in relation to the torts of negligence and nuisance and also the legal perils associated with the liability for the collapse or repair of walls.

(a) **Equipment negligence claims**

In so far as claims stem from the injuries which children in particular may suffer, from use or misuse of equipment in a recreation ground, adventure playground or trim trail, the legal principles have been discussed in the first chapter, in connection with the duties of occupiers to visitors (see paras. 1.004 to 1.013). The situation in law is that the local authority has invited the public to use, for its pleasure and recreation, the sort of equipment mentioned. In those circumstances, the common duty of care rests upon the authority, with all the qualifications which are discussed in that chapter.

(b) **Nuisance**

4.09 The second considerable area of concern to parks managers, at member and officer level, is more specialised. It is the potential liability for nuisance – with a difference.[22] The overriding legal principle which emerges is that a local authority, as owner of land acquired and held for the purposes of section 164 of the Public Health Act 1875, *i.e.* "public walks and pleasure grounds," is not, thereby, in beneficial occupation of that land. "They are incapable by law of using it for any profitable purpose; they must allow the public the free and unrestricted use of it," said Lord Halsbury, Lord Chancellor, in the *Lambeth Overseers* case.[23]

4.10 Following that principle, the local authority in *Hall* v. *Beckenham Corporation*[24] were exonerated from liability for nuisance to a householder who lived near to the public park. The nuisance originated from the flying of model aeroplanes powered by internal combustion engines inside the park. The court accepted the argument that the Corporation could not be liable in nuisance, since they were not, in law, occupiers of the park.

4.11 In the *Beckenham* case, two arguments were advanced by the plaintiff to distinguish the Lambeth Overseers case. Firstly, it was argued that the Corporation could put the recreation ground to a profitable use by appropriating it to another use, *e.g.* a car park, by virtue of their powers under

---

[21] Act of 1907, s.76(4).
[22] See Section B.1, for full discussion.
[23] *The Churchwardens and Overseers of Lambeth Parish* v. *The London County Council* [1897] A.C. 625 at p. 631. Also *infra* at para. 4.37.
[24] [1949] 1 K.B. 716.

the Local Government and Town and Country Planning Acts. This argument did not prevail with Finnemore J. He relied on the view taken in the intervening case of *North Riding County Valuation Committee* v. *Redcar Corporation*.[25] There, a distinction was drawn between certain facilities in a park, such as a boating lake, a car park, a pavilion, which were used to yield income and of which the Corporation were held to be in occupation, and other non-profitable parts of the park. These comprised the expanse of grass, woodland and open space and were held to be within the Lambeth Overseers case principle. In other words, appropriation was irrelevant; the power to obtain income was available to the authority as a parks authority.

The second argument was that the control exercised by the local authority over the park in closing it at night and on certain days throughout the year, legally affected the role and status of the Corporation. However, the court held that these control measures were merely incidental to the role of the Corporation under section 164 of the Public Health Act 1875. They could not have a critical effect on the legal status of the local authority.

This brought the Court to the position that the Corporation could be liable to the plaintiff in nuisance as an occupier, despite the Lambeth principle, but only if they had powers sufficiently extensive by way of management control, that they could prevent the nuisance:

> "They have the right to make by-laws for (the park's) proper conduct and they have express power, if they make by-laws which are confirmed, to eject from the ground those who infringe them. They have no general power to turn people out because they do not like them or because they are doing something of which a particular park keeper may not approve. They can only act against people in the park who offend against their by-laws or who commit some offence or crime for which criminal action can be taken.
>
> It seems plain that if they go beyond those powers, their officer and therefore they themselves will be liable for an action, for example, for assault or false imprisonment, if they lay hands on someone and forcibly put him outside the park."[26]

It was by this process of reasoning that the Beckenham leading case laid down that, not being legally the occupiers, the local authority were not liable in nuisance to the aggrieved neighbouring householder.

By making comprehensive by-laws, a local authority may therefore, bring themselves into the position of occupiers of the whole park and subject to actions in nuisance.

(c) **Nuisance: the general principle**

It is worth restating here the principle that liability to a neighbouring property owner for a nuisance on one's own land arises in law if the nuis-

---

[25] [1943] K.B. 114.
[26] [1949] 1 K.B. 716 at p. 727.

4.15 ance has been adopted or continued on your own land. This is illustrated in the classic case of *Sedley-Denfield* v. *Callaghan*,[27] where flooding of the neighbour's land occurred due to an inadequate culvert on the defendant's land. The burden of the case was to ascertain that the defendant must have known of the nuisance and thus, in law "adopted or continued" it. The defendants were found liable because, in the words of Lord Porter, "with knowledge that a state of things existed which might at any time give rise to a nuisance, they took no steps to remedy that state of affairs."[28]

4.15 So if, in the circumstances discussed above, there is in the park a tree dangerous to the neighbour because it is overhanging, or due to its spreading roots, or there is a tottering wall, or a group of stone-throwing boys,[29] and the park warden and his department do nothing, the authority are liable in nuisance. It is emphasised that it is not the creation of the potential nuisance that is critical – it was a trespasser who did it in the Sedley-Denfield case – it is the ability to stop it, after knowing of it. The other test, the test of reasonableness, comes into play once the nuisance is made out as above and the court considers what was done to prevent the nuisance. "The standard ought to be to require of the occupier what is reasonable to expect of him in his individual circumstances," Lord Wilberforce said in the case of *Goldman* v. *Hargrave*.[30]

(4) *Walls and Fences*

4.16 Walls and fences are a frequent problem for those managing public parks. This is partly due to the sheer expense of repair, so that liability is worth detailed attention and often keen discussion. It is also because it is often desirable to maintain walls and fences, despite the growth of the school of thought which favours open parks. A practical approach, stemming from the legal principles involved, could be on the following lines:
  1. If someone is responsible for damaging the wall or fence, hold him responsible.
  2. If it is age or some non-human agency which has caused the damage or collapse:
     (a) The title deeds are the first guide to responsibility. Their clauses about repair and any "T" marks on the deed plan are the necessary starting point in determining legal liability. Of course, it can be frustrating to find from the deeds that Mr. Wiseacre built the wall but left the document silent on the question of maintenance.
     (b) Trace the history of repairs. Was it last done on the basis of accepted liability or was it "without prejudice"?
     (c) What does an inspection of the wall reveal?
        (i) By its construction, smooth outside and rough within, is it

---

[27] [1940] A.C. 880.
[28] *Ibid.* at p. 920.
[29] *Att. Gen.* v. *Corke* [1933] Ch. 89.
[30] [1967] 1 A.C. 645 at p. 663 E.

clear that it was a park boundary wall, that it was fencing *in* the park?
or
(ii) Is it a fence wall, built on land at the same level on both sides? Is it thus what perhaps 75 per cent. of boundary walls are, namely, party walls, where each landowner owns an unsevered half, has a right of support from the other person's half and maintenance costs are shared equally?
or
(iii) Is it, on the other hand, partly a retaining wall, with earth against a greater number of courses on one side than the other? This might be a highway embankment or the end of a house garden, where that structure needed the retaining wall for its own stability. Again, does history help? If not,
A. If the adjoining property is a highway, that authority should accept the retaining portion of the wall as part of the highway and then they will discuss responsibility for the surmounting fence wall as a separate item.[31]
B. Otherwise, the owner who is higher needs the retaining wall for his own support whilst his neighbour needs the wall to keep out the adjacent soil. The interest in having that sort of wall in that position might be agreed as one to be shared equally. These problems tend to go into court infrequently but there are several such cases which assist in establishing some of the above three points.[32]

3. Finally, there are three statutory provisions which are sometimes relevant to this question of liability for walls and fences.
   (a) The Highways Act 1980 gives power to the highway authority to serve notice upon a property owner adjoining a street and at his own expense he must then fence adequately any part of his property which is a source of danger to persons using the street.[33] The authority have default powers should the owner take no action.
   (b) Under the Burial Act 1900,[34] an obligation rests on the owner of a cemetery to keep the fences in good order and condition. Since disused burial grounds occasionally are transferred to the local authority, this initial obligation of a Parochial Church Council could become one in which the parks department of a local authority is obliged to take a close interest.[35]
   (c) By virtue of the Limitation Act 1980, a party taking legal action

---

[31] See *Att. Gen.* v. *Todmorden B.C.* (1937) 4 All E.R. 588 for a useful case showing (*inter alia*) that the highway authority need only keep the retaining wall in a state of repair sufficient to support the highway. Any better standard must be met by agreement with the adjacent landowner.
[32] See a useful article in (1909) 73 J.P.R. 285 about retaining walls.
[33] s.165.
[34] s.10.
[35] Local Government Act 1972, s.215 deals with closed churchyards.

4.17 PARKS AND RECREATION GROUNDS

based on the terms of a deed, must do so within 12 years of his cause of action arising.[36] If the deed contained a covenant to erect a fence, then the twelve years would run from the date of the deed.

(5) Metal Detectors

4.18 These, also, are of interest to those responsible for parks and open spaces and will be found discussed in Chapter III in relation to museums. This follows the development of relations by metal detector clubs with museums directors, due to mutual interest in treasure below the ground. (A museums department is invariably consulted when Treasure Trove is found.)

(6) Trespass

4.19 This is now the subject of the Occupiers' Liability Act 1984 and will be found discussed in Chapter 1, with other general legal principles.

(7) Closure of Parks

Shows

4.20 When a local authority grants permission for the holding of an agricultural, horticultural or other show, to be held in one of their parks, or grants the use of a park to a charity or other institution, then the authority will wish to be able to close that park for normal public use. They may also wish to allow the temporary occupiers to make charges for admission to the show. The law allows such closure on a maximum of 12 days in a year, provided that not more than six of such days are consecutive.[37] Closure is not permitted on Sundays. Finally, whilst closure can now take place on public holidays, this power is qualified. On any bank holiday,[38] Christmas Day, Good Friday, or a day appointed for national thanksgiving or mourning, the power of closure can only be used if three quarters of the total area of the parks of that authority is still open to the public.

The local authority has discretion to permit charges for admission to the event in question, to be made whilst the park is closed to the public as a park.[39]

Public entertainment

4.21 An extension to this power of closure is now contained in the Local Government Act 1972, s.145(2). This allows a local authority to close a park when they wish to provide entertainment of any nature, or facilities

---

[36] s.8.
[37] Act of 1890, s.44, and Act of 1961, s.53.
[38] See Bank Holidays Act 1871 and Holidays Extension Act 1875.
[39] Act of 1907, s.44, and Act of 1961, s.53.

THE CREATION, MANAGEMENT AND DISPOSAL OF PUBLIC PARKS **4.21**

for dancing. For this purpose they can enclose or set apart any part of a park or pleasure ground under their control.

A similar power of closure is available when a person is to provide entertainment in a theatre, concert hall, dance hall or other premises for entertainment, dance, or arts and crafts, under agreement with the parks authority; that authority can add part of their park to that letting.

In each instance, the authority must take care not to breach a condition or covenant entered into with the donor of the park or indeed, any other person who is entitled to enforce such terms.

(8) *Car Parks*

The pressing need for car parks near certain popular public parks drives local authorities to consider occasionally whether part of the park itself cannot sensibly be set aside for use as a car park. **4.22**

In law, there is now the specific statutory authority to do this.[40] Even so, a local authority can still meet the kind of problems encountered in, *e.g. Attorney General* v. *Southampton Corporation*.[41] When the local authority wished to set aside two areas of a common as car parks, objection was successfully taken to the move. The grounds advanced by the objectors were that the car parks would not be ancillary to the public park, *i.e.* Southampton Common, but rather would afford desirable car parking for an adjacent public house and an adjacent zoo. The case was complicated by the law relating to commons, when government consents became obligatory, and also Local Acts and open space considerations. Nevertheless, the judgment of Foster J. gave as a basis for his decision the view that the local authority held the common "under the Act of 1875 for the purpose of being used as public walks and pleasure grounds and under the Act of 1906 to allow enjoyment of it by the public as an open space. (It) can only exercise the powers given to it by those Acts, if such exercise is consistent with or ancillary to those purposes."[42] The judge was not satisfied that the car parks were reasonably necessary to enable the public to enjoy the common as an open space or to be used as public walks or pleasure grounds. Thus the Corporation were held to be in breach of their duties if they proceeded with their proposals.

Though the Act of 1976 has clarified the power to provide car parks, which is now available to a local authority, there is but a minor change in the test accepted by the court in the *Southampton* case. Would the car parking be a facility, says the modern court, "in connection with other recreational facilities?", *i.e.* that the authority was providing.[43] Thus the link

---

[40] Act of 1976, s.19 (1) (*f*).
[41] (1978) 21 P. & C.R. 281.
[42] (1978) 21 P. & C.R. 281 at p. 290. A curious anomaly relating to car parks is the generous power of providing car parks from this source available to rural parishes (s.46 of Road Traffic Regulation Act 1967) but not to cities or the Greater London Council.
[43] Act of 1976, s.19(1)(*f*).

4.22   PARKS AND RECREATION GROUNDS

between the proposed car park and enhanced use of the public park or pleasure ground, sought but not found by the court in the *Southampton* case, is still the cardinal test today.

(9) *Local Acts or Deeds of Transfer*

4.23   Public parks have frequently passed into local authority ownership as gifts or as friendly transfers from local property owners of substance. In those circumstances it is not uncommon to find Local Act provisions touching on these properties. A century ago, such Acts were used more frequently to achieve land acquisition or schemes of improvement than is necessary now, when a wider range of public general Acts is available.

A sample list from Local Acts selected at random illustrates the recognition given to the donor's rights, in relation to adjoining land or otherwise. This element can often affect park maintenance and must be taken into account.[44]

Examples of third party restrictions on public parks or open spaces

4.24
1. Waltham Holy Cross U.D.C. Act 1958

    Marshes were created as public parks under section 164 of the Act of 1975, with ample powers to provide recreational facilities. Yet these were not to prevent the digging for or taking of stone sand or gravel from Hall Marsh, Waltham Marsh or Cheshunt Marsh (s.14).

2. Bournemouth Corporation Act 1960

    Power was conferred upon the Corporation to provide in their parks a zoo, botanical gardens, a boating lake and facilities for games. But all these were subject to there being no contravention of private trusts which affected the land in question (s.44).

3. Durham County Council Act 1968

    This authorised the provision of golf courses on lands of the local authority but included a similar proviso about private trusts as in the Bournemouth Act (*supra*) (s.58).

4. Hertfordshire County Council Act 1960

    This Act contains a section (s.7) stemming from the requirement of the law of property that the person seeking to enforce a restrictive covenant should own adjacent land which benefits from that covenant. In order, therefore, to give efficacy to such a covenant in an earlier statute (being one affecting public parks or open space), this provision acknowledged in this authoritative form that there

---

[44] One park in Halifax, West Yorkshire has a Protector, to be consulted as of legal right on changes affecting the character of the park. He is this generation's descendant of the Protector appointed over a century ago. The arrangement has been working harmoniously in recent years.

was adjacent land of the Council which would benefit from such a covenant.

(10) *Park Wardens*

Management need wardens in their parks. Earlier statutes referred to them as officers, though an ancient power to have them sworn in and granted warrants to act as constables is out of harmony with present police practice.[45]

4.25

These wardens are usually needed to enforce park by-laws, which are regularly used to control conduct in parks. The wardens can be particularly useful to spot or discourage mischievous or dangerous conduct in recreation grounds. The legal liabilities of local authorities to children or other visitors to parks are dealt with elsewhere; clearly, evidence from alert wardens about the state of machinery in the play equipment, the frequency of its inspection, the location of any warning notices and any special features in the parks which later assumed legal significance—all these are areas of their work where good wardens can be invaluable to an authority.

3. Disposal or Changed Use of Parks

Background

The assembly by local authorities of lands for their public parks represents an historical phase. Urbanisation proceeded apace in the Victorian era and later, and the parks were a healthy outlet for the townsfolk. Recreation in every form was necessary and the parks met one part of that need.

4.26

The legal framework within which such land was owned by local authorities stemmed from that period. Parliament intended the land to be stamped with the trusts and obligations which were appropriate to its character. Thus in 1972 the land variously acquired by local authorities as public walks and pleasure grounds or as public open space[46] was designated as "public trust land"[47] and restraints placed upon its use for purposes other than those for which it was acquired. Local government reorganisation was the occasion for this re-classification and, ironically, it may be that the attention thus given to these lands later led to the significant relaxing of controls over them.

Certainly a new historical phase is now in being, when local authorities, as a matter of dire financial and legal necessity, review their land hold-

---

[45] Act of 1907, s.77, and Act of 1961, s.52. There are exceptions, *e.g.* at Brighton with 2,500 acres of open space to oversee, where it has been found that the "Parks Police" and "Parks Constables" have a role worth maintaining. The staff in question have been sworn in as constables pursuant to Local Act powers which will lapse before long. Recourse to the more limited powers under the Act of 1907, s.77 then becomes necessary.
[46] Act of 1875, s.164, and Act of 1906.
[47] Local Government Act 1972, s.122 (6).

4.26   Parks and Recreation Grounds

ings.[48] They are under pressure to release land not needed beneficially. Thus parks, as well as schools, blocks of flats, and of course derelict sites, can from time to time come into that group. The movements of central area population can also be a social reason for wishing to abandon a park. The legal restraints upon this sort of action have, in recent years, been eased considerably but, in the absence of codification, it is necessary to set these out piecemeal.

(1) Restrictive Covenants

4.27 Sometimes the free use of park land is hindered by a restrictive covenant: no games on Sundays: no drinks in the pavilion: no building nearer than 100 yards to the southern boundary. History has moved along, the circumstances giving rise to these provisions have altered, and it is now, happily, possible in law to challenge these covenants. The procedure, under the Law of Property Act 1925,[49] is worth consideration by anyone responsible for managing parks and restrained by this type of covenant.

The basic submission to be made to a court by a landowner is:

(i) by reason of changes in the character of the property or the neighbourhood, the restrictive covenant has become obsolete; or

(ii) it is obstructive in that it impedes the reasonable use of the land for public or private purposes; or

(iii) it is contrary to the public interest and the modification or discharge can be adequately compensated in money; or

(iv) the persons entitled to the benefit of the covenant have agreed to the modification or discharge and the court – it is currently the Lands Tribunal which exercises this jurisdiction – is satisfied that no injury will be thereby caused to those persons.[50]

(2) Local Acts

4.28 Reference has been made above to the types of restraint upon public parks found in Local Acts.[51] A local authority is in a good position to judge whether one of these restraints has become otiose and should be removed. It may then be that an opportunity can be found to use a Local Act to insert an amending provision. Such a procedure would involve discussion with the government department, usually the Department of the Environment,

---

[48] See Local Government Planning and Land Act 1980, Pt. X, when reviews of land banks by local authorities are obligatory at the behest of the Secretary of State for the Environment.

[49] s.84, modified by Lands Tribunal Act 1949, Administration of Justice Act 1932, Landlord and Tenant Act 1954, and Law of Property Act 1969. A Law Commission report No. 11 of 1967, achieved, via the Law of Property Act 1969, a considerable widening of powers in this area.

[50] The recent Court of Appeal case of *Gilbert* v. *Spoor* [1982] 3 W.L.R. 183, is a useful corrective to any view that release of a restrictive covenant is simple, once planning permission has been given for the use which depends on that release.

[51] Para. 4.23, *et seq*.

THE CREATION, MANAGEMENT AND DISPOSAL OF PUBLIC PARKS **4.28**

whose general support to the proposed change would in any event, with the procedure of a Local Act, be necessary in order to achieve success.[52]

(3) *Appropriation or Disposal*

There are several statutes which specifically exclude open spaces from those lands which can be acquired compulsorily to be used for the purposes of those Acts, *e.g.* housing, allotments, drainage works or agricultural purposes. **4.29**

Having said that, appropriation is, in local government, the normal way in which to authorise resources to be placed behind a new use for land in the ownership of the local authority. An initial form which appropriation might take is to planning purposes, by virtue of the Town and Country Planning Act 1962, s.83. This deals with the development of such land, despite former restrictions placed upon it. Such a course would open up internal discussion about the zoning and permitted uses available for such land and the advice of town planning staff would be vital.

The Local Government Planning and Land Act 1980 marked a revolution in general powers for public parks to be disposed of or put to other public uses. The important provisions may be summarised as follows[53]: **4.30**

(a) The land in question – specifically held under section 164 of the Act of 1875 or section 10 of the Open Spaces Act 1906 – must be "no longer required for the purposes for which it is held."[54]

(b) Then a principal council[55] may appropriate such land to a purpose for which they are authorised to hold land.

(c) The land will then be released "from any trust arising solely by virtue of its being land held in trust for enjoyment by the public in accordance with the said section 164 or, as the case may be, the said section 10."

(d) Nonetheless, the land will still be subject to the rights of other persons in, over or in respect of, the land concerned.[56]

As appropriations are governed by the principles set out above, so disposals, as a more radical step in relation to the land, are covered by the following[57]: **4.31**

(a) Consent is required from the Secretary of State.

---

[52] The beguilingly wide power in the Act of 1961, s.82, for the Secretary of State to repeal, by Order, certain local Act provisions, is limited, in relation to the subject of this section at least, to the subject matter of the three sections relating to parks in the Act of 1961; ss.52, 53 and 54.

[53] ss.122 and 123.

[54] It has been held that the question whether this is so is wholly for the local authority to decide, acting in good faith, and not for the court. *Att. Gen.* v. *Manchester Corporation* [1931] 1 Ch. 254 and *Dowty Boulton Paul Ltd.* v. *Wolverhampton Corporation No. 2.* [1976] Ch. 13.

[55] Principal local authorities are the metropolitan counties and districts and the non-metropolitan ("shire") counties and districts.

[56] The above power is a general one for local authority land. Commons are the subject of separate restrictions.

[57] See s.123 of the Local Government Planning and Land Act 1980.

4.31 PARKS AND RECREATION GROUNDS

- (b) This consent is not necessary if disposal is effected for the best consideration[58] that can be obtained.
- (c) Public notice and consideration of objections resulting therefrom must take place in the case of "open space" land.
- (d) On disposal, the land is freed from any trust in the same way and to the extent stated at paragraph 4.30 above.
- (e) Capital receipts from such a disposal are subject to directions under the Charities Act 1960.
- (f) The Secretary of State's consent is not necessary for a disposal taking the form of a short tenancy, *i.e.* less than seven years, or an assignment with less than seven years to run.

4.32 Since the land in question was succinctly called "public trust land," local authorities are looked upon as accountable in various ways, as trustees are. The new facilities for appropriation and disposal do not relieve them of that responsibility: they are still accountable to the courts by way of judicial review or, financially, to the Audit Commission or otherwise, if they depart from the new legal framework.

B. PARKS AND RATES

1. The Statutes

4.33 Public parks have generated a steady flow of law cases during the last century on the question of their rateability. At first, the matter in dispute was their status as parks; then it was the effect upon liability to rating of various buildings erected in the parks, or specific uses to which parts of the parks were put. Whilst the present intensive and imaginative use of public parks for new leisure services continues, there is no reason to think that the flow of law cases will diminish.

4.34 In the General Rate Act 1967, the provision about the rating of parks embodies legal principles laid down in the stream of these court cases. This is the section in question:

> **44.**–(1) A park which has been provided by, or is under the management of, a local authority, and is for the time being available for free and unrestricted use by members of the public shall, while so available, be treated for rating purposes as if it had been dedicated in perpetuity for such use.
>
> (2) In this section:
>   (a) references to a park include references to a recreation or pleasure ground, a public walk, an open space within the meaning of the Open Spaces Act 1906, and a playing field

---

[58] See *Buttle* v. *Sanders* (1952) 2 All E.R. 193; also *Caldwell* v. *Sumpters* (1971) 3 All E.R. 892. For an interesting early case on this principle, see *Oliver* v. *Court* (1820) 146 E.R. 1152. (The *Encyclopedia of Local Government Law* (Sweet and Maxwell) also quotes *R.* v. *Essex County Council, ex p. Clearbrook Contractors Ltd.* (1981, unrep.) about the best consideration, in these circumstances. Vol. I, para. 2.283).

PARKS AND RATES 4.34

provided under the (Local Government (Miscellaneous Provisions) Act 1976 section 19);
(b) the expression "local authority" means the council of a county, county borough, London borough, county district, a parish council or parish meeting, the Greater London Council, the Common Council of the City of London or the Council of the Isles of Scilly, or any two or more of them acting in combination.[59]

2. **The Cases**

We will take three parts of section 44 for fuller consideration: 4.35
(1) The extended definition in (2)(a)
(2) "free and unrestricted use" in (1)
(3) "dedicated in perpetuity" in (1)

(1) *The Extended Definition*

The recognition of five different expressions as connoted by "park" in section 44 is a useful acknowledgment of the verbal confusion that can afflict this branch of our subject. "Public parks" is the expression currently in use for these bounded, walking out and recreation areas, yet history has bequeathed to us five other expressions, on each of which hangs the relevant law. Until consolidation comes, composite sections such as section 44 are therefore necessary and indeed welcome. 4.36

(2) *"Free and Unrestricted Use"*

Liability to rates follows occupation of property. Thus the courts, faced with attempts to rate parks, had to ask if those parks could be said to have an occupier. On it being demonstrated that the parks were open to the public, the argument moved to the question whether it was the public rather than the local authority which was the occupier in law. Lord Evershed said in a recent case[60]: 4.37

"Are the premises occupied and if so, by whom?. . . . In the case of (a park or open space), the sensible answer to my mind would be . . .

---

[59] The Local Government Planning and Land Act 1980, s.123A, is very important. It eases disposals of park land which has become unwanted. It modifies the principle of inalienability of that land, as laid down in some of the cases under discussion. But it does not fly in the face of s.44 above; it takes its place as an enabling provision for conveyancers. s.44 is about the qualifying conditions for exemption from rates.
The case of *Bowes Museum Park Trustees* v. *Cutts* (*V.O.*) (1950) 43 R. & I.T. 881, is notable as distinguishing between those who own property by virtue of statute and those whose ownership is by virtue of charter or private conveyance. The trustees in that case were found to be in beneficial occupation and rateable.
[60] *Clayton* v. *Kingston-upon-Hull Corporation* [1961] 1 Q.B. 345 at p. 355. This Court of Appeal decision was confirmed by the House of Lords at [1963] A.C. 28.

that the park or open space is not 'occupied' by anyone; the public have, when the gates are open, free and unrestricted access to the whole of it, save only such buildings as are reserved for the use of the park keepers or custodians."

Lord Evershed then had recourse, as, evidently, does every court deliberating upon this question, to the *Lambeth Overseers* case.[61] The House of Lords had there to adjudicate on an attempt to impose rates on Brockwell Park in London. The park contained buildings, such as residences for its departmental staff, shelters, a tool shed and a public gymnasium. But in the House of Lords, Lord Halsbury (L.C.) said:

"I do not think there is here rateable occupation by anybody. 'The Public' is not a rateable occupier and I think that one sentence disposes of the case. . . . The fact that the park is vested in the county council does not make them the occupiers. . . . It would be absurd to contend that wherever the legal estate is, there is occupation. A road is vested in someone but . . . there is no occupation of it, any more than of a milestone or a direction post."

Lord Herschell, following, described the council as "merely custodians or trustees, to hold it and manage it for the use of the public."[62]

Thus Lord Evershed, in the *Kingston-upon-Hull* case above, followed these principles and looked in the case before him for evidence of the extent of public rights in the property. There was a staff of eight, normal hours of closing, and, as an art gallery, an exclusion of the public as visitors from a significant physical area of the premises. The court concluded that the local authority were in occupation of the property in that case and were, moreover, in rateable occupation.[63]

4.38 The inquiry for the actual occupiers of parks led the courts to consider the significance of occupation by the local authority of small buildings, such as pavilions, kiosks, shelters and conveniences. The principle evolved is that where these are ancillary to the management of the public park, as a public park, then they do not justify the court in derogating from the general principle in the *Lambeth Overseers* case. In other words, the local authority is not rateable because it is not in occupation but is a custodian or trustee for the public.

An example is a case from Sheffield.[64] A pavilion in the park was let on a yearly tenancy to an icecream vendor. He was obliged to be open for business whilst the park was open, save for half an hour; his customers were all people frequenting the park. The agreement clearly gave the tenant exclusive occupation of the pavilion at £225 rent per annum and this feature was argued as adequate to isolate the pavilion from the park and

---

[61] *Lambeth Overseers* v. *L.C.C.* [1897] A.C. 625.
[62] *Ibid.* at pp. 629 and 631.
[63] It was an art gallery and the court rejected a plea that it should be exempt from rating.
[64] *Sheffield Corporation* v. *Tranter* [1957] 1 W.L.R. 843.

PARKS AND RATES   **4.38**

leave it open to separate rating. The court did not accede to this argument. Lord Evershed, four years before the *Hull* case, was clear that as the pavilion "was being so used, not because it was surplus to the requirements of the park, but as part of the park," then the *Valuation Officers'* case to have the pavilion rated, failed. The tenant's activity, said Lord Evershed, "was nothing more than an ancillary activity of the conduct of the park itself." In the same judgment, the court accepted the corollary of the view here described, *i.e.* that where, as with the Thameside Restaurant on the bank of the Thames for the Festival of Britain, a building had been "severed" from the park as a park, and given "independent status" as a restaurant, then that building must be rated separately.[65]

(3) *"Dedicated in Perpetuity"*

The last subsection dealt with the question of the effective *occupier* of some   **4.39**
of the park buildings; the above expression raises for consideration the legal *status* of that property. The courts had said that if there was some third person occupying, *e.g.* the tea pavilion, as in the *Sheffield* case,[66] then it was not a *beneficial* occupation: it was not arranged in order to produce a profit for the local authority.

A striking example is *Blake* v. *Hendon Corporation (No. 2)*.[67] A bowling green in a public park was let exclusively to a bowling club. Was it rateable? All three members of the Court of Appeal used the expression "beneficial occupation" when describing the occupation by the local authority. The following sentence by Harman L.J. in an earlier case[68] found favour:

> "Unless therefore, the Corporation occupy merely as custodians, or, in other words, unless the rights of the public are such as to exclude the possibility of beneficial occupation on the part of the Corporation, then the occupation on the part of the Corporation will be treated as beneficial for rating purposes."

There has been legal debate about whether the *Lambeth Overseers* case   **4.40**
rested on the absence of *occupancy* by the Corporation or upon the absence of *beneficial occupation* by the corporation. A sentence from the judgment of Lord Guest in the House of Lords report of the same case is helpful:

> "When the speeches (of Lord Halsbury and Lord Herschell in the *Brockwell Park* case) are examined, I think it is reasonably clear that the real basis of the decision was that there was no beneficial occupa-

---

[65] *L.C.C.* v. *Robinson* (1955) 48 R. & I.T. 455.
 Another important case where rateability was found made out for a foreshore is *N. Riding of Yorkshire County Valuation Committee* v. *Redcar Corporation etc. Committee* [1943] 1 K.B. 114.
[66] See n.64, *supra*.
[67] (1965) 63 L.G.R. 198.
[68] *Hull Corporation* v. *Clayton* [1961] 1 Q.B. 345 at p. 360. See also *Ryde on Rating* (13th ed., 1976), Chapter XV.

tion, because the property was dedicated for the perpetual use of the public and could not therefore be used for any profitable purpose."[69]

That sentence sums up the judicial requirement for a clear, ongoing non-profitable use of property by the public, in order for it to qualify for rate-free status. In the law, the word "dedicated" has, until recently, been regarded as exclusively reserved for the land set aside to be used as a highway.[70] A wider meaning has now been given the authority of an Act of Parliament. The addition of the words "in perpetuity" is surely superfluous, if "dedicated" has a clear meaning. Certainly the dictionary meaning of "something lasting for ever" is out of place in a field of law where appropriation to other uses has become comparatively easy. The judicial "for the foreseeable future" seems more reasonable.[71]

3. Conclusion

4.41 The most recent relevant reported case is *Smith (V.O.) v. City of St. Albans*.[72] The question before the Lands Tribunal was whether an indoor heated swimming pool, standing within, or near to, a public park at Verulamium, St. Albans, was rateable. It was a recreational amenity, with no physical boundaries separating it from the park area. The Tribunal reviewed the cases from *Brockwell Park* onwards and observed that, since the General Rate Act 1967, it was unnecessary to establish dedication to the public, since section 44 says that this element shall be deemed to exist when free and unrestricted use by the public is demonstrated. The Tribunal reached the point that exemption from rating was possible for the pool, only if the pool was ancillary to the park. "Ancillary buildings," said the Tribunal "seem to me to be those which subserve the enjoyment of the park qua park."[73] The baths, being "a separate and distinct amenity," were not within the exemption afforded to parks. The Valuation Officer's appeal to the Tribunal was thus successful.[74]

C. By-Laws

4.42 By-laws are regulations normally limited to one aspect of the legal powers exercised by the local authority, or other body so authorised. They operate only within its own area or part of that area. They are a normal and

---

[69] *Ibid.* at (1961) 3 All E.R. 118.
[70] See, *e.g.* Stroud *Law Terms Defined* and Jowitt's *Dictionary of English Law* (2nd ed., 1977). The wider meaning appears in the American *Black's Law Dictionary* (5th ed., 1979). For an older protest at the use of the word in relation to local authorities, see Maugham J. in *Att. Gen.* v. *Manchester Corporation* [1931] 1 Ch. 254 at p. 267.
[71] *Burnell* v. *Downham Market U.D.C.* [1952] 2 Q.B. 55, Evershed M.R. at p. 64. The judge could not conceive that Lord Halsbury had meant to lay it down that the characteristic of permanence "as an obligation for all eternity" was essential to the conclusion that the L.C.C. was not rateable for a park.
[72] [1978] R.A. 147.
[73] *Ibid.* at p. 30.
[74] Curiously, only the side heading of s.44 uses the word "exemption."

By-Laws 4.42

recognised form of control of public parks by the management. The legal framework within which by-laws are used is a combination of statute and case law.

1. The Statutes

Individual statutes regularly empower local authorities and other legally constituted bodies to make by-laws. The Forestry Commission and the Water Authority are examples outside local government. The schedule below indicates, within the scope of this book, the wide range of subjects that by-laws cover: **4.43**

Subject	*Statute*	*Confirming body*
Allotments	Small Holdings and Allotments Act 1908, s.28	Dept. of the Environment
Ancient Monuments	Ancient Monuments Consolidation and Amendment Act 1913, s.13 Ancient Monuments Act 1931, s.7	,,
Street Playgrounds	Road Traffic Regulation Act 1967, s.27	,,
Libraries & Museums	Public Libraries and Museums Act 1964, s.19	Dept. of Education and Science
Recreation in Public Parks	Public Health Act 1875, s.164	Dept. of the Environment
Open Spaces	Open Spaces Act 1906, s.15	,,
Nature Reserves	National Parks and Access to the Countryside Act 1949, s.90	Home Secretary
The seashore	Public Health Acts Amendment Act 1907, s.82	,,
Pleasure Fairs	Public Health Act 1961, s.75	,,
Pleasure boats in Parks	Public Health Acts Amendment Act 1890, s.44	,,
Seaside Pleasure Boats	Public Health Act 1961, s.76	,,
Country Parks	Countryside Act 1968, ss.4 and 8	Dept. of the Environment
Commons	Commons Act 1899, s.1	Home Secretary
Promenades	Public Health Acts Amendment Act 1907, s.83	,,
Swimming Baths	Public Health Act 1936, s.223	Dept. of the Environment
Inland Waterways	Transport Act 1968, s.113	,,

4.44 PARKS AND RECREATION GROUNDS

Good rule and government

4.44   In addition, there is a class of by-laws known as good rule and government, which certain local authorities are authorised to make.[75] The authorising statute also uses the expression "the prevention and supression of nuisances," as an additional description of the subject-matter. A qualification is placed upon what may seem to be a wide power; such by-laws are not to be made "if provision for that purpose, as respects that area, is made by, or may be made under, any other enactment."[76] This good rule and government group is in the nature of a residual category for by-laws, after the powers for specific subjects have been exhausted. The broadening sweep of modern legislation, applying to all aspects of urban life, has made the use of good rule and government by-laws less important for a well-managed local authority.

Statutory safeguards

4.45   The grant of by-law making powers to a local authority is hedged about with safeguards. The by-laws themselves, before coming into operation, must be confirmed by the appropriate government department. Furthermore, after they have become operative, they are open to challenge in the courts as being invalid.

The power to make by-laws includes a power to amend or repeal those by-laws. Such a step is often taken in practice when making new by-laws; these then contain a by-law which amends or repeals the earlier ones.[77]

2. The Cases

4.46   This branch of law illustrates well the law-making powers of the courts. The tests of the validity of a by-law are most important and these are illustrated, to a remarkably large extent, in the judgments of the Divisional Court in the case of *Kruse* v. *Johnson*.[78]

As a body to whom law-making powers have been given, a local authority must act within those powers. If it should stray, wilfully or carelessly, outside those powers, it is at risk of challenge by means of judicial review, or some other sanction, because it will be said to have acted *ultra vires*, *i.e.* beyond its powers. In considering challenges made to local authorities over the years on this point, the courts evolved various tests: the case of *Kruse* v. *Johnson* brought them usefully together and developed them. This case is invariably consulted when a problem on the validity of by-laws is met.

In the *Kruse* case, Kent County Council had made a by-law which for-

---

[75] Local Government Act 1972, s.235(1). District councils and London borough councils have this power.
[76] *Ibid.* s.235 (3).
[77] The Interpretation Act 1978, s.14, confers power to revoke or amend without necessarily replacing.
[78] [1898] 2 Q.B. 91.

bade persons from singing or playing music within 50 yards of a dwelling house, after being requested to desist. A person duly convicted of an offence appealed on the ground that the by-law was bad, because it was unreasonable. The Court held the by-law valid and in their judgments laid down guidelines for similar cases. Lord Russell C.J. said that by-laws should be certain, they should be reasonable, they should not be repugnant to other laws and they should be *intra vires* the local authority in question.

The Court emphasised that a benevolent attitude should be taken by the courts to local authorities, as public representative bodies. But if they failed to conform to these tests, then the by-laws must be held invalid.

Against that background, some examples of each of these four tests are now given.

(1) *Certainty*

In a recent leisure services case, a by-law failed to pass this requirement.[79] **4.47**
In prohibiting hang-gliders from being flown in pleasure grounds, it failed to stipulate a minimum height below which a glider must not be flown. A person would not, in those circumstances, know when he was contravening the law. The by-law was, therefore, uncertain, invalid and unenforceable.

The classic example of a by-law held invalid for lack of certainty was in the terms: "No person shall wilfully annoy passengers in the street."[80]

(2) *Reasonableness*

The *locus classicus* is again a passage from the judgment of Lord Russell in **4.48**
Kruse v. *Johnson*:

> "If by-laws were found to be partial and unequal in their operation, as between classes, if they were manifestly unjust, if they disclosed bad faith, if they involved such oppressive or gratuitous interference with the rights of those subject to them, as could find no justification in the minds of reasonable men, the court might well say 'Parliament never intended to give authority to make such rules; they are unreasonable and ultra vires.' But, (continued Lord Russell) it is in this sense and in this sense only, that I conceive that the question of unreasonableness can properly be regarded. A by-law is not unreasonable merely because particular judges may think that it goes further than is prudent or necessary or convenient, or because it is not accompanied by a qualification or an exception which some judges think ought to be there."[81]

---

[79] *Staden* v. *Tarjany* (1980) 78 L.G.R. 614 (Q.B.D.). There were several complicating legal provisions about air traffic regulations but the *ratio decidendi* was as above. The local authority was Adur D.C. and the pleasure ground at Shoreham-by-Sea.
[80] *Nash* v. *Finlay* (1901) 85 L.T. 682.
[81] [1898] 2 Q.B. 91 at p. 100.

4.48   PARKS AND RECREATION GROUNDS

A good recent leisure services example is the case of *Burnley B.C.* v. *England*.[82] The local authority made by-laws under local acts for their parks and these were duly confirmed by the Home Secretary. In particular, these by-laws prohibited persons from causing dogs to enter or remain in certain specified "pleasure grounds." These amounted in total to some 141 acres in extent, out of 795 acres available for recreation in the borough.[83] The parks thus forbidden to dogs were carefully selected, as being ornamental gardens, childrens playgrounds or play areas.

Substantial public protests followed the making of these by-laws. These included a walk through a prohibited park by some 200–300 people, some leading dogs. Similar protests were threatened. The local authority secured an interlocutory injunction to prevent such protest meetings or processions in the parks in question and the hearing for the final injunction followed some time later.

At that hearing, there was a challenge to the validity of the critical by-law, on the ground of reasonableness. It was argued strongly that the by-law should have been more limited in extent – more limited in relation to the people to whom it would cause hardship – and that it did not strike a fair balance between children and the elderly residents in the town.

The court indicated what sort of by-law about the entry of dogs into parks would have been viewed as unreasonable, found no such element in the by-law before the court and granted the final injunction sought by the Council. The court based its approach upon the judgment of Lord Russell (*supra*) and said that it did not find the by-law in question "manifestly unjust or that it was an oppressive or gratuitous interference with the rights of others which a reasonable council would not countenance."[84]

4.49   There are numerous other cases in the reports[85]: one instance will suffice. In *Arlidge* v. *Islington Corporation*,[86] a by-law required landlords of lodging houses to limewash them in April, May or June in each year. Insofar as some of these landlords had no contractual power to enter these occupied houses, the by-law was held unreasonable and bad. A landlord would have had to commit trespass or breach of contract in order to comply with it.

(3) *Consistency with other Laws*

4.50   In the 1955 case of *Galer* v. *Morrissey*,[87] the court had to consider a by-law which forbade the keeping of a noisy animal which was a serious nuisance to nearby residents. The court was asked to say that the by-law was invalid, because it covered the same subject matter as the Public Health

---

[82] (1979) 77 L.G.R. 227.
[83] There was an exception for a guide dog, with a blind person.
[84] (1979) 77 L.G.R. 22, p. 237.
[85] See *e.g.* a useful summary in the *Encyclopedia of Local Government Law* (Sweet & Maxwell) at para. 1–249.
[86] [1909] 2 K.B. 127.
[87] [1955] 1 W.L.R. 110.

Act 1936, s.92, about public nuisances, arising from the conditions under which the animals were kept. Lord Goddard L.C.J. presided and said: "No one doubts that if the statute deals with precisely the same matter, the by-law would be *ultra vires*, because there would be no necessity for it."[88] But he drew distinctions between the subject matter of the two provisions and upheld the by-law.

In a different setting, a canal company in their by-law prohibited traffic on the canal on Sundays.[89] The court held the by-law void. There was existing general legislation about Sunday observance and whilst the canal company was entitled to make bylaws about the orderly use of the navigation, the by-law in question did not purport to achieve that end. "They only say," said Rolfe B. about the canal company, "that it was decorous that the canal should not be used on Sundays."[90] That was outside the company's powers and thus the by-law was void.

4.51

(4) *Intra Vires* [91]

In the old case of *R. v. Wood*,[92] a by-law about the removal of several types of deposit about houses was held bad when, instead of staying within the statutory limits relating to deposits of ashes, rubbish, soil and others, it was sought to use the by-law to secure the removal of snow from footpaths. This was not within the by-law making powers.

4.52

It is important to note that a by-law can be good in part even though bad in part. An instance comes from the Common at Beverley in Yorkshire, where a by-law by the pasture masters imposed a penalty for pasturing a vicious horse on their pastures.[93] The by-law stipulated that the "person so offending and the owner of the said horse shall respectively forfeit" the sum of five pounds. The owner, an attorney's clerk, let a pony onto the pasture, the animal being known as vicious. The pasture masters imposed the £5 penalty on him, as provided by the by-law, and when this was unpaid the matter was taken to the justices, who convicted the owner under the by-law. On appeal, Quarter Sessions confirmed that conviction.

4.53

The owner then took an appeal to the Court of Queens Bench to have the conviction quashed on the ground that the by-law was bad. He argued that it made it possible to convict two persons of the one offence and moreover the owner might be unaware of the action of the herdsman in letting the horse onto the common. Insofar as the owner in this case was himself culpable, this argument was academic, but it drew from the court an important statement. Cockburn C.J. said, maintaining the conviction, "Where a by-law is good in part and bad in part, the objectionable portion may be rejected and the remainder retained and acted upon."

---

[88] *Ibid.* "A by-law cannot, in effect, dot the i's and cross the t's of a statute."
[89] *Calder & Hebble Navigation* v. *Pilling* (1845) 153 E.R. 396.
[90] *Ibid.* at p. 402.
[91] Within their powers.
[92] (1855) 5 E. & B. 49.
[93] *R. v. Lundie* (1862) 8 Jur. N.S. 640.

3. The Practice

(a) Making by-laws

4.54 The procedure to obtain a lawful by-law is laid down for local authorities in the Local Government Act 1972[94] and for other bodies in the parent statutes. It is at all times important and must be followed to the letter. It involves due public notice and the sealing of the by-law, after a period for public inspection and making formal objections. The by-law is then submitted to the confirming authority.

(b) Model by-laws

4.55 That authority may well have a published model by-law and departure from that model will oblige the applicant local authority to make out a local need to depart from the standard by-law. The use of a model is justified by the desirability of consistency and by the reliability in practice of a by-law which is used extensively. Thus the scope for by-laws to be a field for local experiment is in practice severely limited.

(c) Enforcement

4.56 The enforcement of by-laws is in practice left to the authority which made them, though in theory an individual can take steps to do so.[95] The *Burnley park* case, above, is an interesting modern case of successful recourse by a local authority to the procedure of a High Court injunction to enforce a by-law. The unusual circumstances, with mass protests threatened and expected, were held by the courts at interlocutory and final injunction stages, to justify that somewhat rare course of action.[96]

(d) No relaxation

4.57 The production of a printed copy of a by-law, duly certified by the proper officer of the local authority, allows it to be used in court proceedings.[97]

There are no powers to waive or relax the provisions of a by-law. It has become, after confirmation, part of the law of the land for that area in which the relevant public authority operates.[98]

---

[94] s.236.
[95] Though not under the Public Health Act 1936, s.298, which is only for the local authority.
[96] The courts followed *Elkenford Ltd.* v. *Stafford B.C.* 75 L.G.R. 337, a Court of Appeal decision, where Denning M.R. said:
   "Where there is a plain breach of the statute, I do not think that the local authorities concerned need wait for finality. It is open to the court to grant an injunction when the law is plain and there appears an intention to continue with the breach." (p. 341)
   That case concerned a Sunday market.
[97] Local Government Act 1972, s.238. For proper officer, see s.270.
[98] The legal merits of making or not making by-laws are discussed in Chap. 1, in relation to Nuisance, as well as in the shorter discussion at paras. 4.09–4.14 of this chapter. Once by-laws are made, the local authority is seen to have taken control of that area of activity in its park and its legal liability therefor as "occupier" is extended. See *Hall* v. *Beckenham Corporation* [1949] 1 K.B. 716.

D. MISCELLANEOUS AMENITIES

1. **Street Playgrounds**

Recreation grounds have for many years been set apart in public parks; in the same spirit, street playgrounds have been developed as urban recreation areas. They are now the subject of a compact code of law contained in the Road Traffic Acts.[99] This may be summarised as follows: **4.58**
- (i) Highway authorities are empowered to make Orders which will require streets to be kept clear of vehicles, so that children may play safely in them.[1]
- (ii) The Orders require the approval of the Minister of Transport.
- (iii) The Orders, which are called Traffic Regulation Orders, specify the streets, or parts of streets, the days or hours of the week and the vehicles affected by the Orders.[2] These elements may be expected to vary from location to location, according to local circumstances.
- (iv) The Orders must preserve access to premises in the affected streets.[3]
- (v) Offences carry fines of £100.[4]
- (vi) By-laws may be made by the local authorities for the areas in question, relating to the safety of children, the access to the playgrounds and the safety of those playgrounds.[5]
- (vii) Traffic signs designating the street playgrounds are specified.[6]
- (viii) A procedure is set out for the making and confirmation of these Orders.[7]
- (ix) Orders can be varied by the same procedure used to make them.[8]
- (x) For the general liability in tort of those who manage street playgrounds, reference should be made to Chapter 1, which deals with general legal principles.

2. **Diseases**

(1) *Dutch Elm Disease*

The affliction of elm trees by an insidious disease in recent years, has been on such a scale that the Government harnessed the resources of local auth- **4.59**

---

[99] Road Traffic Regulation Act 1967, s.26 (modified by the Transport Act 1968).
[1] *Ibid.* s.84B. Highway authorities for these Orders are county councils outside London, and inside the Greater London Council, London boroughs and the City of London Common Council. The pioneer Act was the Street Playgrounds Act 1938, now repealed.
[2] s.26, *supra.*
[3] See s.84 of the Act of 1967 for the guiding principles in making Orders.
[4] s.26(6) *supra,* and the Road Traffic Act 1974, s.21(1).
[5] s.27, *supra.*
[6] *Ibid.* s.56A.
[7] *Ibid.* s.84C.
[8] *Ibid.* s.84D. Background reading on this subject may be found in two reports of the Department of the Environment: *Recreation and Deprivation in Inner Urban Areas,* (1977 HMSO), and *Leisure Provision and People's Needs,* (1981 HMSO).

orities as part of a national campaign to resist the scourge. Action taken has led to the felling of hundreds of trees and replacement planting. This skilled task has fallen on the Amenities Departments of local authorities, being those with responsibilities for parklands and their forest trees.

The legal framework within which the campaign has been waged stems primarily from the Forestry Act of 1967 and a series of Statutory Instruments made under that Act and two later Forestry Acts of 1979 and 1981. Authority has, however, also been drawn from the Plant Health Act 1967,[9] the European Communities Act 1972[10] and the Agriculture (Miscellaneous Provisions) Act 1972.[11]

There have been two main thrusts, from the purely legal point of view, in this campaign. Firstly, powers were conferred on local authorities and others to deal with the diseased trees where they stand. Secondly, a general restriction was placed upon the movement of those trees from listed areas, until the timber had been rendered safe.

A Diseased trees

4.60 The attack on the diseased trees as they grow required two legal weapons:

(a) The inclusion in the Forestry Act 1967 of a new exception to the general provision in that Act that felling of trees could take place only with a licence from the Forestry Commission. The new exception is in these terms:

> "Felling an elm tree which is so affected by Dutch Elm Disease that the greater part of the crown of the tree is dead."[12]

(b) The conferring of powers on named local authorities to deal vigorously with diseased trees.[13] Those councils should appoint officers to:
   (i) Enter land to inspect trees and examine the bark.
   (ii) Arrange for the service upon the relevant landowner of notices which required him to cut down and then destroy or treat the felled timber. The appointed officer would act in default of compliance, in the period specified in the notice, by the landowner.

B Movement of trees

4.61 Turning, secondly, to the movement restriction, an Order placed an embargo upon the movement of Dutch elm. No branches or felled trees of diseased elm were to be moved across highways or by rail or water, unless

---

[9] s.3 and 5.
[10] s.4.
[11] s.20.
[12] Forestry (Exception from Restriction of Felling) Regulations 1979 (S.I. 1979 No. 792) reg. 4, affects s.9 of the Act of 1967.
[13] Various groups of authorities were listed in successive Orders under the Acts mentioned in the text. See now Dutch Elm Disease (Local Authorities) Order 1984 (S.I. 1984 No. 687).

MISCELLANEOUS AMENITIES **4.61**

the bark had been removed. This embargo was supported legally by powers for Forestry Commission inspectors to inspect books of account and other relevant documents. Persons suspected of transporting diseased elms could have notice served upon them by the Commission inspectors to remove the bark from the diseased timber. That Order put the embargo on 64 districts.[14]

This outline indicates briefly the legal activity generated by one serious disease in one genus of tree. It is of interest to local authorities not only because of the duties imposed on them, but also because of their own role as major landowners with large numbers of trees on their own lands.

(2) *Fire Blight Disease*

Another scourge that has called for legal aid in combating it is Fire Blight. **4.62** This is a bacterial disease that affects fruit trees but also ornamental plants. It has been the subject of a series of Statutory Instruments.

The current one is No. 1966/162 Fire Blight Disease (Amendment) Order. It obliges persons who discover or suspect the presence of the blight to notify the Ministry of Agriculture Fisheries and Food, so that appropriate action can be taken.[15]

3. Wild Animals in Parks

Licensing under the Zoo Licensing Act 1981

A local authority desiring to establish a zoo now comes within the con- **4.63** trols set up by the Zoo Licensing Act 1981. This Act, whilst requiring local authorities to licence the zoos of other persons, allows them to grant licences for their own zoos. They must then supply a copy of that licence to the Department of the Environment, together with a copy of any inspector's report upon the zoo in question. The Secretary of State then has, in relation to the local authority's zoo, the same powers that the local authority exercise over private zoos within their area.[16] This means that he has power to revoke that licence if:

    (a) A reasonable requirement to the zoo management, in consequence of some item in the inspector's report, is not met in the time specified.[17]

---

[14] Dutch Elm Disease (Restriction on Movement of Elms) Order 1984 (S.I. 1984 No. 686) is the current Order.
[15] The initial Statutory Instrument was S.I. 1958 No. 1814, which lists the powers and the offences. The Orders are made under the Destructive Insects and Pests Acts of 1877, 1907 and 1927.
[16] Zoo Licensing Act 1981, s.13.
[17] *Ibid.* s.17(1) (*a*). In the second reading debate on this Private Member's Bill, said to be the result of five years research, the mover described its main purpose as "to lift the standard of the zoo industry." 22 zoos were said then to be directly affected by the Bill, though 60 were said to be under inspection by the Health and Safety Executive. *Hansard.* (16.3.81) Vol. 1000, p. 525.

4.63   Parks and Recreation Grounds

    (b) The zoo has been conducted in a disorderly manner, or so as to be a nuisance or in breach of the conditions in the licence.[18]
    (c) One of the persons responsible for the running of the zoo is convicted of an offence under the Act of 1981 or of a listed offence relating to the ill-treatment of animals.[19]

The licensing procedure to be followed by local authorities under the Act of 1981 requires the authority to consider the views invited from six named bodies, ranging from the police and fire services to any national body active in the area of operating zoos and also persons living in the locality of the proposed zoo. A licence once granted has to be exhibited at public entrances to the zoo. The whole code embodied in this Act is clearly intended to be both comprehensive and also to ensure that the best standards are applied to modern zoos.[20]

Keeping wild animals

4.64   Whilst a zoo is by definition in the above Act a place where the public have access to wild animals – as defined – on seven or more days in a year, in our society persons other than the local authority sometimes keep wild animals.[21] That can only be done lawfully under licence from the local authority, under the Dangerous Wild Animals Act 1976. That Act and the Zoo Licensing Act 1981 are mutually exclusive, in that the Act of 1976 does not apply to persons holding a licence under the Act of 1981.

4. Insurance and Bad Weather

4.65   The parks managements of local authorities from time to time need to take advice about their insurance cover. Third party claims for injury in recreation grounds is certainly one such area of risk.

Another is bad weather. All who organise public events in summer can insure against the risk of loss resulting from bad weather, other things being equal. A show, a procession, a carnival – all can be intended for large crowds and the budgeted break-even point can depend upon the sun.

This category in insurance law is pecuniary loss insurance[22] and cases reaching the courts are few and far between.[23] One case of interest, because of the principle involved, is *London County Cycling and Athletic Club Ltd.* v. *Beck*.[24] A cycling meeting was insured with Lloyd's in the sum of

---

[18] *Ibid.* s.17(1) (*b*).
[19] See s.4(5) for a list of 10 Acts or groups of Acts.
[20] There is power for the Secretary of State to give a dispensation to a zoo too small to be brought within the machinery of the Act. A very important provision is the group of sections about special and periodical inspections, ss.10, 11 and 12.
[21] The Act of 1976 does not apply to a pet shop, a zoological garden, a circus or a place registered for experiments under the Cruelty to Animals Act 1976. A deer park is excluded from the definition of a Zoological garden, s.7, *supra*.
[22] The Insurance Companies Act 1974, s.83(6) defines the expression.
[23] The subject was mentioned in comments about a cricket match, almost in passing, by Scrutton L.J. *Leon* v. *Casey* [1932] 2 K.B. 576 at p. 581.
[24] [1897] 3 Commercial Cases 49.

£250, provided that "the expenses attached to the meeting" were not less than the sum of £250.

When the meeting was held, and resulted in a loss, the Club wished to recover the £250 as covered by the policy. To demonstrate to Lloyd's that the expenses incurred were not less than £250, the Club sought to include as expenses the sum of £21 4s. 0d., being the premium for the policy. This would bring the expenses to £267 12s. 9d. Lloyd's rejected the principle involved but after a court hearing the Club succeeded. "Meeting," said the judge, "must mean not merely the actual meeting while in progress but the whole adventure."

The scope of this type of insurance has developed enormously but the principle is not out of date.

Chapter 5

SPECIAL CASES

*"The little more and how much it is
And the little less and what worlds away"*

Robert Browning
"By the Fireside" xxxix.

A. The National Trust

1. **Introduction**

5.01 The National Trust is a unique national institution. It owns nearly 500,000 acres of land, over 400 miles of this country's coastline and attracted over seven million visitors to its properties in a recent year.[1] Devotion to the purposes initially set out in its founding Act of 1907 and later enlarged has enabled the National Trust to reach its present position affording to many people the pleasures of a major leisure service.

2. **Purposes**

5.02 Its purposes were first legally embodied in the National Trust Act 1907, as follows:

> "Promoting the permanent preservation, for the benefit of the nation, of lands and tenements (including buildings) of beauty or historic interest and as regards lands, for the preservation (so far as practicable) of their natural aspect, features and animal and plant life."[2]

5.03 These were later significantly extended by the National Trust Act 1937, s.3 in three ways:

> "The promotion of
> (a) the preservation of buildings of national interest or architectural, historic or artistic interest and places of natural interest or beauty and the protection and augmentation of the amenities of such buildings and places and their surroundings;

---

[1] Figures taken from the 1983 Annual Report.
[2] s.4. There was a short period of incorporation under the Companies' Acts preceding the National Trust Act 1907. There have been five subsequent Acts: the National Trust Charity Scheme Confirmation Act 1919, the National Trust Act 1937, the National Trust Act 1939, the National Trust Act 1953, and the National Trust Act 1971.

(d) the preservation of furniture and pictures and chattels of any description, having national or historic or artistic interest;
(e) the access to and enjoyment of such buildings, places and chattels by the public."

This enlargement of the legal purposes clearly reflected experience and contains a fuller definition in relation to buildings and places, the first reference to furniture, pictures and chattels and the first reference to "access to and enjoyment of" those features.

The purposes set out in that Act of 1907 were brought before the Chancery Division of the High Court by the National Trust itself in 1916, and held to be charitable in law, in the case of *Re Verrall. National Trust v. Attorney General*.[3] It was necessary to satisfy the court that the purposes came within the legal expression, "other purposes beneficial to the community" and Astbury J. said that they were "plainly public purposes, expressly stated to be for the benefit of the nation."[4]

3. Powers

5.04 The National Trust has extensive statutory powers and these may be summarised as follows:

(1) *General*

(i) Acquire land, buildings and rights and interests therein.[5]
(ii) Maintain and manage:
   (a) lands as open spaces or places of public resort;
   (b) buildings, for public recreation, resort or instruction.
(iii) Accept property in trust for public purposes.
(iv) Act in any trusts for any property devoted to public purposes.
(v) Do all acts and take all proceedings as deemed desirable in furtherance of the objects of the National Trust
(vi) Do anything in relation to their property that may be "beneficial for the property or desirable for the comfort or convenience of persons resorting to or using such property."

(2) *Commons*

5.05 In connection with trust land which is common or commonable land:
(i) Keep it at all times open for the recreation of the public.
(ii) For the purposes in (i), plant, drain, level and improve the land and make temporary enclosures, in the interests of good estate management.

---

[3] [1916] 1 Ch. 100.
[4] There are three specific legal classes of charity in English law: relief of poverty, promotion of religion, support of education. This last, fourth, general class is occasionally chary of accommodating all applicants for the shelter it affords.
[5] The Act of 1907, s.4(2).

5.05   Special Cases

    (iii) Make and maintain paths, ponds and waters.
    (iv) Erect and maintain tool sheds.
    (v) Resist and abate all encroachments.
    (vi) Set apart parts of the property for games, meetings or sport gatherings.[6]
    (vii) The restriction on the power of highway authorities to search for, dig and carry away, gravel, sand and other materials from commons in the Commons Act 1876, s.20, is applied to commons vested in the National Trust Act of 1907, s.36.

(3) *Charges*

To make "reasonable charges" for admission to National Trust property or for its use by the public. (This does not apply to commons.)[7]

(4) *Local Authorities*

In order to give effect to its objects, the National Trust is empowered to "act in concert with and make any arrangements and agreements with any local authority" or, indeed, any committee of residents in the neighbourhood of their property.[8]

(5) *By-Laws*

Buildings

5.06   The powers for which by-laws might be made in relation to its buildings were modelled on those which had been recently granted by Parliament for public libraries.[9] Hence the powers include:
    (i) Regulating its use.
    (ii) Protecting its contents.
    (iii) Taking guarantees from users against loss or injury to the contents.
    (iv) Imposing fines.
    (v) Enabling staff to remove persons who offend against the by-laws or against certain standards of behaviour. Being again imported from the Public Libraries Act 1891, these offences covered staying beyond permitted hours on the property, gaming, eating and drinking in places not set apart for those purposes, and general unsociable behaviour.[10]

---

[6] *Ibid.* s.29.
[7] *Ibid.* s.30.
[8] *Ibid.* s.31.
[9] *Ibid.* s.33.
[10] The Public Libraries Act 1901, s.3, was repealed by the Public Libraries and Museums Act 1964, s.26. S.19 of that Act of 1964 now contains comparable by-law making power for regulating the use of facilities provided and the conduct of persons in the premises. The Interpretation Act 1978, s.17(2)(*a*) allows the use of the powers in s.33 of the Act of 1907 by reference to the Public Libraries and Museums Act 1964.

Lands and property

The powers for these extensive subjects were revised in the latest Act obtained by the National Trust, the Act of 1971.[11] Generally, the powers granted are to make by-laws to regulate and protect the property, to prevent and suppress nuisances; to preserve order and regulate the conduct and secure the safety of visitors.

Specifically, the Act of 1971 then lists nineteen subjects which may be dealt with in the by-laws. These range from turves, sods and gravel, to trees, shrubs and plants; they include fires, missiles and deposits of offensive matter, defacements, notices, snares for birds and game, caravans, cycles and other vehicles, roundabouts and swings, games and horses, boats, bathing and fishing. They are comprehensive.

4. Special Properties

The Act of 1907 listed 29 properties which were declared to be held for the benefit of the nation; they should not be chargeable with any debts or liabilities; and they should be inalienable.[12]

The properties varied from 75 acres at Aira Force and Gowbarrow Deer Park, Cumbria, to a cliff at Barmouth and included the Ruskin monument at Friars Crag Keswick and the Vice-Admiral Hardy monument in Dorset.

In order to vary the provisions of that Act of 1907, it was necessary to include in the Act of 1971, a section authorising the possible disposal of one of those properties, namely Kanturk Castle in County Cork, Eire.[13]

The Wey Navigation and the Godalming Navigation were the subject of special provisions in the Act of 1971, since the assumption of their management by the National Trust departed from provisions in Acts of Parliament in 1670 and 1760.[14] The Act of 1971 allowed the two undertakings to be managed as one.

5. General Properties

There is a general provision in the Act of 1907, which enables a resolution of the Council of the National Trust to confer the same status of inalienability on newly acquired "properties or parts thereof." The resolution must declare that "such properties are proper to be held for the benefit of the nation."[15]

The Act of 1939 allowed the National Trust to accept a mansion house and amenity lands from a tenant for life under a settlement. These properties, also, were given the status of inalienability.[16]

---

[11] s.24.
[12] Sched. 1.
[13] Act of 1971, s.28.
[14] Pt. IV.
[15] s.21(2).
[16] Act of 1939, s.8.

5.08 SPECIAL CASES

By the National Trust Charity Scheme Confirmation Act 1919, a Scheme of the Charity Commissioners for the management of property was confirmed.[17] This was primarily to enable the Trust to grant leases (with the sanction of the Charity Commissioners) of land otherwise inalienable due to the above provisions in the Act of 1907. The grant of easements and rights over National Trust property made inalienable as described above, is valid and effectual, without the sanction of the Charity Commissioners.[18]

Compulsory Purchase and National Trust Property

5.09 Various general Acts of Parliament have included provisions to take account of this special category of property held by the National Trust. It is inevitable that, with such a large landholding, from time to time, a local authority or Government department or other body with compulsory powers, wishes to acquire some portion of National Trust land. Some of these Acts are of interest.

The general enabling Act for compulsory purchase is the Acquisition of Land Act 1981. That Act contains a section providing that a compulsory order which includes inalienable land of the National Trust, in respect of which the Trust has submitted and maintained an objection, shall be subject to Special Parliamentary Procedure.[19]

This is an elaborate procedure applied by the Statutory Orders (Special Procedure) Act 1945. Briefly, it involves:
  (i) Notice in the London Gazette and a local paper.
  (ii) Laying the Order before Parliament.
  (iii) Submission of objections by petition to either House.
  (iv) Consideration of those petitions by the Chairman of Ways and Means and the Chairman of Committees. They deal with the petitions as either general objections to the Order or as seeking amendments to it, and report thereon to their respective Houses.
  (v) Either House may then resolve that the Order be annulled and that ends that particular Order. On the other hand, the Order, petitions and Chairmen's reports may be sent to a joint committee of the two Houses, where detailed consideration ensues.
  (vi) In due course, the Order may be confirmed by the appropriate Minister or taken to be confirmed in a Bill, or if the joint committee so reports, it may not be confirmed until it is confirmed in an Act of Parliament.

5.10 Apart from the above general restrictions, there are express restraints on taking National Trust lands by compulsory purchase for:
  (i) Allotments, under the Land Settlement (Facilities) Act 1919, s.28, and the Allotments Act 1922, s.10.
  (ii) National Parks, under the National Parks and Access to the Coun-

---

[17] *Ibid.* s.12.
[18] *Ibid.*
[19] s.18.

tryside Act 1949, Pts. V and VI, though not under Parts II and II of that Act of 1949, in relation to nature conservation.

(iii) War damaged sites, under the War Damaged Sites Act 1949, s.1. National Trust inalienable land may, however, be the subject of compulsory purchase for forestry purposes, under the Forestry Act 1967, s.40(4) and s.49(1).

Finally, National Trust inalienable land is excluded from that to which rights of enfranchisement were conferred on leaseholds, by the Leasehold Reform Act 1967, s.32.

6. Restrictive Covenants

There is one last legal incident of National Trust landholding that is of interest. In the Natonal Trust Act 1937, there was a provision whereby a person entitled to land might agree with the National Trust to restrictions on his use of the property.[20] This might be described as a future use in a manner the Trust thinks fit or as subjecting the property to conditions in order to restrict the planning development. This agreement was to be legally effective and enforceable, although the National Trust was not the owner of adjacent land. (That condition is the normal requirement for legal enforcement of a covenant which restricts the use of real property in this country.)[21]

A second related provision is to be found in the Act of 1971. This states that when there are restrictions on National Trust[22] inalienable land, which are designed to preserve it, protect or augment its amenities or secure access to or enjoyment of such property for the public, then in each of those instances, the normal legal provision for modification of restrictive covenants shall not apply to those restrictions.[23]

That procedure is used to give effect to changes in the character of a neighbourhood, by relieving property of outdated restrictions. It is thus a mark of the importance attached to National Trust Property that it should be thus exempt.[24]

7. Constitution

The above short account of the purposes, powers and property provisions embodied in the six National Trust Acts of Parliament, has dealt with those items thought to be most relevant to this work. It should be noted that the Acts provide in detail for the constitution of the Trust, its accounts and their auditing and other matters appropriate to a large national organisation, indeed "Britain's premier charity."

---

[20] s.8.
[21] See, *e.g. Marquess of Zetland* v. *Driver* [1939] Ch. 1.
[22] Act of 1971, s.27.
[23] See also, for the position before this provision was secured, *Gee* v. *National Trust* [1966] 1 W.L.R. 170.
[24] See for fuller discussion, Chap. 4, para. 4.27.

5.13   Special Cases

B. The Forestry Commission

Introduction

5.13 It is in the last fifty years that the Forestry Commission has used legal powers to provide recreation facilities for the public. Since the creation of the Commission by the Forestry Act 1919, to stimulate the replenishment of the nation's timber reserves after depletion in the first World War, the Commission has extended its land-holding throughout the country, until two million acres were owned by the mid-nineteen-fifties. These were inevitably used by the public, initially for walking over permitted footpaths. Slowly, other outdoor activities developed.

1. The Countryside Act 1968

5.14 It was the Countryside Act 1968 which crystallised the position and the potential.

> "The Commission may, on any land placed at their disposal by the Minister of Agriculture, Fisheries and Food or the Secretary of State for Wales, provide or arrange for or assist in the provision of, tourist, recreational or sporting facilities and any equipment, facilities or works ancillary thereto."[25]

Some of the interesting facilities authorised in this way were:
(a) Accommodation for visitors.
(b) Camping sites and caravan sites.
(c) Places for meals and refreshments.
(d) Picnic places, places for enjoying views, parking places, routes for nature study and footpaths.
(e) Information and display centres.
(f) Shops in relation to any of the above facilities.
(g) Public conveniences.

The clear assertion of the purpose of the facilities and the extensive list was a welcome development. This provision in the Countryside Act 1968 was supplemented legally by a power to make by-laws.

2. By-Laws

5.15 The Commission was authorised to make by-laws in relation to any of the above seven activities.[26] It had acquired, in the Forestry Act 1967, wide powers of by-law making. These were to prohibit and regulate "anything tending to injury or disfigurement of the land or its amenities"; and also "for regulating the reasonable use of land by the public for the purposes of exercise and recreation."[27]

---

[25] Countryside Act 1968, s.23(2).
[26] Countryside Act 1968, s.23(4).
[27] Forestry Act 1967, s.46.

The subjects have been extended as the Commission has had to meet the enlarged interests and increased ingenuity of its visitors. Thus, new items in the last issue of the Commission's by-laws were for operating a hot-air balloon, setting up bee-hives, using a metal detector, taking birds eggs and evading tolls for car parks or forest roads.[28]

The by-laws are made by Statutory Instrument, having been laid before Parliament in draft. Though extensive, the Commission's by-laws are not to affect any "estate, interest, right of common, or other right of a profitable or beneficial nature in, over or affecting any land, except with the consent of the person entitled thereto."[29] In addition, such by-laws are forbidden to relate to a common which is the subject of a Scheme under the Commons Act 1899, or otherwise. Chapter 2 deals more fully with such Schemes.[30]

In the current by-laws, some relate to the New Forest by reference to an increased speed for vehicles and some to the Forest of Dean, *e.g.* where sheep are to have the owner's registration mark if the sheep are turned on to unenclosed areas. These two forests have their own regulating body, the Verderers, and so the by-laws recite, as obliged by the parent statute,[31] that the Verderers were consulted before the by-laws were made.

There are also, in the current by-laws, some with special reference to the Bedgebury Pinetum in Kent, and some referring to the Westonbirt Arboretum in Gloucestershire, banning, *e.g.* kite flying.

Offences against these by-laws are liable to give rise to fines, as provided, not in the by-laws but in the parent Act.[32] Offenders may also, after due warning, be removed from the Commission's lands. (Prosecution for by-law offences is, after all, the last stage in maintaining visitors' standards on the Commission's land. A Forest Code is currently being prepared to encourage adherence to those standards and thus limit prosecutions).

3. Tree Planting for Amenity

The Countryside Act 1968 also gave a new power to the Forestry Commission in relation to tree planting. This was the authority to plant, care for and manage trees" in the interests of amenity."[33] The Minister was at the same time authorised to acquire land needed to support this policy. Such acquisitions might be partly for afforestation and partly for the cause of amenity.

---

[28] *Ibid.* s.48.
[29] Countryside Act 1968, s.23(5).
[30] Forestry Act 1967, s.46(3)(*a*).
[31] *Ibid.* s.47. The Verderers are also empowered, as if Magistrate's Courts, to enforce the Commissions by-laws in their forests.
[32] *Ibid.* s.46(5). Fines are now determined by level 2 of the standard scale. See Criminal Justice Act 1982, s.39, and Sched. 3.
[33] *Ibid.* s.24. This policy is also added, as a drafting amendment, to s.3 in the Forestry Act 1967, by way of an addition to the Commission's purposes.

4. General and Historical

5.17 This short section has sought simply to give some understanding of the role available to the Forestry Commission, in the light of its legal powers, to provide recreation facilities for the public. It only remains to itemise the statutes which provide the Forestry Commission with its general powers by way of completing the picture, rather than adding significantly to the account of leisure service legal powers.

The Forestry Act 1967 is the consolidating statute for the Forestry Commission's powers and duties. It effectively repealed and replaced Forestry Act of 1919,[34] 1945, 1947 and 1951. Those Acts had contained provisions about the constitution of the Forestry Commission, the control of tree felling, the policy of afforestation and the balance to be sought in the various policies to be pursued by the Commission.

The Act of 1967 restates the duty of the Commission to take directions from the three Ministers with Governmental responsibility for the Commission, *i.e.* the Secretaries of State for Scotland and Wales and the Minister of Agriculture, Fisheries and Food.[35] In this instance, the Secretary of State for Scotland acts as the senior Minister.

Since 1967, Parliament has passed four Acts relating to aspects of forestry, though none alter the main policies and powers described in the body of this section. They are:
1. The Forestry Act 1979, dealing with metrication and also with loans and grants for forestry.
2. The Forestry Act 1981, authorising another Commissioner and giving further powers to dispose of land as well dealing with the transfer of sums out of the Forestry Fund for other Treasury purposes not connected with forestry.
3. The Trees Act 1970.
4. The Wild Creatures and Forest Laws Act 1971.
   This repealed many ancient laws about Royal rights in forests and restricted Royal rights for free game.

5. Conclusion

5.18 The recreational facilities provided by the Forestry Commission are not geographically comprehensive, as forests are not located in all parts of the country and not all forests, for tenure and other reasons, can be made available for recreation.

Since the opening of the first National Forest Park in 1935, the Commission has allowed public access for the quiet enjoyment of its forests, wherever it is able to do so. Its policy now is to satisfy as wide a range of the community as possible by providing appropriate recreational facilities

---

[34] Although an Order-making power was retained in relation to the Destructive Pests Acts 1877–1927 (now the Plant Health Act 1967). This has been used by the Commission, *e.g.* for Fire Blight disease, as mentioned in Chap. 4.

[35] Forestry Act 1967, s.1(4).

THE FORESTRY COMMISSION 5.18

of a high standard of design. In recent years, greater emphasis has been placed on the development of such facilities in woodlands near towns.

C. LONDON AND THE PUBLIC LEISURE SERVICES

Introduction

The aim of this section is to pick out the differences in the legal powers available to the local authorities in Greater London from local authorities in the remainder of the country. Where appropriate, non-local authority providers of such services are considered. 5.19

Not the least of the difficulties for a writer on this subject is the inconsistent treatment of the law for London in Acts of Parliament. The last great reorganisation of London local government was in 1964, following a Royal Commission. There was a plethora of special London legislation and the reorganisation, encouraged by that Royal Commission, began the process of bringing local London legislation into line with the rest of the country. Subsequently, some statutes have referred to "local authorities" and this has included those in London; sometimes, there have been special London provisions.[36] There is a strong tradition in London of annual "General Powers" Acts, promoted by the old London County Council and the Greater London Council, dealing with problems peculiar to the metropolis and, often, paving the way for later national legislation.

The London Government Act 1963 is the present Act of Parliament, which lays down the framework of local authorities for Greater London, as there defined. The City of London, the Greater London Council (or its successors), thirty-two London Borough Councils, and the strange, historic survival, the Inner and Middle Temples, comprise the unique group of thirty-six local authorities for that great metropolitan area.[37]

There is one unique provision in the London Government Act 1963 which merits comment, before turning to the detail of individual services. This empowers a Minister to make an Order to achieve uniformity in the law for an area. The Royal Commission, referred to above, was conscious of the magnitude of the task of attempting a revision of a great variety of bodies with powers of government. Their proposals led to the considerable rationalisation indicated above: this section allows that process to continue with services which would otherwise be anomalous and disjointed. The treatment of open spaces is one example below of the bold use of this power.[38] 5.20

---

[36] The Royal Commission Report, a comprehensive, even inspiring, document on the place of London local government in the national scene, is Cmnd. 1164, Report on Local Government in Greater London. The chairman was Sir Edwin Herbert.

[37] This whole section is written during the interval between "Streamlining the Cities," the Circular (No. 9063) of the Department of the Environment in 1983 which projected the demise of (*inter alia*) the Greater London Council and the Local Government Bill and subsequent Act of Parliament, followed by the presumed arrival of the time when a new distribution of functions, powers and duties for the London local authorities will take effect.

[38] See para. 5.25, below.

5.21 Special Cases

1. **Historic Buildings, Statues and Monuments**

5.21 Listed Buildings in need of repair can be acquired by the Common Council of the City of London (the Common Council) and by the London Borough Councils (in this chapter "the Boroughs"), with the use of compulsory powers.[39] Those powers are also enjoyed by the Greater London Council or its successor authority, referred to for convenience throughout much of this section as "the relevant London authority." For the destination table giving the situation after April 1, 1986, readers are referred to the Note at the front of this book.

When a building is of special architectural or historical interest, it may be acquired by agreement by the relevant London authority, the Common Council or the Boroughs, if:
   (a) it is for immediate use, and
   (b) it is in the authority's own area.
Otherwise, the acquisition can only proceed with the consent of the Secretary of State for the Environment.

With the consent of the Common Council or the Borough, as the case may be, the relevant London authority can effect the acquisition.[40] The consent of the Secretary of State for the Environment can override the absence of consent of the Common Council or the Borough to facilitate acquisition by the relevant London authority. It is that authority that is empowered to acquire such a building if the acquisition would be incidental to a move from Greater London by an industrial or commercial undertaking.[41] The same relevant London authority has power to investigate the history of a listed building and to arrange for the publication of that history.[42] It may also give advice whether preservation of such a building is advisable and, if so, how such work should be done.

5.22 The relevant London authorities may, with the owner's consent, put plaques on buildings, in their areas, to indicate "an event of public interest."[43]

The relevant London authority, the Common Council and the Boroughs are local authorities for the purposes of the Ancient Monuments and Archaeological Areas Act 1979.[44]

The Common Council, the Boroughs and the Temples, for their

---

[39] Town and Country Planning Act 1971, ss.114–117.
[40] If the building is in one of the two Temples, then with the consent of the Temple authority, the G.L.C. or its successor can effect the acquisition.
[41] Town and Country Planning Act 1971, s.119(4)(*d*).
[42] London Government Act 1963, Sched. II, para. 18.
[43] London County Council (General Powers) Act 1959, s.31. The twelve inner London boroughs are: City of Westminster, Camden, Islington, Hackney, Tower Hamlets, Greenwich, Lewisham, Southwark, Lambeth, Wandsworth, Hammersmith and the Royal Borough of Kensington and Chelsea. The twenty outer London Boroughs are: Hounslow, Hillingdon, Ealing, Brent, Harrow, Barnet, Haringey, Enfield, Waltham Forest, Redbridge, Havering, Barking, Newham, Bexley, Bromley, Croydon, Sutton, Merton, Richmond and the Royal Borough of Kingston upon Thames.
[44] s.61.

respective areas, are authorised to provide and maintain public clocks, statues and monuments in streets and public places.[45]

The obelisk adjoining Westminster Bridge, known as Cleopatra's Needle, is under the care of the relevant London authority. An initial list of fifteen statues compiled in 1854, including Nelson's Column, has been added to over the years. All those statues became publicly repairable.[46] The Boroughs have the powers of local authorities in relation to war memorials.[47] Under the Roosevelt Memorial Act 1946, a statue of President Roosevelt was erected in Grosvenor Square, at the instance of the Pilgrim's Society, by the Department of the Environment.

2. Open Spaces and Recreation

(1) *The Greater London Council (or relevant Successor Authority) and the London Borough Councils*[48]

The G.L.C. or its successor authority and the Boroughs have the powers available under the Open Spaces Act 1906, and also powers in relation to Open Space and Recreation from a Local Act. The Minister of Housing and Local Government Provisional Order Confirmation (Greater London Parks and Open Spaces) Act 1967. The extended powers in this Local Act of 1967 may be summarised in this way.

> "Open space" for this purpose means land under the control of a local authority, being a public park, heath, common, recreation ground, pleasure ground, garden, walk, ornamental enclosure or disused burial ground.[49]

Powers to provide for recreation

In relation to such open spaces, there are seven powers[50]:
  (a) To provide facilities of all kinds for swimming and open air recreation, including golf courses, gymnasia and rifle ranges, indoor recreational facilities of all kinds, and centres for the use of clubs, and organisations of a social, recreational and educational nature. Such indoor centres must not unfairly restrict the space available to the public for open air recreation on that particular open space.
  (b) Amusement fairs, entertainments, bands of music, concerts, cinematographic exhibitions, pageants.

---

[45] Public Health Act 1975, s.165; Public Health Acts Amendment Act 1890, ss.42 and 46; London Government Act 1963, s.40; Local Government Act 1972, s.180.
[46] Public Statutes (Metropolis) Act 1854, ss.5 and 7.
[47] War Memorials (Local Authorities' Powers) Act 1923, s.4 and London Government Act 1963, s.4(4)(a).
[48] London Government Act 1963, s.58.
[49] Minister of Housing and Local Government Provisional Order Confirmation (Greater London Parks and Open Spaces) Act 1967, s.6.
[50] *Ibid.* s.7.

5.24   Special Cases

(c) In the winter season, the provision of ice-skating on created ice rinks.
(d) Meals and refreshments for sale.
(e) All supporting equipment in the form of lockers, conveniences, clothing, apparatus, including swings and platforms.
(f) The erection and maintenance of associated buildings and structures to afford accommodation.
(g) The right to set apart portions of the available open space for use in connection with the above.

5.25   The following three limits to the use of these powers are contained in the Act of 1967:

(i) Persons must not be excluded from the open space not specially laid out, whilst games are not taking place.
(ii) In any event, the amount specially set apart for the above facilities should not exceed one acre or one tenth, whichever is the greater.
(iii) Entertainments in the form of a cinematographic film are to be for the advancement of art, education, drama, science, music or literature.

They are not to be films normally shown on the commercial circuit, within twelve months of their general release in Great Britain. When the time for local authority showing arrives, there is to be a charge for customers which is not less than the comparable charge in local cinemas. An exception to this charging stipulation is allowed when the show is for charitable, educational, cultural, social or public purposes.[51]

Powers of letting

5.26   The local authorities may, by licence or letting, grant to other persons the right of exercising the powers set out above; open space land or buildings of the authority may be included in those agreements. The authority may contribute directly or indirectly to the expenses of providing the entertainment in question.[52] Vegetation on an open space may be enclosed, to ensure its cultivation or preservation, in the interests of amenity or of public safety, for such periods and on such conditions as may be deemed expedient.[53]

5.27   There is a flexible power for authorities to charge for the facilities provided as described above. This is subject to a limit for reading rooms.[54]

The Act then sets out certain limitations to be observed by local authorities who use the extensive powers described above. There are four of these:

(i) Not to override a person's legal rights, other than as a member of the public, except with his consent.

---

[51] *Ibid.* s.7.
[52] *Ibid.* s.8.
[53] *Ibid.* s.9.
[54] *Ibid.* s.10.

(ii) Not, by use of its powers, to deny members of the public access, without charge, to some part of each plot of open space land.[55]
(iii) Not to conflict with the terms of a trust relating to such land, unless an appropriate order, allowing a departure from the terms of that trust, has been obtained from the High Court or Charity Commissioners, or, alternatively, by obtaining the consent of a person who is in a position to enforce that trust.[56]
(iv) Not to violate any building by-law, town planning or other relevant legal requirement, in relation to the buildings or enclosures or methods employed to use its powers.[57]

Competitions

Local authorities are granted wide powers of running competitions in relation to "any recreation," provided that they do not, if setting aside land in an open space for spectators at a competition, enclose more than one acre or one tenth of that open space, whichever is the greater.[58]   **5.28**

Transfers among local authorities

Local authorities may transfer open space between themselves, if it will thereby provide a more convenient exercise of their functions. In so doing, they must not depart from private legal trusts or covenants affecting the land in question. If the transfer involves assignment of a lessee's interest in a lease, then the lessor's consent to such an assignment must be obtained in the usual way.[59]   **5.29**

Land exchanges

There is, lastly, a useful power of effecting an exchange of land in an open space with other land or enlargement adjacent but outside the open space, when an improvement or enlargement of the open space will result.[60] One plot will lose its open space character: the other will acquire it.

To facilitate the development of open space, local authorities are empowered to enter into agreements with the owners of land, to secure for

---

[55] *Ibid.* s.11. A special legal protection for Paddington Recreation Ground is contained in this section.
[56] *Ibid.* s.11. A trust under s.10 of the Open Spaces Act 1906 is an exception to this provision.
[57] *Ibid.* s.11(4).
[58] *Ibid.* s.13. "Recreation" is widely defined as any activity for which a local authority have power to provide facilities in an open space. (s.13(1)).
[59] *Ibid.* s.14. This section also preserves the positions under the London Squares (Preservation) Act 1931 and s.16 of the Open Spaces Act 1906, should they be relevant to the site.
[60] *Ibid.* s.15. Compensation may be paid for rights extinguished in such a transaction s.15(2)).

5.29 the local authority the first refusal to acquire that land, when the owner decides to sell his estate or interest in the land.

The circumstances[61] in which part of an open space may be used for street improvements are naturally[62] somewhat complex. The power is nonetheless available.

Local authorities may appoint staff to supervise open space land, in order to secure compliance by the public with by-laws or regulations. The staff can only act as constables if duly sworn in and then in uniform or provided with a warrant.[63]

5.30 In an earlier Act, the London Council (General Powers) Act 1890, it was provided that any by-law which prohibits military drill on a heath or common is ineffective unless approved by the Secretary of State for Defence. Even then such a by-law is not to restrain the right and powers of that Secretary of State over parks and gardens or other open space, in any case of national danger or emergency.[64]

5.31 A power to close public parks on three Sundays in a calendar year is held by the relevant London authority, contrary to the position in the rest of the country.[65] The same authority has legal powers in a number of local Acts in relation to three special estates affording open space facilities to the public. Hampstead Heath, Holland House in Kensington[66] (used by the G.L.C. or its successor authority as a hostel and its grounds as open space), and Crystal Palace (vested in the G.L.C. or its successor authority to be used for the purposes of education, recreation, and the promotion of industry, commerce and art).[67]

(2) *The Common Council of the City of London*

5.32 The Corporation of the City of London, by ancient tradition and sanction from Parliament, manages a number of famous London open spaces that lie outside its administrative area.

(a) **Epping Forest**

The City of London (Various Powers) Act 1977, contains a number of provisions about this forest. Compensation became payable to all persons

---

[61] *Ibid.* s.16.
[62] *Ibid.* s.17.
[63] *Ibid.* s.18.
[64] London Council (General Powers) Act 1890, s.16.
[65] The Greater London Council (General Powers) Act 1978, s.12. Prior notice of such closures is necessary. The same Act incorporates a slight variation in relation to other park closures. Instead of the permitted six consecutive days, (exluding Sundays), under s.44 of the Public Health Acts Amendment Act 1890, and Public Health Act 1961, s.53, the G.L.C. or relevant London authority may close its parks for six consecutive days, including Sundays.
[66] See London County Council (Holland House) Act 1952.
[67] London County Council (Crystal Palace) Act 1951, and London Government Act 1963, s.57(2)(*e*).

who had pastured their cattle in the forest during the previous ten years and who, in view of the new condition, stood to lose their right of pasturage.[68]

The ancient name for the legal managers of Epping Forest was the Conservators. By the Act of 1977, the City of London Corporation, acting through its Epping Forest Committee, were the Conservators. Under this Act of 1977, the above Committee assessed the number of cattle pastured in the open space and thus assessed the compensation under the above provision. There was statutory arbitration where the parties did not agree the amount.[69]

In order to regenerate the Forest and protect it as an open space for the recreation of the public, the Conservators were authorised to take areas of the open space, one by one, none exceeding 100 acres, and by enclosing them, exclude the public.[70] These powers of closure should not close public footpaths nor bridleways. If they interfered with the latter, the Conservators must provide an alternative route. Lastly, these enclosure powers were not to interfere with the apparatus of statutory undertakers.

The Act of 1977 further empowered the Corporation to provide facilities by way of refreshments, car parks, public conveniences and shelters. They could charge for use of these facilities and might also authorise other persons, by agreement, to provide the facilities in question.[71]

Fines for offences under the Epping Forest Act 1878 or those contained in a by-laws made under the Corporation of London (Open Spaces) Act 1878 have recently been increased.[72] The lands of the Conservators have been redefined in the City of London (Various Powers) Act 1956.[73] The by-law making powers of the Conservators in relation to deer sanctuaries in Epping Forest are now to be found in the City of London (Various Powers) Act 1959.[74] The City of London (Various Powers) Act 1967 contains authority for the Conservators to provide buildings suitable for the teaching of biology, ecology, and allied subjects and for the instruction of the children ad also the public generally in the natural history of the Forest and its conservation.[75] In the City of London (Various Powers) Act 1971 are to be found powers recently taken by the Conservators to regulate horse-riding in Epping Forest.[76]

---

[68] s.5.
[69] ss.5 and 6.
[70] s.7.
[71] s.8. The Act includes the common qualification that meals and refreshments are not to be provided by the public body, *i.e.* the Common Council, unless the existing provision in the neighbourhood of the Forest is unsatisfactory.
[72] City of London (Various Powers) Act 1977. The maximum fine for both classes of offence was raised to £200.
[73] s.10. The City of London (Various Powers) Act 1967, ss.26–27, related also to the total City land ownership in this Forest.
[74] s.17.
[75] s.27.
[76] Pt. IV.

5.33 SPECIAL CASES

(b) **Burnham Beeches, Spring Park, West Wickham, West Wickham Common, and Coulsdon Commons**

5.33   The City of London (Various Powers) Act 1977 contains powers for the provision in these open spaces of similar facilities, and subject to the same qualifications as are set out in relation to Epping Forest.[77]

(c) **Highgate Wood, Queens Park in Kilburn, West Ham Park**

These are examples of other open spaces which are maintained by the Common Council of the City of London. These activities of the Common Council proceed from a power contained in the Corporation of London (Open Spaces) Act 1878, to acquire open spaces within 25 miles of the City boundaries and to make agreements "for the assertion and protection" of rights over such spaces.

3. Land

5.34   Under the City of London (Various Powers) Act 1958, the Common Council is empowered not only to acquire and dispose of land for its various functions but also to acquire land in advance of requirements.[78] The G.L.C. inherited the powers and duties of the former Middlesex and London County Councils in relation to Green Belt land.[79] This was initially dealt with in the Green Belt (London and Home Counties) Act 1938 and involves a detailed framework of powers for the designation and protection of lands falling within the huge open spaces known as the Green Belt. The areas include parts of Essex, Hertford, Kent, Surrey, Buckingham and Greater London. The powers allow the G.L.C. or the relevant London authority to acquire land,[80] enter into covenants with owners to preserve the Green Belt status, and compensate for the imposition of restrictions on building, adverse use or alienation.[81] Recreation, camping and agriculture are three uses which encouraged by owners or, if the land is owned by the G.L.C., or its successor, by letting.[82]

4. Commons

5.35   In Chapter 2 we considered the legal framework within which commons fall to be managed in the remainder of this country. In the Greater London area, metropolitan commons have been the subject of legislation for more than a century; there are interesting differences between the making of Schemes for the management of such commons and those outside London, and these legal differences can usefully be tabulated:

---

[77] s.9.
[78] ss.7–10.
[79] London Government Act 1963, s.59.
[80] Green Belt (London and Home Counties) Act 1938, s.3.
[81] *Ibid.* ss.3 and 5.
[82] *Ibid.* s.27.

The Commons Act 1899	The Metropolitan Commons Acts 1866–1899[83]
1. The Scheme is made by the local authority.	1. The Scheme is made also by the commoners or the Lord of the Manor.
2. The procedure begins with a draft prepared, published and submitted to the Department of the Environment.	2. The procedure begins with a memorial presented by one of the bodies in 1. (above) to the Commons Commissioners.
3. The period for objections is three months.	3. The comparable period is two months.
4. If the Lord of the Manor or one third of the commoners object, the Scheme cannot go ahead.	4. There is no such built-in power of objection. The inquiry into objections is in respect of their merits.
5. Confirmation by the above Department is the final step before implementation.	5. A Scheme for the management of a metropolitan common requires confirmation by Parliament.

The G.L.C. or its successor is the registration authority for commons under the Commons Registration Act 1965.[84] The G.L.C. or its successor and inner London Boroughs can make agreements with the Ministry of Agriculture, Fisheries and Food, for the surrender of land from a common for the purposes of a highway improvement. Any land given in exchange becomes part of the common.[85]

Commons are protected against encroachment by buildings or enclosures, by provisions in the Act of 1967 discussed in relation to Open Spaces above. Before such encroachment can proceed, Ministerial consent, if necessary after a public inquiry, is required.[86]

A power in the Countryside Act 1968 is available for the relevant London authority, the Common Council and the Boroughs to provide facilities for a common on land "in the neighbourhood of a common." These include car parks, refreshments, conveniences and shelters. Compulsory powers are available to obtain such adjacent land.[87]

Two cases relating to the validity of by-laws for London commons are of interest:

(a) *Mitcham Common Conservators* v. *Cox*; *The same* v. *Cole*.[88]

A golf club formed two courses, with the agreement and under a letting from the Conservators of Mitcham Common. The Conservators acted

---

[83] Commons Act 1899, ss.1 and 2; Metropolitan Commons Act 1866, ss.6–10.
[84] s.2.
[85] London County Council (General Powers) Act 1960, s.10, as amended by the Local Law (G.L.C. and Inner London Boroughs) Order 1965 (S.I. 1965 No. 540).
[86] See s.12 of Act referred to in n.53, *supra*.
[87] s.6(1), s.9 and Sched. II.
[88] [1911] 2 K.B. 854. A case heard shortly afterwards, *Harris* v. *Harrison* 111 L.T. 534, shows that the Club altered its rules, giving preference for Club members for limited times only and the Court upheld that amended rule.

5.36   SPECIAL CASES

under a Local Act, which allowed a Scheme to be made under the Metropolitan Commons Act of 1866 and 1869; by-laws were then made, duly confirmed by the Local Government Board, followed by regulations, which were not deemed to require such confirmation. Schemes, by-laws and regulations formed the legal framework for management of the two golf clubs and cases came before the King's Bench Divisonal Court to challenge some of these regulations. The court decided:

1. A regulation that no one should play, unless accompanied by a caddie approved by the club, was upheld.
2. However, a regulation was held void which limited those who could play to members of the club and inhabitants of Mitcham.
3. Similarly, the Court held void a regulation which said that no non-members could play on Saturdays. This was "partial," within the principles laid down in *Kruse* v. *Johnson*.[89]

(b) *de Morgan* v. *Metropolitan Board of Works*.[90]

This concerned a by-law which regulated the holdings of meetings on Clapham Common. Speakers had to obtain prior approval from the Board and in this case, the plaintiff preached a sermon, without seeking such permission. He was prosecuted and convicted, and challenged the by-law. The Court upheld the by-law; it was a reasonable way of maintaining limits on the time and space occupied by speakers on a public common.

It is sometimes a surprise to learn how many commons there are in Greater London; the concept of a built-up metropolis does not always allow for this element in the total London scene. It should be remarked that commons are inherited by the modern community: they are not created by them.

5. Squares

5.37   London squares as open spaces have been the subject of legislation and, in particular, the Metropolis Management Act 1855, and the Town Gardens Protection Act 1863. (The former has been amended to take into account the current role of the G.L.C. or its successor and the Boroughs). The aim of this legislation is to facilitate the formation for each square of a committee of the householders whose premises fronted on to the square. The committees were empowered to raise monies to maintain the physical amenities of the square, failing which the local authority would assume that responsibility.

The Common Council and the two Temples are the relevant local authorities for squares in their territories.[91]

---

[89] [1898] 2 Q.B. 91. See Chap. 4.
[90] (1880) 5 Q.B. 155.
[91] Background on these squares is to be found in the report of the Royal Commission on London Squares, Cmnd. 3196, of 1928. The London Squares Preservation Act 1931, is also of interest, in providing the powers to preserve Squares from development.

6. Libraries and Museums

Whilst the Boroughs and the Common Council are the library authorities,[92] they and the G.L.C. or its successor are local authorities for the purposes of the Public Libraries and Museums Act 1964.[93] In addition to books, articles which may be provided and repaired for a library include statuary, sculpture models "and other articles of a similar nature."[94]

The G.L.C. or its successor is authorised to adapt, furnish and maintain the following premises. The purposes laid down to guide these activities are to provide for the accommodation, exhibition, and preservation of works of art or objects of historical, antiquarian or other public interest. The premises are:

(i) The Horniman Museum.
(ii) The Geffrye Museum.
(iii) Kenwood House.
(iv) Marble Hill House, Twickenham.
(v) Rangers House, Greenwich.[95]

The G.L.C. or relevant London authority has powers not only to acquire but to commission works of art and then to erect, maintain and contribute to the maintenance of works of art.[96] It also may make contributions to any society providing a public service by means of cultural activities in the area.[97] The Common Council has power to receive on deposit, or acquire, or commission and erect and maintain, or contribute to the cost of, pictures, sculptures or works of art.[98]

7. The Royal Parks

The Crown Lands Act 1851 lays on Commissioners of Works the duty to manage the royal parks. These are St. James's and Hyde and Green Park, Kensington Gardens, Chelsea Gardens, the Treasury Garden, Parliament Square Garden, Regents Park, Primrose Hill, Victoria Park, Battersea Park, Greenwich Park, Kew Gardens Pleasure Grounds and Green, Kew and Richmond Roads, Hampton Court Gardens, Green and Road, Hampton Court Park, Richmond Park and Green, and Bushey Park.

Regulations govern the conduct of visitors to the parks and constables are used for enforcement. The Acts under which the royal parks are managed are the Parks Regulation Act 1872, the Parks Regulation

---

[92] Local Government Act 1972, s.206. The Common Council is the library authority, not only in the City but also in the two Temples: Temples Order 1971 (S.I. 1971 No. 1732), art. 5.
[93] Public Libraries and Museums Act 1964, s.25.
[94] L.C.C. (General Powers) Act 1958, s.36.
[95] London Government Act 1963, Sched. II, para. 16.
[96] *Ibid.* s.2 and Sched. II, para. 16.
[97] L.C.C. (General Powers) Act 1947, s.59.
[98] City of London (Various Powers) Act 1962, s.5.

5.39 SPECIAL CASES

(Amendment) Act 1926, and the Parks Regulation (Amendment) Act 1974.

8. Entertainment and Licensing

5.40 The G.L.C. or its successor is the licensing authority in Greater London for many forms of public entertainment, including:
  (i) Betting tracks.[99]
  (ii) Public boxing and wrestling.
  (iii) Entertainment licences, which include the former music, singing and dancing licences.[1]
  (iv) Theatres.[2]
  (v) Cinemas.[3]
  (vi) Private places of entertainment.[4]
  (vii) Exhibitions and displays at the Alexandra Palace, the Central Hall Westminster, Earl's Court, Olympia, the Royal Festival Hall, the Royal Horticultural Halls and Seymour Hall.[5]

Sex establishments are licensed by the Boroughs and Common Council after a resolution of the relevant council so to do.[6]

9. Recreation and Sport

(1) The Thames Valley

5.41 Under the Water Act 1973, there was a requirement upon the Thames Water Authority to transfer to the G.L.C. (or its successor) its recreation and amenity functions.[7]

These functions, as described in that Act, comprised:

> "the desirability of preserving natural beauty, conserving flora, fauna and geological or physiographical features of special interest, protecting buildings and other objects of architectural archaeological or historic interest."[8]

Additionally, under the same Act, the Water Authority was placed under a duty to put to the best use for recreation, the water and land associated with water. These were not to be related to any functions of the Authority in relation to navigation.[9]

---

[99] London Government Act 1963, s.53.
[1] Local Government (Miscellaneous Provisions) Act 1982.
[2] Theatres Act 1968, ss.12–14 and s.28.
[3] Cinematograph Act 1909 and London Government Act 1963, s.52.
[4] Private Places of Entertainment Act 1967, s.7, (with the consent of the relevant Boroughs); Local Government (Miscellaneous Provisions) Act 1982, Sched. 2.
[5] Greater London Council (General Powers) Act 1966, s.21.
[6] Local Government (Miscellaneous Provisions) Act 1982, s.2.
[7] Water Act 1973, ss.25 and 36.
[8] *Ibid.* ss.22 and 24.
[9] *Ibid.* s.20.

5.41

The Nature Conservancy is charged with advising any Water Authority if they consider that a Scheme may affect land which, not being classified as a nature reserve, is nevertheless of special interest.[10]

(2) *The Lee Valley*

The Lee Valley Regional Park Authority was set up to develop and improve, preserve and manage an area (partly in Greater London) near the river Lee as a place for leisure, recreation, sport, games, amusements for the provision of nature reserves and the provision and enjoyment of entertainments.[11]

5.42

With a governing body comprising representatives from the relevant London authority, other counties and a number of other local authorities, the Authority was empowered to make by-laws, to enter into agreements to eliminate restrictive covenants[12] and, among many other powers, to remove houseboats which had become "seriously injurious to the amenity of the waterway."[13]

10. **The Countryside**

The G.L.C was empowered to set up a Farm Interpretation Centre at Park Lodge Farm, Hillingdon. It is to be used "for the purposes of education, recreation and leisure."[14]

5.43

Allotments

Whilst the G.L.C. or relevant London authority is a smallholding authority,[15] each of the London Boroughs is an allotments authority.[16] A significant difference from the rest of the country is made by the London Government Act 1963, under which the provision of allotments is a power and not a duty.[17]

---

[10] *Ibid.* s.27.
[11] See Lee Valley Regional Park Act 1966.
[12] *Ibid.* s.26.
[13] *Ibid.* s.38.
[14] Greater London Council (General Powers) Act 1974, ss.3–6.
[15] Agriculture Act 1970, s.38.
[16] Small-Holdings and Allotments Act 1908, s.23.
[17] s.55(4). This also eliminates the right in general laws, for six ratepayers to request consideration of their desire for allotments. (See Chap. 8.)

CHAPTER 6

PUBLIC ENTERTAINMENT

> *As everybody who has anything to do with the law well knows, the path of the law is strewn with examples of open and shut cases which, somehow, were not; of unanswerable charges which, in the event, were completely answered; of inexplicable conduct, which was fully explained; of fixed and unalterable determinations that, by discussion, suffered a change.*
>
> Megarry J. in *John* v. *Rees* (1970)
> Ch. 345 at p. 402.

A. Theatres

6.01 This traditional form of public entertainment has been the subject of various legal controls in the last two centuries. At present the Theatres Act 1968 governs the licensing position, in convenient summary form. The same Act is also the point of reference for the legal limits to the contents of stage performances. In addition to these two matters, those engaged in managing theatres need to take account of the law relating to the safety of buildings where the public gather, the law of contract as it relates to the engagement of artists, legal safeguards imposed for the protection of young persons appearing on the stage, certain items concerning animals and also legal aspects of the provision of refreshments and intoxicating liquor.

1. Licensing of Premises

6.02 Licences, normally renewable annually, are issued by district councils, or, for the London area, by the Greater London Council (or its successor authority).[1] A fee will be payable, unless the licensing authority are satisfied that for specific occasions the performance will be of educational or other like character or is to be given for charitable "or other like purpose."[2] The same Act, the Theatres Act 1968, contains the law about the provisional grant, renewal and transfer of licences, as well as their transmission on death.

A licence will normally contain terms about the safety and good man-

---

[1] Local Government Act 1972, s.204(6).
[2] Theatres Act 1968, s.13, Sched. 1.

agement of the theatre; if deemed oppressive or otherwise inappropriate, the licensee has a right to go back to the issuing authority to seek some variation in those terms.[3] This simple licensing code is fortified by the creation of offences for performing a play at unlicensed premises or for contravening the terms of a licence.[4] The persons liable to be prosecuted include those who let the premises or allow them to be used for the unlawful performance.

Appeals against a refusal of the licensing authority to grant a licence go to the magistrates courts, in accordance with the time limit and other procedures contained in the 1968 Act.[5]

2. The Nature of the Performance

For over 200 years, censorship of plays was in this country exercised by the Lord Chamberlain. The Theatres Act 1968 abolished that practice and in its place laid down standards to which plays and other presentations coming within its definition of "play" should conform, in order to remain within the law.[6] The main provisions are as follows:—

Obscene Performances

(i) A person who, whether for gain or not, directs or presents an obscene performance of a play in public or in private, is liable to prosecution before the magistrates or on indictment.[7] There is a two year time limit on prosecutions on indictment for this offence.[8]

(ii) A performance of a play is obscene, for this purpose, if its effect, taken as a whole, is such as to tend to deprave and corrupt persons likely to attend, having regard to all the circumstances.[9]

(iii) This statutory offence is designed to replace any other common law offence in relation to the character of a play.[10] Wilful exposure of an indecent exhibition—to use the old wording in the Vagrancy Act 1824—is also replaced by the new offence.

The new defence—the public good

(iv) A most important section in the Act is that containing a new statutory defence to a prosecution. For this defence to succeed, it has to be shown that the performance was for the public good, as being in the interests of art or ballet or opera or any other art or of literature or learning.[11]

---

[3] Theatres Act 1968, s.12, Sched. 1, para. 7.
[4] For a recent case testing the terms on the grant of a licence, see *Fisher's Restaurant* v. *G.L.C.* (1980) 18 L.G.R. 672.
[5] Theatres Act 1968, s.14.
[6] Theatres Act 1968, s.18.
[7] Theatres Act 1968, s.2(2).
[8] Theatres Act 1968, s.2(3).
[9] Theatres Act 1968, s.2(1).
[10] Theatres Act 1968, s.2(4).
[11] Theatres Act 1968, s.3.

6.03

This is a wide protection, and judicial construction of the terms it embodies is taking place slowly in the courts. However, as the wording is similar to that applied to obscene publications by the Obscene Publications Act 1959, the view of the court in a case under that Act has relevance when construing the Theatres Act defence. The book *Last Exit to Brooklyn* came before the Court of Appeal in the case of *R. v. Calder & Boyars*.[12] Attention centred upon the correct legal direction to be given to the jury, when they had to consider the defence in question. The Court held that the jury should be told to consider the number of readers they believed might be depraved or corrupted, the strength of the tendency to deprave or corrupt and the nature of the depravity or corruption. On the other hand, the jury ought to consider the merits the book had, literary, sociological and ethical. These factors were to be balanced and the jury had then to decide whether the publication was for the public good.

Allowing for the changed subject matter, similar criteria can be applied to a stage performance.

(v) The onus resting upon the defendant under the Theatres Act is to establish the statutory defence on the balance of probabilities; that on the prosecution when seeking a conviction is heavier, *i.e.* to establish guilt beyond reasonable doubt.[13]

6.04 (vi) An offence is created in the Theatres Act concerning a performance which is likely to stir up hatred against a section of the public distinguished by colour, race, ethnic or national origins. It is committed by the person who directs or presents the performance and he must be shown to have intended to stir up hatred against that section of the public.[14]

(vii) Another offence, couched in similar phraseology, is created for provoking a breach of the peace through the stage performance.[15]

6.05 (viii) Certain exceptions are allowed from the overall operation of the provisions concerning these new offences. These are:

(a) A rehearsal.
(b) A recording or filming or broadcast, provided that the performance was not attended by persons other than those involved in the activity listed above.[16]

(ix) A limited exemption from a threatened prosecution for the basic section 2 offence is also given for a play given on a domestic occasion in a private dwelling.

(x) The Attorney General's consent is necessary to initiate proceedings for the three offences described in paragraphs (i), (vi) and (vii) above.[17]

---

[12] [1969] 1 Q.B.157. In a more recent case, *R. v. Michael Bogdanov* (unreported), the play "The Romans in Britain" was under scrutiny in a prosecution under this Act in London in 1982. The play had been produced at the National Theatre. After a defence submission that there was no case to answer, the judge gave a ruling and stopped the case.

[13] See as a recent case, *Public Prosecutor v. Yuvaraj* [1970] A.C. 913 about this "historic distinction."

[14] Theatres Act 1968, s.5.

[15] Theatres Act 1968, s.6.

[16] See the Theatres Act 1968, s.7, for the detailed qualifications on these exceptions, which also include cable transmission.

[17] Theatres Act 1968, s.8.

6.05

This is clearly a most important Act, for local authorities who manage civic theatres in particular, as well as their employees. Though local authorities are corporate bodies, that status does not relieve them, if managing a theatre, of the various offences in the Act.[18]

3. Professional Contracts

6.06 Theatrical usage will be taken into account when construing contracts for the hire of artists. Making this allowance, those contracts must be clear in their terms, avoid illegality, and conform to the normal requirements of the law of this country relating to contracts. One or two of the most common legal problems arising in practice may usefully be discussed.

(1) *Restraint*

6.07 A contract to engage an artist to perform at a theatre would be expected to contain management provisions imposing restraint upon the artist from performing within a stipulated distance and time from the engagement at the theatre in question. The courts provide a point of reference should difference of opinion arise about the reasonableness of such restraints.

The case in 1914 of *London Theatre of Varieties Ltd.* v. *Evans*[19] concerned a contract for a music hall performer. The contract provided that there should be "no colourable imitation, representation, or version" of his performance within a prescribed radius or time of that dealt with in the contract. When such a version was discovered in a "picture palace" close enough in time and location to constitute a contravention of the contract, the case was taken to the High Court. It was there decided that the performer was not liable for the breach since any performance at the picture palace took place without his permission.

Again, "the only concert by this artist in the month of May in Yorkshire" might be an unreasonable term, having regard to the large population, area and length of time. On the other hand, "the only concert in May in Wiltshire", could be reasonable, in the light of the lesser area and population.

(2) *Non-Performance*

6.08 The law has frequently been invoked to resolve differences arising from non-performance by an artist under contract. Weather, illness, the death of a member of a troupe, the absence of a management provision—say of props or supporting staff or performers—are all the sort of factors which have led to legal disputes. The practice of the courts is, first, to construe the terms of the contract and then to look for a reasonable interpretation in the light of the intentions of the parties and earlier decisions of the courts in relevant circumstances.

---

[18] Theatres Act 1968, s.16.
[19] (1914) 31 T.L.R. 75.

Death or Illness

(i) In *Harvey* v. *Tivoli Manchester Ltd.*[20] the death of one of a troupe of three intimate performers was held to be a good reason for the other two artists avoiding the contract. On the other hand, a contract was held not to be frustrated by the illness of a principal in a larger company. (See *Terry* v. *Variety Theatres Controlling Co.*[21] The contract permitted Terry to provide a substitute in such circumstances and this is what he had done.)

Loss of enhanced reputation

(ii) *Fielding* v. *Moisevitch*[22] was a Court of Appeal case which contains legal appraisal of several practical factors which must arise in theatrical management on failure of an artist to fulfil his contract. It is therefore of general interest.

M. a celebrated pianist, was under contract to the plaintiff, a concert impressario, to perform at the Theatre Royal, Nottingham in 1943 and did not do so. He suffered illness and so informed F. on the day before the concert was to take place. A substitute pianist played at the concert, a loss in box office takings occurred and the plaintiff brought the matter to court, primarily to let the public know that it was not his fault that they had been disappointed. First, the court held that a breach of contract had occurred. In so doing they rejected a contention of the defendant that there was a general custom in the theatre that an artist was released from his contract if he felt unable to perform to his usual standard and without fault on his part. Second, the plaintiff was awarded damages based on the extra expenses of engaging a substitute pianist and also taking into account a loss in box office takings. He was not, however, allowed recompense for alleged lower returns at a later promotion nor for loss of publicity. This last was an important point for theatrical management, since it distinguished an impressario such as Mr. Harold Fielding, the plaintiff, from an actor, who does have that right.

Contract cancelled

6.09   (iii) The actor's right had emerged in the case of *Withers* v. *The General Theatre Corporation Ltd.*[23] again in the Court of Appeal. There, an American artist under contract to perform at the London Palladium, was given notice by that theatre management to cancel his contract, less than a week before he was to perform. Management did so on seeing what they considered an inadequately rehearsed show during the trial run at Portsmouth in the week before the opening, for a three week run, at the Palladium. The plaintiff succeeded in his claim for damages, for loss of that enhanced reputation he would have gained at the Palladium and not

---

[20] (1907) 23 T.L.R. 592.
[21] (1928) 44 T.L.R. 451.
[22] (1946) 175 L.T. 265.
[23] [1933] 2 K.B. 536.

for injury to that reputation which he already possessed. What may seem an over-subtle distinction was made by the Court in the light of earlier House of Lords decisions and allied cases from the field of employment law.

(3) *Management Discretion*

Thirdly, a cause célèbre relating to a ticket for a seat on the first night of a new production, illustrates another area of management where awareness of legal principles is needed. *Said* v. *Butt*[24] concerned the situation created when the management of the Palace Theatre, London, had the plaintiff removed from the theatre, even though he had a valid ticket, on the occasion of the first night of a new play, "The Whirligig." Naturally there was a background. The plaintiff had worked with the defendant on a previous production and serious differences between the two had resulted. Indeed the plaintiff knew that he would not be sold a first night ticket if he went to the Palace box office in person. Thus he arranged for a friend, a Mr. Pollock, to purchase the ticket for him. After the debacle, the plaintiff brought an action for damages for breach of contract. He was met by the defence that, in the circumstances, the person with whom the contract was made was important: that there was a fundamental mistake about that person and thus no legal contract was in existence to be broken. The court was told of the special regard for his audience which a manager has in connection with a first night; he feels entitled to choose the people to whom seats are given for that occasion. It is "a special event with special characteristics," said a witness. The defence succeeded. McCardie J. held that non-disclosure by the friend that the ticket he purchased was intended for the plaintiff was a material fact. A legal contract had not been concluded and could not, therefore, be broken.

4. The Premises

(1) *Safety under the Health and Safety at Work Act 1974*

The subject of the safety of the theatre will be touched on in the licence obtained under the Theatres Act. There are provisions in other statutes which are also relevant to this subject. The Health and Safety at Work Act 1974 affects theatres as places where people at work are entitled to safety and health in their working conditions. The gantry and other potentially dangerous areas behind the front curtain will call for scrutiny, in the light of the extensive duties laid upon the occupiers of premises where people work.

It is important to note that this Act of 1974 has avoided creating rights of legal action in the courts concerning the rights and duties it so clearly defines. Thus, on the one hand, the Act states that it is the duty of every employer, so far as is reasonably practicable, to provide for the health,

[24] [1920] 3 K.B. 497.

6.11   PUBLIC ENTERTAINMENT

welfare and safety at work of all his employees.[25] In particular, this duty extends to the provision and maintenance of plant and systems of work that are, so far as reasonably practicable, safe and without risks to health.[26] But, on the other hand, in a section about civil liberty, the Act states that nothing in the Act shall be construed as conferring a right of action in any civil proceeding in respect of any failure to comply with (*inter alia*) the duties described above.[27] By contrast, an associated sub-section says that breach of a provision under Health and Safety Regulations, as distinct from the Act, is, so far as it causes damage, actionable.[28]

Since this creation by legislation of rights and duties, coupled with the removal of statutory rights of enforcement through the courts, is unusual, there is another sub-section designed to remove any doubts that this is indeed what Parliament intended. This says that the earlier provisions in this important section 47 are "without prejudice to any right of action which exists apart from the provisions of this Act."[29] There are not at present any Health and Safety Regulations specifically about theatres.

(2) *Safety under the Public Health Acts*

Exits and entrances

6.12   There are important provisions in the Building Regulations made under the Public Health Acts, which affect the exits and entrances of a theatre. What those regulations require are:

> "means of escape consisting of exits and escape routes, of such number, size, layout, design and construction as may reasonably be required in the circumstances of the case to enable the occupants to reach a place of safety in the event of fire; and other works to ensure that such means of escape can be safely and effectively used."[30]

This puts the provision of exits and entrances in the context of danger from fire, perhaps the ultimate hazard for a theatre. The requirements have behind them the sanctions common to all the Building Regulations.[31]

(3) *Safety at Common Law*

6.13   Section 47 of the Health and Safety at Work Act 1947 clearly leaves the common law operative in respect of health and safety at work of theatrical

---

[25] Health and Safety at Work etc. Act 1974, s.2.
[26] Health and Safety at Work etc. Act 1974, s.2(2)(*a*).
[27] Health and Safety at Work etc. Act 1974, s.47(1)(*a*).
[28] Health and Safety at Work etc. Act 1974, s.47(2).
[29] Health and Safety at Work etc. Act 1974, s.47(4).
[30] Reg. E 22, Building Regulations 1976, S.I. 1976 No.1676 as slightly amended by S.I. 1981 No. 1338, reg. 21. The requirement to raise and lower the safety curtain in the sight of the audience is an associated provision.
[31] Public Health Act 1961, s.4(6). At present £400 maximum and £50 a day. A specific provision about exits and entrances in theatres in the Public Health Act 1936, s.59, is superseded by the above Building Regulation. See Fire Precautions Act 1971, s.30.

employees. The main obligations resting upon an employer from that part of our law are to provide a proper system of working, to provide competent managers and supervisers for the employees and to provide suitable equipment for their use.

A case showing how this obligation operates in the complexity of a theatre is *Fanton* v. *Denville*.[32] For a production of "Maria Martin or Murder in the Red Barn," the classic melodrama, a drop scene was necessary, when the villain was to be executed by hanging. Though the stage manager successfully demonstrated the required fall onto a mattress, the plaintiff, the principal when the show appeared at Gateshead, unfortunately broke his ankle at rehearsal when trying the drop himself. He proceeded to sue his employer for failing to provide fit and safe plant and machinery and properties and for failing to take reasonable precautions to prevent danger to the plaintiff. In particular, he alleged, a sufficient mattress should have been provided.

The case reached the Court of Appeal, which in its judgment, touched upon other matters but emphasised that the employer's common law duty described above is not an absolute warranty of fitness of buildings and plant. It is rather an obligation to use reasonable care to see that they are fit and this obligation is associated with the duty to appoint competent servants. In the circumstances, there was no personal negligence proved against the defendant.

(4) *Coats of Arms*

A unique incident in theatrical history deserves a brief note. The case of *Manchester Corporation* v. *Manchester Palace of Varieties*[33] describes how the Court of Chivalry was assembled and ruled that the famous Manchester theatre was not entitled to exhibit the coat of arms of Manchester Corporation on a pelmet above its main front of stage curtains, wthout the consent of the Corporation, the grantee of the coat of arms in question. Though the sitting of the Court was special, the question raised is not, since coats of arms of the local authority are often found in civic theatres. It is true that the gravamen of the Corporation's complaint was the further use of its seal by the theatrical company but the judgment of Lord Goddard dealt with the pelmet display of the coat of arms and this is of general interest to those involved with theatres. **6.14**

5. Young Persons Taking Part in Performance

Some basic restrictions on this subject need to be borne in mind by theatre managers and their advisers. **6.15**

(i) No person under 16 years of age is to take part in a performance in which his life or limbs are endangered. "Performance" is defined in the Children and Young Persons Act 1933, s.23, in wide terms.

---

[32] [1932] 2 K.B. 309.
[33] [1955] 1 All E.R. 387.

6.15   PUBLIC ENTERTAINMENT

(ii) An under-12 year old is banned from being trained to take part in performances of a dangerous nature. An under-16 year old can do so only under licence from the local authority.[34]

(iii) An under-16 year old is only to take part in public performances, for which a charge is made, if duly licensed by the local authority.[35]

(iv) A licence under (iii) above is qualified further in the case of a child under the age of 13. Such a licence is not to be granted unless:
1. The licence is for acting and a declaration is made to the licensing authority that only a child of his age can act the part in question; or
2. The licence is for dancing in a ballet, being part of an entertainment which is wholly ballet or opera and a like declaration as in (i) above is made about the part the child is to dance; or
3. The child's part in the performance is wholly or mainly musical. In addition, the nature of the performance must be wholly or mainly musical or consist only of opera and ballet.[36]

(v) When conditions in licences granted for performances described in (iii) and (iv) above are not observed, the licensing authority may vary or revoke the licence. They have to give the licence holder a chance to be heard before taking such action.[37] The Act also sets out the procedure to be followed when a child licensed by one local authority is to take part in a performance in the area of another local authority.

(vi) Sanctions for breaches of these licensing requirements are contained in the Act. They include both fines and imprisonment and the courts are given power to revoke the licences. There is also an offence for knowingly making false statements in the licence application.[38]

(vii) An associated legal provision states that when a performance is for an audience of children, in total or as a majority, and the number of children is more than 100, then duties are laid upon managers about the instruction and stationing of their attendants, in order to cope with such an audience.[39]

6. Animals

6.16   The Performing Animals (Regulations) Act 1925 contains important provisions about the exhibition and training of performing animals. Exhibitors and trainers have to be duly registered with local authorities. In particular, exhibitions or performances accompanied by cruelty to ani-

---

[34] Children and Young Persons Act 1963, s.37.
[35] Children and Young Persons Act 1963, s.37, where details can be studied of the conditions under which no licence is needed. Broadly, these are that the performance is non-commercial, under the aegis of school or local authority and it is an exceptional activity for the performers. For details of the conditions relating to child performances mentioned in this paragraph, see the Children (Performances) Regulations 1968 (S.I. 1968 No. 1728). The 43 regulations cover very important details.
[36] Children and Young Persons Act 1963, s.38.
[37] *Ibid.* s.39.
[38] *Ibid.* s.40.
[39] *Ibid.* s.12.

mals give rise to punishable offences. In a later Act,[40] untrained bulls and unbroken horses are given special legal protection against being used in so-called rodeo performances.

7. Refreshments

(i) **Ice Cream**

Theatres, music halls and concert halls are exempt from a requirement in the Food Act 1984, that premises where ice-cream is sold shall be registered.[41]

6.17

(ii) **Intoxicating Liquor**

The Theatres Act licence has to be produced to the licensing justices when application is made to retail intoxicating liquor in pursuance of the normal excise licence.[42] Section F (para. 6.61 *et seq.*, *post*) deals fully with that subject.

(iii) **Young persons as sales staff**

The Shops Act 1950 controls night employment of young persons, normally under-18 year olds, to discourage exploitation. A work free interval of 8 hours from 10pm to 6am is prescribed in this Act, for this group of people. However the special needs of theatres are recognised in a provision that the 8 hour period shall not start, for their staff, until the evening performance ends.[43]

8. Sunday Observance

The Sunday Theatre Act 1972 introduced an exemption for theatres from the general ban under the Sunday Observance Acts on entertainment for payment on Sundays. In a duly licensed theatre, the presentation of a play is lawful, provided that, outside London, it is not performed between 2am and 2pm.[44]

6.18

B. Cinemas

Historical

Cinemas as a form of public entertainment have gone through various phases. These have given rise to the Cinematograph Acts, which are contained on the statute book at the present time. A tentative control system in the Cinematograph Act 1909 was succeeded by the Cinematograph Act 1952, when the cinema was enjoying a considerable vogue. Certain defects

6.19

---

[40] Protection of Animals Act 1934.
[41] Food Act 1984, s.16.
[42] Licensing Act 1964, s.199(c).
[43] Shops Act 1950, s.3.
[44] The London times are 3am to 2pm.

6.19

in control and practice were dealt with in that 1952 Act. More recently, Parliament has given considerable time to enacting the Cinematograph (Amendment) Act 1982. This was designed, as the Minister attending the debates said, "to bring the Cinematograph Acts into the video age."[45] Whilst the definition of cinematograph exhibition which had been adequate since 1952 used the words "produced on a screen by means which include the projection of light,"[46] a video cassette recorder linked with a television monitor is dependent upon the firing of electrons for the production of the image on the screen. This was one of the changes with which the Act of 1982 had to deal. Other matters included social changes, such as sex cinemas and the growth of cinema clubs.

Throughout the legislation of the last 70 years, there have been four main themes. These are the licensing of the premises, the safety of these premises, the best safeguards for children and young persons and, lastly, the control to be exercised over the films themselves. These are the matters dealt with in this section. It may be remarked, for readers seeking to come to terms with this interlocking legislation, that, subsequent to the parent Act of 1909, later Acts have created amendments to such an extent that the Government has acknowledged the need for a consolidating Act.

1. Licensing of the Premises

6.20 District councils are the licensing authorities for cinemas, since the local government reorganisation in 1974.[47] They may grant licences to such persons as they think fit, to use the premises for the purposes of cinematograph exhibitions. The licence can contain terms imposed by the district council, subject to any restrictions that the Secretary of State may issue, in the form of regulations.[48] Twenty-eight days notice of an application for a licence is required.[49] The Local Government (Miscellaneous Provisions) Act 1982 contains a provision that if a cinema is licensed under the Cinematograph Acts, the music played with or forming part of the cinematograph exhibitions shall not attract the need for an Entertainment Licence under that Act, in respect of the cinema premises.[50]

The Home Secretary has made regulations, under the power referred to above. These relate mainly to safety and are dealt with in the next subsection.

Terms of cinema licensing

The nature of the terms imposed in cinema licences by the present local authorities and their predecessors cannot be dealt with as briefly. There

---

[45] Hansard (1982), Vol. 27, col.564.
[46] The 1952 definition was itself a reform of the 1909 definition which incorporated "the use of inflammable films" as an essential ingredient.
[47] Local Government Act 1972, s.204(5).
[48] Cinematograph Act 1909, s.2.
[49] Cinematograph (Amendment) Act 1982, s.3.
[50] Local Government (Miscellaneous Provisions) Act 1982, Sched. 1, para. 21(*b*).

have been numerous interesting cases in the courts, as variations in the conditions imposed throughout the county have been tested. The main principles which have emerged are as follows:

(i) The licensing authority has a wide discretion and the courts, acting in a judicial and not an appellate capacity, will be slow to alter or quash what they have decided.

(ii) However, the district councils must not deal with applications under a blanket policy. Each application must be dealt with on its merits.[51]

6.21 (iii) The district councils must not themselves flout the law. This may seem obvious but in *R. v. L.C.C., ex parte the Entertainment Protection Association*[52] the Court of Appeal condemned a practice of stating that no action would be taken for Sunday opening, accompanied by payments to charities by the cinema managers in the area of that local authority. An Order was issued by the court to stop the practice. "Has the Theatres Committee ever heard of the Bill of Rights?" asked Lord Justice Scrutton, giving the leading judgment of the court.

(iv) The terms must not be so unreasonable that no reasonable body could have reached them. In the leading case of *Associated Provincial Picture Houses Ltd. v. Wednesbury Corporation*,[53] the Court of Appeal declined to intervene where the term challenged was that "No children under the age of 15 years shall be admitted to any entertainment, whether accompanied by an adult or not." (The actual grant of licence was under the Sunday Entertainment Act 1932, but the principle was the same.) Lord Green said:

> "Nobody, at this time of day, can say that the well-being and the physical and moral health of children are not matters which a local authority, in exercising its powers, can properly have in mind when those questions are germane to what it has to consider."[54]

The Master of the Rolls continued that it would require "overwhelming proof" to say that a decision of a local authority was so unreasonable that no reasonable authority could ever have come to it. The facts in that case, he said, "do not come anywhere near such a thing."

(v) The local authority must not take into account extraneous matters but only those germane to their decision.[55] This was a point emphasised by Lord Greene, in his strong judgment in the Wednesbury case.

(vi) In the interests of completeness, it is worth mentioning that in earlier cases in particular, the courts have stressed that the conditions

---

[51] See for instance, *Ellis v. Dubowski* [1921] 3 K.B. 621, and *R. v. Flintshire C.C. County Licensing Committee* [1957] 1 Q.B. 350.
[52] [1931] 2 K.B. 215.
[53] [1947] 2 All E.R. 680.
[54] *Ibid.*, p.683.
[55] See also *Harman v. Butt* [1944] K.B. 491, approved in the *Wednesbury* case.

6.21   PUBLIC ENTERTAINMENT

must be in the public interest.[56] This term was interpreted widely to cover the health, including the spiritual health, and welfare of the public.

A fee is payable for the licence.[57] A penalty may be incurred for contravention of the licence.[58] An appeal system exists to the Crown Court against refusal of a licence or against the terms in the licence actually granted.[59]

2. Enforcement

6.22   The police, the fire authorities and the district councils are invested with varying powers of enforcement and control.[60]

The police have powers of entry, which have been significantly enlarged by the Act of 1982, to cover not only regular cinemas but also cinema clubs and sex cinemas in occasional or moveable buildings or structures. A search warrant under the Act of 1982 requires the authority of a justice of the peace.[61]

The fire service are to give 24 hours notice of inspection and then may enter to see if the precautions are adequate and if terms laid down are being complied with. The punishment for an unlicensed exhibition has now, under the Act of 1982, increased to a fine not exceeding £10,000.[62]

3. Exempted Exhibitions

6.23   Premises used on not more than six days in the year and only occasionally and exceptionally for cinematograph exhibitions, do not require a licence, provided that seven days' notice of an exhibition is given to a local authority and to the police and the exhibitor complies with the conditions subsequently imposed. If the exhibition is to be in a building of a moveable nature, then two days' like notice is required, and due compliance with conditions imposed. A private dwellinghouse is not within the Acts, provided that no charge is involved, and the show is not for private gain. The major exception provision, contained in the 1952 Act and amended slightly by the Act of 1982, is for non-profit making bodies such as film societies, or indeed, any non-commercial committee, society, institution or other organisation. A certificate, formerly from the commissioners of Custom and Excise but now from the Home Office, is needed and then an exhibition by an "exempted organisation," is not in peril as an unlicensed exhibition, notwithstanding a charge for entrance. (This can, however, only be made on three days out of a period of seven days.)

---

[56] See, *e.g. Theatre de Luxe (Halifax) Ltd.* v. *Gledhill* [1915] 2 K.B. 49, where the dissenting judgment of Atkinson J. is notable, as it was preferred in the *Wednesbury* case.
[57] Cinematograph Act 1909, s.2.
[58] Cinematograph (Amendment) Act, 1982, s.7.
[59] Cinematograph Act 1952, s.6.
[60] See especially ss.5 and 6 of the Cinematograph (Amendment) Act 1982.
[61] Cinematograph (Amendment) Act 1982, s.5(3).
[62] Cinematograph (Amendment) Act 1982, s.7.

4. The Safety of the Premises

The power of the Secretary of State to make regulations was conferred in the Act of 1909.[63] The Act of 1952 then defined that power in relation to the subject of safety as follows:

> " . . . safety, in connection with the giving of cinematograph exhibitions (including the keeping and handling, in premises where other entertainments are being given or meetings held, of cinematograph film used or to be used for the purposes of cinematograph exhibitions or other articles or equipment so used or to be used)"[64]

The relevant regulations,[65] in force since 1955, contain 51 provisions and in the main deal with exits, staff, fire precautions, the structure of projection and re-winding rooms, the design of film projectors, as well as lighting and electrical installations and equipment.

5. The Safety of Children and Young Persons

The Secretary of State has also used his power, mentioned above, to make regulations about children. The 1952 Act defined the ambit of this subject as: "the health and welfare of children in relation to attendance at cinematographic exhibitions."[66] The Regulations were issued in 1955[67] and state that they do not derogate from the terms of licences issued by local authorities. What they do is to:

(i) Prohibit the admission of a child apparently under 5 years of age, unless accompanied by a person over 16 years old;

(ii) Prohibit the admission of an under 12 year old after 7 p.m. unless, first, they are accompanied by a person over 16 years old, and secondly, the film in question has not been shown on that day before 7 p.m.

(iii) Require the provision of attendants, when a show is for children, in he proportion of at least 1 per 1,000 children in respect of the lower floor of the cinema, and 1 per 50 children for the higher floor, and in total, to see that there are at least as many attendants as there are exits to the cinema.

For its part, the licensing authority is placed under a statutory duty to:

> "impose conditions or restrictions, prohibiting the admission of children to cinematograph exhibitions, involving the showing of works designated by the licensing authority or such other body as may be designated in the licence as works unsuitable for children."[68]

The licensing authority, in addition to the above *duty* is also charged to *consider*:

---

[63] Act of 1909, s.7; Act of 1952, s.5; and Act of 1982, s.2.
[64] Act of 1952, s.2(1)(a).
[65] See the Cinematograph (Safety) Regulations 1955 (S.I. No. 1129).
[66] Act of 1952, s.2.
[67] See The Cinematograph (Children) (No. 2) Regulations 1955 (S.I. No. 1909).
[68] Cinematograph Act 1952, s.3.

6.25   Public Entertainment

"what if any conditions or restrictions should be imposed as to the admission of children to other cinematograph exhibitions involving the showing of works designated by the authority or such other body as aforesaid as of such other description as may be specified in the licence."[69]

This "other body" is the British Board of Film Censors. They have classified films available for public exhibition and in 1982 changed the categories hitherto used. From Universal, AA and X, they have become categories relating to age, *i.e.*, under 15, under 18, Universal, plus the use of PG where parental guidance is necessary. This is to place responsibility for viewing by the young with their parents.

Where a special film show for children takes place, then there is reserved, to both the Home Secretary and the licensing authority, power to impose special conditions or restrictions on the necessary consent for such shows. Whilst films shown for children in a private dwellinghouse or shown as part of the activities of an educational or religious institution will be exempted exhibitions, these are special cases.

Generally, films shown for children are not to be treated, by that fact alone, as exempted exhibitions.[70]

6. Regulation of Film Renting and Exhibition

6.26 The Films Act 1960 is an essential point of reference for certain persons working in the distribution and production side of the film industry. It consolidated four earlier Acts and set up a comprehensive control system over standard 35mm films. This was designed to ensure that a quota of British films is shown commercially in this country. The system involves the registration of films, licensing of renters and exhibitors, supervision by the Department of Trade, review by the Cinematograph Films Council, returns of films exhibited to the Department of Trade and, finally, offences in relation to false statements on returns and "quota offences" for breach of prescribed quotas. A detailed account is outside the scope of this book. Cinema managers will find themselves involved in the returns, and the quotas will normally be arranged with their distributors.[71]

C. Local Authorities and Public Entertainment

6.27 It is essential for all engaged in public entertainment to know about the extent of the legal powers and duties of local authorities in that field. There are over 450 such authorities now in possession of the powers in question and the use made of them is a vital part of the provision of public entertainment in this country.

After various national Statutes and local Acts granting powers to local authorities in this field, the Local Government Act 1948 conferred wider

---

[69] Cinematograph Act 1952, s.5(2).
[70] See also the associated Acts of 1966 and 1970.
[71] This is a field where currently reforms are under discussion.

powers than any previously granted. The national stimulus given to public entertainment during the war was part of the background to this step.

1. The Local Government Act 1972

Now the Local Government Act 1972 has included in the functions of local authorities section 145, which embodies all that was in the 1948 Act and at the same time extends it and removes a number of restraints earlier imposed. Section 145 is the effective comprehensive statutory power available for nearly all the activities of local authorities in the public entertainment field:

6.28

"**Provision of entertainments**
145.—(1) A local authority may do, or arrange for the doing of, or contribute towards the expenses of the doing of, anything (whether inside or outside their area) necessary or expedient for any of the following purposes, that is to say—
(*a*) the provision of an entertainment of any nature or of facilities for dancing;
(*b*) the provision of a theatre, concert hall, dance hall or other premises suitable for the giving of entertainments or the holding of dances;
(*c*) the maintenance of a band or orchestra;
(*d*) the development and improvement of the knowledge, understanding and practice of the arts and crafts which serve the arts;
(*e*) any purpose incidental to the matters aforesaid, including the provision of refreshments or programmes and the advertising of any entertainment given or dance or exhibition of arts or crafts held by them.
(2) Without prejudice to the generality of the provisions of subsection (1) above, a local authority—
(*a*) may for the purposes therein specified enclose or set apart any part of a park or pleasure ground belonging to the authority or under their control;
(*b*) may permit any theatre, concert hall, dance hall or other premises provided by them for the purposes of subsection (1) above and any part of a park or pleasure ground enclosed or set apart as aforesaid to be used by any other person, on such terms as to payment or otherwise as the authority think fit, and may authorise that other person to make charges for admission thereto;
(*c*) may themselves make charges for admission to any entertainment given or dance or exhibition of arts or crafts held by them and for any refreshment or programmes supplied thereat.
(3) Subsection (2) above shall not authorise any authority to contravene any covenant or condition subject to which a gift or lease of a public park or pleasure ground has been accepted or made without the consent of the donor, grantor, lessor or other person entited in law to the benefit of the covenant or condition.
(4) Nothing in this section shall affect the provisions of any enactment by virtue of which a licence is required for the public performance of a stage play or the public exhibition of cinematograph films, or for boxing or wrestling entertainments or for public music or dancing, or for the sale of intoxicating liquor.

6.28   PUBLIC ENTERTAINMENT

(5) In this section the expression "local authority" includes the Common Council."

2. Removal of Limitations

6.29 Section 145 is in extremely wide terms. An understanding of the real extent of these powers is assisted by noting the seven areas in which this section releases local authorities from pre-1972 restrictions.

(i) The powers now specifically include the arts and crafts.

(ii) They apply to all local authorities and in particular to county councils and parish and community councils. County councils are those authorities best able to look at art and entertainment provision which straddles the boundaries of district councils, such as the national orchestras or opera companies.

(iii) A local authority can now exercise these powers outside its own area. It is no longer necessary to be able to prove benefit to its own inhabitants. An example of the steps needed to overcome this former legal hurdle is the special Eisteddfod Act 1959, which was passed to allow local authorities in Wales, including Monmouthshire, to contribute to the costs of the famous musical event. A comparable Act was passed in 1967 in connection with the Llangollen International Musical Eisteddfod.

(iv) In exercising these powers, a local authority no longer has to obtain the consent of the local authority for the area where the powers are exercised.[72]

(v) An earlier limit to an annually budgeted item is removed so that longer term financial planning is possible.

(vi) Borrowing monies for activities in this field is no longer subject to special procedures.

(vii) There was formerly a limit upon the proportion of a public park which was to be devoted to public entertainment purposes, such as a concert, open air theatre or dancing. That limit also is now removed.

3. Private Covenants

6.30 Section 145(3) restrains a local authority from contravening "any covenant or condition subject to which a gift or lease of a public park or pleasure ground has been accepted or made without the consent of the donor, grantor, lessor or other person entitled in law to the benefit of the covenant or condition." Though this stipulation is necessary and, indeed, repeats an earlier provision in the Local Government Act 1948, its impact is not always appreciated. Hence one or two examples of the way it works may be useful.

(i) An important local Act in 1980 was the West Midlands County Council Act. This was taken through Parliament not only on behalf of the County Council but also for the City of Birmingham and the other strong

---

[72] This follows the repeal without replacement of s.132 of the Local Government Act 1948.

metropolitan district councils lying within that country. One section in that Act related to the Cannon Hill Park in Birmingham and stated that whilst this could in future be used, free from a number of restraints laid down in the documents which had transferred it to the local authority, the Park was still subject to restraints, set out in those documents, and which concerned among others the sale of intoxicating liquors, the use of boats and playing by bands, on Sundays.[73]

(ii) Again, in a comparable local Act, the West Yorkshire Act 1980, a section relating to the People's Park in Halifax states that it shall be "used as a promenade only and no games or sports, swimming or dancing shall be permitted therein."[74] Even so, musical performances in the park are in order if "the Protector" appointed at the time of transfer to the local authority, so consents. Again, an entertainment for a charitable object is in order, subject again to the Protector's consent. This is an interesting example, since the section, quoted represents the residual legal constraint upon the district council's entertainment provision, after a substantial pruning and redrafting of the legacy of conditions and covenants from the Victorian age had taken place.

(iii) Another Halifax park, subject to restraints upon its use when conveyed to the local authority many years ago, had those restraints modernised in the Act mentioned above. Even so, the condition laid down at the time of transfer still prevails, *i.e.* that any building must be first approved by the President of the County Archeological Society.[75]

(iv) A somewhat quaint survival, in the 1980 section Cheshire County Act is of interest.[76] The Act takes up section 145 with its saving subsection (3) for local Acts and says this is not to apply to the Grosvenor Park, Chester. This means that old conditions are not to be saved. The local Act then says that this repeal shall not extend to an indenture of 1867 so far as it precludes "the erection of buildings or structures, the holding of fairs, the sale of intoxicating liquor or dancing, other than country dancing." Perhaps those last four words exemplify the nice battles joined whenever the combined forces of retention and repeal try to revise this type of legislation.

4. Allied Provisions

Section 145 of the Local Government Act 1972 is available to the local authority in its general capacity. There are three other comparatively minor legal provisions which have a bearing on this topic:

Schools

Under the Education Act 1944, the power to develop further education could extend to schools, theatres, or bands or orchestras and these may be

---

[73] West Midlands County Act 1980, s.85.
[74] West Yorkshire Act 1980, s.71.
[75] *Ibid.* s.70(5).
[76] Cheshire County Council Act 1980, s.16(1).

regarded as part of the general provision of public entertainment in an area.[77]

Swimming Pools

Under the Public Health Act 1936, a swimming pool can be closed in order to assist in the provision of entertainment.[78]

Children

The Children and Young Person Act 1933[79] on the other hand, has to be borne in mind as imposing restrictions on the numbers of attendants when there is an entertainment for children.

5. Conclusion

6.32 In view of their very wide powers, local councillors and their advisers are most likely to ask: What may we not do?, than otherwise. The areas of prohibition, comparatively small though they may seem, can be vital in practice.

Yet the final word in this section must be with the Royal Commission on Local Government when considering their duty to plan for the future of these functions.

> "Local authorities will increasingly be the main and, for the more elaborate facilities, the only providers, and their responsibilities, whether for the larger scale regional sport and recreation centres or for the smaller and more local projects, seem bound to increase."[80]

In their first reference, entertainment was not mentioned with the other two topics but in the subsequent chapter containing the Commission's view of the future, it was so mentioned. That is how the law rests at present and we still await testing in the courts of some of the key expressions in which it is set out.

D. Public Halls

6.33 As managers of public halls in the towns within the enlarged local authorities, district councils find themselves involved in legal provisions governing a variety of forms of entertainment performed in those buildings. The halls are naturally important to local societies and are consequently expected to be available for differing purposes. They often become "multi-purpose halls." Managers have to be tightrope performers themselves on occasion. Disappointment to the promoters of the dog show can perhaps be the sad result of giving pleasure to the baby show committee.

---

[77] s.41.
[78] s.226.
[79] s.12. And see para. 6.25.
[80] Cmnd. 4040, June 1969, para. 67.

Public Halls 6.33

Some of the principal forms of entertainment likely to be provided in these halls are now considered, in the light of current legal requirements for their performance.

1. Entertainment Licences

Music, singing and dancing form a significant part of the usage made of many of our public halls. The law relating to these new licences is therefore vital to all who have to do with their ownership, management, hiring and use. A complete code of law governing the licence is contained in the Local Government (Miscellaneous Provisions) Act 1982,[81] and is summarised below. It effectively supersedes all previous somewhat intermittent legislation about music, singing and dancing licences; it puts the licensing of boxing and wrestling on a uniform basis and it introduces for the first time specific powers appropriate to pop and rock festivals. 6.34

(1) Scope of the Licence

The licence is needed for "public dancing or music or any other public entertainment of the like kind." As such the normal Entertainment Licence does not apply to an open-air entertainment, nor to an entertainment at a pleasure fair, nor to music in a place of public religious worship, nor music performed as an incident of a religious meeting or service.[82]

(2) Pop Festivals

In connection with open air pop and rock festivals, the new licence is called a Special Entertainment Licence and the only conditions for its use are that the event is wholly or mainly in the open air; it is on private land and it is "a public musical entertainment."[83] Without using the words, pop and rock festivals, the purport of this provision is made clear by eliminating one or two other events. These are a garden fete, a bazaar, a sale of work, a sporting or athletic event, exhibition, display or other function or event of a similar character, or a religious meeting or service, merely because music is incidental to it. Finally, it is made clear that the legislation is not directed at a pleasure fair. 6.35

The Special Licence may have terms relating to the following and no other matters:

---

[81] s.1 and Sched. I.
[82] The Private Places of Entertainment Act 1967 remains on the Statute Book. It is adoptive, of limited use and works side by side with the large new legal machinery for public entertainment. The definition in the Act of 1982 raises questions for the licensing authority in relation to music played as incidental background music at, *e.g.* a cafe on a juke box, or at a hairdressers. Is the music merely incidental to the dominant object? Is it public entertainment which does not require a licence? See *Quaglieni* v. *Matthews* [1865] 6 B. & S. 474; *Hall* v. *Green* [1853] 9 Exch. 247. Music for ice skating would seem to be more obviously an essential part of the public entertainment.
[83] The procedure in the Act of 1982 requires a special resolution and two public notices.

6.35   PUBLIC ENTERTAINMENT

(i) The safety of the performers and their patrons.
(ii) Access for fire, ambulance and police to deal with all emergencies.
(iii) Sanitary provision.
(iv) Noise nuisance to the people in the neighbourhood.

(3) The General Entertainment Licence

6.36 Let us turn to the normal and general Entertainment Licence.

(i) The licence is annual, or shorter if stated, and is granted by district councils.

(ii) A licence can be for one or more specified occasions or it can be for a longer period, *i.e.* as in (i) above.

(iii) Transfer of licences rests with the licensing authority.

(iv) The police and fire authorities have to be given notice of an application for a licence, so that their views can be before the licensing authority when considering the application.[84]

(v) A reasonable fee is to be determined by the licensing authority. (No fee can be levied for events at religious buildings or village or county halls. Again the fee can be remitted if the licensing authority consider that the event is of an educational or like character or the performance or event is given for charitable or other like purpose.)

(vi) There is provision for cancellation or transmission on death of the licence holder.

(vii) The licensing authority can make regulations prescribing standard terms and conditions, to be applied to all entertainment licences.

6.37 (viii) Offences are created for unlicensed entertainments and breach of the terms of a licence. A licence can be revoked by a licensing authority after conviction for an offence. A defence is set out in the schedule to the offences described. This is that the person charged proves that he took all reasonable precautions and exercised all due diligence to avoid commission of the offence.

(ix) A special order of exemption for the premises, under the Licensing Act 1964,[85] is a good answer to an alleged offence for breach of the terms of an Entertainment Licence, insofar as the latter may have placed a limit on hours of opening and the exemption order can authorise extended hours.

6.38 (x) Police and fire officers have rights of entry for their respective functions.

(xi) The licensing authority is given the useful power to grant a provisional licence when a building for which it is required is at the plan stage. Once the building is complete in accordance with the plans, the full licence must be granted. Similar powers exist for extensions and alter-

---

[84] When dealing with applications for an Entertainment Licence, a local authority is obliged to inform the applicant of the substance of any objection it has from *e.g.* the police, fire services or members of the public. See Glidewell J. in *R. v. Huntingdon D.C. ex p. Cowan* (1984) 1 All E.R. 58.
[85] s.74(4).

ations. The authority have, in each case, to be satisfied that the licence is held by a fit and proper person.

(xii) The terms of a licence can be varied by the authority.

(xiii) Appeals lie first to the magistrates and secondly to the Crown Court, against (a) refusals by the licensing authority to grant, renew, transfer or vary a licence or (b) against a term in the Licence or (c) against a proposed revocation of the licence.

(xiv) An ice rink dealt with in an Entertainment Licence, does not also have to comply with Public Health Act by-laws, whilst the licence endures.[86]

(4) *Relation to Other Statutes*

In view of the comprehensive character of this legislation, it is important to record, finally, as Schedule 1 does, that the introduction of these Entertainment Licences does not affect: **6.39**

  (i) Theatres licences under the Theatres Act 1968.
 (ii) Cinema licences under the Cinematograph Act 1952.
(iii) Musical entertainment licences, under the Sunday Entertainment Act 1932.
(iv) Fire Certificates, under the Fire Precautions Act 1971.
 (v) Licences for premises, under the Licensing Act 1964.
(vi) Premises of the armed forces, authorised by the Secretary of State for public entertainment or amusement.

(5) *Boxing and Wrestling*

The Entertainment Licence is now available for public displays of boxing and wrestling, as discussed below (para. 6.44). **6.40**

2. Hypnotism

As a form of public entertainment, hypnotism is seen comparatively rarely in this country. It was considered desirable to have a simple form of legal control some 30 years ago and the Hypnotism Act 1952 was enacted. Apart from a technical amendment to adapt it to the new Entertainment Licence system, in the Local Government (Miscellaneous Provisions) Act 1982, the Act of 1952 stands as passed by Parliament and does not, indeed, appear to have been tested in the courts. The legal framework now in force is as follows: **6.41**

(i) It is the premises, not the performer, that are to be licensed. The licence can be either the Entertainment Licence or a specific authorisation

---

[86] Local Government (Miscellaneous Provisions) Act 1982, Sched. 1, para. 18, and Public Health Act 1961, s.75.

6.41   Public Entertainment

from the district council. In either event, special conditions can be imposed.

(ii) Offences are created to prevent a performance in unlicensed premises, or a performance upon a person under the age of 18 years.

(iii) A police constable has a legal right of entry to see that the law is being complied with. He should have reasonable cause to believe that an act is being or may be done in contravention of the Hypnotism Act.

(iv) The essential activity which gives rise to the need for authorisation of the premises is an exhibition, demonstration or performance of hypnotism.

6.42   Hypnotism is defined in the Act to include:

> "Hypnotism mesmerism or any similar act or process which produces or is intended to produce in any person any form of induced sleep or trance in which the susceptibility of the mind of that person to suggestion or direction is increased or intended to be increased."[87]

(v) The definition and the offence are not to include:
   (a) Hypnotism, mesmerism or any similar act or process which is self-induced.
   (b) An exhibition, demonstration or performance, otherwise than at an entertainment, which is for scientific or research purposes, or for the treatment of mental or physical disease.
   (c) An exhibition of hypnotism in a performance of a play, as defined in the Theatres Act 1968.

3. Billiards Licensing

6.43   Public billiards tables are normally regulated by reference in the justices' licences for licensed premises under the Licensing Act 1964 and associated statutes. Billiards tables, with which the law has traditionally associated "bagatelle boards or instruments used in any game of the like kind," are normally found in inns, public houses or licensed hotels or restaurants. Where, however, a saloon for public billiards is independent of such premises, then a Billiards Licence is needed.

Under the Gaming (Amendment) Act 1982, this is now dealt with, so far as grant or transfer is concerned, at the licensing sessions before the justices. Fees are fixed by the Secretary of State. These licences are annual.

The other incidents of a Billiards Licence go back to the Gaming Act 1845. A notice of the premises must record the existence of a Billiards Licence. There is a penalty for breach of the licence or for keeping the tables or boards for public use without a licence. The licence will normally indicate days when the tables are not to be used; these stem from the 1845 Act. Finally, the police have rights of entry to check compliance with these provisions.

---

[87] Hypnotism Act 1952, s.6.

4. Boxing and Wrestling

Legal control over these forms of public entertainment had been local rather than national, until the Local Government (Miscellaneous Provisons) Act 1982 introduced a national code. The London area and local councils which acquired Local Act powers, were the only ones with regulating powers. Croydon, Rochdale and Ipswich are examples of the latter.

The Act of 1982, mentioned above, which brings into existence a comprehensive code of licensing public entertainment, specifically applies that code to:

> "any entertainment which consists of or includes any public contest exhibition or display of boxing, wrestling, judo, karate or any similar sport."

This applies to amateur as well as to professional participants.

The procedure for obtaining an Entertainment Licence from the local authority is now of general application to these sports.

5. Breach of Copyright

Persons managing theatres or halls where copyright music is played, or other artistic performances, such as drama, take place, in which copyright may be present, should be aware of the extent of their potential liability under the Copyright Act 1956. Not only can they be a party to an infringement of copyright if they authorise a breach but they may find that they commit a direct offence themselves. Under section 21 of the above Act, a person who causes a "literary dramatic or musical work to be performed in public, knowing that copyright subsists in the work and that the performance constitutes an infringment of the copyright, "is himself guilty of an offence.

The normal and prudent step to take as a protection against this risk is to take out a licence from the copyright holder, often the Performing Right Society Ltd., or to ensure that the performer holds such a licence.[88]

---

[88] See the discussion of the possible infringement of copyright a hall manager can commit by "authorising" the performance. (Chap. 3, paras. 3.15–3.19 and 3.37). Interested readers are also referred to the following cases: (1) *Performing Right Society Ltd.* v. *Bradford Corporation* (1921) Macgillivray's Copyright Cases p. 21 (Vol. 1917–1923), where Roche J. held the Corporation liable for a breach because they published the programmes of their concerts in their Baths Hall. Disclaimer notices on the premises did not avail them. (2) *Monaghan* v. *Taylor* (1885) 2 T.L.R. 685, where the manager was responsible, since he "took the chance of the songs sung (at a Blackpool music hall) being such as could be lawfully or unlawfully sung." (Bowen L.J.) (3) The Performing Right Society also won in *Performing Right Society* v. *Mitchell and Booker (Palais de Danse)* [1924] 1 Q.B. 762, where McCardie J. called the dance band "a migratory thing" and acknowledged the prudence of the case being brought against the manager of the Hammersmith Palais de Danse. The definition of a "place of entertainment" in s.5 of the Copyright Act 1956 should be noted. It would bring in many multi-purpose halls. See also s.7 of the Performers' Protection Act 1963.

6. **Video Recordings Act 1984**

6.46 The manager of a public hall which is used occasionally for public cinematograph displays will now have to take account of the Cinematograph Acts 1909–1982, insofar as they define the exemptions from general licensing for such displays. As it will become commonplace to display video recordings at society and other meetings, note must also be taken of the new Video Recordings Act 1984, which introduces classification certificates for video recordings.

Under this Act of 1984, the video works themselves will normally be exempt works, under section 2 of that Act, if they are designed to inform, educate, or instruct, or are concerned with sport, religion or music. It is indeed only when such recordings are to be "supplied" that the Act may come into play. However, that word is defined to cover exchange, and loan, as well as hire, and sale. In certain circumstances, therefore, an unlawful activity could occur and the manager might wish to impose a condition of letting that the hiring society comply with the relevant legislation relating to video recordings and indemnify the management in respect of any breach thereof.

E. Outdoor Entertainment

1. **Horseracing**

6.47 The "sport of kings" retains its popularity, and nearly 60 racecourses are currently in operation. The Jockey Club, at one time the national manager for the whole industry, now shares the task of administration with three other bodies but is still the major force in the running of what is undoubtedly a complex enterprise.

The numerous groups of participants are to be licensed, the grounds brought to the right standard at the right time, relations with the Home Office and other major government departments maintained, the technical services involved in dope testing, photo-finishes and other matters kept abreast of the latest technology, and, at certain critical points, an enquiry arranged that will satisfy participants and the courts that standards of "natural justice" have been met.

The four legal institutions mentioned are the Jockey Club, the Horserace Betting Levy Board, the Horserace Totalisator Board and the Bookmakers Committee.

(1) *The Jockey Club*

6.48 Incorporated by Royal Charter, the Club exercises day to day control over horseracing. A racecourse needs an annual licence from the Jockey Club before it can open. This licence is subject to the "Rules of Racing," which maintains the role of the Jockey Club. The other major legal functions of the Jockey Club are:

(i) Licensing of personnel, *i.e.* owners, trainers, flat race jockeys, apprentice jockeys, steeple chase and hurdle race jockeys and the registration of stable employees.

(ii) Through Racecourse Security Services, to keep abreast of technical aids needed for the running of horseraces.

(iii) Control over race meetings. In one year, this involved pre-race horse identification and vaccination checks on 10,000 horses.[89]

(iv) Arranging occasional inquiries into disciplinary decisions that have given rise to formal appeals. The courts have from time to time given rulings on aspects of such hearings and the extent to which the rules of natural justice must be followed.[90]

(2) *The Horesrace Betting Levy Board*

The Levy Board assesses and collects annually money to be devoted to the improvement of horseracing. In the year 1982/83, this was £21 million and the main heads of the allocation were grants for prize money, assistance to race courses, maintaining the integrity of horseracing, assistance for veterinary science and education and, finally, assistance for breeding.[91] **6.49**

Another important role of this Levy Board, under the Betting Gaming and Lotteries Act 1963, is the grant of certificates for betting areas at racecourses.[92] These certificates are not annual but are renewed when there are changes made in the areas in question. This Board also approves the facilities for the Totalisator Board at racecourses.

(3) *The Horserace Totalizator Board*

The Horserace Totalizator Board has the power and the exclusive right to engage in, or authorise others to engage in, pool betting, as amplified in the Betting Gaming and Lotteries Act 1963.[93] The Board has powers to acquire land, borrow money and manage its affairs. Its accounts are open to public inspection.[94] **6.50**

(4) *The Bookmakers Committee*

The Bookmakers Committee is constituted under the Betting Levy (Bookmakers Committee) Regulations 1961.[95] These were made by the Sec- **6.51**

---

[89] The 1982 report of the Jockey Club.
[90] See for instance, *Nagle* v. *Fielden* [1966] 29 B. 633.
[91] Annual report of Horserace Betting Levy Board 1982–83, App.4.
[92] Horserace Totalisator and Betting Levy Boards Act 1972, s.5, and Betting, Gaming and Lotteries Act 1963, s.13. The charge to bookmakers and their assistants for the enclosure is not to be more than five times the maximum charge to the public for admission: s.13 of the Act of 1963. The general restriction on the use of premises for betting does not apply to a racecourse on a day when horseracing is taking place: s.1 of the Act of 1963.
[93] s.14.
[94] *Ibid.* s.31.
[95] S.I. 1961 No. 1546.

retary of State for Home Affairs, under the Act of 1963 and provide a representative body to negotiate with the Levy Board about the categories used to settle the annual levy, as described in (2) above. Under the Regulations, bookmakers are granted a right of appeal to the Betting Levy Appeal Tribunal against the proposed levy categories.[96] This is a further body in connection with which the rules of natural justice fall to be observed in its deliberations.

6.52 These four bodies each operate under the appropriate legal authority. There are two final points in connection with the organisation of this sport.

(a) Racecourse Association Ltd. is the representative body for all the racecourse managers in this country. It provides a useful forum for the Jockey Club and others who wish to enter into negotiations about the many aspects of horseracing.

(b) Racecourse ownership is not on a uniform pattern; some are privately owned, some on lease and some, like Pontefract and Doncaster, are on municipally owned land.[97] There are two large owner groups, nevertheless, which contain the majority of the racecourses currently in use.

2. Greyhound Racing

6.53 A greyhound racing stadium is in law but one of several possible types of premises called "tracks" in the Betting Gaming and Lotteries Act 1963.[98] The legal features associated with its management are as follows:

(i) It requires a licence from the local authority. This is the district council, outside London.[99]

(ii) Betting is permitted on 130 days in the year.[1] These may not include Sundays, Good Friday and Christmas Day. A maximum of 14 days in the month for permitted betting is also laid down in these two statutes. The days selected are to be notified to the local authority.

(iii) A totalisator can be installed to carry on pool betting business on a dog track. It can operate only on notified betting days and only for dog races run on that day.

(iv) The track occupier must provide convenient facilities for bookmakers. The case of *Cutler* v. *Wandsworth Stadium Ltd.*[2] reached the House of Lords and is an authority on this point. The decision went against an

---

[96] S.I. 1963 No. 748.
[97] For Pontefract see the West Yorkshire Act 1982 and for Donaster, the South Yorkshire Act 1980.
[98] s.5(1)(*b*).
[99] Act of 1963, Sched. 2, para. 1(*a*) and Local Government Act 1972, ss.251 and 273.
[1] Act of 1963, s.5 and Betting, Gaming & Lotteries (Amendment) Act 1971, s.1. This is an increase from an earlier figure of 104 days. The Act of 1963 fixed the number of races in any one day on which betting could take place. It also had "special betting days" when a greater number of such races were permitted. Both those numbers were increased by the Betting, Gaming and Lotteries (Amendment) Act 1980, s.1.
[2] [1949] A.C. 398. Followed in *Pole Stadium* v. *Squires* [1982] 1 All E.R. 404.

aggrieved bookmaker on the ground that, although *ubi jus ibi remedium*,[3] the remedy for the right was with the public and not the bookmaker. It was, said the Court, for the benefit of the public that the duty was imposed. An offence of non-compliance by the occupier existed, for which prosecution was available and the occupier should not, under the Betting and Lotteries Act 1934, have to face civil liability as well.

(v) The occupier has the same rights in relation to pool betting as the Horserace Totalisator Board has on a horserace track. (See above.)[4]

(vi) The law has some strict and detailed requirements about the operation of the totalizator on a greyhound track. It must be mechanically or electrically operated to comply with prescribed conditions and in good working order. Rigorous controls on its publicity and on its supervision also exist. An accountant and mechanic appointed by the local authority are to be present when the totalizator is in operation.[5]

3. Athletic and Sporting Tracks

This section relates to tracks for events "at which races of any description, athletic sports or other sporting events take place."[6]

(i) These, like greyhound tracks, require a track betting licence from the district council, if betting is to take place on such events.

(ii) There are restrictions upon betting on these tracks, imposed under the Betting Gaming and Lotteries Act 1963 and associated statutes. One hundred and four days in the year is the maximum for betting and not more than 14 of these shall be in any one month.

(iii) The police have powers of entry.[7]

(iv) The operation of bookmakers is subject to detailed restrictions affecting their licences.

(v) The grant of a track betting licence is legally elaborate. The licence can be refused on several grounds:

(a) It would be injurious to the health and comfort of the residents.
(b) It would be detrimental to schoolchildren in the neighbourhood.
(c) It would seriously impair the amenities of the neighbourhood.
(d) It would result in undue traffic congestion.
(e) It would seriously prejudice the preservation of law and order.[8]

Finally, as a legal hurdle, a licence can be withheld from an applicant with a previous conviction.

(vi) The track betting licence normally lasts for seven years.

---

[3] *Pett v. Greyhound Racing Association* [1969] 1 Q.B. 125. A trainer was summoned before the stewards of the Association on a doping charge. He was denied a legal representative and only permitted a kennelman. The High Court said this was wrong and a legal representative must be allowed; the man's livelihood was at stake, said the court. (The maxim in the text means: Where there is a legal right, there will be a legal means to enforce it.)
[4] Act of 1963, s.17.
[5] See Dog Racecourse (Totalizator) Regulations 1967 (S.I. No. 10).
[6] Act of 1963, s.55.
[7] Act of 1963, s.23.
[8] *Ibid.* s.6 and Sched. 3, para.7.

(vii) It can be revoked if the track is conducted irregularly.[9] From such a decision an appeal lies to the Crown Court.

(viii) The charges which an occupier can make to a bookmaker for his facilities are controlled as for horseracing, *i.e.* they must not exceed five times the highest admission charge to the public.

4. Safety of Sports Grounds

6.55 The main points of the governing Act, the Safety of Sports Grounds Act 1975, are as follows:

(i) The Act is aimed at the sports stadium which will hold more than 10,000 spectators. The provisions in the Act are set in motion when the Secretary of State designates such a stadium as needing a Safety Certificate.

(ii) The local authority is empowered to issue a Safety Certificate on receipt of an application from the stadium proprietor. The certificate will be either for a limited number of occasions or it can be indefinite. It must give a maximum number of permitted spectators and also details of exits, entrances, means of access, crush barriers and means of escape in case of fire. As an option, the certificate may specify different numbers of spectators for different parts of the stadium.

(iii) This short Act contains procedures to tbe followed for the consideration of the application, amendments to a Certificate, appeals against refusals to grant a certificate, alterations and extensions at the premises, entry by the police and by the building authority.

(iv) The Secretary of State has power to make various regulations.

(v) Offences are created for contravening a Safety Certificate and in particular for exceeding the permitted number of spectators. A defence is available, namely to satisfy the court that the holder of the certificate took all reasonable precautions and exercised all due diligence to comply with the Certificate.

(vi) The Act is not to be treated as creating new civil liabilities.

(vii) Whilst a Safety Certificate is in force,[10] certain other statutory requirements are not to apply, *i.e.* (a) the Public Health Act 1936, s.59, where it relates to entrances, exits and passageways; (b) the Public Health Acts Amendment Act 1890, about public platforms (s.37); (c) the Fire Precautions Act 1971, about fire certificates; and (d) any relevant Local Acts. These are not to apply in so far as they would be duplicating matters dealt with in the Safety Certificate.

(viii) A special emergency procedure exists, if a risk to spectators is considered to be so great that an Order should be made at once. The magistrates court has power to make this Order and it can prohibit or restrict spectators until steps are taken to reduce the risks in question.

---

[9] *Ibid.*, Sched. 3, para. 13.
[10] Safety of Sports Ground Act 1975, s.9. The certification of football grounds under this Act was accelerated in August 1985, following the Bradford football stadium fire tragedy. The Sporting Events (Control of Alcohol, etc.) Act 1985 and its Designation Order for Football Association clubs was a parallel measure.

5. Pleasure Fairs

6.56 (i) Local Authorities have powers to regulate pleasure fairs under the Public Health Act 1961 and the Local Government (Miscellaneous Provisions) Act 1976.[11] Under the Act of 1961, they were authorised to make by-laws about ingress, egress, prevention of nuisances, preservation of safety, order, cleanliness and sanitary conditions. The Act of 1976 extended these powers to cover measures to prevent outbreaks of fire, both to the fair stalls and also to the caravans or other sleeping quarters of the fair holders.

(ii) The definition of a fair in the Act of 1961 is interesting. "Pleasure Fair" is the statutory term and there are two components. First, it is the place where one of the following entertainments is provided and an admission charge is made.

Secondly, there is then a long list containing a wide range of outdoor entertainments:

(a) Circuses.
(b) Exhibitions of human beings or performing animals.
(c) Merry-go-rounds, roundabouts, swings, swtichback railways.
(d) Coconut shies, hoop-las, shooting galleries, bowling alleys.
(e) Dodgem cars and like machines.
(f) "Automatic or other machines intended for entertainment or amusement."

This concludes with the somewhat enigmatic

(g) "Anything similar to the foregoing":

The by-law powers are not to apply to a fair held under royal charter or like ancient authority, nor to custom. The statutes impose upon the by-law making councils a duty to consult interested bodies and, particularly, the fire authority. As by-laws, these requirements of course fall to be confirmed by the Secretary of State and he is enjoined by the statutes to be satisfied that the consultations have been adequate.

6. Local Authorities

6.57 The earlier section about indoor entertainment has dealt in detail with the powers placed upon local authorities by section 145 of the Local Government Act 1972. An important set of related powers for local authorities is found in section 19 of the Local government (Miscellaneous Powers) Act 1976. That section is headed "Places of Entertainment" and is concerned wholly with recreational facilities. For the purposes of this book, whilst both recreation and entertainment are regarded as within "leisure services", entertainment has been treated as the right category for sporting, athletic and allied events when taking place primarily for the benefit of spectators. When such events are, on the other hand, primarily for partici-

---

[11] Public Health Act 1961, s.75, and Local Government (Miscellaneous Provisions) Act 1976, s.22.

pation by people who want exercise or recreation, then they have been discussed in the Sport or Open Air Exercise chapters. Clearly such a distinction cannot be universally clear-cut. However, sports centres, ice rinks, swimming pools and riding schools have been treated as sport and recreation, rather than entertainment.

7. Local Government (Miscellaneous Provisions) Act 1976

6.58 There is one small but useful power conferred on local authorities which those concerned with outdoor entertainment should know about. It is power to serve notice requiring sanitary provision at a place where there is to be an entertainment or exhibition. The County Court can deal with appeals against these notices.[12]

8. Ancient Custom

6.59 A brief reference is due to two cases where courts allowed outdoor entertainment and pastimes to continue as established customs.

(i) *Hall* v. *Nottingham and others* involved a custom, claimed and upheld for parishioners in Ashford Carbonell, Shropshire, to go on a field, called Maypole Piece, in the parish, set up a maypole and dance round it "and otherwise enjoy on the land any lawful and innocent recreation at any times in the year."

Since the legal tests for such a claimed custom are that it should be both reasonable and certain, this custom was challenged on the ground that it was not certain. Evidence being that the custom was enjoyed over many years at the holiday seasons, the court upheld the custom, holding that the expression should be interpreted as meaning "at all seasonable times."[13]

(ii) *Fitch* v. *Rawlings*[14] was the second case based on a claim of custom. A right was claimed and upheld by the court to play cricket at Steeple Bumstead in Essex. As in the *Salop* case, the decision was arrived at after the Court had received convincing evidence that there were limits upon the right claimed. In this case, those limits were, firstly, as to the duration—namely only at all seasonable times and, secondly, as to the persons benefitting—namely, only the inhabitants of the parish.

9. **Animals**

6.60 The Protection of Animals Act 1911 is a general point of reference for legal restrictions upon those seeking to offer a dubious form of entertainment by subjecting animals to cruelty. The Act makes it an offence to bait an animal or arrange fights between animals for paying spectators. Likewise, it is an offence to keep a house, pit or other place, in which animals might fight.

---

[12] 1976 Act, s.20.
[13] (1875) L.R. 1 Ex. D. 1.
[14] [1775]–[1802] All E.R. Rep. 571; 2 Hy. Bl. 393.

Cockfighting has an Act to itself, the Cockfighting Act 1952. In addition to the prohibition of the fighting, there is also an offence to possess spurs for cocks—"instruments or appliances."

F. Sunday Observance, Licensing and Catering

Introduction

6.61 The five previous sections have dealt with the present law for some of the most substantial forms of public entertainment. Theatres and cinemas are large groups of business, each of which has been shown to have a significant legal framework within which it works. Apart from their involvement with theatres and cinemas, local authorities are now in the entertainment business and the legal powers available to them are vital, not only for themselves but also for their associates, whether performers, contractors, agents and sometimes too, for their customers. The nine areas of public entertainment grouped in the last two sections as public halls or outdoor entertainment, have collectively covered a large part of the British public entertainment scene. They too have been found to have varying legal structures within which to operate.

In this section we turn to three areas of law which can affect most if not all of the other specific entertainments. Sunday observance, the licensing law and catering, otherwise unrelated, have this in common: they impinge upon the individual forms which public entertainment takes in this country. The law controlling the sale of intoxicating liquor is, for historical and social reasons, more bulky and complex than the other two; all three are important for the country's leisure services.

1. Sunday Observance

6.62 This is a tangled subject, primarily because the law is not yet codified.

The Sunday Observance Act 1780 is still on the Statute Book and provides that:

> "Any house, room or other public place which shall be opened or used for public entertainment or amusement on any part of the Lord's day called Sunday and to which persons shall be admitted by the payment of money, or by tickets sold for money, shall be deemed a disorderly house or place."

A potential fine of £200 upon the keeper of the "house" and £50 upon doorkeppers or servants collecting admission money, is contained in this statute.[15]

Exemptions

6.63 However, the situation is materially affected by three other Acts of Parliament:

---

[15] *Houghton le Touzel* v. *Mecca* [1950] 2 K.B. 612, shows that a company can be liable as a "keeper."

6.63 PUBLIC ENTERTAINMENT

(a) Cinemas are now exempt, by virtue of the Sunday Cinema Act 1972, and subject to licensing authority concurrence.

(b) Theatres are also exempt, under the Sunday Theatres Act 1972, apart from the time restriction from 2am to 2 pm outside London and 3 am to 2 pm in London.

(c) Licensed premises are exempt, under the Licensing Act 1964.[16]

In the result, the problems that remain are as follows:

(i) A limited exception to the Act of 1780 was made by the Sunday Entertainment Act 1932, which provided that the authority granting music, singing and dancing licences could grant such a licence in respect of "a musical entertainment on Sundays" and attach appropriate conditions.[17]

(ii) There is, however, no power to authorise public dancing on a Sunday, where such dancing would contravene this provision.[18]

(iii) For the two main types of public entertainment for which the Sunday Entertainment Act 1932 was passed, *i.e.* musical and cinematographic performances, a liberal interpretation was incorporated about the persons thereby exempted from the peril of conviction under the Act of 1780. The conductor and the persons managing or assisting or otherwise taking part in or attending or advertising those two activities were all exempted.[19]

(iv) Exemption is now given, in the Act of 1932, for other public attractions to open on Sundays. These are museums, picture galleries, zoological gardens, botanical gardens and an aquarium.[20] The views of the courts were once tested about a wedding reception coming within the statutory exemptions; it was held that such a gathering was not exempted.[21]

One can only conclude that a consolidating Act would be welcome for this slightly confused area of law.

2. The Public Leisure Services and the Sale of Intoxicating Liquor

Introduction

6.64 A useful approach to this complex branch of the law may be made with a recognition of the main service points for the sale of intoxicating liquor. These are public houses, clubs, off-licence shops and other premses, restaurants and hotels. The law has followed community practice and its provisions relate to these various buildings. So the classes of licence available under the law include on- and off-licences, new licences, removals, provisionals, transfers and table licences.

---

[16] s.88.
[17] The introduction of the new Entertainment Licence to supersede music singing and dancing licences, in the Local Government (Miscellaneous Provisions) Act 1982, specifically leaves this s.3 position untouched. (See para. 6.39). A "musical entertainment" is there defined as a "concert or similar entertainment, consisting of the performance of music, with or without singing or recitation."
[18] See *R.* v. *Brillon ex p. Newton* (1944) 4 All E.R. 419; Sunday Entertainment Act 1932, s.4.
[19] Sunday Entertainment Act 1932, s.4.
[20] *Terry* v. *Brighton Aquarium Co.* (1875) L.R. 10 Q.B. 306.
[21] *Roe* v. *Harrogate Justices* (1966) L.G.R. 465.

Though the subject is wide, an effort has been made to restrict what is dealt with below to that which is relevant to the provision of public leisure services. A manager of a civic theatre or a civic sports centre will no doubt wish to provide licensed bars in those premises. The limited knowledge of licensing law needed by such persons and their advisers forms the content of this subsection. Certainly for the full law on the Licensing Acts, reference should be made to the standard professional books on the subject.[22]

(1) *Classes of Premises and Licences*

The current law relating to the sale of intoxicating liquor is found in the Licensing Acts 1964 to 1980. The licensing districts for the purpose of the Acts are the petty session areas, as defined by the Magistrates' Courts Act 1980. The basic function rests with the licensing justices, composed of justices who sit in those areas.[23]

Sale

The sale by retail of intoxicating liquor is regulated by a system of justices' on-licences and justices' off-licences. The former authorises the sale for consumption either on or off the licensed premises. The off-licence, on the other hand, only authorises sales for consumption off the licensed premises. Whilst an on-licence may authorise the sale of intoxicating liquor of all descriptions, it can, alternatively, be limited to beer, cider and wine only, or beer and cider only, or indeed wine only. There are only two alternatives with the off-licence. It must be for intoxicating liquor of all descriptions or for beer, cider and wine only.[24]

Licences

Licences may be granted as new licences or by way of renewal, transfer or removal of existing licences. New licences are normally granted subject to conditions about tenure and the justices being satisfied about the suitability of the premises.[25] When it is proposed to construct, alter or extend premises, for which it is intended to apply for a licence, it is possible to obtain a Provisional Licence.[26] This allows the applicant to ascertain if a licence will be granted when the works have been completed. A Protection Order is the name of the justices' order sought when a person seeking the transfer of a licence wants authority to sell intoxicating liquor pending the outcome of the application for the transfer.[27]

A restaurant licence is one granted for premises structurally adapted

---

[22] See, *e.g.* Paterson's *Licensing Acts* and Anthony and Berryman's *Guide to Licensing Law*. Also D. Field and M. Pink, *Liquor Licensing Law* (1983, Sweet and Maxwell).
[23] Licensing Act 1964, s.2.
[24] *Ibid.* s.1.
[25] *Ibid.* s.4. Transfer is to another person on the same premises: removal is to different premises.
[26] s.6.
[27] ss.10 and 11.

and bona fide used to provide habitually a customary main meal at midday or in the evening or both for patrons, and where the liquor is sold or supplied to persons taking meals, as an ancillary accompaniment.[28]

A residential licence is granted for premises used to provide habitually for reward board and lodging, including breakfast, and one other customary main meal. In this case, the liquor must be sold or supplied only to residents or their bona fide friends. A combined residential and restaurant licence can be granted.

Duration

A licence normally runs from the time it is granted until the next April 5. If granted in the last three months of a licensing year, then it runs to the end of the next licensing year. A licence granted by way of renewal, transfer or removal supercedes any existing licence.[29]

Occasional Licences

The holder of an on-licence may apply to the justices for the granting to himself of an occasional licence.[30] This is to allow him to sell any liquor covered by his existing licence at other premises. This licence can cover three weeks at a time and be subject to its own conditions. Occasional licences are also subject to certain special provisions:
  (i) 24 hours notice of the application has normally to be given to the police.
  (ii) Liquor cannot be sold under such a licence on Christmas Day, Good Friday nor any day appointed for a public fast or thanksgiving.
  (iii) Unless an electors' poll is held and produces a majority in favour, then this type of licence does not apply to Wales or Monmouthshire.
  (iv) A public hearing can be avoided by giving one month's previous notice of the application to the clerk to the justices.
  (v) Finally, the name of the licence-holder must normally be displayed over the entrance of the premises where the dinner, dance or other function takes place.

6.68 An addition to this procedure was effected by the Licensing (Occasional Permissions) Act 1983. This enables the application to the licensing justices to be made by "an officer of an eligible organisation," or of a branch of such an organisation. The "occasional permission" can be granted to that applicant, provided that the function in question is in connection with the organisation's activities, that the applicant is a fit and proper person, that the place will be a suitable place and that the sale of intoxicating liquor is not likely to result in a disturbance or annoyance to the residents in the neighbourhood of that place or in any disorderly conduct.

---

[28] Pt. IV.
[29] s.26.
[30] s.180.

The other elements in this new legislation are:

1. There are to be no more than four such permissions in any twelve month period granted to that organisation in respect of the same place.

2. This new procedure does not affect or authorise sales of intoxicating liquor in Wales or Monmouthshire, where the Welsh Sunday Polls procedure must still apply.

3. The organisations which can use this procedure must not be conducted for private gain.

4. The full procedure relating to notices and timetable must be referred to, in section 2 of the new Act of 1983.

5. Significantly, the simple reference to the situation dealt with in this Act of the sanctions contained in the Licensing Act 1964, so far as appropriate, results in 14 such offences being listed in the schedule to the Act of 1983. They should be studied.

6. In perhaps the first case to reach the law reports under the new Act, *R. v. Bromley Licensing Justices, ex p. Bromley Licensed Victuallers Association*,[31] the licensing justices were corrected on two points in a decision. First, for four functions on four nights, albeit by the same organisation, there must be four separate "permissions," since each one is limited to a 24 hour period. Secondly, an objection from persons other than the police is valid and must be heard.

(2) *Obtaining a Licence*

6.69 The licensing justices have discretion to grant to a fit and proper person the licence sought.[32] The licensee will normally be the person who will be selling the liquor. In the case of a local authority or other corporate body, a nominated director or manager can be the licence holder. There has to be a named and accountable individal.

There are certain disqualifying features affecting applicants such as previous criminal convictions.[33] There are also rights of appeal against decisions of the justices and these now go before the Crown Court.[34] Likewise for clubs aggrieved by refusals of applications for registration, there are rights of appeal to the Crown Court.[35]

(3) *Special Hours and Extensions*

6.70 (i) Permitted Hours form a general legal restraint upon holders of both justices' licences and club registration certificates. A person may consume or take away liquor on those two classes of premises only during permitted

---

[31] [1984] 1 W.L.R. 585 (Q.B.D.).
[32] s.3.
[33] s.9.
[34] s.21.
[35] s.50.

hours.[36] These are, for licensed premises, normally on weekdays other than Christmas Day or Good Friday, 11 am to 10.30 pm, with a break of $2\frac{1}{2}$ hours which begins at 3pm. In the London Metropolitan District and any other district where the justices deem it desirable, the time of 10.30 pm. is extended to 11 pm. On Sunday, Christmas Day[37] and Good Friday, the permitted hours are 12 noon to 10.30 pm with a break of 5 hours beginning at 2 pm.

Variation

(ii) Licensing justices, if satisfied that the interests of their district make it desirable, can modify those general hours. They can make the total of permitted hours on any day nine, ending at 10.30 pm or $9\frac{1}{2}$ hours when the closing time has been extended to 11 pm. In those circumstances, the permitted hours may not start before 10 am. If this descretion is exercised, there must be a single break of at least 2 hours in the afternoon.[38]

Clubs

6.71 (iii) Club rules fix permitted hours for the club. The rule to be followed is that the hours fixed shall not on any day be longer, nor begin earlier, nor end later, than the general licensing hours. This can take account of any licensing justices' modifications for the district, as above. The club rules must also ensure that there is a break of not less than 2 hours in the afternoon. Finally, on Sundays, Christmas Day and Good Friday, the break shall include the hours from 3 to 5 pm and there shall not be more than $3\frac{1}{2}$ hours after 5 pm.[39]

Legal Relaxation

6.72 (iv) There are two traditional, and legal, mini-extensions to these permitted hours. Ten minutes drinking-up time is in order for consuming liquor served on the premises and for taking away from the premises liquor not supplied nor taken in an open vessel.[40] Also, half an hour is allowed for the consumption of the accompanying liquor by persons taking meals. A resident at the licensed premises, and his bona fide private friends, are not subject to those restraints.

The licensing justices have power to vary the above standard permitted hours for the provision of either refreshment or entertainment or both. Those extensions can have conditions attached.

Special Hours certificates are also obtainable for both licensed premises and clubs where Entertainment Licences for those premises have been

---

[36] s.59.
[37] s.60.
[38] s.61.
[39] s.62.
[40] s.63(1)(b).

SUNDAY OBSERVANCE, LICENSING AND CATERING 6.72

granted by the local authority under the Local Government (Miscellaneous Provisions) Act 1982.[41]

(4) *Inspection and Alterations*

The Acts contain provisions for inspection of premises before their first registration or licensing. The local authority, the police and the fire authority have rights of inspection; from the point of view of applicants, the clerk to the licensing justices is the main initial point of contact.[42] 6.73

Important provisions in the Licensing Acts require consent to be sought from the justices by licensees for alterations to the licensed premises. This duty arises when:
1. The effect of the works would be to afford increased drinking facilities in the public or common parts of the premises.
2. Their effect would be to conceal from observation a public or common part of the premises used for drinking.
3. The proposed works affect the communication between the parts of the premises where intoxicating liquor is sold and the remaining parts of the premises or any streets or any public way.[43]

Furthermore, justices have the power to require certain alterations to be made to premises, in the interests of the proper conduct of the business, when they are dealing with a renewal of a licence.[44]

(5) *Young Persons*

The holder of a justices' licence must not allow any persons under 14 years to be in the bar of the licensed premises during permitted hours.[45] A bar for this purpose includes any place wholly or mainly used for the sale and consumption of liquor. 6.74

The licence holder and his staff must not sell liquor to any person under 18 years or allow a person under 18 years to consume liquor in a bar.[46]

However, a person who is 16 years of age may buy beer, porter, cider or perry for consumption with a meal in a part of the premises set apart for the service of meals and which is not a bar.[47]

The licence holder will be liable to a fine if any person under 18 years is employed in a bar of licensed premises at any time when the bar is open

---

[41] Licensing Act 1964, s.79. The close relation of the Entertainment Licence and the Special Hours Certificate is exemplified in the provision in the Act of 1982, Sched. 1, para. 13, whereby the daily hours of operation of an Entertainment Licence are effectively extended until the end of the exemption order, granted by the Licensing Justices under s.174(4) of the Licensing Act 1964.
[42] Act of 1964, Sched. 1.
[43] *Ibid.* s.20.
[44] s.19.
[45] s.168.
[46] s.169.
[47] s.169(4).

6.74   Public Entertainment

for the sale and consumption of liquor. (A bar set apart solely to supply table meal customers is outside this restriction.)[48]

(6) *Offences*

6.75 In an Act such as the Licensing Act 1964 with 200 sections and 15 Schedules, and designed to restrain the sale and consumption of liquor in its various forms, there are offences created which are too numerous to tabulate here. Some have been identified above; some can give rise to loss of a licence or club registration, apart from the fines or other punishments which provide the normal sanction for offences in Acts of this sort. Basically, all arise in respect of the breach of requirements laid down in the Licensing Acts.

3. Catering

6.76 Catering is a normal accompaniment to most forms of public entertainment. For local authorities, the main section relied upon is section 145 of the Local Government Act 1972. This empowers local authorities to "provide refreshments," in connection with the very wide range of entertainments listed and quoted in section C (para. 6.27 *et seq.*) of this Chapter.

The Civic Restaurants Act 1947 is the other statutory source for local authorities' powers in this field. Though somewhat curtailed by the Local Government Act 1972, this Act of 1947 empowers councils to "establish and carry on restaurants and otherwise provide for the supply to the public of meals and refreshments . . . and carry on such activities as are reasonably incidental or ancillary,"[49] thereto. The main remaining section in that Act of 1947 lays down guide lines for financial responsibility in respect of those activities.[50]

In providing a catering service, public authorities have to take account of employment law, so far as staff are concerned and also the laws of tort and contract, in connection with relations with their customers and claims resulting from the condition of premises used or provisions supplied. These areas of law are outlined in Chapters 1 and 2.

The other detailed area of law affecting catering is that associated with the Food and Drugs Acts and the highly detailed Regulations, both via the European Economic Community and nationally, about standards for food and drinks of all sorts. For these, interested readers are referred to the specialist text books.[51]

---

[48] s.170.
[49] s.1 of the Civic Restaurants Act 1947.
[50] *Ibid.* s.3. "Best endeavours," it says, are to be used to match income and expenditure.
[51] See Butterworth's *Law of Food and Drugs,* now in six volumes, as the most comprehensive publication. Over 100 individual foods and drinks are now dealt with in the Regulations, which have proliferated in the last two decades, as the law has sought to keep pace with scientific and dietetic advances. Purely as caterers, it behoves the public services to engage management who are familiar with this formidable background.

G. Gambling

1. Introduction

"The English working man is less interested in the equality of men than in the equality of horses." G.K. Chesterton's aphorism comes to mind as one turns to the succession of statutes handed down by Parliament on gambling. A major consolidation Act was passed in 1963, The Betting, Gaming and Lotteries Act. It repealed in whole or part seven earlier Acts. But in the period since 1963, at least twelve further Acts have appeared on the Statute Book, including another two consolidating Acts. The subject is clearly of abiding interest to the British.

The forms in which gambling is legally regulated in this country may be conveniently summarised as Betting, Gaming, Lotteries, Prize Competitions and Amusements with Prizes. (Horse and Greyhound racing are treated as complex forms of betting in this simplification.) Each of these involves some public body to carry out duties mentioned in the Acts referred to above and it may help the reader to scan the total scene initially, by tabulating those bodies and their various spheres of activity:

1.	County Councils	Registration of Pool Promoters (*eg.* football pools)	1963 Act s.4 & Sched.2
2.	Licensing Justices	Betting Office Licences *i.e.* the premises	*Ibid.* s.9 & Sched.1
3.	*Ibid.*	Betting Agency Permits *i.e.* the betting office managers	*Ibid.*
4.	*Ibid.*	Gaming Act licences *i.e.* Clubs	1968 Act, s.11 & Sched.2
5.	*Ibid.*	Bingo Club licences *i.e.* the premises.	*Ibid.* ss.2 & 20, Sched.2, para. 25
6.	*Ibid.*	Gaming machine registration *i.e.* for clubs and miners welfare institutes	*Ibid.* s.30 & Sched.7
7.	District Councils, London Boroughs & City of London	Registration of societies for small lotteries	1976 Act, s.5 & Sched.1
8.	*Ibid.*	Grant of permits for amusements with prizes	*Ibid.* s.16 & Sched.3
9.	*Ibid.*	Permits for amusement machines	1968 Act s.34 & Sched.9

6.77 PUBLIC ENTERTAINMENT

10. Gaming Board	Issue of certificates of approval to persons assisting in gaming	1968 Act, s.19 & Sched.5
11. *Ibid.*	Certificates for gaming by machines.	1968 Act, Pt. III with 1976 Act, Sched.4
12. Home Secretary	Regulations to regulate licensed club premises	1968 Act, ss.21, 22
13. *Ibid.*	Regulations about the sale & supply of machines for gaming	*Ibid.* s.28
14. *Ibid.*	Regulations about gaming machines at non-commercial entertainments	*Ibid.* s.68
15. *Ibid.*	Regulations about records and accounts for gaming machines	*Ibid.* s.35
16. *Ibid.*	Regulations to vary limits on certain fees, prizes and other monies	1980 Acts

(1963 Act – Betting Gaming and Lotteries Act; 1968 Act – Gaming Act; 1976 Act – Lotteries and Amusements Act; 1980 Acts – Gaming (Amendment) Act 1980 and Betting Gaming and Lotteries (Amendment) Act 1980).

2. General Principles

6.78 Before describing and commenting upon the law in each of the five areas identified above, it is important to note certain broad principles
  (i) Local authorities are precluded by law from maintaining or contributing to the maintenance of premises for which a Gaming Act licence is in force.[52]
  (ii) A code regulating the limited nature of advertisements for gaming is contained in section 42 of the Act of 1968. Broadly speaking, this contains a general prohibition on such advertising and then this is modified by exceptions for machines, charities, entertainments and fairs. These exceptions are in each instance carefully qualified and merit close study.
  (iii) A system of inspection is set up, with both the police and Gaming Act inspectors authorised to inspect premises to see that the provisions of the Act are being honoured. Fire authority representatives have the same right in relation to the inspection of requisite fire precautions. There are sanctions by imprisonment and fine for

---

[52] Gaming Act 1968, s.44.

GAMBLING   6.78

failure to provide information sought by the inspectors or, generally, to co-operate with them.[53]
The classes of gambling regulated by law are as follows:

3. **Betting**

(1) *Betting Offices*

Under the Act of 1963, a code of law for Betting Offices was established.[54] 6.79
The manager of the Betting Office must obtain a licence from the licensing justices' committee, after giving due notice to that committee to the police and to the local authority.[55] This is to allow references to be taken and the proposed premises to be inspected. The licence holder has either to be the holder of a bookmaker's permit himself or be accredited by a bookmaker as an agent and be the holder of a betting agency permit from the licensing justices.

The Act, with modifications made by the Betting Gaming and Lotteries (Amendment) Act 1984, contains struct rules for the conduct of Betting Offices. It prohibits the employment of or bets with persons under 18 years of age[56]; regulates radio and television broadcasts received within the Office,[57] the serving of refreshments or the provision of entertainment on the premises[58]; and indeed forbids the licence holder and his staff to "encourage" anyone on the premises to bet.[59] In a Divisional Court case upon this code, it was said by the Court that documents in these offices would have to be kept" in a somewhat austere form and lose a certain amount of glamour . . . That appears to be exactly what the legislation intended." The case showed that a licence holder would not be convicted of "encouraging" a visitor to bet, unless it was shown that he had "incited" him, in the sense that the encouragement "reached the mind" of the visitor.[60] Finally the Act prescribes the notices that may be exhibited and also requires the office to be separated from other premises.[61]

(2) *Sporting Events*

Betting at an approved horse racecourse, greyhound track or other licensed track is dealt with in section E of this Chapter, paras. 6.47 *et seq.*, above.

---

[53] *Ibid.* s.43.
[54] Betting Gaming & Lotteries Act 1963, s.10 and Sched. 4.
[55] s.9 and Sched. 1. Local authorities for this purpose are county districts, London boroughs and the Common Council of the City of London.
[56] Sched. 4, para. 2. Whilst not repealed or amended by the Act of 1984 cited in the text, the facilities for radio, TV, refreshments entertainment and also advertisements, are all to be "more civilised and less spartan," said the mover of this successful Private Bill.
[57] *Ibid.* para. 5.
[58] *Ibid.*
[59] *Ibid.* para. 4.
[60] *Wilson* v. *Danny Quastel (Rotherhithe) Ltd.* [1965] 2 All E.R. 541. Sachs J. at p.544. But see now the Act of 1984 (n.56 *supra.*).
[61] s.10 and Sched. 4 (*supra*), para. 6. See also *re* notices under this code *Windsors (Sporting Investments)* v. *Oldfield* [1981] 1 W.L.R. 1176.

6.79 PUBLIC ENTERTAINMENT

(3) *General*

Betting is prohibited in streets or other public places[62] and, as indicated above, there is strict control over the form of betting at certain places to which the public "resort." That word is deemed by the courts to connote close physical proximity but a clearer definition of that key word still awaits a suitable court case.[63]

4. Gaming

6.80 Gaming is "the playing of a game of chance for winnings in money or money's worth, whether any person playing the game is at risk of losing any money or money's worth or not."[64] The law is codified in the Gaming Act 1968 as amended, in which Parliament has tried to grapple with the current forms taken by this leisure service. Commercialised gaming is regulated primarily by the Gaming Board and is made subject to gaming licence duties. Commercial clubs are brought within a system of licensing, whilst members clubs come into a registration system. Gaming with machines now warrants a Part of the 1968 Act to itself and is subject to a new system of control.

Insofar as these matters relate largely to the private commercial sector of society, or the policy and practice of the Gaming Board, they fall outside the scope of this work. This section will deal with those aspects of the law which fall to be administered by local licensing justices namely, members clubs, bingo clubs and gaming with machines.

(1) *Members Clubs*

6.81 (i) When gaming takes place in club premises, that club must be registered with the local licensing justices.[65] The application can be made at any time and notice that it is being made must also be given to the police and the Customs and Excise authority.[66]

(ii) There are numerous grounds for refusing an application if the club has a bad record; or if gaming appears to be the main purpose of the club (with an exception to cover bridge and whist playing);or if it has less than 25 members, appears to be temporary in character or not to be a bona fide members club.[67]

(iii) This procedure with its application and the service of notice, and the criteria applied to an application are also the ones followed when a miners' welfare institute seeks registration.[68]

---

[62] Act of 1963, s.8.
[63] See *e.g. R. v. Brown* [1895] 1 Q.B. 195.
[64] Gaming Act 1968, s.52(1).
[65] Act of 1968 (*supra*), s.11 and Sched. 3.
[66] *Ibid.* s.1 and Sched. 1. Also the Gaming (Amendment) Act 1982, in relaxing the time at which these applications are made.
[67] Act of 1968 (*supra*) Sched. 3, paras. 7–9.
[68] *Ibid.* ss.1 and 11 and Sched. 3.

GAMBLING   6.81

(iv) Registration of either club or institute premises can include a condition limiting the gaming to part or parts of the premises.[69]

(v) The Crown Court is the designated forum for hearing appeals by applicants against refusals of their applications or the nature of conditions attached to registration.[70]

(vi) The code of procedure includes a further right of appeal to a court, whereby any person can, at any time, apply to the clerk to the licensing justices for the club licence to be cancelled. This gives rise to a formal hearing, the views of both police and Customs and Excise being sought by the court. The schedule incorporates eleven reasons for cancelling the registration and these cover all aspects of mismanagement in the running of the club.[71]

(vii) Registration certificates normally run for one year, with discretion to extend that period up to ten years. Renewal of the registration and payment of prescribed fees is built into the system.[72]

(2) *Bingo Clubs*

Where gaming at a club is limited to bingo, it is subject to certain special conditions: 6.82

1. The aggregate winnings paid in a week shall not exceed the aggregate stakes by more than £250.[73]

2. Persons under 18 years of age may be present, if not playing.

Linked Bingo

3. (i) Games played simultaneously in several premises are regarded as one game, provided that:

---

[69] *Ibid.* Sched. 3, para. 11. Those provisions of the Gaming Act 1968 which affect the registration of members clubs and miners welfare institutes were brought into force on May 1, 1969 by S.I. 1969 No. 549. *Lock* v. *Rank Leisure Ltd., The Times,* February 24, 1984: a club cannot lawfully carry on gaming, in respect of which money, apart from the stake hazarded, was charged, on premises not licensed under Pt. II of the Gaming Act 1968, "unless they were its own premises." A regional competition final of the Top Rank Club took place at the Wembley Conference Centre, which was not licensed or registered under Pt. II of the above Act of 1968. Prizes to the value of £25,000 were given out: there was nothing to pay at Wembley because all the payments by the entrants had been made at their "home" clubs. The Court held that s.40, as amended by the Gaming (Amendment) Act 1973, was meant only for bridge and whist clubs and not for this situation. Section 3 of the 1968 Act had been contravened and there should be a conviction.
[70] *Ibid.* para. 12.
[71] *Ibid.* para. 14.
[72] *Ibid.* para. 20.
[73] Act of 1968, s.20. For Bingo Duty, see Customs and Excise Act 1952, Betting and Gaming Duties Act 1972 and Finance Act 1980, s.8. The Gaming (Amendment) Act 1980 introduced the power for the Home Secretary to vary monetary limits. The maximum for prizes for linked games played on several premises in one week was raised to £3,000 by the Gaming Act (Variation of Monetary Limits) Order 1984 (S.I. 1984 No. 247).

6.82

    (a) Winnings in aggregate do not exceed the stakes in aggregate; and

    (b) A limit fixed by the Secretary of State is not exceeded as the total money paid in winnings for the whole week's bingo at those premises.

  (ii) If the conditions in (i) apply, then the normal member and guest conditions for registered clubs apply too, but the 48 hour entrance condition is relaxed to a period of 24 hours.[73a]

(3) *Gaming with Machines*

6.83 Part III of the Gaming Act 1968 now embodies a legal code about gaming with machines. In outline, it provides

(i) Gaming by machines, outside the terms of the Gaming Act, is unlawful and constitutes an offence. Selling, supplying and maintaining the machines are also offences.[74]

(ii) However, gaming by machines is exempted from this prohibition if certificates and permits granted by the Gaming Board are in force for the persons and premises involved and the machines are used on a pleasure pier or a travelling showman's pleasure fair, or on a pleasure fair devoted wholly or mainly to amusements or, fourthly, are for use on premises to be used wholly or mainly for amusements by means of these machines.[75]

(iii) Again there is exemption, where the premises are registered under Part II or Part III of the Gaming Act. This will usually be a members club or miners' welfare institute. Stringent conditions apply to the use of the machines.[76]

(iv) Two more exemptions are available: first, where machines are incidental to non-commercial entertainment and secondly, where these machines are used primarily for amusement and the value of the prizes is limited.[77]

(v) The number of machines is normally limited to two but this can be increased in certain circumstances.[78]

(vi) Only authorised persons may remove money from the machines.[79]

(vii) Records, accounts and verification can be required of the gaming machine user both by the Gaming Board and by the police for the area.[80]

(viii) Offences carry fines of £400 maximum or two years imprisonment or both.[81]

[73a] See now too the Gaming (Bingo) Act 1985 and regulations made thereunder, on multiple bingo.
[74] Act of 1968, s.38.   [75] Act of 1968, s.27.
[76] *Ibid.* s.31. These for instance, limit the machines to two, limit the prize, also the charge for playing, the minimum percentage of the total charges which must be paid out as prizes, and the need for displaying on the machines a statement of the above amounts. The machines are not to be in use when the public has access to the premises.
[77] *Ibid.* s.33 and Sched. 4 of the Act of 1976.
[78] *Ibid.* s.32 and *R. v. Herrod, ex p. Leeds City Council* [1974] 3 All E.R. 362.
[79] *Ibid.* s.36.
[80] *Ibid.* s.37.
[81] *Ibid.* s.39.

5. Lotteries

The classic definition of a lottery is the distribution of prizes by chance. **6.84** For the main provisions on this subject, one turns to the Lotteries and Amusements Act 1976, where it is laid down that all lotteries which do not constitute gaming are unlawful "subject to the provisions of this Act."[82] Exemptions from this prohibition are then defined and in practice four of these are important.

(1) *Small Lotteries* incidental to entertainments. This expression is defined to cover bazaars and dances, as well as sporting, athletic and other events. Special rules apply to the expenses, the prizes, the limits on sale of the tickets and the meaning given to the word "incidental" in the above phrase.[83]

(2) *Private Lotteries* are those limited to members of a society or people who work together or reside together. Again, there are severe conditions to be met in order to ensure that such a lottery is lawful.[84]

(3) *Societies' Lotteries* are the third class. These are small lotteries promoted on behalf of a society established for purposes which are not commercial nor for private gain. Those purposes must be charitable and to do with athletic sports or games or cultural activities, or more than one of those purposes. The society has to be registered with the local authority and its scheme registered also with the Gaming Board,[85] if the total value of the tickets is to exceed the prescribed limit.

(4) *Local Lotteries* are those promoted by local authorities and they must comply with these points:

   (i) A scheme regulating the lottery must be approved by the local authority.

   (ii) The scheme must be registered with the Gaming Board.

---

[82] Act of 1976, s.1, and see also the Lotteries Regulations 1977 (S.I. 1977 No. 256) for the terms which must go into the schemes prepared by societies or local authorities for the promotion of a lottery. The Lotteries (Amendment) Regulations 1981 (S.I. 1981 No. 109) vary the 1977 Regulations. The various offences in s.2 of the Act of 1976, in relation to unlawful lotteries, have been slightly reduced by the Lotteries (Amendment) Act 1984, which abolished some offences relating to foreign lotteries.

[83] Act of 1976, s.3. The lottery is not to be the only, or the only substantial, inducement, to attend (s.3(*d*)).

[84] *Ibid.* s.4. These forbid sending lottery tickets through the post, limit deductible expenses to printing and stationery and require the balance to be used as prizes or for the purpose of the society. Further, there must be no advert, save on the appropriate premises of the society and on the tickets; the price of all tickets must be the same and stated on the ticket; the ticket must contain the name and address of the promoters, the persons who may take part in the lottery, that the prize can only be given to the holder of the winning ticket, that no ticket must be sold except for the full price and that in no circumstances must any ticket money be returned. Lastly, each branch of a society is, for the purposes of a lottery, "a separate and distinct society," and so a single lottery promoted for members of the main society is unlawful. (*Keehan* v. *Walters* [1948] 1 K.B. 19).

[85] *Ibid.* ss.5 and 11. Total ticket value limit is now £5,000. These conditions include making a return to the local authority of a lottery, with details of proceeds, expenses, prizes and money devoted to the purposes for which the lottery was run.

6.84 PUBLIC ENTERTAINMENT

(iii) The normal powers of delegation available for local authorities under the Local Government Act 1972, s.101, do not apply to approval of these schemes.

(iv) The object for which the Local Lottery is promoted must be one within the powers of the local authority. The object can include section 137 of the Local Government Act 1972, *i.e.* benefit of the inhabitants of the area. Devotion of the proceeds of the lottery to a purpose other than the declared object of the lottery can be made only with the consent of the Secretary of State.

(v) A lottery fund must be set up to take the net proceeds of Local Lotteries and the interest on invested monies in this fund.

(vi) There are not to be more than 52 lotteries in 12 months.

There are prescribed offences for breaches of these conditions. The local authorities who are to oversee these lotteries, and who are charged with the difficult task of deciding when some of the conditions have been breached, are district councils, London boroughs and the Common Council of the City of London[86]

6. Prize Competitions

6.85 It should be noted that prize competitions also are unlawful. The definition in the Act of 1963 incorporates these points

(i) The offence involves conducting the competition in a newspaper or in conjunction with a trade or business or the sale of an article to the public.

(ii) The prizes are for forecasts of a future event or even a past event the result of which is not yet ascertained or generally known.

(iii) It is a condition of a competition being unlawful that success does not depend on skill "to a substantial degree."[87]

(iv) A proviso exempts sponsored pool betting and also a bookkeepers' pool betting operations.

(iv) If it transpired that the competition were a lottery, then there would be a second offence and a risk of prosecution for that also.[88]

---

[86] *Ibid.* s.6 and Pt. II of the Act of 1976.
[87] *Ibid.* s.14 and see *Ladbrokes (Football)* v. *Perret* [1971] 1 W.L.R. 110, for a spot the ball competition in a newspaper held to be unlawful.
[88] Act of 1976, s.14. In *Coles* v. *Odhams Press Ltd.* [1936] 1 K.B. 416, a crossword competition in a newspaper was held to be a lottery. This was because there were alternative appropriate answers to the clues and the solution was determined beforehand. Lord Hewart said it was the opportunity "of blind shots at a hidden target." For a case illustrating the borderline between a lottery and a prize competition, see also *Imperial Tobacco* v. *Att.Gen.* [1979] 2 W.L.R. 805. A "spot cash" scheme of cards in packets of cigarettes was held to be neither an unlawful lottery nor an unlawful prize competitin, in the Court of Appeal. The reasons were the absence of any charge for the cards as such and the lack of any "purposeful striving" by the entrants. The House of Lords, however, in a comprehensive review of cases throughout this country, held the scheme to be an unlawful lottery, though not an unlawful competition [1981] A.C. 718. This scheme contravened s.14 of the lotteries and Amusements Act 1976.

7. Amusements with Prizes and Gaming Machines

6.86 (i) Amusements with prizes has become a technical term in Acts relating to betting, gaming and lotteries. It connotes a lottery, or gaming, or both, but not gaming as, *e.g.* roulette, to which Part II of the Gaming Act 1968 applies.

(ii) Amusements with prizes are lawful at bazaars, sales of work, fetes, dinners, dances, sporting or athletic events and other entertainments of a similar nature, whether limited to one day or extending over two or more days.[89]

(iii) There are two conditions to be complied with in order to secure this exemption from normal legal strictures against lotteries.
   (a) The whole of the proceeds are devoted to purposes other than private gain. It is permitted to deduct expenses, including the cost of prizes, in ascertaining "proceeds."
   (b) The opportunity to win prizes at the event is not the only or only substantial, inducement to people to attend the event.[90]

(iv) The promoter of the event must obtain a permit from the local authority.[91]

(v) Pleasure fairs are granted statutory exemption from this procedure, on not more than 27 days in one year, on one site.[92]

(vi) The Lotteries and Amusements Act 1976, contains monetary restraints on the price of a chance, the total money proceeds, the amount for prizes and a prohibition on one prize becoming the grant of an opportunity to take part in a further amusement with prizes or gaming or a lottery.[93]

(vii) Enlarged powers for local authorities in these matters under the Gaming Act 1968 cover refusals, imposition of conditions and dealing with appeals against refusals.[94]

In relation to amusements with gaming machines, the same two conditions relating to the bazaars and other events described in (ii) above apply as set out in (iii) above. "The whole of the proceeds are devoted to purposes other than private gain" is a key condition in this field.[95] As such, it has been before the courts more than once. The House of Lords had to consider it in the case of *Avais* v. *Hartford Shankhouse & District Workingmens' Social Club and Institute*.[96] The court concentrated attention on the time when, and the extent and manner in which, "takings" were reduced to "proceeds," and when and to what purpose the "proceeds" were applied. The case should be studied by any affected by this point.

---

[89] Act of 1976, ss.3 and 15.
[90] *Ibid.* s.15.
[91] *Ibid.* ss.16, 17, 18 and 24.
[92] *Ibid.* s.16(1)(*c*).
[93] *Ibid.* ss.18(1) and 24(2). For current amounts see Amusements with Prizes (Variation of Monetary Limits) Order 1984 (S.I. 1984 No. 245).
[94] *Ibid.* s.16 and Sched. 3.
[95] Act of 1968, s.33(2).
[96] [1969] 1 All E.R. 130.

6.87 PUBLIC ENTERTAINMENT

8. Competition for Prizes

6.87 This is yet one more refinement in this branch of the law. The expression is defined in the Pool Competitions Act 1971. It involves an allocation of prizes dependant upon the result of sporting events; each competitor having the right to forecast the outcome of those events; and prizes being allocated whether those rights are exercised or not. A scheme of this nature was held to be an unlawful lottery in *Singette* v. *Martin*,[97] and not, as the promoters contended, lawful pool betting. The above Act of 1971 was meant as temporary relief for clubs dependant upon income from schemes of this kind.

The Act lays down a procedure for certificates and licences from the Gaming Board to regulate this area of gambling. Fees, excise duties and the sanction of certain offences are included in the provisions of this important Act.[98]

H. Sex Establishments

6.88 The powers of legal control over the two forms of sex establishments, sex shops and sex cinemas, are adoptive for local authorities and are contained in the Local Government (Miscellaneous Provisions) Act 1982. Due public notice by the local authority in question, of a resolution to adopt these powers, is needed as part of the procedure to bring into operation in its area Part III of this Act.[99] The local authorities for this purpose are district councils, London boroughs and the Common Council of the City of London.

1. Statutory Code

6.89 The legal framework provided by the Act is the same for both sex shops and sex cinemas and is as follows

(i) A licence is needed when premises are to be used as a sex establishment. The licence will remain in force for one year, or less if so prescribed.[1]

(ii) The licensing authority can grant, transfer and renew licences. The procedure includes due public notice of the making of the application, an opportunity for objection by the police and others, and an opportunity to

---

[97] The full title is *Singette Ltd.* v. *Martin* [1970] All E.R. 570 and 3 All E.R. 938.
[98] Initially in force for 5 years, this Act has now been renewed annually by statutory instrument, and is still in force.
[99] Expressions in this new Act are being tested in the courts. An early case in the Court of Appeal was *R.* v. *Chester B.C. ex p. Quietly*, *The Times*, March 22, 1984. The local authority lost on one point of procedure, having wrongly, said the court, taken the hearing of objections before a sub-committee, rather than the full committee which was to take the effective decision on behalf of the Council. The case should be studied for observations on notices under the Act and the need for an actual hearing of objections.
[1] Sched. 3, paras. 6, and 9.

appear before the appropriate committee of the council at the hearing of the application.[2]

(iii) A decision by the licensing authority to refuse one of the above three forms of application must be embodied in a statement giving reasons for the decision and supplied on request to the applicant.[3]

(iv) Licences are not to be granted to
   (a) Persons under 18 years of age.
   (b) Persons legally disqualified. (A person is disqualified for 12 months for this purpose if his licence has been revoked.
   (c) A body corporate not incorporated in the United Kingdom.
   (d) A person who, as an applicant, has had his application for grant or renewal refused within 12 months of the new application.

(v) Grounds for declining to grant these applications laid down in the Act are as follows[4]
   (a) The applicant is unsuitable.
   (b) The person who derives the benefit of the business is not the applicant but a person whose application would be declined if he applied in person.
   (c) The number of sex establishments in the locality is sufficient.[5]
   (d) The character of the locality or the use of premises in the vicinity of the proposed premises or the layout, character or condition of the premises[6] for which the application is made.

(vi) The local authority may make standard conditions, embodied in Regulations, in relation to sex establishments, distinguishing not only sex shops from sex cinemas, but also different types of both businesses. The subject matter of such Regulations is set out in the Act.[7]

(vii) A licence holder may apply at any time for a variation in the conditions attached to his licence.

(viii) Offences are created for using sex establishments whilst unlicensed or disqualified or in contravention of the terms in a licence. There is another offence for making a false statement in connection with an application under this Act to the licensing authority. An additional offence arises where a person under 18 years is employed in one of these

---

[2] *Ibid.* paras. 8 and 10.
[3] *Ibid.* para. 10.
[4] *Ibid.* para. 12.
[5] In a debate on the Bill in Parliament, a Government spokesman said that a local authority could decide that the appropriate number of sex establishments for Art. 12(3)(c) might be nil! *Hansard,* July 2, 1982, col. 1141 .
[6] Sched. 3, para. 12(3).
[7] *Ibid.* para. 13. Inclusion in conditions for a sex shop licence of a condition that the holder will comply with relevant legislation, would seem sufficient, unless new guidance is given by the courts, to take initial account of the Video Recordings Act 1984, s.12. This deals with video recordings bearing a classification certificate under the Act, to the effect that no video recording, containing that work, is to be supplied other than in a licensed sex shop. The section sets out both offences and defences arising from that provision. A licencee of a sex shop who intends to supply video recordings will thus be obliged to ensure that classification certificates have been given for the video recordings he may intend to supply through that shop.

establishments or is permitted to enter one of them. A paragraph in the Schedule adapts the wording to the case of corporate bodies so that they also can be prosecuted. These offences are punishable with fines not exceeding £10,000.[8]

(ix) Powers of entry to the sex establishments to enforce the law are conferred upon police constables and also authorised officers of local authorites. A warrant from a justice of the pease is required before such powers can be exercised.[9]

(x) An appeal procedure to the magistrates courts and, subsequently, to the Crown Courts is afforded to applicants who are refused new licences, transfers, variations or are otherwise aggrieved by local authority decisions in these matters.[10]

(xi) The terms sex shop and sex cinema are fully defined in the Act. The shop has to be used for purveying sex articles and the cinema definition is based on an exhibition of moving pictures. A dwellinghouse to which the public is not admitted is specifically excluded from the sex cinema definition. Films, sound recordings and reading matter devoted to the stimulation of sexual activity are fully defined and brought within the scope of this Act.[11]

2. Relation to Existing Law

6.90 Finally, it is important to note the relation of this new law to existing legislation. In the first place, there is in the 1982 Act no reference by way of repeal, amendment or otherwise, to the Indecent Display (Control) Act 1981. That Act had dealt with indecent displays which were visible from a public place and had repealed an earlier law on that subject, the Indecent Advertisements (Amendment) Act 1970. Some overlap between that Act of 1981 and the code for Sex Establishments in Schedule III of the Act of 1982 is now evident. In debate, the Government spokesman indeed made it clear that the same premises were subject not only to these Acts of 1981 and 1982 but also to the Obscene Publications Act 1959.

Furthermore, it is laid down, in the Local Government (Miscellaneous Provisions) Act 1982, that the powers under three recited provisions are not to be superseded. These three Acts, relating to indecency or obscenity are:

1. The Obscene Publications Act 1959, s.3.
2. The Protection of Children Act 1978, s.5.
3. The Customs and Excise Management Act 1979, Sched. 3.

There is. strangely, no reference to the Cinematograph (Amendment) Act 1982,[12] which, by removing a thirty year old exemption, allows licensing of sex cinemas. An overlap by the two Acts is avoided, in logic at least, by

---

[8] *Ibid.* paras. 20, 21, 22, 23 and 26.
[9] *Ibid.* para. 25.
[10] *Ibid.* para. 27.
[11] *Ibid.* para. 4.
[12] Local Government (Miscellaneous Provisions) Act 1982, Sched. 3, para. 3(2).

a provision that premises licensed or exempt from licensing under the Cinematograph Acts are not to be registered as sex cinemas within the Local Government Act. This does not however resolve all issues created by having two statutes dealing with the licensing of the same premises as cinemas.[13]

---

[13] See *e.g.* analysis of the differences in the two codes by Mr. C. Manchester in *Justice of the Peace*, February 12, 1983.

Chapter 7

SPORT

"A horse is not a reliable mechanical contrivance"
Danckwerts L.J. in *Wooldridge* v. *Sumner* [1963] 2 Q.B. 59

A. Managing Swimming Pools
Introduction

7.01   The original legal code for the provision of swimming pools by local authorities is Part VIII of the Public Health Act 1936. This is now supplemented by the Education Act 1944 in relation to swimming pools for schools and further education.[1] It is also placed in the wider context of public leisure and recreation by the Local Government (Miscellaneous Provisions) Act 1976, where the formal power of provision is now contained.[2]

The legal framework for the provision of public swimming pools is completed by consideration of the by-laws, the legal areas of management risks and comments on two aspects of financial management of swimming pools.

1. Provision

7.02   The power to provide swimming pools is now contained in the Local Government (Miscellaneous Provisions) Act 1976.[3] This replaces the formal power in the Public Health Act 1936 but is still supplemented by the additional sections in Part VIII of the Act of 1936. The items of interest in Part VIII are:

(i) When a swimming bath is under the management of a local authority, it is deemed to be a public and open place for the purposes of the laws against indecency.[4]

---

[1] s.53.
[2] s.19. This means that a local authority may provide swimming pools in their capacity as a public health authority or in their capacity as a leisure services authority.
[3] By s.221 of the Public Health Act 1936, district and parish councils are such authorities. By the Local Government Act 1972, the function is also placed with county councils, London Borough Councils, the Common Council of the City of London, the Inner London Education Authority and the Temples: s.180, and Sched. 14, para. 1.
[4] Act of 1975, s.224. Thus indecent exposure could be a public nuisance in such premises. Serious unsociable behaviour is however best dealt with in the by-laws.

(ii) Public swimming baths may be closed temporarily to facilitate the organisation of aquatic sports, contests or similar entertainments either by the local authority or by schools, clubs or other persons.[5]

(iii) Swimming baths may be closed between the beginning of October and the end of April in the following year and used for other purposes.[6]

(iv) The trustees of a public swimming bath are empowered to sell it to the local authority.[7]

(v) Statutory undertakers are empowered to supply gas, electricity or water on favourable terms.[8]

7.03 Under the Education Act 1944, swimming baths may be provided by local education authorities.[9] The Act provides this power, as one of a number of ways of fulfilling a duty to secure adequate facilities for recreation, and social and physical training; these again form part of the primary, secondary and further education for the area of the authority. The Education Act 1944 requires local education authorities, when providing such facilities, to "have regard to the expediency of co-operating with any voluntary societies or bodies," who might be engaged in similar schemes.[10]

7.04 The Local Government (Miscellaneous Provisions) Act 1976 empowers local authorities to provide a wide variety of recreational facilities. These include swimming pools.[11] The pools may be inside or outside the area of the authority; the power extends to "buildings, equipment, supplies and assistance of any kind"[12]; and the initiating local authority may achieve the provision by contributing to the expenses of another local authority who provide the particular facility or by a grant or a loan to a voluntary organisation which is to provide it.

2. By-Laws

7.05 Power to make by-laws for their swimming baths is conferred on local authorities by the Public Health Act 1936.[13] The general power is described as being for the management of baths, and the regulation of persons using them and this can cover the exclusion of undesirable persons.[14] The by-laws may include penalties for breach and also power for swim-

---

[5] *Ibid.* s.225.
[6] *Ibid.* s.226. This is to facilitate the practice in some places of covering the pool and using the building as a public hall. Licences for those other activities must of course, be obtained.
[7] *Ibid.* s.228.
[8] *Ibid.* s.229.
[9] Education Act 1944, s.53(1).
[10] *Ibid.* s.53(2). In practice, education authorities fulfil this obligation by a combination of their own school swimming pools and hired used of the public pools, rather than those of voluntary societies contemplated some years ago.
[11] Local Government (Miscellaneous Provisions) Act 1976, s.19(1)(*a*).
[12] *Ibid.* s.19(2).
[13] Public Health Act 1936, s.223.
[14] *Ibid.* s.223(1).

7.05

ming pool staff to exclude persons who contravene the by-laws. A copy of the by-laws must be exhibited at the relevant premises.[15]

In practice, by-laws assist in regulating day-to-day matters in the running of a swimming pool and only if controversial do they attract publicity. One would expect the by-laws to deal with serious unsociable conduct in the pool or its surrounds, obedience to the directions of the attendants and due hygiene by swimmers.

3. Areas of Management Risk

7.06 The managers of a swimming pool owe to their employees, by the employment law outlined in Chapter 1, the various obligations there set out and to the visitors to the pool, whether patrons, caterers, workmen or the public generally, the common duty of care also discussed in Chapter 1.

The complex range of activities at a swimming pool encourages an analysis of other areas of legal risk. Some have been highlighted by past cases in the courts; to draw attention to others may help to minimise similar cases in the future.

(1) *The Water*

7.07 The temperature is regulated to accommodate persons with normal susceptibilities; to other persons, the management incur legal liability for mishap only when they are negligent. This arises where the duty of reasonable care to swimmers is breached by some action or inaction which reasonable foresight should have avoided. From time to time, an inexperienced swimmer no doubt ventures into a pool and alert management will try to prevent a mishap. The eggshell skull principle obliges a defendant in an action for breach of duty in tort to compensate his successful plaintiff for whatever injury is suffered, though greater than expected. "Take the plaintiff as you find him," is the summary. But in the absence of negligence, management do not enter into this area of risk.[16] Apart from the temperature of the water, the chemicals added in order to purify the water are a matter in the control of management and again afford scope for negligence and consequent legal risk.

(2) *Tickets*

All patrons of the swimming pool may expect to receive a ticket as receipt for payment on admission to the premises. The impact of the Unfair Contract Terms Act 1977 on such a situation was considered in Chapter 1. Briefly, liability as a result of negligence cannot be excluded by such a

---

[15] *Ibid.* s.223(2). For the general law about by-laws see Chap. 4. The by-laws may deal with the use of the hall during any closed period of the pool.

[16] See, *e.g. Smith* v. *Leech Brain & Co. Ltd.* [1962] 2 Q.B. 405 and *Dulieu* v. *White and Sons Ltd.* [1901] 2 K.B. 669, where the unusually weak heart was added to the eggshell skull class and is perhaps a little more relevant to swimming pool accidents.

ticket, if it is in respect of death or personal injury.[17] In other cases, perhaps damage to swimmers personal rings or other property, the test of reasonableness by both parties, the plaintiff and the defendant, is imported by the above Act of 1977.[18]

(3) *The Surround*

In law, the surround to the swimming pool is simply part of the premises which patrons are invited to use. The common duty of care and its qualifications, as discussed in Chapter 1, are relevant. Thus the notices or by-laws about running or horseplay are also relevant; so is any contributory negligence by the swimmer. Any hazard due to negligent cleaning, before the pool was opened to the public, would of course give rise to legal risk if an accident ensued.

7.08

(4) *The Pool*

The two areas of legal risk to which the swimming pool itself gives rise are any unusual features in its construction below water level and also dangerous objects on the bottom. When the level of the bottom of the pool varies, as with the diving area, the management discharge their legal duty of care by informing swimmers of this feature in the notices about the varying depths of water. This is normal and reasonable.

7.09

No swimmer expects to find broken glass or other hazards on the bottom of the pool; still less, sharp projections round its edge. Management are expected to be reasonable and to have some system of inspection which tries efficiently to guard against hazards like broken glass.[19] Other hazards like a jagged tile at the side of the pool ought to be seen on inspection but if present when swimming takes place, can hardly fail to give rise to legal liability for any ensuing injury.

(5) *The Diving Boards*

These are mentioned separately from the pool since, by their nature, they involve greater risk for those using them and hence call for greater care than ordinary swimming. The defence *volenti non fit injuria*—there is no legal liability to the person who has willingly accepted the risks—was discussed in Chapter 1 as one of the available defences in tort. The diver is a "volunteer" within that maxim: he decides to climb and dive. He accepts a risk but he does not expect to find a trap, nor any hazard which is not

7.10

---

[17] Unfair Contract Terms Act 1977, s.2.
[18] *Ibid.* s.2(2).
[19] For the paddling pool equivalent, see *Ellis* v. *Fulham Corporation* [1938] 1 K.B. 212. No reported cases on swimming pools have been found; the relevance of a system of inspection to the hazards in each local situation has been considered by the courts in relation to slipping on spilt yoghurt in a supermarket and tripping over an uneven paving stone in a busy highway (*Griffiths* v. *Liverpool Corporation* [1967] 1 Q.B. 374 and *Whiting* v. *Hillingdon L.B.C.* (1970) 68 L.G.R. 437).

obvious on inspection.[20] Any unusual feature of any sort must, therefore, be the subject of warning notices.

(6) *Children*

It should also be borne in mind that children call for greater warning. "An occupier must be prepared for children to be less careful than adults," says the Occupiers' Liability Act 1957,[21] in language that the brothers Fowler could approve. This is the legal background for the frequent practice of restricting the use of the high diving boards to persons over a certain age.

(7) *The Supervisors*

7.11 Staff trained in life saving, with effective equipment available, will be on duty when the public use a swimming pool. They are the ears and eyes of management and their negligence becomes the negligence of management. The staff who supervise swimming, control the number of swimmers allowed in the pool at one time; they are also expected to be alert for any signs of group danger or individual danger. The test of reasonable foresight is relevant to a situation, where the alleged negligence of a supervisor has given rise to a situation leading to a legal claim for damages.

(8) *The Spectators*

7.12 Statute has not yet provided specific guidance for swimming pool managers on their duties to spectators. The Safety of Sports Grounds Act 1975 has been passed by Parliament to impose a safety inspection system on many sports grounds with large numbers of the public congregating on or near stands. Swimming pools are not normally of a size to attract such numbers and the legal duties of management fall to be framed from the common law and due compliance with such requirements as result from inspection under the Fire Service Acts. Thus the managers again have an ordinary occupier's duty of common care, under the Occupiers' Liability Act 1957, to spectators or other visitors. That duty is to "take such care as in all the circumstances of the case is reasonable to see that the visitor will be reasonably safe in using the premises for the purposes for which he is invited or permitted by the occupier to be there."[22]

A quotation from Diplock L.J. in *Wooldridge* v. *Summer*, the horse trials case, is helpful:

"A person attending a game or competition takes the risk of any

---

[20] Occupiers' Liability Act 1957, s.2(3)(*a*). The same Act places in statutory form the maxim *volenti non fit injuria* as a defence for occupiers to their visitors, who accept risks of which they are aware. The section below on participatory sports discusses this aspect in some detail.
[21] Occupiers' Liability Act 1957, s.2(2).
[22] *Ibid.*

damage caused to him by any act of a participant done in the course of and for the purpose of the game or competition, notwithstanding that such act may involve an error of judgment or a lapse of skill, unless the participant's conduct is such as to evince a reckless disregard of the spectator's safety."[23]

The common duty of care is always present for the safety of the premises, the staircases, the seats, the ceiling, the floor and the lighting. At a swimming competition, the risk of injury from participants may be slight and thus no reported law case has been traced. The risk remains with the distance of the spectator seating from the participants being the initial critical element.

The legal consequences of personal injury suffered by a spectator are not invalidated by any disclaimer on the ticket of admission.

(9) *Saunas*

Sauna baths are often found at modern swimming pools and carry an added legal liability for management; the risks are different due to the specialist equipment upon which they depend. Management may reasonably expect their equipment suppliers and service arrangements to protect them from the more obvious hazards to users of the sauna. Even so, managers cannot avoid certain duties resulting from the common duty of care; they are expected also to have competent staff and a reasonable system of inspection of the equipment. **7.13**

Users should be clearly warned of any dangers they might incur by staying for an excessive time in the different parts of the sauna.

(10) *Sales*

Sales of food and drink as part of a cafeteria at a swimming pool, or from vending machines, are subject to the general laws about the sale of goods (see Chapter 1) and the standards to be found in the Food Act 1984. **7.14**

(11) *Loans of Swimming Equipment*

The supply to users of a swimming pool of costumes, towels or other equipment for use on the premises and return, is a separate activity in respect of which legal risks may attach to management. The loan transaction is essentially a separate contract, governed by the law of contract. **7.15**

This basic contractual relationship of swimmer and manager does not oust the duty in tort. That is the duty of care for the legal neighbour, as defined in *Donoghue* v. *Stevenson*.[24] Clothing sold featured in an early case applying the principle in Donoghue, *i.e. Grant* v. *Australian Knitting Mills*.[25]

---

[23] [1962] 2 All E.R. 978 at p. 989. It was a horseriding competition where the cameraman was injured by a horse.
[24] [1932] A.C. 562.
[25] [1936] A.C. 85.

The duty is akin to that attaching to clothes hire firms, namely to see that the clothes are safe and suitable for their purpose.

(12) *Lockers*

7.16 When a swimmer's own clothing is placed in the management's locker or other receptacle, the clothing passes for a time into the care of that management. The notice to place valuables in a place of separate protection is normal and reasonable; it does not ensure that all swimmers will do so; nor does it avoid a normal bailee's legal duty to look after the goods in his custody. (See Chapter 3.)

Management will be liable to the swimmer if they are careless in their duty; they lessen this risk if they have good staff and an efficient system. Even so, from time to time something will go wrong and they must expect to recompense the patron, who suffers through no fault of his own.

(13) *Car Parks*

7.17 The management of a swimming pool will nowadays normally also be in charge of an associated car park. (If it is a public car park, it falls to be managed by the highway authority or district council under the Road Traffic Acts and that is outside the scope of this work.)

The legal problems resulting from that responsibility usually centre upon the sanctions available to remove the cars belonging either to persons who do not use the pool or the cars of those who overstay or otherwise misuse the parking facility.

In these respects, the management are in no different position from the management of any other private car park. This means that normal commercial prudence is the main resource. It can take the form, *e.g.* of a charging system which is heavily weighted in favour of the swimming pool user; again, it could be an attendant controlled system.

(14) *Private Swimming Instructors*

7.18 Occasionally, management permit private swimming instructors to use the pool for private lessons. Such an arrangement calls for a simple but comprehensive contract which will cover (1) payment, (2) duration, (3) acceptance of liability for all accidents by the instructor, (4) submission of proof of adequate insurance to cover that risk by the instructor, (5) advertising, permitted on terms set out or prohibited.

4. Finance

7.19 The financial aspect of management of a swimming pool calls for comment in two respects only. These are the subjects of admission charges and the extent of sales.

(1) *Admission Charges*

The Local Government (Miscellaneous Provisions) Act 1976, s.19, empowers local authorities to provide swimming pool facilities "for use by such persons as the Authority thinks fit, either without charge or on payment" of such sums as the authority thinks fit.[26]

Insofar as this confers discretion, that discretion is to be exercised on the principles laid down in *Associated Picture Houses Ltd.* v. *Wednesbury Corporation.*[27] In other words, the discretion is to be used reasonably and not to take into account extraneous factors.

When management is prompted to admit groups of patrons without charge or at a nominal charge, the case of *Prescott* v. *Birmingham Corporation*[28] has some relevance. The municipality in that city wished to grant free travel on its transport undertaking to some 70,000 old age pensioners. The Court of Appeal upheld Vaisey J. at first instance and held such a scheme to be *ultra vires*. The principle applied, as stated by Jenkins L.J. is as follows:

> "They (*i.e.* the local authority) are not entitled, merely on the strength of a general power to charge different fares to different passengers or classes of passengers, to make a gift to a particular class of persons of rights of free travel on their vehicles, simply because the local authority concerned are of opinion that the favoured class of persons ought, on benevolent or philanthropic grounds, to be accorded that benefit."[29]

The court cited in support the leading case of *Roberts* v. *Hopwood*.[30] The specific power to admit without charge is of course a feature in the above Act of 1976, which distinguishes it from *Prescott's* case; the duty to discharge a discretion responsibily is one that never departs, when a public body like a local authority is concerned.

(2) *Sales*

The Act of 1976 now empowers specifically the sales of food and drink as part of the facilities at swimming pools. For other sales, a local authority

---

[26] s.222. The Public Health Act 1936 ia also relevant.
[27] [1948] 1 K.B. 223.
[28] [1955] Ch. 210.
[29] p. 235.
[30] [1925] A.C. 578. The House of Lords disallowed special payments to a class of municipal employees, to mitigate their economic difficulties at the time. The text deals only with the general ongoing legal situation. The grant of free or special facilities for the unemployed is currently common in our society and may well be a practice that would not be challenged. What ultimate limit the courts may place upon the statutory discretion in s.19 of the Act of 1976 is yet to be seen. The line of cases stemming from *Liversedge* v. *Anderson* [1942] A.C. 206 under the Defence Regulations, on the test to be applied to the words "as he thinks fit," is a cautionary reminder that absolute, unfettered discretion, akin to that of even a benevolent despot, is rarely to be found in our law when Parliament is granting powers to local authorities, who are always trustees for their ratepayers.

7.20 SPORT

relies on the powers in the Local Government Act 1972, s.111, to do that which is incidental to their authorised duties. In those circumstances, whilst the sale of items related to the use of the swimming pool is clearly within their powers, it is possible that any wider range of sales would be outside those powers and thus unlawful.[31]

B. Managing Sports Centres

7.21 Sports centres are now to be found in nearly every town. Statutory recognition of their place in the public leisure services scene was given in the Local Government (Miscellaneous Provisions) Act 1976. They form today the active sportsman's equivalent of the "compendium of games," which housed draughts, ludo, halma and the like in close proximity. The sports centre can now often provide space for archery, indoor cricket, badminton, swimming and a host of other sports under one roof.

Nevertheless, the legal problems associated with sports centres are not essentially different from those discussed in some detail in relation to swimming pools. Here, two legal aspects are noted; then the Gateshead thumb-nail sketch is a vivid summary of this key leisure activity.

1. Provision

7.22 The statutory provision is the same as that for swimming pools, *i.e.* the Local Government (Miscellaneous Provisions) Act 1976.[32] The section also details the powers to provide staff, and supporting facilities in the following terms:

> "(*e*)staff, including instructors, in connection with any such facilities or premises as are mentioned in the preceding paragraphs and in connection with any other recreational facilities provided by the authority;
> (*f*)such facilities in connection with any other recreational facilities as the authority considers it appropriate to provide including, without prejudice to the generality of the preceding provisions of this paragraph, facilities by way of parking spaces and places at which food, drink and tobacco may be bought from the authority or another person;

and it is hereby declared that the powers conferred by this subsection to provide facilities include powers to provide buildings, equipment, supplies and assistance of any kind."[33]

As the same statute enables a local authority to provide the premises for the use of clubs having athletic, social or recreational objects, it would be

---

[31] The full text, in the Act of 1972, is the power to do anything "which is calculated to facilitate or is conducive or incidental to, the discharge of a local authority's functions."
[32] s.19(1). This lists some of the main sports as follows: "pitches for team games, athletic grounds, swimming pools, tennis courts, cycle tracks, golf courses, bowling greens, riding schools, camp sites and facilities for gliding."
[33] s.19(1)(*e*) and (*f*).

possible to combine such premises with a sports centre building, if it were locally expedient to have that sort of collaboration.

Since there is no specific power to make by-laws for sports centres, managers can have by-laws made for their pools, as described in the last sub-section, and domestic regulations for the remainder of the centre. The power of charging for admission implies a power of control over admission.

2. Running the Sports Centre

7.23 The legal responsibilities for unsafe premises and equipment have been considered in Chapter 1, in relation to the Occupiers' Liabilities Acts 1957 and 1984 and also in relation to swimming pools (above at paragraphs 7.08–7.10). Those principles apply also to sports centres and their patrons.

The principles of contract, too, apply to sports centres. The existence of a contract does not eliminate liability also in tort for, *e.g.* negligence by managers and their staff.

Bars and cafeteria are subject to the same considerations mentioned in relation to swimming pools. Licensing law is to be found in Chapter 4.

Hire of equipment is extensive in sports centres; the legal principles were considered in the last sub-section.

Hire of rooms to clubs is likely to feature in management of a sports centre. The legal elements in the agreement have been touched on in Chapter 1 in relation to property as well as contract.

For a series booking by a club or an individual room booking, a well-drawn hire agreement will cover:

(i) Hiring fee and times for payment;

(ii) Dates, times and duration of the occupancy. (Perhaps closed on certain public holidays);

(iii) Permitted use;

(iv) No nuisance or damage;

(v) Hirer responsible for order in the hired premises;

(vi) Cancellation of booking, financial consequences, retention of deposit or otherwise;

(vii) In a series booking for, *e.g.* martial arts, insurance by the club against claims by its members would be prudent and the sports centre management would be entitled to know, by the production of premium receipts or otherwise, that such an arrangement was in operation and was effective.

It is common to have a special provision at sports centres for use by the unemployed. Useful guidance on this aspect is to be found in the Sports Council's publication "Sport for the Unemployed."[34]

---

[34] A research working paper by S. Glyptis and A.C. Riddington, available from the Sports Council at 16, Upper Woburn Place, London WC1H OQP.

3. **Cameo of a Sports Centre**

7.24 Gateshead International Stadium enjoys well merited support from the public. It embodies many of the features and thus encounters the legal problems touched on above in relation to sports centres. It also exemplifies the pattern of recent years for certain centres to stage national and international sporting events and thus become hosts to very large numbers of spectators. The older fame of Crystal Palace has by this development been shared by Billingham, Hastings, Reading, Sheffield, Preston and Gateshead and doubtless other provincial centres which have, one by one, won acclaim as hosts of specialist sports and leisure pursuits.

Gateshead's provision covers ladies' recreation, coaching at all levels, childrens' play activities, local community events, weight training, as well as the sports of tennis, boxing, fencing, gymnastics, volleyball, badminton, football, basketball, disabled sports, table tennis, cricket, judo, netball, hockey and, of course, athletics. An imaginative cross-country course outside the Stadium is a major asset and was the venue for the 1983 World Cross Country Championships. A five-a-side football area outside has proved very popular and the newly installed full size floodlit synthetic pitch and warm-up strip is proving equally attractive.

The Stadium also houses a Centre of Excellence, supported by the local authority, the Governing Body and the Sports Council, to cover middle distance running, hammer, discus, long jump, pentathlon and high-jump training.

This summary is to illustrate a significant trend among provincial centres. Its extension and the implications, in a possible application of the Safety of Sports Grounds Act 1975 to other sports stadia, will be watched with interest.[35]

C. Participatory Sports

7.25 A recent annual report of the Sports Council listed over fifty sports in which that body took some interest. All would be styled participatory. Some of the legal areas of interest and risk to providers of swimming pools and sports centres have already been considered. These are both clearly attractions for those seeking participatory sports. In the discussion of the law of nuisance in Chapter 1, it was convenient to introduce that consideration in the context of cricket grounds.

The great participatory sports of our country, golf, football (both kinds), tennis, cricket and athletics, have from time to time given rise to cases in the courts and we shall now attempt to gather together the legal principles which govern them. There is no sign that the Law Commission or any other body is proposing to present Parliament with a draft code of

---

[35] s.15 of the Act of 1976 empowers the Secretary of State to make Orders for that purpose. At the time of going to press, no such Orders have been made. In view of the Bradford football stadium fire tragedy and the Popplewell inquiry, significant use of this power and possibly additional legal controls are envisaged.

law on this subject; it is a day to day matter for many people and the law to be applied is the common law.[36] There would seem to be at least seven areas of legal interest:
1. The parties:
   (i) The players and the organisers.
   (ii) The spectators.
2. The place for the maxim *volenti non fit injuria*.
3. The premises.
4. Nuisance.
5. Comparative Commonwealth cases.
6. The Safety of Sports Grounds Act 1975.
7. Private clubs.

1. The Parties

(1) *The Players and the Organisers*

The players willingly accept the risks associated with their particular sport, within the rules. Those risks may be regarded as twofold. In a case about rugby football, the court described that acceptance in terms of "risks which are by no means small, because it is a game involving great physical effort by one side or the other." A footballer also "willingly accepts all the risks of playing a game on such a field as complies with the by-laws laid down by the governing body of the game."[37]

In other words, the risks accepted are, first, those arising from engagement with other players and, secondly, those resulting from the nature of the ground, pitch, court, course or other physical arena used for his or her sport. What the player does not thus accept is the unreasonable danger, the extreme peril, the unjustified tackle or assault. In addition to some of the actions which can be described in these ways as contravening the laws of the sport, they may also contravene the laws of the land.

The organisers are considered with the players, since in the somewhat sporadic law cases in this country, they have been sued, together with the players, by aggrieved spectators.

We turn to some examples to illuminate from the sometimes colourful instances of sport, the principles outlined so far.

Simms v. *Leigh R.F.C.*[38]

In a rugby football match, a player was tackled and fell; in the course of this accident, his leg was broken. In an action against the ground

---

[36] In *Participatory Sports and the Law* (Sunday Telegraph), Mr. E. Grayson has drawn together many instances of sports cases in the courts; the author is indebted to that work for illustrating the extent to which the law has reached into the details of sporting life. Mr. Grayson's main aim, he says, is to show "the manner in which the law of the land transcends and supplements the laws of the game." His book includes draft clauses for a Bill about participants and spectators.
[37] *Simms* v. *Leigh R.F.C.* [1969] 2 All E.R. 923 at p. 927 i.
[38] [1969] 2 All E.R. 923.

organiser, he alleged that his injury was due to his being struck by a concrete wall, which was too near the pitch. After a full hearing, the court was not satisfied that the wall was involved in the accident and the plaintiff failed. A broken leg was treated as an accepted risk in rugby football.

Harrison v. Vincent[39]

A motorcycle racing circuit near Scarborough was the scene of a motorcycle and sidecar combination race. In a six-lap race, the accident occurred in the fifth lap, when, at a hairpin bend, the plaintiff was the passenger in the sidecar and the defendant his driver. The defendant needed to brake down from 100 m.p.h. to about 30 m.p.h. for this bend and the brakes produced only reduced power for this emergency. Missing the change of gear, the defendant did not have the benefit of added braking power from his engine. He went off the track and struck a standing vehicle on a side road. The plaintiff was injured.

The case was brought against the motorcycle rider and his employers and also against the race organisers, based on the inadequate inspection of the brakes before the race and also the layout of the course. The case reached the Court of Appeal. That court had to consider whether the accident and injuries were reasonably foreseeable by the defendants. On that point, the court said that they preferred the way the test was framed in the *Wagon Mound* case[40] to the way it was put in *Simms'* case (above). The preferred phrasing was:

> "A person must be regarded as negligent, if he does not take steps to eliminate a risk which he knows or ought to know is a real risk and not a mere possibility which would never influence the mind of a reasonable man."

Also, the qualification in the *Wagon Mound* case:

> "It is justifiable not to take steps to eliminate a real risk if it is small and if the circumstances are such that a reasonable man, careful of the safety of his neighbour, would think it right to neglect it."

The court referred with approval to the Australian case of *Rootes* v. *Shelton*[41] and put their judgment in favour of the passenger in the following way:

> "The acceptance of risks by the passenger did not extend to the risk of injury in the avenue of escape, following an involuntary departure from the race track."

Latchford v. Spedeworth International Ltd.[42]

This recent case by a participant against the stadium owner related to hot rod motor racing at Wimbledon Stadium in London. The plaintiff, a racing driver, familiar with the track, knew that two concrete flower beds,

---

[39] [1982] 1 R.T.R. 8.
[40] *The Wagon Mound(No. 2)* [1967] 1 A.C. 617 at p. 642.
[41] *Rootes* v. *Shelton* (1967) 116 C.L.R. 383.
[42] (1984) 134 New L.J. 36.

near to the inner edge of the track, were potentially dangerous to drivers. The defendant, the stadium owner, had for some months used small tyres on the ground as a form of boundary marking. These indicated the boundary near to the flower beds. In fact, small tyres were hazardous for this use and large tyres would have been safer, for demarcation purposes.

The case arose because of injuries suffered by the plaintiff in a race on this track. The preceding car struck some of the small tyres, propelling some onto the track and one jammed under the rear axle of the plaintiff's car. This catapulted the car sideways out of control and the plaintiff suffered a head-on collision with the concrete flower beds.

The interesting judgment of the court in favour of the plaintiff, was to the effect that though the plaintiff had an objective awareness of the flower beds and thus could be said to have accepted the risk thereby created, he did not, using the test of Watkins J. in *Harrison* v. *Vincent* (above), have a "full appreciation of the nature and extent of the risk, because of his ignorance of the peril created by the use of the small tyres." The defence of *volenti* failed and the plaintiff succeeded in his claim.

Brown v. Pelosi and St. Johnstone

The clearest instance of a player's legal rights is perhaps that of a football player recovering damages for injuries resulting from a foul tackle. **7.29**

Brown v. *Pelosi and St. Johnstone*[43] related to two Scottish football players and the case was settled out of court. The case is nonetheless of persuasive interest as the principle is that applied in the courts in this country. The essence of the claim was damages for injury due to a reckless assault over and beyond the inherent risks of the game. The defendant player had been sent off for his conduct and this provided strong supporting evidence for the plaintiff.

For a century there have also been convictions in the criminal courts of footballers for unlawful assaults, which gave rise to broken limbs in their opponents.[44]

(2) *The Spectators*

Whilst it is helpful to identify the separate roles of players, organisers and spectators and then the differing legal rights and obligations of each of these parties, in the limited number of English law reports on these subjects, the three are often found together. **7.30**

Hall v. Brooklands Auto-Racing Club[45]

A racing car broke through the barrier between track and spectators after a collision at high speed. Two spectators were killed and others

---

[43] The case was widely reported in the English press in December 1983, when £30,000 was said to be the amount of the claim.
[44] See E. Grayson, *supra*, pp. 32–33.
[45] [1933] 1 K.B. 205.

7.30

injured. In 23 years, no accident had occurred. An action by an injured spectator against the drivers was dismissed, negligence not being proved. An action against the ground organiser was successful at first instance but in the Court of Appeal, the court said that the findings of the jury could not be supported. The ground occupiers had done all that reasonable care and skill could do to make the course free from danger. They were not insurers against dangers which were inherent in the sport, which any reasonable spectator could foresee and of which he took the risk.

Murray v. Harringey Arena Ltd.[46]

A boy spectator was injured by a puck flying from the pitch during an ice hockey game at Haringey Stadium. He failed in an action for damages based on the negligence of the stadium organisers. The barriers and other protection they had provided were not regarded by the Court of Appeal as betraying any negligence. Further, the flying puck was one of the dangers inherent in the game.

Wooldridge v. Sumner

A photographer was injured whilst a spectator at the National Horse Show at the White City Stadium. An experienced horseman, taking part in a competition for heavy hunters, galloped at speed down a straight, with the result that his horse could not take the approaching corner without a wide sweep. This took the horse off the course down a line of shrubs, where the plaintiff photographer was watching. He tried to pull a lady out of the path of the horse and succeeded in doing so but was then himself struck and hurt by the horse.

His action for damages against the horseman was dismissed by the Court of Appeal. The court said that the horseman's actions both in relation to speed and recovery of the horse to the course were not negligent but at most the speed was an error of judgment. (The action against the ground owner had been dismissed at the first hearing.) The judgment included the following passage about spectators and the law:

> "A person attending a game or competition takes the risk of any damage caused to him by any act of a participant done in and for the purposes of the game or competition, notwithstanding that such act may involve an error of judgment or a lapse of skill, unless the participant's conduct is such as to evince a reckless disregard of the spectator's safety." *per* Diplock L.J.[47]

Wilks v. Cheltenham Car Club[48]

7.31 The plaintiffs were spectators at a motorcycle scramble. They were injured when a machine left the track and crossed two barrier ropes.

---

[46] [1951] 2 Q.B. 529.
[47] [1963] 2 Q.B. 44 at p. 68.
[48] [1971] 1 W.L.R. 668.

There was no explanation for this conduct of the motorcycle: it suddenly veered to one side.

In legal proceedings, the ground organisers were exonerated. No negligence was found against them. The plaintiffs did succeed at first instance against the motorcycle rider but in the Court of Appeal the rider's appeal against that decision was upheld. The Court considered both the *Wooldridge* case and comments upon it and laid down a modified standard expected of both competitors and players. It was in these terms:

> "The competitor's duty in relation to the spectators was not to cause injury by an error of judgment which a reasonable competitor, being a reasonable man of the sporting world, would not have made and which could not, in the stress of the circumstances, reasonably be regarded as excusable" *per* Edmund-Davies L.J.[49]

White v. *Blackmore*[50]

This case arose from an accident at a jalopy race in Gloucestershire. A field was laid out and the track roped round the boundary but all the stakes and ropes were linked to one master stake. During the race, a jalopy car got caught on a rope and as its rear wheel rotated, this acted as a winch, pulling up all the stakes with the rope rapidly. One man standing against the rope was catapulted into the air and later died of his injuries. His estate brought a successful action against the organisers of the race meeting.

The case had special points of interest, in that the deceased was at one time during the meeting a rider and thus a competitor and, at the time of the accident, he was a spectator, though not standing on the spectators' side of the barrier ropes. A further point was that the Court of Appeal rejected the ground on which the court of first instance had dismissed the claim of *volenti non fit injuria, i.e.* no legal liability to one who willingly accepts risks. The Court of Appeal held, that the deceased had not appreciated all the risks, due to the way in which the barrier ropes and stakes were fixed. He was not, therefore, *volenti*. This important qualification on the application of this maxim was elaborated in *Latchford*'s case (above).

2. The Place of the Maxim: Volenti Non Fit Injuria

It will be apparent that the defence of *volenti non fit injuria* is raised regularly in these cases brought by spectators against players and organisers or by players against organisers. It is said, with some evident justification, "You cannot complain: there are always risks, whether you come as a player or as a spectator, to these games or events."

Two Irish race cases, one concerning horses and the other cars, embody the typical use of the maxim. In *Callaghan* v. *Killarney Race Co. Ltd.*[51] a

7.32

---
[49] *Ibid.*
[50] [1972] 2 Q.B. 651.
[51] [1958] I.R. 366.

7.32

horse jumped over the wing of a race hurdle and injured the plaintiff spectator. The case was withdrawn from the jury: the occurence was simply a danger inherent in racing. There was no evidence of breach of duty by the organisers. Again, in *McComisky* v. *McDermott*,[52] plaintiff and defendant were respectively passenger and driver in a car in a motor rally. To avoid an unexpected obstruction in the road, the defendant drove his car into a ditch. It overturned and injured the plaintiff. On the dashboard of the car was a notice saying that passengers drove at their own risk. The Court of Appeal, upholding the exoneration of the defendant, discussed also the evidence about the extent to which the passenger, who was also the driver's navigator in the rally, had agreed to abandon his legal claims if injured by the driver's negligence. How far was he *volenti*? The court decided that the evidence on that point before them was tenuous.

On the other hand, in the case of the jalopy race, *White* v. *Blackmore*,[53] the circumstances ruled out the application of that maxim. The accident was due to the linkage of stakes and barrier ropes and this was something the deceased knew nothing about. All three judges agreed that in those circumstances the rule was not relevant. "It cannot be said that the deceased had full knowledge of the risk he was running" (Buckley L.J.)[54]; "Never willingly accepted the risk due to this default" (Denning M.R.)[55]; "the risk of which the deceased man was not and could not be aware" (Roskill L.J.).[56]

7.33   The use of the maxim is not as relevant where contributory negligence by the plaintiff exists, said Lord Reid in *I.C.I. Ltd.* v. *Shatwell*.[57] He instanced the case of a disobedient servant's act being the sole cause of his injury and said it did not matter whether the defence of *volenti* was raised or whether 100 per cent. contributory negligence was alleged. If substantiated, the result would be the same.

The maxim has limited use in any claim by a spectator against a player, since in the absence of negligence, the maxim does not apply.[58]

However, as the cases set out in this section show, there are still some where the maxim is useful and operative. Its fuller use was discussed in the section about defences to an action in tort, in Chapter 1, at paragraph 1.123.

3. The Premises

7.34   Management of sports grounds has, in our age, been subject to public nuisances, protests or other disturbances which raise legal questions.

"Public place" is an expression used in the Public Order Act 1936, s.5,

---

[52] [1974] I.R. 75.
[53] See n. 50, *supra*.
[54] *Ibid.* at p. 169(a).
[55] *Ibid.* at p. 164(d).
[56] *Ibid.* at p. 173(e).
[57] [1965] A.C. 656 at p. 672.
[58] See headnote to *Wooldridge*'s case, n. 47, *supra*, at p. 45.

in defining an offence for causing a breach of the peace; "or other public place" is the collective expression used in the section after a number of particular locations have been listed. What is "a public place"?

In *Cooper* v. *Shield*,[59] Lord Parker C.J. and his court had to consider how far the railway station at West Kirby in Cheshire was a public place, in relation to the above Act of 1936. The arguments related to the entry by ticket only, the proportion of buildings, the platform and the general layout. In due course, the court held that buildings were excluded from the definition of "public place" in that Act. Further, that even though the platform was open, it was all part of the station, which was not a public place.

But at the end of the judgment, Lord Parker said:

> "The position may be very different when one is considering what ordinarily one would call open spaces and asks oneself the question whether they cease to be open spaces because incidental to their use, there happen to be buildings. One immediately thinks of a race course and stands, one thinks of a football ground with stands. It seems to me that in these circumstances, it is perfectly apt to describe the complex as an open space."[60]

So when in *Cozens* v. *Brutus*[61] a demonstration took place on a court at Wimbledon during Wimbledon fortnight, and the above section was used for prosecution, the persons prosecuted, even though employing every possible argument in three hearings (the last being in the House of Lords), conceded, as being beyond argument, that the tennis court was a public place.[62]

In the case of *Cawley* v. *Frost*,[63] a breach of the peace at a football ground in Halifax between rival supporters gave rise to a prosecution under the above Act of 1936. The point taken by the defence was that the location of the fracas was a speedway track, which lay between the football stands and the pitch and that this was not a public place as far as the football spectators were concerned. The Crown Court had accepted this point and dismissed the case but on appeal the Divisional Court took a different view.

> "Where you have an establishment which is set up for the public, such as the Halifax Town Football Club or Wembley Stadium, one ought to approach it on the basis that it is a public place in its entirety." (Lord Widgery L.C.J.)

4. Nuisance

This is an important point for sports organisers and sports have been closed at some grounds on its account; there is a full discussion in Chapter

---

[59] [1971] 2 Q.B. 334. "Open space" is considered, since "public place" in the Act is defined as any "highway, etc. . . . and includes any open space to which for the time being the public have or are permitted to have access, whether on payment or otherwise."
[60] *Ibid.* at p. 340.
[61] [1973] A.C. 854.
[62] *Ibid.* at p. 857.
[63] (1977) 64 Cr. App. Rep. 20.

7.35 SPORT

1 and a further consideration of this subject in Chapter 4, in relation to nuisance in public parks.

5. Comparative Commonwealth Cases

7.36 It has been remarked that there is an almost complete dearth of judicial authority about the duty of care owed by the actual participants in sports and pastimes to their spectators.[64] Speculating on this feature, Professor A.L. Goodhart inferred that the number of sports accidents involving spectators in this country was minimal, as major spectator sports are rarely dangerous to spectators.[65] In those circumstances, it is instructive and interesting to look briefly at the cases in the Commonwealth law reports. These deal with perhaps more robust sports, viewed from sometimes more rudimentary grandstands. The conclusions in these reports are of persuasive authority only in the precedence accorded to judicial decisions in this country. Yet recent reports in other branches of our own law show a readiness by our courts to turn to Commonwealth decisions, when legal authorities in the United Kingdom are difficult to find.[66]

Payne & Payne v. Maple Leaf Gardens Ltd., Stewart and Marucci[67]

During a professional hockey game, two players on opposing sides dropped their hockey sticks on the ice. Play proceeded away from them as they sought to pick up their sticks. One player, Stewart, thought the other player Marucci had his stick. Stewart thus got hold of the stick and was resisted by Marucci who knew that the stick was his own. This struggle took the two men to the side of the ice, where boards four feet high separated the pitch from the front row of spectators, who were two feet away from the boards. When Marucci suddenly released the stick, it flew into the air, over the boards, and struck in the face a lady spectator in the front row of seats. The game was stopped and Stewart was penalised by the referee for violation of the rules.

An action for personal injury was brought by the spectator and her husband, season ticket holders, against the stadium owners for inadequate protection for the spectators and against the two players for assault or negligence arising from their illegal struggle during the game.

The Ontario Court of Appeal dismissed the case against both the stadium owners and against Marucci and held Stewart to be liable for negligence to the spectator and her husband for damages and for loss. The court's reasoning in relation to the owners is of particular interest:

> "Such an occupier is under a duty only to see that reasonable skill and care have been used to make (the premises) safe. He is obliged to guard spectators,

---

[64] Diplock L.J. in *Woodridge* v. *Sumner* [1962] 3 W.L.R. 616 at p. 631.
[65] A.L. Goodhart, "The Sportsman's Charter" (1962) 78 L.Q.R. 490.
[66] See *e.g.* copyright decisions in Chapter 3 (paras 3.17–3.18) of this book or the recent French turkey case (*Bourgoin S.A.* v. *Ministry of Agriculture Fisheries and Food, The Times,* October 4, 1984).
[67] [1949] 1 D.L.R. 369.

not against every possible danger, but only against those which may reasonably be assumed possible to happen."⁶⁸

That court cited with approval *Hall* v. *Brooklands Auto Racing Club*.⁶⁹ There had been, said the court in the *Maple Leaf Gardens* case, evidence of pucks escaping among the spectators but no evidence of this kind of incident. "The misadventure was of so unusual and unexpected a kind that it could not reasonably have been expected."⁷⁰ With regard to the negligent player Stewart, the court said he showed "reckless disregard for the safety of the spectators."⁷¹ He knew or ought to have known that the people in the front row were in danger of injury, if he continued his struggle with Marucci. It was also, said the court, "not without importance that at the time of the accident, Stewart was not engaged in the course of play."⁷²

With regard to the spectators, the court said they were taken to have assumed the risk of injury from known accidents, when no player was at fault. But the case in question was not that sort of case.

Rootes v. *Shelton*⁷³

The plaintiff and two others were being towed by the defendant in his boat for water skiing. The plaintiff and the other two skiers had tow ropes of different lengths, so they could do "cross-overs" with one another. On one of these operations, the plaintiff struck a boat in the river where this sport was taking place. He was injured and sued the boatman for negligence in failing to take due care of his speedboat and for failing to warn the plaintiff of the presence of the stationary boat. (The plaintiff said he was temporarily blinded from being able to see the stationary boat by spray.)

The High Court in Australia, on appeal from the Supreme Court of New South Wales, upheld the plaintiff's claim. He had assumed risks by participating in the sport, said the court. But those risks were the ones inherent in the sport. By doing so, the duty of care by one participant to another was not eliminated.⁷⁴

Reese v. *Coleman and 27 others*⁷⁵

A snowmobile race was held in Saskatchewan, where such races are a frequent occurrence. The plaintiff was one of about 500 spectators who

---

[68] Laidlaw J.A. *Ibid.* at p. 371.
[69] [1933] 1 K.B. 205.
[70] The *Maple Leaf Gardens* case (*supra*) at p. 371.
[71] *Ibid.* at p. 372.
[72] *Ibid.* at p. 373.
[73] (1967) 116 C.L.R. 383.
[74] Barwick C.J. *Ibid.* at p. 383. The court also made some useful observations on the relation of the rules of a sport to the rules of the relevant law. "Non-compliance with such rules is one consideration to be attended to upon the question of reasonableness; but it is only one and it may be of much or little or even no weight in the circumstances." (Killo J.) *Ibid.* at p. 389.
[75] [1976] 3 W.L.R.739.

had paid for admission. The track was oval and had been scraped out of snow to allow the participating machines to make their circuits. Because the machines might come off the track at the curves at the ends of the oval, spectators were not allowed there. But at the sides, called "the straightways," spectators watched on foot or in cars. Here also was the pit where machines were adjusted or repaired for the races.

The injury occurred when a snowmobile went out of control, left the track, came through the pit area at about 30 m.p.h. and struck the plaintiff. He was thrown through the air. The plaintiff recovered damages against the snowmobile driver and the judgment of the court concentrated on the liability of the club, the organisers of the races. The court adopted the principles laid down in the English *Brooklands* case and the Canadian *Maple Leaf Gardens* case, above, and said that the promoter was not liable for "injuries to paying spectators resulting from such risks as by the nature of the spectacle, the spectator must have understood and be presumed to have assumed."[76] The club had made a rule that a racer should not go through the pits; the court held that this meant that the club had by implication promised the plaintiff that by standing in the pits, he was standing in a safe area. The club's failure to protect this area was a breach of its duty to the plaintiff.

Magee v. *Prairie Dusters Motor-cycle Club, Laurence & Dunn*[77]

A racing competition was held by the defendants in a hilly area on a course more than a mile long. Spectators along the route were not protected by barriers, nor were they prevented from entering the track area, nor motor cycles from leaving it.

The plaintiff sold refreshments to the spectators and was injured when struck by the defendant on a motor cycle which went out of control. The plaintiff was just inside the track area when struck. The plaintiff failed in an action against the club and against the driver of the motor cycle. The court said the club was not negligent in not providing barriers. The defendant was a skilled driver and no excessive speed or lack of care was alleged against him. The case of *Wilks* v. *Cheltenham Home Guard Motor Cycle and Light Car Club* was applied. (See para. 7.31, *supra*.)

Klyne v. *Bellegarde Lloyd and Indian Head*[78]

In a game of ice hockey, in an arena owned by the defendant, in the town of Indian Head, the plaintiff suffered injury to an eye from being struck with the hockey stick of one of the players. He was standing in an aisle next to the ice rink boards round the arena at the time. The aisle had to be used by spectators for exit and entrance and they were not required to use the seats available. There were no protective shields over the boundary boards.

[76] MacPherson J. *Ibid.* at p. 742.
[77] [1975] W.W.D. 165 (Western Weekly Digests, Saskatoon, No. 579, 24/9/75).
[78] *Klyne*'s case [1978] 6 W.W.R. 743.

The plaintiff sued the club for negligence and succeeded in his claim. The club, said the court, should have foreseen injury by a player with his stick to a spectator and put protective guards above the boards. However, as the spectator was also negligent in standing where he did, damages were reduced by two-thirds. The case of *Reese* v. *Coleman* (above) was applied. The court said that the owner's liability was "not to ensure safety but to use reasonable care." (Halvorson J.)[79] The court made an interesting point about technical development. At the time of *Payne*'s case, transparent guards, in plexiglass or a similar material, were not available or economically feasible. "The predicament of the arena owner was thus considered favourably."[80] But the changed situation allowed the court to say that he should have put up some protective guards. "Custom is lagging behind technical and engineering capacity."[81]

The risk of a flying puck at a game of ice hockey was one accepted by the spectators, said the court. This did not mean that the spectators accepted the risk of being hit over the head by a hockey stick.[82]

The regular reference in each of these cases, not only to earlier sporting accidents considered in their own Commonwealth countries but also to the leading English reports, has clearly contributed to the even development of this branch of the law, both in this country and in the Commonwealth countries concerned.

6. The Safety of Sports Grounds Act 1975

This Act is discussed generally in Chapter 6. Since 1975, nine designation Orders have been made for various grounds. The Safety of Sports Grounds Regulations 1976 (S.I. 1976 No. 1263) contain full details of the procedure to be followed in applying for a Safety Certificate. This includes the hearing of the application, the inspection of the ground, the notices to be served on interested parties and the rights of appeal to the Secretary of State, both for general and for special Safety Certificates.

7. Private Sports Clubs

There are no doubt thousands of sports clubs in this country which fall into the category, in law, of unincorporated associations. They handle business contracts of all kinds, for catering, sports supplies, or building; they host competitions where large sums of money are involved. Yet not being local authorities or limited companies, they are simply groups of individuals, banded together as sports clubs. They have their rules, they agree that the committee can act for the members. But when it comes to legal action in the courts, the club dissolves. "Such a fluid or anonymous aggregate is not a fit party to sue or be sued," said an Australian legal

---

[79] Halvorson J. *Ibid.* at p. 746.
[80] *Ibid.* at p. 747.
[81] *Ibid.* at p. 747.
[82] *Ibid.* at p. 748.

7.38 Sport

writer.[83] He was troubled by the gap between the law and the real world, where such clubs exist and discharge their day to day duties effectively. Four comments are offered on this situation, particularly since local authorities regularly act in close liaison with such clubs in providing the leisure facilities sought by the public.

(i) Such clubs can and do appoint trustees from their members to act in land transactions, as conveyances or leases. This arrangement is effective. Yet the trustees are still acting for the club, for the association and not for themselves. "As long as they act *intra vires* the trustees are purely nominal holders, with a full right to indemnity from the club fund."[84]

(ii) When the committee itself is brought into the legal action, it is to enable the club to sue and be sued.[85]

(iii) Such a members club can be a "voluntary association" with which a local authority can deal when making grants or loans, under the Local Government (Miscellaneous Provisions) Act 1976.[86]

(iv) When the above Act of 1976 empowers a local authority also to make available the various sporting facilities for the use of clubs and societies, this by implication accepts licences or leases as the necessary and normal legal machinery for effecting such arrangements.[87]

D. Riding

7.39 The popular sport of riding, for many years a private leisure activity, becomes part of the public leisure services, partly because Parliament has, in two Acts, put reins on the riding establishments in the Riding Establishment Acts of 1964 and 1970, the provisions of which may be summarised as follows:

(1) Local authorities are required to license riding establishments.[88] As part of that process, they are to obtain and consider a report of a veterinary surgeon on the establishment.

(2) The authority has to be satisfied on seven points, covering the stabling, its ventilation and drainage, fire risk, adequacy in relation to dis-

---

[83] Prof. S. Stoljar, "Sporting Clubs and Corporate Theory," Melbourne Law Review (1982) Vol. 13, p. 491.
[84] *Ibid.* at p. 495.
[85] See *Carlisle and Silloth Golf Club* v. *Smith* [1913] 3 K.B. 75, where the club as a club was held liable for tax on gate and green fees. The recent case of *Miller* v. *Jackson* [1977] 3 W.L.R. 21, the cricket club case, was typical in that the chairman and secretary of the club were sued by the aggrieved neighbours "on their own behalf and on behalf of all the other members of the club." *Ibid.* at p. 22. (See Chap.1.)
R.S.C. Ord. 15, r. 12, provides the High Court machinery for such representative actions.
[86] s.19(3). This opinion treats such a club as "a person carrying on an undertaking otherwise than for profit," within the section.
[87] The limit on the length of such a lease, without Ministerial authorisation, is seven years: Local Government, Planning and Land Act 1980.
[88] Act of 1964, s.1. This means District Councils, the Common Council of the City of London and London Boroughs. There are four exemptions from the licensing requirements, *i.e.* Defence Department premises, police premises, premises of the Zoological Society of London or a university which provides an approved course for veterinary students.

ease, pasture, and food as well as the applicant's experience in horse management.[89] This first list in the Act of 1964 was significantly extended in the later Act of 1970, to refer to care for the horses and the availability of the Fire Service telephone number.

(3) A provisional licence for three months was a device introduced in the later Act. This allowed fuller deliberation by the authority and more time by the applicant to install all necessary facilities.[90]

(4) The basic licence is for 12 months, renewed annually.[91]

(5) Against refusal there lies an appeal to the magistrates' court.[92]

(6) A riding establishment must never be left in the charge of a person under 16 years of age.[93]

(7) The licence holder must have an insurance policy to cover the risks undertaken by his riders.[94]

(8) He must also keep a register of his horses.[95]

(9) A series of offences is set out in the Acts. These cover concealing horses from inspectors, defective equipment, as well as unsatisfactory keeping of the horses. The Act of 1970 also tightened the law about those horses which were not to be the subject of hiring.[96]

The three classes are:
   (i) Any horse aged three years or under.
   (ii) Any mare heavy with foal.
   (iii) Any mare within three months of foaling.[97]

E. Water Recreation

1. Boats

(1) Provision

The public leisure services charter, that is to be found in the Local Government (Miscellaneous Provisions) Act 1976, s.19, includes boats.[98] This takes up and extends a power that was granted to local authorities a century ago, to provide boats in their lakes, in their parks or pleasure

---

[89] *Ibid.* s.1(4) and s.2 of the Act of 1970.
[90] Act of 1970, s.1.
[91] Act of 1964, s.1(7).
[92] Act of 1964, s.1(5).
[93] Act of 1970, s.2, becoming s.4A of the Act of 1964.
[94] *Ibid.*
[95] *Ibid.*
[96] Act of 1970, s.3, as amended by the Act of 1964, s.3, being seven offences in all.
[97] The basic definition relates to the carrying on of a business of keeping horses to let them out on hire for riding, or for use in providing instruction in riding for payment, or both.
[98] s.19(1)(c): "facilities for boating" is the expression, which is taken to include not only the boats but the waterway or lake, any jetty or landing stage needed for the public use. "Boats" are in law for use in inland waters, "ships" for the sea. "Hovercraft" becomes a ship when used at sea and a boat when used on inland waters or harbours—Hovercraft Act 1968, ss.3 and 4(3).

7.40 SPORT

grounds.[99] The modern power is in relation to inland and coastal waters. In coastal waters, there are many privately managed boating facilities which fall within the scope of the Merchant Shipping Acts as the guide for management.

Boats for use in pleasure grounds are currently dealt with in the Public Health Act 1961.[1]

(2) *Licensing of Pleasure Boats and Boatmen*

7.41 The Public Health Acts Amendment Act 1907 grants to local authorities the power to grant licences, on such terms as they think fit, for the pleasure boats and also for the boatmen.[2]

The boats

The pleasure boats and pleasure vessels thus regulated, are those to be let for hire to the public or used for carrying passengers for hire. The licences incur annual fees to the licensing authority. The licences may be suspended or revoked by the licensing authority, when they deem such action to be necessary in the public interest. The existence of this power must be plainly stated in the licence. A right of appeal against this action is granted to the licence holder in the Act of 1907.[3]

It is an offence to let for hire a boat or pleasure vessel, when not duly licensed. Guidance is given in the Act of 1907 about some of the contents of a boat licence. For instance, the licensee has to paint his own name and the number of permitted passengers on a conspicuous part of the boat or vessel. Vessels licensed by the Board of Trade under the Merchant Shipping Acts are exempted from this licensing procedure. Again, no licence is required under the above Act of 1907 for pleasure boats or pleasure vessels on any canal owned or managed by the British Waterways Board.[4] The section of the Act of 1907 about the licensing of both boats and boatmen, operates only in those districts approved by Order of the Secretary of State.[5]

The absence of a definition of "pleasure boat" has given rise over the years to doubts about the application of these licensing provisions to specific situations. It seems evident that a boat can be a pleasure boat, for the purposes of section 94 of the above Act of 1907, when used for enjoy-

---

[99] Public Health Act 1875, s.172, now repealed; Local Government Planning and Land Act 1980, Sched. 34, Pt. XVI.
[1] Public Health Act 1961, s.54. The power covers associated buildings, and facilities as well as letting of the management of the boating lake.
[2] Act of 1907, s.94. This was amended in certain important respects by the Local Government (Miscellaneous Provisions) Act 1976, s.18, and again by the Local Government Planning and Land Act 1980, s.186.
[3] Act of 1907, s.94(7).
[4] Act of 1908, s.186.
[5] Act of 1907, s.3.

ment and pleasure trips, even if at other times, the boat is used for commercial fishing work.

The boatmen

The licensing requirements of the Act of 1907 extend also to the boatmen. These are defined as "the boatmen or persons in charge of or navigating such boats or vessels."[6] These licences also carry an annual fee. Powers of suspension or cancellation are available to the licensing authority for them, as for those licences relating to the boats. The wording of the offence committed by the person, who carries passengers for hire in an unlicensed pleasure boat, was revised in 1976 so that it now reads[7]:

> "No person shall carry or permit to be carried passengers for hire in any pleasure boat or vessel unless:
> (*a*) the boat or vessel is so licensed and the licence is not suspended; and
> (*b*) the person in charge of the boat or vessel or any other person navigating it is so licensed and his licence is not suspended and the conditions of his licence are complied with."

When the boat or vessel is licensed by the Board of Trade, as above, it is not necessary to have a boatman's licence, under the Act of 1907.[8]

(3) By-laws

The local authority which licenses boats and boatmen under the above Act of 1907 may also make by-laws for regulating the use of such boats.[9]
The by-laws may:
(i) Regulate the specification of the pleasure boats.
(ii) Regulate their use, in order to prevent navigation in a dangerous manner or without due care and attention and without reasonable consideration for other persons.
(iii) Require the use of effectual silencers, on pleasure boats propelled by internal combustion engines.

The Secretary of State is the confirming authority for such by-laws. These by-laws can be effective, not only within the area of a local authority, but also within a distance seawards, not more than 1,000 yards from low water mark of ordinary spring tides; they are of no effect, to the extent that they are in conflict with by-laws made by bodies manning the docks or piers in the district of the local authority in question.

Since the subject matter of the by-laws is limited by the Act of 1961, the local authority wishing to impose additional requirements is left to include them in the licences. These might cover carrying capacity, the range of activity or the qualifications of the boatmen. Insofar as the boats towing

---

[6] Act of 1907, s.94.
[7] Act of 1976, s.18.
[8] *Ibid.*
[9] Public Health Act 1961, s.76.

7.43   Sport

water skiers are also pleasure boats, by-laws framed to keep within section 76 of the Public Health Act 1961 above, could deal with their use too, though not their construction.

(4) *Application*

7.44   An interesting case arose in the courts in 1979 when an injunction was obtained in the Court of Appeal against a motor boat racing club, on account of the noise it created. The case was *Kennaway* v. *Thompson*,[10] and the location was a man-made lake of some 38 acres in Gloucestershire. The injunction was obtained by the owner of an adjoining house. At the first hearing, nuisance was proved and the judge considered damages for the past nuisance and for the diminution in the value of the house (£1,000 and £15,000 respectively) to be a satisfactory award for the successful claimant. The householder, being aggrieved not to obtain an injunction, appealed and thus the main issues in the Court of Appeal were the merits and otherwise of damages and an injunction. In due course, the Court of Appeal decided that an injunction was appropriate. However, in view of the plaintiff's knowledge when her house was being built that some motor racing took place on the lake, the injunction was qualified. At the time of the hearing, racing every week-end from March to November was proved and noise levels touching 100 decibels measured.

The limits in the court injunction were interesting and as follows:
  (i) International events—one per season—duration three days.
  (ii) National events—two per season—duration two days. Spacing between these three major events—four weeks.
  (iii) Club events—duration one day, with three week spacings from the other events.
  (iv) Limits on the decibels.
  (v) Limits to other club activities, including water skiing.

This order resulted from the Court's approach, as Lawton J. said, "There must be a measure of give and take and live and let live."[11]

2. Fishing

Introduction

7.45   The sport of fishing is, in the context of this work, one where limits have to be imposed. The subject, in legal terms, extends from Common Market policy to the niceties of the question of when a fish has been appropriated to the ownership of a fisherman, so that trespass and poaching may be defined and controlled.

Fishing in the sea and tidal waters has given rise to a considerable amount of legislation, of which the Sea Fisheries Regulation Act 1966, and

---

[10] [1981] Q.B. 88.
[11] *Ibid.* at p. 94D.

the Sea Fisheries Act 1968 are recent examples. Fishing in inland waters is the subject of the Salmon and Freshwater Fisheries Act 1975, a recent consolidating measure, which greatly eases the task of those who wish to see a broad picture of legislation in that field.

Seals and whales have attracted legislation on their own account and lead the reader to ancient laws on the Royal Prerogative, in relation to whales and sturgeon.

Lastly, the land law of this country, is the basis for the law about fishing waters, since ownership of the soil carries with it ownership of the water and all within it, until Parliament or the agreements of men lead to variants.

Against this background, a work attempting to select the law of the public leisure services must omit sea fishing, as being primarily commercial and also seals and whales, for the same reason, and will therefore concentrate on:

(1) The Salmon and Freshwater Fisheries Act 1975.
(2) Land law, so far as it bears upon fishing as a leisure pursuit.

(1) *The Salmon and Freshwater Fisheries Act* 1975

This is a consolidating Act of 43 sections and 5 Schedules. It repeals five earlier Acts and it is convenient to consider its provisions in relation to unlawful practices, licensing, by-laws, Water Authority duties and offences.

7.46

Unlawful practices and obstructions

Parts I and II of this Act of 1975 list the prohibited implements and methods of fishing, *i.e.* firearms, otter lath or jack, wire or snare, a crossline or set line, a spear, gaff or stroke haul; a snatch or similar instrument, a light, stone throwing or use of other missiles to take or kill salmon, trout or other freshwater fish.

The Act proceeds to outline the prohibited techniques of fishing in relation to roe, spawning or unclean fish, namely nets, poisonous matter and polluting effluent, explosives, poisons, dams, and electrical devices. "Obstructions" is a general term used in the Act of 1975, when listing prohibited methods of fishing, *i.e.* fixed engines, fishing weirs, fishing milldams, new dams without fish passes, boxes and cribs in weirs and dams, taking salmon or trout above or below obstructions or mill races, except as permitted in the Act.[12] These prohibitions are supplemented by the creation of an offence for obstructing a legally authorised person who is engaged on work on fish passes or Water Authority gratings. These safeguard water flow, as distinct from that "frequented by salmon or migratory trout."[13]

---

[12] Salmon and Freshwater Fisheries Act 1975, s.17.
[13] *Ibid.* s.15(1)(*a*).

Licences

7.47 The licensing of fishing falls upon nine Water Authorities set up by the Water Act 1973.[14] The fish in question are salmon, trout and (unless excused by the Ministry of Agriculture, Fisheries and Food) also all other freshwater fish and eels.[15] A licence defines the area, the duration and the name of the licensee. It is personal, except that the licensee's servant or agent can use the licence in defined circumstances.[16] The person or association entitled to an exclusive right to fish, may be granted a general fishing licence by the Water Authority. This entitles any other person, duly authorised by the secretary of the association or the individual licence holder, also to enjoy the right of fishing in the inland waters in question.[17] Licence duties are regulated by Schedule 2 of the Act of 1975. The fishing licence does not authorise the erection of structures or the use of installations or instruments which would otherwise be illegal.

The number of fishing licences granted by a Water Authority for any part of their area can be limited by Order confirmed by the Minister.[18] The limit will take the form of an annual maximum number and the arrangement is not to be made for more than ten years. The licences in question are those for salmon and trout (other than rainbow trout), with any instrument specified, other than rod and line. The Act contains a procedure for determining the number of licences thus limited; that procedure is designed to hold the balance between "the conservation of the fishery"[19] and those persons who have held a fishing licence previously and are "dependent on fishing for their livelihood."[20]

It is an offence to fish in regulated inland waters without a licence.[21] Part II of the Act of 1975 and Schedule 1 contain the various close seasons for salmon, trout, other freshwater fish and eels. Those parts of the same Act also set out restrictions on the export and the consignment of salmon and trout.[22]

By-laws

7.48 The Act of 1975 authorises the making of by-laws by Water Authorities. The procedure is contained in Schedule 7 of the Water Act 1973. Such by-laws require confirmation by the Minister (or Ministers, in the case of Wales).

---

[14] *Ibid.* s.25. The authorities are listed in the Water Act 1973, Sched. 1 and their areas for fishing functions in Sched. 2, para. 4.
[15] Act of 1975, s.41(2), (acting with the Secretary of State for Wales, as appropriate).
[16] *Ibid.* Sched. 2, paras. 9–14.
[17] *Ibid.* s.25(7).
[18] *Ibid.* s.26.
[19] *Ibid.* s.26(5).
[20] *Ibid.* s.26(4). A recent case on this phrase confirmed its latent scope for argument. "How dependent?" was the issue in *R.* v. *S.W. Water Authority, ex p. Cox, The Times,* January 2, 1982.
[21] *Ibid.* s.27.
[22] *Ibid.* ss.23 and 24.

The Act of 1975 sets out 18 purposes with which the by-laws may deal. They are all aspects of regulating fishing in the waters of the Authorities.[23]

Duties of the Water Authorities

The Act of 1975, in section 28, sets out the duties of the Water Authorities as being:
  (a) To maintain, improve and develop the salmon fisheries, the trout fisheries, the freshwater fisheries and the eel fisheries in its area.
  (b) To establish advisory committees of persons interested in the fisheries of that area and consult them on the various duties set out in (a) above.

There are regional advisory committees set up under these powers in Water Authority areas and these are supplemented by local Advisory committees when necessary.

The Ministers may make Orders by way of Statutory Instrument to regulate the above groups of fisheries in particular areas.[24]

Offences

The offences created by the Act of 1975 are set out in Schedule 4 of the Act, with corresponding fines or terms of imprisonment.

The Water Authorities are entitled to appoint water bailiffs to enforce the law and detect these manifold and often cunning offences, armed, as may be necessary, with search or other warrants for that purpose.[25]

(2) *Land Law and Fishing*

A right to fish goes in law with the ownership of the soil over which the water lies, be it stream, lake, pool, or river.

Because a fishery is a profit of the land, as distinct from an estate in the land, it can be sold or bequeathed or otherwise transferred separately from the land.

There are a number of technical terms which are used in land law:
  (i) A *several fishery* is an exclusive right of fishing in a given place.
  (ii) A *common of fishery* is a right of fishing in another person's water, in common with other persons.

A fishery may be kept with the land to which it relates. When transferred separately, a lease or licence can be used, depending on the nature and duration of the right the owner wishes to give.

In a non-tidal river, the law presumes ownership of the fishery by a riparian owner to the middle of the water. This can be varied by the two riparian owners so that one may own the fishery over the whole water.

---

[23] *Ibid.* s.28 and Sched. 3.
[24] *Ibid.* s.28(3) and (4).
[25] *Ibid.* ss.31–36.

7.51   Sport

A right to use the river bank for fishing can be acquired by prescription, *i.e.* twelve years' uninterrupted use for that purpose.

The Theft Act 1968[26] creates an offence for unlawfully taking or destroying any fish in water which is private property or in which there is a private right of fishing. The offence is absolute.

3. Canals

7.52   In 1947, 18 listed canals were taken into public ownership by the Transport Act 1947.[27] Initially the property of the Transport Commission, they came, in due course, under the authority of the British Waterways Board, which currently manages them. They are used for both commercial and leisure service purposes; this account is limited to the statutes and common law relating to the leisure service use. That use has been extended and the Board has been involved in opening for this use lengths of disused or blocked canals.

The British Waterways Board is placed under a duty by the Transport Act 1962 in wide terms:

> "To provide, to such extent as they may think expedient, [. . .] services and facilities on the inland waterways owned or managed by them."[28]

Part VII of the Transport Act 1968 provides the main group of statutory law about the canals of this country. It divides canals into commercial, cruising and the remainder. "Cruising" waterways are those "principally available for cruising, fishing or other recreational purposes."[29] These canals are separately listed in Schedule 12 of the above Act of 1968. They now number 28 and are described in detail. The description is qualified only by the words: "the main navigable channels of the following waterways." The duty of the Waterways Board in relation to the cruising canals is:

> "to maintain the cruising waterways in a suitable condition for use by cruising craft, that is to say, vessels constructed or adapted for the carriage of passengers and driven by mechanical power."[30]

A standard is included in the section, for the vessels for which the Board is to provide canals as above, *i.e.* those which customarily used that waterway during the nine months between April and December 1967.[31]

It is of interest that the guideline generally given to the Waterways Board about a commercially meritorious management policy, "in the

---

[26] Sched. I, para. 21.
[27] s.12 and Sched. 3. Others not nationalised were referred to as "independent inland waterway undertakings." Transport Act 1962, s.52.
[28] Transport Act 1962, s.10(1)(*a*).
[29] Transport Act 1968, s.104.
[30] *Ibid.* s.105.
[31] *Ibid.* s.105(2). The Minister is empowered by Order to vary that duty on the Board, if the development of design for cruising vessels makes it desirable to do so: *Ibid.* s.105(3).

most economic manner possible and to secure the best possible financial return," is not laid down in relation to the cruising canals.[32]

The Transport Act 1968 set up the Inland Waterways Amenity Advisory Council of persons with knowledge and interest in the use of inland waterways for amenity or recreational purposes including fishing. This Council advises the Board and the Minister on these aspects of their duties.[33] The Act of 1968 authorises local authorities to assist other persons to maintain or improve waterways in or accessible to their areas for amenity or recreational purposes, including fishing.[34] The Board is granted extensive powers to make by-laws.[35]

Towpaths

A towpath alongside a canal is often a public highway, though the soil remains in the canal owners. The dedication for highway use may be specific or the result of prescription (*i.e.* 20 years uninterrupted user). It can even then be defined as a use which recognises the rights of the canal undertakers to use the same towpath for their own legitimate purpose, *e.g.* the horse and its rope.[36] The by-law making powers of the Board include the prohibition of passing along a towpath without the consent of the Board.[37]

7.53

4. Inland Waters

Boating and fishing are the main leisure service activities associated with the inland waters of this country. This subsection gathers together other legal provisions affecting inland water recreation; these can be conveniently grouped about those relating to the National and Country Parks, those about other inland waters and, thirdly, the bearing of the common law on these matters.

7.54

(1) *National and Country Parks*

As National and Country Parks comprise the main scenically attractive parts of the country, it is not surprising that among their statutory controls are a number about water recreation.

A local planning authority, whose area includes the whole or part of a National Park, may stimulate the enjoyment of bathing, boating, fishing,

7.55

---

[32] *Ibid.* s.107.
[33] *Ibid.* s.110.
[34] *Ibid.* s.114.
[35] British Transport Commission Act 1954, s.16.
[36] See, *e.g. Grand Junction Canal Co.* v. *Petty* [1888] 21 Q.B. 273. "The public must be taken to have accepted it as a limited dedication . . . . If the horse or the towrope and the foot passengers are in one another's way, the foot passenger must look out for himself and get out of the way." Though this may speak of another age, it underlines the dual use likely on towpaths.
[37] s.16, see n. 35, *supra*.

7.55   Sport

sailing and other forms of recreation in the waters on its boundary.[38] Similar powers are available for a local authority in relation to a Country Park in its area.[39]

The use of land for such activities may depend on negotiation with owners, unless an Access Order or Agreement, as discussed in Chapter 8, has facilitated that use.[40]

The local authority has powers to make by-laws about the matters described above.[41]

Lakes in National Parks are the subject of a separate section in the Countryside Act 1968. This authorises by-laws to prohibit or restrict traffic on those lakes.[42] The purposes of those by-laws are to be:

(a) To ensure the safety of the persons resorting to the lake.
(b) To regulate sports and in particular the use of boats and other vessels.[43]
(c) To conserve the natural beauty of the lake and its surrounding area.
(d) To prevent damage or nuisance, especially in relation to excessive noise.

The local planning authority must consult the Countryside Commission about such by-laws and act in the context of the two main guidelines for National Parks in sections 1 and 5 of the National Parks and Access to the Countryside Act 1949.[44]

Such by-laws cannot relate to the lakes of a statutory undertaking or a river authority. They cannot override private property rights. They may be jointly enforced by any other local authority with property from its area in that National Park.

7.56   The draftsmen of the National Parks and Access to the Countryside Act 1949 had water recreation in mind when they defined land as including land covered with water, for the purposes of that Act.[45] "Waterway" was a generic term then introduced as meaning "any lake river canal or other waters," being (in any case) waters suitable, or which can be rendered suitable, for sailing, boating, bathing or fishing.[46] "Open country" was another expression carefully defined to give full scope to water, whether it were canal, river or some other expanse of water.[47] In making provision for access orders and agreements, which would enable the public to enjoy

---

[38] National Parks and Access to the Countryside Act 1949, s.13, and Countryside Act 1968, s.12. Local authority action of the sort described is authorised only when such existing facilities are inadequate. Local authorities are encouraged to agree on joint public action. The Minister can require them to act if necessary. *Ibid*. Act of 1949, s.13.

[39] Access orders and agreements are made under Pt. V of the above Act of 1949, s.74 of which says that access arrangements apply to waterways.

[40] *Ibid*. Act of 1949, s.12(5).

[41] Countryside Act 1968, s.8.

[42] *Ibid*. s.13.

[43] "Boat" includes hover vehicle or craft. *Ibid*. s.49.

[44] See Chapter 8 on Open Air Activity.

[45] The above Act of 1949, s.114.

[46] *Ibid*. s.114(1).

[47] Countryside Act 1968, s.16.

the open country, the Act of 1949, supplemented by the Countryside Act 1968, contained detail to ensure that, *e.g.* small boat users could have full and satisfactory access to a waterway. So if they had to carry a small boat "to circumvent obstacles or obstructions on the water by passing round on foot with their boats,"[48] this was a situation that local authorities and the Commission had to consider when framing their access documents. Another example is the case of "obtaining access from a highway to a convenient launching place for small boats."[49]

(2) *Other Inland Waters*

Reservoirs are frequently made available for water recreation. The statutory provision on this point is the Countryside Act 1968, s.22, supplemented by the Water Act 1973, s.20. The Water Authority is to "take steps to secure the use of water and land associated with water for the purposes of recreation." They have a duty to put "their rights to use the water and any land associated with water to the best use for those purposes."[50]

The water undertaker, *i.e.* the Water Boards may provide buildings and other facilities to support this recreational use. They can make charges. They can enter into tenancies. They can make by-laws which will not only regulate the various forms of recreation but also prohibit use by unregistered boats and deal with pollution to the waterway.[51] If the reservoir is a "large raised reservoir," being over five million gallon capacity and above ground level, then whether called a dam or a reservoir, it comes within the regulatory provisions of the Reservoirs Act 1975, since this Act deals with artificial lakes not used for water supply purposes. A register of such undertakings is kept by the Greater London Council and county councils; an engineer's certificate is needed every ten years about its safety and if it should be abandoned or the water level lowered, statutory safety precautions must be observed. If the Rule in *Rylands* v. *Fletcher*, discussed in Chapter 1, is the response of the Common Law to the evident danger in a large raised reservoir, then this is the current statutory complement, in terms of safety regulations.

The Water Authority is not to interfere with navigation which is subject to the control of a harbour authority[52] or a navigation authority.[53] The Welsh Authority, as the equivalent regional authority for parts of Wales, is to confer with the Severn-Trent Water Authority to prepare a plan for the recreational use of water and associated land in Wales.[54] The National Water Council, appointed under the Water Act 1983, has the duty of advising the Secretary of State on policy and its execution in relation to

---

[48] *Ibid.* s.16(4).
[49] *Ibid.* s.16(4).
[50] *Ibid.* s.22.
[51] *Ibid.* s.22.
[52] Harbours Act 1964.
[53] Water Resources Act 1963.
[54] Water Resources Act 1973, s.21.

7.57

the use of water for recreation and amenity in England. This must be expected to involve consultation with the Countryside Commission, the Sports Council, the English Tourist Board and other bodies concerned with sport and recreation.[55]

Additionally, the same Commission is charged with advising the Sports Council and the Water Authorities on the discharge of their duties relating to water recreation.

(3) *The Common Law and Water Rights*

7.58 This may be a suitable point to take note of certain fundamental common law principles relating to rights concerning water.

Water flowing in defined or undefined channels is not, at common law, capable of ownership; it is when the water has been taken into possession, in reservoirs, pools, tanks or pits, for instance, that it can be "owned." The owner of the land on which the water stands is then also the owner of the water; if the pool stands on land with two owners, one on each side, then the water also is owned by those two landowners in proportion to their land holdings.

Whilst flowing water is not owned, it can be used. The Water Resources Act 1973 has considerately modified the common law on this point and under the Act of 1973, a licence is required from the Water Authority for the abstraction of water, except where taken for domestic purposes or for agricultural purposes other than spray irrigation.[56]

Unless there is evidence to the contrary, the common law presumes that the owners of the banks or sides of non-tidal waters own the land forming the bed of the waters to the centre line of the water.[57] If one person owns land on both sides of, say, a river, he will be the presumed owner of all the river bed.[58]

7.59 In general, there is no public right of navigation in a non-tidal river or inland lake; these are under the control of the riparian owners.[59] However, a right of navigation can arise by grant from those riparian owners, by statute or by prescriptive use, similar to the creation of a highway over land.

Where a right of navigation does exist, it does not extend to landing on the banks of the water, to towing along the bank, to mooring or to fishing: the consent of the owner is required for any of these purposes.

Statute is now involved in the regulation of rights in many non-tidal waters, particularly where public expense assisted in the formation of improved navigation. With docks and harbours, statute is usually the paramount legal governing factor.

---

[55] Water Act 1983, s.3.
[56] Water Resources Act 1973, s.24.
[57] *Lamb* v. *Newbiggin* [1844] 1 Car. & King 549.
[58] *Blount* v. *Layard* [1891] 2 Ch. 681.
[59] *Hargreaves* v. *Diddams* [1875] L.R. 10 Q.B. 582.

5. The Seaside

(1) Bathing

A local authority may make by-laws to regulate public bathing at the seaside.[60] The power is now in the Public Health Act 1936.[61] The by-laws may deal with areas of bathing, the times for bathing, the location of bathing huts or tents, the provision of life-saving appliances and the navigation of pleasure boats in relation to bathing areas. The by-laws may also regulate "so far as decency requires," the costumes to be worn by bathers.[62]

(2) The Foreshore

The foreshore is that part of the seashore which lies between the high and low water marks of ordinary spring tides. Seabed, lying below low water mark of medium tides, is Crown Estate property and the Crown's proprietary jurisdiction extends to the limit of territorial waters. The foreshore itself, around the coasts of the United Kingdom, is also in great part in the Crown Estate. The important exceptions include the counties of Cornwall and Lancaster, where the respective Duchies own the foreshore. The other exceptions are lengths of coast where grants have been made to individuals or other bodies, such as the National Trust, especially in some of the major estuaries.[63]

The term "foreshore" is a legal technical term.[64] "Seashore" has been treated, judicially, as equivalent[65] but "beach" was looked on as vague. It became important to define this area of land and its ownership when reclamation of land from the sea was undertaken in the sixteenth century. A subsequent treatise on the law of the sea in the seventeenth century supplied our modern definition of the foreshore.[66]

Baxendale v. *Instow P.C.*[67] raised a practical point about the definition of the foreshore in North Devon, under the Commons Registration Act 1965. The estate owners had a conveyance of 1855 which, in detailed wording and with the aid of a plan, identified a plot of land which "lay between high water mark and low water mark and (is) covered with water at ordin-

---

[60] For an academic discussion of whether a right to bathe in the sea exists, see *Brinckman* v. *Matley* [1904] 2 Ch. 313.
[61] s.231. (The power extends to rivers and lakes.) The purpose, 150 years ago, was to segregate the sexes. The wording has altered with successive Acts to that in the Public Health Act 1936, which seems a little out of date now. The model by-laws keep abreast of social mores.
[62] *Ibid.* s.231(1)(d).
[63] See The Crown Estate, HMSO 1980, annual report, para. 74. There are many examples of industrial development on the foreshore, given in this report.
[64] See *Tito* v. *Waddel (No. 2)* [1977] 2 W.L.R. 496 at p. 644, *per* Megarry V.-C.
[65] *Mellor* v. *Walmsley* [1905] 2 Ch. 164 at pp. 174, 175, 177 and 179.
[66] *De Jure Maris*:-Sir Matthew Hale. The Local Government Act 1972 describes local government areas on the coast as stretching at least to "the low water mark" (s.72), whilst the Countryside Act 1968, s.8, refers to country parks "bounded by the sea."
[67] [1981] 2 W.L.R. 1055.

ary tides." Since 1855, the sea had receded and left this plot standing above high water mark. Was the "high water mark" that which was inscribed on the 1855 conveyance or the mark to be seen on the ground by beachcombers in the 1960s?

The Devon County Council registered this strip of old foreshore as waste land of a manor under the Commons Registration Act 1965, *i.e.* as common land. Sir R. Megarry V.-C. ruled against the local authorities when this action was challenged in his Chancery court. The conveyance was so precise, he said, that it did not allow for the use of any rule about moveable freeholds. The land must be taken off the register, since the objection had been made and sustained by the successors of the 1855 conveyance.

Taking shingle

7.63   *Laird* v. *Briggs*[68] concerned an action by the tenant in possession of part of the foreshore at Margate to stop the defendant removing shingle from the shore. The defendant claimed 40 years prescription at first and he made the same claim for a right to place bathing huts on the beach. In the course of the case this claim was abandoned and the plaintiff won. The case is a simple illustration of the rights of a foreshore owner, here the Marquis of Conyngham, to charge for the rights enjoyed by others on the foreshore.

This case involved a personal plaintiff and a personal defendant. Some cases have related to the efforts of groups of persons to establish rights over the foreshore. The inhabitants of a village or of a parish are examples of these sorts of actions. As with other customary rights noted in Chapter 6, these foreshore claims have foundered if the class of persons making the claim has been fluctuating and thus undefinable.[69]

Taking mussels

7.64   *Loose* v. *Castleton*[70] related to a person who took mussels from a mussel scalp or bed on the coast of the Wash. Action in the courts was successful in bringing this practice to a stop. The plaintiff was the lessee of the alleged rights of shellfishery on that foreshore. The case turned on the historical merits of the plaintiff's claim. Though not precisely traceable to the time of Henry II, the title was, said the court, "in due course of law and must have been created before legal memory." There was evidence, said the court, of a lost grant of free fishery "almost if not completely without a break to the 11th century." (The Norfolk county archivist produced records of two manorial lordships for this purpose.)

7.65   *Brighton Corporation* v. *Packham*[71] was a case where the foreshore owner

---

[68] [1880] Ch.D. 440.
[69] *Beckett Ltd.* v. *Lyons* [1967] 1 All E.R. 833, where a claim to recover sea coal in the name of "the inhabitants of the County Palatine of Durham" was held to be too vague.
[70] (1978) 41 P. & C.R. 19 (C.A.).
[71] *Ibid.*

secured an injunction to restrain the defendants from holding religious meetings on the foreshore. There had been complaints by residents of nuisance and the Corporation took action accordingly. A defence that the practice had been followed from time immemorial was not made out. This was not a claim based on prescription, said Warrington J.; that would have to be by an individual. It was not based on custom: that would have to be a defined group of inhabitants. It was said to be a right of "the public" but the court said: "A right to hold public meetings on private property is not known to the law."

Llandudno U.D.C. v. *Woods*[72] is a useful case in defining rights on the foreshore. It is in line with all those above. The only rights of the public, said Cozens-Hardy J., were for navigation and fishing. Public meetings, similar to those in the Brighton case above, were therefore disallowed. The judge treated the matter as too trivial to justify the issue of an injunction: he simply granted a declaration. He also said: "The plaintiffs are entitled to treat every bather, every nursemaid with a perambulator, every boy riding a donkey and every preacher on the shore at Llandudno as a trespasser."

Lord Fitzhardinge v. *Purcell*[73] was in essence a successful claim by the owner of a foreshore to prevent the defendant from shooting and taking wild duck from that foreshore. It was memorable however for two reasons:

(a) The foreshore was not on the seacoast but in the tidal waters of the River Severn. It demonstrated a common application of the common law to both classes of foreshore.

(b) The defendant set up four heads of claim to shoot and take the wild duck:
   (i) As a prescriptive right of his ancestors: this failed due to lack of supporting evidence.
   (ii) As a trust implied in the original grants of the manors in favour of the inhabitants: this too failed for lack of evidence.
   (iii) As a member of the public, as being a right for all the King's subjects over the foreshore of a tidal navigable river: the court held that the public have no rights in such a place, except rights of navigation and fishing and rights ancillary thereto.
   (iv) As an inhabitant of the manors, by custom: this failed since a *profit à prendre* cannot be claimed by cusom.

The 30 page report is full of interest on the historical background of the law of the foreshore.

7.66

Conclusion

The position at common law is not always the position to be found in practice. The ownership or rights in the foreshore have from time to time

7.67

---

[72] [1899] 2 Ch. 705.
[73] [1908] 2 Ch. 139. The location of this case was Slimbridge in Gloucestershire. The drama of the leisure services has moved on from this first Act eighty years ago to the second Act, in which this is part of the home of the Wildfowl Trust, and wild ducks may fly, without fear, to its welcoming lagoons.

been granted to local authorities to enable them to be used for the benefit of the public resorting to the foreshore. Attention has earlier been drawn to the rights of local authorities to make by-laws regulating conduct on the seashore and adjoining promenades and esplanades. What this survey of the common law shows, is that the purely legal rights of the public on the foreshore may be limited, but local authorities, on behalf of the public, have scope to take initiatives to afford access to part of the country's finest leisure territory.

(3) Beach Activities

7.68 By way of conclusion, note is taken of three common beach activities, in the light of the body of law and history discussed above.

Deck chairs

The local authority may be the owners of the foreshore, in addition to the promenade at the top of the sea wall, the cliff top greens, gardens and walks. It may be that the authority are troubled about the growing habit of visitors to bring their own deck chairs and avoid payments to the authority's own hire service. To regulate the practice under local authority control, as they may wish, the authority will have to make by-laws. They need this specific legal sanction, before they can deal with those who might be inclined to challenge some more general legal claim to make charges.

Donkeys

7.69 When are donkeys on the beach part of a riding establishment? The earlier account of the Riding Establishment Acts of 1964 and 1970, showed that "hiring" was the essential feature of the practice, if the law is to bring such a business under the licensing system. If a youngster on a beach donkey is never allowed to ride it himself, it would seem that the animal has never been put into his possession and thus not "hired." This is the situation when the "donkey-boy" holds the bridle for the whole beach walk. If, however, the pony is hired out and the rider goes along the beach himself, the legal situation is different and, subject to other tests, the law about riding establishments is relevant.

Lobster catching

7.70 The law also monitors lobster catchers. For instance, on England's eastern coast nowadays, this leisure pursuit can only be safely followed under the aegis of the local District Fishery Committee, operating under the Sea Fisheries Regulation Act 1966. The duty of the Committee is to conserve stocks of lobsters and it has to work within the EEC Common Fisheries Policy. Hence Acts and Orders have prescribed minimum sizes of lobster that are catchable and, to complement that stipulation, other regulations about the size of the mesh for the lobster net.

Chapter 8

OPEN AIR ACTIVITY

"The timorous may stay at home"
Cardozo J.

INTRODUCTION

This chapter deals with a group of open air leisure activities. The largest, in legislative provision and in terrain, are the national and countryside parks. With them can conveniently be considered footpaths, caravans, and picnic sites, which have their own legislation.
The other subsections will deal with allotments, wildlife preservation and light railways.

8.01

A. Allotments

There are some half million allotments in this country,[1] forming part of what a Government spokesman recently described as "recreational gardening."[2] They are governed by a body of statute law, extending generally from 1908 to 1950, supported by very few cases in the law reports. Perhaps allotment gardeners have little time to spare for litigation!
The legal framework is easy to summarise, dealing as it does with the definition of allotments, their provision, the terms of letting, the basis for termination, compensation on yielding up allotments and the established legal bodies involved.

8.02

1. **Historical**

Allotments were originally small areas of land let by parish officers to the poor of the parish for cultivation. Alternatively, they were plots "allotted and awarded," under the Inclosure Acts, for the benefit of the poor.

8.03

---

[1] House of Commons debate on Local Government, Planning and Land Bill in Committee D, February 12, 1980. Mr. T. King col. 46. About one quarter of these are privately owned (Departmental Committee of Enquiry into Allotments, 1969 Cmnd. 4166, para. 320).
[2] *Ibid.* A Bill to confirm the status of a recreation for allotment gardening is currently in Parliament.

8.03

Another group were called "fuel allotments," since the rent derived from their letting by the parish was applied for the purchase of fuel for poor parishioners.[3] In one form or another, allotments were incidental to the administration of the Poor Law. As time passed, they were considered to be better managed on their own; when they numbered twenty or more under a vestry or trustees, then separate managing trustees were required.[4] Eventually, in 1894, management passed to local authorities.[5] The Small Holdings and Allotments Act 1908 marks the start of the modern era in legal control over allotments; by that Act, earlier ones were repealed and a general code of management prescribed.

An allotment is, by reference to the definitions in the Allotments Acts of 1922 and 1925, "an allotment garden, not exceeding 40 poles in extent, which is wholly or mainly cultivated by the occupier for the production of vegetables or fruit crops, for consumption by himself or his family."[6] Not being used for trade or business, the allotment is not agricultural land.[7]

2. The Statutes

8.04 The Allotment Acts 1908 to 1950 comprise the Small Holdings and Allotment Act 1908 (so far as it relates to allotments), the Land Settlement (Facilities) Act 1919 (with the same qualification), the Allotment Acts respectively of 1922 and 1925, as much of the Agricultural Land (Utilisation) Act 1931 as relates to allotments and the Allotments Act 1950.[8]

By the Emergency Laws (Miscellaneous Provisions) Act 1953, s.5, local authorities are empowered to let to tenants or tenants' associations, for allotments, land initially occupied by local authorities[9] under Defence Regulation 62A of the Defence (General) Regulations 1939.

A duty to provide and let allotments is laid upon the local authorities, which since the Local Government Act 1972 are the allotments authorities. These are district councils and, where the parish decides to exercise the function, the parish councils.[10] This duty arises where the authority are of the opinion that "there is a demand for allotments."[11] It involves acquiring land and if this cannot be obtained by agreement, compulsory powers are available.[12]

---

[3] Allotments Act 1832, s.8.
[4] Poor Allotments Act 1873, ss.3–4.
[5] Local Government Act 1894, s.33.
[6] Act of 1922, s.22; Act of 1925, s.1.
[7] Agriculture Act 1947, s.109.
[8] Plainly this miscellany of statutes is in need of codification and the Government has indicated that such a measure is at the planning stage (n. 1 *supra*).
[9] *i.e.* City of London, metropolitan and other district councils and county councils.
[10] See DOE Circular 121/72, Local Government Act 1972 Sched. 29, Pt. II, and Act of 1908, s.23. Where the population is more than 10,000, the Act of 1950, s.9, limits the duty of provision to allotments not exceeding one eighth of an acre in extent.
[11] A representation by 6 or more registered electors for allotments in the locality is to be one recognised as calling for due consideration: s.23, *ibid*.
[12] The powers are in the Allotments Act 1908 s.25.

There are certain lands which cannot be taken for this purpose. These are part of a public park, garden or pleasure ground; part of a home farm, occupied with a mansion house; property of the National Trust; woodland or land required for the amenity of a dwellinghouse.[13] Certain other limits are placed on taking farm land, which might displace workers or which, being less than 50 acres, would take away an occupier's principal means of livelihood.[14]

3. Terms of Letting

With some of the Poor Law lettings were requirements that the occupier should "cultivate to preserve in a due state of fertility." A local authority managing allotments has power under the Allotments Acts to improve the land, with drainage, fencing, roads and suitable buildings.[15] The statutory provisions bearing upon lettings are as follows[16]:

(a) Avoid undue preference in lettings.
(b) Comply with the Allotments Rules (Model Rules are available[17]).
(c) Sub-letting is forbidden without local authority consent, as landlords.[18]
(d) Clauses in a tenancy agreement purporting to restrict the keeping of hens and rabbits are forbidden.[19]
(e) It is permitted to let allotments to an association or to persons working on a co-operative basis, provided that the division of profits among members is forbidden or restricted.[20]
(f) The rent charged must be "such as a tenant may reasonably be expected to pay for the land, taking into account the proposed terms."[21] Not more than one quarter of the rent can be made payable in advance, except where the rent is below a stipulated amount.
(g) The allotment is rate free.[22]

4. **Offences**

The Allotment Acts prescribe offences for damaging growing crops, fences or buildings. To support a prosecution, there must be a notice about these offences on display on the site.[23]

---

[13] Act of 1908, s.41, and Act of 1919, ss.16 and 28.
[14] Act of 1908, s.41; Act of 1919, s.16.
[15] Act of 1908, s.26.
[16] *Ibid.* s.28.
[17] *Ibid.*
[18] *Ibid.* s.28(4).
[19] Allotments Act 1950, s.12.
[20] Act of 1908, s.27(6).
[21] Act of 1950, s.10.
[22] General Rate Act 1967, s.263.
[23] Act of 1922, s.19.

5. Termination

8.06 A notice to quit for 12 months or more, is required to terminate the letting of an allotment. This must expire in the winter or close season, *i.e.* September 29 to April 6.[24]

The above is the normal situation. An exception is permitted in that three months is legally sufficient if such is provided in the tenancy agreement for a reason which is realised. This is that the land is needed for building or mining or some industrial use or for roads or sewers.[25] A similar exception is available when it is a housing use that is stipulated and realised.[26]

The last exception of this nature is when some other non-agricultural use is stipulated in the tenancy agreement as a contingency which might result in the land being needed on short notice. Then at least three months notice is needed "except in emergency."[27]

There is also the traditional basis for terminating any tenancy, *i.e.* that the rent has fallen into arrear, or that there is a breach of covenant or that bankruptcy or, in the case of a company, liquidation, has taken place. Re-entry by the landlord is allowed.[28] These provisions are necessary in law for special situations: the reality is that many allotment tenancies last for life.

Reference should be made to the situation where the local authority is itself the tenant of land used for allotments. An indication of the protection Parliament wished to give to allotments is seen in the provision, that if notice to quit is served upon the local authority, as tenant, the authority can serve counter notice and go to arbitration, if desired, on whether the termination has been put in hand in good faith.[29]

6. Compensation

8.07 On determination of an allotment tenancy, compensation is payable by the landlord in respect of:
    (i) Growing crops and fertilisers upon the land.[30] The basis is their value to an incoming tenant. This is on the footing that the tenancy has been duly terminated by re-entry or notice to quit.
    (ii) In respect of the disturbance, a sum equal to one year's rent.[31]

The tenant may remove bushes, fruit trees, and associated huts or sheds he has been using.

For his part, the landlord is legally entitled to counter-claim from the

---

[24] Act of 1922, s.1, and see *Wombwell U.D.C.* v. *Burke* [1966] 2 Q.B. 149, where the question of effectiveness of such a notice reached the Court of Appeal.
[25] Act of 1922, s.1(1)(*b*).
[26] *Ibid.* s.1(1)(*d*).
[27] *Ibid.* s.1(1)(*c*).
[28] *Ibid.* s.1(1)(*e*).
[29] *Ibid.* s.11.
[30] *Ibid.* s.2.
[31] Act of 1950, s.3.

tenant for deterioration, if he can make out a claim that the land has not been maintained in a good condition of cultivation and fertility.[32]

7. Administration

The Secretary of State for the Department of the Environment is the Minister with responsibility for allotment regulation. **8.08**

Local authorities are encouraged to promote allotment societies and associations.[33] It is normal for them to run annual prize competitions for well kept allotments. Local authorities are empowered to make financial advances to allotment societies.[34]

Such societies have the right to the free use of school rooms to facilitate meetings on allotment problems.[35]

A local authority has power to make Rules about allotments.[36] They will be made and confirmed like by-laws.

Allotment management is a function which a parish council is empowered to undertake. If it does, then in its area, the district council does not do so.[37]

8. The Present Day

In the case of *Harwood* v. *Borough of Reigate and Banstead*,[38] an allotment tenant successfully challenged an increase of his annual rent of more than 300 per cent. The case was said to be the first in thirty years on the section in the Allotments Act 1950 which stipulates that the rent should be "such as the tenant may reasonably be expected to pay."[39] **8.09**

The facts were simply that an increase in the plaintiff's annual rent for his allotment in 1976–77 from 90p to £3, was followed in 1977–78 by a proposed new rent of £10. In his case, the plaintiff drew attention to the provisions in the Act of 1950 and other Allotment Acts, which gave guidance on what Parliament had implied by "reasonably" in the above section 10. The section provided that the local authority as landlord "can charge less if the circumstances of that person (*i.e.* the tenant) warrant it."[40]

Another section in the Act of 1950 indicated the latest step by Parliament in the financing of allotments. In the Act of 1908, it was provided

---

[32] *Ibid.* s.4.
[33] Act of 1908, s.49. A proposal by the Government to amend s.8 of the Act of 1908 and abandon the role as final arbiter, on a proposal by a local authority to dispose of allotment land for other use, was withdrawn after combined opposition resistance. (See debate referred in n. 1, *supra*).
[34] Act of 1908, s.49.
[35] Education Act 1944, ss.9 and 120, and Act of 1908, s.35.
[36] Act of 1908, s.28.
[37] Local Government Act 1972, s.251.
[38] (1980) 43 P. & C.R. 336.
[39] Act of 1950, s.10.
[40] *Ibid.*

8.09 OPEN AIR ACTIVITY

that allotments should not be a burden on the rates. In 1922, the Allotments Act was requiring income and expenditure to balance. By 1950, however, the Allotments Act was placing a maximum rate product on the monies to be spent in providing allotments.[41] From this, the court in *Harwood's* case accepted the argument of the plaintiff, that Parliament expected allotments to be subsidised, like other recreational activities. This was the crucial item in the eventual decision of that court in the plaintiff's favour. A significant change in Government thinking was noted. The decision of the court was as follows:

(1) The rent sought under section 10 should be that appropriate from a notional rather than an actual tenant.

(2) All relevant circumstances should be taken into account, in a broad common-sense way, using the expression about settling a "reasonable rent" used by Lord Greene, M.R. in an earlier case.[42]

(3) The evidence was accepted that allotment gardening was a recreational activity, to be subsidised like other such activities.

(4) An increase in rent should be in line with the annual increase for other recreational activities. It was not for the court to determine the new rent. It had been asked for a declaration about the legal basis on which rent under section 10 should be assessed and that declaration was given, on the lines here set out.[43]

B. WILDLIFE PRESERVATION

8.10 This section considers the current legal protection available for birds, animals and plants in this country. The present Act is the Wildlife and Countryside Act 1981 and this consolidated certain Protection of Birds Acts, so that provisions of a similar nature might be brought together. Whilst there are points at which this protective legislation touches on aspects of the national conservation policies and laws, these are best considered separately.

1. Protection of Birds

8.11 The Act of 1981 re-enacts the Protection of Birds Acts 1954–1967, so that it is an offence intentionally:
   1. To kill, injure or take away any wild bird.
   2. To take, damage or destroy its nest whilst in use.
   3. To take or destroy an egg of a wild bird.
   4. To disturb such a bird, whilst building its nest or in its nest, whilst

---

[41] *Ibid.* s.11, duly converted by the Decimal Currency Act 1960 to O.8p in the pound. The same Act repealed s.11(1) of the 1950 Act as superfluous, leaving the effective control in the Act of 1922.

[42] The sentence comes from *Cumming* v. *Danson* (1943) 112 L.J.K.B. 145, as quoted in *John Kay Ltd.* v. *Kay* [1952] 2 Q.B. 258 at p. 264.

[43] The case illustrates the changed social status and popularity of allotments.

containing eggs or young, or to disturb the dependent young of such a bird.[44]

Some seventy or more wild birds are listed in a Schedule to the Act of 1981. For the above offences committed in relation to such birds, a "special penalty" is enacted, *i.e.* a fine not exceeding £1,000, as compared with a normal maximum fine of £200.

Exceptions are made for actions outside the close season[45] (generally, February to September, inclusive), in relation to these birds and also for authorised persons,[46] who include the owners and occupiers of the land where the birds are, in relation to a second short list of thirteen common birds which are thought to do damage. These include crows, gulls, magpies and house-sparrows and their killing is not an offence when in the interests of public health, preventing the spread of disease, or preventing serious damage to livestock, crops or agricultural needs.

Certain *methods* of killing or taking wild birds are forbidden, as traps or electrical stunning devices and various specified guns or other weapons and equipment, the use of decoys and other devious methods and the use of vehicles for chasing wild birds. Again, there are exceptions for authorised persons and, in the case of wild ducks and game birds, for particular circumstances.

The sale or offer for sale or advertising in relation to these protected birds, or their eggs, is another offence. It is also an offence to enter them in competitions.

Certain captive birds can be registered and marked in circumstances prescribed in Regulations but associated offences relate to the conditions in which such birds may be kept. Poultry are excluded from this group of exceptions.

2. Protection of Animals

The Act re-enacts the Conservation of Wild Creatures and Wild Plants Act 1975. It also effects amendments to the Deer Act 1963, the Badgers Act 1973 and the Conservation of Seals Act 1970.

Some forty animals, ranging from the toad to the swallowtail butterfly and from otters to snails and grass snakes, are protected by a series of provisions similar to those summarised above in relation to birds. The intentional killing, injuring or taking of these animals are the basic offences and then associated offences are contained in the Act of 1981 in connection with the sale, offer for sale, advertisement with a view to disposal, and also the intentional spoliation of the dens, lairs or shelters of these animals. Again, there are exceptions on the same lines as for the birds described above and a list of forbidden methods and devices for killing and taking these animals.

---

[44] *Ibid.* s.1(5).
[45] *Ibid.* s.2,
[46] *Ibid.* s.27. This includes the owner, the occupier, a person authorised by the local authority, the water authority or the Nature Conservancy Council. In these last three groups, however, the authorisation does not confer any legal right of entry to the land.

3. Protection of Plants

8.13 The essential offences are the picking, uprooting or destroying of some sixty listed wild plants. There are also offences for selling or advertising for sale these plants when either dead or alive.

In any legal proceedings, a plant is deemed in law to have been a wild plant within the Act, until the contrary is proved.

4. New Species

The Act of 1981 creates an offence for introducing into the wild an animal which is not ordinary resident in, and not a regular visitor to, Great Britain, in a wild state. A list is then given of some forty illustrative animals, from the coypu and the gerbil to the porcupines and the zander, though this is not exhaustive.

There is a defence in the statute, in this instance, that all reasonable steps were taken and all due care exercised to avoid the commission of this offence.

5. General

8.14 There are exceptions in the Act of 1981 for various classes of scientific work, whether taking the form of photography, education, conservation or other ways. Licences to protect such operations are obtainable from the Secretary of State or other appropriate minister or from the Nature Conservancy Council.

There are offences in relation to false statements made in order to obtain such licences. The Secretary of State has the responsibility of establishing advisory bodies in the specialised fields described above. The Secretary of State is empowered to vary the schedules of birds, animals and plants, to take account of changing scientific information and advice. Police constables have powers of arrest for certain suspected offences listed above.

The Nature Conservancy Council is made responsible for advising the Secretary of State on the animals and plants considered suitable for inclusion in the Schedules to the Act of 1981. Background legal information about that Council is found in the Nature Conservancy Act 1973, where it is given a special responsibility for the maintenance and management of nature reserves in National Parks. The Council's statutory function is particularly in relation to the conservation of flora, fauna, geological or physiographical features. It has to produce annual reports about its work and is subject to directions from the Secretary of State. Once a nature reserve is brought into being, it becomes an offence to harm its features without prior consent from the Council.

Local authorities are to bring to the notice of the public and particularly schoolchildren the Part of this Act and Orders made under it which affect their own area. Local authorities also have power to take proceedings for the offences under this Act of 1981.

C. Light Railways

8.15 There are some fifty private railways in use in this country at the present time, which use the standard gauge or the narrow gauge. These are not all used for leisure pursuits; some are in use industrially, in association with factories, quarries or docks. There was an instance in the Conway Mussel Fishery Light Railway Order in 1975. But many are for holiday-makers, in conjunction with railway enthusiasts. Examples are to be found in the attractive scenery of the North Yorkshire Moors railway in its National Park or the Worth Valley railway in West Yorkshire.

It is the Light Railways Acts of 1896 and 1912, which form the legal framework for this comparatively small leisure service. Those Acts were passed to simplify the legislative requirements for authorising the construction of these railways, which were of a local nature. It was in the rural, sparsely populated areas that such railways were needed and the likely amount of traffic was not thought to justify full Parliamentary proceedures and their expenses.

The legal procedures then devised have, fortunately, been found suitable for the private light railways of our day; though in the leisure context, it is not necessary to raise all the commercial and land questions that the Ministry of Transport would investigate otherwise.[47]

8.16 When appraising a new application for an Order under the Light Railways Acts, to authorise a leisure service line, the Ministry, under the terms of these Acts, enquire about:

1. The safety of the public.
2. Objections to the application.
3. The attitude and location of nearby residents.
4. The financial prospects of the application.

Certainly, if there is some clearly foreseeable danger, the application will be declined.[48]

The legal framework, within which the application is studied, is contained in the Acts of 1896 and 1912 (as amended) and in the rules of procedure, laid down in 1927 and revised in 1962[49]:

 1. A light railway company includes any person or body of persons, who are authorised to construct, or who are the owners or lessees of, any light railway authorised by the Light Railways Act 1896, or who are working that railway under a working agreement.[50]

---

[47] "Light railway," as such, is not defined in the Acts. This gave rise, at one point, to strenuous argument whether a tramway might not be a "light railway," at least for certain rating benefits. See *Wakefield Corporation* v. *Wakefield and District Light Railway Co.* [1908] A.C. 293 and especially in the Court of Appeal [1907] 2 K.B. 257.

[48] Railways Act 1921, s.68(1)(*b*): "take all such matters into consideration." And see *Rother Valley Rail Co. Ltd.* v. *Ministry of Transport* [1971] Ch. 515 C.A. Also Act of 1896, s.9.

[49] Ministry of Transport (Light Railways Procedure) Rules 1927 (S.R.O. 1927 No. 196), and Ministry of Transport (Light Railways Procedure) (Amendment) Rules 1962 (S.I. 1962 No. 1806).

[50] Light Railways Act 1896, s.28.

2. A promoter can be a local authority, a corporation, a company or an individual.[51]

3. An application must go before the Ministry of Transport; a century ago it went to three Light Railway Commissioners. The pattern of the procedure has not altered significantly.[52] The Railway Acts apply as far as appropriate in relation to standards of operation and safety.[53] The Department of Trade and Industry has to concur in any approval; there must be available finance and amenity considerations must also be met.

4. The successful application results in the making of a Light Railway Order by Statutory Instrument, under the Acts of 1896 and 1912.[54]

5. As mentioned above, local authorities may be associated with an application and in fact, several such authorities have done this, in liaison with the promoters. Few have been active operators themseles.[55]

6. The Acts contain an offence for operating a light railway in contravention of any of the conditions attached to a consent by the Minister of Transport.[56]

7. The most recent Act of Parliament, with a short direct reference to this subject, is the Transport Act 1968.[57]

D. NATIONAL PARKS AND ACCESS TO THE COUNTRYSIDE

Historical background

8.17   As a social counterweight to the industrialisation of this country in the last century, amenity societies began to emerge. On the one hand, vast areas of hitherto open and pleasant land were gathered into the growing towns and coalescing urban areas, whilst on the other, groups of people created new associations, which sought the preservation and protection of the remaining countryside. The Commons Preservation Society, the Ramblers Association, the Council for the Preservation of Rural England and the National Trust become powerful lobbies for their various causes. They can take great credit for awakening fellow citizens and a series of Governments to the need for, and the value of, open space and open air recreation.

The first aims of successive governments in the face of the tremendous growth in population and in urban life were high standards of public sanitation, control over diseases and building construction. Attention then

---

[51] *Ibid.* s.2(*b*).
[52] *Ibid.* ss.2, 7 and 9.
[53] *Ibid.* s.12.
[54] It was the Railway Act 1921 which transferred the approving function from the Light Railway Commissioners to the then Ministry of Transport. The power is currently with the Department of the Environment, by virtue of S.I. 1970 No. 1681.
[55] Act of 1896, s.3. There are 5 at the time of going to press, which include s.3 in their Orders, though a private company is the operator, under lease. These are, by reference to their Orders, the Midland Centre, the Shackerstone and Bosworth, the Isle of Wight (Havenstreet and Wooton), the Loughborough and Birstall and the British Railways Board (Minehead Branch).
[56] Regulation of Railways Act 1868, s.28.
[57] s.121(4). The latest Order is the Severn Valley Light Railway Order 1984.

NATIONAL PARKS AND ACCESS TO THE COUNTRYSIDE   **8.17**

turned to increasing the nation's housing stock and to town and country planning.[58] By the middle of the nineteenth century, central government was actively encouraging the concept of the countryside for air and exercise. The pendulum has now swung so far in this direction that a number of statutory duties are imposed on public bodies requiring them, in the performance of those functions, to take into account "the desirability of conserving the natural beauty and amenity of the countryside."

The Statutes

The Countryside Act 1968 imposes a duty on every Minister, government department and public body to have regard in the exercise of their functions to this objective.[59] The Act also requires all Ministers, the Countryside Commission, the Nature Conservancy Council and local authorities in the exercise of their functions under the National Parks and Access to the Countryside Act 1949 (the Act of 1949), to have due regard to the needs of agriculture and forestry and to the economic and social interests of rural areas.[60] The Wildlife and Countryside Act 1981, (the Act of 1981) imposes on the Minister of Agriculture, Fisheries and Food, the duty, when giving free advice under an earlier Act,[61] to include advice to persons carrying on agricultural businesses, about the conservation and enhancement of the natural beauty and amenity of the countryside, as well as the other benefits to the rural economy.[62]   **8.18**

A similar principle is enshrined in the procedure for a farm capital grant under the Agricultural Act 1970; if a grant is refused, because the local authority has objected to the proposal for which the grant was sought, on the grounds that it would have an adverse effect on the natural beauty or amenity of the countryside or its enjoyment by the public, then the local authority must offer to enter into a management agreement with the applicant.[63]

Water authorities, in the discharge of their functions, must have regard to the conservation and enhancement of natural beauty and the conservation of flora, fauna and geological or physiographical features of special interest. They are also to have regard to the desirability of protecting buildings and other objects of archaeological, architectural or historic interest.[64]

1. The Countryside Commission

The main body of law on access to the countryside is now to be found in these Acts of 1949, 1968 and 1981, as amended by other major statutes   **8.19**

---

[58] A useful account can be found in Sir Desmond Heap, *Outline of Planning Law*, Ch.1 (8th ed., 1982, Sweet and Maxwell).
[59] The Act of 1968, s.11.
[60] *Ibid.* s.37.
[61] The Agriculture (Miscellaneous Provisions) Act 1944, s.1.
[62] The Act of 1981, s.41.
[63] Agriculture Act 1970, s.29, and see below, para. 8.42.
[64] Act of 1981, s.48 (amending Water Act 1973, s.22).

8.19   Open Air Activity

such as the Water Act 1973 and the Nature Conservancy Council Act 1973. The Act of 1949 established the National Parks Commission, whose title was changed by the Act of 1968 to the Countryside Commission.[65] The Commission is a corporate body not to be regarded as a Crown agent or holding property on behalf of the Crown.[66] The Chairman and members are appointed by the Secretary of State; a separate Committee of the Commission is appointed for Wales.[67] In its obligatory annual report, the Commission is to give a statement of action taken to promote the interests of disabled persons in the countryside.[68] Whilst the Commission may acquire land for their functions, land occupied by the Commission is to be regarded for rating purposes as land or property occupied by the Crown.[69]

8.20   The main general duties of the Commission under the above three Acts are:

(a) the preservation and enhancement of natural beauty in England and Wales, particularly in designated National Parks and in areas of outstanding natural beauty,

(b) encouraging the provision or improvement of facilities for persons resorting to National Parks, and

(c) promoting the enjoyment of the Parks and of the opportunities for open air recreation and study of nature.[70]

The Minister may give directions to the Commission for the exercise of their functions.[71] Those functions were enlarged by the Act of 1968 to include wider responsibilities for the conservation and enhancement of the natural beauty and amenity of the countryside and for encouraging the provision and improvement of facilities for the enjoyment of the countryside and of open air recreation.[72]

The Commission may charge for its services. It may also accept gifts and contributions which assist its work. It is also empowered to do anything conducive or incidental to its functions.[73]

The Commission is required to hold a watching brief over all countryside matters and to advise and assist all persons who submit proposals to them. It must also confer with local planning authorities.[74]

Where special problems arise, the Commission may arrange for their own staff, or consultants engaged by them, to be available to the local authorities or other persons who are submitting proposals. The Commission can provide publicity and other information services.[75] The Com-

---

[65] Act of 1981, s.47 and Sched. 13 now govern the constitution of the Countryside Commission.
[66] *Ibid.* Sched. 13, para. 2.
[67] *Ibid.* para. 5.
[68] *Ibid.* para. 13.
[69] *Ibid.* paras. 14 and 15.
[70] Act of 1949, ss.5 and 6.
[71] Act of 1949, s.3.
[72] Act of 1968, s.1.
[73] *Ibid.* s.1.
[74] *Ibid.* s.2.
[75] *Ibid.* s.2(5).

mission also have the power to engage in experimental schemes in the performance of their functions. In these, they are enjoined to consult with local or other interested authorities; they are given power to acquire land, erect buildings, carry out other works and, with the approval of the Minister, undertake the management of the project.[76]

2. **National Parks**

(1) *Designation*

One of the prime functions of the Countryside Commission is the designation of National Parks. These comprise extensive tracts of countryside in England and Wales where it appears desirable to the Commission that steps should be taken to promote their enjoyment by the public.[77] The factors to be taken into account by the Commission in designating such areas, are their natural beauty and the opportunities they afford for open air recreation by reason of their character and their situation, in relation to centres of population.

The procedure for the designation of a National Park is set out in the Acts of 1949 and 1981.[78] The local planning authorities in the area must be consulted; there are extensive requirements, about publication of the proposal; should objections be received, then a resulting public inquiry must receive ample publicity, as must the confirmation of the Designation Order in due course, if that result should follow.

Well known National Parks include the Lake District, the Peak District, the Yorkshire Dales, Dartmoor, Snowdonia, Pembrokeshire and the Brecon Beacons.

(2) *Duties in a Park*

The more important duties of the Commission in a designated Park are as follows[79]:

1. To make recommendations to the local authorities in the Park and the Minister of appropriate action to promote its enjoyment by the public.
2. To keep the objectives in paragraph 8.20, above, under review.
3. To advise the relevant planning authorities of ongoing arrangements for the management of the Park.
4. To provide information about the Parks, their access, accommodation and facilities.[80]
5. To provide facilities to enable people to learn about the history and natural features of the Park.

---

[76] *Ibid.* s.4, as amended by the Act of 1981, s.40. The former need for the consent of the Secretary of State has been removed.
[77] Act of 1949, ss.5, 6 and 7.
[78] *Ibid.* s.7.
[79] *Ibid.* s.6.
[80] *Ibid.* s.86.

8.22   Open Air Activity

6. To publish recommended codes of conduct in the countryside.

7. To maintain regular liaison with local planning authorities and the Minister about planning applications affecting the Park.

(3) Long Distance Routes

8.23   A related function of the Commission is the creation of long distance routes, for the making of extensive journeys on foot, horseback or by bicycle (not motorised).[81] The Commission is required to submit reports to the Minister on the possible provision of such routes, and dealing with matters such as the maintenance or improvement of existing public paths and roads used as public paths, and the provision of new paths, ferries and facilities for accommodation, meals and refreshments. Suggestions may also be made for the restriction of traffic on existing routes. The estimated capital and revenue costs of the Commission's proposals are also to be included. The Commission must consult any affected Joint Planning Boards, and the county and district councils whose areas will be traversed by the route. The Ministers, after considering the report, may approve a proposal relating to a long distance route with or without modifications, or reject it and must inform the local authorities of his decision.[82]

Highway authorities

It becomes the duty of the highway authorities, through whose areas the route passes, to enforce the public's right to use the route. Penalties are provided for putting up any notice containing false information with a view to deterring the public from using the route. The highway authorities on either side of water crossed by the route may provide a ferry service or make arrangements for another person to provide one but the exercise of this power is not to prejudice any other ferry operator.

The local planning authorities along the route may provide, or make arrangements to provide, accommodation, meals and refreshments (including intoxicating liquor) but authorities may only provide these services themselves if the existing ones are not satisfactory or adequate.[83]

(4) Local Planning Authorities

8.24   As stated above, local planning authorities are to confer with the Countryside Commission in the preparation of development plans. Further, county planning authorities, whose areas include a National Park, are required to publish maps which show areas of moor and heath, which are especially important to conserve.[84] In respect of such areas, the Depart-

---

[81] *Ibid.* ss.51–57.
[82] *Ibid.* s.52.
[83] Act of 1949, s.54. Howard Hill, *Freedom to Roam* (1980, Moorland Publishing) is a fascinating study of the history of the ramblers clubs as a force for the creation of some of these routes.
[84] Act of 1981, s.43.

ment of the Environment for Wales and the same department in conjunction with the Ministry of Agriculture, Fisheries and Food, in respect of England, can make Orders:
  (i) To stop ploughing into agricultural land of such areas, if 20 years have passed since that land was last used for agricultural purposes.
  (ii) On the other hand, to forbid any agricultural operation or forestry work which would be likely to change the character and appearance of the moor or heath.[85]

Landowners have certain legal rights of representation and objection during the procedure to be followed before such Orders are final.

(5) *Powers of the Minister*

In addition to the powers in relation to moor and heath, the Minister has power to acquire land in a Park. He is expected, however, to transfer it to other bodies or trusts.[86] The Minister additionally has power to acquire land to afford public access to a Park.[87] His important power to give directions to the Countryside Commission has already been noted above.

(6) *Administration of a National Park*

The administration of a National Park is the responsibility of a Special Planning Board, in the case of the Peak District and the Lake District. For the other National Parks, a National Park Committee is appointed, in accordance with procedure in the Local Government Act 1972. County and district councils are both involved in the appointment of members of the Committees.[88]

8.25

It falls to these committees, under the Local Government Act 1972 to produce and review every five years National Park plans, embodying their ongoing policy for managing the respective Parks and fulfilling their statutory objectives.[89]

Wardens may be appointed in respect of any land or waterway for which by-laws may be made and in respect of land within a National Park to which section 193 of the Law of Property Act 1925 applies.[90]

8.26

There is a wider power to appoint wardens in respect of land in a National Park or in the countryside, to which the public are allowed access and where wardens may not be appointed under the provisions of the 1949 and 1968 Acts. In such cases the only function of the wardens is

---

[85] Act of 1981, s.42.
[86] Act of 1949, s.14.
[87] *Ibid.* s.77.
[88] Local Government Act 1972, Sched. 17 and Act of 1981, s.46. With these should be read D.O.E. Circ. 63/73 on Local Government Act 1972 and the Administration of National Parks. This explains the areas for agency arrangements by National Park Committees with district councils and planning authorities. The earlier Circular 65/74 contained extensive guidance on the National Park Plans.
[89] Act of 1949, s.92 (amended by ss.41/42 of the Act of 1968).
[90] *Ibid.*

8.26 to advise and assist the public. Wardens may also be appointed for footpaths and bridleways.[91]

8.27 Local planning authorities may, at the request of and in accordance with terms prescribed by the Countryside Commission, make arrangements for securing the provision in their areas of study centres and other facilities for enabling the public to learn about the features of the National Park and its associated facilities.[92]

8.28 Where any part of a National Park is bounded by the sea or a waterway, the local planning authority is empowered to carry out such works and do other things for facilitating the use of the waters and it has additional powers to regulate the use of waters with by-laws.[93]

3. Areas of Outstanding Natural Beauty

8.29 Apart from these extensive duties in relation to National Parks, the Commission has a general duty to advise on natural beauty and to advise the Minister on matters which could prejudice the natural beauty of this country.[94] Orders designating areas of outstanding natural beauty may be made by the Commission and powers are available, similar to those for National Parks,[95] for their protection. These are normally smaller areas and examples of the many areas thus designated are the Malvern Hills, the Quantock Hills, the Forest of Bowland, Cannock Chase, Anglesey, the Solway coast and the Wye Valley.

By-laws, access agreements and plans for any development, in or affecting such areas, would normally follow the making of these Orders.

4. Country Parks

8.30 The Act of 1968 extended the access of the public to open land, by creating the concept of Country Parks. The underlying principle is the provision or improvement of opportunities for the enjoyment of the countryside by the public.[96] Local authorities[97] are to have regard to the location of the relevant area, in relation to an urban or built-up area and to the availability and adequacy of existing facilities for the enjoyment of the countryside by the public. These powers are available within and outside the area of the local authority exercising them.[98]

8.31 A local authority has power to provide a Country Park, defined as a park or pleasure ground to be used as a country park, on any suitable site

---

[91] Act of 1981, s.62.
[92] Act of 1968, s.12.
[93] Act of 1968, s.13. See also Chap. 7.
[94] Act of 1949, s.85.
[95] *Ibid.* ss.87/88.
[96] Act of 1968, s.6.
[97] *i.e.* County and District councils, the Greater London Council (or its successor authority), the City of London Common Council, the London Borough Councils and a National Park Joint Planning Board.
[98] Act of 1968, s.6(3).

in the countryside.[99] The authority may manage and maintain the park in particular by erecting buildings, carrying out works, providing facilities for meals, refreshments, parking and sheltering and facilities and services for open air recreation (not including organised games). Accommodation, meals and refreshments can only be provided by the local authority if no other satisfactory facilities exist. Local authorities have extensive powers to acquire land for the purpose of creating a country park but their powers may be exercised in respect of land in the ownership of another person with his agreement. The power may also be exercised in respect of an existing park or pleasure ground already owned by the authority, subject to the terms of any trust affecting it.[1] Similarly, a Country Park can be designated for any land acquired under Part V of the 1949 Act for access to open land. A country park is not subject to any of the enactments which regulate public parks and pleasure grounds as described in Chapter 4, namely[2]:

Section	Act
164	Public Health Act 1875
44	Public Health Acts Amendment Act 1890
76 & 77	,, ,, ,, ,, ,, 1907
56	,, ,, ,, Act 1925

Apart from the general powers given to provide facilities in country parks, local authorities are given specific powers in respect of waterways situated in country parks.[3] These powers are dealt with in Chapter 7. Reference has already been made in Chapter 2 to the powers of local authorities in respect of land taken out of the common.land.[4]

5. Access Arrangements and Local Authorities

General administration

The 1949 Act created opportunities for public access to and enjoyment of open land in private ownership by giving local planning authorities a range of powers to secure access to open country for open air recreation.[5]

8.32

For the purposes of Part V of the Act, "open country" means any area appearing to the authority with whom an access agreement is made, or to the authority by whom an access order is made or by whom the area is acquired, as the case may be, to consist wholly or predominantly of mountain, moor, heath, down, cliff, or foreshore, (including any bank, barrier, dune, beach, flat or other land adjacent to the foreshore).[6] To this definition was added by the 1968 Act, woodlands in the countryside. Rivers

---

[99] *Ibid.* s.7.
[1] *Ibid.* s.7(5).
[2] *Ibid.* s.7(7).
[3] *Ibid.* s.8, as part of water recreation.
[4] *Ibid.* s.9.
[5] See Act of 1949, Pt. V, as amended by the Acts of 1968 and 1981.
[6] Act of 1949, s.59.

8.32   OPEN AIR ACTIVITY

and canals in the countryside were also added by the 1968 Act, except in relation to reservoirs owned or managed by statutory undertakers or a river authority and canals owned or managed by the British Waterways Board. Where land outside a National Park is adjacent to a river or canal and the local authority proposes to make an access agreement or order in relation to it, the authority should consult with and obtain the agreement of the river authority and such other authorities as the Minister may direct. By section 74, these provisions of Part V of the 1949 Act apply to waterways in a National Park as they apply to open country.[7] The provisions relating to access do not apply to Epping Forest, Burnham Beeches or to National Trust land.[8]

(1) Reviews

8.33   Local planning authorities are under a duty to review their areas to ascertain whether any open country needs to be opened up to public access for their own inhabitants or for persons not living in their areas.[9] If a local authority, after a review, are of the opinion that there are no, or no appreciable, areas of open country or that no action needs to be taken to provide access, they have to inform the Minister of the fact and publish a notice in the London Gazette of their findings.[10] Otherwise, the authority must prepare a map showing such areas and a statement of their proposed action to afford public access.[11]

(2) Access Orders and Agreements

8.34   Access to open land in private ownership can be obtained with the agreement of the owners of the land or, alternatively, by means of an access order.

An access agreement may be irrevocable or subject to such conditions as may be agreed between the authority and the land owner.[12] These may provide for the payment of contributions for the facilities made available. The Countryside Commission must be consulted, if the access affects a National Park.[13]

An access order can be made if the authority find that an access agreement or a series of access agreements proves impracticable. Both access agreements and orders may provide for new means of access as well as maintaining existing ones.[14] The access order cannot relate to land which is in an already concluded access agreement.[15]

---

[7] *Ibid.* s.74.
[8] *Ibid.* ss.112–113.
[9] *Ibid.* s.61.
[10] *Ibid.* s.62.
[11] *Ibid.* s.63.
[12] *Ibid.* s.64.
[13] *Ibid.* s.65. The Commission may ask the local authority to make an Access Order, under s.65(5).
[14] Act of 1949, s.51.
[15] Act of 1949, s.65(2).

National Parks and Access to the Countryside 8.34

A local authority can enforce these agreements for access, not only by default action in respect of works, but also by court proceedings, after failure by an owner to comply with a notice relating to the provision of an access or the removal of some physical obstruction to an access. This enforcement applies to access orders, as well as access agreements.[16]

(3) Land for Access

Where necessary to facilitate access to the open country, local planning authorities may acquire land. This does not include excepted land as defined in (3)(a) below, but it can include adjoining land to that acquired for access.[17] The legal duty laid upon the acquiring authority is to manage the land in question with due regard to any dangers it may contain, as well as the public need for open air[18] recreation. The Minister also has similar powers of acquisition and he, like local planning authorities, has compulsory powers available as a last resort.[19] 8.35

A person who enters land covered by an access agreement or order, for the purpose of open air recreation, and without damaging any wall, fence, hedge or gate, is not to be treated as a trespasser or incur any other liability, by reason only of being on the land. (This right to be on the access land is, however, subject to any other legal provision or prohibition which may be applicable).[20]

(a) **Exclusions**

Certain lands, called excepted lands, are not included in this right of access. These are as follows: 8.36
1. Agricultural land (other than rough grazing).
2. Nature reserves as declared by the Nature Conservancy Council.
3. Land covered by buildings, or the curtilage of such land.
4. Land used as a park, garden or pleasure ground, at the time the access arrangement was made.
5. Land used for surface mineral extraction.
6. Railways, golfcourses, racecourses or aerodromes.
7. Land covered by statutory undertaker's works.
8. Land affected by the public's rights under the Law of Property Act 1925, s.193.[21]

Land does not become excepted land if planning permission is needed for its development and either consent has not been given or there is a

---

[16] *Ibid.* s.69.
[17] *Ibid.* s.76.
[18] *Ibid.* s.77.
[19] *Ibid.* ss.76 and 77.
[20] s.60 of Act of 1949.
[21] Excepted land is dealt with in the Act of 1949, s.60. The Law of Property Act provision is the one dealt with in Chap. 2 in relation to commons, which allow access by the public for air and exercise. The procedure of the Act of 1949 is not to supercede that under the Law of Property Act 1925.

8.36   OPEN AIR ACTIVITY

breach in any condition attached to such consent. The Act of 1968 enables restrictions to be imposed in access agreements to prevent land becoming excepted land.[22]

(b) **Public duties in access areas**

8.37   The second Schedule of the Act of 1949 contains a number of general restrictions to be observed by persons enjoying access to open country by virtue of Part V of that Act. By flouting these restrictions, a person loses the protection of section 60 of the Act of 1949 (whereby he was not to be treated as a trespasser). These restrictions are as follows:

GENERAL RESTRICTIONS TO BE OBSERVED BY PERSONS HAVING ACCESS TO OPEN COUNTRY OR WATERWAYS BY VIRTUE OF PART V OF THE ACT

1. Subsection (1) of section sixty of this Act shall not apply to a person who, in or upon the land in question,—
    - (*a*) drives or rides any vehicle;
    - (*b*) lights any fire or does any act which is likely to cause a fire;
    - (*c*) takes, or allows to enter or remain, any dog not under proper control;
    - (*d*) wilfully kills, takes, molests or disturbs any animal, bird or fish or takes or injures any eggs or nests;
    - (*e*) bathes in any non-tidal water in contravention of a notice displayed near the water prohibiting bathing, being a notice displayed, and purporting to be displayed, with the approval of the local planning authority;
    - (*f*) engages in any operations of or connected with hunting, shooting, fishing, snaring, taking or destroying of animals, birds or fish, or brings or has any engine, instrument or apparatus used for hunting, shooting, fishing, snaring, taking or destroying animals birds or fish;
    - (*g*) wilfully damages the land or anything thereon or therein;
    - (*h*) wilfully injures, removes or destroys any plant, shrub, tree or root or any part thereof;
    - (*i*) obstructs the flow of any drain or watercourse, opens, shuts or otherwise interferes with any sluice-gate or other apparatus, breaks through any hedge, fence or wall, or neglects to shut any gate or to fasten it if any means of so doing is provided;
    - (*j*) affixes or writes any advertisement, bill placard or notice;
    - (*k*) deposits any rubbish or leaves any litter;
    - (*l*) engages in riotous, disorderly or indecent conduct;
    - (*m*) wantonly disturbs, annoys or obstructs any person engaged in any lawful occupation;
    - (*n*) holds any political meeting or delivers any political address; or
    - (*o*) hinders or obstructs any person interested in the land, or any person acting under his authority, in the exercise of any right or power vested in him.
2. In the application of the foregoing provisions of this Schedule to waterways,—
    - (*a*) for references to land there shall be substituted references to a waterway;

---

[22] Act of 1968, s.18.

(b) Sub-paragraphs (a) and (b) of paragraph 1 of this Schedule shall not apply; and
(c) Sub-paragraph (f) of the said paragraph 1 shall have effect as if the words from "or brings" to the end of the sub-paragraph were omitted.

(c) Rights and duties of landowners in access areas

Because of the acceptance or imposition of public rights over his land, the legal rights of the landowner or other affected person need to be adjusted. This is done by the following provisions: **8.38**

(i) No person interested in the land may carry out any works (apart from works to make the land into excepted land), whereby the rights of the public under an access agreement or order are substantially reduced.[23]

(ii) The right of the public not to be treated as trespassers, under section 60 of the Act of 1949, does not increase the liability[24]—it does not absolve them completely—of those interested in the land under the general law, in respect either of the state of the land or of anything done or omitted to be done thereon.

(iii) In relation to covenants affecting the land, any liability for breach of covenant may be the subject of compensation.[25]

(iv) The possibility of a way created by an access agreement or order becoming a highway is countered by the provision that the period when the land is affected by such access is to be disregarded, so far, that is, as any prescription period is concerned.[26]

(v) If the Minister is satisfied, on the application of any person interested in the land, that by reason of exceptional weather conditions or the risk of fire, that the rights of access should not apply, he may suspend them.

(vi) Compensation is payable where the value of the interest of any person in the land is depreciated in consequence of an access order.[27] The compensation, which is payable by the local planning authority, is claimable five years after the order has come into operation. This is to allow a realistic appraisal of the effect of the order upon the land, in the light of experience gained in that period. The compensation is calculated to allow for this inbuilt delay.[28]

(4) Maps

Local planning authorities, whose areas are included in access arrangements, whether by order, agreement or land acquisition, are required to **8.39**

---

[23] Act of 1949, s.66.
[24] See now the Occupiers Liability Act 1984 on duty to trespassers.
[25] Act of 1949, s.70.
[26] Under the Highways Act 1980, s.32, 20 years unchallenged use would otherwise form the legal basis for a presumption of a public highway.
[27] Act of 1949, s.70.
[28] *Ibid.* ss.72 and 73.

prepare and maintain maps.[29] These maps are to show land and also excepted land, as explained above, and also land from which the public are excluded (*e.g.* for reasons of danger).[30] Copies of the maps have to be available for public inspection and may be displayed where the public have access to the land. Boundary notices may also be displayed on land subject to public access.

6. Other General Local Authority Powers in Relation to the Countryside

8.40 The Acts of 1949, 1968 and 1981 give many powers to local authorities in National Parks and generally in respect of the countryside. Local planning authorities have power under the 1949 Act to "take all such action" as appears expedient and for the accomplishment of the purpose of preserving and enhancing the natural beauty of any part of their areas within a National Park.[31] The conferment of specific powers elsewhere in the 1949 Act is not to affect the generality of this broad power. They may make arrangements for the provision by themselves or by other persons, of accommodation, meals and refreshments, camping sites and parking places. Accommodation, meals and refreshments may only be provided direct by the authority if there are no other satisfactory or adequate facilities. The facilities may also be provided on land in the neighbourhood of a National Park. Land required for these purpose may be acquired compulsorily.[32]

Section 13 gives power to local planning authorities to improve waterways for the purposes of open air recreation.[33]

Nature reserves may be established by local authorities other than on land held by or managed in accordance with an agreement entered into with the Nature Conservancy Council.[34]

8.41 For the purpose of preserving or enhancing the natural beauty of any land in their area local planning authorities may plant trees. They may carry out works to bring into use or improve the appearance of land which is derelict, neglected or unsightly, where the land is owned by them or by some other person with his consent. Powers of compulsory purchase are available.[35]

By-laws

Wide by-law making powers are given to local planning authorities in respect of land in their area and ownership comprised in a National Park,

---

[29] *Ibid.* s.78.
[30] *Ibid.* s.81.
[31] *Ibid.* s.11.
[32] *Ibid.* s.12.
[33] *Ibid.* s.13.
[34] Act of 1949, s.21.
[35] *Ibid.* s.89.

area of outstanding natural beauty or subject to access by the public under Part V of the 1949 Act and for country parks.[36] By-laws may be made for the preservation of order, the prevention of damage and the maintenance of order in the interests of persons resorting to the land.[37] The Minister has default powers to make by-laws when the authority fail to comply with his requirement to make them.[38]

Management agreements

County planning authorities in respect of land in a National Park, the Greater London Council (or its successor authority) and the London Borough Councils in respect of land in London and local planning authorities for other land, may make management agreements with land owners and occupiers for the purpose of conserving or enhancing the natural beauty or amenity of any land in the countryside and within their area, for promoting its enjoyment by the public.[39] Management agreements may include restrictions on the use of the land by the owner or occupier and may confer power on the local authority to carry out works for the purpose of their functions under the Acts. The Acts contain a number of powers enabling the local planning authorities to give financial assistance to other persons and bodies carrying out work in furtherance of conserving and enhancing natural beauty in the countryside or incidental thereto. This includes making contributions to persons putting up boundary notices, warning notices, displaying maps, and providing public facilities in a National Park.[40] **8.42**

Facilities and services provided by local authorities under the 1968 Act are to be made available as readily for persons who live outside their areas as for their own residents. They are given powers to make reasonable charges for facilities and services which they provide and may authorise other persons providing facilities and services for the authority to make reasonable charges.[41] **8.43**

E. Footpaths

Found in public parks, National Parks and generally throughout any open air recreational area, footpaths are one important part of the law of highways. For the purposes of this work, we shall deal with their nature, the ways in which they come into existence, how to divert them, how to close them and, finally, how to deal with questions of their maintenance and obstruction. **8.44**

---

[36] *Ibid.* s.90.
[37] Act of 1968, s.41. The Litter Act 1983 reinforces such by-laws in one respect.
[38] Act of 1949, s.91 and Act of 1981, s.49.
[39] Act of 1981, s.39.
[40] Act of 1949, ss.82 and 99; Act of 1968, s.20; and Act of 1981, s.44.
[41] Act of 1968, s.43.

8.44   Open Air Activity

1. Nature

A footpath is a highway on which the public can pass and repass on foot. This distinguishes the footway from highways on which vehicles may freely move[42]; it also implies a distinction from the bridleway, which is a highway for use by foot and by horse and, since the Countryside Act 1968, also by pedal bicycle.[43] Cyclists are, by the terms of the above Act, to give way to pedestrians and to persons on horseback.

The law places no measurement on the minimum width of a footpath; nor does it prescribe the nature of its surface. The fact that footpaths serve an infinite variety of terrain is a good reason for that measure of restraint. All that the law requires is that the way should be reasonably passable.

2. Origins

8.45   Public footpaths may come into existence because they have been clearly dedicated for use in that way. Another method is for them to be presumed to be public footpaths after 20 years enjoyment as such by the public.[44] Thirdly, a statutory record of these and other rights of way has been brought into existence since 1949 and appearance on that record will produce evidence of the footpath in law.[45]

One way in which direct dedication occurs is when a new highway is made, perhaps in the course of creating a turning circle for buses or simply to serve newly built houses. There is no place for argument or inference: there is a document which supplies the evidence that the owner intended to create that highway as a new footpath, the work was done, and by usage the new way came into being.[46]

There are many footpaths, however, where things are not as simple. For them the Highways Act 1980 provides a statutory presumption that a way actually enjoyed by the public as of right and without interruption for a full period of 20 years is deemed to have been dedicated as a highway, unless there is sufficient evidence that there was no intention during that period to dedicate it.[47]

---

[42] Known since the Wildlife and Countryside Act 1981 s.54 as 'byways'—"a byway open to all traffic" is a classification for a road used as a public path. The section provides that the old expression—"road used as a public path"—shall not be used for such highways.
[43] Countryside Act 1968, s.30.
[44] Highways Act 1980, s.31.
[45] Wildlife and Countryside Act 1981, s.56(1).
[46] Highways Act 1980, s.25, for district councils, county councils, the National Park Planning Board, the Greater London Council (or its successor authority) or a London Borough Council. Highways Act 1980, s.30 for local councils. The document may be a Public Path Creation Agreement under this section. Alternatively, it may be a builder's agreement wih the local authority, under s.38 of the Act of 1980, whereby the carriageways and footways on the new estate become maintainable public highways. The same Act, s.26, deals with creation orders, when compulsory powers are used to create a footpath.
[47] Highways Act 1980, s.31.

Such a contrary intent would be the placing of a chain or some other physical form of closure annually by the landowner to prevent the 20 year period from running. Again the placing of a notice at the end of the footpath bearing words such as "Private Path. No public right of way" would serve the landowner's purpose of preventing the above statutory presumption from operating.[48]

8.46 The third way is the definitive map and statement. A record by map and by written statement was required of local authorities under the National Parks and Access to the Countryside Act 1949. This was to show all public rights of way. It was comprehensive, almost a Domesday Book approach to this important element in knowledge of the use of the land. But it broke down because of the weight of work it imposed at certain critical points, for instance on the Ministry in dealing with objections and on the local authorities, in organising periodic reviews. The Act was amended and simplified. Definitive maps are now prepared and these can be modified to keep them up to date with known changes. The reason for referring to this system as a third way in which footpaths come into being, is that the immense community research, by specialist societies and in town halls at officer and member level, has revealed footpaths and the history of footpaths that were not hitherto known. In so far as that was its aim, it succeeded.[49]

3. Diversion and Closure

8.47 Diversion of a public footpath may be required for the convenience of the owner of nearby property. A farmer may be putting up a new barn, a new highway may cross the existing footpath, a new building in the village may be better sited if the footpath were re-routed.

There are three legal procedures available for this common situation. One is under the Town and Country Planning Act 1971, and is by way of an Order made by the local planning authority to facilitate development. It will be done when the alternative route is agreed and the land of that route can be dedicated as a footpath. It will also take into account the physical work in constructing the new footpath and responsibility for paying for that work.[50]

The second legal method is by a magistrate's court order under the

---

[48] Also s.31(6); somewhat academic and little used. It allows a landowner to deposit with the highway authority a map and statement of the ways over his land which he admits are public highways. It is renewable every six years. On this and many practical details, the new book *Rights of Way* by P. Clayden and J. Trevelyan (Ramblers Association and Open Spaces Society (1983)) is helpful.

[49] It was then the role of county and county borough councils. The Countryside Act 1968, Sched. 3, was one effort to speed the process. The Wildlife and Countryside Act 1981 contains the method now in use. Section 53 shows the way modifications are made to a definitive map. Section 54 relates to the duty in relation to footpaths, and the Wildlife and Countryside (Definitive Maps and Statements) Regulations 1983 (S.I. 1983 No. 21) have the detail.

[50] Town and Country Planning Act 1971, s.210.

8.47   OPEN AIR ACTIVITY

Highways Act 1980. As the statute says that the diverted way is to be "more commodious" to the public," this condition may in the circumstances be an obstacle to using that method.[51] The section sets out other details of the procedure, concerning public notice in various forms. If for one reason or another, this method is inappropriate, then the local authority may turn to a Public Path Diversion Order, under another section of the Highways Act 1980.[52] This is slightly more intricate and the legal requirements for confirmation of such an Order by the Secretary of State, when objection has been raised, are a little more formidable. There are, in substance, four of them, namely:

(i) The diversion is expedient.
(ii) The path will not be substantially less convenient to the public in consequence of the diversion.
(iii) Consideration has been given to the effect the diversion would have on public enjoyment of the path as a whole, and
(iv) Consideration has been given both to the effect the diversion will have on the old route and land held with it and also to the new route and land held with it. (This last point is one that might be seen in the light of arrangements made for payments by or between the landowner and the local authority.)

The procedure for confirmation of such an Order is in the Sixth Schedule to the Highways Act 1980 and may involve a local inquiry to hear objections.

8.48   The procedure for the closing of a public path is similar to that described above for its diversion. Thus an extinguishment order under the Town and Country Planning Act 1971 is available. When there are no objections to the public notices, the local authority may make the Order; when objections appear, the draft Order goes to the Secretary of State. Again, under the Highways Act 1980, closure may be made after application to the magistrates court for an order. This is available only if the court is satisfied that the path to be closed is "unnecessary." This unvarnished word has been the stumbling block for not a few applications. So, if the interested parties turn to the third possibility, a public path extinguishment order, they meet a form of words in the Statute to the effect that it is "expedient" that the path be stopped up on the ground that it is "not needed for public use." The procedure is as indicated for the diversion order.[53]

4. Maintenance and Obstruction

8.49   Under the Highways Act 1980, the highway authority are under a duty to maintain a highway maintainable at the public expense.[54] This is a duty

---

[51] Highways Act 1980, s.116.
[52] *Ibid.* s.119. D.O.E. Circular 1/83 *Public Rights of Way* para. 21, encourages the use of ss.118, 119 and 120, rather than s.116.
[53] *Ibid.* s.120.
[54] *Ibid.* s.41.

that a district council can undertake, in place of the county council, the highway authority.[55] Apart from that possibility, the duty is one that can be enforced by court order.[56] Adequacy of maintenance is occasionally a matter for argument; suffice it to say that the standard will be that appropriate to the locality and user.

Obstruction of a footpath is common. Again, as with maintenance, the highway authority has a duty to prevent an obstruction and this duty is enforceable against that authority.[57] A temporary obstacle is unlikely to be accepted by the courts as an obstruction within the Highways Act meaning. "Anything which substantially prevents the public from having free access over the whole of the highway, which is not purely temporary in nature, is an unlawful obstruction" were the words of Parker L.C.J. in *Seekings* v. *Clarke*.[58]

5. **Danger from Bulls**

In Part III of the last major Act to deal with public rights of way, *i.e.* the Wildlife and Countryside Act 1981, is a section which deals with the situation when a bull is in a field crossed by a public footpath. **8.50**

It is made an offence to keep a bull at large in such a field and this is punishable by fine in a magistrates' court.[59] However, the action is subject to certain important exceptions:
1. Bulls less than 10 months old.
2. A bull which is not of a recognised dairy breed and is at large with cows or heifers. (The breeds in question are Ayrshire, British Friesian, British Holstein, Dairy Shorthorn, Guernsey, Jersey and Kerry.)

F. Picnic Sites

The provision of picnic sites is now an authorised function of local planning authorities and district councils. They may "provide in their area . . . picnic sites for motorists and others using the roads, with space for parking vehicles and a means of access to and from the road."[60] **8.51**

Additionally, these authorities may do anything appearing to them to be desirable in connection with the provision of such a site, especially "services or facilities for their health or convenience."[61]

Since land is needed, the councils are empowered to acquire land, compulsorily if necessary, that is required for this service. They may take the

---

[55] *Ibid.* s.42.
[56] *Ibid.* s.56.
[57] *Ibid.* s.130(3).
[58] (1961) 59 L.G.R. 268.
[59] Wildlife and Countryside Act 1981, s.59.
[60] Countryside Act 1968, s.10.
[61] *Ibid.*

8.51   OPEN AIR ACTIVITY

site on lease or lease it to someone to act as the council's agent in providing the service.[62]

Lastly, they can charge for the service or they can permit their lessee to charge similarly.

This is a summary of the simple legal code associated with the provision of these sites. The policy, the planning scene, the design skill and the practical common sense in managing them are touched on in the Sandford Committee report on National Parks and government circulars on the same wide subject.[63]

G. LITTER

8.52 The Litter Act 1983 consolidates earlier Litter Acts of 1958 and 1971, together with associated sections in the Public Health Act 1961[64] and the Control of Pollution Act 1974.[65] It maintains as an offence the leaving of litter in any place in the open air to which the public are entitled or permitted to have access without payment. It is necessary, in order to constitute the offence that the result of this action should be "the defacement by litter of any place in the open air."[66] The penalty is a fine not exceeding, at the present time, £400. Local authorities are authorised to counter the anti-social behaviour at which the Act is aimed, by due publicity.[67]

H. CARAVANS

1. Site Licensing

8.53 Caravan sites came of legal age in 1960, when the Caravan Sites and Control of Development Act 1960 introduced legal site licensing. Previously there had allegedly been 3,000 unlicensed sites in this country and some form of regulation was needed.

Caravans have become a feature of national parks and they are discussed in recent authoritative documents on that subject.[68]

The main features of the regulatory system contained in the above Act of 1960[69] are as follows.

A caravan site licence always follows the grant of planning pemission for that use.[70] Indeed, without planning permission, a site licence must not be issued. A second recognition of the close relation between these two

---

[62] *Ibid.* s.43.
[63] See above n. 88, and below n. 68.
[64] Public Health Act 1961, s.51.
[65] s.24.
[66] Litter Act 1983, s.1.
[67] This includes all local authorities with the exception of the Greater London Council (or its relevant successor authority).
[68] The Sandford Committee Report 1974 (National Park Policies Review Committee) and D.O.E. Circular 4/76 (see especially paras. 41–46).
[69] Pt. I is about caravans; Pt. II, now repealed, was about general development control.
[70] Act of 1960, s.3(3).

legal steps is the provision that if the planning permission is limited in time, then the site licence will lapse at the same time.[71] Apart from this, a caravan site licence is not to be issued for a limited period only.

A site licence is issued by a local authority, which for this purpose is a district council or the Common Council of the City of London.[72]

The site licence is primarily about the internal management of the caravan site. The planning permission deals with the prior question of its suitability for use by caravans. All site licences will not be in the same terms; they must be appropriate for the particular site. The Act of 1960 suggests the following subjects as those that might be considered by those responsible for drawing up the site licence[73]:

1. A time limit for caravans on the site.
2. A limit on the total number of caravans on the site.
3. Control over the types of caravans permitted, though not about the materials of which those caravans are made.[74]
4. The position of the caravans on the site and restraints on the positions of tents, vehicles and other structures.
5. The amenity of the site, including the planting of bushes and trees.
6. Fire fighting. This important subject is amplified in the Model Standards issued by the Department of the Environment.[75]
7. Sanitary arrangements.
8. The display of the licence on the site.[76]

The case of *Esdell Caravan Parks Ltd.* v. *Hemel Hempstead U.D.C.*,[77] provided useful guidance on the extent to which site licence conditions could go. A challenge to a limit of 24 caravans in the licence, was made by a site occupier, who wanted to have 78 caravans on the site. He lost. The court accepted the view that educational, transport and shopping aspects of the caravan population in relation to the locality, were reasonable matters to be considered. The court did not favour restricting conditions on a site licence to public health ones, or what Winn L.J. called "the meretriciously simple test" of "an inward looking view."[78]

Again, the case of *Mixnam's Properties* v. *Chertsey U.D.C.*[79] in the House of Lords, shows that conditions about the rent for the caravan sites, the security of tenure of the occupants, and their personal and social activities, were too wide to go into site licence conditions. They were all held *ultra vires*. Lord Radcliffe said "permissible conditions must relate to the

---

[71] *Ibid.* s.4.
[72] Local Government Act 1972, Sched. 29, para. 14.
[73] Act of 1960, s.19.
[74] *Ibid*, s.5(2).
[75] See *e.g. Encyclopaedia of Planning*, Vol. I, 2–368, and ss.3A and 3B, added by the Local Government (Miscellaneous Provisions) Act 1982, s.8.
[76] Act of 1960, s.5(3). There is an interesting legal stipulation in s.5(5), that a condition is valid notwithstanding that it requires the site owner to do something which he cannot do "as of right." This might conceivably involve obtaining an easement from the adjoining owner.
[77] [1965] 3 All E.R. 737.
[78] *Ibid.* at p. 752B.
[79] [1965] A.C. 735.

user of the licensed site, not to the user of the licensee's legal powers of letting or licensing caravan spaces." Lord Upjohn found that the conditions in question involved "oppressive and gratuitous interference with the rights of the occupier." They were, he said, "wholly unnecessary for the good governance of the site."

As these cases show, the site owner has a right of appeal against conditions in the site licence. That appeal goes to a magistrates court, which has the limited duty of considering whether the condition in question is "unduly burdensome."[80] The local authority, for its part, may alter the conditions, provided that it gives the site owner an opportunity to make representations on the matter before a decision is reached.[81]

8.56 A local authority can send its officers to inspect a site, but must give 24 hours prior notice. It is an offence to obstruct the officers in their reasonable task.[82]

Breaches of conditions in a site licence can be prosecuted by a local authority and a third conviction of such an offence can give rise to revocation of the site licence. Insofar as a condition requires works to be done, the local authority may carry out those works, in default of compliance by the site owner. The cost of such work can then be recovered by the local authority.[83]

The Act of 1960 provides for the transfer of site licences when the legal occupier of the site changes. The local authority must be informed and its consent is needed for the transfer to be lawful.

2. Exemptions

8.57 There are a number of situations where a site licence is not needed. (It should be noted that planning permission for these cases is a separate question. The General Development Order does grant such permission for many but not all of these cases.) They are listed in the First Schedule to the Act of 1960 and are as follows:
   1. When the caravan is sited within the curtilage of a dwellinghouse and is incidental to the enjoyment of that use.
   2. Use of land for not more than two nights when travelling with a caravan. This is subject to that land not being used for more than 28 days in the twelve month period, which ends on the day on which the caravan is brought onto the land.[84]

---

[80] Act of 1960, s.7. The case of *Llanfyllan R.D.C.* v. *Holland* (1964) 62 L.G.R. 459, illustrates justices allowing an appeal on this statutory ground, when they agreed that a site licence condition about drainage connections to individual caravan standings was unreasonable. The High Court upheld the justices on appeal by the local authority, since they had applied the right test.
[81] Act of 1960, s.8.
[82] *Ibid.* s.26.
[83] *Ibid.* s.9.
[84] s.12 of the Act should be studied by any concerned with a breach of his licence or tenancy by a tenant in letting a caravan site develop on his land. This is essentially a landlord and tenant dispute.

CARAVANS   8.57

3. When a site not exceeding *five* acres does not have more than *three* caravans in total thereon for more than *28* days in a year. (These three numbers are variable by Order of the Secretary of State.)
4. Sites occupied and supervised by exempted organisations.[85]
5. A site which is duly certified by such an exempted organisation for not more than five caravans and for not more than one year.
6. Meetings by such exempted organisations for not more than five days.
7. Agricultural and forestry workers, engaged on such work on land in the same occupation.
8. Caravans on building and engineering sites, occupied by persons employed on those sites.
9. Travelling showmen, accompanying their equipment and transports.
10. Sites occupied by the licensing authority itself.
11. Sites occupied by a county council as accommodation for gypsies.
12. There is a reserve power to deal with an individual site by Order of the Secretary of State, on the application of a local authority.

3. General

The Act has several provisions about existing, *i.e.* pre-1960, sites.   **8.58**
Local authorities are required to keep registers of site licences and these must be open for public inspection.[86] The Act applies to land normally considered as Crown land, when the occupier is not the Crown.[87] A district council can make an Order in relation to a Common in their area, prohibiting wholly or partly the stationing of caravans upon it for the purposes of human habitation.[88] It is an offence to contravene that Order. There are certain legal formalities to be complied with in taking such a step, in connection with consultation, and public notice and hearing representations.[89]

---

[85] At the time of going to press, there are 11 of these, listed in D.O.E. Circ. 17/65, *e.g.* Caravan Club, Boy Scouts Assocation, Caravan Tourists Association.
[86] Act of 1960, s.25.
[87] *Ibid.* s.28.
[88] *Ibid.* s.23.
[89] *Ibid.* See Sched. 2.

Chapter 9

AVAILABILITY OF FINANCE

*"If our decision is inconvenient, it cannot be helped.
Convenience and justice are often not on speaking terms."*
– Lord Atkin in *General Medical Council* v. *Spackman* [1943] A.C. 627 at p.638.

Introduction

9.01 The public leisure services, as surveyed in this book, have a strong base in the local authorities of this country. They are not, however, confined to those authorities but extend into a series of public boards, commissions, trusts and quangos. This Chapter considers the finance available for the public leisure services and must, therefore, look at local authorities to some extent. The finances available from non-local authority sources are, nevertheless, of considerable practical interest.

After comments in the first section on local government finance in general, we turn to current capital expenditure controls, followed by some detail on the Government grant system. This leads to a section above five specific grants, of interest to the leisure services. Then, turning from local government, we deal finally, with the relation to the public leisure services of the Tourist Board, the Arts Council and the Sports Council and the role of private trusts.

By selecting this context, it is hoped to avoid too detailed an excursion into the strictly specialist territory of local authority finance[1] and, at the same time, to portray realistically the quiverful of financial aid that is available for the leisure services.

A. LOCAL GOVERNMENT FINANCE

9.02 There are two kinds of expenditure in local government:
(i) **Capital expenditure**, which has been described as all expenditure

---

[1] See the dictum of Ackner L.J. in the Brent L.B.C. case on R.S.G. control, *i.e. R.* v. *Secretary of State for the Environment, ex p. Brent LBC* [1982] Q.B. 593: "The rate support grant system is a complex one and a simple account is not possible. While anxious to avoid a thesis on the subject, there is no escape from a somewhat lengthy exposition on a subject, which few will find rivetting."

on an object, for which the local authority concerned could reasonably expect to obtain a loan sanction.

This is regardless of the way in which the object is actually financed. It excludes true deferred charges, such as those a local authority might incur when presenting a Local Act.

Typical classes of expenditure which would normally be capital expenditure are the acquisition of land and existing buildings, the construction or improvement of buildings, the civil engineering works, including the fees and the cost of the authority's own professional staff, connected with those works, the acquisition, renewal, or replacement of vehicles, major plant, furniture and equipment, vessels or similar items, and, lastly, research and development expenditure, within limits.

(ii) **Revenue expenditure**, which is simply all the annual running costs, plus the costs of repaying any borrowing carried out to finance capital expenditure.

9.03 The methods of financing capital expenditure are by borrowing, by the use of unapplied capital receipts, by leasing or even direct from revenue. There are, however, detailed restraints on a local authority's freedom to spend what it likes. These are:
  (i) The capital expenditure controls, which control the initial spending; and
  (ii) The effects of the Block Grant and its penalty provisions, which can make the consequential running costs and borrowing repayments difficult to afford.

It will, accordingly, be helpful to turn first to current capital expenditure controls.

B. Capital Expenditure Controls

9.04 The Local Government, Planning and Land Act 1980, Part VIII, now contains the legal framework for Government controls on local authority capital expenditure. The Act has been supplemented by Regulations and Circulars[2] and the resulting position is summarised, so far as is necessary to put into perspective the controls over monies to be used for the public leisure services.

The local authorities thus affected are county councils, district councils, London borough councils, the Common Council of the City of London and the joint and special planning boards for National Parks.[3]

The expenditure thus controlled is called "prescribed expenditure" and is listed under thirteen heads, none of which relates specifically to leisure services except expenditure on capital grants and advances to private owners of historic buildings.

The scheme is to give each local authority annually an expenditure allo-

---

[2] Local Government (Prescribed Expenditure) Regulations 1983 (S.I. 1983 No. 296) referred to in the rest of this chapter as "the Regulations." (Circular 9/83 of the Department of the Environment.)
[3] Local Government, Planning and Land Act 1980, s.71.

9.04 AVAILABILITY OF FINANCE

cation containing five service blocks: Housing, Education, Transport, Personal Social Services and Other Services. Once given, these blocks can be aggregated by a local authority, according to its own priorities at the time. (There are, though, specific parts of the allocation, as for coast protection, not to be transferred.)

9.05 In addition to this block allocation, a local authority is entitled to spend any or all of the following:

(i) An additional 10 per cent. of that allocation or such proportion as may be specified, being either unspent from the previous year or anticipated from the next year.

(ii) Any special additional Government allocation received during the year.

(iii) A transferred allocation from any other local authority.

(iv) An amount equal to capital receipts or, as the case may be, the prescribed proportion of those receipts.

(v) An amount equal to the local authority's entitlement to the profits of a trading undertaking.[4]

Trading undertakings, in this context, have some special interest as they include an exhibition hall, or complex, and an undertaking for the provision of entertainment under the Local Government Act 1972, s.145.

The prescribed proportions of capital receipts are contained in the Regulations, which should be consulted for detail. The only itemised one within the ambit of the public leisure services, is the net proceeds of Local Lotteries. That item rates at 100 per cent. permitted use. For many of the others, the rate is 50 per cent. Local authorities may agree to share prescribed expenditure and virement can be arranged.[5]

9.06 Borrowing by local authorities is the subject of a general approval annexed to the main Circular[6] about the Regulations and the Act of 1980. Repayment periods of 10, 20, 40 and 60 years are used for different classes of expenditure. The approved purposes of borrowing include land purchase, improvement and reclamation and the construction and improvement of buildings. There are, within the general approval, qualifications and conditions attached to the precise limits of borrowing. There are separate controls in force for the Greater London Council, the City of London and parish and other local councils. Breach of these controls can give rise to a direction from the Minister to restrain expenditure on contracts for new construction and other items which would have taken the authority's expenditure over the limit.[7]

Projects of national or regional importance

The last item is one which may affect the public leisure services. It concerns projects of regional or national importance. For these, there is the

---

[4] *Ibid.* s.72.
[5] *Ibid.* s.77. This is calculated on a current cost accounting basis.
[6] See n.2, *supra.*
[7] *Ibid.* s.78.

CAPITAL EXPENDITURE CONTROLS   **9.06**

machinery to make special allocations of prescribed expenditure to the participating local authorities.[8] The Minister has to be persuaded of the importance of the project and may approve expenditure also, which, though "not itself of national or regional importance, is part of a project which is of such importance."[9]

C. Government Grants

Successive governments have made financial grants to local authorities. **9.07** Some were to stimulate expenditure on special services, such as road improvement. A grant of a percentage of monies spent by the local authority on that service was a simple way to link the grant to the service. Such percentage grants go back over a hundred years.

Even with those grants, the reasonable desire of central government to pay only what was proper, led to the concept of "approved" local authority expenditure ranking for grant. It was only a short step to defining a standard of local authority expenditure which was acceptable to central government, when considering liability for grant payments.

As an example, see the Local Government Act 1966. After earlier sections had described the general rate support grants payable by Government, the Act turned to the circumstances when these grants might be reduced:

> "If . . . the appropriate Minister
> (a) is satisfied that the authority . . . have failed to achieve or maintain a reasonable standard in the discharge of any of their functions, regard being had to the standards maintained by other authorities [. . .], and
> (b) is of opinion that by reason of the failure a reduction should be made in the amount of any elements of rate support grant payable to the local authority . . . ."[10]

Since then, in successive statutes, this relation between government grant and "reasonable standard" has been gradually refined. In the formula used to settle grant, there has always been a compound of subjective, if executive, judgment at Ministerial level and objective analysis of a local situation which, inevitably, was ever-changing. Different names have been used for the grants, as the above Act of 1966 was succeeded by the Local Government Act 1974, the Local Government, Planning and Land Act 1980, the Local Government Finance Act 1982 and the Rates Act 1984. (The Local Government Act 1972, which sought to lay the legal foundations for the reformed local government system of April 1974, also contained certain financial provisions which have some bearing on the above sequence.)

The present grant is called a Rate Support Grant and is composed of a

---

[8] *Ibid.* s.73.
[9] *Ibid.* s.73(2)(b).
[10] Local Government Act 1966, s.4.

9.07   AVAILABILITY OF FINANCE

domestic rate relief grant and a block grant, which is at present some ten times greater. That financial relationship may well be reflected in the respective descriptions of the two grants, which now follow.

1. Domestic Rate Relief Grant

9.08 The domestic rate relief grant is designed to compensate local authorities for the amount by which they are required to reduce the rate poundage charged to domestic ratepayers.[11] This requirement is contained in the General Rate Act 1967[12] and the aim of the section in that Act has been to keep down the rate liability of the domestic occupier. The present legal provision is therefore a continuation of existing practice and policy. The only slight change is one of terms: the amount of the reduction to be made by the local rating authorities is now called "the standard amount."[13]

The aggregate amount of this grant is to be determined by the Secretary of State. The grant payments are to be taken into account by the local authorities, as if they were payable on account of rates.[14] The grants are not payable to the Greater London Council, the Inner London Education Authority nor County Councils, not being rate levying authorities. (They do, however, apply to the expenditure of these authorities.)

2. The Block Grant

9.09 The amount of Block Grant for a year is the balance left after deducting the amount of Domestic Rate Relief Grant from the aggregate amount of Rate Support Grants.[15]

The objective of the Block Grant is usually described as being to give authorities sufficient grant to be able to provide a similar standard of service for a similar rate in the pound.[16]

A single grant is paid to each authority, instead of the previous two components, the Needs and Resources elements, of the Rate Support Grant. The Block Grant is, in theory, a sum equal to the difference between an authority's "total expenditure" and the amount the authority is deemed to be able to raise by charging a rate (on its gross rateable value at a prescribed date), equal to a specified "grant related poundage."[17]

---

[11] Local Government, Planning and Land Act 1980, s.55, and Sched. 9. It is equivalent to the domestic element, so called, in the R.S.G. under the former Local Government Act 1974.

[12] General Rate Act 1967, s.48.

[13] The standard amount is the amount specified for that area in the R.S.G. report (Act of 1980, s.60) or prescribed for the year for the rating authority's area, Local Government Act 1974, Sched. 2, para. 5.

[14] The Act of 1980, ss.1 and 4.

[15] *Ibid*. s.56(1).

[16] See, as an illuminating commentary on the whole rate support grant system, the *Brent* case (n.1, *supra*). That court was specifically interested to identify the areas in the system where the Secretary of State had scope to exercise his discretion; to achieve this aim, the Court was obliged to analyse the total system and this may be found in a characteristically pellucid judgment of Ackner L.J.

[17] Act of 1980, s.56(6).

GOVERNMENT GRANTS 9.09

The critical element of the system is the measure of service levels, as it is this which determines the appropriate "grant related poundage." This measure is reached by comparing an authority's "total expenditure" with the expenditure which, it is claimed, all authorities with similar characteristics would be expected to incur in providing a "typical" standard of service.[18] This standard of service, or yardstick, is called the Grant Related Expenditure. The Secretary of State sets a "grant related poundage," which is the same for all authorities of the same type, provided that their "total expenditure" is the same as their "grant related expenditure."[19]

If an authority's "total expenditure"[20] is *less* than its "grant related 9.10 expenditure," then the poundage it is expected to levy is the basic poundage, mentioned above, reduced by a poundage equal to the difference between its "total expenditure per head" and its "grant related expenditure per head," multiplied by a specified factor.[21]

If an authority's "total expenditure" is *greater* than its "grant related expenditure," then the basic poundage is increased by the difference between "total expenditure per head" and "grant related expenditure per head," multiplied by a specified factor.[22]

If "total expenditure" is greater than "grant related expenditure," the specified factor, referred to above, is increased for any excess of "total expenditure per head" above a specified limit, known as the "threshold."[23]

The specified factor

The purpose of this change in the specified factor, is to make the grant related poundage increase more quickly, in respect of all spending above the threshold, with the result that the amount to be met from rates (as opposed to grant) also increases at a greater rate. This is the "tapering effect," which is intended to encourage authorities to restrict their spending to their assessed spending need.[24] The "grant related poundage," once established for an authority, is applied to its rateable value and, consequently, authorities with a high rateable value will be deemed to raise more from the rates than those with a low rateable value but having the same "grant related poundage."

Summary

To summarise: the relationship between "total expenditure" and 9.11 "grant related expenditure" and the "threshold," determines the "grant related poundage" for any local authority and the application of the

---
[18] *Ibid.* s.56(8) for the definition.
[19] *Ibid.* s.57(1).
[20] *Ibid.* s.56(8) for the definition.
[21] *Ibid.* s.59.
[22] *Ibid.* s.59 and Pt. II of the Local Government Finance Act 1982.
[23] *Ibid.*
[24] Act of 1980 s.59.

9.11 AVAILABILITY OF FINANCE

"grant related poundage" to the authority's rateable value determines the rate income which an authority is deemed to raise. This deemed rate income is deducted from the "total expenditure," to give the amount of the grant entitlement.

However, this entitlement is not quite the end of the story. It may, in its turn, be reduced by either or both of two further mechanisms, set out below.

It is worth noting that the "total expenditure" is not actual expenditure, and, for this and other technical reasons, the "grant related poundage" is not the actual poundage that will be levied. The grant "curve" of individual local authorities obviously varies and some authorities will have a curve which means that, for spending above a certain point, the actual grant will not only fail to grow but will actually be less in total than would be received on a smaller total expenditure. This is why readers might have heard of "the negative grant curve."

Reductions in grant entitlement

9.12 The total amount of rate support grant to be distributed throughout the country is pre-determined. This is known as the "closed-end." Consequently, if the total of all grant entitlements is more than the pre-determined sum, then all entitlements will be scaled down.[25] This adjustment is known as *clawback*. This and the fact that the final grant entitlements will depend on actual expenditure, mean that there is a great deal of uncertainty, at budget time, about the amount of grant any local authority will eventually receive.

Penalties

The second cause of a reduction in grant entitlement is a penalty which will be imposed upon those authorities which fail to keep their total expenditure within specially constructed target. The target for each authority is determined by a complex formula. At ratepayer level (which means when rate and precept levies are conbined), any spending over the target will attract a grant reduction at rates which increase in severity for each percentage point of overspend. Over recent years, the penalty for overspend has become more severe with each Rate Support Grant settlement.[26]

9.13 As a mechanism for distributing a pre-determined amount of grant, the new system is regarded by experts as a pleasing theoretical device. Unfortunately, it is claimed to be much more than that. It is said to be a means of distinguishing, in a fair and objective fashion, between "good" (*i.e.* responsible) local authorities and "bad" (*i.e.* profligate) local authorities. This it cannot do, insofar as the basis of that distinction is the subjective judgment and assessment of spending need. Indeed, even in its simpler role of endeavouring to force local authorities to spend close to their

---

[25] *Ibid.* s.62.
[26] *Ibid.* s.59 and also Pt. II of the Act of 1982.

assessed need, (whether or not that assessment is fair), it is experiencing difficulties, due to the nature of some of the grant "curves."[27]

The statutory Rate Support Grant Report

The legal machinery for this complex system includes the statutory report, called the Rate Support Grant Report, which the Secretary of State submits to Parliament. It is only when that Report is approved by the House of Commons, that payment of Rate Support Grant can lawfully be made by the Government. This Report follows detailed consultation and, after approval, a copy is given to each local authority.[28]

It is in this report that the principles are set out which are used in setting the "grant related expenditure" and "grant related poundage," as explained at paragraph 9–09, above.[29]

One safeguard available to the Secretary of State is the power to bring forward a Supplementary Rate Support Grant Report, with a new set of determinations compiled as in the initial Report.[30]

9.14

Adjustment of total

The Secretary of State also has a final safeguard in his power to adjust the Block Grant total in any year, to achieve correspondence with the aggregate available for grant in that year. This adjustment may affect each local authority and is to be carried out by substituting the actual total expenditure of the local authority for the estimated total expenditure on which the grant for that year was earlier based.[31]

3. **Rate Capping**

The system described above is mainly contained in the Local Government, Planning and Land Act 1980 and the Local Government Finance Act 1982. These two Acts have now been supplemented in certain important respects by the Rates Act 1984. Divided into three Parts, this Act may be summarised as follows.

9.15

(1) *Selective Limitation of Rates and Precepts*

The Secretary of State may designate authorities in respect of whom the proposes to prescribe a maximum for the rate they make or the precept

---

[27] The authoritative report on the above system by the Audit Commisssion—"Impact on Local Authorities' Economy, Efficiency and Effectiveness of the Block Grant Distribution System," H.M.S.O. Aug. 1984—calls for major changes, in the light of seven listed weaknesses. It would seem, in this instance more than others, that we may be describing but a passing system.
[28] The Act of 1980, s.60. The Secretary of State for Transport has a distinct responsibility for that part of the R.S.G. report which relates to transport (s.60(3)).
[29] Act of 1980, s.57(2).
[30] *Ibid.* s.61.
[31] *Ibid.* s.61(7).

9.15

they issue, as the case may be. This designation is effected by individual notice to the authority and by inclusion in a report placed before the House of Commons.[32]

This designation can only be made when the total expenditure of the authority is likely to exceed its grant related expenditure or £10 million, whichever is the greater and to be "excessive having regard to the general economic conditions."[33]

The interest of this work in the Rate Support Grant in general, is in its indirect effect on the availability of finance for the maintenance and development of the public leisure services. For the details of this new system, the interested reader must be referred to the Act of 1984. Those details relate to Government consistency of principle in dealing with designated authorities, to a requirement that a statement of those principles should go in a report to be placed before the House of Commons; to the opportunity for a designated local authority to request a re-determination of the level of total expenditure, in the light of information supplied to the Government[34]; to the power of the Secretary of State to impose requirements in relation to the expenditure and financial management of an authority, with the sanction, behind such requirements, of designation in a further financial year; and the imposition upon the Secretary of State of a duty to take note, in his approval of a local authority's expenditure, of the extent to which contributions to registered charities form parts thereof.

This designation procedure for selected local authorities also includes guidance in the Act of 1984 about the method of determining the maximum rate or precept of those authorities, the use of an interim maximum in certain circumstances[35] and finally, the need for the eventual rate notices in the press and rate demands to occupiers of property, to include a statement about due compliance of the rate thus fixed with the maximum prescribed by the Secretary of State.[36]

(2) *General Limitations*

9.16 The Act of 1984 also contains provisions, in Part II, about a general limitation of rates and precepts, in contrast to the specific limits described above. The Act allows exemption of authorities who have complied with the Government's financial guidelines for three succeeding years. The Secretary of State is to use this power to impose general limits by statutory instrument, which can be annulled by resolution of the House of Commons.[37]

---

[32] Rates Act 1984, ss.1 and 2.
[33] *Ibid.* s.2.
[34] *Ibid.* s.3.
[35] *Ibid.* s.5.
[36] *Ibid.* s.7.
[37] *Ibid.* ss.9, 10 and 11.

GOVERNMENT GRANTS 9.16

(3) *Prescribed Consultations*

Lastly, the Act of 1984 gives the Secretary of State power to issue guidance to local authorities designated under Part I of the Act, about consulting representatives of industrial and commercial ratepayers in their area about their financial budget proposals. This guidance can be incorporated in, and thus have the authority of, formal regulations.[38]

D. SPECIFIC GRANTS

The above account of the general rate support system should indicate the welter of local detail in which, progressively, the national grant calculation has become involved. Clearly, so far as the public leisure services expenditure of a local authority is concerned, it is only after the above process is complete, and all adjustments done, that the feasibility of proceeding with the new sports centre, swimming pool or library, may be known. However, there are one or two places in the total exercise which can now be pinpointed, as being of special relevance for the leisure services. 9.17

1. **Caravan Sites for Gypsies**

Under the Local Government, Planning and Land Act 1980,[39] the Secretary of State may make grants, towards capital expenditure, only in relation to the expenditure by local authorities on caravan sites for gypsies. That expenditure arises under the Caravan Sites and Control of Development Act 1960,[40] in the provision of sites and the acquisition of land and cost of services for the sites. 9.18

2. **National Parks**

A deduction from the gross amount available for grants, in order to reach the net amount available for Rate Support Grant, consists of those monies used for grants to county councils for expenditure on National Parks. In the Local Government Act 1974,[41] a duty is laid upon the Secretary of State to make grants towards county councils in relation to expenditure on so much of any National Parks as lie within their areas. These supplementary grants, determined by the Secretary of State, after consultation with the Countryside Commission, are to be on such a basis for sharing the aggregate amount of monies available for these grants, as may be duly determined. This grant covers management and administration. 9.19

---

[38] *Ibid.* s.13. Other provisions in ss.14 and 15 relate to the greater information for ratepayers about the local authority's past and present financial performance and also, for occupiers of non-rated houses, information similar to that given to rate-paying occupiers.
[39] s.70.
[40] Caravan Sites and Control of Development Act 1960, s.24, and see Chapter 8.
[41] s.7. The grant *was* 75 per cent. of "desirable expenditure on relevant items."

3. Local Lotteries

9.20 A third source of money for leisure services, if so decided, is the product of local lotteries under the Lotteries and Amusements Act 1976.[42] This is mentioned in the Rate Support Grant legislation, dealing with the calculations, as an item to be set aside from the computation of "relevant expenditure" by a local authority, when preparing that figure for its annual discussion with the Department of the Environment about entitlement to Rate Support Grant.

4. Derelict Land and National Parks

9.21 Under the Derelict Land Act 1982,[43] the Secretary of State can make a grant for expenditure to reclaim or improve land which is derelict, neglected or unsightly. If the land is in a development or intermediate area and a local authority is the applicant, the grant is 100 per cent. Otherwise it is 75 per cent. This grant can also be made to bring such land into use. An additional final category of land for which these grants are available is that which passes into one of these classes, by an actual or apprehended collapse of the surface associated with mining operations.[44]

Where the land in question is in a National Park, or in an area of outstanding natural beauty, and the applicant for grant is a local authority, the Government grant is to be 75 per cent. of the approved expenditure. In other circumstances, it is to be 50 per cent. of that expenditure.[45]

5. Countryside

9.22 The Countryside Act 1968 is an enabling Act for a group of Exchequer grants for different aspects of the countryside. The list is as follows[46]:
1. In a country park, land, buildings, works, litter control or discontinuance of adverse uses.
2. Facilities over or near common land.
3. Facilities for camping sites, caravan sites or picnic sites.
4. Study centres in relation to National Parks.
5. Provision of access to the countryside.
6. Compensation related to Tree Preservation Orders.
7. Expenditure on tree planting.
8. Wardens.
9. The cost of removal of "things disfiguring the countryside."[47]

The Act of 1968 limits the grant to 75 per cent. of the approved expendi-

---

[42] s.8(3).
[43] ss.1 and 5.
[44] See definition in s.1(11) *ibid.*
[45] *Ibid.* s.1(6). (This general provision was initially in the National Parks and Access to the Countryside Act 1949, s.97, and amended by the Countryside Act 1968, s.36.)
[46] ss.33, 34 and 36.
[47] s.34(1). These are capital grants.

SPECIFIC GRANTS   9.22

ture. The approval, by the Department, can be limited to items, or classes of the expenditure or to "expenditure incurred in specified circumstances."[48] Close consultation with the Countryside Commission is enjoined in the Act of 1968 in relation to those grants.[49]

6. Fees and Charges

The impact of fees and charges as a useful form of revenue, must never be overlooked. With some popular seaside resorts, for instance, this can be a very significant figure.   9.23

E. NON-LOCAL AUTHORITY FINANCE

1. The Arts Council

The Arts Council of Great Britain is an important grant making body for those engaged in the public leisure services. It was founded by Royal Charter in 1946. In a recent operating year, the Arts Council made grants of some £77 million to a considerable range of persons and societies in the fields of arts and culture. It is not surprising that the organisation through which such a large sum is dispensed is complex; this note simply indicates the broad picture of an important component of the British public leisure services scene.   9.24

(1) *Aims and Objects*

The objects for which the Arts Council of Great Britain is established are (i) to develop and improve the knowledge, understanding and practice of the arts; (ii) to increase the accessibility of the arts to the public throughout Great Britain; (iii) to co-operate with government departments, local authorities and other bodies to achieve these ends.[50]   9.25

(2) *Organisation*

The central Council consists of a Chairman and not more than eighteen others. The Vice-Chairman is chosen from those others and the Chairman is appointed by the Secretary of State for Education and Science. The Secretary of State for Education and Science is the point of liaison with the Government; he has an assessor attached to the Council. The Treasury are involved in appointments. The Secretary of State for Wales is the point of liaison for the Welsh Arts Council, which interlocks with the British one.[51]   9.26

---

[48] *Ibid.* s.36(3).
[49] *Ibid.* s.36(6).
[50] Article 17 of the Charter of Incorporation of February 7, 1967.
[51] There is also a Scottish Arts Council, of which the Chairman too is a member of the British Arts Council.

9.26   Availability of Finance

There are twelve Regional Arts Councils through which the national Council works. The Arts Council also has its own framework of advisory panels, groups or committees, on drama, arts films, photography, art, dance, housing the arts, literature, music, and training. In Wales, some of these arts are also represented by specialist groups; in addition, there is a group to advise on crafts.

(3) Grant Aided Leisure Services

9.27 In a recent year,[52] when some £77 million was distributed, the broad totals and divisions of the beneficiaries were as follows:

(a) £26m—Four national companies: the English National Opera, National Theatre Board, Royal Opera House Covent Garden Limited and the Royal Shakespeare Theatre.
(b) £10m – Twelve Regional Arts Associations
(c) £6m – Music
(d) £5m – Touring
(e) £11½m – Drama
(f) £2½m – Dance
(g) £3m – Art
(h) £¾m – Literature
(i) £0.6m – Arts centres and community projects
(j) £0.66m – Training in the Arts
(k) £1.6m – Housing the Arts.

To gauge the range of Arts Council grants, it should be noted that within the above totals, is a block grant to the 1,200 strong National Federation of Music Societies, which distributes to its members. It has been further estimated that the twelve Regional Arts Associations make grants to some 7,000 separate persons or societies or local authorities.

The address of the Arts Council is 105 Piccadilly, London W1V 0AU.

2. The Sports Council

9.28 This also is an important grant making body in the field of public leisure services. One of its annual reports affords evidence of the large number of activities it supports and the considerable benefit it provides for participants in over fifty sports and pastimes.

(1) Aims

Founded by Royal Charter in 1972, the primary aims and legal objects of the Sports Council are "fostering the knowledge and practice of sport and

---

[52] It may be of interest that the comparative figures in the same year (1982–83) for Wales was £6.7m (within the above £77m) and for Scotland £10½m.

physical education among the public at large and the provision of facilities therefore."

The Charter also enjoins the Council to "encourage the attainment of high standards in conjunction with governing bodies of sport and physical recreation."[53]

These broad objects have led over the years to detailed projects, targets and schemes for the various sports in which the Council is involved.

(2) Grants

The figures taken from a recent annual report show that the main areas through which the Sports Council channelled its financial support, in the form of grants and loans, were as follows:

(i) Grant Aid to governing bodies of sport for administration, coaching, competitions and other ongoing commitments—£8.3 million.
(ii) Capital grant aid for regional and local facilities—£9 million.
(iii) Revenue and capital support for the six national sports centres of the Sports Council—£3.6 million.[54] These are Bisham Abbey, Lilleshall Hall, Plas y Brenin, Cowes, Crystal Palace and Holme Pierrepont, situated and designed to provide emphasis on climbing, sailing, athletics, tennis or other sports but not limited by that speciality; they provide a stimulus for the whole country and are being regularly developed to meet changing fashions and needs.

(3) Organisation

The Sports Council devolves detailed grant making for certain levels to its Regional Councils, of which there are nine. It attaches great importance to the national sports centres, *i.e.* the six listed above and also Harrison Rocks, each of which has its own managing committee.

The Regional committees are paralleled by regional conferences for sport and recreation. The Council has ten panels and groups attached to it in order to receive specialist advice on areas of activity. These include trade and industry, coaches, drug abuse, physical education, fitness and health, medical services, sports science, recreation management and community sports leadership training. There is a separate Sports Council for Wales.

(4) Conclusion

There is ongoing research in the field of countryside and water recreation; there is a major project in hand currently for a new canoe slalom course at the national water sports centre at Holme Pierrepont; in fact, the Sports

---

[53] See, *e.g.* pp. 32 and 3(36) of the latest annual report of the Sports Council, for the year 1983/84.
[54] *Ibid.* at p. 32.

9.31 AVAILABILITY OF FINANCE

Council provides stimulus for many of the public leisure pursuits dealt with in this work. Apart from the Safety of Sports Grounds Act 1975,[55] it is difficult to identify items of statute law, still less cases in the courts, in which the Council, as distinct from players, clubs, coaches and referees and associated sports supporters of all kinds, have been involved. The address of the Sports Council is 16 Upper Woburn Place, London WC1H 0QP.

3. The Tourist Board

9.32 The public leisure services are all, to greater or lesser degrees, involved in this country's tourist trade. This makes them a natural partner of the British Tourist Authority and associated Tourist Boards, who legally and in every other way have a prime role in this field. As the Tourist Authority has power to provide financial assistance for suitable projects, a note about its legal status is appropriate.

(1) The Development of Tourism Act 1969

This Act establishes the British Tourist Authority and the English, Scottish and Welsh Tourist Boards. The chairmen of the three national Boards are on the board of the British Tourist Authority, together with six others appointed by the Secretary of State for Trade.[56]

(a) The function of all four bodies is to encourage people to visit Great Britain and people living in Great Britain to take their holidays there; and

(b) encourage the provision and improvement of tourist amenities and facilities in Great Britain."

"Tourist amenities and facilities" are, "in relation to any country, amenities and facilities for visitors to that country and for other people travelling within it on business or pleasure."[57]

The British Tourist Authority may "prepare schemes for the giving of financial assistance (by the three above national Boards) for the carrying out of projects of such classes as may be specified in the schemes, being schemes which will, in the opinion of the Authority, provide or improve tourist amenities or facilities in Great Britain."[58] Assistance is by a grant or loan or by a combination of those methods.[59] A scheme is to be submitted to the Department of Trade, who may "by order confirm it with or without modification" and if a scheme is so confirmed, it shall thereupon

---

[55] See Chapter 6.
[56] Development of Tourism Act 1969, s.1 and S.I. 1974 No. 692.
[57] *Ibid.* s.2(9).
[58] *Ibid.* s.3(1). The annual report of the B.T.A. for 1983/1984 says that 266 such schemes were then running (p. 21). Sched. II to the Act of 1969 sets out the conditions to be attached to a grant pursuant to s.3 schemes.
[59] Development of Tourism Act 1969, s.3(3).

have effect.[60] Any Order made by the Department of Trade, approving such a scheme, is to be by statutory instrument. The order requires Treasury consent and a draft to be approved by each House of Parliament.[61]

In addition to the above procedure about schemes, a Tourist Board has power to give financial assistance for a project which will improve or provide tourist amenities or facilities which will improve or provide tourist amenities or facilities in the country for which the Tourist Board is responsible.

The relevant Minister and the Treasury must approve; the assistance may be in the form of a grant, a loan or by subscribing to or otherwise acquiring shares or stock in a company, if the project is to be carried out by a company incorporated in Great Britain.[62]

(2) *Hotel Development*

Under the 1969 Act, loans and grants to assist hotel development can be made by the three Tourist Boards. This assistance is subject to directions from the Minister about matters on which the Board must be satisfied before making a loan[63]; the terms and conditions subject to which loans are to be made; and the conditions to be imposed when making a grant under a scheme.

(3) *Local Authorities*

The Local Government Act 1972 included a provision to stimulate tourism through initiatives by local authority. Local authorities, alone or jointly with some other person, might "encourage persons, by advertisement or otherwise, to visit their area for recreation, for health purposes, or to hold conferences, trade fairs and exhibitions in their area and provide and improve facilities for these purposes."[64]

Fourteen years later[65] the word "recreation" was removed from the three purposes. This followed the much wider concept of recreation embodied in the Act of 1976 and in respect of which wide new powers were conferred on local authorities.

The Local Government Act 1972, also empowered local authorities to contribute to any organisation approved by the Secretary of State for the purposes of the section, as stated above, and being an organisation established for the purpose of encouraging persons to visit the United Kingdom or any part thereof. The address of the British Tourist Authority is Queen's House, 64 St. James Street, London SW1A 1NF.

---

[60] *Ibid.* s.3(2).
[61] *Ibid.* s.3(6).
[62] *Ibid.* s.4.
[63] *Ibid.* s.19.
[64] s.144.
[65] Local Government (Miscellaneous Provisions) Act 1976, s.81(1), Sched. 2.

9.35 AVAILABILITY OF FINANCE

4. Private Trust Funds

9.35 The leading directory of charitable trusts, in this country, with some 2,300 entries, shows a significant proportion with powers to assist the leisure services in all their range.[66]

Music and the arts, physical fitness, the preservation of the environment and the architectural heritage, the promotion of recreation, all figure in the quoted items of reference of many of the listed trusts.

It is true that these bodies vary greatly in their resources and some confine their donations to certain parts of the country. Additionally, the current edition of the directory indicates that some trusts can take no new applications for the time being, being committed with existing assistance for some time to come.

Having made these qualifications, it is evident that many hundreds of trusts have resources to deploy in the field covered by this book. They thus furnish another avenue for financial assistance to those leisure services with funding difficulties for new projects.[67]

---

[66] *Directory of Grant-Making Trusts* 1983. (Published by Charities Aid Foundation, Tonbridge).

[67] Over 200 entries relate to parks and playing fields, over 250 to sport and recreational facilities, over 200 to adventure centres and playgrounds, over 500 to the preservation of amenities, over 600 to music and the theatre, over 400 to museums, over 300 to painting and sculpture and over 300 to films.

Index

References throughout are to paragraph numbers. Those followed by "n" (e.g. 2.09n.) are to footnotes.

ABATEMENT. *See* REMEDIES.
AGRICULTURAL TENANCIES, 1.042–1.045
AGRICULTURE,
 definition of, 1.042
ALCOHOL,
 licences for sale of, 6.67–6.69
 sale of, 6.64–6.75
  hours for, 6.70–6.74
  young persons, sale to, 6.74
ALLOTMENTS, 8.02–8.09
 administration, 8.08
 compensation, 8.07
 compulsory purchase of land, for, 5.10
 history, 8.03
 London, in, provision of, 5.43
 offences, 8.05
 statutes, 8.04
 termination of letting, 8.06
 terms of letting, 8.05
AMENITIES,
 parks, in, 4.07
AMUSEMENTS WITH PRIZES, 6.86
ANCIENT MONUMENT, 3.78–3.80
 definition of, 3.78n.
ANIMALS,
 outdoor entertainments, 6.60
 performing, 6.16
 protection of, 8.12
 wild, 4.63–4.64
APPROPRIATION,
 land, of, meaning, 2.35n.
ARCHEOLOGICAL IMPORTANCE,
 areas of, 3.80–3.81
ARCHIVES,
 libraries as repository, 3.38
AREAS OF OUTSTANDING NATURAL BEAUTY, 8.29
ART GALLERIES, 3.39–3.43
 charge for admission, 3.39
 pictures loaned for exhibition, 3.40
ARTS COUNCIL, 9.01
 address, 9.27
 grants from, 9.24–9.27
 objects, 9.25
 organisation, 9.26
ASSIGNMENT,
 business tenancy, of, 1.046
 contract, of, 1.150–1.151
ATHLETIC TRACKS,
 licence for, 6.54
ATTORNEY GENERAL,
 prosecutions, consent to, 6.05

ATTORNEY GENERAL—*cont.*
 public nuisance,
  legal process for, 1.033
BAILMENT,
 museum collection of, 3.72 *et seq.*
 professional standard of care, 3.76n.
BETTING, 6.79
 offices, improvements in, 6.79n.
BILLIARDS,
 licence for, 6.43
BINGO, 6.82
BIRDS,
 protection of, 8.11
BOATING POOL,
 watercourse, interference with, 4.06n.
BOATS, 7.40–7.44
 boatmen,
  licensing of, 7.42
 by-laws regulating use of, 7.43
 injunction restraining use of, 7.44
 meaning of, 7.40n.
 nuisance, 7.44
 pleasure,
  licences for, 7.41
BOOKMAKERS COMMITTEE, 6.47, 6.51–6.52
BOXING MATCH,
 licence for, 6.40, 6.44
BREACH OF CONTRACT, 1.153–1.155
 limitation periods, 1.154
BRITISH BOARD OF FILM CENSORS, 6.25
BRITISH TOURIST AUTHORITY, 9.32
 address, 9.34
BRITISH WATERWAYS BOARD, 7.41, 7.52, 7.53, 8.32
BROADCASTING,
 copyright and, 3.34
BRIBERY. *See* CORRUPTION.
BUILDING,
 listed. *See* LISTED BUILDING.
BUILDING BY-LAWS,
 duty of local authority in relation to, 1.108
BULLS,
 danger from, 8.50
BURIAL GROUNDS,
 development of, 2.41, 2.54
BUSINESS,
 definition of, 1.046
BUSINESS TENANCIES, 1.046–1.051
 assignment of, 1.049
 excluded businesses, 1.046
BY-LAWS,
 boats, 7.43

Index

BY-LAWS—cont.
countryside, protection of, 8.41
enforcement, 4.56
freshwater fishing, 7.48
making of, 4.54
model, 4.55
museums, for, 3.47
parks, 4.13, 4.42–4.57
seaside boating, 7.60
swimming pools, 7.05
ultra vires, 4.46
validity, test for, 4.47 *et seq.*
waiver of, 4.57
And see LOCAL AUTHORITY.
BYWAY,
meaning of, 8.44n.

CANALS, 7.52–7.53
British Waterways Board duties, 7.52
towpaths, 7.53
CANNON HILL PARK, BIRMINGHAM, 6.30
CAR PARKS,
swimming pools, 7.17
CARAVANS, 8.53–8.58
common land, on, 2.78
holiday,
code of practice, 1.167
register of licences, 8.58
site licensing, 8.53–8.56
exemptions, 8.57
CARE,
common duty of, 1.004 *et seq.*
CEMETERY,
fences, liability of owner for, 4.17
CHARITY,
legal classes of, 5.03n.
National Trust as a, 5.03
CHARITY COMMISSIONERS, 2.51
CHILD POVERTY ACTION GROUP, 2.09n.
CHILDREN,
liability of occupier to, 1.013
CHURCH LAND,
development of, 2.41
CINEMAS, 6.19–6.26
enforcement, 6.22
exempted exhibitions, 6.23
licensing of premises, 6.20–6.21
regulation of films, 6.26
safety of children and young persons, 6.25
safety of premises, 6.24
CINEMATOGRAPH FILMS COUNCIL, 6.26
CITY OF LONDON,
open space management by, 5.32–5.33
CLEOPATRA'S NEEDLE, 5.23
CLOCKS,
public, London, in, 5.22
COMMISSION FOR RACIAL EQUALITY, 1.089, 1.092

COMMON LAND, 2.60–2.79
building on, 2.75
caravans on, 2.78
customary rights over, 2.76
definition of, 2.68
development of, 2.42
facilities for public, 2.79
foreshore, 2.77
history of, 2.61–2.72
inclosure of, 2.63
local authority appropriation of, 2.35–2.37
local authority disposal of, 2.38
London, in, 5.35–5.36
management of, 2.66–2.67
National Trust and, 5.05
objection to registration, effect of, 2.71n.
protection of, 2.64–2.67
registration of, 2.69–2.72
rights of public over, 2.73–2.79
traditional rights, 2.60n.
COMMONS COMMISSIONER, 2.70, 2.76
COMMONS PRESERVATION SOCIETY, 8.17
COMPANY,
capacity to contract, 1.148
COMPETITIONS,
prize, 6.85, 6.87
COMPULSORY PURCHASE,
countryside, in, 8.41
local authority, by, 2.33–2.34
National Trust property, of, 5.09–5.10
parish council, by, 2.40
parks, exclusion of, 4.29
CONCERT HALLS. *See* THEATRES.
CONDITIONS. *See* TERMS.
CONSIDERATION. *See* CONTRACT.
CONSUMER,
protection of, 1.164–1.175
CONSUMER PROTECTION ADVISORY
COMMITTEE, 1.165, 1.166
CONSUMER SAFETY,
dangerous goods, 1.168–1.170
CONTEMPT OF COURT,
museum curator, 3.67–3.70
observations of ombudsman in, 2.14
CONTRACT, 1.001
acceptance, 1.135
actors, etc.,
hire of, 6.06–6.10
non-performance, 6.08–6.10
restraint, 6.07
assignment, 1.150–1.151
breach, 1.153–1.155. *See also* BREACH OF
CONTRACT.
company, capacity of, 1.148
consideration, 1.135
corporations, capacity of, 1.147
damages, 1.153
duress, 1.141
foundation of, 1.134–1.135

Index

CONTRACT—*cont.*
  frustration of, 1.152
  "illegal," 1.143
  jurisdiction of courts, ousting, 1.144
  legally enforceable relations, 1.135
  liability, limitation of, 1.155
  minors, capacity of, 1.146
  misrepresentation, 1.139–1.140
    definition, 1.139
    rescission for, 1.140
    remedies, 1.140
  mistake, 1.136–1.138
    mutual, 1.136
    unilateral, 1.137
    signing of documents, 1.138
  performance of, 1.152
  privity, 1.149
  quantum meruit, 1.152, 1.153. *See also* REMEDIES.
  restraint of employees, 1.145
  restraint of trade, in, 1.144
  restrictive trading agreements, 1.142
  sale of goods, for, 1.156–1.163
  sale of land, need for writing, 1.135
  specific performance, 1.153
  unfair terms, 1.155
  void, 1.142, 1.144
  wagering, 1.142
CONTRACT OF SERVICE,
  definition, 1.175
CONTRIBUTORY NEGLIGENCE, 1.121–1.122
  sports, 7.33
COPYRIGHT,
  broadcasting, in, 3.34
  building construction, 3.31
  copying of documents, 3.18, 3.20–3.25
  definition of, 3.26–3.27
  EEC and, 3.35–3.36
  enforcement, 3.32
  European concept of, 3.36n.
  fair dealing, 3.30
  libraries and, 3.14–3.36
  permitted acts, 3.29
  public halls and breach of, 6.45
  schools and, 3.34
  statutory prohibitions, 3.27–3.28
CORONER,
  treasure trove, duty in respect of, 3.53
CORPORATION,
  capacity to contract, 1.147
CORRUPTION, 1.093–1.097
  enforcement, 1.096
  offences, 1.095
  onus of proof, 1.097
COUNCIL FOR THE PRESERVATION OF RURAL ENGLAND, 8.17
COUNTY PARK, 2.59
  provision of, 8.30–8.31

COUNTRYSIDE COMMISSION, 1.002, 7.57, 8.18, 8.19–8.20, 9.22
  areas agreement, 8.34
  areas of outstanding natural beauty, 8.29
  national parks, 8.21 *et seq.*
COVENANTS,
  parks, in relation to, challenge of, 4.27
CROSSWORD COMPETITION,
  lottery, as, 6.85n.
CRICKET MATCH,
  private nuisance, and, 1.026–1.027
CROWN,
  foreshore, ownership of, 2.77, 7.61
  local authority, control of, 2.10
  open space land, 2.48n.
  Royal Prerogative, whales and sturgeon, 7.45
  Royal rights in forests, restriction of, 5.17
  treasure trove, 3.50–3.53
  whales, 3.58
  wrecks, ownership of, 3.54
CRYSTAL PALACE, 5.31
CUSTOM,
  law deriving from, 1.001
  outdoor entertainments, 6.59
CUSTOMS AND EXCISE,
  copyright, role in enforcement, 3.32
  gaining, 6.81
  import and export of works of art, 3.42

DAMAGE,
  remoteness of, 1.001
  negligence, for, 1.110 *et seq.*
  See also REMEDIES.
DEED,
  limitation period, 4.17
DEFAMATION, 1.001
DEFECTIVE PREMISES,
  duty of care owned, 1.109
DEFENCES,
  dangerous goods, in relation to, 1.169
  trade descriptions, 1.183
DEFINITION,
  metal detector, 3.65
DICKENS, CHARLES, 3.14
DISABLED PERSONS, 1.086–1.092
  employment quota, 1.087
  mental disorders, 1.087
DISCRIMINATION, 1.001, 1.076–1.085
  local authority, duty of, 1.092
  race, 1.088–1.092
    codes of practice, 1.092
    definition, 1.090
    exclusions from legislation, 1.091
    racial group, 1.090
  sex, on grounds of, 1.078–1.085
    advertising and, 1.083
    emforcement, 1.085
    examples of, 1.081

Index

DISCRIMINATION—*cont.*
  sex, on grounds of—*cont.*
    exclusions from legislation, 1.080
    liability of principal, 1.083
    swimming pools and, 1.082
    training of recruits, 1.084
DISEASES,
  Dutch elm, 4.59–4.61
  fire blight, 4.62
DISMISSAL,
  employees, of, 1.064–1.072
  employees outside regulations, 1.071
  national security, 1.071
  relevance of strike, 1.071
  unfair, 1.065
  valid reasons for, 1.070
DISRAELI, BENJAMIN,
  copyright, on, 3.26
DUCHY OF CORNWALL,
  foreshore, ownership of, 7.61
DUCHY OF LANCASTER,
  Chancellor of, public library service, 3.03, 3.06
  foreshore, ownership of, 7.61
  open space land, 2.48n.
DURESS. *See under* CONTRACT.
DUTY OF CARE, 1.004 *et seq.*

EASEMENT,
  National Trust property, owner, 5.08
ECONOMIC LOSS,
  negligence, as result of, 1.106–1.108
EMPLOYEE,
  conditions of work, 1.073–1.099
  dismissal of, 1.064–1.072
  dismissal, valid reasons for, 1.070
  duties of, 1.062
  duty of, health and safety at work, 1.075
  licence to occupy residence, 1.038 *et seq.*
  restraint of, 1.145
  swimming pool, 7.06
  theft by, 1.098–1.099
  trade union activities, dismissal in relation to, 1.066–1.067
EMPLOYER,
  duties of, 1.063
  duty of, health and safety at work, 1.074
  secrets, protection of, 1.062
EMPLOYMENT, 1.001
  collective bargaining, 1.058, 1.059
  collective redundancies, 1.059
  contract, of, 1.061–1.072
    equality provision in, 1.077
  EEC, 1.059
EMPLOYMENT PROTECTION,
  excluded jobs, 1.061n.
ENGLISH TOURIST BOARD, 7.57
ENVIRONMENT,
  Department of, listed buildings, 1.054

ENVIRONMENT—*cont.*
  Secretary of State for the, 4.26n., 4.31, 4.63, 7.57
  allotments, 8.08
  ancient monuments and, 3.78–3.80
  areas of archeological importance and, 3.80–3.81
  commons, 2.65
  compulsory acquisition of land by, 2.34
  control of local authorities, 2.10
  local government finance, 9.08, 9.09, 9.14, 9.15, 9.16, 9.18, 9.19, 9.21
  local ombudsman, 2.11n.
  open space land, 2.48n.
  protection of common land, 2.65
  wildlife preservation, 8.14
  wrecks, 3.55, 3.56
EPPING FOREST, 8.32
  commons registration, 2.72
  management of, 5.32
EQUAL OPPORTUNITIES COMMISSION, 1.078, 1.085, 1.089
EUROPEAN COMMISSION ON HUMAN RIGHTS, 1.059
EUROPEAN COURT OF JUSTICE,
  copyright law, 3.35–3.36
EXCLUSION CLAUSE,
  dangerous goods, 1.169

FAIR TRADING,
  Director General, of, 1.165, 1.167
  Office of, 1.164, 1.167
FENCES,
  parks, of, 4.16–4.17
FILM,
  performers' protection, 3.37
FINANCE,
  capital expenditure controls, 9.04–9.06
  government grants, 9.07–9.16. *See also* GRANTS.
  local government, 9.02–9.03
  non-local authority, 9.24–9.35
FISHING,
  freshwater,
    by-laws, 7.48
    licenses for, 7.47
    offences, 7.50
    unlawful practices, 7.46
    water authority duties, 7.49
  land law, 7.51
  salmon and freshwater, 7.46–7.50
  sea, 7.45
FOOTPATHS, 8.44–8.50
  bulls, danger from, 8.50
  closure, 8.48
  creation, 8.45–8.46
  division, 8.47
  maintenance, 8.49
  meaning, 8.44

Index

FOOTPATHS—cont.
  obstruction, 8.49
FORESHORE, 2.59, 2.77
  rateability of, 4.38n.
FOREST,
  National Trust land, 5.10
FOREST OF DEAN, 2.72, 5.15
FORESTRY COMMISSION, 1.002, 4.43,
    5.13–5.18
  by-laws, 5.15
  creation of, 5.13
  Dutch elm disease, 4.61
  inspectors, 4.61
  public facilities, 5.14
  tree planting for amenity, 5.16

GAMBLING, 6.77–6.87. *See also* BETTING;
    GAMING; LOTTERIES; COMPETITIONS.
  general principles, 6.78
GAMING, 6.80–6.83
  meaning of, 6.80
  machines, with, 6.83
  registration of clubs, 6.81
GAMING MACHINES, 6.86
GATESHEAD INTERNATIONAL STADIUM, 7.24
GOODS AND SERVICES,
  contract for, 1.171–1.175
GRAMOPHONE RECORDS,
  lending of, 3.15 *et seq.*
  performers' protection, 3.37
GRANTS,
  Arts Council, from, 9.24–9.27
  block, 9.09–9.10
  clawback, 9.12
  countryside, for, 9.22
  derelict land, 9.21
  domestic rate relief, 9.08
  gypsy caravan sites, 9.18
  national parks, 9.19, 9.21
  rate support, 9.07, 9.12, 9.14, 9.15, 9.20
  penalties, 9.12–9.13
  rate capping, 9.15–9.16
  Sports Council, from, 9.28–9.31
  Tourist Board, from, 9.32–9.34
GREEN BELT LAND,
  London, in, 5.34
GREYHOUND RACING, 6.53
GROSVENOR PARK, CHESTER, 6.30
GUARANTEE, 1.155

HADRIAN'S WALL, 3.78
HAMPSTEAD HEATH, 5.31
HIGHWAY,
  obstruction of,
    public nuisance, on, 1.033
  property owner adjoining, liability of,
    4.16–4.17
HIGHWAY AUTHORITY,
  footpaths, duties over, 8.49

HIGHWAY AUTHORITY—cont.
  long distance routes, 8.23
HISTORIC BUILDINGS AND MONUMENTS
    COMMISSION FOR ENGLAND, 1.056n.
HOLLAND HOUSE, 5.31
HORSERACE BETTING LEVY BOARD, 6.47,
    6.49
HORSERACE TOTALISER BOARD, 6.47, 6.50
HORSERACING, 6.47–6.52
HUMAN RIGHTS,
  European Convention on, 1.059
HYPNOTISM,
  definition of, 6.42
  licence for, 6.41

INDUSTRIAL TRIBUNAL,
  precedent, 1.071n.
INJUNCTION,
  boats,
    restraining use of, 7.44
  See also REMEDIES.
INLAND WATERS, 7.54–7.58
  National and County Parks, 7.55–7.56
  reservoirs, 7.57
INLAND WATERWAYS AMENITY ADVISORY
    COUNCIL, 7.52
INSURANCE COVER,
  grants, for, 4.65
INTOXICATING LIQUOR. *See* ALCOHOL.
INVITEE, 1.005

JOCKEY CLUB, 6.47, 6.48, 6.52
JUDICIAL REVIEW,
  meaning of, 2.08

KEW GARDENS, 1.056n.

LAW COMMISSION, 1.014n., 1.155, 1.171,
    1.174n.
  parks and recreation grounds, 4.01
  participatory sports, 7.25
LAW REFORM COMMITTEE, 1.022n.
LEASE, 2.45
  National Trust property, on, 5.08
LEE VALLEY,
  regional park authority, 5.42
LIBRARIES, 2.03
  archives, storage of, 3.38
  by-laws, 3.09
  charge for services, 3.05
  copyright and, 3.14–3.36
  duty of public authority, 3.03–3.04
  gramophone records,
    lending of, 3.15 *et seq.*
  legal aspects of provision, 3.07–3.09
  legal copying categories, 3.20–3.25
  London, in, 5.38
  National Trust and, 5.06
  offences committed in, 3.08

Index

LIBRARIES—*cont.*
  periodicals,
    copying of, 3.20
  powers of public authority, 3.06
  provision and management, 3.03–3.09
  public lending right, 3.10–3.13
  publication of original work, 3.24–3.25
  published works,
    copying of, 3.21–3.22
  tax on gifts and bequests, 3.43
  typographical arrangements,
    copying of, 3.23
LICENCE,
  alcohol, for sale of, 6.67–6.69
  athletic tracks, 6.54
  betting office, for, 6.79
  billiards, for, 6.43
  bingo club, 2.03
  boats, 7.42
  boxing match, for, 6.44
  caravan site, 8.53–8.56
  cinemas, 6.20–6.21
  entertainment,
    public halls, for, 6.34–6.40
  freshwater fishing, for, 7.47
  greyhound racing, for, 6.53
  horseracing, for, 6.48
  hypnotism, for, 6.41
  keeping of wild animals, for, 4.63–4.64
  meaning of, 2.43
  occasional, 6.67–6.68
  restaurant, for, 6.67
  sex establishments, for, 6.89
  theatre premises, for, 6.02
  wrestling match, for, 6.44
  young persons in theatres, for, 6.15
LICENSEE. *See* INVITEE.
LICENSED PREMISES,
  inspections and alterations, 6.73
  obtaining a licence, 6.69
  offences, 6.75
  opening hours, 6.70–6.72
  young persons, 6.74
LICENSING. *See* LICENCE.
LIMITATION PERIOD,
  deed, based on, 4.17
  defence, as, 1.129–1.131
  trade descriptions offences, in, 1.185
LISTED BUILDING, 1.053–1.056
  criteria related to age, 1.054n.
  definition of, 1.053
  immunity certificate, 1.054n.
  London, in, 5.21
  meaning of, 1.054
LITTER, 8.52
LOCAL AUTHORITY,
  access agreement/order, 8.34
  access to countryside, 8.32–8.39
    excepted land, 8.36

LOCAL AUTHORITY—*cont.*
  access to countryside—*cont.*
    landowners' rights and duties, 8.38
    public duties, 8.37
  acquisition of land, 2.33–2.37
  acquisition of open space land, 2.49–2.53
  allotments, 8.08
  budget of, 2.17
  building by-laws,
    duty to ensure compliance with, 1.108
  by-laws, 2.28, 2.31
    open space land, 2.55
  capital expenditure controls, 9.04–9.06
  caravan sites, 8.55–8.56
    register of licences, 8.58
  catering,
    powers in relation to, 6.76
  common land, 2.60 *et seq.*
  control by audit, 2.21
  country parks, 8.30–8.31
  countryside,
    powers in relation to, 8.40–8.43
  disposal of land, 2.38–2.39
  finance, 9.02–9.03
  functions of, 2.02
  government grants, 9.07–9.16
  internal rules, 2.05
  land transactions, 2.32–2.45
  libraries,
    provision of. *See* LIBRARIES.
  library authority, as, 2.03, 2.16
  negligence of, 2.04
  open space land,
    duty in relation to, 2.54–2.55
  outdoor entertainments, 6.57–6.58
  parks,
    accountability, 4.32
    powers of appropriation and disposal,
      4.30–4.31
  planning,
    access to countryside, 8.33, 8.35, 8.38
    countryside management, 8.42
    footpaths, 8.47, 8.48
    maps of access areas, 8.39
    national parks and, 8.23, 8.24, 8.27, 8.28
    picnic sites, 8.51
  power to limit statutory functions, 2.05
  powers,
    adoptive acts, from, 2.26
    by-laws, from, 2.28
    provisional orders, from, 2.27
  public entertainment, 6.27–6.32
    arts and crafts, 6.29
    children, 6.31
    Eisteddfod, 6.29
    parks, 6.29
    private covenants, 6.30
    schools, 6.31
    statutory control of, 6.28–6.30

INDEX

LOCAL AUTHORITY—*cont.*
  public entertainment—*cont.*
    swimming pools, 6.31
    legal process for, 1.033
    rating purposes, for,
      meaning of, 4.34
  sanctions against, 2.06
    breach of statutory duty, 2.07
    judicial review, 2.08–2.09
    local government commissioners, 2.11–2.14
    ministerial control, 2.10
  statutory nuisance,
    responsibility for, 1.032
  territory of, 2.16
  tourism, development of, 9.34
  treasurer,
    duty of, 2.22
  ultra vires,
    bad faith and, 2.19
    doctrine of, 2.15–2.23
    estoppel and, 2.20
    statutory exceptions, 2.18
  wildlife preservation, 8.14
LOCAL GOVERNMENT,
  Royal Commission on, 6.32
Locus Standi,
  "aggrieved person," 2.09n.
LONDON,
  commons, 5.35–5.36
  competitions in, 5.28
  Green Belt land, 5.34
  letting of land or buildings,
    local authorities, by, 5.26–5.27
  libraries and museums, 5.38
  open space, 5.24
  public leisure services in, 5.19–5.43
  public park,
    closure of, 5.31
  recreation and sport, 5.41–5.42
  recreation in,
    powers to provide for, 5.24–5.25
  Royal Parks, 5.39–5.40
  squares, 5.37
LOTTERIES, 6.84
  local, 9.05

MAPS,
  access areas, 8.39
MERCHANTABLE QUALITY,
  implied term as to, 1.174
METAL DETECTORS, 3.61–3.65
  archeological area,
    use of in, 3.81
  control of use, 3.63
  definition of, 3.65
  parks and open spaces, 4.18
  use in "protected place," 3.65
MINOR,
  capacity to contract, 1.146

MISREPRESENTATION. *See* CONTRACT.
MISTAKE. *See* CONTRACT.
MONOPOLIES AND MERGERS COMMISSION, 1.145
MONUMENT,
  London, in, 5.22
MUSEUMS, 3.44–3.81
  by-laws, 3.47
    enforcement of, 3.47n.
  charges for admission, 3.49
  collections, 3.71–3.81
  duty of local authority towards, 3.45
  finance, 3.46
  grants to, 3.48
  London, in, 5.38
  main national, 3.49
  metal detectors, 4.18
  range of work, 3.44
  standard of care, 3.75–3.77
  Treasure Trove, 4.18
  whales, 3.57–3.60
  wildlife protection, 3.66–3.69
  wrecks, 3.54–3.56
MUSIC HALLS. *See* THEATRES.

NATIONAL GALLERY, 3.40
NATIONAL HERITAGE MEMORIAL FUND, 1.056
  museums, arrangements with, 3.48
NATIONAL PARKS, 8.21–8.28
  administration, 8.25–8.28
  compulsory purchase of land for, 5.10
  Countryside Commssion, duties of, 8.22
  designation, 8.21
  grants, 9.19, 9.21
  inland waters in, 7.55–7.56
  local authority powers, 8.40–8.42
  long distance routes, 8.23
  occupier,
    liability of, 1.009
  wardens, 8.26
  waterways in, 8.32
NATIONAL THEATRE,
  strike at, 1.072
  "The Romans in Britain," 6.03n.
NATIONAL TRUST, 1.017, 5.01–5.12, 8.17
  allotments, 8.04
  by-laws, 5.06
  charge for entry to property, 5.05
  common land and, 5.05
  constitution, 5.12
  foreshore,
    ownership, of, 7.61
  land, 8.32
  powers of, 5.04–5.06
  property of,
    compulsory purchase, 5.09–5.10
    grant of right over, 5.08
  purposes of, 5.02–5.03

347

Index

NATIONAL TRUST—*cont.*
  restrictive covenants, 5.11
  special properties, 5.07
NATIONAL WATER COUNCIL, 2.11n., 7.57
NATURE CONSERVANCY, 5.41
NATURE CONSERVANCY COUNCIL, 8.11n., 8.14, 8.18, 8.36, 8.40
NAVIGATION,
  right of, 7.58
NEGLIGENCE, 1.001, 1.100–1.131
  breach of duty, 1.104n.
  burden of proof, 1.117–1.118
  common law liability for, 1.021–1.022
  contributory, 1.121–1.122
  current knowledge, 1.103
  damages for, 1.110 *et seq.*
  deafness, 1.103
  defective premises, 1.103, 1.109
  defences, 1.119–1.130
  definition of, 1.100
  degree of care, 1.102–1.103
  economic loss, 1.106–1.108
  "egg-shell skull" rule, 1.116, 7.07
  employer, of, 6.13
  forseeability,
    fact of, 1.113, 1.115
  liability for,
    restriction on exclusion of, 1.155
  limitation periods, 1.129–1.131
  local authority, liability for, 2.04
  meaning,
    standard of care and, 3.75–3.77
  negligent statement, 1.106–1.108
  nervous shock, 1.114–1.115
  party, management of, 4.08
  reasonable man, 1.104
  remoteness of damage, 1.111–1.113
  res ipsa loquitur, 1.117–1.118
  statutory defences, 1.128
  swimming pool, 7.07 *et seq.*
  volenti non fit injuria, 1.123–1.127, 7.10, 7.12, 7.32–7.33
  rescue cases, 1.125–1.126
NELSON'S COLUMN, 5.23
NERVOUS SHOCK, 1.114–1.115
NEW FOREST, 2.72, 5.15
NUISANCE, 1.001, 1.025–1.034
  boats as, 7.44
  contributory negligence as defence, 1.122
  limitation period, 1.129–1.131
  neighbouring property owner, liability to, 4.14–4.15
  parks, 4.09 *et seq.*
  participatory sports, 7.35
  private, 1.025–1.031
    abatement or remedy, 1.031
    cricket matches, 1.026–1.027
    damages as remedy, 1.026, 1.031
    degree of damage, 1.025

NUISANCE—*cont.*
  private—*cont.*
    injunction or remedy, 1.026, 1.031
    malice, relevance of, 1.030
    occupier, necessary to be, 1.031
    trees, 1.028–1.029
  public, 1.033–1.034
    Attorney-General and, 1.033
    criminal offence as, 1.033
    legal process for, 1.033
  statutory, 1.032
  statutory defences, 1.128

OCCUPIER,
  "business" liability, 1.012n.
  liability of, 1.003 *et seq.*
    children, 1.013, 7.10
    contributory negligence as defence, 1.122
    dangerous activities on land, 1.020
    exclusion and limitation, 1.011, 1.012
    independent contractor, 1.023–1.024
    National Parks, 1.009
    negligence, 1.021–1.022
    people enjoying easement, 1.018
    people exercising their calling, 1.019
    swimming pools, 7.12
    trespassers, 1.014–1.017
    under contract, 1.010
  parks,
    rating purposes, for, 4.37 *et seq.*
    residential lettings, 1.038–1.041
OFFENCES,
  alcohol, role of, 6.75
  allotment, in, 8.05
  ancient monuments, 3.79
  animals, 6.60
    protection of, 8.12
  birds, protection of, 8.11
  bribery and corruption, 1.095
  caravans, 8.56, 8.58
  copyright, breach of, 3.32
  hypnotism, 6.41
  library, committed in, 3.08
  licences, affirming of, 8.14
  litter, 8.52
  lotteries, 6.84
  metal detectors, 3.65
  new species, introducing, 8.13
  plants, protection of, 8.13
  prize competitions, 6.85
  public halls, 6.37
  safety of sports grounds, 6.55
  sex establishment, 6.89
  street playgrounds, 4.58
  theatres, 6.03, 6.04
    obscene performance in, 6.03
    racial hatred, 6.04

INDEX

OFFENCES—*cont.*
  theft,
    employment, 1.098–1.099
    trade descriptions, 1.177, 1.179, 1.180, 1.181–1.187
  wrecks, protection of, 3.56
OIL,
  washed onshore,
    public nuisance, as, 1.033
OMBUDSMAN,
  annual report, 2.11n.
  local, 2.11–2.14
OPEN SPACE,
  Crown Court, 2.48.
  definition of, 2.48, 5.24
  London, in,
    exchanges, 5.29–5.31
    transfers between local authorities, 5.29
  metal detectors, 4.18
  parks as, 4.04
  Royal Parks, 2.48n.
  third party restrictions on, 4.24
  And see PARKS.
OPEN SPACE LAND, 2.46–2.59
  acquisition by local authority, 2.49–2.53
  development of, 2.42
  duty of local authority, 2.54–2.55
  foreshore, 2.59
  housing estates, 2.56
  local education authorities, 2.57–2.58
  management of, 2.54–2.55
  town and country planning, 2.59
OUTDOOR ENTERTAINMENTS,
  ancient custom, 6.59
  animals, 6.60
  athletic and sporting tracks, 6.54
  greyhound racing, 6.53
  horseracing, 6.47–6.52
  local authority powers, 6.57–6.58
  pleasure fairs, 6.56. *And see* PLEASURE FAIRS.
  safety of sports grounds, 6.55

PARISH COUNCIL,
  powers over land, 2.40
PARLIAMENT,
  private bill procedure, 2.30
PARKS,
  acquisition of, 4.02–4.04
  amenities, 4.07
  appropriations,
    local authority powers, 4.30
  by-laws, 4.13, 4.42–4.57
  car parks, provision for, 4.22–4.23
  change of use, 4.26–4.32
  charges for admission, 4.20
  closure, powers of, 4.20–4.21
  country, 4.04
  covenants, challenge of, 4.27

PARKS—*cont.*
  disposal of, 4.26–4.32
  insurance cover, 4.65
  local authority, recoverability of, 4.32
  local authority, powers, 4.31
  management of, 4.05–4.25
  metal detectors, 4.18
  negligence in management, 4.08
  nuisance, tort of, 4.09 *et seq.*
  occupier,
    rating purposes, for, 4.37 *et seq.*
  open space as, 4.04
  policing of, 4.25, 4.25n.
  Protector, 4.23n., 6.30
  public entertainment, 6.29
  rates, 4.33–4.41
  rating purposes, for,
    meaning of, 4.34, 4.36 *et seq.*
  sport, 4.06
  third party restrictions on, 4.24
  trespass, 4.19
  walls and fences, 4.16–4.17
  wardens, 4.25
  wild animals, in, 4.63–4.64
  See also PUBLIC PARK.
PAY,
  equal, 1.077
PENALTIES,
  attached, sale of, 6.75
  birds, protection of, 8.11
  bribery and corruption, 1.096
  cinemas, 6.21, 6.22
  contempt of court, 3.67
  gambling, 6.78
  gaming with machines, 6.83
  grants, 9.12–9.13
  litter, 8.52
  sex establishments, 6.89
  street playgrounds, 4.58
  Sunday observance, 6.62
  trade descriptions, 1.184, 1.185
  wrecks, protection of, 3.56
PEOPLE'S PARK, HALIFAX, 6.30
PERFORMERS' PROTECTION, 3.37n.
PERFORMING RIGHTS SOCIETY, 6.45
PERFORMING RIGHTS TRIBUNAL, 3.33–3.34
PICNIC SITES,
  provision of, 8.51
PLANTS,
  protection of, 8.13
PLAQUE,
  building in London, on, 5.22
PLAY. *See* THEATRES.
PLEASURE FAIRS,
  local authority powers, 6.56
  meaning of, 6.56
POP FESTIVALS,
  licence for, 6.35
  public nuisance, as, 1.033

349

Index

PREMISES,
  definition of, 1.006
PREROGATIVE ORDERS,
  meaning of, 2.09n.
PRINCIPAL,
  agent and,
    liability for sex discrimination, 1.083
PRIVATE BILL,
  procedure, 2.30
PRIVILEGE,
  ombudsman protected by, 2.14
PRIVITY,
  contract, of, 1.149
PROOF,
  burden of,
    negligence, 1.117–1.118
PUBLIC ENTERTAINMENT,
  entertainment licence, 6.63n.
  incidental music, 6.34n.
PUBLIC HALLS, 6.33–6.46
  billiards licencing, 6.43
  copyright, breach of, 6.45
  entertainment licences, 6.34–6.40
    boxing and wrestling, 6.40, 6.44
    general, 6.36–6.38
    pop festivals, 6.35
    hypnotism, 6.41–6.42
  video recordings, display of, 6.46
PUBLIC LENDING RIGHT, 3.10–3.13
PUBLIC PARK,
  London, in,
    closure of, 5.31
    See also PARKS.
PUBLIC PLACE,
  meaning of, 7.34n.
PUBLIC POLICY,
  local authority infringement of individual rights, 2.09
PUBLICATION OF ORIGINAL WORKS,
  libraries, by, 3.24–3.25

QUARRYING,
  public nuisance, of, 1.037

RACING,
  greyhounds, 6.53
  horses, 6.47–6.52
RAILWAYS,
  light, 8.15–8.16
RAMBLERS ASSOCIATION, 8.17
RATE CAPPING, 9.15–9.16
RATES,
  parks, 4.33–4.41
REASONABLE MAN, 1.104
RECKLESSLY,
  advertising services, 1.181n.
RECREATION,
  London, in,
    powers to provide for, 5.24–5.25

REMEDIES,
  abatement, 1.031
  bailment, 3.73–3.74
  breach of contract, for, 1.163
  copyright, breach of, 3.31, 3.32
  damages, 1.153, 1.163
    local authority, against, 2.07
    private nuisance, for, 1.026, 1.031
  equitable,
    laches, 1.184
  injunction, 1.154
    private nuisance, for, 1.026, 1.031
  recission for misrepresentation, 1.140
  specific performance, 1.153, 1.163
  statutory duty, for breach of, 1.169
RESERVOIRS, 7.57
RESTAURANT,
  licence for, 6.67
RESTRICTIVE COVENANTS,
  National Trust land, 5.11
RESTRICTIVE TRADE PRACTICES COURT,
  1.145, 1.167
RESTRICTIVE TRADING AGREEMENTS, 1.142
RIDING, 7.39
ROYAL PARKS,
  London, in, 5.39–5.40
  open space land, 2.48n.
RYLANDS v. *FLETCHER*,
  rule in, 1.001, 1.034, 7.57
  defences, 1.120, 1.122

SALE OF GOODS, 1.001, 1.156–1.163
  acceptance by buyer, 1.161
  condition, 1.157
  delivery, 1.161
  description, 1.158
  fit for purpose, 1.158
  future goods, 1.156
  merchantable quality, 1.158
  passing of property, 1.159
  price, 1.156
  remedies, 1.163
  rights of unpaid seller, 1.162
  sample, 1.158
  specific goods, 1.156
  time of essence, 1.157
  title, 1.158
  transfer of goods, 1.156
  transfer of title, 1.160
  warranty, 1.157
SAUNAS, 7.13
SCHOOL PLAYING FIELDS,
  use of, 2.57–2.58
SCHOOLS,
  copyright,
    special provisions in relation to, 3.34
SEASIDE, 7.60–7.70
  bathing, 7.60
  deck chairs, 7.68

Index

Seaside—*cont.*
  donkeys, 7.69
  foreshore, 7.61–7.62
    taking mussels, 7.64–7.66
    taking shingle, 7.63
  lobster catching, 7.70
  contract of,
    definition, 1.175
Services and Goods,
  contract for, 1.171–1.175
Sex Establishments,
  local authority powers, 6.88–6.90
Sir John Soame's Museum, 3.41
Specific Performance. *See* Remedies.
Sports,
  parks, in, 4.06
  participatory, 7.25–7.39
    nuisance, 7.35
    players, liability for, 7.26–7.29
    premises, 7.34
    private sports clubs, 7.38
    safety certificates, 7.37
    spectators, liability for, 7.30–7.31
    "*volenti non fit injuria*," 7.32–7.33
Sports Centres,
  by-laws, 7.22
  Gateshead International Stadium, 7.24
  management of, 7.21–7.24
  See also Swimming Pools.
  provision of, 7.22
Sports Council, 7.57, 9.01
  address, 9.31
  grants from, 9.28–9.31
  objects, 9.28
  organisation, 9.30
Sports Grounds,
  safety of, 6.55
Squares,
  London, in, 5.37
Statement,
  negligent, 1.106–1.108
Statue,
  London, in, 5.22
Statute,
  interpretation of, 2.24
  local, 2.29–2.30
Street Playgrounds, 4.58
Sunday Observance, 6.62–6.63
  exempt premises, 6.63
Swimming Pools,
  by-laws, 7.05
  car parks, 7.17
  closure of, 7.02
  education authorities, 7.03
  employees, 7.06
  equipment, loan of, 7.15
  finance, 7.19–7.20
  management of, 7.01–7.20
  negligence, liability for, 7.07 *et seq.*

Swimming Pools—*cont.*
  provision of, 7.02–7.04
  public entertainment, for, 6.31
  sale of, 7.02
  supervision, 7.11

Tate Gallery, 3.40, 3.41
Temple,
  local authority, as, 5.19, 5.37
  open space land, 2.48n.
Tenancy,
  agricultural, 1.042–1.045
  business, 1.046–1.051. *See also* Business Tenancies.
Tenant,
  agricultural,
    protection of, 1.043–1.045
  business,
    protection of, 1.048
  occupier's duty to, 1.035–1.051
Terms,
  implied, in contract for work and materials, 1.173
Thames Valley,
  water authority,
    duty of, 8.41
Theatres, 6.01–6.18
  animals, 6.16
  censorship, 6.03
  licensing of premises, 6.02
  obscene performance, 6.03
  premises, 6.11–6.14
  professional contracts, 6.06–6.10
  refreshments sold in, 6.17
  safety in, 6.11–6.13
  Sunday Observance, 6.18
  "the public good," 6.03
  young persons,
    restrictions on performance, 6.15
    restrictions on work, 6.17
Theft, 1.098–1.099
  dismissal of employee for, 1.098–1.099
Tied Cottage,
  occupier and, 1.036, 1.038
Title,
  implied term as to, 1.174
Tourist Board, 9.01
  grants from, 9.32–9.34
  hotel development, 9.33
Tower of London, 3.49n., 3.78
Town and Country Planning,
  open space land, 2.59
Trade Descriptions, 1.176–1.185
  definition of, 1.178
  enforcement, 1.184
  false price, 1.180
  false statements about services, 1.181–1.182
  limitation periods, 1.185

Index

Trade Descriptions—*cont.*
  offences, 1.177
  "offer to supply,"
    meaning of, 1.177
  statutory defences, 1.187
Trade Union,
  membership of, as reason for dismissal,
    1.065–1.066
Travel Agents,
  code of practice, 1.167
Treasure Trove, 3.50–3.53, 4.18
  compensation of finder, 3.53
  coroner to decide, 3.53
  gold or silver, 3.52
  hidden, 3.51
Treaty of Rome,
  article 85, 1.142
  article 118, 1.059
  copyright and, 3.35
  free movement of workers, 1.060n.
Trees,
  private nuisance, and, 1.028–1.029
Trespass, 1.001
  parks, 4.19
Trespassers,
  Law Commission recommendation,
    1.014n.
  liability of occupier to, 1.014–1.017

Ultra Vires,
  by-laws, 4.46
  doctrine of,
    local authority and, 2.15–2.23
    And see Local Authority.
Unfair Dismissal, 1.065
  pregnancy and, 1.069
  redundancy and, 1.068

Verderers, 5.15
Victoria and Albert Museum, 1.056n., 3.49n.
Video Recordings,
  public display of, 6.46

Video Recordings—*cont.*
  sex shop and, 6.89n.

Walls,
  parks, of, 4.16–4.17
War Memorial,
  London, in, 5.23
Warranty. *See* Terms.
Water,
  common law rights relating to, 7.58
Water Authority,
  conservation, 8.18
  duties of, 1.002, 7.49, 7.57
  making of by-laws, 7.48
Water Recreation, 7.40–7.70
  boats, 7.0–7.44. *And see* Boats.
  canals, 7.52–7.53. *And see* Canals.
  fishing, 7.45–7.51. *And see* Fishing.
  inland waters, 7.54–7.58. *And see* Inland
    Waters.
  seaside, the, 7.60–7.70. *And see* Seaside.
Waterway,
  meaning of, 7.56
Wardens,
  parks, in, 4.25
Whales,
  Royal ownership of, 3.57, 3.60
Wildfowl Trust, 7.66n.
Wildlife,
  preservation of, 8.10–8.14
  protection of, 3.66–3.69
Work,
  conditions of, 1.073–10.099
  health and safety at, 1.001, 1.073–1.075
    codes of practice, 1.075
Work and Materials,
  contract for, 1.171–1.175
Wrecks,
  definition of, 3.54
  hovercraft as, 3.54n.
  protection of, 3.56
  receiver of, 3.55
Wrestling Match,
  licence for, 6.40, 6.44